IMPLEMENTING
THE AMERICANS
WITH DISABILITIES ACT

IMPLEMENTING THE AMERICANS WITH DISABILITIES ACT

Rights and Responsibilities of All Americans

edited by

Lawrence O. Gostin, J.D.

Executive Director, American Society of Law, Medicine & Ethics
Boston University School of Law
Boston, Massachusetts

and

Henry A. Beyer, J.D.

Director, The N. Neal Pike Institute on Law and Disability
Boston University School of Law
Boston, Massachusetts

·P·A·U·L·H·
BROOKES
PUBLISHING CO.

Baltimore • London • Toronto • Sydney

Paul H. Brookes Publishing Co.
P.O. Box 10624
Baltimore, Maryland 21285-0624

Typeset by Brushwood Graphics, Inc., Baltimore, Maryland.
Manufactured in the United States of America by
Rose Printing Company, Inc., Tallahassee, Florida.

Library of Congress Cataloguing in Publication Data
Implementing the Americans with disabilities act : rights and responsibilities of all
 Americans / edited by Lawrence O. Gostin, and Henry A. Beyer.
    p.   cm.
 Includes bibliographical references and index.
 ISBN 1-55766-119-7
 1. Handicapped—Legal status, laws, etc.—United States. 2. Discrimination against
the handicapped—Law and legislation—United States. 3. Handicapped—Employment—Law and legislation—United States. I. Gostin, Lawrence O. (Lawrence Ogle-
thorpe) II. Beyer, Henry A.
KF480.I47 1993
346.7301′3—dc20
[347.30613]
                                   93-14711
                                        CIP

British Library Cataloguing-in-Publication data are available from the British Library.

Contents

Contributors

Elmer C. Bartels, Ph.D.
Commissioner
Massachusetts Rehabilitation Commission
27–43 Wormwood Street
Fort Point Place
Boston, Massachusetts 02210-1606

Henry A. Beyer, J.D.
Director
The N. Neal Pike Institute on Law and Disability
Boston University School of Law
765 Commonwealth Avenue
Boston, Massachusetts 02215

Judi Chamberlin
Program Coordinator
Ruby Rogers Advocacy & Drop-In Center
2336 Massachusetts Avenue
Cambridge, Massachusetts 02140

Justin W. Dart, Jr., M.A.
Chairman
President's Committee on Employment of People
  with Disabilities
Suite 300
1331 F Street, NW
Washington, DC 20004-1107

Chai R. Feldblum, J.D.
Associate Professor of Law
Legislative Clinic Director
Georgetown University Law Center
600 New Jersey Avenue, NW
Washington, DC 20001

Marilyn Golden
Policy Analyst
Disability Rights Education and Defense
  Fund, Inc.
2212 Sixth Street
Berkeley, California 94710

Lawrence O. Gostin, J.D.
Executive Director
American Society of Law, Medicine & Ethics
Boston University School of Law
765 Commonwealth Avenue
Boston, Massachusetts 02215

Stanley S. Herr, J.D., D.Phil.
Associate Professor
University of Maryland Law School
Clinical Law Office
510 West Baltimore Street
Baltimore, Maryland 21201-1786

Judith E. Heumann, M.P.H.
Co-Founder and Vice President
World Institute on Disability
510 16th Street
Suite 100
Oakland, California 94612-1500

Steven Hitov, J.D.
Greater Boston Legal Services
68 Essex Street
Boston, Massachusetts 02111

I. King Jordan, Ph.D.
President
Gallaudet University
800 Florida Avenue, NE
Washington, DC 20002-3695

Linda Kilb, J.D.
Managing Director
Disability Rights Education and Defense
  Fund, Inc.
2212 Sixth Street
Berkeley, California 94710

Arlene Mayerson, J.D.
Directing Attorney
Disability Rights Education and Defense
    Fund, Inc.
2212 Sixth Street
Berkeley, California 94710

Bonnie Milstein, J.D.
Judge David L. Bazelon Center for Mental
    Health Law
1101 15th Street, NW
Suite 1212
Washington, DC 20005-5002

Wendy E. Parmet, J.D.
Professor of Law
Northeastern University School of Law
400 Huntington Avenue
Boston, Massachusetts 02115

John Parry, J.D.
Director
Commission on Mental and Physical Disability
    Law
Editor-in-Chief
Mental & Physical Disability Law Reporter
American Bar Association
1800 M Street, NW
Washington, DC 20036-5886

Leonard S. Rubenstein, M.A., J.D.
Director
Judge David L. Bazelon Center for Mental
    Health Law
1101 15th Street, NW
Suite 1212
Washington, DC 20005-5002

Karen Peltz Strauss, J.D., LL.M.
Supervising Attorney
National Center for Law and Deafness
800 Florida Avenue, NE
Washington, DC 20002-3695

Guy Stubblefield
Executive Director, Retired
International Association of Machinists Center for
    Administering Rehabilitation and Employment
    Services
9000 Machinist Place
Upper Marlboro, Maryland 20772-2687

Sara D. Watson, M.P.P., Ph.D.
Director, Washington Office
Berkeley Planning Associates
1100 17th Street, NW #330
Washington, DC 20036

Jane West, Ph.D.
Program Officer
Milbank Memorial Fund
1 East 75th Street
New York, New York 10021

Irving Kenneth Zola, Ph.D.
Mortimer Gryzmish Professor of Human Relations
Brandeis University
Sociology Department
Waltham, Massachusetts 02254

Dedication

One of the most effective advocates for individuals with disabilities, and a leading architect of the Americans with Disabilities Act, is missing from this volume's list of contributors. In October 1991, attorney Timothy M. Cook, an extraordinary disability rights advocate, who agreed to write the transportation chapter, was claimed by cancer before he could complete the task. From the time of his graduation from the University of Pennsylvania Law School in 1978 through a number of positions leading to his role as President and Executive Director of the National Disability Action Center, Mr. Cook worked tirelessly and effectively for persons with disabilities, addressing issues of education, employment, health services, institutionalization, housing, public benefits, and, most notably, transportation. His passion was always the full and unstinting inclusion of individuals with disabilities in all aspects of American life. As Senator Tom Harkin remembered, "Tim taught us that segregation affects one's heart and mind in ways that may never be undone. Separate but equal is inherently unequal." To the memory of Tim Cook, in gratitude for his incalculable contributions to the full integration of Americans with disabilities into our society, this book is dedicated.

This book is also dedicated to the treasured memory of Dr. Rosemary Ferguson Dybwad and to Professor Gunnar Dybwad, her surviving partner in a worldwide campaign for human rights and human dignity. For over 60 years, they were equal partners in a movement to ensure that people come first. Their work in international and national arenas to declare and uphold egalitarian principles for persons with mental retardation and persons with other disabilities is legendary. Rosemary brought together an international network of advocates committed to community integration and to the participation of persons with disabilities in all facets of life. Ushering in a new civil rights era, Gunnar testified with eloquence and total moral and intellectual conviction in courtrooms and legislatures around the nation. Together, the sum of their work—their legacy of deeds, legal landmarks, and courageous leadership—offers inspiration to all in the disability rights movement. The Americans with Disabilities Act expresses the values Rosemary and Gunnar have lived by: justice, equality, and community.

Acknowledgments

This book would not have been possible without the expertise and energy of Merrill Kaitz, Director of Publications of the American Society of Law, Medicine & Ethics, and Managing Editor of *The Journal of Law, Medicine & Ethics*. Mr. Kaitz oversaw and managed the development of the manuscript.

The editors also are grateful to Sarah B. Cheney, Acquisitions Editor, of the Paul H. Brookes Publishing Company. Ms. Cheney saw the possibilities for the book early on, encouraged the book, and nurtured it.

In addition, thanks are due the two sponsoring organizations of the national conference from which this book developed. The American Society of Law, Medicine & Ethics is the largest organization in North America devoted to medicolegal education on an interdisciplinary basis. The society brings together attorneys, physicians, health care administrators, nurses and other allied health professionals, bioethicists, judges, insurers, and teachers who are concerned with the interrelationships of law, medicine, and health care. Ongoing efforts include the publication of two quarterly journals: *The Journal of Law, Medicine & Ethics* (formerly *Law, Medicine & Health Care*) and the *American Journal of Law & Medicine*. In addition, the Society houses an extensive medicolegal library, sponsors a variety of educational conferences, maintains a Speakers' Bureau, and administers the Health Law Teachers, Ethics Consultants, and Nurses Sections.

The N. Neal Pike Institute on Law and Disability at Boston University School of Law was founded in 1983 by Neal Pike, a 1937 graduate of the Law School, who has been blind since age 7. The Institute seeks to advance development and public understanding of disability law through a variety of activities: conferences, including the Emily Rose Peeke Lecture Series; publications, including the bimonthly *Disability Advocates Bulletin*; television and radio presentations, including the biweekly "Disability Law News and Commentary"; the annual awarding of the N. Neal Pike Prize, recognizing outstanding service to individuals with disabilities; teaching; research; and public service. The Institute has been directed since its founding by Henry A. Beyer, a graduate of the Harvard Law School.

Preface

The Americans with Disabilities Act (ADA) is the most important piece of federal legislation since the Civil Rights Act of 1964. The ADA represents the culmination of a series of federal statutes prohibiting discrimination against persons with disabilities. The ADA does not replace, but supplements, the large body of disability law that already exists. Other disability legislation includes the Federal Rehabilitation Act, Fair Housing Amendments Act, and Individuals with Disabilities Act, as well as state disability statutes.

The corpus of disability legislation adopts the visions of *both* equal treatment and special treatment. The law treats persons with disabilities as if their disabilities did not matter by requiring businesses, public accommodations, public services, transportation, and telecommunications authorities not to discriminate. This concept of equal treatment is powerfully articulated in the law. No qualified or eligible person with a disability can be subject to discrimination.

At the same time disability law also requires special treatment. The law requires covered entities to adopt a concept of affirmative action that *focuses* on the persons' disabilities as well as on societal barriers to equal treatment. The law requires reasonable accommodations or modifications designed to enable or empower the person with disabilities to take his or her rightful place in society. The law, therefore, insists on special treatment when that is necessary to allow a person to perform a job, enter a public building, or receive public service.

The ADA arises out of the honorable tradition of civil rights law. Like other civil rights laws, the ADA views persons as unique individuals with strengths and weaknesses. The act treats persons with disabilities as individuals of inherent worth, equal to all others. The act therefore perceives discrimination on the basis of disability much in the same way that civil rights law views African-Americans, women, and religious minorities. In each case the law will not allow different treatment based on a status or immutable condition.

Disability law stands for this proposition: A person's disabilities have little to do with his or her inabilities. Often it is society's reactions to the person with disabilities or society's structural barriers that disable the person. The mandate of civil rights law is to destroy those negative reactions and dismantle those barriers in order to restore equal opportunity and full participation in daily life activities with dignity, not charity.

The ADA, as the following chapters make abundantly clear, significantly affects not just persons with disabilities and persons charged with respecting and enforcing human rights, but virtually every segment of our society—*all* Americans. The far-reaching effects of the ADA have become apparent within only a few months of the initial implementation of the act: a Little League baseball rule that banned coaches in wheelchairs from the field during games was suspended by a federal court in Arizona; the Bush administration denied Medicaid approval to the Oregon health care rationing plan because it classified prospective health care recipients by their disabilities; and lawsuits were filed against theaters, shops, the Empire State Building, and New York City's "911" emergency response system for discrimination against persons with disabilities. The ADA is likely to transform the way Americans order their lives and will challenge existing assumptions and stereotypes about the meaning of disability in America.

In anticipation of the ADA's ubiquitous impact, the American Society of Law, Medicine & Ethics and the N. Neal Pike Institute on Law and Disability held a national conference in May 1991, entitled: "The Americans with Disabilities Act: What it Means for All Americans." A week earlier the then–Attorney General, Richard Thornburgh, delivered an address for the Pike Institute under the same title. The conference, attended by participants from 24 states and three foreign countries, affirmed our belief in the importance of the ADA and demonstrated the widespread interest in its implementation on the part of industry, trade unions, public services, and persons with disabilities. So that all Americans may share in the information, insights, and visions discussed at the conference, the faculty and an impressive array of other leaders in the disability rights field have joined with us in preparing this work.

Scope of the Book

We are privileged to have had two extraordinary people write the Introduction and the Foreword for this book—Justin Dart, the chair of the President's Committee on Employment of People with Disabilities, and I. King Jordan, the president of Gallaudet University. The Prologue to the book by Irving Zola places into perspective the magnitude of the impact of the ADA. Zola shows how pervasive disabilities are in American society, ranging from distinct physical disabilities to chronic diseases and deteriorating health. In a sense, most of us have had, currently have, or will have a disability some time in our lives.

Part I of the book is concerned with the modern history of the enactment of the ADA, together with the legal framework. Jane West, Arlene Mayerson, and Sara Watson chronicle the extraordinary efforts and alliances that led to the enactment of the ADA. They do so from the perspective of legislative strategists on Capitol Hill, as well as the disability rights movement. Chai Feldblum places the ADA in the context of antidiscrimination law.

The ADA is divided into four Titles, each of which is discussed in detail in Part II of the book. John Parry examines the legislative provisions, as well as prior case law, relating to Title I of the ADA concerning employment. Elmer Bartels explores the role of vocational rehabilitation programs under Title I, and Guy Stubblefield provides the perspective of labor and the trade union movement. Linda Kilb and Marilyn Golden both write on implementing Title II, Public Services. Kilb examines the role of state government because the ADA covers services and activities of state and local government; Golden is concerned with Title II, Subpart B, Public Transportation. Wendy Parmet explains and assesses the provisions and likely effects of Title III, Public Accommodations. Public accommodations are broadly defined and will cover not only theaters, stadiums, and restaurants but also health care offices. Karen Peltz Strauss explores the detailed provisions of Title IV, Telecommunications. The ADA is likely to have a profound impact on the accessibility of communication systems for persons with disabilities.

Discrimination in housing is not expressly covered in the ADA. The federal Fair Housing Amendments Act, however, continues to remain in force and provide strong antidiscrimination protection to persons with disabilities who are seeking a place to live or are already residing in a home or apartment. Bonnie Milstein and Steven Hitov present a national perspective on housing discrimination.

The ADA is often thought of as legislation that remedies obvious forms of discrimination, seeking to redress years of benign neglect or bigotry. Many people, therefore, view the ADA as providing access for persons with mobility impairments to public and private buildings; changing the physical plant or equipment in the workplace in order to provide equal opportunities in employment; or ensuring the availability of reading assistance to persons with vision impairments or text telephones to persons with hearing impairments. The ADA, to be sure, will accomplish these goals, but the legislation promises much more. Part III of the book examines the innovative side of the ADA, and tries to predict the future impact. Larry Gostin has written two chapters evaluating the diverse ways that the ADA will affect the health care system. The first chapter reviews the duties of health care providers to treat patients in need of services; the responsibilities of employers not to discriminate in screening, medical examinations, and health care benefits for employees; and the obligation of public health departments to comply with the "significant risk" standard in the ADA. The second chapter looks to the future of the National Human Genome Project and assesses whether the ADA is adequate in preventing and redressing genetic discrimination.

Leonard Rubenstein and Judi Chamberlin write on the impact of the ADA on the mental health system. Persons with mental illness have suffered from misunderstanding, prejudice, and discrimination since ancient history. Rubenstein looks through the lens of an experienced thinker and litigator in mental health court cases, and Chamberlin looks at the ADA through the lens of a consumer and nationally prominent advocate.

Stanley Herr takes on a dual role in his chapter. He analyzes the implications of the ADA for persons with developmental disabilities. As an internationally respected scholar and advocate, Herr also places the ADA in the context of international human rights. The ADA is consistent with the United Nations Declaration on the Rights of Persons with Disabilities. It also provides a legislative model for other countries to consider in national efforts to combat discrimination against persons with disabilities.

The ADA, as we all know, still leaves a great deal to do in truly defending and promoting the rights and inherent dignity and worth of all persons with disabilities. Judith Heumann reminds us, at the conclusion of the book, of the disability rights agenda that still remains.

The book also includes the amended text of the Americans with Disabilities Act itself, which is reproduced in the Appendix.

Prologue

The Sleeping Giant
in Our Midst
Redefining "Persons with Disabilities"

Irving Kenneth Zola

Depending on who is speaking, the estimate of people with a disability may range from 25 to 60 million. The number varies depending on the definition and thus the measurement of disability. Important as this number is for policy, the very debate may unwittingly perpetuate some questionable assumptions: that the figure, whatever it is, is relatively stable—some fixed ratio of persons with disabilities to those without disabilities—and that the condition measured (i.e., disability) is itself finite and static. I present data to demonstrate that quite contrary assumptions are likely, with quite different implications for the development of specific policies.

REFLECTIONS ON THE COUNTING OF DISABILITY

Although epidemiologists have noted for decades a shift in "health problems" from acute to chronic diseases, vital statistics traditionally have been concerned with mortality; they have measured such categories as total death rate, infant and maternal mortality, condition-specific death rates, and life expectancy. Only recently has there been an attempt to measure morbidity systematically. The figures themselves add nuance to the debate about numbers.

Typical is the quite detailed and systematic study of Wilson and Drury (1984). Reviewing 20-year trends (1960–1981) in 15 broad categories of chronic illness in the United States, they found that the prevalence of seven conditions had more than doubled, two had increased their prevalence from 50% to 99%, five had increased by up to 50%, and only one condition had become less prevalent. The so-called graying of the population did not explain this, because a similar pattern was observed for persons age 45–64. For this latter group—the core of the working population—these chronic conditions translated into activity limitation, with a more than doubling (from 4.4% to 10.8%) of the number of males in this two-decade period who claimed that they were unable to work because of some illness or disability.

Looking at two subsets—the young and the old—is particularly instructive. Whereas the absolute number of children (under 17) is not expected to increase, the proportion of those with a disability will. The United States National Health Interview Survey (Newacheck, Budetti, &

Halfon, 1986) indicates that the prevalence of activity-limiting chronic conditions among children doubled between 1960 and 1981 from 1.8% to 3.8%, with the greatest increase in the last decade. Although much of this increase may be due to the survival of lower weight newborns with various impairments, the major increase may well be due to shifting perceptions on the part of parents, educators, and physicians. Changing educational concerns are making learning disabilities (e.g., dyslexia) the fastest growing category of disability in the country (Faigel, 1985).

In absolute numbers, all census data affirm that the fastest growing segment of the U.S. population is made up of those over the age of 65. In 1880 their number was less than 2 million (3% of the total population), but by 1990 there were nearly 32 million persons over age 65 (at least 12% of the population). By the year 2030 an estimated one in four or five citizens (20%–25%) is likely to be over 65 (Gilford, 1988). Put another way, throughout most of history only 1 in 10 people lived past 65; now nearly 80% do. This traditional use of the age of 65 as a benchmark, however, is deceptive, because the most phenomenal growth will be in even older age groups, particularly those over 85. This age group, while constituting 1% of the total population in 1980, is projected to be 3% in 2030 and over 5% in 2050. At that time they could represent nearly one quarter of all elderly people (Gilford, 1988). The service implications are worth noting; whereas only about 5% of those ages 65–74 require assistance in one or more basic activities of daily living, nearly one third do so by age 85 (Feinstein, Gornick, & Greenberg 1984; Fulton, Katz, Jack, & Hendershot, 1989). Moreover, even these estimates of disability and service needs may be conservative. The most detailed compilation of future trends (Haan, Rice, Satariano, & Selby, 1991) indicates not only that the over-85 age group is likely to get even older but that, under current "medical policy," people are requiring progressively "more care" (however defined) in the last year of life. Thus, no matter how one defines it or measures it, the number of people in the United States with conditions that interfere with their full participation in society is steadily and dramatically increasing.

THE CONTINUALLY CHANGING FACE AND BODY OF DISABILITY

For years infant mortality has steadily decreased, in large part because of improvements in standards of living and prenatal care. Recently, these improvements have been supplemented by advances in the specialization of neonatology. Although the numbers are as yet small, it is clear that progressively more low birth weight, premature, and ill infants are surviving into childhood and beyond with manifest chronic impairments. With advances in medical therapeutics, many children who would have died (e.g., from leukemia, spina bifida, or cystic fibrosis) now are surviving into adulthood or longer. Diagnostic advances, as well as some life-extending technologies, allow many young people to survive with so-called terminal illnesses. A simple way of illustrating this phenomenon is to think of anyone you know with any of these diseases. *That* person is likely to be among the longest lived with this condition.

There is a similar trend evident in the young adult group. Although trauma still continues to be a major cause of mortality in this group, there is a major turnaround in the survival rates of people with spinal cord injuries. As recently as the 1950s, death was likely in the very early stages or soon after because of respiratory and other complications. In World War I only 400 men with wounds that paralyzed them from the waist down survived *at all*, and 90% of them died before they reached home. In World War II, 2,000 veterans with paraplegia lived and 1,700—over 85% of them—were still alive in the late 1960s (President's Committee on the Employment of the Handicapped, 1967). Each decade since has seen a rapid decline in the death rate and thus an increase of long-term survival—first of those with paraplegia, then those with quadriplegia, and now, in the 1990s, those with head injuries. The changing inpatient census in all our hospitals directly reflects this.

This is only the most dramatic example. Many chronic diseases once thought inevitably to cut short the life span (e.g., diabetes) are now, with diet and therapeutics, having almost negligible effects. In addition, life-extending interventions seem to be available for many other persons, from those with cancer and heart disease to those with multiple sclerosis, muscular dystrophy, and AIDS.

The aging population itself will be even more "at risk" for what were once considered "natural" occurrences (e.g., decreases in mobility, visual acuity, and hearing) and for other musculoskeletal, cardiovascular, and cerebrovascular changes whose implications are only beginning to be appreciated. Moreover, they very likely will have more than one chronic condition (Verbrugge, 1990)—what is coming to be known as comorbidity, an event almost certain to exacerbate disease in nonlinear ways (Verbrugge, Lepkowski, & Imanaka, 1989).

Still another unappreciated aspect of most chronic conditions is that, although permanent, they are not necessarily static. We do, of course, recognize at least in terminology that some diseases are "progressive," but we are less inclined to see that there is no one-time, overall adaptation/ adjustment to the condition. Even for a recognized progressive or episodic disorder, such as multiple sclerosis, attention only recently has been given to the continuing nature of adaptations (Brooks & Matson, 1987). The same also is true for end-stage renal disease (Gerhardt & Brieskorn-Zinke, 1986). With the survival into adulthood of people with diseases that once were fatal come new changes and complications. Problems of circulation and vision for people with diabetes, for example, may be due to the disease itself, the aging process, or even the original life-sustaining treatment (Turk & Speers, 1983).

Perhaps the most telling example of a new manifestation of an old disease is the current concern over the so-called postpolio syndrome (Laurie & Raymond, 1984). To most of the public, to clinicians, and certainly to its bearers, polio had been considered a stable chronic illness. Following its acute onset and a period of rehabilitation, most people had reached a plateau and expected to stay there. For the majority this may still be true, but for at least one quarter it is not. Large numbers of people are experiencing new problems some 20–40 years after the original onset. The most common are fatigue, weakness in muscles previously affected and unaffected, muscle and joint pain, breathing difficulties, and intolerance to cold. Whether these new problems are the mere concomitant of aging, the reemergence of a still-lingering virus, a long-term effect of the early damage or even of the early rehabilitation programs, or something else is still at issue (Halstead & Wiechers, 1985). Whatever the etiology of this type of phenomenon, there likely will be many more new manifestations of old diseases and disabilities as people survive decades beyond the acute onset of their original diseases or disabilities (Funne, Gingher, & Olsen, 1989; Sato, 1989). Thus, the dichotomy between those people with a "progressive" condition versus those with a "static" one may well be, generally speaking, less distinct than once thought.

CONCLUSION

What may have looked initially like a methodological debate—what is the "real" number of people with disabilities—has become one that goes to the heart of current policy formulation. The latter has been built on the notion of people with disabilities being another oppressed statistical minority like people of differing racial, ethnic, and gender backgrounds. I am arguing that people with disabilities do not represent a statistical minority. It is not merely, as the cliche states, that everyone is only a slip away. The empirical reality is that everyone, unless they experience sudden death, will in fact acquire one or more disabilities with all their consequences. This is the reality on which future conceptualization, measurement, and policy must be based—truly the sleeping giant in our midst.

REFERENCES

Brooks, N., & Matson, R. (1987). Managing multiple sclerosis. In J. Roth & P. Conrad (Eds.), *Experience and management of chronic illness* (pp. 73–106). Greenwich, CT: JAI Press.

Faigel, H. (1985). When the learning disabled go to college. *Journal of American College Health, 43*, 18–22.

Feinstein, P.H., Gornick, M., & Greenberg, J.N. (1984). The need for new approaches in long-term care. In P.H. Feinstein, M. Gornick, & J.N. Greenberg (Eds.), *Long-term care financing and delivery systems: Exploring some alternatives.* Washington, DC: Health Care Financing Administration.

Fulton, J.P., Katz, S., Jack, S.S., & Hendershot, G.E. (1989). Physical functioning in the aged: United States, 1984. *Vital and Health Statistics, 10* (167 DHHS Publication No. PHS 89-1595). Hyattsville, MD: National Center for Health Statistics.

Funne, K.B., Gingher, N., & Olsen, L.M. (1989). *A survey of the medical and functional status of the adult network of the Spina Bifida Association.* Rockville, MD: Spina Bifida Association of America.

Gerhardt, U., & Brieskorn-Zinke, M. (1986). Normalization of hemodialysis at home. In J. Roth & S.B. Ruzek (Eds.), *The adoption and social consequences of medical technologies* (pp. 271–317). Greenwich, CT: JAI Press.

Gilford, D.M. (Ed.). (1988). *The aging population in the twenty-first century: Statistics for health policy.* Washington, DC: National Academy Press.

Haan, M.N., Rice, D.P., Satariano, W.A., & Selby, J.V. (Guest Eds.). (1991). Living longer and doing worse? Present and future trends in the health of the elderly [Special issue]. *Journal of Aging and Health, 3*, 133–307.

Halstead, L.S., & Wiechers, D. (1985). *Late effects of poliomyelitis.* New York: Symposia Foundation.

Laurie, G., & Raymond, J. (Eds.). (1984). *Proceedings of Rehabilitation Gazette's 2nd international post-polio conference and symposium on living independently with severe disability.* St. Louis: Gazette International Networking Institute.

National Center for Health Statistics. (1983).

Newacheck, P.W., Budetti, P.P., & Halfon, N. (1986). Trends in activity-limiting chronic conditions among children. *American Journal of Public Health, 76*, 178–183.

President's Committee on Employment of the Handicapped. (1967). *Designs for all Americans* (p. 5). Washington, DC: Author.

Sato, H. (1989). Secondary disabilities of adults with cerebral palsy in Japan. *Disability Studies Quarterly, 9*, 14.

Turk, D.C., & Speers, M.A. (1983). Diabetes mellitus: A cognitive-functional analysis of stress. In T.G. Burish & L.A. Bradley (Eds.), *Coping with chronic disease* (pp. 191–217). New York: Academic Press.

Verbrugge, L.M. (1990). The iceberg of disability. In S.M. Stahl (Ed.), *The legacy of longevity* (pp. 55–75). Newbury Park, CA: Sage.

Verbrugge, L.M., Lepkowski, J.M., & Imanaka, Y. (1989). Comorbidity and its impact on disability. *Milbank Quarterly/Health and Society, 67*, 450–484.

Wilson, R., & Drury, T. (1984). Interpreting trends in illness and disability: Health statistics and health status. *Annual Review of Public Health, 5*, 83–106.

Introduction

The ADA
A Promise To Be Kept

Justin W. Dart, Jr.

Throughout all of reported history until recent decades, people perceived as having significant disabilities have been treated as subhumans. At worst they were killed or left to die as beggars/ outcasts; at best they were cared for through subsistence welfare, usually in the most demeaning circumstances. During the last 150 years this oppression actually has been magnified in many "developed" nations through the enforced segregation of people with disabilities in institutional settings where individuality is smothered by authoritarian paternalism, and too often there also is mental and physical abuse.

With the development of modern medicine, standards of living, and social responsibility, increasing millions of 20th-century humans have survived previously fatal conditions to live on with significant disabilities. These individuals have a great potential to be happy, productive members of their communities. However, our best efforts to fulfill this potential have been limited severely by a massive residue of ancient prejudice and paternalism. Our society still is infected by an insidious, now almost subconscious, assumption that people with disabilities are less than fully human and therefore are not entitled to the respect, the opportunities, and the services and support systems that are available to other people as a matter of right.

More than two decades ago many leaders of the disability movement decided that certain rights and independence-oriented services must be guaranteed by law. These pioneer patriots began to work with a handful of friends in Congress to pass, over a period of years, a series of historic laws that protected rights and provided supports in key areas such as medical and vocational rehabilitation, federal operations, public education, and residential institutions. There were pockets of very substantial progress, including considerable legislation of such solid civil rights sophistication that it fits well into the total mandate for equality that was completed by the Americans with Disabilities Act (ADA). However, public knowledge and the implementation and enforcement of the new laws were, and remain, limited. Each of those laws covered relatively limited areas of social process and thus did not convey a message of total equality. Obsolete attitudes and practices were slow to change. The basic assumption of inequality remained intact. The great majority of people with severe disabilities remained isolated, unemployed, impoverished, and dependent.

Around 1980 it became clear to me that we would never overcome the barriers to mainstream participation until the message of our full humanity was communicated into the consciousness and political process of America by a strong, highly visible, comprehensive civil rights law. It was equally clear that no meaningful mandate for equality could be passed or implemented until our tiny, fragmented disability community movement united, expanded, and matured in the political process.

A decade ago there was little demand for comprehensive disability rights legislation among the national leaders of our movement: "We can't even enforce Section 504 [of the Rehabilitation Act], why waste our time talking about more?" "The day of civil rights is gone, there will never be another major civil rights law passed." The consensus was for advocating legislation that provided services and partial rights in incremental steps.

Although I was by no means confident that a law like the ADA could be passed in this century, I felt strongly that the project must become the central focus and passion of our movement. To Americans, total equality is a sacred concept of transcending power and majesty. "We hold these truths . . ." and "I have a dream . . ." are far easier to communicate than partial rights and particular services. No matter how long it took to pass and implement a comprehensive disability rights law, every day of advocacy for total equality would unite and strengthen our movement and would contribute to the kind of public consciousness of our equality that is absolutely essential to the achievement of all our goals. In addition, the process would provide an ideal context for advocating particular services and rights.

I determined to devote my life to this project. My role would be: 1) to attempt to bring the groups and individuals of our community together and 2) to promote united advocacy and bipartisan political and public support for a strong legal mandate for full equality. I would not debate the details of civil rights, services, or turf, except to insist on the principle of full equality and full participation in every area of social process for all who suffered discrimination on account of disability. If I lived to see the enactment of an authentic civil rights law, which I seriously doubted would come to pass, I would then advocate a comprehensive empowerment policy that would make equality real in daily life.

In 1982 National Council on the Handicapped (NCH) chair Joe Dusenbury authorized me, as vice chair of the Council, to gather input for disability policy recommendations. In 1983, after I had held meetings with disability community leaders in every state, we published a "National Policy for Persons with Disabilities." One of the recommendations was that "Congress should act forthwith to include persons with disabilities in the Civil Rights Act of 1964 and other civil and voting rights legislation and regulations." On January 5, 1984, President Reagan endorsed this document: "I agree with you that . . . 'people with disabilities have an absolute right and responsibility to participate fully and equally in society . . .'." Subsequently we of the NCH decided—correctly, I believe—that disability discrimination is distinctive and requires a separate civil rights law. Under the leadership of then–NCH chair Sandra Parrino, NCH Director Lex Frieden, and disability rights attorney Bob Burgdorf, the ADA became the flagship recommendation of our historic 1986 report to Congress and the President, *Toward Independence*. A version of this approach to the ADA was introduced in Congress by Senator Lowell Weicker in April of 1988, mainly to secure endorsements during the election year. A good many members of Congress signed on as sponsors, and both Vice President Bush and Governor Dukakis endorsed the bill in concept.

In support of the ADA, I visited every state from 4 to 20 times, dialoguing with groups of from 3 to 6,000 persons, from nursing home residents to the President and members of Congress. I sent thousands of united advocacy messages to Congress and to a national network of more than 1,000 disability community leaders. As chair of the ADA-focused Congressional Task Force on the Rights and Empowerment of Americans with Disabilities (1988–1990), I held 63 public forums, at least one in every state, Guam, and Puerto Rico. We provided numerous reports to the Congress, the administration, and advocates.

After extensive consultation with leaders of the disability and business communities, Congress, and the administration, Bob Silverstein, the Director of the Senate Subcommittee on the Handicapped, wrote a much-improved version of the ADA. This was introduced in 1989 by Senator Tom Harkin and Congressman Tony Coelho and other members of both parties.

During the entire time that the ADA was before the Congress, the disability community was represented in negotiations principally by Pat Wright and a group of veteran advocates from the Disability Rights Education and Defense Fund (DREDF) and the Consortium of Citizens with Disabilities (CCD). In a unique example of the power of democracy, the CCD convened the representatives of the major disability constituencies from one to three times a week. We received accurate reports on the issues and negotiations of the hour from Pat and her colleagues. We hammered out consensus positions for them to take on our behalf and we received our marching orders for advocacy from Pat's field marshals, Liz Savage, and CCD chair Paul Marchand. We went forth in passionate unity to communicate positions and strategy by telephone, fax, computer, and mail to the nationwide grass roots networks of the CCD, the Congressional Task Force, and individual organizations. Congress was deluged with adamant, unified calls, telegrams, letters, cards, and visits, sometimes within minutes of each other. All this occurred with no central office and no central fund, with each of us or our organizations paying for stamps, calls, paper, trips, and printing.

Dialogue and advocacy—especially through the efforts of Presidential Counsel Boyden Gray and disability rights attorney Evan Kemp—led to the August 1989 endorsement of the Senate version of the ADA by President Bush. After months of inspired negotiation led by Senators Harkin, Kennedy, Hatch, and Dole, by Congressmen Hoyer, Bartlett, Mineta, Brooks, and others, and by Bob Silverstein and other staffers and, of course, Pat Wright, the ADA was passed on July 13, 1990. The final, one-sided votes for the ADA in the House and the Senate were misleading. There was massive opposition by some of the most powerful political forces in the nation, such as the National Federation of Independent Business, the U.S. Chamber of Commerce, the entire public transportation community, the *New York Times*, and the *Wall Street Journal*.

Although there was never much doubt that the ADA could be passed in some form, there was very strong support for amendments that would have destroyed it as a mandate for equality. Amendments were proposed that virtually would have eliminated legal remedies and exempted important constituencies, such as people with mental illness and AIDS, from protection. Amendments also were proposed to exempt vast areas of social process from important requirements of equality—for example, public and private bus and rail transportation and small businesses.

During the early stages of the Congressional debate, some of our community leaders believed that one or two such amendments would have to be accepted in order to secure passage of the ADA and seemed willing to support an amended law. Many of us, however, argued that amendments of this nature would legalize discrimination, possibly for generations. We stated that, although we could be flexible in terms of time limits, remedies, and cases of undue hardship, we would publicly oppose an ADA that included any significant permanent exemptions of coverage or "separate but equal" "Jim Crow" provisions. We knew, of course, that no law could effect total equality. What we wanted was a law that society would interpret as a firm statement that "people with disabilities are equal, period!"

The latter view prevailed. On July 26, 1990, President Bush signed the ADA into law. There were some amendments, but none that significantly compromised the principle of equality. In terms of its concrete impact on specific areas of social process, the ADA and its companion rights laws probably form the most comprehensive package of federal civil rights legislation in the history of

America. The ADA is an absolutely essential legal tool to achieve equality, but it does not guarantee equality. It is a promise to be kept. What is that promise? Whatever the act says legally, the clearly communicated promise of the ADA is that all people with disabilities will be fully equal, fully productive, fully prosperous, and fully welcome participants in the mainstream.

Keeping the promise of the ADA is not going to be quick or easy. Civil rights laws have brought about great progress for many groups in America, but not all. Thanks to many of the authors of this book and hundreds of others, pioneering initiatives in rehabilitation, independent living, education, employment, and advocacy have proven absolutely that people with severe disabilities can be fully independent, productive, and prosperous. However, the magnificent experimental progress of the last few decades has not been implemented on a society-wide basis. In 1970, 3 years before the passage of the Rehabilitation Act (PL 93-112) with its prohibitions on discrimination in employment (Section 504), the employment rate among persons with disabilities was 41%. In 1988 it was 33%. Employment has risen in absolute numbers and in quality, but has not kept pace with the population explosion and changes in the nature of work. People with disabilities remain the poorest of the poor, and they are falling further behind every year.

The time has come for our movement, for our nation, to face an important reality. In today's society of exploding change and complexity, we are not going to solve our massive social and economic problems simply by fine-tuning and implementing the legal requirements of civil rights laws or by waiting for the free market to overcome magically the problems of the people who operate it. Real solutions are going to require expanding the definition and process of civil rights—and indeed the definition of democracy itself—to include as its central focus a concept of empowerment, a policy of empowerment, and a science of empowerment.

Government must accept the responsibility to coordinate, and citizens must accept the responsibility to execute, a revolution of empowerment—a profound change of attitudes and a massive reallocation of public and private resources from conspicuous consumption, paternalism, and dependency to the empowerment of all people to be productive in terms of quality of life. We must replace obsolete models and processes. We must refine, systematize, and utilize on a society-wide basis the very successful experiments in scientific, civil rights, and free enterprise empowerment that have been developed in rehabilitation, independent living, business, politics, sports, space travel, and other areas.

A serious science of empowerment must be constructed on certain foundational concepts:

1. The legitimate purpose of civil rights, human society, and its governments is not simply to guarantee equal opportunity to *pursue* life, liberty, and happiness, but to *empower* all people to make those free choices and to take those concrete actions that actually *produce* life, liberty, and happiness—lives of quality. Empowerment achieved must be the standard by which civil rights, productivity, and all public and private activities are measured—by government, by the courts, by schools, by the media, by business, and by us, the people, as we make daily decisions. Public policy must be empowerment policy.

2. Productivity must be measured not only in terms of raw dollars but also in terms of the extent to which individuals are maximizing their own quality of life, and that of society. It is self-evidently irrational to say that creating $1 million worth of cigarettes or television programs that promote violence is productivity in the same sense as creating $1 million worth of automated farm machinery or quality health care.

3. There should be no distinct "disability" policy, only public policy. With the advance of modern medicine and technology, disability has become a normal characteristic of the human process. There is a virtual certainty that any family of currently able-bodied persons will eventually include persons with disabilities who have significant potential to function in society. As people within the normal spectrum of human differences, we who have disabilities have the same

inalienable rights and the same inalienable responsibilities as other people. Therefore, society must create processes that empower us just as normally as people without disabilities. In such a society the government agency that I head would not exist.

4. The locus of empowerment is the individual. The illusion that paternalistic government can give quality of life to its subjects has resulted in a dependency that has debilitated the people it promised to empower. Empowerment can be supported, but it cannot be given or imposed. Empowerment in interdependent human society occurs through the will, perceptions, ability, and cooperative action of each individual to produce lives of quality for all persons, or it does not occur at all. However, complex modern society cannot be operated efficiently without strong government. Government should be strengthened and should be held absolutely accountable for leadership that produces positive results. This must occur through the temporary delegation of authority by citizens who are willing to subject themselves to the disciplines of the leaders they have chosen and who accept full responsibility to take the creative personal actions that are the substance of quality culture.

5. Civil rights and free enterprise are not in conflict; they are two sides of the same cultural currency. Working in combination, they have powered American democracy to miracles of productivity, self-realization, and quality of life that have revolutionized the political, economic, and cultural processes of the world. The effort and creativity of people who *know* that they possess guaranteed equal opportunity to participate freely and to profit fairly has been the driving force of free enterprise. The fruits of the extraordinary resulting productivity have given meaningful substance to paper civil rights. Civil rights and free enterprise are the means to an end, and the end is empowerment.

Empowerment occurs when we perceive that we have a basic vested interest in the success of each other. Empowerment is suppressed when we perceive—even subconsciously—that we have a vested economic or psychological interest in the subservience of others. Too often government officials, company executives, welfare workers, teachers, and many others—even parents—act to protect the status quo, rather than to empower. Empowerment occurs when we decide that achieving a particular goal is important enough for us to junk out-of-date systems and create environments and relationships that enable us to do whatever it takes to accomplish the task.

Empowerment policy cannot be the traditional quick fix, pork barrel bargain to buy votes in the next election. America is faced with the dangerous results of successful systems having become obsolete: a widening poverty gap, an increasing inadequacy of basic social and commercial services, dangerously increasing public and private debt, and potentially catastrophic international and ecological problems. Keeping the promise of the ADA and keeping the promise of democracy in this context will require comprehensive policy for empowerment undertaken with a passionate unity of purpose.

I advocate lifelong education for empowerment, and lifelong human services and community supports for empowerment—including rehabilitation, independent living, transition, supported employment, transportation, communication, and personal assistance services. I advocate financial services, public and private media communication, business leadership, full legal services, and technology for empowerment, incentives rather than disincentives for productivity, housing as a base for empowerment, aggressive prevention, and quality, affordable insurance and health care for all. And, yes, I advocate totally new attitudinal and physical environments and completely new types of communities and relationships created to utilize the resources and meet the needs of human beings in the 21st century.

I have presented an ambitious agenda. Some will suggest that it is politically impossible and unaffordably expensive, especially in a time of budget crisis. These are tired, adolescent excuses for failure to undertake a demanding but self-evidently necessary investment in the future of human life. Former President Bush estimated the economic cost of excluding two thirds of Americans with disabilities from the mainstream to be about $200 billion annually.

Our irresponsible status quo is the cause of the budget crisis. The empowerment of society is the solution. We are spending hundreds of billions of dollars to support obsolete public and private systems that isolate millions in ghettos and waste the talents of all. Lack of money is not the basic problem. Advocacy, government, and business as usual are not the solution.

What is required is courageous, unifying leadership for empowerment. The president, the administration, the Congress, and government at all levels must provide leadership for the creation of an empowered society as a first priority for America. Special entities should be created at every level of government to coordinate a society-wide mobilization of resources.

More importantly and far more difficultly, the private sector—business, religion, nonprofit service providers, the public media, families, and individuals—must become absolutely committed to the arduous self-discipline and decisive action required to implement empowerment. An empowered society will not occur until we understand that the responsible leaders are all of us, that "the disabled and the disadvantaged" are all of us, and that the productive self-realization and quality of life of the person with mental illness or the single mother in the ghetto are just as important to our pocketbooks and our happiness as the productivity of the president of Coca-Cola and the quarterback of the Redskins.

Most important is dynamic leadership by the disability community. Equality, prosperity, and empowerment have never been handed down to disadvantaged people by an entrenched status quo. United advocacy is the fundamental basis of power for any group in any form of society. Real-life empowerment occurs only through the consistent advocacy, action, and vigilance of those who seek it.

We of the disability community have a responsibility to keep the promise of the ADA—to take the lead in initiating the revolution of empowerment. We cannot complete the revolution alone, but we can struggle to ensure that it will include all people because, to the extent that it is exclusive, it will fail for all.

We must maintain the united disability community advocacy that carried us to victory for the ADA. We must mobilize all of our forces to monitor and ensure the implementation of the ADA at the national, state, and local levels. We must reach out to all people with all disabilities and their potential advocates. We must educate them about their ADA rights and motivate and train them to be effective advocates for implementation.

We must reach out to employers, operators of public facilities, and government at all levels to inform them of their ADA responsibilities and of their ADA opportunities. We must embrace them in positive partnership for full and harmonious compliance, with minimal expense, minimal litigation, and maximal profit for business, for people with disabilities, and for all Americans.

Inevitably, situations will arise in which we must resort to lawsuits to establish, to define, and to communicate dramatically our new ADA rights. However, these lawsuits must be carefully selected cases in which ADA rights have been obviously, blatantly infringed, where we have the resources to win, and where the facts of our case can be utilized to communicate powerful messages of equality through the media into the public consciousness. An avalanche of unplanned, unfocused, poorly funded and researched lawsuits—many of which we would lose—would simply deplete our resources, escalate hostility toward people with disabilities, and create a backlash that would be a tragedy for all concerned.

We must create united coalitions and cross-disability organizations with millions of activist members, with state-of-the-art offices and technology. We who occupy positions of leadership must overcome self-defeating tendencies to protect our modest power. We must expand that power through the aggressive recruitment and training of new leaders who combine our principles, passion, and pioneer wisdom with highly refined skills to organize and to compete for attention and money in the major leagues of 21st century social, political, and commercial action. We as a movement must take immediate steps to develop a consensus empowerment policy and a consensus plan to launch the revolution of empowerment.

We must reach out aggressively beyond our movement to become the catalyst for a powerful new coalition for empowerment that includes not only traditional minorities but also business, labor, the churches, taxpayers, elderly people, and all groups sharing an immediate interest in solving the problems of adolescent democracy. Also, we must unite with our colleagues in every nation to create a worldwide revolution for the establishment of strong civil rights laws and empowerment policies. We have much to communicate and much to learn. Only through worldwide solidarity will we establish and maintain our humanity. Half a billion voices raised in unison for independence and empowerment will not be denied.

We must become far more effective politicians at the national, state, and local levels in both parties—millions of us. The politics of equals at the highest levels of public decision making requires a sophistication, a quid pro quo, and a patient toughness that is quite different from the politics of impoverished recipients of paternalistic tokenism.

We must become far more dynamic and sophisticated communicators because, no matter how well we enforce civil rights laws, we will not be equal in real life until we communicate the simple message of our equality to the more than 240 million Americans who will never read any law, but whose thoughts and actions will define our humanity every hour of every day. We must learn to access the power of the public media to communicate empowerment. We must graduate from charity telethons, human interest stories, and slow-day news coverage to consistent coverage as serious news and serious participants in all aspects of social process. Our political, economic, educational, and social data should be reported regularly along with those of other significant segments of society. We must learn to dominate the news when necessary, as we did during the Gallaudet revolution.

We as individuals must learn to utilize more fully the real power that drives our movement: loving reverence for human life—the fundamental truth that life and its quality are the ultimate values of being human. We must transcend the superficial friendliness, toughness, and cynicism that is the language of a society whose values are dictated by television news and commercials. We must speak increasingly to the heart and conscience of the world with simple truth, simply stated in words and especially actions that express profound love. Our movement does not yet have a Martin Luther King, but each one of us can be a truly powerful celebrant and promoter of human rights and empowerment every day in every place. The real heroes of history are not necessarily the brightest, the bravest, the strongest, or the most moral. They are the individuals who accept the responsibility to humankind that destiny thrusts on them and who will themselves to expend every available physical and psychological resource, including life itself, to fulfill that responsibility.

Just what is the magnitude of responsibility of the American disability movement in 1993? We are responsible for keeping the promise of the ADA, to lay the foundation for the empowerment of 43 million Americans with disabilities as well as more than half a billion people in other nations. Once again, America is watching. Because this is America, the world is watching. If we succeed in keeping the promise of the ADA, the world will follow. If we fail, the world will follow, and it will be a tragedy beyond words or tears.

We know what to do. With a faith born of loving association with individuals of transcending passion and responsibility for life, I believe that we will unite, that we will act—that we shall overcome!

Foreword

Reflections on a New Era

I. King Jordan

On July 26, 1990, President Bush signed into law the Americans with Disabilities Act (ADA: PL 101-336), closing a significant gap in the federal statutes governing civil rights. Previous legislation limited protection against discrimination on the basis of disabilities to entities within the executive federal sector or to those receiving federal support in excess of $2,500. With the signing of the ADA, Americans with disabilities gained a new sense of dignity and self-worth. This marked the end of a long struggle on the part of committed individuals who conceived, nursed, and championed the ADA to its final form, and the beginning of new challenges for our nation.

I remember the day I sat in the visitors' gallery of the House of Representatives with many other deaf people watching the last debate and final vote on the ADA. At the end, when the votes had been tabulated and the ADA bill had passed, Representative Steve Gunderson, who is a Congressional member of our Gallaudet Board of Trustees, looked up at me and signed, "You should be very proud and very happy." This was a memorable event for me and for those who were there with me. I felt I was a member of a winning team. There, in the House of Representatives, was a Congressman signing and speaking a language I and my deaf colleagues easily understood.

In a sense, this is what the ADA is to those of us with disabilities. It speaks OUR language. It is a law we all helped write and it leads to a door of access, to a freedom most of us have been denied for most of our lives.

Since the passage of the act and its signing into law, I have given much thought to the meaning of the ADA in my life and in the lives of my colleagues with and without disabilities. As I read what others have written and published in regard to the ADA, like some of what appears in this volume, I comprehend more fully that the process of understanding what the ADA really is has only begun. In fact, none of us can really be sure of the full meaning of this monumental law until 20, 30, or 50 years from now. It is left for jurisprudence and actual practice to add to the meaning of the ADA, guided by the recorded intent of the Congress. At the same time that I appreciate all the work that has gone into the ADA, its formation, and the accompanying regulations, I am keenly aware, as are my colleagues with disabilities, of the great gap that still remains. This is a gap that no amount of legislation can possibly surmount, the age-old problem of attitude. This is a problem that all of us must work on together to resolve or reduce.

Disabilities take many forms. Some of us cannot see and we therefore make use of auxiliary aids like dogs or books written in braille. Some of us cannot hear. We use sign language or oral interpreters, telecommunication devices (e.g., text telephones), and relay services to make phone calls. Some of us cannot walk and use wheelchairs to get around and ramps to give us access to buildings. Some of us use personal assistants. The list goes on. Each of us is a unique and significant human being who wants to contribute to the society in which we live and to reap benefits from life, just like everyone else. Of course, we will require some accommodations along the way. We are entitled to them as members of an egalitarian society!

The ADA establishes by law our right to these accommodations. This is the bottom line, the heart of the ADA. It is a legal guarantee to equal rights for those of us with disabilities. Although I wish I could say that the ADA has thrown the door of equality wide open, we know by experience that is not the case. Instead, we have collectively been ushered to the door of opportunity. We now stand at the threshold of a new era for all Americans, those of us with disabilities and those of us without. The ADA is our license to access, which is the birthright of every citizen. Together we will lead the world so that people of other nations one day will have the same opportunities.

How can we make the ADA work? This challenge faces each of us singly and collectively. If we are going to change attitudes about people with disabilities, we first of all must be convinced that it can be done. I know it can. I believe that what is required is a personal commitment on our part to the reeducation of all Americans about their perception of "disabilities." By bringing human relations skills to bear on this process of working the ADA into the legal foundation of our society, all of us will enhance the law's effectiveness.

The human relations part is ours to enact. We need not be lawyers, rehabilitation counselors, or specialists in any particular profession to help others to understand what we have to offer. To succeed, we must become our own salespeople and take the lead in educating others about the capabilities of persons with disabilities. One way to do this is by sharing information. I have met individuals who told me that, up to a certain point, they had no idea of how to talk to persons with disabilities, either about themselves and their lives or about their disabilities. If we make the first move, show that we accept our own disabilities and share how we constantly learn new ways to deal with them, we begin to paint a clearer picture of our being, our realities, and our dreams. Sharing who we are and how we live with those we meet will instill greater awareness and help to weave the ADA indelibly into the tapestry of a better America. The key to understanding is first-hand knowledge, not the presumption of knowledge.

I would like to note that, as a man with a disability, I do not presume to understand the particular needs of another individual's disability, even those of another person who is deaf. Although I recognize that we might share similar needs or concerns, I cannot for one moment think that I understand how his or her life activities are shaped by his or her unique abilities. Thus, we are reminded that, in respecting others' individualities, we must also understand that we do not know the very personal, internal experiences and beliefs with which each of us lives. This is a key to working together, to being able to advocate for each other. We are humans, facing the conditions of life that all humans face. We are all the same and we are all different. Just as we understand and respect the sameness, we must acknowledge and respect the difference. Our best hope in the success of this effort is to join forces, recognize our sameness and differences, and work together for the empowerment of all of us.

Welcome to an exciting, challenging new era!

IMPLEMENTING
THE AMERICANS
WITH DISABILITIES ACT

PART I

MODERN HISTORY
AND THE LEGAL FRAMEWORK

Chapter 1

The Evolution of Disability Rights

Jane West

As a declaration of equality for persons with disabilities, the Americans with Disabilities Act[1] (ADA) sends a clear message about what society's attitudes should be toward persons with disabilities—attitudes of respect, inclusion, and support. The ADA is the result of 2 decades of efforts, mainly by the disability rights movement and its allies, to change policies based on different attitudes: attitudes of pity, patronization, and exclusion toward persons with disabilities. In establishing equality of opportunity, full participation, independent living, and economic self-sufficiency as the nation's proper goals for persons with disabilities (42 U.S.C. §12101[a][8]), the ADA reflects attitudes of respect, inclusion, and support.

This chapter examines the social and policy contexts of the ADA in terms of the evolution of attitudes toward persons with disabilities. It considers societal attitudes toward persons with disabilities and the attitudes persons with disabilities hold toward themselves. It examines these attitudes through three lenses: the experience of disability in America, the changing language of disability, and the history of federal disability rights legislation over the past 20 years. It considers how our public policies and our language—both the results of negotiation—have defined and reflected the changing relationships between persons with disabilities and the society at large. This chapter documents a gradual change in attitudes, of which the ADA is the latest outcome.

CURRENT STATUS OF PERSONS WITH DISABILITIES

Only since the 1980s have we begun to consider persons with disabilities as a distinct minority group—one that can be described in terms of demographic characteristics and in relation to other minority groups. Although the limited data that we have for this purpose often raise more questions than they answer, many significant descriptive statements can be made.

When compared to other minority groups, persons with disabilities are distinguished in virtually every category by their disadvantaged status. As the ADA notes, "census data, national polls, and other studies have documented that people with disabilities, as a group, occupy an in-

This chapter was written with the support of the Milbank Memorial Fund. The original article from which this chapter is adapted is entitled "The Social and Policy Context of the Act" and appears in *The Americans with Disabilities Act: From Policy to Practice*, published by the Milbank Memorial Fund.

[1]The Americans with Disabilities Act of 1990 (PL 101-336) is published in *Statutes at Large* (104 Stat. 327) and codified in the *United States Code* (42 U.S.C. §§12101–12213 [Supp. II 1990]). References to various portions of the Act within this chapter cite the specific section of the Code.

ferior status in our society, and are severely disadvantaged socially, vocationally, economically and educationally" (42 U.S.C. §12101[a][6]). A few specific examples illustrate the status of persons with disabilities in the late 1980s:

Fifty percent of adults with disabilities had household incomes of $15,000 or less. Only 25% of persons without disabilities had household incomes in this bracket (U.S. Senate Committee on Labor and Human Resources, 1989, p. 9).

Two thirds of all Americans with disabilities between the ages of 16 and 64 were not working at all. Sixty-six percent of these would have liked to work (Louis Harris and Associates, Inc., 1986).

Whereas only 15% of all adults age 18 and over had less than a high school education, 40% of all persons with disabilities age 16 and over had not finished high school (Louis Harris and Associates, Inc., 1986).

Whereas 56% of all students participated in postsecondary education programs, only 15% of students with disabilities did so (Wagner, 1989).

Persons with disabilities participated in society in social events (e.g., dining out, movies, attending sporting events) far less frequently than did persons without disabilities (Louis Harris and Associates, Inc., 1986).

Furthermore, the situation for persons with disabilities has become worse since the 1970s—at least in terms of economic well-being. A recent study concluded that in the mid-1960s persons with disabilities had income levels close to those of persons without disabilities. Their relative well-being declined in the next decade, reaching a low in the recession of the early 1980s. Since then people with disabilities have regained most of the ground they lost, but those gains are very unevenly distributed, and increases in household incomes have come mainly from increased wage earnings by household members who do not have disabilities. Persons who have disabilities and also are nonwhite or not well educated are the worst off (Burkhauser, Haveman, & Wolfe, 1990).

DISCRIMINATION AGAINST PERSONS WITH DISABILITIES

It is generally accepted that discrimination plays a significant role in the outcomes described above. Congress believes that the elimination of discrimination will facilitate the achievement of the goals of equal opportunity, full participation, independent living, and economic self-sufficiency. The establishment of "a clear and comprehensive national mandate for the elimination of discrimination against individuals with disabilities" (42 U.S.C. §12102[b][1]) is the ADA's contribution toward meeting these goals.

Discrimination against the estimated 43 million persons with mental and physical disabilities has been documented repeatedly (Arangio, 1979; English, 1971; Livneh, 1982; Presidential Commission on the Human Immunodeficiency Virus Epidemic, 1988; U.S. Commission on Civil Rights, 1983; U.S. Senate Committee on Labor and Human Resources, 1989). Findings in the ADA hold that society has tended to isolate and segregate persons with disabilities (42 U.S.C. §12102[a][2]) and that discrimination continues to be pervasive in virtually all aspects of life (42 U.S.C. §12102[a][3] and [5]). The ADA states that persons with disabilities have been "subjected to a history of purposeful unequal treatment, and relegated to a position of political powerlessness" primarily because of the stereotypical assumptions that society holds (42 U.S.C. §12102[a][7]). Persons with disabilities who are members of other groups frequently encountering discrimination, such as African-Americans and women, may encounter dual discrimination (Brown, 1981; Burkhauser et al., 1990), leaving them to wonder on which basis they were being rejected.

Discrimination against persons with disabilities has much in common with discrimination against other groups of people; however, there are also unique features. Discrimination against persons with disabilities might be considered in two aspects: *prejudice* and *barriers*. It is the experience of being the target of prejudiced, or "pre-judged" attitudes, that persons with disabilities share with other groups that have been targets of discrimination. However, many of the barriers confronted by persons with disabilities are unlike those confronted by other minority groups.

Prejudice

Prejudice is an attitude that distorts social relationships by overemphasizing some characteristic such as race, gender, age, or disability (U.S. Commission on Civil Rights, 1983). A range of prejudicial attitudes is examined later in this chapter, but it suffices now to note that prejudice often gives birth to myths, stereotypes, and stigmas that are associated with a negative exaggeration of the impairment of the individual to the exclusion of other attributes of the individual. Persons with disabilities have long encountered a generic stereotype that holds that "you are less of a person if an aspect of your functioning is impaired." There is a generalization that links impaired functioning to impaired personhood.

Because of unfounded assumptions about the capabilities of persons with disabilities, certain opportunities have been closed to them. An employer might not consider hiring a receptionist who is blind, assuming he or she would be incapable of performing the tasks of the job. A training program for dentists may refuse to admit a candidate who cannot hear, assuming he or she would be unable to understand the instructors or communicate with patients.

Women and other minority groups share the experience of being the recipients of prejudiced attitudes and concomitant discriminatory policies and practices. One of the many damaging effects is that many may come to believe what they hear and internalize the experiences of discrimination they confront, resulting in beliefs of inadequacy and low self-esteem.

Barriers and the Accommodation Imperative

The other aspect of discrimination against persons with disabilities is the existence of barriers. Many barriers encountered by persons with disabilities are unique to them as members of a minority group. Barriers include *any aspects of the social or physical environment that prohibit meaningful involvement by persons with disabilities* (e.g., stairs for a person in a wheelchair; lack of a telecommunication device [TDD] for a person who cannot hear who is seeking to use the phone; a health service that does not provide an alternative way to communicate for a person who cannot speak).

It is this second aspect of discrimination against persons with disabilities—barriers—that generates an *accommodation imperative* when the exercise of their civil rights is at issue. The accommodation imperative requires that efforts be undertaken to provide an environment that makes an experience available in a meaningful way to the person with a disability. Without the accommodation imperative, the notion of equal opportunity for persons with disabilities may not be viable. In many cases, an opportunity is not equal if there is no accommodation or accessibility. A job on the third floor of a building with no elevator is not an equal opportunity for a person in a wheelchair. An educational program that does not offer an alternative reading method, such as braille or a reader, is not an equal opportunity for a student who is blind.

In order to avoid discrimination, society enters into a contract with a person with a disability. Society agrees to structure or manipulate the social and physical environment in every reasonable way possible with the goal of creating an experience that is a meaningful equal opportunity for the individual with the disability. This obligation may involve an allocation of resources or an expenditure of funds. The person with a disability agrees to make the same effort at citizenship that we expect from everyone else.

The ADA affirms that it is not enough to hang up a sign and say "we do not discriminate on the basis of disability." In order for an opportunity to be truly equitable, more is required from society than a passive commitment to "equal opportunity." Whereas simply eliminating exclusionary policies may at times be sufficient for other protected groups (e.g., racial and ethnic minorities and women), it is not sufficient for persons with disabilities.

It is often a stated goal of nondiscrimination policy for persons in other stigmatized groups to be treated in a neutral fashion or "just like everyone else." The goal may be to "forget" that the individual is a woman or an African-American as standards are applied. It is often said that the law should be administered in a "color-blind" fashion. This is not the goal in providing equal opportunity to persons with disabilities; in fact, the goal may often be the opposite: a recognition of the functional impairment and an effort to adapt an environment or situation so that functioning is enhanced and/or alternatives are discovered that will yield meaningful involvement. The ADA requires a view of the environment as a medium that can provide opportunities to ameliorate the results of functional impairments rather than a series of obstacles that exacerbate an impairment. It requires society to develop alternatives that enable accomplishment of the particular task.

One of the most significant aspects of the accommodation imperative is that it must be individualized. Although persons with disabilities are a group and may be considered a "protected class" for purposes of civil rights, or a set of people defined by particular characteristics in terms of eligibility for certain services and programs, people with disabilities are individuals first. The uniqueness of each person with a disability in terms of how that disability may affect his or her functioning, and in what circumstances, is an essential aspect of considering discrimination against persons with disabilities.

Unlike race and gender, moreover, disability is often a dynamic characteristic. A disability may require no accommodation in one situation and complex technological intervention in another situation. Furthermore, some disabilities change in intensity from day to day or week to week and may require different accommodations at different times. The same impairment often affects different individuals differently. A critical aspect of accommodations is that they be flexible.

Whereas ordinary citizens and national leaders may have a definitive sense of what it means not to discriminate against a racial minority, this is not the case for persons with disabilities. Until recently such persons have been a notably silent and nonvisible minority in society. The addition of the accommodation imperative to the concept of civil rights requires a change in how we think about civil rights.

ATTITUDES TOWARD PERSONS WITH DISABILITIES

Being the target of discrimination and negative attitudes may be the one experience that diverse persons with disabilities have in common. Research documents that persons with disabilities are perceived by persons without disabilities with a range of negative attitudes (English, 1971). Although the percentage of persons in society without disabilities who perceive persons with disabilities negatively is not known precisely, and probably never will be, studies about attitudes toward persons with disabilities have been undertaken since the 1950s.

Several studies have indicated that males have more negative attitudes toward persons with disabilities than do females (English, 1971). Persons in higher income groups and with higher educational levels generally have more favorable attitudes toward persons with disabilities than those in lower income groups and those with lower educational levels (Livneh, 1982). Studies have indicated that mental disabilities are the most negatively perceived of all disabilities (Arangio, 1979). The sources of negative attitudes toward persons with disabilities are many, including sociocultural conditioning and childhood influences (Livneh, 1982). The terms *handicappism, physicalism,* and *normalism* have been offered as disability correlates to *racism* and *sexism* when referring to prejudiced attitudes toward persons with disabilities (Longmore, 1985).

Persons with disabilities have documented and described a number of second-class relationships with society. They have articulated the experience of being invisible or ignored; of engendering discomfort; of being objects of pity; of being adulated as inspirational for overcoming seemingly insurmountable obstacles; of negotiating a bargain with society.

The experience of being repeatedly ignored or unnoticed has been described as one of *disconfirmation*—being denied recognition as a person (Golfus, 1989). Disconfirmation comes in many forms: being deserted by former friends after sustaining an impairment or being dismissed by a receptionist who is too busy with "real work" and "important people." Disconfirmation comes frequently from the very individuals and programs designed to support people with disabilities. Persons with disabilities experience rejection from both services and individuals (e.g., counselors, educators, therapists) because they do not fit into a prescribed mold of behavior or symptoms. The message is: "There's nothing wrong with the program, there's something wrong with you."

Both research studies and individuals with disabilities have frequently described discomfort and embarrassment experienced by persons without disabilities when interacting with persons with disabilities (U.S. Commission on Civil Rights, 1983). People without disabilities may feel unsure as to how to act around a person with a disability. (Should they offer help? Should they ignore the disability? Should they comment on the disability?) The discomfort could reflect an awareness that persons without disabilities are vulnerable to death, injury, and disease—a vulnerability most of us are eager to forget. A person without a disability can become a person with a disability virtually in a matter of seconds. Finally, discomfort may come from a concern about what other people will think about someone who associates with a person with a disability: Will that person be considered second-rate by association? Feelings of discomfort have caused proprietors to reject persons with disabilities from restaurants, movie houses, zoos, and other public places. Proprietors may believe that people with disabilities will drive other customers away because they engender discomfort and even revulsion.

Persons with disabilities are frequently looked on with pity (U.S. Commission on Civil Rights, 1983). This is most clearly seen in fund-raising efforts by nonprofit organizations, which may depict individuals with disabilities in a pity-invoking manner in hopes of appealing to charitable instincts. Feeling pity toward an individual is rarely accompanied by respect or by recognition of the person's dignity. It is grounded in the belief that "I am better than you are." Attitudes of pity and patronization rarely contribute to independence and empowerment; they are more likely to foster dependence and low self-esteem.

Persons with disabilities have often been looked on with horror. Portraying having a disability as a "fate worse than death" sends a clear message to persons with disabilities. This attitude is often utilized to sell insurance policies or to "scare" people with certain conditions into getting treatment so they do not regress and reach this state "worse than death." For example, a recent memo from the general manager of an insurance agency to agents included a photo of a body next to a wrecked car. The memo said: "Do you think he's dead? He's not, but he might have been better off if he were. He is dead from the waist down. He'll never walk again." The memo was intended to inspire agents to sell disability insurance ("Special Issue," 1990).

Many persons with disabilities resent being viewed as heroes or heroines, as remarkable "overcomers," or as inspirations for the average person with average problems. Persons with disabilities may be described as "courageous" or "inspirational" because they accomplish things when they have disabilities, or in spite of the disabilities. Commenting on being repeatedly described as "courageous," Stephen Hawking, the brilliant Cambridge University scientist who has Lou Gehrig's disease (amyotrophic lateral sclerosis), noted his aversion to being repeatedly labeled a superhero because he has a disability. Readers of the *Disability Rag,* a voice of the disability rights movement, noted that being described as "courageous" was the one thing they hated most about how people with disabilities are portrayed in the media ("Special Issue," 1990). Being viewed as courageous does not signify respect or equality but rather holds people with disabilities in a category separate from others.

Many of these attitudes are reflections of a widely held conviction in our society that we should strive for youth, beauty, and success at virtually any cost. This conviction leaves little tolerance for persons with disabilities and little room for an affirmation that persons with disabilities are equal. Furthermore, these attitudes define persons with disabilities from a perspective of society at large, not from the perspective of persons with disabilities themselves.

To negotiate this imposed identity, persons with disabilities have struck a bargain, according to one disability rights activist (Johnson, 1989). Society agrees to accept marginally a person with a disability as long as that person cheerfully strives to be normal. The more normal that person becomes, the more acceptance that person gains. This bargain is an uneasy one for many persons with disabilities and has in part spurred the disability rights movement, which holds that the identity of persons with disabilities will be defined by individuals with disabilities themselves.

Changing attitudes toward persons with disabilities is a long, slow process. Because attitudes are learned and conditioned over many years, changes in those attitudes will take many years. The disability rights movement has initiated changes in recent years to begin that process.

PERSONS WITH DISABILITIES AS A MINORITY
GROUP AND THE DISABILITY RIGHTS MOVEMENT

It has been suggested that the ultimate test of a minority group is self-identification (Hahn, 1985). Persons with disabilities, like other oppressed groups, move to claim the power to define themselves, to develop their own identity, their own culture, their own pride. This movement toward self-identification can be seen in the growth of the disability rights and independent living movements, the evolving political sophistication and power of the disability interest groups in Washington, the changes in language we use to talk about people with disabilities, and the changes in public policies affecting people with disabilities.

Seventy-four percent of people with disabilities surveyed in the 1986 Louis Harris and Associates, Inc., survey said that they feel at least some sense of common identity with other people with disabilities. Forty-five percent said that they feel that people with disabilities are a minority group in the same sense as African-Americans and Hispanics. Those who were younger and who had disabilities beginning at earlier periods in their lives were more likely to see people with disabilities as a minority group.

Persons with disabilities, however, face unique challenges in solidifying as a minority group. Whereas persons with disabilities have the negative experiences of encountering discrimination and demeaning attitudes in common with other minority groups, many of the positive minority group experiences are lacking for them (Johnson, 1987; Kriegel, 1969). Unlike other minority groups, persons with disabilities have generally grown up in isolation from each other, and there is no sense of a subculture or of positive shared experiences with which they can identify (Johnson, 1987; Zola, 1988). Emphasis on functional limitation has encouraged persons with disabilities to "overcome" rather than identify with their disabilities (Hahn, 1985). Some have noted that there is a case to be made for segregated schools for youngsters with disabilities in terms of fostering disability identity and culture (Johnson, 1987; Thomas, 1989).

The trademarks of minority pride, such as slogans, rituals, clothing, hairstyles, and songs, are in their infancy in the disability community. The equivalent of "Black is Beautiful" or "Sisterhood is Powerful" has yet to emerge from the disability community (Zola, 1988). The challenge of turning stigmas into pride is at the heart of solidifying persons with disabilities as a minority. One disability rights commentator noted, "If we neglect the cultural aspects of our movement, we will fail" (Johnson, 1987, p. 9).

Although the emergence of persons with disabilities as a cultural minority is just beginning, the disability rights movement has grown considerably in the last decade. Leadership of disability organizations and interest groups is more and more in the hands of persons with disabilities themselves rather than persons without disabilities. Federal programs that affect persons with disabilities more and more often are being administered by persons with disabilities. The success of advocacy and lobbying efforts by disability interest groups reflects the increased empowerment of persons with disabilities.

At the heart of the emergence of the disability rights movement is the philosophy of independent living. The independent living philosophy emerged in the 1960s, bolstered by the civil rights movement for African-Americans, the women's rights movement, and the tenor of the times, which challenged the status quo. Persons with severe disabilities were seeking alternatives to institutionalization, segregated programs, and service delivery systems that offered limited alternatives and limited support for self-determination. Independent living is a set of values dedicated to self-determination and personal control over one's own life. Equal opportunity to participate in all aspects of society, including freedom of choice and risk taking, is a tenet of the independent living philosophy (DeJong, 1979; Lachat, 1988).

The independent living movement is at the center of the civil rights movement for people with disabilities. The movement is dedicated to liberation for people with disabilities—liberation from limited and second-rate options. The independent living movement has rejected the role of patient for persons with disabilities and embraced consumer-controlled decision making instead. The fact that many disabilities are conditions that may be lifelong has led to a rejection of the medical model, which sets a goal of palliation or cure, and instead calls for a management approach that seeks maximum independence. Living in the community as other members of society do, and not in institutions and segregated settings, is another trademark of independent living.

This consciousness of independent living that has evolved over the last 2 decades has been a significant contributor to the development of a sense of a disability community and a call for civil rights reforms. Independent living has also evolved as an important service delivery model, with hundreds of centers for independent living currently providing services all over the country. The independent living consciousness has shepherded in a gradual shift in policy focus from custody to cure to care to rights.

THE LANGUAGE OF DISABILITY

A recent article in the *Wall Street Journal* about the ADA was entitled "Disabilities Act Crippled by Ambiguity" (Weaver, 1991). In a recent effort to raise money for persons with disabilities, Jerry Lewis described a wheelchair as "that steel imprisonment that long has been deemed the dystrophic child's plight" ("Special Issue," 1990, p. 30).

Contrast these statements with some current posters recently issued by the National Easter Seal Society. In one, a person in a wheelchair sits at the bottom of a flight of stairs and the caption reads: "For some people the search for an apartment is all uphill." Another poster pictures a person's hand meeting another person's hook (prosthetic device) for a handshake. The caption reads "Sometimes the worst thing about having a disability is that people meet it before they meet you" ("Kudos," 1991, p. 36).

The differences in the language of these statements are indicative of efforts to move away from patronizing and stigmatizing descriptors to empowering and respectful terminology. The language also reflects the thinking that the particular impairment of the individual is less of a difficulty than the way in which the individual is received by society at large. In testifying before Congress in 1989 in support of the passage of the ADA, Governor (formerly Senator) Lowell Weicker of Connecticut noted that the biggest obstacle for people with disabilities was not so much what God hath wrought, but rather what man has imposed by custom and law (U.S. Senate Committee on Labor and Human Resources Subcommittee on the Handicapped, 1989).

The language used in the ADA, and throughout this book, is what is often called the "people first" language (e.g., individuals with disabilities or persons with disabilities). This terminology evolved as a rejection of descriptors that focus on the impairment, not the person (e.g., the deaf, the blind, the disabled, cripples).

The terminology *disabled* and *disability* is generally preferred to *handicapped* and *handicap*. In proposing changing the name of the U.S. Senate Subcommittee on the Handicapped to the U.S. Senate Subcommittee on Disability Policy, Senator Tom Harkin (Iowa) noted that the term *handicapped* has a negative connotation and that it was the responsibility of the Subcommittee to do the opposite of what the name implied. "It is our responsibility to develop public policy which removes the barriers in this society for people with disabilities and enables them to pursue their independence in an environment of respect and support," he noted (Newsletter Staff, 1989).

Other important national organizations have also changed their names in recent years. The National Council on the Handicapped is now the National Council on Disability. The President's Committee on Employment of the Handicapped is now the President's Committee for the Employment of People with Disabilities. The American Association of Mental Deficiency is now the American Association on Mental Retardation.

In 1991 a New York foundation—the National Cristina Foundation—sponsored a contest offering a $50,000 reward to whomever could come up with a word or phrase for the abilities of people with disabilities. This phrase is intended to convey a positive empowering message about persons with disabilities rather than the negative, demeaning messages so much of the terminology implies. The winning phrase was "people with differing abilities."

There are differences of opinion about the proper language of disability in the disability community and elsewhere. Some believe that the energy spent on determining the proper language is better spent on "real" issues, such as accessing personal assistant services ("Special Issue," 1990). Some people with disabilities see their disabilities as central features of their identities and choose to call themselves "deaf people" or "cripples" (Zola, 1988). To them, to consider the disability as a secondary feature is not being true to their identity. Some see preoccupation with particular language and terminology as evasive, euphemistic, and eventually engendering a backlash. In fact, one entry to the contest sponsored by the National Cristina Foundation was "severely euphemized" ("Special Issue," 1990, p. 14).

LEGISLATIVE BUILDING BLOCKS FOR THE ADA

The ADA is the culmination of years of legislative action. Legislation for people with disabilities can be thought of in at least three categories: programs and services, income maintenance, and civil rights. Numerous pieces of civil rights legislation promoting the full participation and independence of persons with disabilities predate the adoption of the ADA. In addition, numerous programs and service delivery systems that provide education, training, and support services for persons with disabilities have been established by the federal government. Although some of these programs have been criticized for promoting dependence rather than independence (Berkowitz, 1987), many are intended to support the goals of the ADA.

Since the 1970s a number of federal laws have made incremental changes that created the possibility of enacting the ADA. These laws are grounded in the core concepts that pervade the ADA: full participation and independence. Although bills have been repeatedly introduced since the mid-1960s to amend generic civil rights laws to include persons with disabilities (Burgdorf, 1990), none of them received serious legislative consideration. In 1977 the White House Conference on Handicapped Individuals recommended amending all titles of the Civil Rights Act of 1964 to include discrimination on the basis of disability. Legislation introduced in the mid-1980s to provide antidiscrimination protection for persons with HIV infection and AIDS were likewise unsuccessful in gaining serious legislative consideration.

In 1986 the National Council on Disability, a presidentially appointed disability policy agency, issued a report to the President entitled *Toward Independence* and recommended the enactment of comprehensive antidiscrimination legislation for people with disabilities. This report was followed up in 1988 by another report, *On the Threshold of Independence* (Farbman, 1988), which included a draft of the legislation. At that same time the Presidential Commission on the Human Immunodeficiency Virus Epidemic (1988) issued its final report calling for similar legislation.

The National Council asked then-Senator Weicker, the historical legislative champion of disability rights, to introduce the legislation. Senator Weicker agreed. With the unique opportunity of a civil rights initiative emanating from a Republican administration agency, the well-organized disability interest groups, joined by the newly emerging AIDS interest groups, seized the opportunity for action. It was at this point that Congress seriously began to consider comprehensive antidiscrimination protection for persons with disabilities.

The following federal laws could be considered legislative building blocks for the ADA.

The Architectural Barriers Act

The Architectural Barriers Act of 1968 mandated that all buildings constructed, altered, or financed by the federal government after 1969 be accessible to and usable by persons with physical disabilities. In 1973, The Architectural and Transportation Barriers Compliance Board (ATBCB) was established to develop guidelines and accessibility standards and to enforce these standards. The guidelines took effect in September 1982.

The Rehabilitation Act

In 1973, Sections 501, 503, and 504 were enacted as part of the Rehabilitation Act. Section 504 prohibits discrimination against otherwise qualified persons with disabilities in any program or activity receiving federal funds and in executive agencies and the Postal Service. Sections 501 and 503 require affirmative action plans for the hiring and advancement of persons with disabilities in the federal government and by any contractors receiving contracts over $2,500 from the federal government.

Section 504 is the most significant building block for the ADA. Its 17-year history of implementation has delineated many of the core concepts of the ADA, such as *reasonable accommodation* and *undue burden*. Numerous court decisions have examined questions raised by Section 504, such as how to determine when a person with a disability is "otherwise qualified," how to determine when a reasonable accommodation crosses the line and becomes an undue burden, and how to determine when a person with a disability presents a threat to the health and/or safety of others. The implementing regulations for Section 504, which emanate from every federal agency and are voluminous, have offered definitions of key terms such as who is and is not considered a person with a disability.

In 1987, Section 504 was amended by the Civil Rights Restoration Act. This legislation overturned the Supreme Court's *Grove City College v. Bell* (1984) decision and defined coverage of Section 504 as broad (e.g., extending to an entire university) rather than narrow (e.g., extending just to one department of the university) when federal funds were involved.

This amendment to Section 504 was particularly significant as a building block for the ADA because of the Humphrey–Harkin provision. This provision incorporated the standards and approach of the Supreme Court's *School Board of Nassau County, Fla. v. Arline* (1987) decision and clarified that, if an individual with a disability posed a "direct threat" to the health or safety of others, that individual was not covered by Section 504. The amendment was written in response to concerns that employers might be required to hire a person with a contagious disease or infection, especially AIDS or HIV infection, when that individual posed a direct threat to others. The "direct threat" language is incorporated in the ADA.

The Education for All Handicapped Children Act

In 1975, the Education for All Handicapped Children Act (PL 94-142) was enacted. Now called the Individuals with Disabilities Education Act (1990) this law mandates a free, appropriate public education for all children with disabilities. It requires that they be educated in the "least restrictive environment," or with their nondisabled peers to the maximum extent appropriate. The integration of students with disabilities is often called mainstreaming. Over 4 million students with disabilities are currently in programs receiving federal support.

The Developmental Disabilities Assistance and Bill of Rights Act

The Developmental Disabilities Assistance and Bill of Rights Act was enacted in 1975 also. This legislation includes a small federal grant program administered by state Developmental Disabilities Councils that is intended to coordinate and fund services for persons with developmental disabilities or severe long-term disabilities the onset of which is prior to age 22, and whose needs are likely to be lifelong. Largely in response to substandard and abusive situations in institutions for persons with mental retardation, the Bill of Rights declared that persons with developmental disabilities have a right to appropriate treatment, services, and habilitation that maximize the developmental potential of the person and are provided in a setting as nonrestrictive as possible to the person's personal liberty. Although not enforceable, the Bill of Rights is a statement of Congressional intent.

The Developmental Disabilities Act also established a system of Protection and Advocacy organizations in every state. These organizations are independent of any service-providing organization and advocate for and represent the rights of persons with developmental disabilities. In addition, they provide information and referral services.

The Civil Rights of Institutionalized Persons Act

In 1980, Congress passed the Civil Rights of Institutionalized Persons Act authorizing the U.S. Department of Justice to sue states for alleged violations of the rights of persons living in institutions, including persons in mental hospitals or facilities for persons with mental retardation.

The Voting Accessibility for the Elderly and Handicapped Act

In 1984, Congress enacted the Voting Accessibility for the Elderly and Handicapped Act. The law requires that registration and polling places for federal elections be accessible to persons with disabilities.

The Air Carriers Access Act

In 1986, Congress acted to overturn a Supreme Court decision that held that air carriers operating at federally funded airports were not subject to Section 504. The Air Carriers Access Act of 1986 prohibits discrimination against persons with disabilities by all air carriers and provides for enforcement under the U.S. Department of Transportation.

The Fair Housing Amendments Act

Although housing was originally included as a part of the first version of the ADA, it was dropped when the opportunity to include persons with disabilities in the Fair Housing Amendments Act of 1988 materialized. This act added persons with disabilities to the list of groups protected from discrimination in housing. This was the first time the antidiscrimination mandate for persons with disabilities was extended into the private sector. The law mandates accessibility standards for all new housing construction for multifamily dwellings and requires that persons with disabilities be able to adapt their dwelling places to meet their needs. Many of the provisions that appear in the ADA come directly from this legislation.

GROWTH OF DISABILITY INTEREST GROUPS

The progression of disability rights legislation is reflected by the remarkable growth and increasing sophistication of the disability interest groups in Washington, D.C., over the last several years. The interest groups are organized as a coalition called the Consortium for Citizens with Disabilities (CCD). When the CCD was first established in 1973, there were 18 members. Their focus was to promote the enactment of the Developmental Disabilities Act of 1975. Today there are over 90 members. They are organized into task forces concerned with topics ranging from the budget to health research to transportation to social security to taxes. The growth in both volume and breadth of issues addressed by the CCD is noteworthy.

Perhaps even more impressive than the growth in numbers and substantive issues considered by the CCD is the growth in sophistication, lobbying skill, and credibility of these organizations. In the early 1980s, virtually all disability legislation was scrutinized at the subcommittee and committee levels of Congress but never by the whole membership of the Senate or the House of Representatives. Generally the legislation was what was referred to as "greased" by the time it came up for consideration on the floor of either body. In fact, this was the goal. Examination by the full Senate or House usually meant that bases had not been covered and that trouble was brewing.

This situation changed dramatically with consideration of the Civil Rights Restoration Act of 1987 and the Fair Housing Amendments Act of 1988. Both these pieces of legislation were large civil rights coalition bills, and the disability interest groups joined generic civil rights groups—for minorities, women, and elders—to lobby for one piece of legislation. The participation by disability groups in a generic civil rights coalition meant participation in mainstream public policy, which brought with it a more central position on the policy agenda and greater public scrutiny.

The disability interest groups learned how to play hardball politics in the big league—how to lobby every member of Congress, not just members of committees, who were often, by definition, advocates. They learned how to manipulate Senate and House floor procedures and count votes. They learned strategies from the more experienced traditional civil rights groups about how to gain support for legislation and undermine the opposition. They learned how to be a part of a mammoth coalition.

In turn, the general civil rights groups learned that disability rights is an equal partner in the civil rights movement. They learned what a reasonable accommodation is and how it redefines our traditional thinking about what antidiscrimination protection means. They got to know people with disabilities and saw discrimination from a new vantage point. Everyone learned about the new disability—AIDS.

The ADA was the result of a rich history of legislation, lobbying, and advocacy. A strong foundation was in place in terms of both policy and politics.

CONCLUSIONS

The ADA has received impressive accolades since its enactment. It has been called the Declaration of Independence for People with Disabilities, the Emancipation Proclamation for People with Disabilities, and the most significant piece of civil rights legislation enacted since 1964.

The legislative history of the ADA represents the most comprehensive examination of the experience of being a person with a disability that has ever been undertaken by the U.S. Congress. It is also a spectacular affirmation of the rights of persons with disabilities. The ADA was examined by five full committees in Congress. It was debated at length by the entire bodies of both the Senate and the House of Representatives. It was the subject of prolonged debate and negotiation with the highest level officials at the White House. It was considered by the tax-writing committees in Congress when a tax credit was added to subsidize small businesses for ADA-related expenses. The ADA was personally endorsed and promoted by the President, complete with a signing ceremony at the White House. All of these are dramatic firsts for disability legislation. They all took place within 15 months.

In 1987, Edward Berkowitz began his book *Disabled Policy* with the statement that "America has no disability policy." He went on to describe the many contradictory, uncoordinated, and disparate programs and policies intended to serve persons with disabilities—some promoting dependence and segregation and others supporting independence and integration. With the enactment of the ADA, we can say that America at last has chosen the goals and some of the methods of its disability policy. We have chosen independence over dependence and integration over segregation. The goals for the nation articulated by the ADA will serve as standards against which we can measure and modify other disability policies, programs, and services for persons with disabilities.

The ADA is not expected to be a panacea. The ADA is a law that sends a clear message about what our society's attitudes should be toward persons with disabilities. The ADA is an orienting framework that can be used to construct a comprehensive service delivery system. As some have said, "The ADA will not get you out of bed in the morning." The ADA is intended to open the doors of society and keep them open, but its effect will be limited unless we are as strongly committed to providing adequate education, training, and support services as we are to eradicating discrimination.

REFERENCES

Air Carriers Access Act of 1986, 49 U.S.C. app. §1374(c) (1986).

Arangio, A.J. (1979). *Behind the stigma of epilepsy: An inquiry into the centuries-old discrimination against persons with epilepsy.* Lanham, MD: Epilepsy Foundation of America.

Architectural Barriers Act of 1968, 42 U.S.C. §§4151–4157 (1968).

Berkowitz, E.D. (1987). *Disabled policy: America's programs for the handicapped.* Cambridge, MA: Cambridge University Press.

Brown, D. (1981). Jobs and disabled women: Double discrimination and little help from the women's movement. *Disabled USA* (President's Committee for Employment of Persons with Disabilities) *4*(8).

Burgdorf, R.L. (1990). History. In *The Americans With Disabilities Act: A practical and legal guide to impact, enforcement and compliance* (pp. 9–34). Washington, DC: Bureau of National Affairs.

Burkhauser, R.V., Haveman, R.H., & Wolfe, B.L. (1990). *The changing economic condition of the disabled: A two-decade review of economic well-being.* Washington, DC: National Council on Disability.

Civil Rights Act of 1964, codified as amended in scattered sections of 42 U.S.C. (1988).

Civil Rights of Institutionalized Persons Act of 1980, 42 U.S.C. §1997 *et seq.* (1980).

Civil Rights Restoration Act of 1987, 20 U.S.C. §168 *et seq.*, 29 U.S.C. §706, 42 U.S.C. §2000 (1987).

DeJong, G. (1979). *The movement for independent living: Origins, ideology, and implications for disability research.* East Lansing: Michigan State University.

Developmental Disabilities Assistance and Bill of Rights Act of 1975, 42 U.S.C. §§6000–6081 (1975).

Education for All Handicapped Children Act of 1975, 20 U.S.C. §§1232, 1401, 1405–1420, 1453 (1975).

English, R.W. (1971). Correlates of stigma towards physically disabled persons. *Rehabilitation Research and Practice Review, 2*(4), 1–17.

Fair Housing Amendments Act of 1988, 42 U.S.C. §§3601–3619 (1988).

Farbman, A. (Ed.). (1988). *On the threshold of independence.* Washington, DC: National Council on Disability.

Golfus, B. (1989, November/December). Disconfirmation. *Disability Rag,* pp. 1, 4–8.

Grove City College v. Bell, 465 U.S. 555 (1984).

Hahn, H. (1985). Disability policy and the problem of discrimination. *American Behavioural Scientist, 28,* 293–318.

Individuals with Disabilities Education Act of 1992, 20 U.S.C. §1400 *et seq.* (1991).

Johnson, M. (1987, January/February). Emotion and pride: The search for a disability culture. *Disability Rag,* pp. 1, 4–6.

Johnson, M. (1989, September/October). The bargain. *Disability Rag* pp. 5–8.

Kriegel, L. (1969). Uncle Tom and Tiny Tim: Some reflections on the cripple as Negro. *American Scholar, 38,* 412–430.

Kudos. (1991, March/April). *Disability Rag,* p. 36.

Lachat, M.A. (1988). *The independent living service model: Historical roots, core elements and current practice.* Hampton, NH: Center for Resource Management, Inc.

Livneh, H. (1982). On the origins of negative attitudes toward people with disabilities. *Rehabilitation Literature, 13,* 338–347.

Longmore, P. (1985). A note on language and the social identity of disabled people. *American Behavioural Scientist, 28,* 419–423.

Louis Harris and Associates, Inc. (1986). *Disabled Americans' self perceptions: Bringing disabled Americans into the mainstream.* New York: Author.

National Council on Disability. (1986). *Toward independence.* Washington, DC: Author.

National Council on Disability. (1988). *On the threshold of independence.* Washington, DC: Author.

Newsletter Staff. (1989, November 11). Resolution introduced to change Senate Subcommittee name. *National Association of Rehabilitation Facilities Rehabilitation Review* p. 4.

Presidential Commission on the Human Immunodeficiency Virus Epidemic. (1988). *Report of the Presidential Commission on the Human Immunodeficiency Virus Epidemic.* Washington, DC: U.S. Government Printing Office.

Rehabilitation Act of 1973, 29 U.S.C. §§791–794 (1988 & Supp. I 1989).

School Board of Nassau County, Fla. v. Arline, 107 S.Ct. 1123 (1987).

Special issue: We wish we wouldn't see . . . . (1990, Winter). *Disability Rag.*

Thomas, R. (1989). Testimony before the National Council on Disability, June 8, 1989. In *The education of students with disabilities: Where do we stand? Hearings before the National Council on Disability* (pp. 260–265). Washington, DC: National Council on Disability.

U.S. Commission on Civil Rights. (1983). *Accommodating the spectrum of individual abilities.* Washington, DC: Author.

U.S. Senate Committee on Labor and Human Resources. (1989, May 9, 10, 16; June 22). *Hearings on S. 933, the Americans with Disabilities Act of 1989 (S. Hrg. 101–156).* Washington, DC: U.S. Government Printing Office.

U.S. Senate Committee on Labor and Human Resources Subcommittee on the Handicapped. (1989). *Hearings on S. 933, Act of 1989 (testimony of Lowell W. Weicker) (S. Hrg. 101–156).* Washington, DC: U.S. Government Printing Office.

Voting Accessibility for the Elderly and Handicapped Act of 1984, 42 U.S.C. §1973 (1984).

Wagner, M. (1989). *The transition experience of youths with disabilities: A report from the National Longitudinal Transition Study.* Menlo Park, CA: SRI International.

Weaver, C.L. (1991, January 31). Disabilities act cripples through ambiguity. *The Wall Street Journal.*

Zola, I.K. (1988). The language of disability: Problems of politics and practice. *Journal of the Disability Advisory Council of Australia, 1*(3), 13–21.

Chapter 2

The History of the ADA

A Movement Perspective

Arlene Mayerson

The history of the Americans with Disabilities Act (ADA) began long ago in cities and towns throughout the United States when people with disabilities began to challenge societal barriers that excluded them from their communities, and when parents of children with disabilities began to fight against the exclusion and segregation of their children. It began with the establishment of local groups to advocate for the rights of people with disabilities. It began with the establishment of the independent living movement, which challenged the notion that people with disabilities needed to be institutionalized and which fought for and provided services for people with disabilities to live in the community.

The ADA owes its birthright not to any one person or any few, but to the many thousands of people who make up the disability rights movement—people who have worked for years organizing and attending protests, licking envelopes, sending out alerts, drafting legislation, speaking, testifying, negotiating, lobbying, filing lawsuits, and being arrested—doing whatever they could for a cause in which they believed. There are far too many people whose commitment and hard work contributed to the passage of this historic piece of disability civil rights legislation to be able to give appropriate credit by name. Without the work of so many—without the disability rights movement—there would be no ADA.

Over the last couple of decades, the disability rights movement has made the injustices faced by people with disabilities visible to the American public and to politicians. This required reversing the centuries-long history of "out of sight, out of mind" that the segregation of persons with disability served to promote.

The disability rights movement adopted many of the strategies of the civil rights movements before it. Like the African-Americans who sat in at segregated lunch counters and refused to move to the back of the bus, people with disabilities sat in federal buildings, obstructed the movement of inaccessible buses, and marched through the streets to protest injustice. In addition, like the civil rights movements before it, the disability rights movement sought justice in the courts and in the halls of Congress.

SECTION 504—CLASS STATUS AND ANTIDISCRIMINATION

From a legal perspective, a profound and historical shift in disability public policy occurred in 1973 with the passage of Section 504 of the 1973 Rehabilitation Act.[1] Section 504 (29 U.S.C. §794), which banned discrimination on the basis of disability by recipients of federal funds, was modeled after previous laws that banned race-, ethnic origin–, and sex-based discrimination by federal funds recipients.

For the first time, the exclusion and segregation of people with disabilities was viewed as discrimination. Previously, it had been assumed that the problems faced by people with disabilities—such as unemployment and lack of education—were inevitable consequences of the physical or mental limitations imposed by the disabilities themselves. Enactment of Section 504 evidenced Congress' recognition that the inferior social and economic status of people with disabilities was not a consequence of the disabilities themselves, but instead was a result of societal barriers and prejudices. This shift in public policy is well portrayed in this statement made by Senator Williams prior to the enactment of the 1973 Rehabilitation Act:

> For too long, we have been dealing with [the handicapped] out of charity . . . . This is medieval treatment for a very current problem . . . . Most of us see the handicapped only in terms of stereotypes that are relevant for extreme cases. This ancient attitude is in part the result of the historical separation of our handicapped population . . . . I wish it to be said of America in the 1970's that when its attention at last returned to domestic needs, it made a strong and new commitment of equal opportunity and equal justice under law . . . . The handicapped are one part of our Nation that have been denied these fundamental rights for too long. It is time for the Congress and the nation to assure that these rights are no longer denied. (U.S. Senate, 1972, pp. 3321, 3322)

As with racial minorities and women, Congress recognized that legislation was necessary to eradicate discriminatory policies and practices. As stated in the Senate report accompanying the 1974 amendments:

> Section 504 was patterned after, and is almost identical to, the anti-discrimination language of section 601 of the Civil Rights Act of 1964 [prohibiting race discrimination in federally funded programs] and section 901 of the Education Amendments of 1972 [prohibiting sex discrimination in federally funded education programs]. The section therefore constitutes the establishment of a broad government policy that programs receiving federal financial assistance shall be operated without discrimination on the basis of handicap. (U.S. Senate Committee on Labor and Human Resources, 1974, p. 39)

Section 504 was also historical because for the first time people with disabilities were viewed as a class—as a minority group. Previously, public policy had been characterized by addressing the needs of particular disabilities by category based on diagnosis. Each disability group was seen as separate, with differing needs. Section 504 recognized that, although there are major physical and mental variations in different disabilities, people with disabilities as a group face similar discrimination in employment, education, and access to society. People with disabilities were seen as a legitimate minority, subject to discrimination and deserving of basic civil rights protections. This "class status" concept has been critical in the development of the movement and advocacy efforts. The coalition of people with disabilities has been constantly put to the test by attempts to remove protections for particular groups. The history of the ADA is a testament to the movement's commitment to solidarity among people with different disabilities.

After Section 504 established the fundamental civil right of nondiscrimination in 1973, the next step was to define what nondiscrimination meant in the context of disability. How was it the

---

[1]In addition to the 1973 Rehabilitation Act, Congress enacted several other pieces of legislation designed to promote equal opportunity and integration of people with disabilities into the mainstream of American life. Chronologically, these statutes included the Architectural Barriers Act of 1968 (42 U.S.C. §4141 *et seq.* [1968]), which required federally funded or leased buildings to be accessible, and the Urban Mass Transportation Act of 1970 (49 U.S.C. §1612 [1970]), which required eligible jurisdictions to provide accessibility plans for mass transportation.

same as or different from race and sex discrimination? The U.S. Department of Health, Education, and Welfare (DHEW) had been given the task of promulgating regulations to implement Section 504 that would serve as guidelines for all other federal agencies. These regulations became the focus of attention for the disability rights movement for the next 4 years. During this time the movement grew in sophistication, skill, and visibility. The first task was to assure that the regulations provided meaningful antidiscrimination protections. It was not enough to remove policy barriers; it was imperative that the regulations mandated affirmative conduct to remove architectural and communication barriers and to provide accommodations.

The second step was to force a recalcitrant agency to get the regulations out. All over the country people with disabilities staged sit-ins at DHEW buildings. The longest sit-in was in San Francisco, lasting 28 days (Craib, 1977). A lawsuit was filed, hearings before Congress were organized, testimony was delivered to Congressional committees, negotiations were held, and letters were written. The disability community mobilized a successful campaign using a variety of strategies, and on May 4, 1977, the Section 504 regulations were issued (DHEW, 1977). It is these regulations that form the basis of the ADA (Mayerson, 1991, p. 499).

In the early 1980s the disability community was called on to defend the hard-fought-for Section 504 regulations from attack. After taking office, President Ronald Reagan established the Task Force on Regulatory Relief under the leadership of then–Vice President George Bush. The mission of the Task Force was to "deregulate" regulations that were burdensome to businesses. The Section 504 regulations were chosen for deregulation (Babcock, 1982). This news sent a current throughout the disability movement across the country, which quickly mobilized a multitiered strategy to preserve the regulations.

For 2 years, representatives from the disability community met with administration officials to explain why the various deregulation proposals must not be adopted. These high-level meetings would not have continued or been successful without the constant bombardment of letters to the White House from people with disabilities and parents of children with disabilities around the country protesting any attempt to deregulate Section 504.

After a remarkable show of force and commitment by the disability community, the Administration announced a halt to all attempts to deregulate Section 504 (Barringer, 1983). This was a tremendous victory for the disability movement. Those 2 years proved to be invaluable in setting the stage for the ADA. Not only were the Section 504 regulations—which form the basis of the ADA—preserved, but it was at this time that high officials of what later became the Bush administration received an education on the importance of the principles of nondiscrimination contained in the Section 504 regulations in the lives of people with disabilities.

DISABILITY RIGHTS AND THE SUPREME COURT

Civil Rights Legislation

During much of the 1980s, the disability community's efforts in Washington were focused on reinstating civil rights protections that had been stripped away by negative Supreme Court decisions. The longest legislative battle was fought over the Civil Rights Restoration Act, first introduced in 1984 and finally passed in 1988. This act sought to overturn *Grove City College v. Bell* (1984), a Supreme Court decision that had significantly restricted the reach of all the statutes prohibiting race-, ethnic origin–, sex-, or disability-based discrimination by recipients of federal funds. Because the court decision affected all of these constituencies, the effort to overturn the decision required a coalition effort. For the first time, representatives of the disability community worked in leadership roles with representatives of minority and women's groups on a major piece of civil rights legislation.

Working in coalition again in 1988, the civil rights community promoted the passage of the Fair Housing Amendments Act (1988) to improve enforcement mechanisms, and for the first time disability antidiscrimination provisions were included in a traditional civil rights statute banning race discrimination. During these years, alliances were forged within the civil rights community that became critical in the fight for the passage of the ADA. Because of its commitment to disability civil rights, the Leadership Conference on Civil Rights played an important role in securing passage of the ADA.

Antidiscrimination Legislation

During the 1980s it also became clear to the disability community that it should play a very active role in Supreme Court litigation under Section 504. The first Section 504 case that was decided by the Supreme Court, *Southeastern Community College v. Davis* (1979), revealed what was at best a lack of understanding and at worst a hostility toward even applying the concept of discrimination to exclusion based on disability. In that case, a woman with hearing impairment was seeking admission to the nursing program of Southeastern Community College. The court found that Ms. Davis's hearing impairment rendered her unqualified to participate in the program because she would not be able to fulfill all of the clinical requirements. However, the Court did not limit itself to the fate of Ms. Davis, but included within the decision several very broad negative interpretations of Section 504. In fact, the *Davis* decision cast doubt on whether those entities covered by Section 504 would be required to take any affirmative steps to accommodate the needs of persons with disabilities. Contrary to established Court doctrine, the Section 504 regulations that had been issued by the DHEW were given little deference by the Court. Ironically, the Court attributed this lack of deference to the fact that the DHEW had been recalcitrant in issuing the regulations.

After the *Davis* decision, it was clear that the Supreme Court needed to be educated on the issue of disability-based discrimination and the role that it plays in people's lives. Moreover, it was clear to the disability community that the focus of its efforts in any future Supreme Court litigation must be to reinforce the validity of the 1977 DHEW regulations. In the next case to be granted review by the Supreme Court, *Consolidated Rail Corporation v. Darrone* (1984), the disability community focused its efforts on educating the Court and bolstering the validity of the DHEW regulations interpreting Section 504. The issue in *Consolidated Rail Corporation* was whether employment discrimination was covered by the antidiscrimination provisions of Section 504. In order to educate the court on the pervasive role of discrimination in the unemployment and underemployment of persons with disabilities, the Disability Rights Education and Defense Fund (DREDF) filed an *amicus* brief on behalf of 63 national, state, and local organizations dedicated to securing the civil rights of persons with disabilities. This *amicus* brief served not only to educate the Court on discriminatory employment policies and practices, but also to demonstrate to the Court that these issues concern the millions of Americans affiliated with the organizations that filed the brief. DREDF also worked very closely with the lawyer representing the plaintiff in the lawsuit in order to present to the court the best legal arguments on the validity of the 1977 DHEW regulations, which had included employment discrimination within the coverage of Section 504. The decision in *Consolidated Rail Corporation v. Darrone* marked a significant victory for the disability rights community. The Court found that employment discrimination was in fact prohibited by Section 504 and, equally importantly, that the regulations issued in 1977 by the DHEW were entitled to great deference by the courts. It is these regulations, elevated by the Court in *Consolidated Rail Corporation*, that formed the basis of the ADA.

The disability community continued its active involvement in Supreme Court cases involving Section 504 throughout the 1980s. In 1987, the Court was presented with the issue of whether people with contagious diseases are covered by Section 504. Although the case involved a woman with tuberculosis, it became clear throughout the country that the Court's decision in this case would be critical for protecting people with HIV infection against discrimination. The disability rights community worked closely with the lawyers representing the woman with tuberculosis and filed numerous *amicus* briefs in the Supreme Court, including a congressional brief by DREDF that set forth the legislative history that served as the foundation of the Court's decision. The Court's decision in *School Board of Nassau County, Fla. v. Arline* (1987) became the basis for coverage of people with AIDS under Section 504 and the ADA. Working on the *Arline* case also provided a critical opportunity for lawyers in the disability rights community and lawyers in the AIDS community to work together closely and form alliances that would prove critical in the battle to secure passage of the ADA.

During the 1980s the disability community was also successful in overturning by legislation several disability-specific negative Supreme Court rulings. Legislation was passed to reinstate the application of antidiscrimination provisions to all airlines (Air Carriers Access Act of 1986, overturning *U.S. Department of Transportation v. Paralyzed Veterans of America* [1986]); the right to sue states for violations of Section 504 (Civil Rights and Remedies Equalization Act of 1986, overturning *Atascadeco State Hospital v. Scanlon* [1985]); and the right of parents to recover attorney fees under the Individuals with Disabilities Education Act (The Handicapped Children's Protection Act of 1986, overturning *Smith v. Robinson* [1984]). These legislative victories further advanced the reputation of the disability community and its advocates in Congress. The respect for the legal, organizational, and negotiation skills gained during these legislative efforts formed the basis of working relationships with members of Congress and officials of the administration that proved indispensable in passing the ADA. By friend and foe alike, the disability community was taken seriously—it had become a political force to be reckoned with in Congress, in the voting booth, and in the media.

THE FINAL STEPS TOWARD THE ADA

The ADA as we know it today has gone through numerous drafts, revisions, negotiations, and amendments since the first version was introduced in 1988. Spurred by a draft bill prepared by the National Council on Disability (Farbman, 1988), an independent federal agency whose members were appointed by President Reagan, Senator Weicker and Representative Coelho introduced the first version of the ADA in April 1988 in the 100th Congress.

The disability community began to educate people with disabilities about the ADA and to gather evidence to support the need for broad antidiscrimination protections. A national campaign was initiated to write "discrimination diaries." People with disabilities were asked to document daily instances of inaccessibility and discrimination. The diaries served not only as testimonials of discrimination, but also to raise consciousness about the barriers to daily living that were simply tolerated as a part of life. Justin Dart, chair of the Congressional Task Force on the Rights and Empowerment of People with Disabilities, traversed the country holding public hearings that were attended by thousands of people with disabilities, their friends, and their families documenting the injustice of discrimination in the lives of people with disabilities.

In September 1988, joint hearings were held before the Senate Subcommittee on Disability Policy and the House Subcommittee on Select Education (U.S. Senate Committee on Labor and Human Resources Subcommittee on the Handicapped and U.S. House of Representatives Committee on Education and Labor Subcommittee on Select Education, 1988). Witnesses with a wide variety of disabilities, such as blindness, deafness, Down syndrome, and HIV infection, as well as parents of children with disabilities, testified about architectural and communication barriers and the pervasiveness of stereotyping and prejudice. A room that seated over 700 overflowed with persons with disabilities, parents, and advocates. After the hearing, a commitment was made by Senator Kennedy, chair of the Labor and Human Resources Committee, Senator Harkin, chair of the Subcommittee on Disability Policy, and Representative Owens of the House Subcommittee on Select Education, that a comprehensive disability civil rights bill would be a top priority for the next Congress. At the same time, both presidential candidates, Vice President Bush and Governor Dukakis, endorsed broad civil rights protections for people with disabilities. The disability community was determined to ensure that President Bush would make good on his campaign promise and invoked it repeatedly during the legislative process.

On May 9, 1989, Senators Harkin and Durrenberger and Representatives Coelho and Fish jointly introduced the new ADA in the 101st Congress. From that moment, the disability community mobilized, organizing a multilayered strategy for passage. A huge coalition was assembled by the Consortium on Citizens with Disabilities that included disability organizations, the Leadership Conference on Civil Rights, and an array of religious, labor, and civic organizations.

A team of lawyers and advocates worked on drafting regulations and on the various and complex legal issues that were continually arising. Top-level negotiators and policy analysts strategized with members of Congress and their staffs. Disability organizations informed and rallied their members, and a lobbying system was developed using members of the disability community from around the country. Witnesses came in from all over the country to testify before Congressional committees. Lawyers and others prepared written answers to the hundreds of questions posed by members of Congress and by businesses. Task forces were formed, networks were established to evoke responses from the community by telephone or mail, and demonstrations were planned—the disability rights movement coalesced around a single goal: passage of the ADA.

From the beginning, the "class" concept prevailed—groups representing specific disabilities and specialized issues vowed to work on all of the issues affecting all persons with disabilities. This commitment was constantly put to the test. The disability community as a whole resisted any proposals made by various members of Congress to exclude people with AIDS or mental illness or to otherwise narrow the class of people covered.

Even at the 11th hour, after 2 years of endless work and a Senate and House vote in favor of the act, the disability community held fast with the AIDS community to eliminate an amendment that would have excluded food-handlers with AIDS (Fullwood, 1990; Kenworthy, 1990a; U.S. House of Representatives, 1990), running the risk of indefinitely postponing passage or even losing the bill. Likewise, even if it was an issue that did not particularly affect their constituencies, all of the groups held fast against amendments to water down the transportation provisions (Kenworthy, 1990b).

The underlying principle of the ADA was to extend the basic civil rights protections covering minorities and women to people with disabilities. The 1964 Civil Rights Act prohibited employment discrimination by the private sector against women and racial and ethnic minorities and banned discrimination against minorities in public accommodations. Before the ADA, no federal law prohibited private sector discrimination against people with disabilities, absent a federal grant or contract.

The job of the disability rights movement during the ADA legislative process was to demonstrate to Congress and the American people the need for comprehensive civil rights protections to eradicate fundamental injustice—to demonstrate not only how this injustice harms the individual subjected to it, but also how it harms our society.

The first hearing in the 101st Senate on the new ADA was a historical event and set the tone for future hearings and lobbying efforts. It was kicked off by the primary sponsors talking about their personal experiences with disability. Senator Harkin spoke of his brother, who is deaf; Senator Kennedy spoke of his son, who has had a leg amputation; and Representative Coelho, who has epilepsy, spoke about how the discrimination he faced almost destroyed him.

The witnesses spoke of their own experiences with discrimination. A young woman who has cerebral palsy told the Senators about a local movie theater that would not let her attend because of her disability (U.S. Senate Committee on Labor and Human Resources Subcommittee on the Handicapped, 1989, p. 64, statement of Lisa Carl). When her mother called the theater to protest that this attitude "sounded like discrimination," the theater owner stated "I don't care what it sounds like." This story became a symbol for the ADA and was mentioned throughout the floor debates and at the signing. The members of Congress and the President related this story to demonstrate that America "*does* care what it sounds like" and will no longer tolerate this type of discrimination.

A Vietnam veteran who had been paralyzed during the war and came home using a wheelchair testified that when he got home and could not get out of his housing project, on the bus, or off the curb because of inaccessibility and could not get a job because of discrimination, he realized he had fought for everyone but himself—and he vowed to fight tirelessly for passage of the ADA (U.S. Senate Committee on Labor and Human Resources, 1989, pp. 62–64, statement of Perry Tillman).

The President of Gallaudet University gave compelling testimony about what life is like for someone who is deaf, faced with pervasive communication barriers. The audience was filled with Gallaudet students who waved their hands in approval (U.S. Senate Committee on Labor and Human Resources, 1989, pp. 11–14).

A woman testified that, when she lost her breast to cancer, she also lost her job and, as a person with a history of cancer, could not find another one (U.S. Senate Committee on Labor and Human Resources Subcommittee on the Handicapped, 1989, pp. 24–25, statement of Mary Pesapio). Parents whose small child had died of AIDS testified about how they could not find an undertaker who would bury their child (U.S. Senate Committee on Labor and Human Resources Subcommittee on the Handicapped, 1989, pp. 102–103, statement of Betty and Emory Corey). The committee also received boxes loaded with thousands of letters and pieces of testimony that had been gathered in hearings across the country the summer before from people whose lives had been damaged or destroyed by discrimination.

At this Senate hearing and in all of the many hearings in the House, members of Congress heard from witnesses who told their stories of discrimination. With each story, the level of consciousness was raised and the level of tolerance to this kind of injustice was lowered. However, the stories did not end in the hearing room. People with disabilities came from around the country to talk to members of Congress, to advocate for the bill, to explain why each provision was necessary, and to address a very real form of discrimination. Individuals came in at their own expense, sleeping on floors by night and visiting Congressional offices by day. People who could not come to Washington told their stories in letters, attended town meetings, and made endless phone calls.

It was a long haul. After the spectacular Senate vote of 76 to 8 on September 7, 1989, the Bill went to the House, where it was considered by an unprecedented four Committees: Education and Labor, Judiciary, Public Works and Transportation, and Energy and Commerce. (The bill also had to go to the Rules Committee.) Each Committee had at least one subcommittee hearing, and added more amendments to be explained, lobbied, and defeated. Grass roots organizing became even more important because by this time many business associations had rallied their members to write members of Congress to oppose or weaken the bill. The perseverance and commitment of the disability movement never wavered. Through many moments of high stress and tension, the community stayed unified. For every hearing the hearing room was full, and for every proposed amendment to weaken the bill, letters poured in and the halls of Congress were canvassed.

CONCLUSION

As the effective dates for the individual Titles of the ADA passed, public awareness of the ADA and its requirements heightened. For the first time in the history of our country, or the history of the world, businesses must think about access to people with disabilities. If the ADA means anything, it means that people with disabilities will no longer be out of sight and out of mind. The ADA is based on a presumption that people with disabilities want to work and are capable of working, and want to be and are capable of being members of their communities; exclusion and segregation cannot be tolerated. Accommodating a person with a disability is no longer a matter of charity but rather a basic issue of civil rights.

Although some in the media portray this new era as falling from the sky unannounced, the thousands of men and women in the disability rights movement know that these rights were hard won and are long overdue. The ADA is radical only in comparison with a shameful history of outright exclusion and segregation of people with disabilities. From a civil rights perspective the Americans with Disabilities Act is a codification of simple justice.

REFERENCES

Air Carriers Access Act of 1986, 49 U.S.C. app. §1374(c) (1986).

Atascadeco State Hospital v. Scanlon, 473 U.S. 234 (1985).

Babcock, C.R. (1982, March 4). Handicapped policy undergoing a rewrite. *Washington Post*, p. A27, col. b.

Barringer, F. (1983, April 12). How handicapped won access rule fight. *Washington Post*, p. A8.

Civil Rights and Remedies Equalization Act of 1986, 42 U.S.C. §2000d–7 (1988).

Civil Rights Restoration Act of 1987 (PL 100-259), 20 U.S.C. §168 *et seq.*, 29 U.S.C. §706, 42 U.S.C. §2000 (1988).

Consolidated Rail Corporation v. Darrone, 465 U.S. 624 (1984).

Craib, R. (1977, April 29). The disabled win fight with HEW. *San Francisco Chronicle*, p. 1.

Fair Housing Amendments Act of 1988, 42 U.S.C. §§3601–3619 (1968).

Farbman, A. (Ed.). (1988). *On the threshold of independence*. Washington, DC: National Council on Disability.

Fulwood, S., III. (1990, May 23). Broad disabled rights bill ok'd. *L.A. Times*, pp. A1, A20.

Grove City College v. Bell, 465 U.S. 555 (1984).

Handicapped Children's Protection Act of 1986, 20 U.S.C. 1415(f) (1986).

Individuals with Disabilities Education Act of 1992, 20 U.S.C. §1400 *et seq.* (1992).

Kenworthy, T. (1990a, May 18). House adds AIDS amendment to measure for disabled. *Washington Post*, pp. A12, col. 5.

Kenworthy, T. (1990b, May 23). House votes new rights for disabled. *Washington Post*, pp. A1, A10.

Mayerson, A. (1991). Title I—Employment provisions of the Americans with Disabilities Act. *Temple Law Review, 64*, 499–521.

Rehabilitation Act of 1973, 29 U.S.C. §§791–794 (1988 & Supp. I 1989).

School Board of Nassau County v. Arline, 480 U.S. 273 (1987).

Smith v. Robinson, 468 U.S. 992 (1984).

Southeastern Community College v. Davis, 442 U.S. 397 (1979).

U.S. Department of Health, Education and Welfare. (1977, May 4). [Title of regulations.] *Federal Register, 42*, 22676–22702.

U.S. Department of Transportation v. Paralyzed Veterans of America, 477 U.S. 597 (1986).

U.S. House of Representatives. (1990, July 12). *House conference report no. 101-596, to accompany S. 933 (101st Congress, 2nd session)*. Washington, DC: U.S. Government Printing Office. (Reprinted in *United States Code Congressional and Administrative News, 4*, 565–600 [1990]).

U.S. Senate. (1972, February 9). Hearings on S.J. Res. 202. A joint resolution to express the sense of Congress that a White House Conference on the Handicapped be called by the President of the United States. *Congressional Record 118*, S3320–S3322.

U.S. Senate Committee on Labor and Human Resources. (1989, August 30). *Senate report no. 101-116, to accompany S. 933 (101st Congress, 1st session)*. Washington, DC: U.S. Government Printing Office.

U.S. Senate Committee on Labor and Human Resources Subcommittee on the Handicapped. (1989, May 9, 10, 16; June 22). *Hearings on S. 933, the Americans with Disabilities Act of 1989 (S. Hrg. 101–156)*. Washington, DC: U.S. Government Printing Office.

U.S. Senate Committee on Labor and Human Resources Subcommittee on the Handicapped and U.S. House of Representatives Committee on Education and Labor Subcommittee on Select Education. (1988, September 27). *Joint hearings on S. 2345, the Americans with Disabilities Act of 1988 (S. Hrg. 100-926)*. Washington, DC: U.S. Government Printing Office.

U.S. Senate Committee on Labor and Human Resources. (1974). *Senate report no. 1297 (93rd Congress, 2d session)*. Washington, DC: U.S. Government Printing Office. (Reprinted in *United States Code Congressional and Administrative News*, 6390).

Chapter 3

A Study in Legislative Strategy

The Passage of the ADA

Sara D. Watson

In 1988 Congress began considering a sweeping civil rights bill that would prohibit discrimination on the basis of disability in the areas of employment, transportation, public communications, and public facilities: the Americans with Disabilities Act (ADA). Despite the fact that this bill came after disability advocates had worked for years to pursue increased services and equal rights for people with disabilities, there were no indications that this was an especially propitious time to launch such a venture, and, indeed, even advocates were not universally optimistic about the bill's chances for passage. Almost singlehandedly, and in the short span of about 2 years, the disability lobby changed the bill from one with little chance of passage to one that virtually no one could oppose. In 1990, the bill passed by overwhelming margins in both Houses of Congress and was signed by President Bush in an elaborate White House ceremony. Behind this transformation lies a story of legislative skill and the evolution of a social movement.

A HOSTILE ENVIRONMENT

To understand the magnitude of the legislative achievement, it is important first to examine the environment into which the idea for this bill was introduced. We can examine the obstacles facing the disability lobby by looking at the legislative history in two stages: placing the bill on the political agenda and achieving its passage.

When the bill was introduced in Congress, there was little reason to consider that it would be a welcome addition to the political agenda. For the preceding 8 years, the Reagan administration had constantly sought to cut services for this population and to reduce government's role in society generally. President Reagan's Task Force on Regulatory Relief had tried to eviscerate the most significant antidiscrimination bill up to that time, the Rehabilitation Act of 1973 (PL 93-112). Furthermore, the ADA expanded the concept of civil rights beyond that in the Civil Rights Act of 1964, which was not a popular mission in that political climate.

Not only was the political environment hostile, but there was no reason to think it would change. Issues often come to the forefront of the public agenda based on a precipitating event. In this case,

The author would like to thank Elizabeth Savage of the Disability Rights Education and Defense Fund for her comments and suggestions.

however, no public opinion poll had highlighted disability discrimination as a major issue; no new publication had captured the public's attention; no crisis had emerged to spur legislators to action; no data had suddenly emerged to indicate a dramatic increase in problematic behavior; and no media exposé had taken place. (Students at Gallaudet University had gained media attention early in 1988 for their movement to have a deaf president. This event might have educated some legislators about the disability movement, but it alone was not enough to prompt the passage of such a sweeping bill.) In sum, in a seemingly hostile environment, there was no reason to think the agenda would make room for such a significant piece of legislation.

Even after the bill was introduced, there were numerous obstacles to its passage. The requirements were quite broad, affecting the majority of small businesses in the United States. Opponents of the bill, ranging from the U.S. Chamber of Commerce to the American Public Transit Association, had political action committees (PACs), strong connections with their federal legislators, and substantial lobbying funds. By contrast, disability groups, like most consumer organizations, were not as well funded for advocacy efforts.

The media was not particularly friendly either. The disability lobby did stage its share of good photo opportunities, such as one demonstration in March 1990 in which activists left their wheelchairs and crawled up the steps of the U.S. Capitol building. However, editorials from the major newspapers were mixed, with one *New York Times* editorial encapsulating a common concern in its title "Blank Check for the Disabled?" (1989). Finally, the original sponsors of the bill in both the House and the Senate left office shortly after the bill was introduced, one because he was not reelected (Sen. Lowell Weicker) and one voluntarily because of acknowledged errors in judgment (Rep. Tony Coelho). On the face of it, the bill seemed to have little chance for passage. There were none of the classical factors that place issues on a legislative agenda, it contradicted the policies of the most popular President in recent history, and its sponsors had left Congress for two most undesirable reasons.

Yet within the space of 2 years, the disability community had achieved passage of the ADA. Furthermore, the bill was far from being a watered-down version. With the exception of eliminating provisions that prohibited discrimination in health insurance and required extensive retrofitting of public buildings, and delaying mandates for the acquisition of accessible long-distance buses, the disability lobby had defeated virtually every proposal to weaken the original version of the act.

By exploring the legislative strategy used to engineer passage of the ADA, this chapter attempts to explain how the disability lobby achieved this coup.

HOW DID IT HAPPEN?

The factors behind the passage of the ADA can be divided into three categories. First, several characteristics of the bill itself facilitated its passage. Second, the disability rights movement had reached a point at which a window of opportunity would be opened for the public to be receptive of its message. Third, the disability lobby demonstrated remarkable skill in framing and managing the debate. Each of these factors is considered in turn.

Factors within the ADA

Certainly, several obvious characteristics of the bill itself made passage easier. Probably the most necessary—although not sufficient—condition was the fact that it carried a low federal price tag. The ADA requires the covered entities to pay for workplace accommodations and alterations to make facilities accessible; the costs for new telecommunications services for people with hearing and speech impairments are spread among the public; and accessible transportation services will be financed through a combination of state and federal funds. Virtually the only other federal costs are for enforcement and tax credits to help businesses pay the costs of accommodations. Furthermore, the ADA could be expected to reduce federal benefit expenditures through the reduction of the number of people receiving Supplemental Security Income and Social Security Disability Insurance.

The bill would also be expected to generate a certain amount of support because of the public's natural desire to help people with disabilities. However, there are many such groups warranting this sentiment who are not the beneficiaries of such comprehensive legislation. Although the ADA benefited from each of these conditions, none of them is sufficient to explain its success.

Evolution of a Movement

The story is actually much more complex and partly reflects the evolution of a social movement in our society. The success of the disability lobby built on two decades of social change and legislative initiatives that had laid the necessary groundwork for the ADA. The disability rights movement began in earnest in the 1970s when activists began demanding equal access to all facets of society for people with disabilities—employment, education, public facilities, housing, and the like. The movement also began to transform the concept of a person with disabilities from a passive patient with an overwhelming medical condition to an active person with characteristics that sometimes required social support services. Leaders rejected the idea that persons with disabilities should simply be grateful to be alive and argued that they had a right to as high a quality of life as modern technology and services could support. The result was enactment of laws such as the Rehabilitation Act of 1973 and the Education for All Handicapped Children Act of 1975 (PL 94-142). Almost every state also passed laws or enacted policies akin to the ADA that prohibited at least some forms of discrimination on the basis of disability, especially in employment and access to public facilities (Holbrook & Percy, 1992). For example, Massachusetts prohibits discrimination on the basis of disability in an amendment to the state constitution (Pfeiffer, 1991).

The movement and the legislation it engendered served five goals that were important to the success of the ADA. First, they introduced the idea that people with disabilities are an identifiable and disadvantaged constituency in the same way as are women and minorities. The passage of civil rights laws solidified the disability constituency's claims for civil rights protections equal to those of other minority groups. These parallels with other populations were crucial in passing a law that was based on the Civil Rights Act of 1964 and emphasized access as a matter of right instead of charitable obligation.

Second, they enabled people with disabilities to enter the mainstream of society in all stages of their lives, so that persons without disabilities became more accustomed to living, going to school, and working alongside those with disabilities (J. Kemp, Executive Director of United Cerebral Palsy Associations, personal communication, February 1992). The disability movement constantly emphasizes that attitudes can be a bigger barrier than physical obstacles. Familiarity began to remove the fear that hindered true access. Another consequence of mainstreaming has been that an entire generation of people with disabilities (and their friends and families) has come to expect that the full range of opportunities in life would be open to them. The Education for All Handicapped Children Act resulted in students without disabilities getting to know, and become friends with, students with disabilities, as well as students with disabilities coming to expect the accessibility and services after age 22 that they had found in their schools. The "Deaf President Now" movement at Gallaudet University in 1988 illustrated this heightened expectation. Students vehemently rejected the idea that there were no deaf persons qualified to lead their university and demanded a president who could be a role model for them (Gannon, 1989). As a result of these events, more people with disabilities did not hesitate to claim equal access, and there were more persons without disabilities who understood and supported this claim.

Third, the early disability rights movement and legislation helped disability organizations change their missions to support the concept of the ADA and disability lobbyists to build their legislative expertise and their local and federal networks. Most of the big disability organizations

(United Cerebral Palsy, National Easter Seal Society, Association for Retarded Citizens, etc.) were established as service organizations that provided assistance to their constituencies. However, the disability movement began to change these organizations' concept of their mission. By the time of the ADA, these organizations had recognized the importance of advocacy efforts and established a strong Washington lobbying presence. A cluster of younger, smaller, more activist disability organizations, such as the Disability Rights Education and Defense Fund (DREDF), the Mental Health Law Project, and Americans Disabled for Accessible Public Transit (ADAPT), had also become well versed in using legal means as well as public demonstrations to pursue and preserve civil rights for people with disabilities. Furthermore, both types of organizations had an entire generation of seasoned leaders who were well known in the community, had experience lobbying on the federal, state, and local level, and had a clear vision of the type of society they wanted to build with this law. These leaders and their organizations had established vast networks of local constituents—people with disabilities, family members, teachers, and other supporters—whom they could mobilize. Both types of skills—federal lobbying and grass roots organization—would be needed.

A fourth consequence of the early political battles in the disability movement was that legislators had come to understand and appreciate the growing power of the disability constituency (E. Savage, Director of Training for DREDF, personal communication, March 1992). Advocates of the ADA constantly used (and thereby legitimated) a figure of 43 million Americans with disabilities—by no means a small constituency. Although President Bush had indeed chaired a task force that attempted to weaken the Rehabilitation Act, he learned from that experience that disability organizations were formidable opponents, with passionate investments in their programs and extensive grass roots networks (Kosterlitz, 1989).

Fifth, disability groups benefited from the fact that the movement had evolved to precisely the point at which a window of opportunity appeared. The concept of providing civil rights protections for people with disabilities had advanced far enough to make itself palatable but not so far that it had become unpopular or even objectionable. This concept warrants some attention.

Sections 503 (29 U.S.C. §793) and 504 (29 U.S.C. §794) of the Rehabilitation Act of 1973 required federal contractors to take affirmative action toward people with disabilities and prohibited federal grantees from discrimination against people with disabilities. This federal law, as well as other state laws, helped people with disabilities attain status as a protected group similar to that of other constituencies. However, this recognition was at least 10 and perhaps closer to 20 years behind that given to women and minorities. It was also less pervasive, not only because of the limited reach of legislation such as the Rehabilitation Act, but also because of its lessened impact on societal consciousness. The societal attention given to affirmative action for this population was far less than that given to minorities and women. For example, employers, consumer watchdog organizations, and columnists routinely monitored and commented on the percentage of women and minorities in management positions in various corporations, but these same reports almost never mentioned people with disabilities. (This is not to imply a deliberate slight; there are substantial reasons why it is more difficult to measure the advancement of people with disabilities, including many persons' reluctance to identify themselves as such.)

Unlike advocacy of the rights of people with disabilities, civil rights protections for minorities and women have existed long enough and been extensive enough to have gone through cycles of popularity. The recent publication of books such as *Reflections of an Affirmative Action Baby* (Carter, 1991) indicates that this policy has evolved to the point at which there exists a widespread recognition of the perceived stigma of affirmative action for blacks (and perhaps for women). Furthermore, whereas such policies once were supported for many of the same reasons that are used to support employment opportunities for people with disabilities (past discrimination, current attitudes), they are now generating a backlash, including perceptions that nondiscrimination practices are taking jobs away from nonprotected classes.

By and large, this perceived stigma of affirmative action and this impression of job usurpation have not touched people with disabilities. Even though the ADA does not include an affirmative action component, some of its other requirements could have generated a backlash if the attitudes toward people with disabilities were the same as those toward other protected groups. For example, the ADA requires employers to invest in reasonable accommodations. If the disability movement were at the same stage in its evolution as the civil rights movement, such requirements might have jeopardized the bill's chances for success.

Another advantage of the timing of the ADA initiative was that scholars and analysts outside the relevant interest groups had not yet studied disability programs to the extent that they had scrutinized other large social programs, such as welfare or food stamps. As a result, there were no well-known, comprehensive, competing proposals on how to change the obvious discrimination faced by people with disabilities. There were also relatively few competing data on the costs of employing people with disabilities—most studies showed it to be cost-effective. The most widely cited study, conducted by Berkeley Planning Associates (1982), concluded that most accommodations cost nothing and more than 80% cost less than $500. It was unusual that the consumer lobbies were well supplied with information, whereas opponents of the ADA had few comparable studies of their own to contradict disability activists' assertions that the ADA would be inexpensive for employers. Because legislators were largely unfamiliar with disability issues and had few sources of information that were as well prepared as the disability groups, they tended to rely on the disability lobby to educate them on the merits of its proposals.

Strategies and Tactics

The existence of certain helpful characteristics within the bill and a changing societal environment would not have been enough to spur Congress to enact so sweeping a bill. The most important reason for the passage of the bill was the success of numerous strategies and tactics developed and deployed by the major disability community lobbyists, led by Patrisha Wright of the DREDF.

Framing the Debate   The disability community's most powerful accomplishment was its success in framing the debate immediately and lastingly. There were three important aspects to this strategy. First, the disability lobby established the bipartisan nature of the bill, giving both Republicans and Democrats reasons to support it. Second, it established the need for the bill, leaving no room to question the existence of disability discrimination. Third, it established the basis for the bill's approach (i.e., that its protections were an issue of civil rights rather than a charitable obligation or some other rationale).

From the beginning, the bill was presented and received as a bipartisan proposal that all stripes of the political spectrum could support. It appealed not only to liberals' sense of government's duty to protect a disadvantaged population, but also conservatives' sense of the importance of self-reliance. One of the keys to establishing the bill as a bipartisan effort was its early history (E. Savage, personal communication, March 1992). The original bill was proposed and written by the National Council on Disability, an independent federal agency whose members at that time were appointed by President Reagan (National Council on Disability, 1986). This bill was more stringent than the subsequent versions; for example, whereas the current law requires employers to make only "reasonable" accommodations, the original would have required businesses to make accommodations unless they would have jeopardized the financial viability of the firm (Farbman, 1988). Having a Reagan-appointed body decry a social problem and propose dramatic steps to rectify it made it difficult for opponents to refute the existence of disability discrimination and the need for some sort of measures to combat it. As Bob Silverstein, chief counsel for the Senate Subcommittee on Disability Policy, described the source of the bill, "We're not talking leftwing crazies here" (Yost, 1989).

The original bill was introduced in April 1988 with no real hope of passage in that Congress but rather as a vehicle for discussion and to establish the original parameters for debate (Shapiro, 1993). It did not pass out of committee, but the second version was introduced in May 1989 as S. 922 and H.R. 2273. For this version, the disability and business lobbyists relatively quickly compromised on areas of disagreement, with the disability lobby eliminating jury trials for certain offenses and the business lobby accepting a broad definition of public accommodations. These compromises induced President Bush to endorse the new bill, which virtually guaranteed its passage through the Senate (Yost, 1989).

The particular tactics the disability lobby used to make clear the level of discrimination people with disabilities faced every day is discussed below. The lobby recognized that its first task was to establish conclusively the magnitude of the discrimination problem. That they were successful in doing so is reflected in the fact that even the opponents of the ADA did not dispute the need for protections. Numerous statements from political leaders or business groups critical of the bill nevertheless started with the acknowledgment that people with disabilities experienced discrimination and required some measures to remedy their situation (McCollum, 1989; U.S. House of Representatives Committee on the Judiciary Subcommittee on Civil and Constitutional Rights, 1989).

The third part of the battle was establishing the debate as a civil rights issue. A traditional rationale for providing services to people with disabilities has been charitable obligation, but the disability movement has rejected that motivation. Two other rationales were used as needed. One was enlightened self-interest—the idea that anyone could become disabled and would expect the protections and accessibility offered by the ADA. As the chair of the National Council on Disability put it during her testimony, "Advancing age, economic circumstances, illness or accident will someday, according to reputable statistics, put all of us, or a loved one, in the category of a person with a disability" (U.S. Senate Committee on Labor and Human Resources Subcommittee on the Handicapped and U.S. House of Representatives Committee on Education and Labor Subcommittee on Select Education, 1988). Another was cost-effectiveness, which could be considered in two ways. First, the ADA was cost-effective for society because it would allow people with disabilities to become taxpayers instead of tax beneficiaries. ADA advocates used this argument constantly during the debate (Rasky, 1989). Another way of looking at the cost-effectiveness of the ADA was that covered entities would recoup their financial outlays through improved employee recruiting and productivity or through an increased customer base. However, it was clear that this cost-effectiveness argument would not work for the entire population because the ADA could require expensive modifications or accommodations. So, to keep the focus on civil rights regardless of cost, some advocates rejected the use of that version of the cost-effective argument entirely (M. Johnson, editor, *Disability Rag*, personal communication, July 22, 1992).

The dominant argument used during the debate over the ADA was that the bill was a civil rights law that would finally provide people with disabilities with the same protections as those given to minorities and women (DREDF, 1992). This strategy was somewhat risky given the civil rights climate and given the fact that this was a new concept for many in Congress and elsewhere. However, the disability lobby had little choice because any other strategy would have pushed the entire disability rights movement backward. Furthermore, the other rationales simply were not powerful enough to warrant changes of this magnitude. This strategy worked because of the new climate for civil rights for people with disabilities and because of the variety of other grass roots tactics (explored below) used by the disability lobby to convince legislators of the merits of its claim for equal protections.

In fact, disability activists were so thorough at framing the debate and publicizing the level of discrimination faced by people with disabilities that it became extremely difficult for anyone to oppose this bill outright. Even the major coalition of employers opposing the bill called itself the "Disability Rights Working Group." The debate began with what kind of bill should be enacted, not whether discrimination existed or if it should be combatted.

Policy Advocates   The disability lobby's second major strategy was organizing and galvanizing policy advocates in and out of Congress. Kingdon (1984) and others have termed advocates using this strategy *policy entrepreneurs*, but actually the ADA experience broadens this concept. Although the ADA advocates did share with the policy entrepreneur model the ability and drive to place an issue on the agenda and move it to passage, their motivation for selecting the issue was new. As described by Kingdon, policy entrepreneurs may support legislation not only out of a deep-rooted personal conviction but also because it would establish their reputations as experts in important policy areas. By contrast, most of the key ADA supporters were already known as disability advocates. Furthermore, simply enhancing this reputation in disability policy would not generate the widespread publicity that entrepreneurship in a different policy area, such as education or environmental issues, would generate. Disability policy is not as well known or understood as other policy areas. Until the ADA, at least, the mainstream media, policy organizations, and think tanks had not recognized disability programs as venerable targets of reform in the way that they had social security or welfare. Therefore, becoming a leader in this field was not yet a reliable means to national prominence.

Rather, the legislators who pushed the ADA through had intense personal motivations to assume their roles. Sen. Lowell Weicker, the original Senate sponsor of the bill, has a son with mental retardation. Rep. Tony Coelho, the original House sponsor, has epilepsy. Sen. Weicker's successor was Sen. Tom Harkin, whose brother is deaf and whose nephew has quadriplegia. Rep. Coelho's successor was Rep. Steny Hoyer, who has a family member with a disability. Other leaders were Senator Edward Kennedy, whose son lost his leg to cancer and whose sister had mental retardation; Senator Orrin Hatch, whose brother-in-law had polio; and Senator Robert Dole, who has a disability from a World War II injury (Shapiro, 1989).

The ADA also benefited from the activities of policy advocates outside Congress. A Republican disability activist, Justin Dart, spent his own funds to travel across the United States, sponsoring his own hearings on the need for the ADA. These hearings were given the stamp of endorsement through his chairmanship of a "Task Force on the Rights and Empowerment of Americans with Disabilities," sponsored by Rep. Major Owens, chair of the House Education and Labor Committee's Subcommittee on Select Education. These hearings served as key mechanisms to keep legislators focused on the experiences of their constituents.

Working Congress   A combination of good politicking and serendipitous logistics also helped the bill move very quickly through one part of Congress. In the Senate, the bill had to pass through only the Labor and Human Resources Committee, chaired by disability advocate Sen. Edward Kennedy. The relevant subcommittee, the Subcommittee on the Handicapped (later renamed the Subcommittee on Disability Policy) was chaired by Sen. Tom Harkin—the main Senate sponsor of the bill. The ranking minority member of the committee was Sen. Orrin Hatch. Outside the committee, Senate Minority Leader Robert Dole, as well as a surprising number of other members, such as Sen. Robert Kerrey and Sen. Daniel Inouye, also had personal experiences with and commitments to disability issues. Part of the reason for the bipartisan support for the bill was the skill of the disability lobby, but part must be explained by the pervasiveness of disability in society, including the lives of an astounding number of senators. The bill breezed through the Senate with relatively little scrutiny, so swiftly that opponents had little time to mobilize substantial opposition. The ADA passed the Senate 76 to 8 on September 7, 1989.

The situation in the House was altogether different. The easy Senate passage alerted the business and public transportation lobbies to the significance of the bill, and their lobbying efforts began to increase. Furthermore, the scope of the bill required that it pass through four committees: Education and Labor, Energy and Commerce, Judiciary, and Public Works and Transportation. There were fewer natural allies in the House, with the considerable exceptions of Rep. Steny Hoyer and Rep. Major Owens. Former Rep. Coelho did continue to play a role behind the scenes, and

Rep. Hoyer's position as chair of the Democratic Caucus and his immense personal investment in the bill were major factors (E. Savage, personal communication, March 1992). The other elements described in this chapter helped the disability lobby wend its way through this logistical and political maze; the bill passed the House of Representatives by a vote of 403 to 20 on May 22, 1990. The final, reconciled version passed the House on July 12, 1990, by a vote of 377 to 28 and the Senate the next day by a vote of 91 to 6.

Building Coalitions   A third important strategy was activists' ability to build and hold together coalitions diverse by the nature of their disabilities, primary interests, and politics. Although other civil rights groups have pursued similar strategies, disability advocates refined this art.

The first type of coalition included people with all types of disabilities. In 1970, disability organizations began to organize into an informal confederation that would eventually be called the Consortium for Citizens with Disabilities. Contrary to popular perception, people with disabilities are even less homogeneous than are other minority groups. Yet organizations representing people with literally dozens of different disabilities focused on the ADA as their legislative priority and threw their weight behind a single lobbying team in Washington (DREDF, 1992). This cohesion represented a significant change from earlier battles. During the debate over public transportation policy in the 1970s and early 1980s, disability groups were splintered between those that supported paratransit services and those that wanted access to mainline transportation (Katzman, 1986). As a result, it was much more difficult for the lobbyists credibly to maintain a solid coalition. However, during the ADA debate there was relatively little public dissension. Even though many of the advocates had worked together on the Rehabilitation Act of 1973 and other subsequent legislation, the ADA represented a new level of cohesion for the disability lobby.

The second type of coalition was formed of groups that had never worked on disability issues and perhaps had never thought of themselves as obvious allies. Lobbyists from the Leadership Conference on Civil Rights worked alongside longtime disability advocates. Gay rights organizations joined the disability forces not only out of a sense of solidarity on civil rights but also out of the knowledge that people with AIDS would need this bill. Conservative legislators tried to induce disability groups to exempt people with AIDS and HIV infection from coverage under the bill, but the coalition hung together, forging a compromise in the last days before final passage.

Equally interesting, however, were the organizations that did not provide high-profile support for the ADA. For example, several major organizations, such as the American Cancer Society and the American Lung Association, had constituencies that would be helped by the ADA, but either their constituencies did not want to think of themselves as "disabled," or for other reasons they did not consider the ADA within the scope of their legislative agenda. These organizations did not take an active, public stance in support of the bill (or did not do so until well into the debate). It is all the more remarkable that the ADA passed despite the lack of support from these giant organizations.

A third coalition involved people from across the political spectrum. Even though Democrats might be expected to support such a bill, it passed because an array of Republicans endorsed its principles as well. The bill was originally written by a government agency headed by Republican appointees and endorsed by a Republican president, who signed it in the same summer he vetoed another civil rights bill that probably would have had less impact than the ADA (the Civil Rights Restoration Act). The Republican Attorney General, Richard Thornburgh, lobbied for it (U.S. House of Representatives Committee on the Judiciary, 1989), as did Senate Minority Leader Robert Dole (U.S. Senate Committee on Labor and Human Resources, 1989).

The bipartisan appeal of the substance of the bill has been noted, but there is yet another reason for its broad support: the diffuse incidence of disability in society. It is unlikely that well-to-do political leaders will become welfare recipients, and impossible that white political leaders will become black. However, disability is born into and may occur in any family. Numerous examples of this have already been offered; another is that President Bush has one son with a learning disability and another with a colostomy. It is also quite likely that the sudden entrance of former press secretary Jim Brady into the ranks of people with disabilities and his emergence as a disability activist reinforced this point.

Mobilizing the Grass Roots At least as important as the other political strategies mentioned earlier was the mobilization of sustained grass roots support. The bill passed largely because national, state, and local organizations, such as the National Council on Independent Living, used the profound appeal of the ADA to ensure that persons with disabilities, as well as their families, teachers, colleagues, and friends, pressured their state representatives in greater force than did local small business owners. Disability organizations staged several protest marches and numerous visits to Capitol Hill (Holmes, 1990). The obvious presence of people with visible disabilities ensured that people who merely saw them in the halls and in the streets were reminded of the bill.

National groups also found means to communicate the local impact of discrimination to federal lawmakers. Persons with disabilities kept "discrimination diaries" that were presented to lawmakers in hearings and individual meetings. These diaries recorded everyday examples of discrimination on the basis of disability, whether it was a movie theatre manager who refused to admit them, a store with steps, a public bus with no wheelchair lift, or an employer who refused to make an accommodation. These copious records vividly illustrated the grinding nature of society's ubiquitous discriminatory attitudes and actions.

CONCLUSION

The pasage of the ADA was the culmination of decades of societal change toward people with disabilities, but this gradual change was only a necessary (not sufficient) condition to effect passage of one of the most sweeping civil rights bills in America's history. The story behind the passage is a classic saga involving the strategic use of both federal lobbying skills and grass roots pressure in the face of tremendous odds.

REFERENCES

Berkeley Planning Associates. (1982). *A study of accommodations provided to handicapped employees by federal contractors: Final report to the U.S. Department of Labor, Employment Standards Administration.* Washington, DC: U.S. Government Printing Office.

Blank check for the disabled? [editorial]. (1989, September 6). *The New York Times,* p. A24.

Carter, S. (1991). *Reflections of an affirmative action baby.* New York: Basic Books.

Civil Rights Act of 1964, codified as amended in scattered sections of 42 U.S.C. (1988).

Disability Rights Education and Defense Fund. (1992). *ADA gala.* Washington, DC: Author.

Education for All Handicapped Children Act of 1975, 20 U.S.C. §§1232, 1401, 1405–1420, 1453 (1975).

Farbman, A. (Ed.). (1988). *On the threshold of independence.* Washington, DC: National Council on Disability.

Gannon, J. (1989). *The week the world heard Gallaudet.* Washington, DC: Gallaudet University Press.

Holbrook, T.M., & Percy, S.L. (1992). Exploring variations in state laws providing protections for persons with disabilities. *Western Political Quarterly, 45,* 201–220.

Holmes, S. (1990, March 13). Bill barring discrimination against disabled hits snag. *The New York Times,* p. A20.

Katzman, R. (1986). *Institutional disability: The saga of transportation policy for the disabled.* Washington, DC: Brookings Institution.

Kingdon, J. (1984). *Agendas, alternatives and public policies.* Glenview, IL: Scott, Foresman and Co.

Kosterlitz, J. (1989, January 28). Joining forces. *The National Journal,* pp. 194–199.

McCollum, W. (1989, May 5). "Dear Colleague" letter written by Rep. William McCollum (R-FL).

National Council on Disability. (1986). *Toward independence.* Washington, DC: Author.

Pfeiffer, D. (1991, August 29). *The rise of the disability movement.* Paper presented at the annual meeting of the American Political Science Association, Washington, DC.

Rasky, S. (1989, September 17). How the disabled sold Congress on a new bill of rights. *The New York Times,* p. E5.

Rehabilitation Act of 1973, 29 U.S.C. §§791–794 (1988 & Supp. I 1989).

Shapiro, J. (1989, September 18). A liberation day for the disabled. *U.S. News & World Report,* pp. 20–24.

Shapiro, J. (1993). *No pity: The story of the disability rights movement and how it is changing America.* New York: Random House/Times.

U.S. House of Representatives Committee on the Judiciary. (1989, October 12). *Hearings on H.R. 2273, the Americans with Disabilities Act of 1989 (testimony of Richard Thornburgh, Attorney General) (H.R. Hrg. 101-485* Part 3*)*. Washington, DC: U.S. Government Printing Office.

U.S. House of Representatives Committee on the Judiciary Subcommittee on Civil and Constitutional Rights. (1989, October 12). *Hearings on H.R. 2273, the Americans with Disabilities Act of 1989 (testimony of Robert Dale Lynch, Architect/ AIA) (H.R. Hrg. 101-485* Part 3*)*. Washington, DC: U.S. Government Printing Office.

U.S. Senate Committee on Labor and Human Resources. (1989, May 10). *Hearings on S. 933, the Americans with Disabilities Act of 1989 (testimony of Sen. Robert Dole) (S. Hrg. 101-156*)*. Washington, DC: U.S. Government Printing Office.

U.S. Senate Committee on Labor and Human Resources Subcommittee on the Handicapped and U.S. House of Representatives Committee on Education and Labor Subcommittee on Select Education. (1988, September 27). *Joint hearings on S. 2345, the Americans with Disabilities Act of 1988 (testimony of Sandra Swift Parrino, Chair, National Council on Disability) (S. Hrg. 100-926*)*. Washington, DC: U.S. Government Printing Office.

Yost, P. (1989, August 7). Tedious meetings, testy exchanges produced disability-rights bill. *The Washington Post,* p. A4.

Chapter 4

Antidiscrimination Requirements of the ADA

Chai R. Feldblum

The purpose of this chapter is twofold. First, it gives the reader a basic sense of *who* is covered under the Americans with Disabilities Act[1] (ADA) and, generally, *what* is prohibited by the law. Thus it discusses the concept of "person with a disability," as defined by the ADA, and defines in general terms the employment and public accommodation requirements of the law. Other chapters in this book discuss in greater detail the substantive requirements of the ADA in these areas as well as others (see Part II, Key Provisions).

Second, this chapter is intended to introduce the reader to two different concepts of antidiscrimination protection that are embodied in the ADA. The first concept is a traditional one, familiar to many through the antidiscrimination protections established by the Civil Rights Acts of 1964 (PL 88-352) and 1968 (PL 90-284). As a general matter, this concept of antidiscrimination assumes that characteristics such as race, religion, national origin, or sex are either always or often irrelevant to competent performance of a job or enjoyment of a business good or service. I say "always or often" because Title VII of the Civil Rights Act of 1964 presumes that there may be a "bona fide occupational qualification" that will prevent an individual from adequately performing a job because of the person's gender, religion, or national origin (see 42 U.S.C. §2000e-2[e]). In addition, Title VII requires an employer to make affirmative accommodations to a person's religious practices and beliefs (see 42 U.S.C. §2000e[j]). However, the antidiscrimination provisions of such laws, as a general matter, prohibit taking such characteristics into account when making employment decisions or in serving customers (See, e.g., 42 U.S.C. §2000e-2[a][1]: "It shall be an unlawful employment practice for an employer—(1) to fail or refuse to hire or to discharge any individual with respect to his compensation, terms, conditions or privileges of employment, because of such individual's race, color, religion, sex or national origin"; and 42 U.S.C. §2000a: "All

This article is adapted from Feldblum, C.R. (1991). Employment protections. In J. West (Ed.), *The Americans with Disabilities Act: From policy to practice* (pp. 81–110). New York: Milbank Memorial Fund.

The author thanks Teresa Jakubowski for her excellent research assistance in preparing this chapter.

[1]The Americans with Disabilities Act of 1990 (PL 101-336) is published in *Statutes at Large* (104 Stat. 327) and codified in The *United States Code* (42 U.S.C. §§12101–12213 [Supp. II 1990]). References to various portions of the act within this chapter cite the specific section of the Code.

persons shall be entitled to the full and equal enjoyment of goods, services, facilities, privileges, advantages, and accommodations of any place of public accommodation, as defined in this section, without discrimination or segregation on the ground of race, color, religion, or national origin").

This traditional concept of antidiscrimination underlies much of the ADA's antidiscrimination requirements. It is premised on the same assumption articulated in traditional civil rights discourse that the particular characteristic at issue—here, the characteristic of "disability"—is often irrelevant in an employment or business setting (see Traditional Civil Rights Protection, below).

There is a second concept of antidiscrimination, however, that is equally prominent in the provisions of the ADA. This concept presumes that a person's disability is often *very relevant* to the person's ability or inability to perform a job adequately or to enjoy a particular good or service. The concept further presumes, however, that such inability may not be viewed in a vacuum. Rather, the inability must be viewed in the context of the *interaction* between societal realities and choices and the individual's disability, rather than in the context of the individual's disability per se.

For example, one could probably state with some confidence that a person who is completely blind is not competent to be a truck driver, purely as a result of the physical ramifications of his or her disability. By contrast, one could not state with confidence that a person who uses a wheelchair is not competent to be the vice president of a bank solely because of his or her disability. That person, in fact, may have difficulty performing certain aspects of the vice president's job—because the bank decided 5 years ago to build a building with many steps and inaccessible rest rooms and because other entities in society chose, over the years, to build inaccessible airline terminals and restaurants. The interaction between disability and society is succinctly set forth in a short article entitled "Quality of Our Lives" (1985). In that article, the author notes:

> Average people, who have no disabilities yet, look at our lives and see deprivation. But they misunderstand its cause.
> They discover we can't get into their cars to go out in the evenings. They see that we have to be helped up and down curbs, that we can get into only a few nice restaurants without help. They've heard from us that the college we attended held its classes up steps we had to be carried up and down. They notice that we still don't have a job, even though we earned a degree . . . .
> We must tell them in a way that will make them see that the problem is not our personal disabilities, but the design of those cars, city sidewalks, restaurants, university classrooms, office buildings and condominiums. When they're not designed for us to use, of course they can't give our lives "quality!" (Anonymous, p. 8)

Under the second concept of antidiscrimination, therefore, the roles that various *societal decisions* play in determining the real-life ramifications of a person's disability are scrutinized and, in a sense, "called to account." That is, the law requires employers and businesses to take affirmative steps that will "undo" the barriers that have been set up by society, often unintentionally, to keep people with disabilities out of employment and out of the enjoyment of goods and services. These requirements are termed making *reasonable accommodations* in the employment area (42 U.S.C. §12112[b][5]) and are termed modifying *policies, practices, and procedures,* providing *auxiliary aids and services,* and making physical access changes in the area of providing goods and services (42 U.S.C. §§12182[b][2][A][ii]–[iv], 12183).

The jurisprudential justification for such affirmative requirements is the same for both employment and public accommodations. The premise is that barriers to people with disabilities have been established because members of society have not historically viewed people with disabilities as part of the *societal norm.* Thus, no effort has been made to ensure that barriers to people with disabilities are not built into the structural frameworks of society. (By the term *structural* I mean both physical structures and policy structures [see, e.g., U.S. Commission on Civil Rights, 1983, pp. 17–27].) The second antidiscrimination concept of the ADA is presumed on the assumption that people with disabilities have a *civil right* to be considered part of the societal norm. This approach is itself revolutionary because it contrasts sharply with the traditional approach of "doing special things" for people with disabilities based on a charity model. (See, e.g., U.S. Commission on Civil Rights 1983, pp. 17–22, describing the charity approach; compare Hannaford, 1985, rejecting the charity model.) Indeed, one of the striking aspects of the second concept of anti-discrimination is that it requires affirmative activities on the part of employers and businesses *not* as part of a "help the handicapped" program, but rather as a response to the legitimate demands of a group whose civil rights have traditionally been denied.

The judgment was made by those of us seeking to pass the ADA that the most politically feasible manner in which to achieve the civil rights of people with disabilities at this time was to require individual employers and businesses to make the necessary modifications and adjustments at their own expense, and to build in flexibility based on the size and resources of the business. That is, the judgment was made to pattern the ADA after Section 504 of the Rehabilitation Act of 1973, which had already incorporated both concepts of antidiscrimination within its implementing regulations and case law, through placing such affirmative obligations on recipients of federal funds.

The ADA is thus essentially the "offspring" of two preexisting federal civil rights laws (Feldblum, 1991a, pp. 521–531). The substantive provisions of the ADA are drawn primarily from Sections 501, 503, and 504 of the Rehabilitation Act of 1973. These sections of the Rehabilitation Act prohibit discrimination on the basis of handicap by the federal government, by entities that receive federal funds, and by federal contractors. Politically, the goal of the drafters of the ADA was to draw as much as possible from the 15 years of experience under the Rehabilitation Act in order to demonstrate that a workable and understandable law could be achieved (see Feldblum, 1991a, pp. 523–528). Thus issues such as who is a person with a "disability," what constitutes "discrimination" on the basis of disability, and what is required as a "reasonable accommodation" were derived by the drafters of the ADA from similar substantive requirements that had been established under the Rehabilitation Act and its implementing regulations. These regulations had incorporated both concepts of antidiscrimination: first, that disability should not be taken into account in most circumstances, and second, that antidiscrimination requires, in some circumstances, the taking of affirmative steps that acknowledge and accommodate a person's disability.

The procedural requirements of the ADA, by contrast, were drawn primarily from the Civil Rights Act of 1964 (see 42 U.S.C. §§2000e to 2000e-17 [1988]; 42 U.S.C. §§2000a to 2000a-6 [1988]). Title VII of that law prohibits discrimination on the basis of race, sex, religion, or national origin on the part of employers with 15 or more employees (see 42 U.S.C. §§2000e[b], 2000e-2 [1988]). Title II of that law prohibits discrimination on the basis of race, religion, and national origin in selected private businesses (see 42 U.S.C. §2000a[b] [1988]). Thus the procedural requirements of the ADA, such as which entities are covered under the law and what remedies are available, are largely, although not exclusively, drawn from the Civil Rights Act of 1964. This approach was taken because one of the goals of the ADA was finally to establish parity in federal civil rights laws for people with disabilities and other minorities and women.

One significant difference in coverage between the ADA and Title II of the Civil Rights Act of 1964 concerns the type of public accommodations subject to the two laws. Title II of the Civil Rights Act prohibits discrimination on the part of hotels and other places of lodging, restaurants and other places that sell food, and recreational facilities (42 U.S.C. §2000a [b][1]–[2] [1988]) (See Whalen & Whalen, 1985, describing the struggle over coverage of public accommodations in the Civil Rights Act of 1964). By contrast, the ADA covers a wide range of businesses, including all sales and retail establishments and service providers (see 42 U.S.C. §12181[f]; see also Feldblum, 1991a, p. 528, explaining the "deal" between Senate sponsors of the ADA and the Bush administration that resulted in extensive coverage of public accommodations under the ADA).

WHO IS COVERED UNDER THE LAW?

To understand the ADA, one must first understand who is protected under the law. The ADA prohibits discrimination against an "individual with a disability" (see, e.g., 42 U.S.C. §§12112,
12132, 12182). The definition of "disability" under the ADA is derived substantially from the definition of "handicap" under the Rehabilitation Act. Although the Rehabilitation Act protects individuals with *handicaps* against discrimination (see 29 U.S.C. §794 [1988]), people with disabilities and their advocates prefer to use the term *disability* rather than handicap. In recognition of that
preference, the term disability is used throughout the ADA. The definition of disability, however, is
the same as the definition of handicap under Title V of the Rehabilitation Act with the exception of
the exclusion of current users of illegal drugs and certain other individuals (see pp. 41–42 in this
chapter; see also Feldblum, 1991b). Under the ADA, a "person with a disability" is someone who:
1) has a physical or mental impairment that substantially limits that person in one or more major life
activities, or 2) has a record of such a physical or mental impairment, or 3) is regarded as having
such a physical or mental impairment (42 U.S.C. §12102[2]).

First Prong of the Definition

The first prong of the definition of a person with a disability is someone who has a "physical or
mental impairment that substantially limits one or more of the major life activities of such individual" (42 U.S.C. §12102[2][a]). The regulations issued by the government agencies[2] to implement
the ADA explain that a "physical or mental impairment" is:

> any physiological disorder or condition, cosmetic disfigurement, or anatomical loss affecting one or
> more of the following body systems: neurological; musculoskeletal; special sense organs; respir
> atory, including speech organs; cardiovascular; reproductive; digestive; genito-urinary; hemic
> and lymphatic; skin; and endocrine [or] any mental or psychological disorder . . . . (29 C.F.R.
> §1630.2[h] [EEOC, 1992b], 28 C.F.R. §36.104 [DOJ, 1992a])

The various committee reports accompanying the ADA note the same definition for "physical or
mental impairment" (U.S. House of Representatives Committee on Education and Labor, 1990,
p. 51; U.S. House of Representatives Committee on the Judiciary, 1990, p. 28; U.S. Senate Committee on Labor and Human Resources, 1989, p. 22).

Neither the Rehabilitation Act regulations nor the ADA regulations attempt to set forth a list of
specific diseases or conditions that would make up physical or mental impairments. The reason is
simple: it would be impossible to ensure the comprehensiveness of such a list given the variety of
possible physical and mental disorders that may exist. The DOJ regulations, however, give some
examples of conditions that would be covered, including:

> contagious and noncontagious diseases and conditions such as orthopedic, visual, speech, and hearing
> impairments, cerebral palsy, epilepsy, muscular dystrophy, multiple sclerosis, cancer, heart disease,
> diabetes, mental retardation, emotional illness, specific learning disabilities, HIV disease (whether
> symptomatic or asymptomatic), tuberculosis, drug addiction and alcoholism. (28 C.F.R. §36.104[1][iii])

The committee reports accompanying the ADA included a similar list of examples (see U.S. House
of Representatives Committee on Education and Labor, 1990, p. 51; U.S. House of Representatives
Committee on the Judiciary, 1990, p. 28; U.S. Senate Committee on Labor and Human Resources,
1989, p. 22). The House Judiciary Report correctly notes that, although drug addiction is a recognized physical disorder, the currently illegal use of drugs is not protected under the ADA (see U.S.
House of Representatives Committee on the Judiciary, 1990, p. 28, note 17). This illustrative list of

---

[2]Equal Employment Opportunity Commission (EEOC) and U.S. Department of Justice (DOJ) regulations are codified
at 29 C.F.R. part 1630 (1992) and 28 C.F.R. part 36 (1992), respectively. References to various portions of these regulations
within this chapter cite the specific section of the regulations.

physical and mental disorders is derived from the U.S. Department of Health and Human Services (DHHS) regulations implementing Section 504 of the Rehabilitation Act (see 45 C.F.R. pt. 84, app. A[3]; DHHS, 1991, pp. 376–377).

An impairment, therefore, is some physiological or mental disorder. It does not include simple physical characteristics such as eye or hair color (29 C.F.R. app. §1630.2[h]; 28 C.F.R. app. §36.102). Having a physical or mental impairment, however, is only the first part of the definition. The impairment must also be one that "substantially limits" the person in a "major life activity." The EEOC and DOJ regulations both set forth an illustrative, nonexhaustive list of "major life activities." These included functions such as "caring for one's self, performing manual tasks, walking, seeing, hearing, speaking, breathing, learning, and working" (29 C.F.R. §1630.2[i]; 28 C.F.R. §36.104[2]). These are just examples of significant life activities. For example, the EEOC (1992a) notes that other life activities would include sitting, standing, lifting, and reaching (29 C.F.R. app. §1630.2[i]). The point is that the physiological or mental disorder must be a type that substantially limits the person in a significant life activity.

The meaning of "substantially limits" is also quite broad. A person is substantially limited in a major life activity if: 1) the person cannot do the activity at all; or 2) the person is limited in the "condition, manner, or duration" in which he or she performs the life activity (29 C.F.R. §1630.2[j]). For example, a completely deaf person would be substantially limited in the life activity of hearing because he or she is not able to hear at all. A person who uses artificial legs and is able to walk would also be substantially limited in the life activity of walking because he or she is restricted in the *condition* or *manner* in which he or she engages in that activity (see 29 C.F.R. app. §1630.2[j]). In determining whether a person is "substantially limited" in a life activity, the potential limitation must be analyzed without regard to the existence of mitigating devices or medicines. For example, a person with diabetes who is performing all life activities without difficulty because he or she is taking insulin is covered under the *first* prong of the definition of disability because *without* insulin that person would be limited in various life activities (see 29 C.F.R. app. §1630.2[h], [j]).

Most serious medical conditions do have a substantial impact on basic life activities. For example, someone with emphysema will have substantial difficulty in breathing; someone who is a paraplegic will have substantial difficulty in walking; and someone with dyslexia will have substantial difficulty in learning. As the acting Assistant Attorney General, Office of Legal Counsel, of the Department of Justice pointed out in a legal memo on Section 504, another significant life activity is that of procreation and intimate personal relations, in which people infected with HIV are substantially limited (Kmiec, 1988, p. 9). Both the EEOC and DOJ regulations note that people with HIV infection, asymptomatic and symptomatic, are covered under the first prong of the definition of disability (see 29 C.F.R. app. §1630.2[j]; 28 C.F.R. app. §36.104). The term *people with disabilities,* therefore, is not limited to what has sometimes been termed *traditional disabilities.* The ADA covers a wide range of individuals—from people who use wheelchairs, to people who have vision or hearing impairments, to people with epilepsy or cerebral palsy or HIV disease or lung cancer or manic depression. A relatively exhaustive list of disabilities that have been covered under the Rehabilitation Act and that would similarly be covered under the ADA can be found in *de la Torres v. Bolger* (1986). A list of approximately 50 examples of impairments covered under the Rehabilitation Act and citations to cases can also be found in Burgdorf (1990, pp. 77, 82–83).

Second Prong of the Definition

The second prong of the definition of disability covers a person with a "record" of an impairment (42 U.S.C. §12102[2][B]). A person with a record of an impairment is defined as someone who: 1) had a physiological or mental disorder that substantially limited them in a major life activity but *no longer* has that impairment, or 2) someone who was simply *misclassified* as having such an impairment (29 C.F.R. §1630.2[k]; 28 C.F.R. §36.104[3]). The EEOC and DOJ regulations explain that frequently occurring examples of the first group are people who have histories of mental or emotional illness, heart disease, or cancer. Such individuals may no longer have the impairment, but *had* the impairment at some point in the past. A frequently occurring example of the second group are people who have been misclassified as having mental retardation or learning disabilities (29 C.F.R. app. §1630.2[k]; 28 C.F.R. app. §36.104).

The point of the second prong of the definition is that people who have *recovered* from a physiological or mental disorder often face discrimination simply because of the stigma or the fear associated with such impairments when an employer or business discovers they have a history of such a disorder. The employer or other entity may discover this fact through educational, medical, or employment records. If any of these records indicates that the individual had a substantially limiting physiological or mental disorder, and the employer discriminates against the person based on that record, that person is covered under the second prong of the definition (29 C.F.R. §1630.2[k]; 28 C.F.R. §36.104[3]).

Third Prong of the Definition

The EEOC and DOJ regulations lay out in detail the individuals who are covered under the third prong of the definition of disability. The regulations explain that a person is regarded as having such an impairment if:

1. The person has a physical or mental impairment that does *not* substantially limit a major life activity, but is *treated* by an entity covered by the law as constituting such limitation.
2. The person has a physical or mental impairment that substantially limits a major life activity *only as the result of* the attitudes of others toward the impairment.
3. The person does *not* have a physical or mental impairment, but is treated by the entity covered by the law as having a physical or mental impairment that substantially limits a major life activity. (29 C.F.R. §1630.2[l]; 28 C.F.R. §36.104[4]).

These three examples are different aspects of the same concept. The underlying common theme is that the law prohibits discrimination against an individual who is treated *as if* he or she has a disability—that is, as if he or she has a physiological or mental disorder that limits him or her in a major life activity.

The first two examples provided in the regulations deal with situations in which an individual has some physiological or mental impairment, but that impairment does not actually limit the person in any life activity. The person's impairment, however, is treated by an employer or business as substantially limiting the person in some major life activity.

This type of treatment may occur, for example, if an employer or business has certain assumptions about what a person with a particular impairment is or is not capable of doing, or if the employer or business is reacting to the fears or concerns of others. For example, assume that a person has slightly high blood pressure that does not actually limit him or her in any life activity. If an employer is nevertheless afraid that the person's blood pressure level will make him or her incapable of performing any stressful jobs, or a business owner believes that the person's high blood pressure makes him or her incapable of enjoying the business's service, and the employer refuses to hire the person or the business owner refuses to serve the person on that basis, that individual is covered under the third prong of the definition (29 C.F.R. app. §1630.2[k]; 28 C.F.R. app. §36.104).

As a second example, assume that a person has a significant physiological cosmetic disorder that does not, in fact, substantially limit the person in any way. If an employer, however, views that disorder as substantially limiting the person's ability to work because of potential adverse reactions from co-workers or customers and refuses to hire the person on that basis, or a business views the disorder as making other customers uncomfortable and refuses to serve the person on that basis, that person is covered under the third prong of the definition (29 C.F.R. app. §1630.2[k]; 28 C.F.R. app. §36.104).

The third situation referred to in the regulations deals with a person who has *no* impairment at all, but who is treated by an employer or business owner as if he or she has a physiological or mental disorder that substantially limits the person in a life activity. For example, assume that a person does not have either AIDS or HIV infection, but is perceived by an employer or a business owner as having AIDS or HIV infection and is fired or refused services on that basis. That individual would be covered under the third prong of the definition (29 C.F.R. app. §1630.2[l]; 28 C.F.R. app. §36.104).

The scope and purpose of the third prong of the definition of disability may not be intuitively obvious to all (see, e.g., U.S. House of Representatives Committee on the Judiciary, 1989, pp. 70–75). Yet this prong reflects a basic fact of disability discrimination: many instances of discrimination occur not because of any inherent difficulty that an *impairment* causes an individual with regard to a major life activity, but rather because of difficulties created as a result of the *reaction* of others to an actual or perceived physical or mental impairment.

Thus, in all of the examples noted above, it is the discriminatory *action* of an employer or business owner that operates to *create* coverage for individuals who would otherwise not be covered under the law. That is, the third prong of the definition of disability specifically encompasses individuals whose impairments are not particularly severe (i.e., they are not covered under the first prong of the definition because they do not constitute actual limitations in life activities) or who have no impairments at all. It is an action by *another,* based on fears and presumptions, that creates antidiscrimination protection for such individuals.

Specific categories of people with various disabilities received special attention during the passage of the ADA—either to emphasize their inclusion or to establish their exclusion (for a more explicit discussion of the coverage and exclusion of such individuals, see Feldblum, 1991b, pp. 18–25). For example, people who currently illegally use drugs are excluded from the definition of disability under the ADA (42 U.S.C. §12114[a]; 29 C.F.R. §1630.3[a]; 28 C.F.R. §36.209[a][1]). Individuals who have recovered from such use or are erroneously regarded as drug users remain covered under the law (42 U.S.C. §12114[b]; 29 C.F.R. §1630.3[b]; 28 C.F.R. §36.209[a][2]). People with various sexual and behavior disorders are excluded from the definition of disability (42 U.S.C. §12211[b]; 29 C.F.R. §1630.3[d]; 28 C.F.R. §36.104[5]). The excluded disorders are pedophilia, exhibitionism, voyeurism, gender identity disorders that are not the result of physical impairments, other sexual behavior disorders, compulsive gambling, kleptomania, pyromania, and psychoactive substance use disorders resulting from the current illegal use of drugs. Transvestism and transsexualism, which are still defined as mental impairments by the American Psychiatric Association, are also included in this list of exclusions. (This list of exclusions was added to the ADA by the Senate in the waning hours of the Senate's consideration of the ADA.)

Congress specifically affirmed that homosexuality and bisexuality are not physical or mental impairments and hence not covered under the ADA (42 U.S.C. §12211[a]). However, although sexual orientation is not a disability protected under the ADA, a gay man, lesbian, or bisexual person who has a disability covered under the law is protected from discrimination on the basis of the covered disability. Thus, for example, a homosexual or bisexual person who has HIV disease, uses a wheelchair, or is blind is protected against unjustified discrimination based on those covered disabilities. Moreover, if a gay man, lesbian, or bisexual person is discriminated against by an employer or a business owner because the person is *regarded* as having AIDS or HIV infection, that person is protected under the third prong of the definition of disability. In addition, Congress specifically noted that people with AIDS and asymptomatic HIV infection are covered under the ADA's definition of disability. The term *HIV disease,* which is the term used in the legislative history to the

ADA, includes everything from asymptomatic HIV infection to full-blown AIDS. Thus "HIV disease" is used as a single term to describe the spectrum of manifestations of HIV-related illness covered under the definition of disability (see 29 C.F.R. app. §1630.2[j]; 28 C.F.R. §36.104[1][iii]; see also U.S. House of Representatives Committee on Education and Labor, 1990, p. 52; U.S. House of Representatives Committee on the Judiciary, 1990, p. 28, note 18; U.S. Senate Committee on Labor and Human Resources, 1989, p. 22). For an explanation of the term, see U.S. House of Representatives (1990b, 1990c, 1990d) and U.S. Senate (1990).

The ADA also prohibits discrimination against an individual because the individual *associates* with a person who has a disability (42 U.S.C. §§12112[b][4], 12182[b][1][E]; 29 C.F.R. §1630.8; 28 C.F.R. §36.205). For example, an employer could not refuse to hire an applicant simply because the applicant's wife or husband uses a wheelchair or because the applicant lives with a person who has AIDS (29 C.F.R. §1630.8 & app.). Similarly, a movie theater could not refuse entrance to a person with cerebral palsy and to his or her friends simply because they are accompanying the person with cerebral palsy (28 C.F.R. §36.205 & app.). Although protection for people who associate with people with disabilities does not appear in the Rehabilitation Act, it is not a new concept. When Congress passed the Fair Housing Amendments Act of 1988, in which protection against discrimination was extended to people with disabilities in the sale or rental of private housing, Congress added protection for people who associate with people with disabilities (see 42 U.S.C. §3604[f][1]–[2]). Such protection was added because people who are friends or relatives of people with disabilities are often discriminated against simply because they associate with a person with a disability.

The ADA does not limit the forms in which the "association" with the person with a disability takes place. Thus individuals who associate with a person with a disability through a range of activities—through being a friend, spouse, domestic partner, relative, business associate, advocate, or caregiver—are all covered under the association provision (29 C.F.R. §1630.8; 28 C.F.R. §36.205). Indeed, there were various efforts made during the legislative process to restrict the coverage of this provision to individuals who associate with people with disabilities through marriage, blood, or caregiving relationships. These various restrictive efforts failed (see, e.g., U.S. House of Representatives Committee on the Judiciary, 1990, p. 38).

WHAT IS PROHIBITED UNDER THE LAW?

Traditional Civil Rights Protection

Like most other civil rights laws, the ADA sets forth general prohibitions against discrimination in areas such as employment (42 U.S.C. §12112[a]) and public accommodations (42 U.S.C. §12182[a]). As a basic rule in employment, the ADA provides that no "covered entity" may discriminate against a qualified person with a disability, because of the disability of such individual, in a range of employment decisions: job application procedures; the hiring, advancement, or discharge of employees; employee compensation; job training; and other terms and conditions of employment (42 U.S.C. §12112[a]). The term *covered entity* includes employers, employment agencies, labor organizations, and joint labor–management committees (42 U.S.C. §12111[2]). (The definition of *employer* is drawn from Title VII of the Civil Rights Act of 1964; see 42 U.S.C. §2000e[b].) Essentially, every type of employment decision is covered. The Section 504 regulations, the legislative history to the ADA, and the EEOC regulations include a more detailed list of employment decisions in which disability discrimination is prohibited (29 C.F.R. §1630.4; see also U.S. House of Representatives Committee on Education and Labor, 1990, pp. 54–55; U.S. House of Representatives Committee on the Judiciary, 1990, p. 35; U.S. Senate Committee on Labor and Human Resources, 1989, p. 25). The basic requirement is that a qualified person with a disability may not be discriminated against on the basis of his or her disability in terms of hiring, firing, promotions, recruitment, conditions of the employment position, or any other aspect of employment.

As a general rule in public accommodations, the ADA similarly provides that no individual shall be discriminated against on the basis of disability "in the full and equal enjoyment" of the "goods, services, facilities, privileges, advantages, or accommodations" of any place of public accommodation (42 U.S.C. §12182[a]). This prohibition applies to any entity that owns, leases, leases to, or operates a place of public accommodation. The DOJ regulations define a place of public accommodation to mean a facility that falls within one of the 12 designated categories in the law. A *public accommodation* is then defined as a private entity that owns, leases (or leases to), or operates a place of public accommodation (see 28 C.F.R. §36.104 [1992]). Thus, for example, a covered entity under the public accommodations section would include the owner of a building in which a restaurant was located, the owner of the restaurant, the operator of the restaurant, and a group that leased the restaurant for a particular function.

The ADA sets forth a list of 12 broad categories of private establishments that are considered public accommodations. The categories include, among others, all sales and rental establishments, all service establishments (from shoe repair services to lawyers' offices to doctors' offices), all places of education, all places selling food or providing lodging, and all places of recreation (42 U.S.C. §12181[7]). All businesses that fall within these 12 categories are covered regardless of the number of employees that work in the business. This parallels the absence of a limit based on employee size in Title II of the Civil Rights Act of 1964. There is a longer phase-in period, however, before the public accommodations section of the ADA becomes effective for small businesses.

Unlike most other civil rights laws, the ADA then sets forth *specific constructions* of what it considers "discrimination" on the basis of disability to encompass. In both employment and public accommodations, the law's constructions of antidiscrimination include the traditional concept of civil rights as well as the newer, more affirmative concept of civil rights (see Affirmative Aspects of Antidiscrimination Protection, below).

For example, in the employment context the ADA states that the prohibition on discrimination means that an employer may not limit, segregate, or classify applicants or employees on the basis of disability in a way that adversely affects the opportunities or status of such individuals (42 U.S.C. §12112[b][1]). This is a relatively straightforward application of the traditional antidiscrimination concept. Under this approach an employer is not permitted to treat a person with a disability differently simply because of the person's disability. For example, an employer may not have all employees with disabilities work in a separate, segregated section of the workplace or pay its employees with disabilities on a lower pay scale for work equivalent to that peformed by other employees (29 C.F.R. app. §1630.5).

Similarly, in the public accommodations arena, the ADA specifies that discrimination includes: denying a person with a disability the *opportunity* to participate in or benefit from a good or service; providing a person with a disability a benefit or service that is *not equal* to that provided others; or providing a person with a disability a *different or separate* benefit or service from that provided others (42 U.S.C. §12182[b][1][A][iii]). Again, these prohibitions represent straightforward applications of the civil rights principle that disability is a characteristic that should not be taken into account in providing services or goods or in providing unequal or separate services or goods.

For example, with regard to denying a person the opportunity to enjoy goods or services, a restaurant could not refuse to serve a person with cerebral palsy; a video store could not refuse to rent videos to a blind person; and an accountant could not refuse to provide services to a person with AIDS (see generally 28 C.F.R. §36.202[a]). With regard to providing unequal goods or services, a hotel could not refuse to rent suites with a good view to people with muscular dystrophy and a beauty shop could not require that deaf people be served only by "junior" beauticians (see generally

28 C.F.R. §36.202[b]). Finally, with regard to providing separate services, a restaurant could not require that people who have amputated limbs sit in only one particular section of the restaurant; a bank could not require that people who are blind be served only by a special designated teller; and a day camp could not require that all children with learning disabilities attend a separate, special section of the camp (see generally 28 C.F.R. §36.202[c]). (See Separate Services under the ADA, below, for qualifications on these requirements.)

In both the employment and public accommodations arenas, the ADA also explicitly provides that the employer or public accommodation may not enter into a contractual arrangement that has the effect of subjecting the employer's employees or the public accommodation's customers to discrimination (42 U.S.C. §§12112[b][2], 12182[b][1][A][i]–[iv]). In other words, an employer or a public accommodation may not do indirectly through a contract or a license what it may not do directly under the ADA. In the employment context, this provision means that, if an employer contracts with another entity to provide training for its employees, the training must be provided in a place and manner that is accessible to any employees with disabilities. Similarly, if the employer holds an annual retreat or convention for its employees, the employer must pick a site that is accessible to its employees with disabilities (see 29 C.F.R. §1630.6); see also U.S. House of Representatives Committee on Education and Labor, 1990, p. 60; U.S. House of Representatives Committee on the Judiciary, 1990, p. 37). These would be the type of reasonable accommodation requirements the employer would bear if it were acting directly. Similarly, in the area of public accommodations, a day camp could not contract with another company to perform its application procedures for the camp and then allow that company to screen out all children with AIDS (28 C.F.R. §36.202). Again, such provisions are a basic application of the traditional civil rights concept—they prohibit an entity from taking disability into account either directly or through the use of contractual or licensing arrangements.

Affirmative Aspects of Antidiscrimination Protection

Apart from the traditional antidiscrimination prohibitions, the ADA also sets forth constructions of antidiscrimination that embody the second concept of antidiscrimination. That is, the law explicitly provides that discrimination includes *not* taking certain *affirmative steps* to make changes and modifications.

Employment   In the employment arena, the ADA provides that discrimination includes a failure to provide "reasonable accommodations" to the known physical or mental limitations of a person with a disability who is otherwise qualified to perform a particular job (42 U.S.C. §12112[b][5][A]–[B]). A person with a disability is often perfectly able to perform a job—*if* some adjustment is first made in the job structure, job schedule, physical layout of the job, or job equipment. For example, a person who uses a wheelchair may need a table adjusted for height or may need a ramp built to allow access. Persons with varying degrees of hearing impairments may need a telephone amplifier or an interpreter. Someone with a chronic physical condition may need some time off each week for medical treatments. If these adjustments or modifications—which are called reasonable accommodations—are made, a person with a disability might *then* be qualified for the particular job he or she seeks.

Reasonable Accommodations   The ADA mandates that employers provide these reasonable accommodations to both applicants and employees with disabilities. The ADA requires that employers provide reasonable accommodations to a person with a disability who is "otherwise qualified" to perform a particular job. What this means is that an applicant or employee must *first* show that he or she meets all of the employer's job-related selection criteria *except* those criteria that he or she cannot meet because of the disability but that could be met if a reasonable accommodation were provided. An initial job-related criterion would be, for example, possessing a certain educational degree. If the individual meets these job-related criteria and is thus "otherwise qualified" for the job, the employer must then provide a reasonable accommodation to allow the person to be fully qualified for the job (42 U.S.C. §12112[b][5][A]; 29 C.F.R. §1630.9 & app.; U.S. House of Representatives Committee on Education and Labor, 1990, pp. 64–65).

The law provides examples of modifications that fall within the framework of reasonable accommodations (42 U.S.C. §12111[9]). These include:

1. Making modifications to the physical layout of a job facility so as to make it accessible to individuals who use wheelchairs or who have other impairments that make access difficult (29 C.F.R. §1630.2[o][2][i]).
2. Restructuring a job so as to enable the person with a disability to perform the essential functions of the job. Job restructuring may include eliminating nonessential elements of the job, exchanging assignments with other employees or redesigning procedures for task performance (29 C.F.R. app. §1630.2[o]; U.S. House of Representatives Committee on Education and Labor, 1990, p. 62).
3. Establishing a part-time or modified work schedule (e.g., to accommodate people with disabilities who have treatment needs or fatigue problems) (29 C.F.R. §1630.2[o][2][ii]; U.S. House of Representatives 1990b, 1990c; U.S. House of Representatives Committee on Education and Labor, 1990, p. 62).
4. Reassigning a person with a disability to a vacant job. An employer is not required to create a new job for an employee with a disability who is no longer able to perform his or her present job. However, if a vacant job exists that the person is qualified to perform, reassignment to that job would be a required reasonable accommodation (29 C.F.R. §1630.2[o][2][ii] & app.; see also U.S. House of Representatives Committee on Education and Labor, 1990, p. 63).
5. Acquiring or modifying equipment or devices (such as buying a telephone amplifier for a person with a hearing impairment) (29 C.F.R. §1630.2[o][2][ii] & app.).
6. Adjusting or modifying exams, training materials, or policies (such as giving an application examination orally to a person with dyslexia or modifying a policy against dogs in the workplace for a person with a service dog) (29 C.F.R. §1630.2[o][2][ii] & app.).
7. Providing qualified readers or interpreters for people with vision or hearing impairments (28 C.F.R. §1630.2[o][2][ii] & app.). Personal assistants for people with disabilities is another possible from of reasonable accommodation (see 29 C.F.R. §1630.2[o] & app., noting coverage of travel attendants as a reasonable accommodation; U.S. House of Representatives Committee on Education and Labor, 1990, p. 64; U.S. Senate Committee on Labor and Human Resources, 1989; p. 33).

These are simply examples of types of accommodations that might be required. The basic characteristic of a reasonable accommodation is that it is designed to address the particular, unique needs of a person with a particular disability. Thus the accommodation needed by the person might be one that falls within one of the above categories, or it might be a different type of accommodation personally identified by the person with a disability or by the employer. The underlying goal is to identify aspects of the disability that make it difficult or impossible for the person with a disability to perform certain aspects of a job and then to determine if there are any modifications or adjustments to the job environment or structure that will enable the person to be qualified to perform the job (42 U.S.C. §12111[9]; 29 C.F.R. app. §1630.2[a]). It should be noted that discrimination also includes refusing to hire a person with a disability simply because the person will require a reasonable accommodation (42 U.S.C. §12112[b][5][B]).

Undue Hardship   As can be imagined, some accommodations are quite inexpensive and are easy to institute, whereas others are quite costly and are difficult to implement. In light of that fact, the ADA set a limitation on the employer's obligation to provide a reasonable accommodation. Under the law, an employer need not provide an accommodation if doing so would impose an "undue hardship" on the employer. An accommodation is considered to rise to the level of an undue hardship if providing it would result in a "significant difficulty or expense" for the employer (see 42 U.S.C. §§12111[10], 12112[b][5][A]). This limitation on an employer's responsibilities is similar to the limitation that exists under Section 504 of the Rehabilitation Act of 1973 (45 C.F.R. §84.12).

Whether an accommodation is considered to impose a "significant difficulty or expense" on the employer depends on a series of factors about the particular business. The ADA sets forth the following factors that must be weighed:

1. What is the nature of the needed accommodation and how much will it cost?
2. What are the financial resources available to the employer, how big is the employer (i.e., how many individuals are employed), and what effect will the accommodation have on the employer's expenses, resources, or other areas?
3. What is the type of operation and type of work force run by the employer and what impact will the accommodation have on that operation and work force?

The factors for undue hardship in the ADA were taken primarily from those set forth in the DHHS regulations implementing Section 504 (45 C.F.R. §84.12[c]). The EEOC regulations explicate the factors for undue hardship (29 C.F.R. §1630.2[p]). One modification made, however, was to take into account "site-specific" concerns.

There were extensive negotiations surrounding the ADA during its consideration by a Senate Committee and four separate House Committees, including the House Education and Labor Committee and the House Judiciary Committee (see Feldblum, 1991a, pp. 523–531, detailing the political chronology of the development of the ADA). During negotiations on the ADA in both the House Education and Labor Committee and the House Judiciary Committee, those representing business owners raised the concern that the unique needs of a facility that was operating on the margin or at a loss but was part of a larger parent company might not be taken into account with regard to the provision of reasonable accommodations. The specific fear expressed was that a parent company might choose to close a marginally profitable facility, rather than have the facility provide an expensive accommodation (see U.S. House of Representatives Committee on Education and Labor, 1990, p. 68; U.S. House of Representatives Committee on the Judiciary, 1990, pp. 40–41). These were termed *site-specific concerns*.

To address these concerns, the undue hardship factors were modified to clarify that, if a large entity operated several facilities, a court was to weigh the financial resources of *both* the small facility *and* the parent company and was to analyze the relationship between the two. In other words, a court was to examine the regular practices of the parent company in providing services and resources to its facilities in the area of employee benefits, services, and hiring in order to determine what resources were reasonably available to the local facility from the parent company (see U.S. House of Representatives Committee on Education and Labor, 1990, pp. 68–69; U.S. House of Representatives Committee on the Judiciary, 1990, p. 40; see also 29 C.F.R. §1630.2[p][2][ii]–[iii] & app.). Thus the small facility of a large company would not be treated like an independent small business because the parent company's resources would be taken into account—but hardships unique to the small facility would be considered as well.

As reflected in the statutory language, the ADA's approach to undue hardship was to require that the nature and cost of the accommodation be assessed in light of an employer's financial resources, workplace, and operations. The undue hardship standard is thus a *relative* standard. An accommodation that would rise to the level of an undue hardship for one employer in light of that employer's size, financial resources, or structure would not necessarily be an undue hardship for another employer (see U.S. House of Representatives Committee on the Judiciary, 1990, p. 41 ["Only those accommodations which would require significant difficulty or expense when considered in light of the size, resources, and structure of the employer would be considered an undue hardship"]; U.S. House of Representatives Committee on Education and Labor, 1990, p. 67; U.S. Senate Committee on Labor and Human Resources, 1989, pp. 35–36; 29 C.F.R. app. §1630.2[p]: "The 'undue hardship' provision takes into account the financial realities of the particular employer or other covered entity"; see also the individualized approach in determining undue hardship in the case of *Nelson v. Thornburgh* [1983]).

The fact that the ADA's undue hardship standard is a flexible one caused some concern to representatives of the business community during passage of the ADA. Understandably, businesses want certainty; it is hard for an employer to imagine providing reasonable accommodations if the employer can never be "sure" whether a particular accommodation would ultimately be required under the law or not.

Although this desire for certainty is understandable, various alternatives to the flexible approach could severely undermine the civil rights aspect of the reasonable accommodation requirement without aiding employers in any significant manner. For example, a requirement that employers spend up to 10% of their gross income on reasonable accommodations would not take into account the employer's other expenses or whether those expenses have been particularly heavy in a specific year. A requirement that employers spend up to 10% of their net income on accommodations would allow employers to allocate all of their income to other expenses (including discretionary expenses) before any resources would be considered for accommodations for people with disabilities. An approach that tied the accommodation limit to a certain percentage of an employee's salary would mean that a wide range of accommodations that would be reasonable to expect large employers to provide as a matter of civil rights would not be required simply because the person with a disability was in a low-paying job. Indeed, the House of Representatives rejected an amendment that would have created a presumption of undue hardship if a reasonable accommodation cost more than 10% of the annual salary of the employee requesting it (House of Representatives, 1990a).

In the final analysis, therefore, Congress chose to continue the flexible "undue hardship" approach that had been used under the Rehabilitation Act for over 15 years. This approach ensures that the different resources and needs of small companies, as compared to large companies, are taken into account in each individual case while still providing the essential protection of reasonable accommodations to people with disabilities.

Public Accommodations In the area of public accommodations, the ADA lists three categories of affirmative steps that must be undertaken by private businesses to ensure that people with disabilities are effectively able to enjoy the goods and services being offered. Failure to take such steps constitutes discrimination against people with disabilities. These three requirement areas, covering modifications, auxiliary aids and services, and accessibility, are basically identical to the reasonable accommodation requirement in the employment arena, but the decision was made by those drafting the ADA to divide the requirement into three separate categories.

Modifications The ADA provides that a public accommodation must modify its policies, practices, and procedures if such modifications are necessary for a person with a disability to enjoy the goods and services being offered (42 U.S.C. §12182[b][2][A][ii]). For example, a restaurant that has a "no pets" rule must modify that policy to allow a person who uses a guide dog to keep the dog with him or her while eating at the restaurant (28 C.F.R. §36.302[c] & app.).

Auxiliary Aids and Services A public accommodation must provide "auxiliary aids and services" to a person with a disability if doing so would enable the person to benefit from the goods or services (42 U.S.C. §12182[b][2][A][iii]). For example, a doctor's office may have to provide an interpreter for a patient who is deaf, and a bank may have to ensure either that its written materials are available in braille for blind individuals or that a person is available to read the materials to blind customers (28 C.F.R. §36.303). The DOJ regulations make clear that the provision regarding auxiliary aids and services applies solely to making goods and services available to individuals with disabilities affecting hearing, vision, or speech (28 C.F.R. app. §36.303). As the DOJ guidance explains, a business is required to ensure that individuals with other disabilities can effectively enjoy the business's goods and services through its obligations regarding modifications of policies and practices and physical barrier removal.

Again, there are limits to the requirements placed by the ADA. For example, a modification of a policy or practice need not be undertaken if doing so would "fundamentally alter the nature" of the goods or services being offered (42 U.S.C. §12182[b][2][ii]). For example, assume that a person with a vision impairment needs bright lights in order to see. A night club that kept its lights down low for ambience purposes would not have to change that policy because doing so would fundamentally alter the nature of the service being provided (28 C.F.R. §36.303[a]). (It is interesting to note that there is no *financial limit* placed on this obligation, although such limits are placed on most other obligations of businesses under the law.)

Similarly, a public accommodation need not provide an auxiliary aid or service if doing so would either fundamentally alter the nature of the goods or services being offered or impose an "undue burden" on the accommodation (42 U.S.C. §12182[b][2][A][iii]). Like undue hardship in employment, an undue burden is defined in the DOJ regulations as an action requiring "significant difficulty or expense" on the part of the public accommodation (28 C.F.R. §36.303[a]). Again, like undue hardship in employment, whether provision of an auxiliary aid would impose a significant difficulty or expense will depend on a range of factors, including the size and financial resources of the business (28 C.F.R. §36.104).

Accessibility   Public accommodations are also required to take various affirmative steps to make their facilities accessible to people with disabilities. The limitations on these requirements vary depending on the *status* of the building—that is, whether the building is an existing one, is undergoing renovations, or is newly constructed.

In an existing building the law places a relatively low burden on a public accommodation in order to achieve nondiscrimination: the public accommodation must make physical access changes that are "readily achievable" (42 U.S.C. §12182[b][2][A][iv]). The ADA defines readily achievable as an action that is "easily accomplishable . . . without much difficulty or expense (42 U.S.C. §12181[9]). Examples would include installing ramps; making curb cuts in sidewalks and entrances; repositioning shelves; rearranging tables, vending machines, display racks, and other furniture; repositioning telephones; widening doors; eliminating a turnstile or providing an alternative accessible path; repositioning the paper towel dispenser in a bathroom and installing a full-length mirror; and creating designated accessible parking spaces (28 C.F.R. §36.304[b]).

The standard for determining whether an action is readily achievable is again a relative one, depending on the size and financial resources of the business. (42 U.S.C. §12181[9] lists factors to weigh in determining whether an action is readily achievable.) The *factors* listed in the law (such as the cost of the action, the financial resources of the business, and site-specific concerns) are identical to those set forth in the law to determine whether a reasonable accommodation in the employment setting represents an undue hardship and those set forth in the DOJ regulations to determine whether providing an auxiliary aid in a public accommodation setting represents an undue burden. The difference lies in the *standard* against which those factors are applied. That is, the standard for undue hardship and undue burden is "significant difficulty or expense." By contrast, the standard for readily achievable is "easily accomplishable and able to be carried out without much difficulty or expense."

If a public accommodation chooses to renovate a building, it must ensure that the renovated area is fully accessible. For example, the public accommodation may not build steps into the newly renovated area and would have to remove any steps that existed prior to the renovation in the area (42 U.S.C. §12183[a][2]). The only limitation in this regard is that the renovated area must be made accessible "to the maximum extent feasible (42 U.S.C. §12183[a][2]). Almost all accessibility changes will meet this standard. The DOJ regulations provide that, in circumstances in which the nature of an existing facility makes it "virtually impossible" to comply fully with applicable accessibility standards, the alteration shall provide the maximum physical accessibility feasible (28 C.F.R. §36.402[c]).

If a public accommodation renovates a "primary function area" of its building, it incurs more extensive access requirements. A primary function area includes any area in which a primary function of the business takes place (28 C.F.R. §36.403[b]). For example, the customer service area of a bank is a primary function area, as is the dining area of a cafeteria, the meeting rooms in a conference center, and the offices and other work areas in which the activities of the public accommodation using the facility are carried out. Most major service or employment areas in a building will meet the definition of a primary function area. Areas that would not be covered include such places as mechanical rooms, boiler rooms, supply storage rooms, employee lounges or locker rooms, janitorial closets, entrances, corridors, and rest rooms. In renovating a primary function area, the public accommodation must ensure that not only the renovated area itself but also the "path of travel" to the area is accessible (42 U.S.C. §12183[a][2]). In other words, the path that a person would travel from the *entrance* of the building *to the renovated area* must be made barrier free (28 C.F.R. §36.403[e]). In addition, the facilities serving the area, such as rest rooms, telephones, and water fountains, must be made accessible as well (42 U.S.C. §12183[a][2]).

An explicit financial limit, however, is afforded public accommodations in this area. That is, the path of travel and facilities serving the area do not have to be made accessible if the cost of doing so would be disproportionate to the cost of the initial renovation (42 U.S.C. §12183[a][2]). The DOJ has decided that "disproportionate" means any amount greater than 20 percent of the cost of the initial renovation (28 C.F.R. §36.403[f]). Thus if a public accommodation spends $100,000 on a renovation, it is required to spend up to, but not more than, $20,000 in making the path of travel to the renovated area and the facilities serving the area accessible (28 C.F.R. §36.403[g]). There is also an exemption that elevators need not be installed in buildings with fewer than three stories or less than 3,000 square feet per floor (42 U.S.C. §12183[b]; 28 C.F.R. §36.404).

Finally, if a public accommodation builds a new building, it must meet stringent requirements of accessibility: the building must be "readily accessible to and usable by" people with disabilities (42 U.S.C. §12183[a][1]). This means that people with disabilities must be able to enter the building, get around in the building, and use the building's facilities. Although it is not necessary that every rest room or, in some situations, every room be fully accessible, this standard requires a very high degree of accessibility throughout the building (U.S. House of Representatives Committee on Education and Labor, 1990, p. 118; U.S. House of Representatives Committee on the Judiciary, 1990, p. 60). In addition, there is no financial limitation on this requirement. Rather, a new building must be built accessible unless doing so would be "structurally impracticable" (42 U.S.C. §12183[a][1]; 28 C.F.R. §36.401[c]). Full compliance is structurally impracticable solely when the "unique characteristics of the terrain *prevent* the incorporation of accessibility features" (emphasis added).

Affirmative Requirements and Concomitant Limitations   In the areas of both employment and public accommodations, the ADA thus places affirmative obligations on employers and businesses to remove barriers to the employment of people with disabilities or to the ability of people with disabilities to enjoy goods or services—whether those barriers are caused by physical impediments or by policy impediments. In each case, however, the civil right of the individual with the disability to encounter a society free of barriers is not carried to its logical conclusion. That is, in each case, a *limit* is placed on the employer's or public accommodation's obligation to make changes or modifications. These limits take into account both financial and operational concerns of the employer or business.

Some might say the incorporation of financial and operational limitations in the law ensures that the civil rights of people with disabilities are not carried to their "extreme conclusion." I believe that the second concept of antidiscrimination, which rests on the premise that people with disabilities have a civil right to be *included* within the *societal norm*, does not inherently (nor should it) include a limitation based on cost or operational difficulty. Thus I believe that the civil rights of people with disabilities have not been taken to their "logical" conclusion in the ADA.

I also believe, however, that as a practical and political matter, Congress would not have passed the ADA without these particular limitations (see, e.g., Feldblum, 1991a, pp. 523–531). That is, I believe that *Congress* viewed establishing affirmative requirements on businesses and employers without including concomitant limitations based on cost and operational difficulty as taking the civil rights concept for people with disabilities to an "extreme" rather than a "logical" conclusion. Accepting this premise within the law was thus a necessary precondition to ensure that the bill actually became a law.

Qualification Standards and Eligibility Criteria: A Combination of the Civil Rights Concepts

The ADA sets forth explicit requirements regarding qualification standards in employment and eligibility criteria in public accommodations that incorporate both concepts of antidiscrimination. In employment the ADA provides that discrimination includes having qualification standards, employment tests, or other job selection criteria that "screen out or tend to screen out" people with disabilities (42 U.S.C. §12112[b][6]). For example, an employer may not have as a qualification standard for a job the requirement that applicants must be able to stand for 5 hours at a time or must have a driver's license, because such standards would screen out, or tend to screen out, people whose disabilities preclude them from standing for long periods of time (e.g., people with various medical conditions) or from obtaining drivers' licenses (e.g., some people who use wheelchairs or who have epilepsy).

This requirement is an application of the traditional concept of civil rights. That is, just as an employer may not directly deny employment to a protected group of individuals (e.g., have a policy that says: "no people with any hearing impairments need apply"), the employer also may not have a qualification standard that screens out, or tends to screen out, people with certain disabilities. This is analogous to the "disparate impact" discrimination prohibited under Title VII of the Civil Rights Act of 1964, initially through judicial interpretation and now codified in statute (see, e.g., Civil Rights Act of 1991 [PL 102-166]; *Griggs v. Duke Power Company*, 1971). Section 102(b)(3)(A) of the ADA also refers to this aspect of discrimination by prohibiting the use of "standards, criteria or methods of administration that have the *effect of discrimination* on the basis of disability" (emphasis added).

There is also a necessary and logical limitation to this prohibition. Under the ADA, an employer *may* have a qualification standard, test, or criterion that directly screens out, or that tends to screen out, people with disabilities if that standard or criterion is "job-related and consistent with business necessity" (42 U.S.C. §12113[a]). (For a brief political history of the motivation for adoption of these particular words, see Feldblum, 1991a, pp. 538–540.) In other words, an employer may apply a physical or mental qualification standard that precludes a person with a disability from obtaining a job if the employer demonstrates that the standard is, in fact, necessary for the person's performance of the job.

This allowance for the employer recognizes that a person's disability sometimes *is* relevant to performance of a job. In other words, the concept of civil rights for people with disabilities does not mean that a person with a disability has the *right* to *any* job he or she seeks. Rather, it means that the person has the right to be judged on his or her *merits* and not to be judged on the basis of myths or stereotypes regarding the person's particular disability.

However, the concept of civil rights also means something more for the person with a disability. The allowance for the employer is not open ended: it comes with an *obligation* that reflects the second concept of antidiscrimination. That is, an employer must prove not only that a qualification standard that screens out a person with a disability is job related but also that it is "consistent with business necessity" and that performance of the job by the applicant or employee "cannot be accomplished with reasonable accommodation" (42 U.S.C. §12113[a]; see also 29 C.F.R. §1630.15[b][1]). In other words, the employer must scrutinize its standard to see if there are lesser discriminatory alternatives than the one it has chosen (see, e.g., *Davis v. Frank*, 1989; *Prewitt v. United States Postal Service*, 1983) and whether there are societal barriers that the employer can remove through *reasonable accommodations* that will enable the person with a disability to perform the job (see, e.g., *Davis v. Frank*, 1989; *Hall v. United States Postal Service*, 1988; *Nelson v. Thornburgh*, 1983).

The same concepts of antidiscrimination appear in an analogous requirement in the public accommodations section of the ADA. Under the law a public accommodation may not have an "eligibility criterion" that screens out, or that tends to screen out, a person with a disability (42 U.S.C. §12182[b][2][A][i]). This is basically a straightforward explication of the prohibition that goods and services may not be denied to people with disabilities. It is based on the premise that disability is a characteristic that should be irrelevant to the provision of goods or services. For example, a fitness club may not require that all clients be able to hear the spoken word because that would directly screen out deaf people from the club's facilities. Similarly, a business could not have a "neutral" requirement that all customers must display a valid driver's license in order to make purchases because that would tend to screen out people with certain disabilities.

As can be expected, there is an "unless" to this prohibition as well. That is, a public accommodation *may* have an eligibility criterion that screens out persons with disabilities *if* the business proves that the criterion is "necessary" for the provision of the goods or services (42 U.S.C. §12182[b][2][a][i]; 28 C.F.R. §36.301). For example, a rental car company may require that customers show valid driver's licenses because that would be necessary for the business's provision of the service. In other words, if disability *is* directly relevant to the provision of goods or services, it may be taken into account.

Again, however, the second concept of antidiscrimination is interwoven within this requirement. Although a business may impose legitimate eligibility criteria, it must also first ensure that there are no modifications of policies or procedures and no provision of auxiliary aids or services that would enable the person with a disability to meet the criteria and enjoy the goods and services (28 C.F.R. §36.301–303). That is, the business owner must examine whether there are any *societal* barriers that prevent a customer or client from meeting a particular eligibility criterion before imposing the criterion to exclude the individual.

These requirements are explicitly spelled out in the area of health or safety threats to others. The ADA recognizes that a business may require that a customer or client not pose a "direct threat" to the health or safety of others. Such a requirement is explicitly recognized as a valid eligibility criterion (42 U.S.C. §12182[b][3]). There is an analogous requirement in the employment arena (42 U.S.C. §12111[3]). The law in such situations explicitly defines direct threat to mean: "a significant risk to the health or safety of others that cannot be eliminated by *a modification of policies*, practices, or procedures, or by the *provision of auxiliary aids* or services" (42 U.S.C. §12182[b][3], emphasis added; see also 28 C.F.R. §36.208). In other words, if a customer's disability would cause a significant threat to the health or safety of others, that is a relevant concern that can justify the denial of services to that individual. However, *before* services may be denied, the business owner must ensure that there are no affirmative steps that can be taken by the business to eliminate the harm or reduce it to an acceptable level. The same requirement exists in the employment setting (42 U.S.C. §12111[3]), where a direct threat is defined as "a significant risk to the health or safety of others that cannot be eliminated by reasonable accommodation."

Separate Services under the ADA

As can be discerned from the two previous sections, three conceptual premises operate simultaneously within the ADA: 1) that disability is irrelevant in most cases, 2) that disability *is* relevant in certain circumstances, and 3) that the relevance of a disability may not be evaluated in a social vacuum and that employers and business owners have an affirmative obligation to "undo" barriers caused by society (what I have called the "second concept of antidiscrimination" embodies these latter two conceptual premises). The interplay between these premises is graphically displayed in the ADA's requirement regarding "separate" services for people with disabilities in the area of public accommodations.

As noted above, the ADA prohibits offering goods and services to people with disabilities in a special or separate format (42 U.S.C. §12182[b][1][a][iii]). The law also provides, however, that it is not discriminatory for a public accommodation to offer different or separate services if doing so would be "necessary" to provide the individual with a good or service that is as "effective" as that provided to others. For example, a day camp could legitimately set up a special section in the camp for emotionally disturbed children if specially trained counselors and special accommodations in the programs were necessary to provide the children with a day camp experience that was effective for them.

The ADA also emphasizes that, if a public accommodation sets up a separate program (which meets the requirements of a legitimate separate program) for people with certain disabilities, that does not allow the public accommodation to *preclude* a person with a disability from participating in the mainstream, nonseparate programs (42 U.S.C. §12182[b][1][C]). The public accommodation may require, of course, that the individual meet the necessary eligibility criteria for the mainstream, integrated program (28 C.F.R. §36.301[a]). The business, however, bears the responsibility for providing any necessary modification of policies or provisions of auxiliary aids that will enable the person to enjoy the mainstream services, up to the limits established by the law (see Affirmative Aspects of Antidiscrimination Protection, above).

The ADA's treatment of separate services thus graphically illustrates the interdependency among the three conceptual premises of the ADA. The law precludes treating a person with a disability as if the disability were relevant to the person's enjoyment of goods and services by offering the person a different or separate service—*except* when the person's disability *is* relevant. In that case, a separate good or service that enables the person to enjoy the good or service in a more effective manner may be offered. The public accommodation, however, may not foist this separate good or service on the person; the individual must be allowed to participate in the integrated good or service. The business retains the right, however, to ensure that the person meets necessary and legitimate eligibility criteria—albeit with modifications of policies or provisions of auxiliary aids if necessary.

CONCLUSION

In setting forth detailed, explicit forms of prohibited discrimination, the ADA differs from most other civil rights laws. The majority of civil rights laws simply set forth a general prohibition on discrimination. The regulations issued to implement such laws and the cases brought under such laws subsequently fill out the types of action that are considered to be "discrimination" (see, e.g., Title II, Title VII, and Title VIII of the Civil Rights Act of 1964 [42 U.S.C. §§2000a, 2000e, 2000f (1988)], which cover public accommodations, employment, and housing, respectively).

Section 504 of the Rehabilitation Act follows this classic civil rights law model. It has a general prohibition that states, "[n]o otherwise qualified individual with handicaps . . . shall, solely by reason of his or her handicap, be excluded from the participation in, be denied the benefits of, or be subjected to discrimination under any program or activity receiving Federal financial assistance . . . " (29 U.S.C. §794[a] [1988]). The regulations to Section 504 and the subsequent case law then set forth specific examples of the prohibited discrimination (see, e.g., 45 C.F.R. pt. 84).

The detailed form of the ADA, by contrast, is critical in that it sets forth explicitly within the law the second concept of antidiscrimination. The detailed form of the ADA can be traced to two separate factors. First, it took significant time and effort for regulations to be issued by the relevant federal agencies, in the mid-1970s, to implement Section 504 of the Rehabilitation Act of 1973 (Burgdorf, 1990, pp. 22–23; Scotch, 1984). Those regulations, when they were finally issued, represented strong requirements and incorporated the concept of affirmative obligations as part of Section 504's antidiscrimination principle (see, e.g., 45 C.F.R. pt. 84). This principle was then further explicated in a series of judicial cases brought under Section 504 (see, e.g., *Davis v. Frank*, 1989; *Hall v. United States Postal Service*, 1988; *Nelson v. Thornburgh*, 1983; *Prewitt v. United States Postal Service*, 1981).

Those of us working on the ADA were thus interested in having the law be as explicit as possible with regard to the prohibited forms of discrimination (Feldblum, 1991a, p. 524). We expected this explicitness to be beneficial on two levels. First, it would ensure that implementation of the ADA would not be excessively dependent on the issuance of new regulations by various federal agencies. Second, it would ensure that the antidiscrimination principle of the law would explicitly include the second concept of antidiscrimination—that of affirmative obligations on the part of employers and businesses.

The second major factor dictating the detailed structure of the law came from what could be perceived as "the opposite corner." There were extensive negotiations over the ADA with a range of interested parties—including Democratic and Republican members of both the Senate and the House of Representatives, the Bush administration, the business community, and the disability and civil rights communities (see Feldblum, 1991a, pp. 525–531). Members of the Bush administration were key players in these early negotiations. As reflected in testimony to the Senate Labor and Human Resources Committee delivered by then–Attorney General Richard Thornburgh, the administration's stance was to support legislation that would simply extend the requirements of Section 504 of the Rehabilitation Act of 1973 to the private sector (U.S. Senate Committee on Labor and Human Resources Subcommittee on the Handicapped, 1989; see also Feldblum, 1991a, pp. 527–528). This position accommodated the political goal of reassuring members of the business community that the new law would not be any more radical or sweeping than what had already been in place for over 15 years (Feldblum, 1991a, pp. 522, 527).

Thus a major principle guiding the negotiations between administration officials and Senate sponsors of the ADA during the early stages of the ADA's progress was to draw on existing Section 504 regulations and case law for guidance and direction. As part of the negotiations, many detailed Section 504 regulations were transported, almost verbatim, into the ADA (see Feldblum, 1991a, pp. 527–528, describing the political process of the negotiations, and pp. 541–548, explicating how that process affected the development of specific statutory language). The result was to enhance the specific, detailed requirements that already existed in the law. This focus on using the detailed Section 504 regulations as a basis for the ADA's statutory language remained a constant factor throughout the various negotiations on the ADA (Feldblum, 1991a, 529–530, noting negotiations with four different House Committees). (A weakening of reliance on Section 504 case law occurred during negotiations between disability advocates and members of the House Energy and Commerce Committee, when both parties to the negotiation developed a new approach to accessibility in rail transportation.)

Thus concerns on the part of the disability community on the one hand and on the part of the business community on the other resulted in a form of statutory explicitness that has not traditionally been present in civil rights laws. The result is that affirmative obligations on the part of employers and business owners, which represent a newer and more radical aspect of civil rights, have become clearly explicated in a federal statute. The long-term ramifications—for other minority groups as well as for people with disabilities—of imposing such obligations as a matter of *civil rights* is something to be followed and analyzed as the courts begin to implement the ADA across this country.

REFERENCES

Anonymous. (1985, March/April). Quality of our lives. *Disability Rag,* p. 8.

Burgdorf, R.L., Jr. (1990). Legal analysis. In *The Americans with Disabilities Act: A practical and legal guide to impact, enforcement and compliance* (pp. 77–139). Washington, DC: Bureau of National Affairs.

Civil Rights Act of 1964 (codified as amended in scattered sections of 42 U.S.C.).

Civil Rights Act of 1968 (codified as amended in scattered sections of 18 U.S.C., 25 U.S.C., and 42 U.S.C.).

Civil Rights Act of 1991, 105 Stat. 1071 (1991) (codified in scattered sections of 2 U.S.C. and 42 U.S.C.).

Davis v. Frank, 711 F.Supp. 447 (N.D. Ill. 1989).

de la Torres v. Bolger, 781 F.2d 1134, 1137 (5th Cir. 1986).

Equal Employment Opportunity Commission. (1992a). *Interpretive guidance on Title I of the Americans with Disabilities Act.* In *Code of Federal Regulations* (29: Labor, pp. 404–428). Washington, DC: U.S. Government Printing Office.

Equal Employment Opportunity Commission. (1992b). Regulations to implement the equal employment provisions of the Americans with Disabilities Act. In *Code of Federal Regulations* (29: Labor, pp. 395–404). Washington, DC: U.S. Government Printing Office.

Fair Housing Amendments Act of 1988, 42 U.S.C. §§3601–3619 (1988).

Feldblum, C.R. (1991a). Medical examinations and inquiries under the Americans with Disabilities Act: A view from the inside. *Temple Law Review, 64,* pp. 521–549.

Feldblum, C.R. (1991b). The Americans with Disabilities Act definition of disability. *Labor Lawyer, 7,* 11–26.

Griggs v. Duke Power Company, 401 U.S. 424 (1971).

Hall v. United States Postal Service, 857 F.2d 1073 (6th Cir. 1988).

Hannaford, S. (1985). *Living outside inside: A disabled woman's experience.* Berkeley, CA: Canterbury Press.

Kmiec, D.W. (1988, September 27). Memorandum on Section 504 of the Rehabilitation Act of 1973.

Nelson v. Thornburgh, 576 F.Supp. 369 (E.D. Pa. 1983).

Prewitt v. United States Postal Service, 662 F.2d 292 (5th Cir. 1981).

Rehabilitation Act of 1973, 29 U.S.C. §§791–794 (1988 & Supp. I 1989).

Scotch, R.K. (1984). *From good will to civil rights: Transforming federal disability policy.* Philadelphia: Temple University Press.

U.S. Commission on Civil Rights. (1983). *Accommodating the spectrum of individual abilities.* Washington, DC: U.S. Government Printing Office.

U.S. Department of Health and Human Services. (1991). Nondiscrimination on the basis of handicap in programs and activities receiving federal financial assistance, appendix A. In *Code of Federal Regulations* (45: Public Welfare. Washington, DC: U.S. Government Printing Office.

U.S. Department of Justice. (1992). Nondiscrimination on the basis of disability by public accommodations and in commercial facilities. In *Code of Federal Regulations* (28: Judicial Administration, pp. 457–629). Washington, DC: U.S. Government Printing Office.

U.S. House of Representatives. (1990a, May 17). Debate on H.R. 2273, rejecting amendment offered by Rep. Olin. *Congressional Record, 136,* H2470.

U.S. House of Representatives. (1990b, July 12). Debate on H.R. 2273, statement of Rep. Edwards. *Congressional Record, 136,* H4624.

U.S. House of Representatives. (1990c, July 12). Debate on H.R. 2273, Statement of Rep. Owens. *Congressional Record, 136,* H4623.

U.S. House of Representatives. (1990d, July 12). Debate on H.R. 2273, Statement of Rep. Waxman. *Congressional Record, 136,* H4626.

U.S. House of Representatives Committee on Education and Labor. (1990, May 15). *House report no. 101-485(II), to accompany H.R. 2273 (101st Congress, 2nd session).* Washington, DC: U.S. Government Printing Office. (Reprinted in *United States Code Congressional and Administrative News, 4,* 303–444 [1990])

U.S. House of Representatives Committee on the Judiciary. (1989). *Hearings on H.R. 2273, the Americans with Disabilities Act of 1989 (exchange between Chai R. Feldblum and Rep. William Dannemeyer)* Washington, DC: U.S. Government Printing Office.

U.S. House of Representatives Committee on the Judiciary. (1990, May 15). *House report no. 101-485(III), to accompany H.R. 2273 (101st Congress, 2nd session).* Washington, DC: U.S. Government Printing Office. (Reprinted in *United States Code Congressional and Administrative News, 4,* 445–511 [1990])

U.S. Senate. (1990, July 13). Debate on S. 933, statement of Sen. Kennedy. *Congressional Record, 136,* S9697.

U.S. Senate Committee on Labor and Human Resources. (1989, August 30). *Senate report no. 101-116, to accompany S. 933 (101st Congress, 1st session).* Washington, DC: U.S. Government Printing Office.

U.S. Senate Committee on Labor and Human Resources Subcommittee on the Handicapped. (1989). *Hearings on S. 933, the Americans with Disabilities Act of 1989 (testimony of Richard Thornburgh, Attorney General) (S. Hrg. 101-156).* Washington, DC: U.S. Government Printing Office.

Whalen, C., & Whalen, B. (1985). *The longest debate: A legislative history of the 1964 Civil Rights Act.* Arlington, VA: Seven Locks Press.

PART II

KEY PROVISIONS

Chapter 5

Title I—Employment

John Parry

Title I, Employment, may be the single most important title of the Americans with Disabilities Act[1] (ADA) because employment is the key to independence. This chapter examines Title I in light of other civil rights measures and then discusses the employment provisions in detail, concentrating on those areas that are likely to generate the most controversy and using the regulations issued by the Equal Employment Opportunity Commission (EEOC) as a reference point. Because the EEOC regulations are well organized and are likely to be the single most important interpretive tool for many of the ADA's employment provisions, most of the chapter follows the organizational pattern established by those regulations (EEOC, 1991b).

COMPARISON WITH OTHER CIVIL RIGHTS LAWS

The ADA charts its own course with regard to discrimination and affirmative action, both building on and diverging from the familiar approaches found in other civil rights measures. This dichotomy is particularly striking in Title I (42 U.S.C. §§12111–12117). Title I follows other civil rights laws in prohibiting discrimination and supporting disparate impact analysis to ascertain whether discrimination exists. In calling for affirmative action measures, however, Title I is quite different from other civil rights laws, particularly in embracing the notions of reasonable accommodations and undue hardships while precluding quotas and trying to back away from preferences altogether. (Although there are repeated statements in the legislative history that there is no affirmative action requirement in Title I, the provisions themselves mandate that certain affirmative steps be taken with respect to providing reasonable accommodations and accessible premises.) According to the EEOC:

> The ADA seeks to ensure access to equal employment opportunities based on merit. It does not guarantee equal results, establish quotas, or require preferences favoring individuals with disabilities over those without disabilities.
>
> When an individual's disability creates a barrier to employment opportunities, the ADA requires employers to consider whether reasonable accommodation could remove the barrier. (1991b, p. 35739)

---

[1]The Americans with Disabilities Act of 1990 (PL 101-336) is published in *Statutes at Large* (104 Stat. 327) and codified in the *United States Code* (42 U.S.C. §12101–12213 [Supp. II 1990]). References to various portions of the act within this chapter cite the specific section of the Code.

A major aspect of the ADA is that an applicant or employee with a disability is entitled to any reasonable accommodation that allows the person to carry out essential job duties or enjoy job benefits equal to those of someone who does not have a disability as long as the accommodation does not place an undue hardship on the employer. The ADA attempts to fit individuals with disabilities into specific positions by compelling all but the smallest businesses to make reasonable modifications of those positions and the surrounding work environment. The individual employee is the primary focus of reasonable accommodations. The primary focus of undue hardship is the individual employer, with particular reference to the specific facility or site.

The test of employability under the ADA is the ability to carry out all essential job functions. Reasonable accommodations are intended to remove barriers that would prevent employees with disabilities from properly performing their duties. If the applicant or employee still is unable to carry out those essential functions with reasonable accommodation, the individual is not qualified for the position.

Previous civil rights statutes (except those dealing with persons with disabilities) do not individualize the affirmative action process by mandating reasonable accommodations or making exceptions for undue hardship. Instead they rely on broader affirmative action measures that favor or provide quotas or preferences to specific categories of individuals. Designated minority groups are the primary focus of these preferences. Thus the real difference between the ADA and other civil rights laws is not that there can be no affirmative action under the ADA, but that the ADA's affirmative action is directed at individual concerns rather than quotas or group preferences. In some ways, the ADA's affirmative measures go further than other civil rights laws.

Time will tell which approach works best in which situation. To understand Title I, however, it is important to remember that, compared with other civil rights laws, there are as many fundamental differences in the ADA's employment provisions as there are similarities.

HOW TO INTERPRET THE EMPLOYMENT PROVISIONS

The ADA has been criticized as being confusing and hard to interpret (Weaver, 1991). Title I is a particular target of such criticism and, to a certain extent, such criticism is justified. Two things must be understood, however, in evaluating such criticism. First, the type of criticism aimed at the ADA is very similar to the general criticism aimed at all social legislation. Second, by its nature, effective civil rights legislation is difficult to implement. In order to create something valuable, one normally must give up something. Thus what often occurs with civil rights legislation is that the more certain the law the less individualized its application, and the more individualized the law the more uncertain its application.

The ADA's employment provisions score high in individualizing remedies and score less well when it comes to certainty. Overall, however, the trade-off—fairness for certainty—is a good one, especially when one considers the interpretive tools, which ameliorate much of the unnecessary uncertainty, that are available to implement this law.

The statutory language is, of course, the place to begin interpreting Title I. A number of other sources of information are going to be critical in interpreting that language. In order of importance, these tools are:

1. The regulations published by the EEOC, and the interpretive appendix and other accompanying explanations written by the EEOC staff (EEOC, 1991a, 1991b, 1991c)[2]
2. The legislative history, particularly the Senate and House committee reports (U.S. House of Representatives Committee on Education and Labor, 1990; U.S. Senate Committee on Labor and Human Resources, 1989)

---

[2]The EEOC regulations are codified at 29 C.F.R. part 1630. References to various portions of these regulations within this chapter cite the specific section of the regulations.

3. Case law and regulations interpreting similar provisions of Section 504 and other sections of the Rehabilitation Act of 1973 (34 C.F.R. pt. 104; Office for Civil Rights, U.S. Department of Education, 1992)
4. An ADA compliance manual that the EEOC and the Department of Justice have published (EEOC and U.S. Department of Justice, 1991)

It also is important to remember that the EEOC has stated that discrimination claims, and thus new law in this area, will be decided on a case-by-case basis (EEOC, 1991b, p. 35740). This means that each dispute must be evaluated on its own terms, and new precedents probably will flow more slowly and be more narrowly conceived than might otherwise occur. (A number of important precedents already have been established under Section 504 of the Rehabilitation Act.) Despite outcries from businesses and employers, this type of incremental legal development is consistent with the approach favored by the most conservative Supreme Court justices. Moreover, much of the law is in place from precedents that already have interpreted similar language in previous federal discrimination laws.

It should be noted that this chapter does not cover the employment enforcement provisions. Enforcement under Title I (42 U.S.C. §12117) is the same as under Title VII of the Civil Rights Act of 1964 and its amendments (42 U.S.C. §§2000e-4, 2000e-5, 2000e-6, 2000-8, 2000e-9), including the recently enacted Civil Rights Act of 1991, which changed the enforcement provisions (*Congressional Monitor*, 1991). Moreover, enforcement under the ADA is an area of sufficient scope and complexity that it is best covered separately.

SECTION 1630.1: PURPOSE, APPLICABILITY, AND CONSTRUCTION

The purpose of Title I is to provide "equal employment opportunities for qualified individuals with disabilities" (29 C.F.R. §1630.1[a]). In construing this title, two points are crucial. First, Title I's standard encompasses the standard in Title V of the Rehabilitation Act of 1973 (29 U.S.C. §§790–794) and its regulations (29 C.F.R. §1630.1[c][1]). Stated another way, employees and applicants for employment enjoy all the protections found under the Rehabilitation Act as interpreted by its regulations and court decisions as well as additional protections found in Title I and its regulations. Second, Title I does not preempt any federal, state, or local laws that provide greater or equal protection for persons with disabilities (29 C.F.R. §1630.1[c][2]). Title I does preempt laws that provide less protection than Title I (EEOC, 1991b, p. 35740).

SECTION 1630.2: DEFINITIONS

Many of Title I's basic concepts are set out in the definitions section. The most important are discussed here.

Who Is Bound by Title I?

Title I covers employers, employment agencies, labor organizations, and joint labor–management committees (29 C.F.R. §1630.2[b]). As with Title VII of the Civil Rights Act, state governments, governmental agencies, and political subdivisions also are considered employers under Title I.

Title I creates two exclusions. First, small businesses are exempt from coverage if they have fewer than 25 employees during the 2-year period beginning July 26, 1992, or fewer than 15 employees after July 25, 1994 (29 C.F.R. §1630.2[e]). Second, the term *employer* does not include the federal government (which is covered by the Rehabilitation Act), tax-exempt private clubs, and Indian tribes (29 C.F.R. §1630.2[e][2]).

Note the following anomaly: Because the Rehabilitation Act, but not the ADA, covers the federal government, there will be instances in which the federal government will be held to a less rigorous standard than other employers (29 C.F.R. §1630.1[c]). In addition, the ADA establishes special rules for the Senate and House of Representatives (42 U.S.C. §12209; see also Government Employee Rights Act of 1991), which allows each house to establish its own compliance rules.

Who Is Protected by Title I? (Definition of Disability)

Title I protects persons with disabilities, and the term *disability* parallels the definition of "handicapped individual" under Title V of the Rehabilitation Act. Thus, precedents from Section 504 case law and regulations are particularly relevant to this definition. Terminology is the major difference between the two definitions. "Handicapped individual" is no longer considered appropriate and has been replaced by "person or individual with a disability" under the ADA and the Rehabilitation Act. The meaning of the terms *handicap* and *disability* remains the same.

The ADA defines disability using the same three prongs as the Rehabilitation Act (see Feldblum, chap. 4, this volume). The first prong sets the standard around which the other two prongs are organized and states that *disability* means "a physical or mental impairment that substantially limits one or more of the major life activities of that individual" (29 C.F.R. §1630.2[g][1]). A *physical impairment* refers to a disorder, condition, disfigurement, or anatomical loss that affects at least one body system, such as the respiratory or neurological system (29 C.F.R. §1630.2[h][1]). A *mental impairment* refers to "any mental or psychological disorder, such as mental retardation, organic brain syndrome, emotional or mental illness, and specific learning disabilities" (29 C.F.R. §1630.2[h][2]). The EEOC's interpretive analysis that accompanies the regulations indicates that Title I excludes two types of impairments: predispositions to illness or disease and pregnancy. In addition, it seems clear that a physical characteristic such as being overweight or short is not an impairment unless it substantially limits a major life activity, such as walking or breathing (Feldblum, 1991, p. 7). Also, although "[a]dvanced age, in and of itself, is . . . not an impairment . . . various medical conditions commonly associated with age, such as hearing loss, osteoporosis, or arthritis . . . constitute impairments (EEOC, 1991b, p. 35741).

One criticism of the regulation is that it lists some types of impairments but does not provide a complete list. Thus, as one commentator has pointed out, "employers will have to make very fact-specific determinations as to whether particular individuals are sufficiently impaired to be entitled to ADA protection (Shaller, 1991, pp. 431, 432). This is not a critical problem, however, because Section 504 case law addresses many borderline impairments as well as what constitutes a substantial limitation of a major life activity (see, e.g., *Daley v. Koch*, 1989; *Forrisi v. Bowen*, 1986; *Jasany v. United States Postal Service*, 1985; *Thornhill v. Marsh*, 1989).

Major life activities include, but are not limited to, "caring for oneself, performing manual tasks, walking, seeing, hearing, speaking, breathing, learning, and working (29 C.F.R. §1630.2[i]). These are activities that most people do every day. The more difficult concept is determining what constitutes a *substantial limitation* of a major life activity. The regulations identify two measures: an inability to perform an activity that an "average person in the general population can perform" (29 C.F.R. §1630.2[j][1][i]), and "significantly restricted . . . as compared to the condition, manner, or duration under which the average person in the general population can perform the same major life activity" (29 C.F.R. §1630.2[j][1][ii]). The regulation sets out three relevant, but not required, factors: an impairment's nature and severity, its duration, and its permanent or long-term impact (29 C.F.R. §1630.2[j][2][i]–[iii]).

The regulations explain that substantial limitation in working means a significant restriction of one's ability to perform work "as compared to someone having comparable training, skills and ability." Such an assessment must take into account the geographical area and other jobs the individual's impairment disqualifies him or her from taking (29 C.F.R. §1630.2[j][3][i]–[ii]).

Individuals are not substantially limited merely because they are unable to perform one "particular job or profession requiring extraordinary skill, prowess or talent" (EEOC, 1991b, p. 35742;

see also *E.E. Black Ltd. v. Marshall*, 1980; *Forrisi v. Bowen*, 1986; *Jasany v. United States Postal Service*, 1985). At the same time, individuals need not be totally unable to work in order to be protected. Under Title I, individuals are considered substantially limited in working in two situations: if they have a disability with respect to any major life activity (EEOC, 1991a, p. 35728) or they are "significantly restricted in the ability to perform a class of jobs or a broad range of jobs in various classes, when compared with the ability of the average person with comparable qualifications to perform those same jobs (EEOC, 1991b, p. 35742).

Finally, the EEOC notes that, in determining whether an impairment substantially limits a major life activity, the decision must "be made without regard to the availability of medicines, assistive devices, or other mitigating measures" (EEOC, 1991b, p. 35742; see also U.S. House of Representatives Committee on Education and Labor, 1990; U.S. Senate Committee on Labor and Human Development, 1989). In other words, individuals who function better because of such assistance are not excluded from coverage.

The second prong of the disability definition focuses on the person who "has a history of, or has been misclassified as having" a disability (29 C.F.R. §1630.2[k]). The key is to identify a record the employer relied on that indicates the applicant or employee has "a physical or mental impairment that substantially limits one or more of the individual's major life activities (EEOC, 1991b, p. 35742). People in this category include those who no longer have a qualifying disability or were incorrectly classified as having a qualifying disability. Under the ADA, as under the Rehabilitation Act, such persons are protected from employment discrimination.

The third prong of the disability definition focuses on people who do not have a qualifying disability but are treated as if they do. Early on, a federal court held that the Rehabilitation Act's coverage of persons who are "regarded as having such an impairment" protects individuals against an employer's perception of a handicap even where a handicap does not exist (*E.E. Black Ltd, v. Marshall*, 1980). Years later, the Supreme Court affirmed this line of reasoning, noting that Congress intended the concept of a handicapping condition to include instances in which persons with disabilities were being handicapped by erroneous perceptions, myths, or stereotypes (*School Board of Nassau County, Fla. v. Arline*, 1987).

The new EEOC regulations identify three variations in which a person may be regarded as having an impairment (29 C.F.R. §1630.2[l]). In the first two variations the person has some type of physical or mental impairment but does not have a qualifying disability as defined in the act. The person qualifies, however, because either: 1) the employer treats the person as having such a qualifying disability or, 2) other people's attitudes toward the impairment create a substantial limitation of a major life activity. In the third variation the person has no mental or physical impairment as defined in the regulations but is treated as if he or she has a substantially limiting impairment. Individuals are covered under the third variation when they are treated as having a substantially limiting impairment whether or not the impairment is specifically listed in the regulations.

Who Is Qualified To Be Employed?

The Supreme Court ruled in *Southeastern Community College v. Davis* (1979) that, under the Rehabilitation Act, "otherwise qualified" does not mean that entities subject to the law cannot establish job qualifications, but only that the qualifications must be reasonable. To be qualified as an individual with a disability under Title I, the person must have the "requisite skill, experience, education and other job-related requirements of the employment position" and be able, with or without reasonable accommodation, to "perform the essential functions of the position" (29 C.F.R. §1630.2[m]).

Skill, experience, and education are not the only permissible qualifications. As the EEOC points out, "other types of job-related requirements may be relevant to determining when an individual is qualified for a position (EEOC, 1991d, p. 35728) and may be imposed by employers. Also, the legislative history indicates that an employer is free to select the most qualified applicant or employee as long as reasonable accommodations are made or considered in making the selection (U.S. Senate Committee on Labor and Human Resources, 1989, p. 26). At the same time, the legislative history indicates that a person's qualifications must be ascertained at the time of the employment decision and cannot be based on speculation regarding the individual's future ability to perform (U.S. Senate Committee on Labor and Human Resources, 1989, p. 26).

The regulations view *essential functions* as fundamental, as opposed to marginal, job duties. What is essential is to be determined on a case-by-case basis. Three indicators are mentioned specifically (29 C.F.R. §1630.2[n]):

1. Does the position exist to perform one job function and is that particular function the one that is being evaluated?
2. Are there only a limited number of employees available who can perform each function?
3. Does the function require special expertise?

A positive answer to any of these inquiries indicates the function may be essential.

In addition, the regulations list seven relevant factors that may be used to determine whether a particular function is essential (29 C.F.R. §1630.2[n][3]): the employer's judgment, job descriptions written before applicants are interviewed, the amount of time an employee must spend performing that function, the consequences of someone else performing that function, the terms of any applicable collective bargaining agreement, the work experience of persons who have held that job, and the work experience of persons who have held similar jobs.

Although it is clear that all seven factors should be considered if available, the list is not intended to be exhaustive (EEOC, 1991a, p. 35729). With respect to written job descriptions specifically, they are to be viewed as one type of relevant evidence, but employers are not required to prepare such descriptions in order to avoid findings of illegal discrimination (EEOC, 1991a, p. 35729). Finally, although the employer's judgment is evidence of which functions are essential, a rebuttable presumption in favor of the employer's judgment is not intended. In fact, the House Committee on the Judiciary specifically rejected such a presumption (EEOC, 1991a, p. 35729).

What Is a Reasonable Accommodation?

In *Southeastern Community College v. Davis* (1979), the U.S. Supreme Court rejected the notion that Section 504 of the Rehabilitation Act requires affirmative action. Instead, the Court determined that reasonable modifications are required if they do not impose "undue financial and administrative burdens." Since then, the notion of *reasonable accommodation* has been accepted instead of quotas and preferences in disability discrimination cases (Shaller, 1991). The ADA generally and Title I specifically incorporate the regulations and case law under the Rehabilitation Act pertaining to reasonable accommodations.

The regulations note that there are three general types of reasonable accommodation. In the job application process, reasonable accommodations are "modifications or adjustments . . . that enable a qualified applicant with a disability to be considered" for the position for which he or she is applying (29 C.F.R. §1630.2[o][1][i]). In the work environment or the performance of a job, reasonable accommodations are "modifications or adjustments . . . that enable a qualified individual with a disability to perform the essential functions of that position" (29 C.F.R. §1630.2[o][1][ii]). Reasonable accommodations also include "modifications or adjustments that enable a[n] . . . employee with a disability to enjoy equal benefits and privileges of employment as are enjoyed by . . . similarly situated employees without disabilities" (29 C.F.R. §1630.2[o][1][iii]). The regulation uses "equal" instead of "the same" to emphasize that, although individuals with disabilities must have equal access to benefits and privileges, this does not mean they necessarily will enjoy the same results from those benefits and privileges or even be given precisely the same benefits and privileges (EEOC, 1991a, p. 35729).

The regulations refer to two descriptions to explain what employers must do to comply with Title I's reasonable accommodation requirement. First, employers must make "existing facilities used by employees readily accessible to and usable by individuals with disabilities" (29 C.F.R. §1630.2[o][2][i]). This provision refers to architectural or structural changes and covers both the employee's immediate work area and public nonwork areas such as lunchrooms, rest rooms, and conference rooms. Second, in appropriate circumstances employers must be willing to do things such as restructuring jobs, offering part-time or modified work schedules, reassigning employees with disabilities to vacant positions, acquiring or modifying equipment or devices, modifying exams or policies, and providing readers or interpreters (29 C.F.R. §1630.2[o][2][ii]).

The regulations also indicate that, in determining what is a reasonable accommodation, the employer may have to "initiate an informal, interactive process" with the employee (29 C.F.R. §1630.2[o][3]). The legislative history sets out a four-step problem-solving approach when the appropriate accommodation is not obvious to the parties involved (U.S. House of Representatives Committee on Education and Labor, 1990, p. 66; U.S. Senate Committee on Labor and Human Resources, 1989, pp. 34–35). The employer and employee would identify the precise limitations that affect the employee's performance, identify possible accommodations, assess the reasonableness of those possible accommodations based on their effectiveness and any undue hardship, and implement the most appropriate accommodation. The Senate report notes that, when two effective means of accommodation are available, the employer may choose the one that is less expensive or easier to implement. In determining which accommodations are effective, however, the employee's preference is to be considered primary (U.S. Senate Committee on Labor and Human Resources, 1989, pp. 34–35).

The regulations clearly anticipate that the law in this area will be developed on a case-by-case basis. This makes employers nervous because they would prefer more precision, but a great number of situations, including many of the most common, already are addressed either in the EEOC's analysis of its regulations or in the case law.

As was noted earlier, neither the Rehabilitation Act nor Title I requires quotas or group preferences. Thus, although an employer had to take reasonable steps to find another job for an employee who developed a disability that disqualified the employee from his or her present position, the employer did not have to create a job for the employee or hire him or her for another position unless he or she was the most qualified (*Clarke v. Shoreline School District No. 412*, 1986; *Dean v. Municipality of Metropolitan Seattle-Metro*, 1985).

Another area of concern to employers is the provision of attendant care as a form of reasonable accommodation. The case law makes it clear that such an accommodation is required if it is needed to help an applicant or employee "with specified duties related to the job" (*Clarke v. Shoreline*, 1986; *Dean v. Municipality*, 1985). What is not required is an attendant who performs the job for the person with a disability. Thus, courts have required part-time qualified readers and interpreters but not full-time assistants (*Nelson v. Thornburgh*, 1983). Also, the EEOC does not interpret reasonable accommodation to require employers to provide attendants to assist with personal hygiene, toileting, or eating. This interpretation is, however, one of the most disappointing outcomes for the disability community. Although the EEOC's interpretation probably is on solid legal ground, there are significant negative implications for persons with severe disabilities who, if they need attendants, will have to pay for them or lose their jobs.

Similarly, employers must provide aids and equipment that will help an employee or applicant carry out specified job duties. For example, under the Rehabilitation Act a woman with a hearing and speech impairment was entitled to preprinted cards and expanded use of a teletype electronic keyboard to allow her to communicate sufficiently to meet the requirements of her clerical position (*Davis v. Frank*, 1989). Also, under the Rehabilitation Act, a job applicant with dyslexia had to be allowed to take an oral exam where a written test was not an essential part of the job application process (*Stutts v. Freeman*, 1983). The EEOC also points out that, even if an employer does not have to provide available aids, equipment, or services because they would constitute an undue financial hardship, the employer still must treat such assistance as a reasonable accommodation if employees choose to pay for it (EEOC, 1991a, p. 35729).

Clearly, employers must make existing facilities accessible if employees use them to perform essential job functions. In addition, as mentioned earlier, the EEOC's analysis indicates that making nonwork areas, including rest rooms, accessible also may be required as a reasonable accommodation under Title I (EEOC, 1991a, p. 35729).

Job restructuring, including "changing when and how an essential function is performed," may be required reasonable accommodation (EEOC, 1991a, p. 35729). Or, a nonessential job function may be reassigned. Thus, under the Rehabilitation Act, a nurse who was recovering from a drug addiction could expect that her job would be restructured so that someone else would administer drugs to her patients (*Wallace v. Veterans Administration*, 1988). Similarly, job schedules may have to be modified to accommodate an employee with a disability who needs to change shifts (*Rhone v. United States Department of the Army*, 1987), to accommodate an employee with cancer who needs to receive treatment during regular work hours (*Fisher v. Superior Court*, 1986), or to allow a full-time employee to return to work part-time while he or she recuperates from a serious back injury (*Perez v. Philadelphia Housing Authority*, 1987). What is not required is a reallocation of essential job functions to another person (EEOC, 1991b, p. 35744).

In certain instances employers may have to reassign employees with disabilities to any position for which the employee is qualified, but both the regulations and case law indicate that reassignments need only be made to vacant positions (29 C.F.R. §1630.2[o][2][ii]; *Coley v. Secretary of the Army*, 1987). The EEOC also notes that an employer need only wait a reasonable amount of time for a vacancy to arise and does not have to maintain the employee's salary at the same level unless the salaries of persons without disabilities would be maintained (EEOC, 1991a, p. 35730).

It should be noted that any type of job restructuring, shift changes, or reassignments may conflict with collective bargaining agreements (*Carter v. Tisch*, 1987; *Hurst v. United States Postal Service*, 1986). The EEOC states, however, that this is to be considered as *evidence* of undue hardship, not undue hardship per se (EEOC, 1991a, p. 35727).

What Is an Undue Hardship?

An accommodation is not considered reasonable if it creates an undue hardship for the employer. The regulations do not include undue hardship in the definition of reasonable accommodation, however, because undue hardship is considered a defense to, not an element of, reasonable accommodation. The EEOC views this as a technical differentiation that "does not affect the obligations of employers or the rights of individuals with disabilities (EEOC, 1991a, p. 35729).

An *undue hardship* with respect to the provision of a reasonable accommodation is a "significant difficulty or expense" (29 C.F.R. §1630.2[p][1]). Five factors are to be considered:

1. The accommodation's "nature and net cost . . . taking into consideration the availability of tax credits and deductions, and/or outside funding"
2. The overall financial resources devoted to the reasonable accommodation, the number of persons employed, and the effect of the accommodation on expenses and resources
3. The overall financial resources of the employer and overall size of the business
4. The nature of the workplace and the "geographic separateness and administrative or fiscal relationship of the facility or facilities in question to the covered entity"
5. The accommodation's impact "upon the operation of the facility, including the impact on the ability of other employees to perform their duties and the impact on the facility's ability to conduct business" (29 C.F.R. §1630.2[p][2][i]–[v])

These five factors are not exclusive. For example, the legislative history refers to the number of employees benefiting from an accommodation as an additional factor that can be considered in determining undue hardship (U.S. House of Representatives Committee on Education and Labor, 1990, p. 68).

The legislative history describes an undue hardship as an action that is "unduly costly, extensive, substantial, disruptive, or that will fundamentally alter the nature of the program" (U.S. House of Representatives Committee on Education and Labor, 1990, p. 67; U.S. Senate Committee on Labor and Human Resources, 1989, p. 35). The most notable distinction is drawn between so-called *de minimis* costs or burdens, which Congress specifically rejected, and truly significant costs and burdens (Gardner & Campanella, 1991, pp. 39–40).

Once a plaintiff establishes a *prima facie* case of illegal discrimination, the employer has the burden of proving that an accommodation is unreasonable because it causes an undue burden. Proof cannot be based on hypothetical situations. Rather, actual costs and burdens must be referenced in order to prevail. The chief justifications for placing the burden of proof on the employer are the employer's superior knowledge of the job essentials and possible experience with other employees who have similar disabilities (*Prewitt v. United States Postal Service*, 1985).

In many respects cost is the most important, although certainly not the only, factor in assessing undue hardship (Gardner & Campanella, 1991, p. 43). Cost is somewhat elusive, however, because it depends on the totality of the circumstances and must be measured on a case-by-case basis. As was mentioned earlier, an employer need not hire an assistant who carries out the essential job functions for an employee who has a disability. One might determine whether providing a part-time assistant is an undue hardship by examining such factors as the job duties of the assistant, the assistant's impact on the employee's job, the cost of the assistant, and what funding might be available to help offset the employer's cost (*Arneson v. Heckler*, 1989). Presumably, if the impact of the assistance to the employee is substantial and the overall cost to the employer is reasonable when compared with the position's value to the business, then such assistance would be required. Thus an interpreter for a young man who flips hamburgers at McDonald's probably would not be reasonable, whereas a reader for a partner in a law firm probably would be. Of course, McDonald's still would be required to provide other types of reasonable accommodations.

Courts have consistently ruled that an employer does not have to create a new position for an employee with a disability because that would constitute an undue financial or administrative hardship (*Clarke v. Shoreline School District No. 412*, 1986; *Davis v. Meese*, 1988; *Dean v. Municipality of Metropolitan Seattle-Metro*, 1985). This does not mean, however, that it would always be unreasonable to require the creation of a new position. If a position would have minimal value to a business, there is little doubt that its creation would not be required. However, if the new position fills a clear need and/or would result in other measurable savings, a business might not be unduly burdened by having to create that position. The distinction between creating a new position and changing an existing position, which courts have mandated (*Ackerman v. Western Electric*, 1986; *Wallace v. Veterans Administration*, 1988), may be more a matter of degree than a substantive difference. The case-by-case approach leaves room for further litigation.

The EEOC's analysis and the ADA's legislative history emphasize that, where cost is a primary factor in measuring undue hardship, an unreasonable accommodation can be made reasonable if the individual with the disability is willing to pay "the portion of the cost that constitutes an undue hardship" (EEOC, 1991a, p. 35730, citing U.S. House of Representatives Committee on Education and Labor, 1990, p. 69, and U.S. Senate Committee on Labor and Human Resources, 1989, p. 36). Also, although employers wanted Congress to specify in monetary terms what constitutes an undue hardship, Congress refused to peg undue hardship to a fixed ratio, such as comparing an accommodation's cost to the employee's salary and benefits (EEOC, 1991a, p. 35730, citing U.S. House of Representatives Committee on Education and Labor, 1990, p. 41).

Finally, according to the case law under the Rehabilitation Act, employers may not use the morale of other employees as evidence of an undue administrative or financial burden. The fact that other employees may be envious of or in other ways disapprove of an accommodation does not justify withholding that accommodation (*Anderson v. General Dynamics*, 1978; *Davis v. Frank*, 1989). Note that an exception may exist if a collective bargaining agreement incorporates such employee feelings into a preexisting agreement that limits the types of accommodations that can be used. Employers cannot, however, evade their Title I obligations by instigating the inclusion of such provisions into a collective bargaining agreement. If such an agreement is to be upheld at all, its concepts must come from the employees, not the employer.

What Constitutes a Direct Threat?

A major debate arose in Title I's enactment concerning whether certain disabilities might pose a direct threat to other employees or the public. The notion of a direct threat has an impact on both an employee's qualifications and an employer's undue hardships. As defined in the EEOC's regulations, a *direct threat* is "a significant risk of substantial harm to the health or safety of the individual or others that cannot be eliminated or reduced by reasonable accommodation" (42 U.S.C. §12111[3]). The regulations make two additions to the language of the act itself (29 C.F.R. §1630.2[r]) by stating that, to be legally significant, the risk must constitute a substantial harm and also by specifying that a threat may be a risk to oneself as well as to others.

The definition of direct threat may be the most controversial aspect of the Title I regulations. In determining how to measure a direct threat, the regulations incorporate the U.S. Supreme Court's interpretation of the Rehabilitation Act concerning the threat posed by a teacher with tuberculosis (*School Board of Nassau County, Fla. v. Arline*, 1987). The regulations state that there should be "an individualized assessment of the individual's present ability to safely perform the essential functions of the job. This assessment shall be based on a reasonable medical judgment that relies on the most current medical knowledge and/or on the best available objective evidence." The most prominent factors in making such a determination are the risk's duration, the nature and severity of the potential harm, the likelihood it will occur, and its imminence (29 C.F.R. §1630.2[r]). As other commentators have pointed out, the Supreme Court's test dispels the too-often-accepted belief that AIDS and other quasi-contagious diseases or mental illnesses automatically create a direct threat (Millstein, Rubenstein, & Cyr, 1991).

The EEOC's regulations and analysis both expand and narrow the notion of a direct threat (EEOC, 1991a, p. 35730). Consistent with the ADA's legislative history and Rehabilitation Act case law, the EEOC includes threats to the health and safety of an individual with a disability as a proper justification for discriminating against that person. A 1985 U.S. Court of Appeals decision ruled that an appropriate qualification for a job applicant who had grand mal seizures was whether there was a reasonable probability she would substantially harm herself (*Mantolete v. Bolger*, 1985). The EEOC's approach, however, is inconsistent with the statutory language, which states that qualification standards "may include a requirement that an individual shall not pose a direct threat to the *health and safety of other individuals in the workplace*" (42 U.S.C. §12113[b], emphasis added). Nothing is said about a threat to oneself. In fact, the definition of direct threat under the Department of Justice public accommodations regulations applies only to threats to others, not threats to onself (U.S. Department of Justice, 1991, p. 35544; see also Tucker, 1991, p. 1).

Moreover, as a matter of policy, the EEOC's approach runs counter to the notion of self-determination by allowing someone else to determine what is or is not a threat to the employee. Also, a so-called threat to the employee can be used to mask the real reason(s) an employer chooses to terminate or not hire a person with a disability.

The EEOC does accept the view that a significant risk must include "substantial harm." A direct threat must be substantial with or without reasonable accommodation, meaning it is much more than the zero harm proposed by some employers. Also, the imminence of the harm is part of any substantial harm determination. If an employer is going to use a direct threat standard in its hiring and other employment practices, the same standard must be applied to all employees, not just those with a disability. Finally, a direct threat must be based on an individualized assessment that measures a person's current ability to perform a job's essential functions safely, not on speculation that the person's disability may present a direct threat in the future.

SECTION 1630.3: WHAT CONDITIONS ARE EXCLUDED FROM COVERAGE?

The regulations describe a number of exceptions to the definitions of who has a disability and who is a qualified individual with a disability under Title I. These exceptions relate to drug use, compulsions, sexual disorders, and sexual preferences, and leave these conditions unprotected primarily because of political considerations.

One major exception relates to people who use illegal drugs (29 C.F.R. §1630.3[a]–[c]), defined as taking controlled substances for unlawful purposes. This includes taking any drug without the required supervision of a licensed health care professional. The regulations make it clear, however, the employers may not deny employment to people who are in or have completed a "supervised" drug rehabilitation program and are no longer engaging in illegal drug use. Similarly, employers may not deny employment to persons who are mistakenly regarded as using drugs. Employers may, however, implement reasonable policies or procedures, including drug testing, to ensure that persons who are in or have completed supervised drug rehabilitation programs are not using illegal drugs.

The EEOC's analysis accompanying its regulations makes two points regarding the drug use standards (EEOC, 1991a, p. 35730). First, included within the rubric of a rehabilitation program are self-help groups, but only those that are "professionally recognized." The problem with this approach is that it leaves unanswered the inevitable questions of who decides what constitutes professional recognition and what standards should be applied to make that determination. Second, the EEOC states that employers may ask that employees take a drug test if they are in or have completed a drug program, but no one else can compel employees to take such tests.

Other excluded conditions are "transvestism, transsexualism, pedophilia, exhibitionism, voyeurism, gender identity disorders not resulting from physical impairments, or other sexual behavior disorders; compulsive gambling, kleptomania, or pyromania; or psychoactive substance use disorders resulting from current illegal use of drugs" (29 C.F.R. §1630.3[d]). Homosexuality and bisexuality also are excluded (29 C.F.R. §1630.3[e]).

SECTIONS 1630.4–1630.13: WHAT TYPE OF ACTIVITIES ARE PROHIBITED?

Title I prohibits discrimination in all aspects of employment, including the application and hiring processes, on-the-job issues, and termination (29 C.F.R. §1630.4).

Limiting, Segregating, and Classifying

It is unlawful for an employer "to limit, segregate, or classify a job applicant or employee in a way that adversely affects his or her employment opportunities or status on the basis of disability" (29 C.F.R. §1630.5). In other words, employers may not use stereotypes and myths about disabilities to restrict employment opportunities, segregate qualified employees with disabilities into special work areas or tracks of employment, or deny equal opportunities and benefits to qualified persons with disabilities. Employers may reduce opportunities or benefits to all employees or categories of employees as long as such reductions are not made for discriminatory reasons (EEOC, 1991b, p. 35746).

What constitutes a discriminatory purpose under the Rehabilitation Act has changed over the years, and the current interpretation is applied to Title I. In *Alexander v. Choate* (1985), involving the application of Tennessee's Medicaid program to persons with disabilities, the U.S. Supreme Court ruled that a discriminatory effect rather than an intent to discriminate will support a cause of action under Section 504 of the Rehabilitation Act. Because it is so difficult to prove an intent to discriminate, the recognition that a discriminatory effect is enough to establish a violation is significant both to employers and employees.

Contractual Arrangements

An employer may not enter into a contract or similar type of relationship that will have the effect of discriminating against either the employer's current employees or persons who apply for employment with the employer. This provision does not cover the other party's employees or people who apply to work for the other party (29 C.F.R. §1630.6).

Administrative Standards

An employer may not use standards, criteria, or methods of administration that in any way further employment discrimination unless they are "job-related and consistent with business necessity" (29 C.F.R. §1630.7).

Association with an Individual with a Disability

An employer may not discriminate against the family, business, or social acquaintances of a person with a disability because of their relationship with the person with the disability (29 C.F.R. §1630.8). However, people who are discriminated against because they associate with people who have disabilities are not entitled to reasonable accommodation.

Reasonable Accommodation

It is impermissible discrimination for an employer to refuse to make a reasonable accommodation for a qualified applicant or employee with a disability unless such an accommodation would impose an undue hardship. It also is unlawful to deny an employment opportunity to a person with a disability based on the employer's obligation to make a reasonable accommodation. Also, employers are not excused from complying with the ADA because they were not awarded technical assistance from the EEOC. However, if employees elect not to accept a reasonable accommodation and thus cannot perform the essential functions of their position, they are not considered qualified for their position (29 C.F.R. §1630.9).

According to the EEOC, employers must provide personal items as reasonable accommodations, but only if the items are specifically designed or required to meet job-related needs. Before an accommodation can be mandated, there must be a nexus between what the employer knows about the individual's disability and the need for that accommodation. Where the need for a requested accommodation is not obvious, employers may ask for documentation, and an employer must allow individuals with disabilities to provide their own accommodations if they so choose (EEOC, 1991a, p. 35731).

Qualification Criteria

It is unlawful for an employer to use qualification criteria that screen out or tend to screen out individuals with disabilities on the basis of their disability unless the criteria are job-related and consistent with business necessity (29 C.F.R. §1630.10). According to the EEOC, a finding of discrimination depends on a nexus existing between the exclusion involved and the disability. In addition, although a direct threat may be a defense to discrimination, its absence is not an appropriate standard or qualification (EEOC, 1991a, p. 35731).

Administration of Tests

Employers must take appropriate steps to ensure that any tests administered to applicants or employees take into account any disability the applicant or employee might have (29 C.F.R. §1630.11). The EEOC's analysis (EEOC, 1991a, p. 35731) adds that the employee should request an accommodation as soon as he or she becomes aware that it will be needed. Also, an employer may test an employee on job-related skills.

Retaliation and Coercion

Employers are prohibited from retaliating against, coercing, harassing, interfering with, or intimidating an employee with a disability with respect to the employee's enjoyment of Title I's protections (29 C.F.R. §1630.12).

Prohibited Medical Exams/Inquiries

Except as Title I specifically permits, employers may not use medical exams or inquiries either before or during employment to ascertain whether an applicant or employee has a disability or even the nature or severity of that disability (29 C.F.R. §1630.13). According to the EEOC, prohibited inquiries include seeking information at the preoffer stage about an individual's workers' compensation history (EEOC, 1991a, p. 35732).

SECTION 1630.14: WHAT KINDS OF EXAMS AND INQUIRIES ARE ALLOWED?

Title I does not prohibit all preemployment and employment exams and inquiries, and allows some that may indirectly supply the employer with medically related information. The permitted inquiries are divided into four categories.

Acceptable Preemployment Inquiries

"A covered entity may make pre-employment inquiries into the ability of an applicant to perform job-related functions, and/or ask an applicant to describe or to demonstrate how, with or without reasonable accommodation, the applicant will be able to perform the job-related functions" (29 C.F.R. §1630.14[a]). According to the EEOC, "an employer may ask an individual whether [and how] he or she can perform a job function with or without reasonable accommodation" (EEOC, 1991a, p. 35732). Also, in administering tests to all employees, the employer may ask candidates who need reasonable accommodation in taking such a test to inform the employer and document the need before the test is administered (EEOC, 1991a, p. 35732). The EEOC does not consider physical agility tests required by law enforcement and other public safety agencies to be medical exams (EEOC, 1991a, p. 35732), and they are not subject to the provisions that limit preemployment inquiries.

Although preemployment inquiries affect all persons with disabilities, these inquiries have been of particular concern for individuals with mental disabilities. Because mental disabilities often are not obvious, employers sometimes have required applicants to undergo medical exams or provide medical histories allowing employers to identify these disabilities (Millstein et al., 1991, p. 1243). Under Title I, such inquiries are illegal. However, the legislative history indicates that federal, state, and local governments may establish legitimate medical requirements that employers must enforce (Millstein et al., 1991, p. 1243, citing U.S. House of Representatives Committee on Education and Labor, 1990, p. 70). Also, employers may establish reasonable medical standards for safety or security reasons. As with other ADA provisions, what is reasonable for governments and employers to require will be determined on a case-by-case basis.

Entrance Exams

Employers may mandate medical exams or medical inquiries once an offer of employment is made and may condition employment on the results of that exam or inquiry as long as "all entering employees in the same job category are subjected to such an examination (and/or inquiry) regardless of disability" (29 C.F.R. §1630.14[b]). The information obtained must be kept confidential and may be shared only in limited circumstances with supervisors, managers, first aid and safety personnel, and government officials investigating compliance with Title I (29 C.F.R. §1630.14[b][1]). Although medical exams generally need not be either job related or consistent with business necessity, if they are used to screen out employees with disabilities, they must meet both these criteria (29 C.F.R. §1630.14[b][3]).

The EEOC adds that information gathered in allowable medical exams or medical inquiries may be submitted to state workers' compensation offices and used for other legitimate insurance purposes (1991a, pp. 35732–35733).

Examination of Employees

As long as the inquiries are job related and consistent with business necessity, employers may require medical exams or medical inquiries, including inquiries into an employee's fitness for duty or ability to perform job-related functions. Again, this information must be kept confidential and may be shared only in limited circumstances with supervisors, managers, first aid and safety personnel, and government officials investigating compliance with Title I (29 C.F.R. §1630.14[c]; EEOC, 1991a, p. 35733).

How broadly "business necessity" may be interpreted under this provision is indicated in a U.S. Court of Appeals decision involving an employer who fired a nurse who refused to take an HIV antibody test (*Leckelt v. Board of Commissioners of Hospital District No. 1*, 1990). Even though the risk of transmission was low, no discrimination was found under Section 504 of the Rehabilitation Act. The employer was justified in protecting its patients, particularly because the nurse, a homosexual, was in a high-risk group and had not always followed Centers for Disease Control safety precautions.

Voluntary Exams/Inquiries

Voluntary exams or inquiries are acceptable if they are part of an employee health program. The same confidentiality guidelines described above for other exams apply (29 C.F.R. §1630.14[d]).

SECTIONS 1630.15 AND 1630.16: WHAT DEFENSES ARE AVAILABLE FOR EMPLOYERS?

The EEOC regulations list a number of possible defenses to discrimination under Title I, including specifically permitted activities. This list is not exhaustive.

Disparate Treatment Charges

As has been decided in a number of Title VII civil rights cases (*McDonnell Douglas Corp. v. Green*, 1973; *Texas Department of Community Affairs v. Burdine*, 1981) and then extended to claims under the Rehabilitation Act (*Prewitt v. United States Postal Service*, 1981), any "legitimate, nondiscriminatory reason" may be a defense of disparate treatment—treating a person differently on the basis of his or her disability (29 C.F.R. §1630.15[a]). Thus, if the employee charges disparate treatment, the employer must show that the discrimination has a reasonable business purpose. A reasonable business purpose will constitute a valid defense unless the employee shows that it was merely a pretext for unlawful discrimination (EEOC, 1991b, p. 35751).

Disparate Impact Defenses

Under Title I, disparate impact occurs when "uniformly applied criteria have an adverse impact on an individual with a disability or a disproportionately negative impact on a class of individuals with disabilities" (EEOC, 1991b, p. 35751). This is true whether or not the employer has an invidious motive. In other words, criteria that are neutral on their face may have a disparate or disproportional effect that works to exclude minorities from certain benefits. Under the Rehabilitation Act, the disparate impact theory was diluted somewhat by a U.S. Supreme Court decision stating that employees are entitled only to reasonable access to whatever benefit was being offered (*Alexander v. Choate*, 1985). The Title I regulations, however, reestablish the full force of the disparate impact analysis (Parmet, 1990, pp. 331, 336) but at the same time create defenses for employers.

Qualifying standards, including requirements that individuals do not pose a direct threat to workplace health and safety (29 C.F.R. §1630.15[b]), and other uniformly applied standards, criteria, and policies (29 C.F.R. §1630.15[c]), are acceptable if they are job related, consistent with business necessity, and applied using reasonable accommodations.

Undue Hardship

As discussed in some detail earlier, a proper defense to not making a reasonable accommodation is proof that such an accommodation will place an undue hardship on the employer's business (29 C.F.R. §1630.15[d]; EEOC, 1991b, p. 35752). Because hardship is measured on a case-by-case basis, what may be a hardship in one set of circumstances may not be a hardship in other circumstances. Also, "a negative effect on morale, by itself, is not sufficient to meet the undue hardship standard" (EEOC, 1991a, p. 35752).

Conflict with Federal Laws

Where another federal law or regulation conflicts with Title I, such a conflict may constitute a defense to discrimination or failure to provide reasonable accommodation (29 C.F.R. §1630.15[e]). The defense will fail, however, if the employee shows either that the employer is using the federal law as a pretext for discrimination or that there was another nondiscriminatory means to comply with the conflicting provision (EEOC, 1991a, p. 35752).

Religious Entities

Religious entities may establish criteria that favor the employment of persons of a particular religion or require that applicants and employees conform to certain religious tenets. The entity cannot engage in prohibited discrimination against a person with a disability who satisfies the religion criteria (29 C.F.R. §1630.16[a]).

Alcohol and Drugs

Employers may take proper steps to control the use of alcohol and illegal drugs in the workplace. Specifically authorized steps include prohibitions against employees using or being under the influence of drugs or alcohol in the workplace, requiring employees to obey the Drug-Free Workplace Act of 1988 and holding employees who use illegal drugs or abuse alcohol to the same qualification standards as any other employee even if their substance abuse causes unsatisfactory performance or behavior. Also, businesses subject to regulations established by the Departments of Defense and Transportation and the Nuclear Regulatory Commission may require employees to obey special regulations regarding the use of alcohol and illegal drugs (29 C.F.R. §1630.16[b]).

As noted earlier, individuals who currently are using illegal drugs are not considered individuals with disabilities under Title I and thus are not protected. Individuals disabled by alcoholism, however, are covered in the same way as any other individual with a disability (EEOC, 1991b,

p. 35752). The extent of their protection is defined by numerous court decisions under the Rehabilitation Act prohibiting discrimination on the basis of alcoholism (*McElrath v. Kemp*, 1989; *Rodgers v. Lehman*, 1989).

Drug Testing

The administration of tests by employers to determine the use of illegal drugs is not prohibited as a medical exam or medical inquiry. The EEOC neither encourages nor discourages the use of such tests. Any information beyond whether illegal drugs are being used that is revealed in such a test must be kept confidential (29 C.F.R. §1630.16[c]).

Smoking

An employer may regulate smoking in the workplace without violating Title I (29 C.F.R. §1630.16[d]).

Infectious and Communicable Diseases

Despite strong pressures from restaurant and related food-handling businesses to exempt all people with infectious and communicable diseases from Title I's protection, a compromise was reached: the ADA allows only limited discrimination against food handlers with infectious or communicable diseases. Each year, the Secretary of Health and Human Services must prepare a list of infectious and communicable diseases that are transmitted through food handling. The final list for 1991 was published August 16, 1991 (U.S. Department of Health and Human Services, 1991, p. 40897). If someone who has such a condition would create a risk of transmission even with all reasonable accommodations, the employer can decide whether or not to assign that person food-handling duties. Also, in the case of a current employee, the employer must at least consider reassigning the person to a non–food-handling position. In addition, Title I does not affect any state or local law that, in accordance with the Secretary's list of infectious and communicable diseases, is designed to protect the public from significant health risks that cannot be eliminated by reasonable accommodation (29 C.F.R. §1630.16[e]).

Insurance and Other Benefit Plans

Title I is not intended to penalize employers and insurers who offer health and life insurance plans that follow accepted practices of risk assessment but is intended to prohibit employers and insurers from denying an employee with a disability equal access to insurance or benefit plans (EEOC, 1991b, p. 35753). Subject to any applicable state laws, the regulations permit entities that administer benefit plans to practice insurance risk assessment and employers associated with the management of benefit plans, or as self-insurers, to administer benefit plans that practice risk assessment (29 C.F.R. §1630.16[f]). Even where these activities limit individuals with disabilities, there is no impermissible discrimination unless the risk assessment activities are used "as a subterfuge" (29 C.F.R. §1630.16[f][4]). The EEOC makes it clear, however, that:

> An employer . . . cannot deny a qualified individual with a disability equal access to insurance or subject a qualified individual with a disability to different terms or conditions of insurance based on disability alone, if the disability does not pose increased risks. [D]ecisions not based on risk classification [must] be made in conformity with non-discrimination requirements [of Title I]. (EEOC, 1991b, p. 35753)

Under Title I, insurers may sell and employers may buy insurance that limits coverage for specific mental and physical conditions, including preexisting condition exclusions, as long as these practices are based on risk tables rather than speculation or prejudice and are applied equally to all employees (Milstein et al., 1991, pp. 1243–1244; U.S. House of Representatives Committee on Education and Labor, 1990).

CONCLUSION

The structure of Title I as set out in the EEOC's employment regulations and accompanying materials is well conceived. This analysis mirrors that structure but also explains what the regulations mean in the context of the EEOC's own view, the legislative history, and court decisions defining similar terms and provisions in other federal antidiscrimination laws.

Title I appears to be an historic document that will move forward the cause of civil rights for persons with disabilities, perhaps surpassing the impact of similar laws for other minority groups. In most respects the EEOC seems committed both to educating employers about these requirements and to enforcing the requirements when necessary. The question remains whether sufficient resources will be used for education and enforcement. At this stage the signs are encouraging.

REFERENCES

Ackerman v. Western Electric, 643 F. Supp. 836 (N.D. Calif. 1986).

Alexander v. Choate, 469 U.S. 287 (1985).

Anderson v. General Dynamics, 589 F.2d 397 (9th Cir. 1978), *cert. denied*, 442 U.S. 921 (1979).

Arneson v. Heckler, 879 F.2d 393 (8th Cir. 1989).

Carter v. Tisch, 822 F.2d 465 (4th Cir. 1987).

Civil Rights Act of 1964, codified as amended in scattered sections of 42 U.S.C. (1988).

Civil Rights Act of 1991, 42 U.S.C. §2000-5, 2000-6, 2000-8, and 2000-9 (1981).

Clarke v. Shoreline School District No. 412, 720 P.2d 793 (Wash. Sup. Ct. 1986).

Coley v. Secretary of the Army, 689 F.Supp. 519 (D. Md. 1987).

Congressional Monitor, (1991, September 3). *27*(131), 2.

Daley v. Koch, 892 F.2d 212 (2d Cir. 1989).

Davis v. Frank, 711 F. Supp. 447 (N.D. Ill. 1989).

Davis v. Meese, 692 F. Supp. 505 (E.D. Pa. 1988), *aff'd*, 865 F.2d 592 (3d Cir. 1989).

Dean v. Municipality of Metropolitan Seattle–Metro, 708 P.2d 393 (Wash. Sup. Ct. 1985).

Drug-Free Workplace Act of 1988, 41 U.S.C. §701–707 (1988).

E.E. Black Ltd. v. Marshall, 497 F. Supp. 1088 (D. Haw. 1980).

Equal Employment Opportunity Commission. (1991a, July 26). Equal employment opportunity for individuals with disabilities; final rule. *Federal Register, 56*, 35725–35739.

Equal Employment Opportunity Commission. (1991b, July 26). Interpretive Guidance on Title I of the Americans with Disabilities Act. *Federal Register, 56*, 35739–35753.

Equal Employment Opportunity Commission. (1991c, July 26), Recordkeeping and reporting under Title VII of the Civil Rights Act of 1964 and the Americans with Disabilities Act (ADA); final rule. *Federal Register, 56*, 35753–35756.

Equal Employment Opportunity Commission and U.S. Department of Justice. (1991). *Americans with Disabilities Act handbook*. Washington, DC: U.S. Government Printing Office.

Feldblum, C.R. (1991). The Americans with Disabilities Act definition of disability. *Labor Lawyer, 7*, 11–26.

Fisher v. Superior Court, 223 Cal. Rptr. 203 (Cal. Ct. App. 1986).

Forrissi v. Bowen, 794 F.2d 931 (4th Cir. 1986).

Gardner, R.H., & Campanella, C.J. (1991). The undue hardship defense to the reasonable accommodation requirement of the Americans with Disabilities Act of 1990. *Labor Lawyer, 7*, 37–51.

Government Employee Rights Act of 1991, 2 U.S.C. §1201–1224 (1991).

Hurst v. United States Postal Service, 653 F. Supp. 259 (N.D. 1986).

Jasany v. United States Postal Service, 755 F.2d 1244 (6th Cir. 1985).

Leckelt v. Board of Commissioners of Hospital District No. 1, 909 F.2d 820 (5th cir. 1990).

Mantolete v. Bolger, 767 F.2d 1416 (9th Cir. 1985).

McDonnell Douglas Corporation v. Green, 411 U.S. 792 (1973).

McElrath v. Kemp, 714 F. Supp. 23 (D.D.C. 1989).

Millstein, B., Rubenstein, L., & Cyr, R. (1991). The Americans with Disabilities Act: A breathtaking promise for people with mental disabilities. *Clearinghouse Review, 24*, 1240–1249.

Nelson v. Thornburgh, 567 F. Supp. 3689 (E.D. Pa. 1983), *aff'd* 732 F.2d 146 (3d Cir. 1984), *cert. denied*, 469 U.S. 1188 (1985).

Office for Civil Rights, U.S. Department of Education. (1992). Nondiscrimination on the basis of handicap in programs and activities receiving federal financial assistance. In *Code of Federal Regulations* (34: Education, pp. 404–437). Washington, DC: U.S. Government Printing Office.

Parmet, W.E. (1990). Discrimination and disability: The challenges of the ADA. *Law, Medicine & Health Care, 18*, 331–344.

Perez v. Philadelphia Housing Authority, 677 F. Supp. 357 (E.D. Pa. 1987), *aff'd*, 841 F.2d 1120 (3d Cir. 1988).

Prewitt v. United States Postal Service, 622 F.2d 1416 (9th Cir. 1985).

Rehabilitation Act of 1973, 29 U.S.C. §791–794 (1973).

Rhone v. United States Department of the Army, 665 F. Supp. 734 (E.D. Mo. 1987).

Rodgers v. Lehman, 869 F.2d 253 (4th Cir. 1989).

School Board of Nassau County, Fla. v. Arline, 481 U.S. 1024 (1987).

Shaller, E.H. (1991). "Reasonable accommodation" under the Americans with Disabilities Act—what does it mean? *Employee Relations Law Journal, 16*, 431–451.

Southeastern Community College v. Davis, 442 U.S. 397 (1979).

Stutts v. Freeman, 694 F.2d. 666 (11th Cir. 1983).

Texas Department of Community Affairs v. Burdine, 450 U.S. 248 (1981).

Thornhill v. Marsh, 866 f.2D 1182 (9th Cir. 1989).

Tucker, B. (1991). The EEOC's safety defense under Title I of the ADA: Valid or invalid? *National Disability Law Reporter, 2*(5).

U.S. Department of Health and Human Services. (1991, August 16). Diseases transmitted through the food supply. *Federal Register, 56*, 40897–40899.

U.S. Department of Justice. (1991, July 26). Nondiscrimination on the basis of disability by public accommodations and in commercial facilities; final rule. *Federal Register, 56*, 35543–35604.

U.S. House of Representatives Committee on Education and Labor. (1990, May 15). *House report no. 101-485(II), to accompany H.R. 2273 (101st Congress, 2nd session).* Washington, DC: U.S. Government Printing Office. (Reprinted in *United States Code Congressional and Administrative News, 4*, 303–444 [1990])

U.S. Senate Committee on Labor and Human Resources. (1989, August 30). *Senate report no. 101-116, to accompany S. 933 (101st Congress, 1st session).* Washington, DC: U.S. Government Printing Office.

Wallace v. Veterans Administration, 683 F. Supp. 758 (D. Kan. 1988).

Weaver, C.L. (1991, January 31). Disabilities act cripples through ambiguity. *Wall Street Journal*, p. 16.

Chapter 6

Employment and the Public Vocational Rehabilitation Program

Impact of the ADA

Elmer C. Bartels

The Americans with Disabilities Act (ADA) is hailed as the "Declaration of Independence for People with Disabilities." It clearly mandates disability policies to include people with disabilities in the economic and community life of the nation. This landmark law has greatly heightened the expectations of people with disabilities that we all can participate fully in the American dream and be financially independent through work. The ADA opens access to public and private sector employment, thus furthering the hopes and dreams of people with disabilities in terms of their ability to pursue their own personal goals.

The ADA was built on the basic premises of the Rehabilitation Act of 1973 and its amendments and on the concepts that are reflected in earlier disability programs and policies. This chapter discusses this foundation and the role the public Vocational Rehabilitation Program can be expected to play in supporting the employment provisions of the ADA.

DEVELOPMENT OF THE PUBLIC VOCATIONAL REHABILITATION PROGRAM

Since 1920 the efforts of the public Vocational Rehabilitation Program have been directed toward services that assist people with disabilities to work. In 1973 the Rehabilitation Act (PL 93-112) enhanced opportunities for individuals with severe disabilities to be considered for services on a priority basis and established their rights to individualized rehabilitation programs that describe each eligible individual's own vocational goal and the specific services that will be required to attain that goal. Title V of the Act prohibited discrimination based on disability and introduced the concepts of program accessibility and the fundamental right to equal employment opportunities in federally funded programs. It also established the Architectural and Transportation Barriers Compliance Board to enforce federal architectural accessibility laws.

The public Vocational Rehabilitation Program was designed as a comprehensive service deliv-

The author would like to thank Ms. Nancy Franklin Earsy, Chief Legal Counsel for the Massachusetts Rehabilitation Commission, for her assistance in developing this chapter.

ery system that enables people with disabilities to achieve their employment goals through the provision of vocational services. The 1973 Rehabilitation Act described more fully the services available for assisting individuals with disabilities to work. In 1978 an amendment to the Act authorized, but funded at only a minimal level, a comprehensive service delivery system for independent living (which has never been funded above $13 million nationally) and a grants program to develop independent living centers (which has not exceeded $25 million nationally). The independent living centers network has begun to expand nationally with the mission of providing community-based services for independent living to assist people with disabilities. Goals for consumers of independent living services may encompass linkages to the public Vocational Rehabilitation Program through the provision of services that support an individual's work goals. Thus the Rehabilitation Act provides the legal basis for a comprehensive service delivery mechanism that is potentially a key resource for implementing the inclusionary goals of the ADA.

As a starting point for this effort, the public Vocational Rehabilitation Program has evolved to become a work program with very open eligibility. For example, before 1973, individuals with impairments that resulted in quadriplegia were not considered employable. The provisions of the 1973 Act prioritized vocational rehabilitation services for individuals with severe disabilities, thereby establishing a legal mandate to provide employment-oriented services that had become possible through advances in technology, medicine, and public attitudes. The Rehabilitation Act Amendments of 1992 simplified the eligibility and service planning process by streamlining the documentation needed for eligibility while retaining the program's focus on an individual's functional capacities for employment and reaffirming the program's purpose of getting people to work. The eligibility process determines the nature of the individual's disability, assets, and liabilities with regard to work. Vocational goals are explored and developed, within the potentials of restoration and assistive technology services, with the planned outcome of employment in a job that reflects a particular individual's goals, talents, and capabilities.

The outcomes of the public Vocational Rehabilitation Program are demonstrated by annual statistics. Nationally, vocational rehabilitation services provided by state rehabilitation agencies in the 50 states and the territories affect about 950,000 individuals with disabilities in their efforts to enter the work force or retain their present employment. In 1992 over 70% of the individuals served by the program were individuals with severe disabilities. In Fiscal Year 1992 more than 668,000 people with severe disabilities were served through the $1.788 billion of federal funds appropriated for vocational rehabilitation services and state funds of more than $460 million, for a total of over $2 billion in federal and state expenditures for the year.

These national results are exemplified by statistics for the Massachusetts Rehabilitation Commission. The Commission's budget for the Vocational Rehabilitation Program in Fiscal Year 1991 was $40 million, of which $16 million was used to purchase services for individuals. Another $14 million paid for direct service personnel—the vocational rehabilitation counselors who assist clients through the rehabilitation process, their supervisors, and the managers who develop programs and options to support the process. In a given year, the Commission serves approximately 32,000 individuals with disabilities. It accepts 4,000 people with disabilities, after receiving 17,000 new referrals. About half of the individuals referred are found eligible for vocational rehabilitation services. Although some individuals who are found eligible do not complete the rehabilitation programs because of illness or changing personal circumstances, the typical individual takes between 2 and 3 years to complete an individual vocational rehabilitation program before going to work. Each year about 4,000 persons with disabilities complete services and get a job. The overall success rate of the Vocational Rehabilitation Program is 65% for all individuals who participate actively in their individualized programs. Approximately 90% of the consumers served by the Commission meet the priority criteria of severe disability, and 93% of those who become employed with the support of vocational rehabilitation services are individuals with severe disabilities.

CONTEMPORARY CHANGES IN REHABILITATION

Today the public rehabilitation programs are operating in a new environment that reflects the policies of the Americans with Disabilities Act to include and integrate persons with disabilities into all aspects of American life, including employment. Increased levels of consumer involvement in state agency policy making and individual service choices were endorsed by the 1992 amendments to the Rehabilitation Act. The 1992 law required every state rehabilitation agency participating in the public rehabilitation program to establish a rehabilitation advisory council with a majority of its membership constituted of persons with disabilities. Congress, public officials, and disability advocacy groups expect the rehabilitation agencies to reach out and include people with severe disabilities who were once considered "unemployable." Just as medical advances, new technology, innovation grants, and legal mandates encouraged state rehabilitation agencies to reach out and provide services to individuals with quadriplegia who wanted to work, educational advances, advocacy, and changing public views about the capabilities of individuals with cognitive impairments began to expand vocational rehabilitation options for this population. In 1986, the Rehabilitation Act was amended to include a "formula grant" program of supported employment. The supported employment program provided special federal funding for each state to create training and work situations in private sector employment settings for persons with severe disabilities who had not previously been provided such opportunities. The program paid for services to program participants so that they could obtain a reasonable level of productivity in the private sector setting. Any support services they required after the termination of the formula-supported work program were to be provided by the employer or other public and private agencies. This method of providing short-term supported employment services expanded the vision and expectations of those in the rehabilitation community about who has the potential for working in a competitive setting. It also assisted people with severe mental disabilities to enter the work force and to become more independent economically and in their personal lives.

Another important change endorsed by the 1986 amendments to the Rehabilitation Act was the mandate for technology assessments within the vocational rehabilitation eligibility and service process. This change, too, expanded the vision of the act to provide practical supports for serving individuals with severe disabilities. The direct use of technology to assess and serve persons with severe disabilities is another tool for breaking down barriers to their employment. The range of technology options increases every day. It includes everything from simple electronic devices such as telephone voice amplifiers for persons with hearing impairments to voice-activated computers and computers with voice output for persons who are blind or have other severe disabilities. Before such technologies were available, these individuals could not work productively in competitive settings. New technology makes possible their inclusion in vocational rehabilitation programs and the workplace. The ever-changing potential of technology to transform the lives of people with disabilities has created public pressures to develop employment options and services for people who once would have been considered incapable of work. For example, an individual with multiple disabilities who is nonverbal can try using communications devices during an eligibility assessment. Successful use of the communication equipment can support the individual in learning new skills, such as data entry, during a period of vocational rehabilitation training and the individual can be transferred to a work situation upon completion of the training when he or she gets a job.

The technology mandate and supported employment program also present new challenges for rehabilitation facilities, community rehabilitation programs, and other private sector vendors. Traditionally, these facilities, programs, and vendors have played a key role in providing work settings for vocational rehabilitation consumers. Rehabilitation facilities have already begun to work with state rehabilitation agencies to place more emphasis on vocational assessment of applicants in the workplace. Some rehabilitation facilities and programs have moved into mainstream workplaces through cooperative partnerships with state rehabilitation agencies and private employers to develop and operate supported employment programs for persons with severe disabilities. Other rehabilitation facilities are still on the sidelines, observing these efforts to link the rehabilitation process with employment in mainstream workplaces.

In the next decade and beyond, employers, rehabilitation facilities, community rehabilitation programs, and state rehabilitation agencies will face the challenge of developing cooperative partnerships to expand work options for individuals with severe disabilities, to increase the availability of competitive work settings in the community, and to open up employment opportunities for persons with disabilities all over America. The development of technology assessment, supported employment, and creative work training options pays off in terms of expanded opportunities for persons with disabilities and a trained labor pool for employers. Work options available within business and industry in this country vary greatly. These new tools for tailoring training to employer needs and specific work sites can support cooperative relationships between the public rehabilitation agencies and private sector employers to achieve the results envisioned by the Rehabilitation Act—gainful, meaningful employment for individuals with disabilities.

FUTURE CHALLENGES IN VOCATIONAL REHABILITATION

As we look to the future in providing services at the state level under the Rehabilitation Act, challenges within the public Vocational Rehabilitation Program occupy the concerns of state rehabilitation agencies. A closer look at the vocational rehabilitation process provides some possible responses to those concerns.

There has long been public concern about the *quality of job placements* and the degree to which those placements relate to an individual consumer's career goals. The Vocational Rehabilitation Program has traditionally looked to entry-level placements as the primary starting point for persons with disabilities. In many ways, this approach to placement reflects the opportunities available to Americans who do not have disabilities. However, when persons with disabilities are going through the vocational rehabilitation process, it is helpful if the relationships between the initial job placement and future career development are clearly identified in planning the individual's rehabilitation program and making the first placement. Such an approach can strengthen the career commitment of the individual consumer, who sees the relationship between the initial job placement and career opportunities in the future. In practice, job placement activities involving an individual consumer depend to a considerable degree on work options that are identified at the beginning of the vocational rehabilitation process. That discussion and exploration occur between the consumer and that individual's counselor in the process of vocational assessment and guidance that lead to an individual rehabilitation plan.

In developing the rehabilitation service plan with consumers, counselors try to maintain a wide vision with regard to work options and not limit consumers to traditional occupations that have been successful for vocational rehabilitation consumers in the past. Because the public Vocational Rehabilitation Program focuses on career development, counselors must be mindful of the fact that some of these traditional jobs may exist at the moment but may not provide appropriate opportunities to assure consumers of a present and future career in the workplace. This objective puts a great deal of responsibility on individual rehabilitation counselors. The professional development programs that are funded through the Rehabilitation Act are an important resource to update current and future counselors with the knowledge and skills necessary to provide services that will enable consumers to develop their own potential to participate in the American workplace now and in the future.

Another mechanism to help consumers with disabilities stay in the workplace after they have completed a rehabilitation program is the option of *postemployment services*, which is endorsed by the Rehabilitation Act. Under this service option, a public rehabilitation agency can provide services to assist the individual with a disability to stay in the work force in a particular job. Alternatively, the individual may be referred to the Vocational Rehabilitation Program in order to reactivate service delivery and provide important services that will support that person's continued employment.

Title I of the ADA is based on the assumption that individuals with severe disabilities want to work and can do so with reasonable accommodations. State rehabilitation agencies are encouraged to provide vocational rehabilitation services to individuals who receive disability benefits from the Social Security Administration, yet some Social Security laws do not support this effort. *National work incentive policies* play a vital role in supporting the work efforts of individuals with severe disabilities. The Supplemental Security Income (SSI) program provides mechanisms to assure that people with disabilities will not precipitously lose their Medicaid coverage as they begin to work and also permits a gradual phase-out of income benefits as recipients earn wages. In contrast, the Social Security Disability Insurance (SSDI) program, uses the concept of "substantial gainful activity," which is based on earning level only. The SSDI program allows a 9-month trial work period for continuation of benefits and then eliminates them entirely. This disparate treatment of wages and abrupt benefit cutoff operates as a disincentive for employment efforts by SSDI beneficiaries. These specific issues and elements of national disability policy are not yet fully consistent with the inclusionary mandates of the ADA and the Rehabilitation Act. Similar disincentives to employment are exemplified by Medicaid policies that provide funding supports for individuals in institutional settings, but do not reimburse or reward community-based services that are essential for living independently in the community and entering employment. Changes in the laws that govern these federal programs are needed to make them consistent with the disability policies of the ADA and the employment focus of the Rehabilitation Act.

EFFECTS OF THE ADA

The public Vocational Rehabilitation Program offers a proven mechanism that enables individuals with disabilities to gain the skills and knowledge they will need in order to achieve the promises of the ADA for economic inclusion and independence. However, unless there is additional funding for the public Vocational Rehabilitation Program, as more individuals with severe disabilities seek services to gain the qualifications they will need for employment, the resources of the program will not be adequate to meet the demand.

Throughout the past 70 years, the public vocational rehabilitation program has been successful politically because it is an accountable, outcome-oriented work program. The state–federal partnership ensures a basic consistency of approach and of results in operating the programs under the Rehabilitation Act. The program's success can be measured in terms of the clients who work and pay taxes. Dependency on benefit programs is reduced or eliminated. At the same time, the programs of the Rehabilitation Act continually must strive to be accountable to the consumers they are mandated to serve. There is considerable flexibility in the public Vocational Rehabilitation Program to enable individuals with disabilities to define and achieve their goals of independent, productive lives with the help of knowledgeable rehabilitation professionals who work in the state agencies. Rehabilitation professionals are constantly challenged to strengthen their own knowledge and creativity in order to work with consumers to develop individualized options for employment in changing workplaces and labor markets. Increasingly, consumers are becoming more empowered to participate fully in their own rehabilitation processes. The 1992 Amendments to the Rehabilitation Act re-endorsed the rights of individuals in developing individualized vocational rehabilitation programs and making choices about services provided in connection with such programs.

The consumer rights movement has also worked to ensure that persons with disabilities are involved in rehabilitation agency policymaking regarding service delivery. Disability advocacy groups played a critical role in shaping the 1992 Amendments and ensured that consumer involvement in policy making would continue at the state level through the new state rehabilitation advisory councils mandated by the Act. In the 1990s and into the new millennium, the dynamics of consumer advocacy will challenge the state rehabilitation agencies to provide innovative services that will reach out to individuals with severe disabilities who are seeking to realize the ADA's promises of independence and economic opportunities. If the agencies can work effectively in partnership with consumers and employers to increase the resources that are essential to this task, vocational rehabilitation services capacity can grow and expand to meet the challenge. However, if the partnerships flounder and advocacy efforts splinter into groups focused on a single disability, the opportunity to achieve shared goals and values will be lost. Cooperation and effective working relationships between the state rehabilitation agencies and their constituencies are crucial to using the public Vocational Rehabilitation Program as a vital catalyst in providing individuals with disabilities with the opportunities and qualifications that they need to enter employment and fulfill the promises of the ADA.

CONCLUSION

Over the next decade and into the new century, the foremost challenges for the public Vocational Rehabilitation Program and the people who provide services through this program will be the delivery of responsive, client-centered services that support inclusionary disability policies. The vision and service delivery structure of the Rehabilitation Act constitute powerful tools to prepare people with disabilities for full participation in work and community life. The Rehabilitation Act, with adequate funding, is a critical public resource for supporting the efforts of hundreds of thousands of individuals with disabilities across this nation to achieve personal and economic independence. The public Vocational Rehabilitation Program and the mutual efforts that it supports can release the talents and energies of all citizens, in the spirit of the ADA, to participate fully and contribute to the country we all share.

REFERENCES

The Rehabilitation Act of 1973, PL 93-112; 29 U.S.C. §§700 *et seq.*
Rehabilitation, Comprehensive Services and Developmental Disabilities Amendments of 1978, PL 95–602. 29 U.S.C. §§791–794 (1978).
The Rehabilitation Act Amendments of 1986, PL 99–506.
The Rehabilitation Act Amendments of 1992, PL 102–569.
Social Security Act, Title II, Federal Old-Age, Survivors, and Disability Insurance Benefits, (SSDI), 42 U.S.C. 401 *et seq.*
Social Security Act, Title XVI, Supplemental Security Income for the Aged, Blind and Disabled, (SSI), 42 U.S.C. 1381 *et. seq.*
U.S. Department of Education, Office of Special Education and Rehabilitative Services, Rehabilitation Services Administration, Annual Report of the Rehabilitation Services Administration on Federal Activities Related to the Administration of the Rehabilitation Act of 1973, as amended, 1990.
U.S. House of Representatives, Appropriations Committee, Subcommittee on Education, Labor and Health and Human Services, testimony on behalf of the Council of State Administrators of Vocational Rehabilitation by Edmund Cortez, Deputy Director, New York Vocational Education Services for Individuals with Disabilities, March 4, 1993.

Chapter 7

Organized Labor's Role in Implementing the ADA

Guy Stubblefield

This chapter examines the implementation of the ADA from two union-oriented perspectives: 1) how labor unions can be used as a resource in the community for implementing the ADA, and 2) how the ADA will affect the relationship between companies with which a collective bargaining agreement exists and the unions that are parties to that agreement.

Labor unions have a tradition of representing the workers: we have historically fought for their rights and for safe and healthy work environments, and advocated for good jobs, good pay, and good benefits. That role has always included assisting union members who had become disabled and were seeking to return to work. That special role was expanded under recent policy changes to include helping persons with disabilities make the initial entry to the job market. The Americans with Disabilities Act (ADA) will further increase that involvement. The ADA is designed to provide significant new opportunities for people with disabilities to engage in employment in an equitable manner in an integrated setting with people without disabilities. The ADA challenges labor unions and employers to take action to eliminate discrimination in the world of work.

Persons with disabilities and their advocates have long recognized that legislative action was necessary in order to provide equitable rights to employment for people with disabilities. The ADA represents a major benchmark in the long progression toward equality, fairness, and justice for persons with disabilities. It presents both a challenge and an opportunity for organized labor as an advocate of workers' rights, in partnership with management, to address the problems of this special population, many of whom have been living without jobs and the acceptable quality of life that can be achieved only with the financial resources that a job provides.

Labor union contracts cover an estimated 17–18 million workers employed in a variety of settings throughout the United States. The unions represent a relatively untapped resource in developing employment for persons with developmental disabilities as well as workers who become ill or injured on the job and lose their job as a result of no accommodation being made for their disability. "The involvement of labor unions in promoting and advocating for jobs for persons with disabilities is encouraged by the leadership of the parent body, the American Federation of Labor–Congress of Industrial Organizations (AFL-CIO)" (Whitehead, 1990). This involvement is strengthened and

A condensed version of this chapter was published earlier in a monograph of the 15th Mary E. Switzer memorial seminar (October 1991), published by the National Rehabilitation Association, 1910 Association Drive, Suite 205, Reston, VA 22091.

given credibility nationwide by the policy that has been adopted by the AFL-CIO. This policy was summarized by AFL-CIO president Lane Kirkland (1989):

> The AFL-CIO firmly supports the rights of workers with disabilities to be treated with dignity and respect in their working lives. The Federation and its 90 affiliated unions work through legislative channels and collective bargaining agreements to assure equal opportunity for all workers with either mental or physical disabilities.

President Kirkland goes on to say that researchers have found that employers are facing a shortage of both skilled and entry-level workers, a shortage that will create new opportunities for work. Persons with disabilities now will gain more easily the job protection and workplace accommodation that has always been the goal of unions. The ADA will encourage workers to take advantage of these opportunities and, to a great extent, fulfill the need of employers.

Additionally, it should be noted that 31 national and international unions affiliated with the AFL-CIO are members of the President's Committee on Employment of Persons with Disabilities. Lenore Miller, the president of the Retail, Wholesale, Department Store Union, is currently a vice chair of the President's Committee. Michael G. McMillan of the Human Resources Development Institute, AFL-CIO, is a member of its executive committee. Charles E. Bradford recently completed a 3-year term on the executive committee. It should also be noted that the Machinists' Union has been an active member of the President's committee on employment of people with disabilities since the establishment of the committee by then President Harry S Truman more than 40 years ago. The labor committee of the President's Committee consists of designated representatives from among these 31 international unions. Beginning in May 1991, I served as chair of this committee until my retirement. There is a very sincere and deep involvement of the labor movement as an advocate for persons with disabilities, an involvement that began even before the ADA became the law of the land.

Both unions and employers should recognize that there are two ways to approach the implementation of the ADA. One approach would be carefully to fulfill the requirements of the law, "even though grudgingly," in an effort to avoid penalties, liability suits, or perhaps prison. A far better way would be to react as good citizens in the communities where we live and, in the words of Justin Dart, chair of the President's Committee on Employment of People with Disabilities, work to do "the fair, the right and just thing in behalf of those persons with disabilities" (1987). That will be easy if we simply remember who the persons with disabilities really are. For some of us they may be spouses, children, or other close relatives; for others, they may be close friends or the friends of friends or neighbors. All of them are human beings for whom we have some moral and now a legal obligation as they strive to become a part of the American work force.

IMPLEMENTING THE ADA—LABOR AS A RESOURCE

There are several areas that present opportunities for a labor union to cooperate with management, to serve as a community resource for implementation of the ADA. Unions could:

Refer qualified job seekers with disabilities through their hiring halls or other referral systems, where they exist.

Serve as liaisons between employers and special placement counselors from the state vocational rehabilitation agency or other specialized employment services organizations.

Sensitize employers (and co-workers) to the benefits and desirability of hiring persons with disabilities.

Encourage outreach to community sources of job seekers who are disabled.

Provide a buddy system to the new entrants to employment—that is, assist qualified candidates in initial access to jobs as well as help workers who have lost their jobs as a result of disability to return to work.

Work with management to identify (current and future) jobs that are an appropriate match to the skills and abilities of persons with physical or mental disabilities.

Promote the use of tax incentives available to employers of persons with disabilities under the Targeted Jobs Tax Credit program.

Encourage and assist employers who have had good experience with workers with disabilities to communicate this information to other employers and to employer associations.

Of course the list above is not by any means a complete list of opportunities to cooperate in implementing ADA in a work place, a company, or a multi-plant situation. Company officials and union representatives are encouraged to use their ingenuity and imagination to discover the areas of cooperation that can be adapted to their respective needs. Above everything else, the parties are encouraged to provide forums for an ongoing dialogue.

Work Site Accommodations

Unions also can be a valuable resource to employers at the administrative and supervisory level regarding accommodations at the work site. Most collective bargaining agreements would prohibit unilateral changes by management that would affect the working conditions and/or the earning opportunities of workers during the term of the agreement. Arbitrators and the courts have held that terms of a collective bargaining agreement is inviolable. The procedure for modifying an agreement during its term has been well established by the National Labor Relations Act of 1947 as amended. Decisions by the National Labor Relations Board and/or the courts have established the guidelines to be followed that are well known and generally acceptable by both union and company negotiators. Some accommodations, such as the following, will require negotiations with the union before changes can be implemented:

Job restructuring
Task simplification
Approval of the use of a job coach or personal assistant
Endorsement of phase-in schedule
Work site alterations

Worker Advocacy

The actions of unions as a resource for the community and for employers are merely an extension of the legal responsibility of unions and the role that they currently play as advocates for all members and particularly for workers with disabilities who are or who will become members. Many unions assume the duty and responsibility to:

Assist the worker in accessing community services, resources, and public assistance programs (e.g., Social Security, disability income support, and medical assistance).

Monitor and assist in resolving the problems of the returning worker with disabilities or the new work force entrant with disabilities.

Work with management to ensure that workers with disabilities are paid wages commensurate with those of workers who do not have disabilities.

Establish state, central, and local committees on rights of workers with disabilities.

Create a climate of acceptance of persons with disabilities among co-workers.

Encourage individual union members to get involved through interaction with co-workers with disabilities in on-the-job support.

Involve workers with disabilities in sensitizing co-workers, union stewards, and business agents.

Monitor employer compliance with affirmative action and nondiscrimination obligations under federal and state laws.

Promote changes and implementation of state and federal laws through political action committees and legislative coalitions that include organizations concerned with persons with disabilities.

Many of the national and/or international unions have as a part of their structure and included in their constitution the establishment of departments of:

Civil Rights
Community services
Safety and health

These departments also often have elected or appointed standing committees at the local union level. Additionally the AFL-CIO has similar departments in their Washington D.C., office and in the state and regional affiliated organizations of the AFL-CIO.

Employment-Related Services

A number of federal, state, and municipal agencies currently fund projects that provide employment-related services to people with disabilities. A number of unions also are involved in providing these services and have considerable experience already in the rehabilitation field. Some of these, to mention only a few, are:

International Association of Machinists, Center for Administering Rehabilitation and Employment Services (IAM CARES), Upper Marlboro, MD
Human Resources Development Institute (HRDI), Handicapped Placement Program, Washington, DC
American Federation of State, County and Municipal Employees (AFSCME), New York, NY
Communication Workers of America (CWA), San Francisco, CA
United Auto Workers (UAW), Detroit, MI, in cooperation with the Pontiac Division of General Motors
The Amalgamated Clothing and Textile Workers Union (ACTWU), New York, NY
Services Employees International Union (SEIU), Seattle, WA

Funding is also provided through various United Way agencies. Private foundations such as the Dole Foundation in Washington, D.C., are also involved. This foundation was developed by Senator Robert Dole of Kansas, who, as a World War II veteran with war-related disabilities has strongly advocated on behalf of persons with disabilities throughout his political career.

The level of funding for employment-related services must be increased by Congress. The programs must be expanded to serve the hundreds of additional persons who will be seeking to enter the labor market as a result of the ADA and to provide at no cost to the employer various and significant services enabling them to implement the new law successfully. Now that federal law mandates such services, it is only fair that financial support for providing the services be forthcoming from Congress and the administration. That support should include a resource of trained and experienced personnel and the financial means to hire and maintain them, as well as to acquire the technological services and implement the mechanical and structural changes that employers and unions will find themselves obligated to provide.

EFFECT OF THE ADA ON COLLECTIVE BARGAINING

Both union and management negotiators are familiar with the language changes made necessary by the passage of the Civil Rights Act of 1964. Similar changes should be considered to indicate recognition of and compliance with ADA. I believe such language changes would protect both parties should complaints of discrimination be filed or when charges of alleged noncompliance with ADA have been made. The language changes would affirm the intent of the parties to comply and eliminate the possibility for either party to use the agreement as a reason for noncompliance.

There are some aspects of the collective bargaining agreement in which special contract language might be needed in order to implement the ADA:

Nondiscrimination
Retention, retraining, or transfer of employees with disabilities
Promotion and transfer
Establishment of joint labor–management affirmative action committees
Training for management and labor representatives by professionals from organizations such as
    IAM CARES

If language to address these issues is to be included in the collective bargaining agreement, union consent will be necessary.

FINAL COMMENTS

A comment or two on the enforcement of the ADA seems appropriate. The powers, remedies, and procedures set forth in Sections 705, 706, 707, 709, and 710 of the Civil Rights Act of 1964 are available to the Equal Employment Opportunity Commission (EEOC), the U.S. Attorney General, or any other person alleging discrimination on the basis of disability in violation of any provisions or regulations of the ADA concerning employment. Thus, the powers, remedies, and procedures available to persons discriminated against based on disability are the same as, and parallel to, the powers, remedies, and procedures available to persons discriminated against because of their race, religion, sex, or national origin. Any amendments to Title VII's provisions on remedies and the like will also be fully applicable to the ADA. I would project, based on my experience, that the regulations will be modified and/or a substantial amount of case law will be developed as challenges to the law and individual acts of discrimination are countered by charges filed with the EEOC and eventually settled in the courts.

REFERENCES

Civil Rights Act of 1964 (codified as amended in scattered sections of 42 U.S.C.).
Commerce Clearing House, Inc. (1990). *CCH's explanation of the Americans with Disabilities Act of 1990.* Chicago.
Dart, J. (1987). Hearing of the Social Security Disability Advisory Council [Testimony]. Washington, DC.
Kirkland, L. (1989, May). Support for enactment of ADA [Testimony]. Washington, DC: Congressional committee.
Whitehead, C.W. (1990). *A manual for labor organizations, employment specialists, job coaches, rehabilitation counselors, and advocates.* Hudson, FL: Employment Related Services Associates.

Chapter 8

Title II—
Public Services, Subtitle A

State and Local Governments' Role

Linda Kilb

Title II, Public Services, of the Americans with Disabilities Act[1] (ADA) (42 U.S.C. §§12131–12165) prohibits discrimination against persons with disabilities in all services, programs, and activities provided or made available by state or local governments. Unless otherwise specified, these requirements went into effect on January 26, 1992 (18 months after the enactment of the ADA).

Many state and local government programs and services were prohibited from discriminating against persons with disabilities before the passage of the ADA, because they were covered by Section 504 of the Rehabilitation Act of 1973 (29 U.S.C. §794), which bars discrimination on the basis of handicap in any programs and activities that receive federal funds. Title II of the ADA extends the nondiscrimination requirements of Section 504 to the activities of *all* state and local governments, regardless of whether they receive federal financial assistance.

Title II is divided into two subtitles. Subtitle A of Title II, which is explained here, covers the activities of state and local governments other than public transit. Subtitle B of Title II, which is discussed in Chapter 9 (this volume), deals with the provision of publicly funded transit.

The Department of Justice (DOJ) published regulations implementing Title II, Subtitle A on July 26, 1991. This explanation of the ADA's state and local government requirements provided in this chapter is drawn directly from the statute, the DOJ's Title II regulations,[2] the DOJ's *Title II Technical Assistance Manual* (January 24, 1992) (DOJ, 1992),[3] and the statute's legislative history. At times, the explanation contains material taken verbatim from these source materials.

---

[1]The Americans with Disabilities Act of 1990 (PL 101-336) is published in *Statutes at Large* (104 Stat. 327) and codified in the *United States Code* (42 U.S.C. §§12101–12213 [Supp. II 1990]). References to various portions of the act within this chapter cite the specific section of the Code.

[2]U.S. Department of Justice regulations are codified at 28 C.F.R. part 35 (1992). References to various portions of these regulations within this chapter cite the specific section of the regulations.

[3]References to various portions of the DOJ's *Title II Technical Assistance Manual* (1992) within this chapter cite the particular page.

WHAT ENTITIES ARE COVERED?

Title II of the ADA covers public entities—that is, entities that are publicly funded (42 U.S.C. §§12102[3], 12131[1]; 28 C.F.R. §§35.102, 35.104). All public entities are covered, regardless of size. The term *public entity* means any department, agency, special-purpose district, or other instrumentality of a state or local government, as well as Amtrak and certain commuter rail agencies. This broad definition is intended to cover every type of state and local government entity, including:

All types of state agencies
Counties
Municipalities and cities
Boroughs
All types of special-purpose districts (public school districts, water and sewer districts, public
    housing authorities, etc.)
Executive, legislative, and judicial branches of state and local governments.

WHAT ACTIVITIES ARE COVERED?

The ADA covers every type of state or local government activity or program (28 C.F.R. §§35.102, 35.104). In employment, state and local governments cannot discriminate against job applicants and employees with disabilities. Unlike private employers, who are only subject to the ADA if they have 15 or more employees, all state and local governments are covered regardless of how many people they employ. For example, even if a city sewage district has only seven employees, it cannot discriminate in employment.

State and local governments that would be large enough to be covered by Title I of the ADA if they were private employers (i.e., that have 15 or more employees) must comply with Title I of the ADA. State and local governments that would not be large enough to be covered by Title I of the ADA (i.e., that have fewer than 15 employees) must comply with the DOJ regulations that implement Section 504 of the Rehabilitation Act (DOJ, 1992a; codified at 28 C.F.R. pt. 41). The requirements set forth in the two sets of regulations are, for the most part, identical.

The state and local government employment requirements, like the rest of the state and local government requirements, went into effect on January 26, 1992.

In addition to employment practices, two other major categories of programs and activities are identified: 1) activities and programs involving general public contact (e.g., communication with the public through telephone contact, office walk-ins or interviews, and the public's use of facilities); and 2) activities and programs directly administered by state and local government for beneficiaries and participants (e.g., programs that provide state or local government services or benefits). The latter include, for example:

Activities of state legislatures
Voting for and election of state and local officials
Activities of state or local courts, including traffic, municipal, superior, appellate, and supreme
    courts, with respect to everything from jury duty to appearing as a witness or a party to a
    lawsuit
Town meetings
Board meetings of a special-purpose district (e.g., a public school district)
Activities of police and fire departments
All planning or advisory boards
Licensure and registration activities (e.g., motor vehicle driver licensure, child care licensure, mar-
    riage licensure, voter registration)
Administration of public benefits and social service programs

The ADA also covers all public school systems' programs and activities, including those not covered by the Individuals with Disabilities Education Act (PL 101-476, which amended and renamed PL 94-142, the Education for All Handicapped Children Act of 1975, 20 U.S.C. §§1400 *et seq.*). These include such activities as programs open to parents or the public, graduation ceremonies, parent–teacher organization meetings, plays, and adult education classes.

RELATIONSHIP TO TITLE III (PUBLIC ACCOMMODATIONS) OF THE ADA

State and local governments are never subject to the public accommodations requirements of Title III of the ADA, because, by definition, public accommodations are privately operated facilities and services, not publicly funded state and local governments. Conversely, privately operated facilities cannot be covered by Title II, because Title II covers state and local governments, which are publicly funded entities. Title II and Title III have somewhat different requirements. However, there are situations in which governments and private entities stand in very close relation to each other, with the result that certain activities may be affected, at least indirectly, by both titles. In general, the Government entity must ensure that the state and local government requirements are met, and the private entity must ensure that the public accommodations requirements are met.

For example, consider a state Department of Parks that provides a restaurant in one of its parks that is operated by a restaurant corporation under contract with the state. Because the restaurant is a place of public accommodation, the corporation is a public accommodation, subject to the public accommodations requirements of the ADA. However, the state Department of Parks is subject to the state and local government requirements of the ADA and, because of the contract, it is obligated to ensure that the restaurant is operated in a manner that meets the state and local government requirements. For this reason, the State Department of Parks should stipulate in the contract that the restaurant must meet certain obligations that the restaurant would not ordinarily need to meet under the ADA if the restaurant did not contract with a government entity.

As a further example, consider a city that owns a downtown office building occupied by its Department of Human Resources. The first floor is leased as commercial space to a restaurant, a newsstand, and a travel agency. The city is the landlord, but because it is a government entity rather than a private entity, it is not subject to the public accommodations requirements, even though a landlord leasing space to a place of public accommodation is normally subject to the public accommodations requirements. Of course, because the city is covered by the state and local government requirements, it still has obligations under the ADA.

Last, assume that a city engages in a joint venture with a corporation to build a new professional sports stadium. The stadium must be built in compliance with the accessibility provisions of both the public accommodations requirements and the state and local government requirements. In cases in which the standards differ, the stadium would have to meet the standard that provides the highest degree of access to people with disabilities.

ELIGIBILITY: WHO IS A "QUALIFIED INDIVIDUAL WITH A DISABILITY"?

The ADA prohibits discrimination by any state or local government against any qualified individual with a disability because of such individual's disability. "A qualified individual with a disability" is defined as an individual who, with or without reasonable modifications to rules, policies, and practices, the removal of architectural, communication, or transportation barriers, or the provision of auxiliary aids or services, meets the essential eligibility requirements for the receipt of services or the participation in programs or activities provided by a state or local government (42 U.S.C. §12131[2]; 28 C.F.R. §35.104).

It is the duty of the state or local government to show that an eligibility requirement is essential. Before a state or local government may conclude that a person with a disability is unable to meet essential eligibility requirements, it must consider whether any of the following measures will enable the person to meet the requirements: 1) modification of the rules, policies, or practices; 2) removal of architectural or transportation barriers; or 3) provision of auxiliary aids and service. If such measures will enable a person with a disability to meet essential eligibility requirements, the person is a qualified individual with a disability.

Where questions of safety are involved, the principles established in the ADA regulations for Title III (which do not require a public accommodation to permit participation by an individual who poses a direct threat to the health and safety of himself or herself and/or others) are applicable.

BASIC PROVISIONS OF TITLE II, SUBTITLE A

General Requirements

No qualified individual with a disability shall, on the basis of disability, be discriminated against, be excluded from participation in, or be denied the benefits of the services, programs, or activities of a state or local government (42 U.S.C. §12132; 28 C.F.R. §35.130). It is discrimination to refuse to allow a person with a disability to participate in a service, program, or activity simply because the person has a disability. For example, it is a violation of the ADA if a person who uses a wheelchair is told she may not use a public park on the basis that the sight of her mobility impairment would upset other picnickers or that the city's insurance policy would not cover her. It is a violation of the ADA if a person who is blind is told he may not enter a city art museum because he cannot enjoy the exhibits.

A state or local government that enters into a contract with a private entity must ensure that the activity operated under contract is in compliance with the ADA. However, the state or local government is not responsible for ensuring that the other activities of the private entity (those not involved in the contract) are in compliance; the state or local government's responsibility extends only to the activity that is the subject of the contract.

Integrated Settings

Integration is fundamental to the ADA, because segregation relegates people with disabilities to second-class status. Therefore, it is a violation of the ADA if a state or local government fails to provide programs and services in the most integrated setting appropriate to the needs of the individual (i.e., in a setting that enables individuals with disabilities to interact with persons without disabilities to the largest extent possible) (28 C.F.R. §§35.130[b][1][iv], 35.130[c], 35. 130[d]). For example, it is a violation of the ADA to segregate seating for persons using wheelchairs to the backs of auditoriums or theaters, or to require such persons to sit near exits.

Program Participation and Accommodations

Participation in Separate Programs   Under the ADA, state and local governments can offer programs that are specifically designed for people with disabilities (28 C.F.R. §35.130[C]). However, even if state and local governments provide such programs, an individual with a disability cannot be required to participate in such a program and cannot be denied the opportunity to participate in programs or activities that are not separate or different (42 U.S.C. §12201[d]; 28 C.F.R. §§35.130[b][2], 35.130[e]; DOJ, 1992, p. 11). For example:

A child with a disability is entitled to swim at a public pool during regular swimming hours, even if
     a separate swimming program for children with disabilities is available.
A person who is blind may decide not to participate in a special museum tour that would allow her
     to touch sculptures in an exhibit, choosing instead to tour the exhibit at her own pace with the
     museum's recorded tour.

A state that provides optional special automobile license plates for individuals with disabilities and requires appropriate documentation for eligibility for the special plates cannot require an individual who qualifies for a special plate to accept a special plate or present documentation if he applies for a plate without the special designation.

Right To Refuse an Accommodation Nothing in the ADA requires an individual to accept an accommodation, aid, service, opportunity, or benefit that the individual chooses not to accept (42 U.S.C. §12201[d]; 28 C.F.R. §§35.130[b][2], 35.130[e]). For example, an individual who is blind may choose not to avail herself of the right to go to the front of a line, even if this privilege is available.

The ban against requiring a person with a disability to accept an accommodation is not to be interpreted as authorizing the representative or guardian of an individual with a disability to decline food, water, medical treatment, or medical services for that individual (28 C.F.R. §35.130[c][2]). The ADA does not alter current federal laws ensuring the rights of individuals with disabilities, who may be unable to express their wishes because of medical reasons, to receive food, water, and medical treatment.

Accommodations in the Regular Program When a state or local government offers a special program for individuals with disabilities, but an individual with a disaiblity chooses to participate in the regular program rather than in the special program, the state or local government still may have an obligation to provide accommodations (e.g., auxiliary aids and services) for that individual to benefit from the regular program (28 C.F.R. §35.130[b][2]; DOJ, 1992, p. 11). The fact that a separate program is offered may be a factor in determining the extent of the state or local government's obligation to provide accommodation in the regular program, but only if the separate program is appropriate to the needs of the particular individual with a disability.

For example, if a museum provides a special tour in sign language, the availability of the signed tour may be a factor in determining whether it would be an undue burden to provide a sign language interpreter for a deaf person who wants to take the regular tour at a different time. However, the availability of the signed tour would not affect the museum's obligation to provide an oral interpreter or an assistive listening device for a different tour if the individual does not use sign language.

Eligibility Criteria that Screen Out People with Disabilities

It is discrimination for a state or local government to apply eligibility criteria or standards that screen out or tend to screen out an individual with a disability or a class of individuals with disabilities from fully and equally enjoying any goods and services, unless such criteria can be shown to be necessary for the provision of the goods and services (28 C.F.R. §35.130[b][8]; DOJ, 1992, p. 12). The wishes, tastes, or preferences of other clients or participants may not be used to justify criteria that would exclude or segregate individuals with disabilities.

For example, a county library cannot require that an individual have a driver's license in order to obtain a library card, because some classes of people with disabilities, such as some persons with seizure disorders or visual impairments, cannot obtain driver's licenses. Other forms of identification also must be allowed. If a county recreation program prohibited persons who use wheelchairs from participating in county-sponsored scuba diving classes because the program's director believed that wheelchair users probably could not swim well enough to participate, this would be a blanket exclusion that would violate the ADA.

State and local governments may impose legitimate safety requirements, even if they tend to screen out people with disabilities. However, these requirements must be based on actual risks and on facts about particular individuals, not on speculation, stereotypes, or generalizations about individuals with disabilities or on the basis of presumptions about what a class of individuals with disabilities can or cannot do. The state or local government has the burden of showing that the criteria are necessary for the provision of the service, program, or activity. Any safety standard must be applied to all clients or participants, and inquiries about it must be limited to matters necessary to carrying out the specific standard. For example, the county recreation program may require that all participants in its scuba program pass a swimming test if the county can demonstrate that being able to swim is necessary for safe participation in the class.

Modification in Policies

State and local governments must make reasonable modifications in policies, practices, and procedures when such modifications are necessary to avoid discrimination on the basis of disability, unless the state or local government can demonstrate that modifying the policy or practice would fundamentally alter the nature of the activities and services offered (28 C.F.R. §35.130[b][7]; DOJ, 1992, p. 13).

Examples of policy modification include the following:

A municipal zoning ordinance requires that, in the central business district, the front entrance be set back 12 feet from the curb, creating a "set-back area." In order to install a ramp to the front entrance of a pharmacy, the owner must encroach on the set-back by 3 feet. Granting a variance in the zoning requirement may be a reasonable modification of policy.

A county general relief program provides emergency food, shelter, and cash grants to eligible individuals. The application process is lengthy and complex, and many persons with mental disabilities cannot complete it on their own. The county has an obligation to modify the application process to ensure that otherwise eligible individuals are not denied needed benefits. Modifications could include simplifying the process or providing individualized assistance for applicants with mental disabilities.

However, modification is not required when it would fundamentally alter the nature of the service, program, or activity. For example, a city-run planetarium darkens the planetarium during a show so the audience can see the representation of the night sky created on the ceiling above. A deaf individual requests that the policy of darkening the planetarium be modified in order to have sufficient light for an interpreter to be seen. If the city can show that modifying its policy would fundamentally alter the planetarium exhibit by preventing the audience from seeing the image on the ceiling, the modification would not be required.

However, the planetarium would be required to make all modifications up to the point of "fundamental alteration." Thus, if it would be a fundamental alteration to have more than one interpreter lighted in different parts of the room, but it would not be a fundamental alteration to have one interpreter lighted in a corner of the room, the practice of dimming all lights would have to be modified to allow for the one interpreter.

The requirement to modify policies, practices, and procedures requires law enforcement agencies to make changes in policies that result in discriminatory arrests or abuse of individuals with disabilities. Law enforcement personnel are required to make appropriate efforts to determine whether behavior that is perceived as disruptive or strange is the result of a disability such as mental retardation, diabetes, cerebral palsy, traumatic brain injury, mental illness, or a seizure disorder rather than criminal activity.

Association

It is discrimination for a state or local government to exclude or deny equal services, programs, or activities to an individual or entity because of the known disability of another individual with whom the individual or entity has a relationship or association (28 C.F.R. §35.130[g]). The term *entity* is included because, at times, organizations that provide services to, or are otherwise associated with, persons with disabilities are subjected to discrimination. The relationship or association need not be a family relationship; any kind of relationship will suffice.

For example, a county recreation center may not refuse to allow someone to participate on a sports team because her partner has AIDS, and a county-sponsored baseball league may not refuse participation by a team made up of volunteers who work with persons with AIDS.

Charges

A state or local government may not impose a surcharge on an individual with a disability or a group of individuals with disabilities to cover the cost of measures taken to comply with the ADA, such as the provision of auxiliary aids or program access (28 C.F.R. §35.103[f]; DOJ, 1992, p. 12). However, the ADA does not prohibit state or local governments from requiring a person with a disability to leave a completely refundable security deposit when using certain auxiliary aids, such as personal receivers that are part of an assistive listening system. Also, a state or local government may pass on the cost of complying with the ADA to all of the individuals who use its programs and services, as long as the cost is not imposed differently on people with disabilities than on other people.

Granting of Licenses and Certifications

A state or local government may not discriminate against a qualified individual with a disability, on the basis of disability, in the granting of licenses and certifications (28 C.F.R. §35.130[b][6]; DOJ, 1992, p. 14). A state or local government may not administer a licensing or certification program in a manner that subjects qualified individuals with disabilities to discrimination on the basis of disability, nor may a state or local government establish requirements for the programs or activities of licensees or certified entities that subject qualified individuals with disabilities to discrimination on the basis of disability.

For example, a state licensing requirement that prohibits child care centers from taking certain children with disabilities is illegal. Also, a state may not prohibit the licensing of transportation companies that employ individuals with missing limbs as drivers, because many persons with missing limbs are qualified to be drivers, with or without accommodations such as hand controls.

However, the requirements of the ADA do not extend to the programs or activities of licensed or certified entities themselves. These programs or activities are not themselves programs or activities of the state or local government merely by virtue of the license or certificate. For example, the fact that the state health department grants an operating license to a meat packing plant does not mean that the plant must comply with the ADA's requirements of state and local governments. (However, the plant may be covered by other parts of the ADA, such as the Title I employment requirements, if it has 15 or more employees.)

Protection Against Retaliation,
Relationship to Other Laws, and Other Miscellaneous Provisions

It should be noted that all of the miscellaneous provisions in Title V of the ADA, including the prohibition against retaliation and harassment and the provisions about the ADA's relationship to other laws, apply to state and local governments as well (42 U.S.C. §§12201–12212).

PROGRAM ACCESS

Program Access in Existing Facilities

Every qualified individual with a disability is entitled to access to the programs, activities, services, and benefits provided by a state or local government (28 C.F.R. §§35.149, 35.150). In existing facilities, a state or local government is required to operate each program so that, when viewed it its entirety, the program is readily accessible to and usable by people with disabilities. If a program can be made accessible by some method other than providing architectural access, providing architectural access is not required.

A state or local government need not provide program access where the government can show that to do so would result in a fundamental alteration of the program or an undue financial or administrative burden. However, even if fundamental alteration or undue burden can be shown, the government is still required to provide program access up to the level of fundamental alteration or undue burden.

Methods for Achieving Program Access

In deciding which methods to use to achieve program access, innovation and creativity are encouraged (28 C.F.R. §35.150[b]; DOJ, 1992, pp. 10, 20–21). The following are possible methods that may be used:

Redesign of equipment
Reassignment to accessible buildings
Use of aides
Home visits
Delivery of services at alternate accessible sites
Use of accessible vehicles
Alteration of existing facilities
Construction of new facilities

Effective access must be provided, and priority is given to methods that ensure integration of people with disabilities into the same programs and activities as persons without disabilities (i.e., that enable individuals with disabilities to interact with persons without disabilities to the fullest extent possible).

Example Case Studies—How To Provide Program Access

Whether methods that do not provide integration are effective depends on a case-by-case analysis of each situation, such as in the following case studies.

Case Study 1   A county has five county hospitals offering a variety of health services. Only three of the hospitals are physically accessible. Is the county health service program, when viewed in its entirety, accessible to people with disabilities? Consider the following possibilities:

A.   Suppose that all of the physically accessible hospitals are located on the south side of the county, so that it takes a person with a disability who lives on the north side an hour to get to an accessible south-side hospital, whereas other north-side residents who do not need architectural access can be at one of the two inaccessible north-side hospitals within 15 minutes. When viewed in its entirety, the program is not equally accessible. In this situation, structural alteration of one of the north-side hospitals would be required.

B.   Suppose that the five hospitals are located throughout the county so that, on average, regardless of where one lives, it takes the same amount of time to get to an accessible hospital as to an inaccessible one. In this situation, the program of health services is equally accessible to people with disabilities, when viewed in its entirety, assuming that the same types and levels of service are available at each hospital.

C.   Suppose that pediatric services are available only at one of the inaccessible hospitals. When the county program is viewed in its entirety, pediatric services are not accessible to people with disabilities. However, the program access requirement would not necessarily mean that the inaccessible hospital must be altered, because there may be other equally effective methods of providing program access. For example, all the pediatric services could be moved to one of the accessible hospitals, or the same level of pediatric services could be offered at one of the accessible hospitals.

D.   Suppose certain services are available at inaccessible hospitals only. Can program access be provided through home visits? The answer depends on several factors. For example, home visits may provide program access for a routine consultation with a doctor, but may not if necessary specialized equipment or testing is only available at the hospital. Furthermore, whether home visits are an effective means of program access also will depend on whether it takes longer to schedule a home visit than to schedule an appointment at the inaccessible hospital. Finally, if the county sponsors a special service such as a prenatal care class in one of the inaccessible hospitals, providing the information in a home visit is not an effective method of providing program access, because interaction between class participants is not available. In this case, reassigning the class to one of the accessible hospitals would be needed to provide program access.

Case Study 2   A state university has library facilities located on the ground floor of an existing building that has not been recently renovated. Architectural access is available to the main entrance of the library, the reading room, and the rest rooms. The library stacks are not wheelchair accessible, but the library staff retrieves books within 10 minutes of a request. Computer users in the reading room can use an on-line browsing program that provides information about all books in the same order the books appear on the stacks. Has program access been provided?

A.   In the situation described above, program access exists and no structural alteration is required, even though the entire library is not physically accessible.

B.   Suppose there are no wheelchair-accessible rest rooms in the library. If rest rooms are provided for library patrons without disabilities, the lack of accessible rest rooms means that, when viewed in its entirety, the library is not accessible to and usable by people with disabilities. As part of the program access requirement, the state university must provide accessible rest rooms if it provides rest rooms for persons without disabilities.

Case Study 3   If a school system has many sites, what must it do to provide program access?

A.   In general, the school system must provide wheelchair access at schools dispersed throughout its service area so that children who use wheelchairs can attend school at locations comparable in convenience to those available to other children.

B.   Where "magnet" schools or schools offering different curricula or instruction techniques are available, the range of choice provided to students with disabilities must be comparable to that offered to other students.

Where structural alteration to existing facilities is required as part of program access, the accessibility standards discussed in Chapter 10 (this volume) will apply. Also, where structural alteration is needed, state and local governments with 50 or more employees must develop a transition plan (see Transition Plans, below).

Generally Unacceptable Means of Accessibility

Carrying   Carrying an individual with a disability is considered an ineffective and therefore unacceptable method for achieving program accessibility (28 C.F.R. §35.150[b][1]; DOJ, 1992, p. 20). Carrying is not permitted as an alternative to structural modifications such as putting in a ramp or a lift.

Carrying is allowed only in very rare and manifestly exceptional cases, such as onto an ocean-going vessel (e.g., a submarine), where physical access either cannot be provided or is prohibitively expensive. Also, when program accessibility in existing facilities may be achieved only through structural alterations, carrying may serve as a temporary expedient until construction is completed. However, even in such rare situations, all persons involved in the carrying must be formally instructed on the safest and least humiliating methods of carrying.

Back Doors and Freight Elevators   Back doors and freight elevators may be used to satisfy the program accessibility requirement only as a last resort and only if they provide accessibility comparable to that provided to persons without disabilities (DOJ, 1992, p. 19). A back door is acceptable only if it is kept unlocked during the same hours the front door remains unlocked; the passageway to and from the door is accessible, well lit, neat, and clean; and an individual with mobility impairment need not travel excessive distances or through nonpublic areas such as kitchens or stockrooms to gain access. A freight elevator is only acceptable if it is upgraded so as to be usable by passsengers generally and if the passageways leading to and from the elevator are well lit, neat, and clean.

Fundamental Alteration and Undue Burden

Although a state or local government is required to make its programs accessible when viewed in their entirety, it is not required to provide program access when this would result in a fundamental alteration in the nature of the program or an undue financial or administrative burden (28 C.F.R. §35.150[a][3]–[3]). However, if measures to provide full program access would result in a fundamental alteration or undue burden, the state or local government is still required to take those measures that would provide as much program access as possible without resulting in the fundamental alteration or undue burden.

The program access standard in Title II, with its limitation of undue burden, is different, and is significantly higher, than the ADA's requirement in Title III that public accommodations remove barriers in every facility if the removal is readily achievable (defined as "easily accomplishable and able to be carried out without much difficulty or expense"). Although Title II does not require removal of barriers in situations where a state or local government is providing program access in some other way, the program access requirement obligates state and local governments to enable individuals with disabilities to participate in and benefit from the services, programs, or activities of those governments.

The ADA anticipates that providing program access will generally not result in undue financial and administrative burdens; such burdens will result only in the most unusual cases.

Procedure for Claiming Fundamental Alteration or Undue Burden   A state or local government has the obligation to prove that providing program access would result in fundamental alteration or undue burden (28 C.F.R. §35.150[a][3]). In determining whether the expenditure required in order to provide access is sizeable relative to the government's budget, all resources available for use in the funding and operation of the service, program, or activity must be considered. The decision that fundamental alteration or undue burden would result must be made by the head of the state or local government or his or her designee, but in any case by a high-level official no lower than a department head, having budgetary authority and responsibility for making spending decisions. The decision must be documented in a written statement that includes the reasons for reaching the conclusion that fundamental alteration or undue burden would result.

Historic Preservation

In providing program access, a state or local government is not required to take any action that would threaten or destroy the historic significance of a historic preservation program in a historic property (28 C.F.R. §§35.104, 35.150[a][2], 35.150[b][2]). "Historic preservation programs" are programs that have preservation as a primary purpose. "Historic properties" are those listed or eligible for listing in the National Register of Historic Places, or designated as historic under a state or local law. Therefore, if a program occupies a historic property but does not have historic preservation as a primary purpose, the special accessibility provisions described below may not be used.

When providing program access to historic preservation programs in historic properties, state and local governments must give priority to methods that provide independent physical access. When physical access is not required because it would threaten or destroy historic significance, alternative methods of providing program access must be provided. However, this exception is to be applied only in those very rare situations in which it is not possible to provide access to a historic property using the special access provisions established by the *Uniform Federal Accessibility Standards* (UFAS) (General Services Administration, 1991) or the *Americans with Disabilities Act Accessibility Guidelines for Buildings and Facilities* (ADAAG) (U.S. Architectural and Transportation Barriers Compliance Board, 1991). In such situations, alternative methods include using audiovisual materials and devices to depict inaccessible portions of a historic property, or assigning aides to guide persons with disabilities through those parts of the historic property that would be inaccessible without the guide. Other innovative alternative methods are also acceptable.

ARCHITECTURAL ACCESS REQUIREMENTS

General Requirements

Existing Facilities   The obligation to provide architectural access to existing state and local government facilities is based on first determining whether program access to government programs and activities can be provided without the need to make structural modifications (28 C.F.R. §35.150[b][1]). If program access cannot be provided without structural modification, such modifications must be made. The technical requirements that apply to facilities that are altered also apply to structural modifications that are undertaken to provide program access.

New Construction   Any facility or part of a facility that is newly constructed by a state or local government must be designed and constructed so that it is readily accessible to and usable by people with disabilities (28 C.F.R. §35.151[a]). This requirement applies to any construction that is begun after January 26, 1992. Facilities that were under design on January 26, 1992, are included if the date that bids were invited for the construction was after January 26, 1992.

Facilities that Are Altered   When alterations will affect the usability of a facility, the altered portion of the facility must, to the maximum extent feasible, be readily accessible to and usable by people with disabilities (28 C.F.R. §35.151[b]). This requirement applies to any alteration that is begun after January 26, 1992. Alterations that were under design on January 26, 1992, are included if the date that bids were invited for the alteration was after January 26, 1992.

Curb Ramps   If a state or local government has authority over roads and sidewalks, it must provide physical access in the form of curb ramps or other sloped areas at existing pedestrian walkways (28 C.F.R. §35.150[d][2]). Pedestrian walkways include intersections and crosswalks as well as locations where access is required for use of public transportation, such as bus stops that are not located at intersections or crosswalks. Providing curb ramps to sidewalks serving facilities covered by the ADA (state and local government buildings, public accommodations, transportation facilities, and places of employment) must be given first priority.

All newly constructed or altered streets, roads, and highways must have curb ramps at any intersection having curbs or other barriers to entry from a street-level pedestrian walkway, and all newly constructed or altered street-level pedestrian walkways must have curb ramps at intersections with streets, roads, or highways.

Existing Parking Lots or Garages   A state or local government should provide an adequate number of accessible parking spaces in existing parking lots or garages over which it has jurisdiction (DOJ, 1992, p. 21).

Accessibility Standards

The original DOJ Title II regulations provided two choices for technical standards to be used in new construction and alterations of state and local government buildings: the UFAS or the ADAAG (28 C.F.R. §35.151[c]). Under the original regulations, a state or local government could comply with either standard. However, a state or local government could not choose to follow the ADAAG on one floor and the UFAS on another floor of a new building; each facility or project was required to follow one standard or the other. Similarly, a state or local government could not choose to follow the ADAAG for one alteration project and the UFAS for another alteration project in the same building; all alterations in the same building were required to be done in accordance with the same standard.

This choice of standards provided by the original Title II regulations differed from the public accommodations requirements of Title III, which refer to only one set of accessibility standards— the ADAAG. The reason that state and local governments were given a choice of standards is that many state and local governments receive federal funding and have been required by Section 504 of the Rehabilitation Act of 1973 to follow the UFAS standard. That standard is therefore familiar to them, and the ADA gave state and local governments the option, an interim period, to follow a standard with which they were familiar. In December 1992, the U.S. Architectural and Transportation Barriers Compliance Board issued a proposed rulemaking to establish ADAAG accessibility standards specifically for state and local governments (57 Fed. Reg. 60612 [December 21, 1992]). Upon issuance of the final rule, it is expected that the DOJ will require state and local governments to use only the ADAAG.

ADAAG Elevator Exemption   If the ADAAG is used instead of the UFAS, the ADAAG "elevator exemption," which applies to private entities complying with Title III of the ADA, does not apply to state and local governments under Title II (42 U.S.C. §12201[a]; 28 C.F.R. §35.151[c]; DOJ, 1992, p. 30). (The elevator exemption provides that elevators are not required in any building that has fewer than three stories or has fewer than 3,000 square feet per story, unless the building is a shopping center, the office of a health care provider, or a transit terminal, depot, or station.)

Clearly Equivalent Access   A state or local government may depart from the specific requirements of the UFAS or the ADAAG where it is clearly evident that equivalent access is provided. For example, compliance with a state or local building code may also comply with Title II, if it is clearly evident that the state or local code provides at least the same level of access as the UFAS or the ADAAG. This provision is intended to ensure that innovative barrier-free design is not discouraged.

Leased Buildings

Buildings leased or rented by a state or local government are not necessarily required to be physically accessible (28 C.F.R. §§35.150–.151; DOJ, 1992, p. 32). However, state or local governments must comply with the program access requirement when they lease or rent buildings. In addition, state and local governments are encouraged to follow the requirements that apply to the federal government under the Architectural Barriers Act of 1968 (42 U.S.C. §§4151 *et seq.;* 36 C.F.R. §1190.34). Under this act, the federal government may not lease a building unless it has:

One accessible route from an accessible entrance to the parts of the building where principal activities for which it was leased take place
Accessible toilet facilities
Accessible parking facilities

Maintenance of Accessible Features

State and local governments must maintain in operable and working condition all features and equipment that are required to be readily accessible to and usable by people with disabilities (28

C.F.R. §35.133). Whereas isolated or temporary interruptions in service or access do not constitute discrimination, allowing obstructions or "out of service" equipment to persist beyond a reasonable period of time would be discrimination, as would repeated mechanical failures resulting from improper or inadequate maintenance.

This requirement applies to features and equipment that provide architectural and physical access, such as elevators, lifts, ramps, and accessible routes, as well as to communications features and equipment such as telecommunication devices and auditory and visual signals. It refers not only to situations in which mechanical or motorized devices are not working, but also to situations in which accessible routes are blocked or accessible doors are locked.

Information and Signage

State and local governments must provide signage at all inaccessible entrances at each of their facilities that directs users to an accessible entrance or to a location with information about accessible facilities (28 C.F.R. §35.163).

COMMUNICATION ACCESS

Equally Effective Communication

State and local governments must take appropriate steps to ensure that communication with people with disabilities is as effective as communication with people without disabilities (28 C.F.R. §35.160[a]; DOJ, 1992, p. 35).

Auxiliary Aids and Services

In order to meet the requirement of equally effective communication, state and local governments must furnish appropriate auxiliary aids and services where necessary to afford an individual with a disability an equal opportunity to participate in, and enjoy the benefits of, a service, program, or activity, unless it would result in a fundamental alteration of the program or an undue financial or administrative burden (28 C.F.R. §§35.104, 35.160[b], 35.164; DOJ, 1992, p. 35).

Auxiliary aids and services include (28 C.F.R. §35.104; DOJ, 1992, p. 35):

Effective methods of making visually delivered materials available to individuals with visual impairments, including but not limited to qualified readers, taped texts, audio recordings, and braille or large-print materials.

Effective methods of making aurally delivered materials available to individuals with hearing impairments, including but not limited to qualified interpreters, note takers, transcription services, written materials, telephone handset amplifiers, assistive listening devices, assistive listening systems, telephones compatible with hearing aids, closed caption decoders, open and closed captioning, and telecommunications devices for deaf persons (TDDs) or videotext displays

Acquisition or modification of equipment or devices

Other similar services and actions

Auxiliary Aid and Service Requirements

Primary Consideration for Request of Person with a Disability   A state or local government must give persons with disabilities the opportunity to request the auxiliary aids and services of their choice (28 C.F.R. §35.160[b][2]; DOJ, 1992, pp. 36–37). That choice must be given primary consideration—that is, the government must honor the choice unless it can demonstrate that another effective means of communication exists, or that use of the means chosen by the person with a disability is not required because it would result in a fundamental alteration or an undue burden.

Provision of Qualified Interpreters A "qualified interpreter" is an interpreter who is able to interpret effectively, accurately, and impartially both receptively and expressively, using any necessary specialized vocabulary (28 C.F.R. §35.104; DOJ, 1992, pp. 37–38). The ADA does not require that the interpreter be certified, although a certified interpreter may be a qualified interpreter. However, it should be noted that even the most skilled interpreter may not be considered qualified if the situation demands more impartiality than use of that interpreter would afford. For example, in a situation between a doctor and a deaf patient at a city hospital, if the deaf patient has a sister who is a certified interpreter, he may yet require another interpreter in order to have an interpreter who can interpret effectively, accurately, and impartially.

It further should be noted that persons with hearing impairments have different communication needs and use different modes of communication. Some use American Sign Language, but others use different sign languages. Some people rely on an oral interpreter who silently mouths words spoken by others to make them easier to lip read. Many people with hearing impairments use their voices to communicate, and some combine talking and signing. The individual should be consulted to determine the most effective means of communication for him or her (28 C.F.R. §35.160[b][2]).

A case-by-case decision is required in order to determine whether an interpreter of some kind is required for effective communication with a person who is deaf, or if other forms of communications, such as writing notes, will be effective (28 C.F.R. §35.160[b][1]). Factors to be considered include the complexity and importance of the communication, its length, the context, and the number of people involved. For example, communications about medical, legal, or financial issues would more likely require the use of an interpreter than a communication about an agency's office hours, obtaining a bus schedule, or checking a book out of the county library.

Provision of Qualified Readers Readers or reading devices are sometimes necessary to ensure access to a state or local government's services, programs, or activities, such as reviewing public documents, examining demonstrative evidence, and filling out voter registration forms or forms needed to receive public benefits (28 C.F.R. §35.160[b][1]).

Provision of Telecommunications Devices for the Deaf

Communication by Telephone When a state or local government communicates with the public by telephone, the ADA requires that TDDs or equally effective telecommunications systems be used to communicate with people who have hearing or speech impairments (28 C.F.R. §35.161; DOJ, 1992, p. 38). "Equally effective communications systems" may include the use of a telecommunications relay service such as that required by Title IV of the ADA. However, where the provision of telephone service is a major function of the entity (e.g., a city hall, a public library, a public aid office), TDDs should be available.

In addition to providing TDDs for use by state and local government employees who must communicate with the public, the ADA technical standards require TDDs to be available in a certain portion of public pay telephones for general use by the public. Clear signage should be posted indicating the location of such TDDs, and directional signage indicating the location of available TDDs should be placed adjacent to banks of telephones that do not contain a TDD (ADAAG, §4.1.3[17]).

Telephone Emergency Services (911) A state or local government is required to provide "direct access" for callers with hearing or speech impairments who use TDDs or computer modems to any telephone emergency services (often known as "911" services) available to callers without disabilities, including fire, police, ambulance service, emergency poison control, and the like (28 C.F.R. §35.162; DOJ, 1992, pp. 38–39).

The requirement for direct access is a stronger requirement than the requirement for equally effective telecommunication systems that applies to offices that communicate with the public.

Whereas telecommunications relay services can be used to accomplish "equally effective" communication, TDDs are required to accomplish "direct access." Access to telephone emergency services through a third party or through a relay service will not satisfy the requirement for direct access. Of course, if an individual places a call to the emergency service through a relay service, the service must accept the call rather than require the caller to hang up and call directly to the emergency service without using the relay.

A state or local government may, however, operate its own relay service within its emergency system, provided that the services for nonvoice calls are as effective as those provided for voice calls in terms of response time and availability in hours. Telephone emergency service systems are not required to be comptabile with all formats used for nonvoice communications. At present, they are only required to be compatible with the Baudot format.

No additional dialing or space bar requirements may be imposed on TDD calls to emergency services. Operators must be trained to recognize incoming TDD signals and respond appropriately. In addition, they must be trained to recognize that "silent" calls may be TDD or computer modem calls and to respond appropriately.

Separate seven-digit emergency call numbers may not be used for TDD instead of 911 if 911 dialing is available for voice calls. Separate seven-digit emergency call numbers would be unfamiliar and more burdensome to use. However, a separate seven-digit line for use exclusively by TDD calls may be provided in addition to direct access on the 911 line. Where such a separate line is provided, callers using TDDs or computer modems would have the option of calling either 911 or the seven-digit number.

If a state or local government provides emergency services through a seven-digit number to all callers, it may provide two separate lines—one for voice calls and one for TDD calls—rather than providing direct access for TDD calls on the same line used for voice calls, so long as the services for TDD calls are as effective as those offered for voice calls in terms of the time it takes to respond to the calls and the hours of operation. Also, the TDD number must be publicized as effectively and be displayed as prominently as the voice number wherever the emergency numbers are listed.

Telephone emergency services are encouraged to install voice amplification devices on the handsets of the dispatcher's telephones to amplify the dispatcher's voice because, in an emergency, a person with a hearing loss may be using a telephone that does not have an amplification device.

Access to Television Programming   Television and videotape programming produced by a state or local government is covered by the requirement for auxiliary aids and services, and must provide access to persons with hearing impairments. Access may be provided by closed captioning (28 C.F.R. §35.160[b][1]).

Provision of Documents in Formats Other Than Print   Written communications provided by state and local governments are subject to the auxiliary aids and services requirement and must, when requested, be available to persons with visual impairments in a usable form (DOJ, 1992, p. 36). Large-print versions of written documents may be produced on a copier with enlargement capabilities. Braille versions of documents produced by computers can be produced with a braille printer. Audiotapes or computer disks of written documents may be provided for individuals who are unable to read large print and do not use braille, but who desire the tape or disk format. Tax documents are just one example of a written communication that must be provided in an alternative form if requested.

Fundamental Alteration and Undue Burden

A state or local government's obligation to provide auxiliary aids and services where necessary to ensure equal access is limited to situations that do not require a fundamental alteration of the nature of the program or activity or an undue financial or administrative burden (28 C.F.R. §35.164) (see, e.g., the discussion of a city-run planetarium above). The ADA anticipates that providing auxiliary aids and services will generally not result in undue financial and administrative burdens; such burdens will result only in the most unusual cases.

NOTICE AND EVALUATION REQUIREMENTS

State and local governments must ensure that people with disabilities are made aware of their rights, and must follow evaluation and planning procedures to ensure that those rights will be protected.

Notice

All state and local governments must give people with disabilities notice of their rights (28 C.F.R. §35.106; DOJ, 1992, p. 44). The following methods are examples of how such notice can be given:

Include ADA information in handbooks, manuals, and pamphlets that are distributed to the public
Put posters in service centers or other public places
Broadcast on radio and television

In providing notice, state and local governments must meet the requirement to provide communication access to persons with hearing and vision impairments.

Self-Evaluation

All state and local governments must perform a written self-evaluation of their current services, programs, and activities, and review all their policies and practices, and the effects thereof, that do not or may not meet the requirements of the ADA (28 C.F.R. §35.105; DOJ, 1992, pp. 40–43). To the extent that modification of any such services, policies, and practices is required, the state or local government must make the necessary modifications. Normally, policies and practices are reflected in laws, ordinances, regulations, administrative manuals or guides, policy directives, and memoranda. Other practices, however, may not be recorded and may be based on local custom.

Under the ADA, all state and local governments were required to complete a self-evaluation that must have been completed by January 26, 1993. However, because the requirements of Title II went into effect on January 26, 1992, even though governments had a year to complete the self-evaluation, they were still responsible for complying with the ADA as of January 26, 1992, and the ADA was enforceable against governments as of January 26, 1992. State and local governments were required to provide interested persons, including individuals with disabilities or organizations representing them, with the opportunity to participate in the self-evaluation process by submitting comments.

For state and local governments that have 50 or more employees, there is an additional requirement. For at least 3 years after the self-evaluation is finished, they must keep the following documents on file and make them available for public inspection:

A list of the interested persons consulted
A description of services, policies, and practices that were evaluated and problems that were identified
A description of any changes that were made to comply with the ADA

All states have at least 50 employees, so all state departments, agencies, and other divisional units are subject to the above requirements. Determining if a local government has 50 or more employees will be based on a government-wide total, rather than on the number of employees of a sub-unit, department, or division of the local government. Part-time employees are included in the determination.

If a state or local government that receives federal funding has already conducted a self-evaluation as was required by Section 504 of the Rehabilitation Act of 1973, the ADA self-evaluation requirement applied only to those policies and practices that were not included in the previous self-evaluation. However, the DOJ encouraged governments to reexamine all of their policies and programs, because old Section 504 self-evaluations may be outdated or insufficient to meet the requirements of the ADA. Government programs covered by Section 504 will still have to meet the requirements of that law even if they are included in the ADA self-evaluation.

Guidance in Conducting Self-Evaluation The self-evaluation requirement mandates careful examination in the following areas:

1. Whether any physical barriers to access existed and what steps needed to be taken to make the programs accessible when viewed in their entirety (if structural changes were determined to be necessary, the state or local government was required to make a transition plan)
2. Whether any policies or practices excluded or limited the participation of individuals with disabilities in programs, activities, or services and what policy modifications needed to be implemented to change them, and complete justifications for any exclusionary or limiting policies that were not going to be modified
3. Whether the state or local government communication with program participants and members of the public with disabilities was as effective as with others, including TDD communication and telephone emergency services
4. Whether readers, interpreters, and other such services were needed, including policies to ensure maintenance of communications equipment in operable order
5. Whether emergency evacuation warnings and procedures were adequate to protect people with disabilities
6. Whether written or audiovisual materials portrayed individuals with disabilities in an offensive or demeaning manner
7. Whether historic preservation programs gave priority to methods that provide physical access to persons with disabilities
8. Whether decisions were made properly and expeditiously about whether compliance with the ADA resulted in an undue burden or fundamental alteration
9. Whether individuals with mobility impairments were provided access to public meetings
10. Whether employment practices complied with nondiscrimination requirements
11. Whether building and construction policies ensured that new construction and alterations conformed to the appropriate standards in the ADA
12. Whether measures had been taken to ensure that employees were familiar with the requirements of the ADA
13. If participation in programs and activities was denied based on drug usage, whether the denial discriminated against former drug users, as opposed to individuals who are currently engaged in the illegal use of drugs

TRANSITION PLANS

Unlike the self-evaluation requirement, which applies to all state and local governments, the transition plan requirement applies only to state and local governments that have more than 50 employees, and only if structural changes are needed to achieve program access (28 C.F.R. §35.150[d][1]; DOJ, 1992, pp. 43–44).

State and local governments subject to the requirement were obligated to develop a transition plan by July 26, 1992, to address structural changes that needed to be made to state or local government facilities (28 C.F.R. §35.150[d][1], [3]). The transition plan must identify physical obstacles that limit program access, describe in detail the methods that will be used to achieve program access, and set out the schedule for making structural changes that are needed. If the time period for the transition is more than 1 year, the schedule must identify the changes that will be made during each year in order to comply with the deadline for completion of all structural changes, which is January 26, 1995. The plan must also identify the state or local government official who is responsible for implementing the plan.

Note that the July 26, 1992, deadline for completion of a transition plan came sooner than the 1-year deadline for completing a self-evaluation. Thus, even though governments had 1 year to do an overall self-evaluation of their programs, larger governments had to determine within 6 months whether structural changes would be needed to provide program access because, if they were, a transition plan had to be developed within 6 months of the effective date of Title II of the ADA. All structural changes that must be made to provide program access must be made by January 26, 1995, but in any event as expeditiously as possible (28 C.F.R. §35.150[c]).

Transition Plan Requirements

State and local governments were required to provide interested persons, including individuals with disabilities or organizations representing individuals with disabilities, the opportunity to participate in the transition plan by submitting comments. Also, a copy of the plan must be made available for public inspection.

If a state or local government that receives federal funding has already made a transition plan that was required by Section 504 of the Rehabilitation Act of 1973, the ADA transition plan requirement only applied to those necessary structural changes that were not included in the previous transition plan. However, the DOJ encouraged governments to include all of their operations in their ADA transition plans, because old Section 504 transition plans may be outdated or insufficient to meet the requirements of the ADA, and because it is simpler to be comprehensive than to try to identify and exclude everything covered by the Section 504 transition plan. Government programs covered by Section 504 will still have to meet the requirements of that law even if they are included in the ADA transition plan.

It should be noted that if a Section 504 transition plan was written but not fully implemented within the Section 504 time frame, the state or local government is out of compliance with Section 504.

Curb Ramps

If a state or local government has responsibility for or authority over roads and sidewalks, its transition plan is required to include a schedule for providing curb ramps at existing pedestrian walkways (28 C.F.R. §35.150[d][2]).

LIMITATIONS ON THE OBLIGATIONS OF STATE AND LOCAL GOVERNMENTS

Personal Devices and Services

A state or local government is not required to provide individuals with disabilities with personal devices, such as wheelchairs; individually prescribed devices, such as prescription eyeglasses or hearing aids; readers for personal use or study; or services of a personal nature, including assistance in eating, toileting, and dressing (28 C.F.R. §35.135; DOJ, 1992, p. 13). However, measures taken as alternatives to structural modification to achieve program access, such as retrieving items from shelves or providing home delivery of services, are not considered personal services and may be required.

Minimal actions that may be required as modifications of policies, practices, and procedures, such as a government benefits counselor assisting a person with a disability in filling out an application form, are not services of a personal nature. Also, the personal services exemption does not preclude the short-term loan of personal receivers that are part of an assistive listening system, which would be required as an auxiliary aid. Furthermore, in the area of employment, personal assistance services may be required as a reasonable accommodation. Of course, if personal services are customarily provided to other participants in a program, such as a hospital or a daycare center, they should also be provided to people with disabilities.

Drug Testing and Illegal Use of Drugs

Persons who currently take drugs illegally are not protected from discrimination or exclusionary action taken by a state or local government because of the illegal use (42 U.S.C. §12210; 28 C.F.R. §35.131; DOJ, 1992, p. 14). A state or local government may adopt or administer reasonable policies and procedures, including but not limited to drug testing, designed to ensure that participants in state or local government programs and activities are not engaging in current illegal use of drugs. However, a state or local government may not conduct inquiries, tests, or other procedures that would disclose the use of substances that are taken under supervision of a licensed health care professional, or other uses authorized by the Controlled Substances Act of 1970 or other provisions of federal law, because such uses are not included in the definition of "illegal use of drugs" (21 U.S.C. §§801 *et seq.*).

ENFORCEMENT

All nonstructural changes required by the ADA had to have been made by January 26, 1992 (28 C.F.R. §35.150[c], [d]; DOJ, 1992, p. 22). For example, this would have included eliminating unnecessary eligibility criteria or making reasonable modifications to policies. Where structural changes are required, they must be made as soon as practicable, but in no event later than January 26, 1995. Self-evaluations must have been completed by January 26, 1993 (28 C.F.R. §35.105). Transition plans must have been completed by July 26, 1992 (28 C.F.R. §35.150[d][1]).

Internal Grievance Procedures

All state and local governments with 50 or more employees must designate at least one employee to coordinate the government's effort to comply with the ADA, and must disseminate information about how to locate the employee (including making the name, business address, and business telephone number[s] of the designated employee[s] available to interested persons) (28 C.F.R. §35.107; DOJ, 1992, pp. 40–44). The designated employee(s) must investigate any complaints that the state or local government has failed to meet the requirements of the ADA. A state or local government with 50 or more employees must adopt and publish grievance procedures providing for prompt and equitable resolution of complaints alleging failure to comply with the ADA.

If a person with a disability does not meet the deadline for filing a formal administrative complaint of discrimination with the federal government because he or she was trying to resolve the problem through the state or local government's internal grievance procedure, that will generally be considered good cause for extending the deadline for filing an administrative complaint with the federal government. It should be noted that use of the internal grievance procedures of a state or local government to resolve a complaint is entirely optional. If a complainant wishes, he or she may proceed directly to filing the complaint with a federal agency, or filing a lawsuit (DOJ, 1992, p. 48).

Filing Administrative Complaints with the Federal Government

To enforce Title II, administrative complaints may be filed with the federal government alleging that a state or local government has not complied with the ADA (28 C.F.R. §§35.170–.174, 35.190; DOJ, 1992, pp. 45–46). A complaint may be filed by an individual with a disability him- or herself, a class of individuals with disabilities, or an authorized representative of an individual or class of individuals with disabilities. Any administrative complaint must be filed within 180 days (6 months) of an incident of discrimination.

A complaint may be filed with any of the following (28 C.F.R. §§35.170[c], 35.171, 35.190; DOJ, 1992, pp. 46–48):

1. Any federal agency providing funding to the state or local government that is the subject of the complaint
2. Any of the eight agencies designated by the ADA for state and local government enforcement
3. The DOJ

If a complaint is submitted to the wrong agency, the agency to which it is submitted will refer it to the DOJ and will notify the complainant that it is doing so. The DOJ will, in turn, refer the complaint to the correct agency.

Similarly, an employment complaint may be filed with any agency listed below or with the Equal Employment Opportunity Commission. Filing a complaint with any federal agency within 180 days of the incident of discrimination will satisfy the requirement for timely filing, even if it is filed with the incorrect agency. Some of the choices of where to file are discussed below.

Federal Agency Providing Funding to the State or Local Government If a state or local government program or activity receives federal funds and is therefore subject to Section 504 of the Rehabilitation Act of 1973, which bars discrimination on the basis of handicap in any program or activity receiving federal funding, a complaint about that state or local government program or activity will be handled by the federal agency with Section 504 jurisdiction over the state or local government program or activity. This has the added advantage that, if noncompliance is found, the potential remedy of withholding the program or activity's funding under Section 504 is possible. Because the Civil Rights Restoration Act of 1987 (PL 100-259) confirmed the application of Section 504 to all of the operations of a state or local government if one of its programs or activities receives federal funds, many programs and activities of state and local governments are already covered by Section 504.

Eight Agencies Designated by the ADA for State and Local Government Enforcement For state and local government programs, activities, and agencies that are not covered by Section 504, the ADA establishes a system of eight federal agencies that are responsible for enforcing the ADA's requirements for state and local governments. Each agency will process complaints about the components of state and local governments that exercise responsibilities most like their own. If two or more agencies have apparent responsibility over a complaint, or if the complaint involves more than one area, the DOJ will determine which one of the agencies shall be the designated agency for purposes of that complaint.

The eight agencies are:

Department of Agriculture, for all programs, services, and regulatory activities relating to farming and the raising of livestock, including extension services.
Department of Education, for all programs, services, and regulatory activities relating to the operation of elementary and secondary education systems and institutions, institutions of higher education and vocational education (other than schools of medicine, dentistry, nursing, and other health-related schools), and libraries.
Department of Health and Human Services, for all programs, services, and regulatory activities relating to the provision of health care and social services, including schools of medicine, dentistry, nursing, and other health-related schools; the operation of health care and social service providers and institutions, including "grass roots" and community services organizations and programs, and preschool and daycare programs.

Department of Housing and Urban Development, for all programs, services, and regulatory activities relating to state and local public housing, housing assistance, and referral.

Department of the Interior, for all programs, services, and regulatory activities relating to lands and natural resources, including parks and recreation, water and waste management, environmental protection, energy, historic and cultural preservations, and museums.

Department of Justice, for all programs, services, and regulatory activities relating to law enforcement, public safety, and the administration of justice, including courts and correctional institutions; commerce and industry, including general economic development, banking and finance, consumer protection, insurance, and small business; planning, development, and regulation (unless assigned to other designated agencies); state and local government support services (e.g., audit, personnel, comptroller, and administrative services); and all other government functions not assigned to other designated agencies.

Department of Labor, for all programs, services, and regulatory activities relating to labor and the work force.

Department of Transportation, for all programs, services, and regulatory activities relating to transportation, including highways, public transportation, traffic management (non–law enforcement), automobile licensing and inspection, and driver licensing.

Addresses of these agencies can be found in the DOJ *Title II Technical Assistance Manual* (1992, pp. 46–48).

Department of Justice   The DOJ is the agency responsible for all state and local government functions not assigned to the other designated agencies. Also, if one is unsure about where to file, one may file the complaint with the DOJ, which will refer the complaint to the proper agency. Complaints may be filed with the DOJ at the following address: Coordination and Review Section, P.O. Box 66118, Civil Rights Division, U.S. Department of Justice, Washington, D.C. 20035-6118.

Administrative Complaint Process   Designated agencies will accept all complete complaints and will promptly notify the complainant of the receipt and acceptance of the complaint (28 C.F.R. §§35.171[a], 35.172–174). A complete complaint is a written statement that contains the complainant's name and address and describes the state or local government's alleged discriminatory action in sufficient detail to inform the agency of the nature and date of the alleged violation. It must be signed by the complainant or by someone authorized to sign on the complainant's behalf. Complaints filed on behalf of classes or third parties shall describe or identify (by name, if possible) the alleged victims of discrimination.

If a designated agency receives a complaint that is not complete, it shall notify the complainant and specify the additional information that is needed to make the complaint complete. If the complainant fails to complete the complaint, the designated agency will close the complaint.

Designated agencies will investigate each complete complaint, attempt informal resolution and, if resolution is not achieved, issue to the complainant and to the state or local government against which the complaint has been filed a Letter of Findings containing findings of fact, conclusions of law, and a description of a remedy for each violation found.

If a designated agency's Letter of Findings finds noncompliance, it will notify the DOJ by forwarding a copy of the Letter of Findings and will initiate negotiations with the state or local government to secure compliance by voluntary means. Where the designated agency is able to secure voluntary compliance, a voluntary compliance agreement will be executed in writing and signed by the parties. This voluntary compliance agreement will:

Address each cited violation.

Specify the corrective or remedial action to be taken, within a stated period of time, to come into compliance.

Provide assurance that discrimination will not recur.

Provide for enforcement by the DOJ.

If a state or local government declines to enter into voluntary compliance negotiations or if negotiations are unsuccessful, the designated agency shall refer the matter to the DOJ with a recommendation for appropriate action. The DOJ may proceed to file a suit in federal district court.

Lawsuits

Lawsuits may be filed against state or local governments at any time, whether or not one has filed an administrative complaint (28 C.F.R. §§35.175–35.178; DOJ, 1992, p. 48). Both individuals with disabilities and organizations representing individuals with disabilities may file lawsuits. The remedies that are available in a lawsuit under Title II of the ADA are the same as the remedies that are available under Section 504 of the Rehabilitation Act of 1973. These remedies include court orders that a state or local government comply with the ADA, and attorney's fees.

Until 1992, federal courts in various part of the country came to different conclusions as to whether compensatory and punitive damages are available under Section 504. However, this issue may have been resolved by the Supreme Court decision in *Franklin v. Gwinnett County Public Schools* (1992), which states that under a similar law—Title IX of the Education Amendments of 1972, which prohibits sex discrimination—courts may award damages. Therefore, it seems very likely that money damage awards are available under Title II of the ADA.

CONCLUSION

Title II of the ADA extends a federal prohibition against discrimination on the basis of disability to all state and local government programs and activities, regardless of their size and regardless of whether they receive federal money. By mandating the modification of discriminatory policies and practices and the removal of physical and communication barriers, and by creating a comprehensive enforcement scheme, Title II ensures access for all persons with disabilities to all aspects of citizenship and public life.

REFERENCES

Architectural Barriers Act of 1968, 42 U.S.C. §§4151–4157 (1968).

Civil Rights Restoration Act of 1988, PL 100-259, codified at 29 U.S.C. §§ 706, 794(b) & (c), 20 U.S.C. §1681 n., §§1688, 1688 n., 1687, 1687 n., 42 U.S.C. 2000d–4a, 6107 Supp. (July 1988).

Controlled Substances Act of 1970, 21 U.S.C. §§801, *et seq.*

Franklin v. Gwinnett County Public Schools, 60 U.S. L.W. 4167 (February 26, 1992).

General Services Administration. Uniform Federal Accessibility Standards originally published at 49 Fed. Reg. 31528 (August 7, 1984), codified at 41 C.F.R. subpart 19.6.

Individuals with Disabilities Education Act of 1990, PL 101-476, amending and renaming the Education for All Children's Act, 20 U.S.C. §§1400 *et seq.*

Section 504 of the Rehabilitation Act of 1973, as amended, 29 U.S.C. §794.

U.S. Architectural and Transportation Barriers Compliance Board. (1991, July 26). Americans with Disabilities Act (ADA) accessibility guidelines for buildings and facilities, originally published at 56 Fed. Reg. 35605, codified at 28 C.F.R. part 36, App. A.

U.S. Architectural and Transportation Barriers Compliance Board. Americans with Disabilities Act (ADA) accessibility guidelines; state and local government facilities; proposed rulemaking, originally published at 57 Fed. Reg. 60612 (Dec. 21, 1992), to be codified at 36 C.F.R. 1191.

U.S. Department of Justice. (1978, January 13). Implementation of Executive Order 12250, nondiscrimination on the basis of handicap in federally assisted programs, originally published at 43 Fed. Reg. 2132, codified at 28 C.F.R. part 41.

U.S. Department of Justice. (1991, July 26). Nondiscrimination on the basis of disability in state and local government services; final rule, originally published at 56 Fed. Reg. 35694, codified at 28 C.F.R. part 36. *Federal Register, 56,* 35693–35723.

U.S. Department of Justic. (1992, January 24). *Title II technical assistance manual.* Washington, DC: U.S. Government Printing Office.

Chapter 9

Title II—
Public Services, Subtitle B

Public Transportation

Marilyn Golden

The transportation provisions in Title II, Subtitle B, of the Americans with Disabilities Act[1] (ADA) (42 U.S.C. §§12161–12165, 12184–12186) represent a great leap forward in transportation policy, far beyond any previous gain. The statute, along with the U.S. Department of Transportation (DOT) regulations (DOT, 1991a, 1991b, 1991c, 1991d, 1991e)[2] (which may be the strongest of all the ADA regulations) and the technical standards written by the U.S. Architectural and Transportation Barriers Compliance Board (1991b, 1992b), form a thorough and advanced blueprint for disability transportation policy in the 21st century.

It would be easy to follow the tendency of many previous commentators on the ADA by saying that implementation is likely to be less satisfactory than the policy looks on paper. Although this is true, it is also inevitable—implementation, a mundane and messy process, is always different from, and less precise than, the pristine detail of theoretical plans. The important question is, how different?

Here, there is some cause for optimism. The advent of the ADA and its transportation rules comes at a time when the disability community in the United States is most highly organized in terms of transportation advocacy. An extremely visible movement, catalyzed by a great deal of activity in the late 1970s and revitalized and led by American Disabled for Accessible Public Transit (ADAPT) in the 1980s, made a lifts-on-all-new-buses policy and all its trimmings a nonnegotiable part of the ADA. Large numbers of Americans with disabilities have argued, organized, fought, and gone to jail for their right to ride the bus. They understand this issue in a far deeper and more cohesive way than most of the other issues in the ADA. They are watching closely and will not be easily fooled by a lack of compliance.

A further cause for optimism in the transportation arena is that, for the most part, the entities that must comply are large, visible agencies that run public bus and rail services, and there is only

---

[1]The Americans with Disabilities Act of 1990 (PL 101-336) is published in *Statutes at Large* (104 Stat. 327) and codified in the *United States Code* (42 U.S.C. §§12101–12213 [Supp. II 1990]). References to various portions of the act within this chapter cite the specific section of the code.

[2]Department of Transportation regulations are codified at 49 C.F.R. parts 27, 37, and 38 (1991). References to various portions of these regulations within this chapter cite the specific section of the regulations.

one (or at the most a few) per community. Although the disability community's resources may be spread thin when monitoring thousands of restaurants and stores, it will be far easier to monitor one or two public transit agencies. Besides, most communities already have established some form of disability participation with (or against) the local transit authority, so its actions will not escape notice easily.

Certainly, accessible mass transit is an idea that is long overdue. It is, and always has been, quite affordable—particularly accessibility of newly purchased buses (which is all the ADA requires—there is no retrofit requirement). Given that lift-type equipment adds only about 5 percent to the cost of a bus, and that the federal government pays for 80% of a new vehicle's capital cost, the cost to cities is quite a bargain.

TRANSIT RIGHTS AND THE ADA

The ADA, as is often stated, is a civil rights law. It is in the area of transit, and particularly of paratransit, that the civil rights nature of the ADA helps explain what would otherwise be strangely limited requirements. As a civil rights law the ADA does not pretend to provide persons with disabilities with everything that they need. What it does provide is a level playing field—access to the same services and privileges available to persons without disabilities.

The Issue of Paratransit

Before the ADA, federal policy made paratransit a substitute for accessible fixed-route transit. Mass transit agencies could choose it as a method of fulfilling their obligation to transport persons with mobility impairment under the infamous policy of "local option." However, paratransit provided under local option was always so inferior to regular service and posed so many service limitations—lengthy advance notice requirements, waiting lists, trip purpose restrictions, few service hours, cumbersome eligibility procedures, limits on the number of rides available per month, and so forth—that it reduced its clients to second-class citizenship.

In a major policy shift, the ADA requires all public transit agencies to provide accessible mass transit gradually as old, inaccessible buses are replaced with new, accessible ones. In addition to, rather than instead of, accessible mass transit, public transit agencies must also provide paratransit. However, paratransit is only required by the ADA for certain persons—those who cannot use fixed-route transit. (It should be noted that transit agencies are certainly permitted to provide service beyond these limitations, but the ADA does not require them to do so.)

The amount of paratransit provided to such persons under the ADA differs, sometimes sharply, from what conventional paratransit service has provided in the past. Lift-equipped vans will no longer pick people up anywhere in town and take them anywhere else. Rather, the service will correspond very closely to fixed bus routes—generally, paratransit vehicles will travel less than a mile from a bus route, although under some circumstances they will travel up to a mile and a half. These restrictions apply only to public transit agencies that provide fixed-route bus service and are required, in addition, to provide paratransit to those people who cannot use the fixed-route service. The restrictions do not apply to other entities, such as private nonprofit paratransit providers.

The civil rights logic is that, if a particular agency provides transportation to the general public, it should also provide specialized transportation to persons who, as a result of their disabilities, cannot use regular fixed-route transit. Those who "cannot use" could mean, for example, persons with mental impairments of such a type or severity that they are unable to learn where to get off the bus, as well as persons who need lifts to ride the bus during the years before their mass transit system becomes lift equipped.

Like fixed-route buses, paratransit vehicles will not go just anywhere to pick up or drop off people who live far from a bus route. In tracking fairly closely to the bus routes, the geographic range of paratranist vehicles under the ADA will replicate the service area in which persons without disabilities would normally walk to the bus.

Persons unfamiliar with the civil rights logic behind these new paratransit rules have sometimes complained about their limits. It should be noted, however, that these new limitations are no greater than the limitations fixed-route bus transit poses on its users without disabilities. As persons who shaped the policy have joked, the ADA offers persons with disabilities "the same lousy mass transit" available to everyone else.

The ADA requires most communities to undergo a major paratransit transition. In the past, the pattern of how much paratransit was provided, and to whom, has varied significantly from community to community, funded by a hodgepodge of federal, state, county, local, nonprofit, and other private sources, generally not pursuant to any legal right but as a service. Today, as mass transit agencies shift into ADA compliance, some persons to whom they have given paratransit rides in the past are no longer receiving them because these persons are not a part of the ADA-mandated minimum eligible group on whom the mass transit agencies are now focusing. In other cases, previous paratransit riders are still eligible but a van will no longer come to their doors because of the new rules about paratransit hewing closely to bus routes. The seeming result to these persons is that "the ADA is taking away my paratransit."

Correcting an Historic Inequity

This tendency to blame the ADA is even greater because the ADA happened to be passed at a time when mass transit's funding problems are at their height. Many transit agencies that would be cutting back paratransit now in any case are doing so and blaming it on the ADA. The ADA actually creates a new civil right to paratransit for persons who, for some disability-related reason, cannot ride the bus. Unfortunately, the landmark nature of this right is not being fully appreciated. The real culprit is not the ADA. The problem predates the ADA by many years and, in fact, is the very reason that people with disabilities needed the ADA in the first place.

After Congress passed Section 504 of the Rehabilitation Act of 1973, which barred any entity receiving federal monies from discriminating against persons with disabilities, the logical transportation policy would have been a mandate for newly purchased mass transit vehicles to be accessible. The DOT put forward such a mandate in its 1979 Section 504 regulations, but this mandate soon went down to a now-famous defeat after the lawsuit *American Public Transportation Association (APTA) v. Lewis* (1981).

The devastating result was more than a decade of unnecessary and unnatural paratransit dependence during which thousands of Americans with mobility impairments who could have used accessible mass transit were denied it and therefore had to rely on door-to-door service. Their understandable indignance about the paratransit cuts in some cities must be seen in the light of this long-deferred dream of accessible mass transit and the havoc it wreaked on the habits and expectations of Americans with disabilities regarding transit systems and the general public.

Of course, our current unnatural paratransit dependence would be far less of a problem in an ideal society where funding was plentiful. The reality is that, at least for the short term, funding for paratransit and for all human needs is and will be scarce.

Financial Limits

Given that paratransit is a very expensive service and that the ADA creates no new funding source for it, Congress placed an additional limit on ADA paratransit, one that is due not to the law's civil rights logic but to economics: public transit agencies are not required to provide paratransit beyond the point at which it will pose an undue financial burden (42 U.S.C. §12143[c][4]).

The original intent of this limit was to give the paratransit requirement some teeth—to require transit agencies to dig deep into their pockets to provide adequate paratransit, even to the point at which they would have to cut back service to the general public somewhat—but not too much. Defining how much was too much became a mind-mangling difficulty for everyone involved in paratransit policy development, particularly during the process of formulating the ADA transportation regulations. Even more difficult was the problem of how to keep the definition meaningful while still making it flexible enough to work in hundreds of diverse communities across the country.

The DOT's initial proposals for how to define undue financial burden in the paratransit context were surprisingly bold. The DOT postulated that perhaps the undue burden limit would be met if a transit agency had to spend more than a certain percentage of its budget on paratransit (figures of 10%, 15%, and 25% were conjectured), or if the transit agency had to cut back service to the general public more than a certain amount (to the tune of 10%, 15%, or 25%), or if the transit agency had to eliminate more than a certain percentage of bus routes (e.g., 10%, 15%, or 25%). These ideas provoked a horrified outcry from the transit industry and were quickly dropped.

The next question, of course, was what should take their place? The DOT's regulators begged input on this question from every possible source, but received very little guidance in the way of good ideas from anyone. National disability leaders, appalled at the prospect of public outrage in every local community if the ADA required massive cutbacks in general public transit service, were as perplexed as the DOT about how to require a substantial amount of paratransit without creating a gigantic and unprecedented backlash against the ADA. Tongue-in-cheek, DOT regulators began to call the definition of undue financial burden in paratransit "one of the great philosophical questions of the age."

The answer to the question, as provided in the final regulations, consists of a general set of factors that the DOT will consider in evaluating whether a transit agency qualifies for an undue financial burden waiver. (The DOT's role as an enforcer is explained at length later in this chapter.) In the meantime, however, the overall limitations on ADA paratransit create an unusual strategy problem for local disability community leaders, whose close involvement with transit agencies in shaping local paratransit policy is clearly required by the ADA.

In the past, it has been the role of leaders of the disability movement always to work toward the greatest possible services, benefits, rights, and so forth. Local paratransit policy will be a different kettle of fish. If disability community leaders push transit agencies to interpret eligibility as broadly as possible, thereby to serve the most people, the amount of service each eligible person can receive will be smaller. Persons who cannot use fixed-route transit at all (the persons for whom the ADA's paratransit provisions were designed) will receive fewer rides. For perhaps the first time, leaders may need to set limits and consider balances rather than automatically going for broke.

Strengths and Problems in DOT Regulations

The ADA statute provided only a lean framework for transportation policy, the substance of which was filled in by the DOT's regulations. Regulations promulgated by the DOT to interpret the ADA were published on September 6, 1991 (DOT, 1991d; see also DOT, 1991a, 1991b, 1991c, 1991e). These regulations include technical standards for buildings and facilities, known as the ADA Accessibility Guidelines, which were published by the Architectural and Transportation Barriers Compliance Board (1991a, 1992a, 1992b). The DOT regulations also include technical standards for vehicles.

Here, mention must be made of how far some of the DOT's policymakers have come since the days when they were ardent advocates of local option. Of course, it helps to be embedded in an administration that supported the ADA. Still, the DOT regulations are noteworthy for their strength in establishing firm rights, as well as for their humor—evidence that policymakers at federal agencies are people too.

There are many examples of what is good in the regulations. There are strict requirements on lift maintenance (49 C.F.R. §§37.161, 37.163); on standees being allowed to use lifts (§37.165[g]); on public agencies that buy over-the-road buses today having to buy accessible ones (§37.77); on barring mandatory transfers (§37.165[e]); on allowing departures from compliance with technical standards only if the DOT approves each one (§37.7); on barring transit agencies from declaring certain bus stops inaccessible (§§37.161, 37.163); on disallowing cost as a factor when agencies buy used or remanufactured accessible vehicles (§§37.73, 37.83); on making wheelchair users paratransit-eligible if *any buses* on the route they need are not yet accessible (§37.121); on abolishing artificial capacity constraints, which have long suppressed paratransit demand and warped its quality (§37.169); and on encouraging paratransit coordination between neighboring agencies (§37.153[c][3]); to name just a few.

It must also be said, however, that there are some real problems in the regulations that tend to operate against the intent and spirit of the ADA. For example, allowing private intercity bus transit companies to require 2 days' advance notice for providing boarding assistance is generally unnecessary and opens the door for these companies to establish the same type of discriminatory policies that many have practiced in the past. It will be important to remind these providers that advance notice may be required only for boarding the person, not the mobility device, and that even if advance notice is not given, the provider must make a reasonable effort to provide boarding assistance anyway.

Also, allowing public transit agencies to forbid wheelchair users from riding outside securement location areas in a bus (49 C.F.R. §37.165[b]) will create serious delays every time a bus with its wheelchair securements already in use passes another wheelchair user waiting at a bus stop, an all-too-frequent occurrence in many cities. In contrast to the general logic in the DOT regulations, which usually limits persons with disabilities only when persons without disabilities face limits as well, this problem has no parallel for persons without disabilities, who simply squeeze onto the bus in greater numbers when crowds develop.

Furthermore, not requiring universities with fixed-route transit systems to provide supplementary paratransit for persons who cannot use the fixed-route service (49 C.F.R. §37.25) is a serious blow to students and other persons with disabilities in campus-dominated communities where university transit, as the regulation itself states, is more or less the only mass transit in town.

The DOT's regulations, of course, are not its last word on the ADA—the DOT has important enforcement responsibilities yet to perform: monitoring paratransit plans (including making decisions on undue financial burden waivers as described above) and processing complaints.

What can we expect from the DOT in this regard? If past performance is any clue, strong enforcement will not be its general practice. Aggrieved persons with disabilities will be well advised to take an assertive stance in dealing with the DOT in enforcement issues and, in situations of clear violations, not to hesitate to file lawsuits with respect to both transit agencies and the DOT itself.

The triumphs and negotiated compromises achieved by the disability community in this remarkable piece of legislation are evident in the following detailed analysis of its provisions.

SUMMARY OF THE ADA'S TRANSPORTATION REQUIREMENTS

The ADA prohibits discrimination in public transportation provided by both publicly funded and privately funded entities. Public transportation means transportation by bus, rail, or any other conveyance (other than air travel) that provides the general public with general or special service on a regular and continuing basis. This includes transportation by boat or ship. Air travel is excluded because it is covered by the Air Carriers Access Act of 1986. The ADA's various transportation requirements have many different effective dates. In general, they went into effect on October 7, 1991, unless stated otherwise below.

Transportation Provided by Publicly Funded Entities (42 U.S.C. §§12141–12161)

Newly Purchased Vehicles   It is discrimination for a public entity to purchase or lease a new fixed-route bus or rail vehicle, for which a solicitation was made later than August 25, 1990 (30 days after the ADA's enactment), if the vehicle is not readily accessible to and usable by individuals with disabilities (49 C.F.R. §37.71). Fixed-route transit systems are defined as those that operate along prescribed routes according to fixed schedules, in contrast to demand-responsive transit service, in which a vehicle is dispatched or routed in response to a potential rider's request.

Public entities (or contractors to public entities) acquiring over-the-road buses must comply with the requirements to purchase accessible vehicles. Over-the-road buses are buses with an elevated passenger deck located over a baggage compartment.

The ADA does not require buses that had already been purchased when the ADA became effective to be retrofitted in order to be made accessible. By establishing such a scheme for bus accessibility, the ADA requires that public transit bus fleets become accessible gradually, as old buses are replaced. Normally, a bus is replaced after 10–12 years, or in some cases after 15 + years.

Used Vehicles   If a public entity purchases or leases a used vehicle after August 25, 1990, the entity must make demonstrated good faith efforts to purchase or lease an accessible vehicle (42 U.S.C. §12142[b]; 49 C.F.R. §37.73). "Demonstrated good faith efforts" means that the public entity must specify the need for acccessible vehicles in all bid solicitations and conduct a nationwide search, not just a search limited to a particular region. The entity must advertise in a trade magazine or contact a transit agency association to determine whether used vehicles are available. Transit agencies must maintain the records of their good faith efforts for 3 years and make these records available to the DOT and members of the public on request.

Remanufactured Vehicles   If a public entity remanufactures a vehicle or purchases a remanufactured vehicle, so as to extend its useful life for 5 years or more, the vehicle must be accessible to the maximum extent feasible (42 U.S.C. §12142[c]; 49 C.F.R. §37.75). A remanufactured vehicle is a vehicle that has been structurally restored and has had new or rebuilt major components installed to extend its service life. This requirement went into effect on August 25, 1990.

Evasion of Requirements through Private Contracts   Although a transit agency may contract out its services, it may not contract away its ADA responsibilities. A private entity that purchases or leases vehicles for use, or in contemplation of use, under contract or other arrangement with a public agency must acquire accessible vehicles in all situations in which the public agency itself would be required to do so (49 C.F.R. §37.21). Also, the public agency must ensure that the percentage of accessible vehicles in the overall fleet (including those of the private entity) is not diminished as a result of the contract.

Providing Nondiscriminatory Service   No public or private transit agency may deny any individual with a disability, on the basis of disability, the opportunity to use the transit agency's service if the individual is capable of using that service (49 C.F.R. §§37.5, 37.161–167, 37.173). Each transit agency must ensure that personnel are trained to proficiency in dealing with persons with disabilities.

Maintenance   Transit agencies must maintain in operative condition those features of facilities and vehicles necessary to make the facilities and vehicles accessible. When an accessibility feature is out of order, the transit agency must take reasonable steps to accommodate individuals with disabilities who would otherwise use the feature. Isolated or temporary interruptions in service or access as a result of maintenance or repairs are not considered discrimination, but a pattern of such interruptions could be considered discrimination.

Publicly funded bus transit agencies must establish a system of regular and frequent maintenance checks of lifts sufficient to determine whether they are operative. The transit agency must ensure that vehicle operators report, by the most immediate means available, any failure of a lift to operate in service. When a lift is discovered to be inoperative, the transit agency must take the vehicle out of service before the beginning of the vehicle's next service day and ensure that the lift is repaired before the vehicle returns to service.

There is an exception to the requirement to remove a vehicle from service to repair it: this is not required in situations in which there is no spare vehicle to take the place of the vehicle to be removed and taking the vehicle out of service will reduce the transportation service available to the general public. In such cases, the transit agency may keep the vehicle in service with an inoperable lift for no more than 5 days (if the transit agency serves an area of 50,000 or less population) or 3 days (if the transit agency serves an area of over 50,000 population) from the day on which the lift is discovered to be inoperative.

If a vehicle is operating on a fixed route with an inoperative lift, and the time before arrival of the next accessible vehicle on the route exceeds 30 minutes, the transit agency must promptly provide alternative transportation (e.g., paratransit) to individuals with disabilities who are unable to use the vehicle because the lift does not work.

Lift and Securement Use All common wheelchairs and their users must be transported in the transit agency's vehicles or other conveyances. Common wheelchairs are those wheelchairs that can fit on a lift that complies with the DOT's technical standards (i.e., a 30-inch by 48-inch lift).

The transit agency is not required to permit wheelchairs to ride in places other than designated securement locations in the vehicle, where such locations exist. The transit agency must use securement systems to ensure that the wheelchair remains in the securement area. However, even if the securement system cannot accommodate a particular wheelchair, transportation cannot be denied to its user. The wheelchair passenger may not be required by the transit agency to use a seat belt unless all other passengers in the vehicle are similarly required to use seat belts. The transit agency may recommend but may not require that a wheelchair user transfer to a vehicle seat.

The transit agency must permit individuals with disabilities who do not use wheelchairs, including standees, to use a vehicle's lift or ramp to enter the vehicle.

Bus Stop Discrimination The transit agency may not refuse to permit a passenger who uses a lift to board or disembark from a vehicle at any designated stop unless the lift cannot be deployed at the stop, or unless the lift will be damaged if it is deployed, or unless *all* passengers are precluded from using the stop because of temporary conditions at the stop that are not under the control of the transit agency.

Paratransit Provision Requirement It is discrimination for a public agency that operates a fixed-route bus system, rapid rail system, or light rail system to fail to ensure that paratransit is provided to individuals with disabilities who cannot use the fixed-route system (42 U.S.C. §12143; 49 C.F.R. §§37.121–155). If the provision of paratransit would be an undue financial burden on the public transit agency, service is not required beyond the undue burden level unless ordered by the DOT.

Public agencies that operate commuter bus systems as the sole form of public transit are exempt from the paratransit requirement. Commuter bus service means bus service that is characterized by service predominantly in one direction during peak periods, limited stops, use of multiride tickets, and routes of extended length, usually between the central business district and outlying suburbs.

Paratransit Eligibility Public transit agencies that provide fixed-route transportation to the general public must ensure the provision of alternate paratransit service to those members of the general public who are unable to use the fixed-route system. This will encompass three categories of eligible persons.

1. *"Can't Navigate the System."* This category includes any individual with a disability who is unable, as the result of a physical or mental impairment (including a vision impairment) to board, ride, or disembark from any vehicle on the system that is readily accessible to and usable by individuals with disabilities. This category includes, for example, some persons with cognitive disabilities who do not know where to get off the bus or how to go to their destina-

tions from the bus stop. It would also include some blind persons who have not had the mobility training required to navigate the routes to their destinations.

2. *"Needs an Accessible Bus."* This category includes individuals with disabilities who can use buses that have wheelchair lifts or other boarding assistance devices when such persons want to travel on routes that are still inaccessible (not served by accessible buses).

3. *"Specific Impairment-Related Condition."* This category includes any individual with a disability who has a specific impairment-related condition that prevents the individual from traveling to a boarding location or from a disembarking location. Architectural barriers not under the control of the transit agency providing fixed-route service and environmental barriers (e.g., distance, terrain, weather) do not, standing alone, form a basis for eligibility under this category. However, the interaction of such barriers with an individual's specific impairment-related condition may form the basis for eligibility if the effect is to prevent the individual from traveling to a boarding location or from a disembarking location.

It should be noted that a person's eligibility for paratransit may be different for different trips. For example, under the first category, a blind individual who has received mobility training on how to get to work every day will not need paratransit for work trips. However, on a day when she must go to a different area of the city to visit a new doctor, she may be unable to navigate the system by finding her way from the bus stop to the doctor's office, and she may need paratransit for that trip. Similarly, under the third category, a particular wheelchair user may be able to negotiate the trip to the bus stop on a summer day but cannot do so during the dead of winter with 2 feet of unplowed snow on the ground.

In addition to persons in the three categories listed above, at least one associate may ride with any recipient of paratransit services.

Paratransit Service Criteria

1. *Service Area:* The transit agency must provide paratransit to origins and destinations within corridors that extend three fourths of a mile on each side of each fixed route (i.e., corridors that are 1½ miles wide). At the end point of each route, the corridor must include an area with a ¾-mile radius. Outside the core service area, the transit agency may designate corridors with widths from ¾ up to 1½ miles on each side of a fixed route (i.e., corridors can be up to a total of 3 miles wide). Service must be provided from any point in any of the corridors to any point in any other corridor.

2. *Response Time:* The transit agency must schedule and provide paratransit service to any person eligible for paratransit under the ADA at any request time on a particular day in response to a request for service made the previous day.

3. *Fares:* Paratransit fares may not exceed twice the fare that would be paid by an individual paying full fare (not discounted fare) for a trip of similar length, at a similar time of day, on the transit agency's fixed-route service. Transfer and premium charges applicable to a trip of similar length, at a similar time of day, may be included. The transit agency, however, is allowed to charge a higher fare to a social service agency or other organization for agency trips that are guaranteed to the organization. This exception allows the transit agency to negotiate any price it can with the other agency or organization because the trips are reserved for the other agency's clients, and the other agency pays for the trips.

4. *No Trip Purpose Restrictions:* Paratransit service may not impose restrictions or priorities based on trip purpose.

5. *Hours and Days of Service:* Paratransit must be available throughout the same hours and days as the transit agency's fixed-route service.

6. *Capacity Constraints:* The transit agency may not limit the availability of paratransit service to

persons eligible for paratransit under the ADA through restrictions on the number of trips, waiting lists, substantial numbers of significantly untimely pickups, substantial numbers of trip denials or missed trips, or substantial numbers of trips with excessive lengths.

Visitors   A visitor is an individual with a disability who does not reside in the jurisdiction(s) served by a particular transit agency (or other transit agencies) within a region in which that transit agency provides coordinated paratransit. Any visitors presenting documentation that they are paratransit eligible under the ADA in the jurisdictions where they reside must be treated by the transit agency as eligible. If a visitor does not have such documentation, the transit agency may require documentation of the individual's place of residence and of the individual's disability, if the disability is not apparent. The transit agency must then provide paratransit service to the individual.

Paratransit Plan Filed by Transit Agency   Transit agencies required to provide paratransit were required to submit and begin implementation of a paratransit service plan by January 26, 1992. An annual update must be submitted by each January 26 thereafter. Each plan must provide full compliance by no later than January 26, 1997, unless the transit agency has received a waiver based on undue financial burden. However, not all transit agencies will be granted the full 5-year time period by the DOT. In developing its plans, the transit agency must comply with extensive requirements for public participation, including outreach, consultation with individuals with disabilities, opportunity for public comment, and holding a public hearing.

A transit agency may request a waiver from some or all of the paratransit requirements based on undue financial burden if it has complied with the public participation requirements. The DOT may or may not grant the request for a waiver.

Communities Operating Demand-Responsive Systems for the General Public   Many suburban and rural communities operate demand-responsive or paratransit-type systems for the general public. To use such a system, an individual (with or without a disability) must request transportation service before it is rendered, distinguishing this kind of system from a fixed-route service.

It is discrimination under the ADA for such a transit agency to purchase or lease a new vehicle after August 25, 1990, that is not accessible, unless the transit agency can demonstrate that such a system, when viewed in its entirety, provides a level of service to individuals with disabilities equivalent to the level of service provided to the general public (42 U.S.C. §12144; 49 C.F.R. §37.77). "When viewed in its entirety" means that, when all aspects of the system are analyzed, equal opportunities for each individual with a disability to use the transportation system must exist. Because every rider must contact the transit agency ahead of time, an accessible vehicle can be dispatched when one is needed. If the response time to pick up an individual with a disability is not greater than the response time to pick up an individual without disabilities, such a service is accessible when viewed in its entirety.

Rail Transit

Intercity Rail (Amtrak)   The ADA requires Amtrak, which operates intercity rail transit in the United States, to have at least one passenger car per train that is readily accessible to and usable by individuals with disabilities as soon as practicable but in no event later than July 26, 1995 (42 U.S.C. §12162; 49 C.F.R. §37.91). Also by July 26, 1995, Amtrak must include on each train a number of spaces not less than one half of the number of single-level rail passenger coaches on the train to park and secure wheelchairs to accommodate individuals who wish to remain in their wheelchairs while traveling on Amtrak. In addition, Amtrak must also include on each of these trains a number of spaces not less than one half of the number of single-level passenger coaches on the train to fold and store wheelchairs to accommodate persons who wish to transfer to coach seats from their wheelchairs. According to this formula, then, Amtrak will make available by July 26, 1995, a total number of potential spaces for people who use wheelchairs equal to the number of single-level passenger coaches on the train.

Furthermore, within 10 years of the enactment date, Amtrak must provide twice that number. That is, they must provide enough spaces to park and secure wheelchairs equal to the number of single-level coaches, as well as the same number of spaces to fold and store wheelchairs for persons who wish to transfer. These spaces must be located in the single-level passenger rail coaches or food service cars. However, not more than two spaces to park and secure wheelchairs or more than two spaces to fold and store wheelchairs may be located in any one car. Cars that have any of these spaces must also have a rest room accessible to individuals using wheelchairs. Also, these cars must be accessible from the station platform by a person using a wheelchair.

Existing intercity rail (Amtrak) stations must be made accessible as soon as practicable, but in any event no later than July 26, 2010. It is discrimination to build a new station for intercity rail use that is not readily accessible to and usable by individuals with disabilities. This requirement went into effect on July 26, 1990.

Commuter, Rapid, and Light Rail At least one car per train on light and rapid rail trains of at least two cars in length must be accessible to individuals with disabilities by July 26, 1995 (42 U.S.C. §12162; 49 C.F.R. §§37.47–53, 37.59, 37.79, 37.85, 37.93). One-car trains are exempted. For commuter rail, one car per train is required to be accessible by July 26, 1995, regardless of the train's length. It is discrimination under the ADA to purchase or lease new passenger rail cars for use in commuter, rapid, and light rail transportation, for which solicitation is made after August 25, 1991, unless the cars are readily accessible to and usable by individuals with disabilities.

Key stations in rapid rail, commuter rail, and light rail systems must be made accessible as soon as practicable, but in any event no later than July 26, 1993. The time limit for rapid and light rail may be extended by the DOT up to 30 years for extraordinarily expensive structural changes to, or replacement of, existing facilities necessary to achieve accessibility. For commuter rail, the time limit for extraordinarily expensive structural changes may be extended by the DOT for up to 20 years. Extraordinarily expensive structural changes means installations of elevators, raising the entire passenger platform, or alterations of similar magnitude and cost within a station. The process of designating key stations should include significant involvement of the disability community. A public hearing should be held during the deliberation process. The deadline for submission of the key stations plan to the appropriate DOT regional office was July 26, 1992.

It is discrimination to build a new station for commuter, rapid, or light rail use that is not readily accessible to and usable by individuals with disabilities. For new rapid and light rail stations, the requirements became effective on January 26, 1992. For new commuter rail stations, the effective date was July 26, 1990.

Paratransit Provision Requirement for Rapid and Light Rail Systems Just as the ADA requires fixed-route bus operators to provide supplementary paratransit for persons who cannot use the fixed-route service, it also places paratransit requirements on operators of rapid and light rail systems. The service area for rail transit will consist of a circle with a diameter of 1½ miles around each station (whether or not it is a key station). At end stations and other stations in outlying areas, the operator may designate service area circles with diameters of up to 3 miles, based on local circumstances. The transit agency is required to provide trips from any point in one circle to any point in any other circle. The transit agency is not required to provide paratransit service between two points within the same circle because a trip between two points in the vicinity of the same station is not a trip that typically would be taken by train.

Eligibility for rail paratransit is the same as for bus paratransit except for the second eligibility category. For this category, an individual is eligible if the individual could use an accessible rail system except for the fact that there is not yet one accessible car per train on the system, or that key stations have not yet been made accessible. For persons in this category, the operator's obligation is only to provide transportation between circles centered on key stations because, even when the key station plan is fully implemented, these individuals will be unable to use nonkey stations.

Enforcement Enforcement provisions for the ADA's requirements for public transit agencies, which are part of Title II, are the same as the enforcement provisions for the rest of Title II (42 U.S.C. §12133).

Transportation Provided by Private Entities (42 U.S.C. §§12182–12188)

Private transit providers are divided into two categories: those that are primarily in the transportation business (e.g., a tour bus company), and those that are not primarily in the transportation business (e.g., a hotel that provides shuttle service to the airport).

Requirements for Private Entities Primarily in the Business of Transportation Private entities primarily engaged in the business of transporting people are prohibited from purchasing or leasing a new vehicle (other than an automobile, a van with a seating capacity of less than eight passengers including the driver, or an over-the-road bus) to be used in a fixed-route system that is not readily accessible to and usable by people with disabilities if the solicitation for the vehicle was made after August 25, 1990 (42 U.S.C. §12184; 49 C.F.R. §§37.29, 37.103–105, 37.107). When these providers purchase or lease a new vehicle that is to be used in a demand-responsive system, the new vehicle need not be accessible if the transit provider can show that the system, when viewed in its entirety, provides a level of service to individuals with disabilities equivalent to the level of service provided to the general public.

In assessing whether a transit system, when viewed in its entirety, provides a level of service to persons with disabilities equivalent to the level of service provided to persons without disabilities, the provider should consider the next potential customer who might need an accessible vehicle (the fact that such persons have never called in the past is irrelevant). If the service is not as available, or as quick, or the like for the next customer (even if the next customer needing an accessible vehicle will be the first such customer), then the next vehicle bought or leased must be an accessible vehicle. If over-the-road buses are used by these systems, they are subject to the special provisions described below.

If a van with a seating capacity of less than eight passengers is purchased or leased, it must be readily accessible to and usable by people with disabilities unless the transit provider can demonstrate that the system for which the van is being purchased or leased, when viewed in its entirety, provides a level of service to individuals with disabilities equivalent to the level of service provided to the general public. Vans and minivans are treated the same way whether they are operated in a fixed-route or demand-responsive system. Owning, or having access to, an accessible minivan or a portable boarding assistance device that can be used in concert with an otherwise inaccessible minivan is required in order to meet the needs of passengers with disabilities on an on-call basis. The van purchase requirement became effective on February 25, 1992.

Operators providing taxi and limousine service may not discriminate on the basis of disability in providing that service. For example, it is a violation of the ADA for a taxi to refuse to pick up a person because of his or her disability or because the driver does not want to lift the wheelchair into the trunk or back seat of the taxi. Nor could a taxi company insist that a wheelchair user wait for a lift-equipped van if the person could use an automobile. Taxi operators may not charge higher fares or fees for carrying individuals with disabilities and their equipment than those charged to other persons, although if a charge is imposed for carrying luggage, a similar charge may be imposed for carrying a wheelchair.

Private rail operators primarily engaged in the business of transporting people may not purchase or lease a new rail passenger car for which a solicitation is made after February 25, 1992, that is not readily accessible to and usable by people with disabilities.

Intercity Bus Service and Over-the-Road Buses Private intercity bus transit generally uses vehicles known as over-the-road coaches or buses. Over-the-road buses are buses characterized by an elevated passenger deck located over a baggage compartment. Greyhound is the most familiar nationwide provider of such service.

The ADA allows intercity transit providers a long implementation period before they must provide accessible service: 6 years for large providers and 7 years for small ones. However, during this period, they must comply with nondiscrimination provisions described below (42 U.S.C. §§12185–12186; 49 C.F.R. §37.169).

During the 6- or 7-year implementation period, a study will be conducted by the federal Office of Technology Assessment to determine the best way to provide access to new over-the-road buses. All possible methods of making intercity bus service accessible will be considered in the study, including equipping the buses with lifts and carrying passengers with disabilities onto the buses. The results of the study will determine the method of accessibility ultimately to be used. The study must be completed by July 26, 1993, and may result in changes to the regulations issued by the DOT to implement the ADA. Additional regulations will be issued within 1 year of the study's completion. These regulations will require that each private entity that uses over-the-road buses provide accessibility to such buses to individuals who use wheelchairs.

During the interim 6- or 7-year period, private intercity transit providers are not required to make physical improvements in their vehicles, but they will be subject to general nondiscrimination requirements. They must permit customers with disabilities to ride their buses. They may not refuse service to passengers who use wheelchairs, including motorized wheelchairs. They may not deny service to a person with a disability, just because he or she does not bring along a nondisabled companion during travel.

Furthermore, private intercity transit providers must assist a passenger with a disability onto the bus if the passenger cannot board the bus independently. The private provider must ensure that personnel are trained to provide this assistance safely and appropriately. The provider may require up to 48 hours advance notice from individuals with disabilities, but only for providing boarding assistance. However, if the individual does not provide such notice, the entity must nonetheless provide the service if it can do so by making a reasonable effort without delaying regular bus service.

Wheelchairs must be accommodated, to the extent that they can be, in areas of the passenger compartment provided for passengers' personal effects. Other mobility aids and devices must be permitted in the passenger compartment. When the bus is at a rest stop, the driver or other personnel must assist individuals with disabilities with retrieval and stowage of this equipment. Wheelchairs and other mobility equipment that cannot be accommodated in the passenger compartment must be accommodated in the baggage compartment, unless the size of the baggage compartment prevents such accommodation.

Furthermore, at any given stop individuals with disabilities must have the opportunity to have their wheelchairs or other mobility equipment stowed in the baggage compartment before other baggage or cargo is loaded. Baggage or cargo already on the bus, however, need not be off-loaded in order to make room for mobility devices or equipment.

Over-the-road buses are exempt from accessible rest room requirements unless such rest rooms can be provided without a loss of seating capacity. However, drivers must stop at accessible stations and/or rest stops to allow persons with disabilities to use the rest room.

Requirements for Private Entities Not Primarily in the Business of Transportation

Special rules apply to private companies that provide the public with transportation but that are not primarily in the transportation business (42 U.S.C. §12182; 49 C.F.R. §§37.101, 37.171). These include, for example, hotel and motel airport shuttle services; shuttle operations of recreational facilities such as stadiums, zoos, amusement parks, and ski resorts; and customer and employee shuttle bus services operated by private companies and shopping centers. Vanpools are not covered by these provisions.

Transit providers covered by this section may not purchase or lease any vehicle (new or used) that carries in excess of 16 passengers (including the driver) for fixed-route service for which a solicitation is made after August 25, 1990, that is not readily accessible to and usable by individuals with disabilities. If such providers purchase or lease a vehicle (new or used) carrying 16 or fewer passengers (including the driver) for use in fixed-route service, the service must be operated such that it offers people with disabilities a level of service equivalent to that provided to the general public, when the system is viewed in its entirety. Automobiles and vans seating less than eight persons are exempt from this requirement.

Each private entity not primarily in the transportation business that provides demand-responsive transportation must provide a level of service to persons with disabilities equivalent to what it provides to the general public when the transit system is viewed in its entirety. The standard for a system, when viewed in its entirety, providing an equivalent level of service is met when an operator has, or has access to, a vehicle (including a vehicle operated in conjunction with a portable boarding assistance device) that is readily accessible to and usable by individuals with disabilities to meet the needs of such individuals on an "on-call" basis. For example, when a hotel provides free shuttle service on a demand-responsive basis to and from an airport, the hotel need not purchase new vehicles that are accessible so long as it makes alternative equivalent arrangements for transporting people with disabilities who cannot ride the inaccessible vehicles. This might be accomplished through the use of a portable ramp or by making arrangements with another organization that can make an accessible vehicle available to provide equivalent shuttle service.

If over-the-road buses are used by these private entities, they are subject to the special requirements of over-the-road vehicles described above.

Enforcement Enforcement of the ADA's requirements for privately funded transportation providers, which are part of Title III, are the same as the enforcement provisions for the rest of Title III (42 U.S.C. §12188) (see Parmet, chap. 10, this volume).

REFERENCES

Air Carriers Access Act of 1986, 49 U.S.C. app. §1374(c) (1986).

American Public Transportation Association (APTA) v. Lewis, 485 F. Supp. 811 (D.D.C. 1980), 655 F.2d 1272 (D.C. Cir. 1981).

Rehabilitation Act of 1973, 29 U.S.C. §§791–794 (1973).

U.S. Architectural and Transportation Barriers Compliance Board. (1991a, September 6). Americans with Disabilities Act (ADA) accessibility guidelines for buildings and facilities; transportation facilities; amendment to final guidelines and amendments to part 1191—accessibility guidelines. *Federal Register, 56,* 45499–45527.

U.S. Architectural and Transportation Barriers Compliance Board. (1991b, September 6). Americans with Disabilities Act (ADA) accessibility guidelines for transportation vehicles; final guidelines. *Federal Register, 56,* 45529–45581.

U.S. Architectural and Transportation Barriers Compliance Board. (1992a). Americans with Disabilities Act (ADA) accessibility guidelines for buildings and facilities. In *Code of Federal Regulations* (36: Parks, Forests and Public Property, pp. 623–715). Washington, DC: U.S. Government Printing Office.

U.S. Architectural and Transportation Barriers Compliance Board. (1992b). Americans with Disabilities Act (ADA) accessibility guidelines for transportation vehicles and appendix to part 1192—advisory guidance. In *Code of Federal Regulations* (36: Parks, Forests and Public Property, pp. 716–751). Washington, DC: U.S. Government Printing Office.

U.S. Department of Transportation. (1991a). Americans with Disabilities Act (ADA) accessibility specifications for transportation vehicles. In *Code of Federal Regulations* (49: Transportation, pp. 532–566). Washington, DC: U.S. Government Printing Office.

U.S. Department of Transportation. (1991b). Nondiscrimination on the basis of handicap in programs and activities receiving or benefitting from federal financial assistance. In *Code of Federal Regulations* (49: Transportation, pp. 267–307). Washington, DC: U.S. Government Printing Office.

U.S. Department of Transportation. (1991c, December 9). Transportation for individuals with disabilities (amendment to final rule). *Federal Register, 56,* 64214–64215.

U.S. Department of Transportation. (1991d, September 6). Transportation for individuals with disabilities; final rule. *Federal Register, 56,* 45583–45641.

U.S. Department of Transportation. (1991e). Transportation services for individuals with disabilities (ADA). In *Code of Federal Regulations* (49: Transportation, pp. 355–532). Washington, DC: U.S. Government Printing Office.

Chapter 10

Title III—Public Accommodations

Wendy E. Parmet

Most of us, most of the time, take much of the world for granted. Stores are stores, schools are schools, and movie theaters are movie theaters. Of course, things change, but they usually do so slowly and haphazardly, without conscious design. It is unusual for laws to challenge that givenness. Laws regulate, laws alter, but usually the change they command is incremental. Rarely do laws suggest that the given world should look, feel, and sound completely different from the way it does. Rarely do they open up all of the status quo ante for debate.

Title III of the Americans with Disabilities Act[1] (ADA) (42 U.S.C. §§12181–12189), the so-called public accommodations provision, comes close to doing just that. It challenges the most basic, the most inherent assumptions that underlie the organization of our society. It seeks not only to end discrimination against people with disabilities but also to re-create the public world, to make it more accessible and more inclusive. In order to understand how it attempts to do so, and assess the likelihood of its success, a brief overview of the title's scope and provisions is first in order.

BREADTH OF COVERAGE

Going far beyond any prior law, Title III of the ADA prohibits discrimination against individuals with disabilities in a wide array of privately owned facilities and services. In many ways, Title III is modeled after Title II of the Civil Rights Act of 1964. That landmark legislation, born of the battles of the great civil rights movement, prohibited "discrimination or segregation on the grounds of race, color, religion or national origin" in "public accommodations" affecting commerce (42 U.S.C. §2000a *et seq.*). Striking Jim Crow at its jugular, Title II changed the nation's landscape.

Although the impact of Title II has been profound, it was actually a fairly simple and narrow statue. Far from prohibiting discrimination in all parts of public life, Title II only applied to a select number of facilities many of which were traditionally regulated for public benefit under common law. Inns, hotels, and other places offering transient lodging, facilities offering food consumption on the premises, and places of entertainment were the only public accommodations actually regulated by the 1964 act (42 U.S.C. §2000a[b][1–4]). Moreover, Title II's concept of discrimination

The author wishes to thank Mary O'Connell for her useful criticism. Anne Gillespie, Liz Stillman, and Jim Shorter provided outstanding research assistance. Kathy Gabriel, as always, provided untiring secretarial assistance.

[1]The Americans with Disabilities Act of 1990 (PL 101–336) is published in *Statutes at Large* (104 Stat. 327) and codified in the *United States Code* (42 U.S.C. §§12101–12213 [Supp. II 1990]). References to various portions of the act within this chapter cite the specific section of the Codes.

was fairly straightforward: individuals could not be barred access, segregated, or granted unequal benefits simply because of their race, religion, or national origin. Thus under the act all that had to change were explicit exclusionary or separatist policies based on the prohibited criteria.

Title V of the Rehabilitation Act of 1973, the most important federal disability rights law prior to the ADA, was similarly limited in its scope. Although it came to impose a sophisticated conception of nondiscrimination that included a requirement for making reasonable modifications, it applied only narrowly to recipients of federal money. It did not cover the vast majority of private programs and facilities, even those that were covered with respect to race, religion, and ethnicity by the 1964 Civil Rights Act. Moreover, the Rehabilitation Act's requirement to provide reasonable accommodations comes not from the literal language of the statute itself but from U.S. Department of Health and Human Services regulations (1990; 45 C.F.R. 84.3[k][1]), which was approved by the Supreme Court in *Southeastern Community College v. Davis* (1979).

Title III of the ADA, in contrast, sweeps broadly and does so complexly. Most obviously, its concept of public accommodations is dramatically wider than was that of Title II. Rather than providing a narrow definition, the ADA provides a list of 12 broad categories of public accommodations:

(A) an inn, hotel, motel, or other place of lodging . . . ;
(B) a restaurant, bar, or other establishment serving food or drink;
(C) a motion picture house, theater, concert hall, stadium, or other place of exhibition or entertainment;
(D) an auditorium, convention center, lecture hall, or other place of public gathering;
(E) a bakery, grocery store, clothing store, hardware store, shopping center, or other sales or rental establishment;
(F) a laundromat, dry-cleaner, bank, barber shop, beauty parlor, gas station, office of an accountant or lawyer, pharmacy, insurance office, professional office of a health care provider, hospital, or other service establishment;
(G) a terminal, depot, or other station used for specified public transportation;
(H) a museum, library, gallery, or other place of public display or collection;
(I) a park, zoo, amusement park, or other place of recreation;
(J) a nursery, elementary, secondary, undergraduate, or postgraduate private school, or other place of education;
(K) a day care center, senior citizen center, homeless shelter, food bank, adoption agency, or other social service center establishment; and
(L) a gymnasium, health spa, bowling alley, golf course, or other place of exercise or recreation. (42 U.S.C. §12181[7])

This listing effectively regulates many of the facilities and services in the world around us. Indeed, other than residential housing, which is covered by the Fair Housing Amendments Act of 1988, commercial air travel, which is covered by the Air Carriers Access Act, and governmental services regulated by Title II of the ADA and/or the Rehabilitation Act, it is difficult to think of many facilities or services left uncovered. Perhaps the only significant exceptions are facilities owned by religious organizations or private clubs (42 U.S.C. §12187) and the federal courts (Tucker, 1991). In other words, most of the public world in which we operate as consumers, patrons, clients, and patients is covered.

Title III, however, is even more encompassing than its own broad definition would indicate. Although many of its provisions apply only to public accommodations, its critical construction and alteration provisions also apply to all "commercial facilities," a category that covers all "facilities that are intended for nonresidential use and whose operations will affect commerce" (42 U.S.C. §12181[2]). Privately operated transportation facilities (42 U.S.C. §§12182[b][2][B–D], 12184) (see Golden, chap. 9, this volume) and courses and examinations relating to applications or certification for advanced study or career certification (42 U.S.C. §12189) are also covered by specific provisions. Thus Title III effectively covers most of the world around us. Its mandate of non-discrimination runs wide and it is nothing less than public life itself that the law seeks to reach.

However, it is not only the scope of covered entities that is extraordinarily wide. Like the rest of the ADA, Title III uses a broad and expansive definition of disability (42 U.S.C. §12102). This wide definition covers a whole range of impairments, from arthritis to diabetes, HIV infection to blindness, severe depression to spinal cord injuries (see U.S. Department of Justice, 1992; 28 C.F.R. §36.104).[2] (Some conditions were specifically excluded by Congress from coverage under the ADA in general [see 42 U.S.C. §§12208, 12210, 12211]. For a discussion of these exclusions, see Burgdorf [1991b, pp. 413, 451–452].) Moreover, the reach of the title is broadened by its prohibition of discrimination based on one's association with a disabled person (42 U.S.C. §12182[b][1][E]). It is therefore unlawful for a public accommodation to discriminate against an individual because his or her friend, lover, spouse, or family member is disabled.

It is not, however, the scope of Title III alone that makes it such an extraordinary piece of legislation. Rather, it is the ways in which Title III challenges the givenness of the world. To understand what is at stake and to assess its meaning, a brief examination of the title's requirements is necessary.

A BRIEF DESCRIPTION OF TITLE III

Title III's uniqueness is obscured in layers of detail. In order to see how novel the title is, some technical description is required.

The starting point for understanding Title III is the recognition that it employs a temporal vision of discrimination. Whereas most antidiscrimination laws simply prohibit discrimination on the act's effective date, Title III envisions an evolving process. Nondiscrimination meant one thing as of January 26, 1992, when the title became generally effective. It obtains another meaning as time passes and facilities are altered or constructed (see Physical Spaces, below). Although this postponement of the act's more stringent demands resulted from a political concession to small business interests (Burgdorf, 1991a, pp. 183, 203), it may have the unanticipated consequence of suggesting that nondiscrimination is not a fixed but rather an ever-changing concept, one that evolves with the passage of time.

The act's immediate nondiscrimination mandate is found in Section 302(a). It provides a broad and majestic statement:

No individual shall be discriminated against on the basis of disability in the full and equal enjoyment of the goods, services, facilities, privileges, advantages, or accommodations of any place of public accommodation by any person who owns, leases (or leases to) or operates a place of public accommodation. (42 U.S.C. §12182[a])

Section 302's proclamation is given meaning by a further series of general and specific prohibitions. The general prohibitions clarify that the denial of participation and the provision of an unequal or separate benefit through contractual, licensing, or other arrangements constitutes discrimination (42 U.S.C. §12182[b][1][A]). They also require that goods, services, and benefits be provided in the "most integrated setting appropriate to the needs of the individual" (42 U.S.C. §12182[b][1][B]).

The heart of Title III, however, lies in the specific provisions of Section 302(b)(2) (42 U.S.C. §12182[b][2]). According to the implementing regulations of the Department of Justice (DOJ), these provisions supersede the more general provisions whenever there is conflict or uncertainty

---

[2]Department of Justice Title III regulations are codified at 28 C.F.R. part 36 (1992). References to various portions of these regulations within this chapter cite the specific section of the regulations.

(DOJ, 1992; 28 C.F.R. §36.213). Briefly, these critical provisions prohibit eligibility criteria that tend to screen out persons with disabilities except where such criteria "can be shown to be necessary for the provision of the goods, services . . ." (42 U.S.C. §12182[b][2][A][i]). They also require public accommodations to make reasonable modifications unless doing so would fundamentally alter the service provided (42 U.S.C. §12182[b][2][A][ii]). Similarly, public accommodations must provide auxiliary aids except in such cases where they would fundamentally alter or place an undue burden on the public accommodation (42 U.S.C. §12182 [b][2][A][iii]).

Both Title III's general and specific provisions are limited by Section 302(b)(3), which states that a public accommodation is not required to permit a person to participate in its services when the individual poses a "direct threat to others" (42 U.S.C. §12182[b][3]). This provision, which parallels a similar provision in the ADA's employment title (42 U.S.C. §12113[b]), as discussed by Parry (chap. 5, this volume), was clearly meant to address concerns arising in those rare instances when a disability may actually create a risk for others if an individual participates in a public accommodation. For example, a student with active, contagious tuberculosis might pose a direct threat to other students. According to the DOJ (1991b, p. 35560) and the legislative history (U.S. House of Representatives, 1990, p. 77), the section establishes a "strict standard." A direct threat is a significant risk that cannot be eliminated by a modification of policies or the provision of auxiliary aids (DOJ, 1991b, p. 35560). The explanatory notes to the Title III regulations state that:

> The determination that a person poses a direct threat to the health or safety of others may not be based on generializations or stereotypes about the effects of a particular disability; it must be based on an individual assessment . . . based on reasonable judgment that relies on current medical evidence or on the best available objective evidence to determine: The nature, duration and severity of the risk; the probability that the potential injury will actually occur; and whether reasonable modifications of policies, practices, or procedures will mitigate the risk. (DOJ, 1991b, p. 35560)

The test is derived from the Supreme Court's opinion in *School Board of Nassau County, Fla. v. Arline* (1987). For a further discussion of the test, see Gostin (1991, pp. 268, 276–280).

Title III's last major set of requirements deal with privately owned transportation facilities that are not covered by the ADA's public services provisions in Title II. Here, again, the section provides a set of general and specific requirements that parallel the provisions applying to public accommodations more generally (42 U.S.C. §12184) (see Golden, chap. 9, this volume). As with public accommodations generally, the act limits its most stringent criteria to newly purchased or leased vehicles. Detailed requirements are provided by the statute and are amplified in the regulations of the Department of Transportation (1991).

Except with respect to its transportation provisions, Title III relies to a large extent on DOJ regulations to provide meaning for its terms (42 U.S.C. §12186[b]). (The DOJ promulgated final regulations on July 26, 1991 [DOJ, 1991b, 1992].) As with Title II of the 1964 Civil Rights Act, the DOJ also has primary enforcement responsibility. The DOJ is required to investigate alleged violations and periodically review compliance by covered entitites (42 U.S.C. §12188[b][1][A]]i]). Where the Attorney General has reasonable cause to believe that there is a pattern or practice of discrimination, or a single cause of discrimination raises an "issue of general public importance," he or she may commence a civil action seeking equitable relief and civil damages (42 U.S.C. §12188[b][1][B]). Individuals who are aggrieved may bring a civil action in federal district court seeking an order to cease and desist the discrimination (42 U.S.C. §12188[a][1]). (The statute incorporates the remedies available under Title II of the 1964 Civil Rights Act [42 U.S.C. §2000a-3].)

MANDATING A NEW WORLD

Hidden within the detail and complexity of Title III's many provisions is an extraordinarily bold statute, one that will profoundly alter the world about us and take civil rights laws in new directions. Several features of the statute are particularly important and warrant special discussion. This section considers the statute's unusual detail. Title III's presumption of "qualification" and its treatment of preexisting criteria is considered below.

Title III's most obvious innovation is its detail and specificity. Typically, civil rights statutes have been simple and concise, prohibiting discrimination and leaving the ascertainment of what that means to administrative agencies and the courts. Title II of the Civil Rights Act of 1964 is a perfect example of that. It states simply that "all persons are entitled to the full and equal enjoyment" of the goods and benefits provided by public accommodations and shall not be discriminated against or segregated on the basis of race, color, national origin, or religion. Exactly what that meant was not considered problematic, and any ambiguities were easily left to judicial determination.

Title III, like Title I, of the ADA departs from this simplicity. Title III contains a myriad of detailed provisions stating just what constitutes discrimination and under just what circumstances. Some of this specificity is no doubt attributable to the inherent difficulties of delineating just what constitutes discrimination on the basis of disability—discrimination that can be eliminated only through positive steps to eliminate physical and programmatic barriers, not merely by changing attitudes. As Burgdorf, one of the bill's initial drafters, has noted, some of the specificity may also reflect a realization by Congress that short and simple bills may provide invitations to administrative agencies and the courts to limit the scope of protections (1991b, p. 511). The Supreme Court has certainly done so in the past with respect to disability rights laws (see *Southeastern Community College v. Davis*, 1979). The Supreme Court's recent tendency to construe uncertainty against civil rights plaintiffs (Parmet, 1990, pp. 331, 336–337) may well have prompted Congress to remove as much ambiguity as possible.

Title III's unusual specificity, however, may also reflect a growing recognition that the old model of antidiscrimination legislation, which in effect simply said "stop excluding and segregating," is inadequate to ensure meaningful participation and equality. Instead, a different type of statute, one that not only says "stop" but also alters the conditions that make stopping difficult, is needed. Title III's detail enables it to challenge preexisting conditions in a variety of ways that are considered below.

The Presumption of Qualification

Title III begins the task of remaking the public world with Section 302(a), its general anti-discrimination statement (42 U.S.C. §12182[a]). Taken alone, this bold statement looks much like prior statutes and parallels the general provisions found in the employment and public sector titles of the ADA as well as Section 504 of the Rehabilitation Act (29 U.S.C. §794). Looked at more closely, however, Section 302(a) is radically different from prior disability discrimination statutes.

For example, Titles I and II of the ADA as well as Section 504 of the Rehabilitation Act apply only in the case in which a person with disabilities is "qualified" for the particular activity at issue. They thus accept the notion that, at least in some instances, a person with a disability might not be qualified, perhaps because of the disability, to do the job or receive the service at stake. This requirement of qualification has been central to past disability discrimination law. Under the Rehabilitation Act, for example, the concept of qualification has been the key to fitting disability discrimination law into an equal opportunity paradigm (Parmet, 1987). As long as the law requires that the individual be qualified to do the job or receive the service, disability discrimination law can be seen as merely removing artificial and prejudicial barriers, giving individuals with disabilities their chance to become independent and productive citizens. The problem, of course, is that qualifications themselves can form the barriers. As long as these qualifications go unquestioned, true equality can remain elusive. After all, an individual cannot be "qualified" for a job if he or she cannot get into the office because the door frame is too narrow for a wheelchair.

Section 504 of the Rehabilitation Act and Titles I and II of the ADA deal with this problem through the requirement that covered entities provide "reasonable accommodations." With a simple reasonable accommodation such as the installation of a ramp, people with disabilities often are able to meet all other qualifications, and accessibility can be realized.

Thus Titles I and II of the ADA, following Section 504 of the Rehabilitation Act, do envision some alteration of the preexisting requirements of jobs and programs in order to enable persons with disabilities to be qualified. Nevertheless, those statutes all keep the qualification requirements. What this means, technically, is that a plaintiff with a disability must still prove as part of his or her *prima facie* case, qualification, albeit with reasonable accommodations, for the particular job or benefit at issue. As a result, the plaintiff with a disability still has the stigmatizing burden of disproving the stereotypical assumption that he or she simply is not qualified because of the disability (e.g., *Severino v. North Fort Myers Fire Control District* [1991] discussing the plaintiff's burden under Section 504 of the Rehabilitation Act). Theoretically, Titles I and II, like Section 504, accept the legitimacy of much of the givenness of the world, not to mention stereotypical thinking, and demand that the plaintiff prove otherwise.

Title III departs dramatically from this framework. Neither its general nor its specific provisions apply only to "qualified persons with disabilities." Instead, the general provision is truly general—it applies to all persons with disabilities. Of course, this does not mean that Congress did not recognize that there will be cases in which an individual's disability makes it difficult for that person to receive the benefits or services of a particular public accommodation. However, rather than place a general "qualification" requirement on all persons with disabilities, Title III deals with the issue through its specific provisions that construe the general mandate. Each of these provisions in Section 302 contains some exceptions that explicitly exempt public accommodations from the antidiscrimination mandate in cases in which nondiscrimination would require a "fundamental alteration" of or place an "undue burden" on the facility.

This relegation of the qualification requirement to the exceptions to the specific provisions is extraordinarily significant. As a practical matter, this change makes it probable that Title III plaintiffs will not have to bear the often difficult and always stigmatizing burden of proving that they are qualified to participate in a public accommodation. Although neither the act nor the regulations so specify, the structure of each suggests that in Title III alone the lack of qualification effectively becomes an affirmative defense, which means that the defendant will bear the burden of proof.

More fundamentally, the deletion of a general qualification requirement creates the presumption that all persons, with or without disability, are qualified for public accommodations. The public world is to be open to all, and there is no need for individuals with disabilities to prove their qualifications. Thus in a very profound and radical way, Title III suggests that the public world belongs to all of us. Its vision is one of inclusiveness.

Modifications and Disparate Impact

Title III, however, does not stop with symbols alone. The ADA seeks to realize its vision of an inclusive public world in a number of other ways. Only by actually requiring the alteration of the public world can meaningful access to public accommodations be assured (Parmet, 1990). Here is where the specific provisions come into further play.

Two key concepts underlie the specific requirements of Section 302(b)(2). One is that a public accommodation is under an affirmative obligation to ensure that the goods or services of the facility be provided to a person with disabilities. Thus Title III, unlike Title II of the Civil Rights Act of 1964, does not simply require that the public accommodation cease exclusion or segregation. Rather, Title III recognizes that public accommodations may need to be reconsidered or altered in order to make access meaningful. The act prohibits a "failure to make reasonable modifications" in policies, practices, or procedures when such actions are necessary to provide such goods, services, facilities, privileges, advantages, or accommodations to persons with disabilities except when the reasonable modification would "fundamentally alter" the public accommodation (42 U.S.C. §12182[b][2][A][ii]). In other words, although the ADA does not require the fundamental alteration of the public world, it does require public accommodations to take significant steps toward making their facilities and services more meaningfully available to people with disabilities (DOJ, 1992; 28 C.F.R. §§36.402 *et seq.*).

Similarly, Section 302(b)(2)(A)(iii) requires public accommodations to

> take such steps as may be necessary to ensure that no individual with a disability is excluded, denied services, segregated or otherwise treated differently than other individuals because of the absence of auxiliary aids and services, unless the entity can demonstrate that taking such steps would fundamentally alter the nature of the good, service [or facility] . . .

or impose an undue burden (42 U.S.C. §12182[b][2][A][iii]). The regulations clarify that such "auxiliary aids and services" may include, among other things, the provisions of qualified interpreters, written materials, braille materials, or amplifiers. Thus once again, a public accommodation will need to rethink and alter what it provides (DOJ, 1992a; 28 C.F.R. §36.304). Past assumptions about how things are done in movie theaters, parks, stores, and all other public accommodations are no longer sufficient.

Finally, the ADA requires all public accommodations, as of January 1992, to "remove architectural barriers, and communication barriers that are structural in nature" where so doing is "readily achievable," a term that is defined as meaning "easily accomplishable" without much difficulty or expense (42 U.S.C. §§12182[b][2][A][iv], 12181[9]). Therefore, although the ADA does not require that public accommodations immediately make physical alterations that are difficult to accomplish, it does require some affirmative reconstruction of facilities.

The second critical way in which the specific provisions require the remaking and restructuring of public accommodations is by their adoption of disparate impact analysis. Disparate impact analysis looks not to the discriminatory intent behind actions and policies but rather to their effect, whether they disproportionately harm a protected group.

In the case of disability discrimination, disparate impact analysis can be critical. As has long been recognized, persons with disabilities are often barred from full participation in society not because of malign intent but because of "indifference and thoughtlessness" (*Alexander v. Choate*, 1985). In other words, it is not evil thought but the way in which society is shaped—the fact that buildings are built without ramps, that signage lacks braille—that causes much of the problem. Only when society recognizes that those preexisting structures that exclude are discriminatory, regardless of the intent behind them, can people with disabilities achieve meaningful access.

The ADA recognizes and wholeheartedly adopts disparate impact analysis (U.S. House of Representatives Committee on Education and Labor, 1990, p. 61). Despite the current controversy over disparate impact in cases of race and gender discrimination and the Supreme Court's rejection of the concept in those areas (see *Wards Cove v. Antonio*, 1988, and *Washington v. Davis*, 1976, rejecting disparate impact analysis under the 14th Amendment), Title III prohibits the "imposition or application of eligibility criteria that screen out or tend to screen out an individual with disability" unless that policy or criteria can be "shown to be necessary" (42 U.S.C. §12182[b][2][A][i]). Intent is thus irrelevant. What matters is whether the criteria have a tendency to harm individuals with disabilities. The result is that many criteria, many of the givens of the world, may come under scrutiny. If they tend to screen out persons with disabilities, they may be prohibited. Criteria must be rethought.

Taken together, these specific provisions of Title III will go far beyond prior law in calling for a reimagining and reinvention of the public world. Title III does not simply call for a cessation of invidious action. It mandates change, modification, and a testing of all that is given. It requires that, as time passes, as structures are altered and constructed, greater accessibility must be achieved.

The world must be altered to be inclusive. We must ask, however, what would a world in compliance with Title III look like?

THE REIMAGINED WORLD

Physical Spaces

What will the public world look like when Title III is fully implemented? What will its vision entail? It is certainly too early to know for sure. The very breadth and boldness of Title III guarantees that the changes it will make will extend beyond the simple and knowable.

The most predictable set of changes will occur in the design and construction of public accommodations and commercial facilities. Just as Title II of the Civil Rights Act of 1964 focused on eating and lodging services, Title III of the ADA most specifically affects the physical layout of public accommodations.

The title's emphasis on physical design and construction is apparent in its initial definitional listing of public accommodations. Title III states, for example, that it is the "office of a health care worker" that constitutes a public accommodation (42 U.S.C. §1218[7][F]). Technically, it is not the *service* of the worker that falls within the definition. Similarly, insurance offices are covered, although a different section of the ADA exempts many insurance underwriting practices from nondiscrimination mandates, at least to the extent that they comply with state law (42 U.S.C. §12201[c]). (For somewhat different interpretations of the impact of this exemption, compare Burgdorf [1991b, pp. 247–249] to Parmet [1990, p. 340].)

Title III and its regulations are at their most detailed when they consider the design and construction requirements of buildings and transportation vehicles (42 U.S.C. §12183; DOJ, 1992a; 28 C.F.R. §36, Appendix A). This should not be surprising. For many people with disabilities, physical barriers to accessibility have been among the most formidable. Without a ramp, a rest room that can accommodate an individual using a wheelchair, or a place to park a van, little else matters to these individuals. For many people with disabilities physical accessibility is the sine qua non of meaningful accessibility, and the ADA's drafters rightly saw it as the first step toward creating a more inclusive public world.

Moreover, in emphasizing design and construction, the drafters of both the ADA and the regulations had a rich history on which to draw. Since the enactment of the Rehabilitation Act of 1973, the U.S. Architectural and Transportation Barriers Compliance Board (ATBCB), an independent federal agency, has been developing standards to ensure that federal facilities are physically accessible to persons with disabilities. The ATBCB's standards, known as Minimum Guidelines and Requirements for Accessible Design (MGRAD), have paralleled nongovernmental standards promulgated by the American National Standards Institute's ANSI A117 Committee, a group consisting of 42 organizations representing individuals with disabilities, architects and designers, building owners and managers, building product manufacturers, model code groups, and government officials (ATBCB, 1991, p. 35410; DOJ, 1992; 28 C.F.R. §36.304[b]). These standards, not surprisingly, have focused primarily on architectural and design barriers to physical access and equal utilization by persons with mobility, hearing, and sight impairments. Thus, although there was no federal requirement prior to the ADA that all public accommodations be designed for accessibility, there at least has been a tradition of standard setting in this area (ATBCB, 1991, p. 35410; DOJ, 1992; 28 C.F.R. §36.304[b]).

Title III builds on that foundation. The statute itself has several specific provisions pertaining to architectural and design issues. These provisions envision an evolutionary process. As of the ADA's effective date, all public accommodations have been required to remove architectural and communications barriers where doing so is "readily achievable." As was noted above, the statute defines readily achievable as "easily accomplishable and able to be carried out without much difficulty or expense" in light of the nature and cost of the action, the financial situation of the particular public accommodation, and the type of operation at issue (42 U.S.C. §12181[9]). The regulations offer the following examples of readily achievable removal of barriers: installing ramps; making curb cuts; repositioning shelves; rearranging tables, chairs, vending machines, and display racks; and repositioning telephones (DOJ, 1992; 28 C.F.R. §36.304[b]). Ultimately, however, this requirement is not particularly stringent. According to the DOJ, "[Barrier removals] are not readily achievable to the extent that they would result in a significant loss of selling or serving space . . . " (1991b, p. 35568). Thus, although Title III does not take the physical design of public accommodations as set in stone, it does not require that significant alterations be made imminently. In the short run, much of the public world will continue to look and be physically much as it has always been.

The more profound alterations of physical space will occur only as public accommodations and, more broadly, commercial facilities undergo construction or alteration. (Title III's construction and alteration provisions apply not only to public accommodations but also more broadly to commercial facilities, which are defined as facilities "that are intended for nonresidential use; and whose operations will affect commerce" [42 U.S.C. §12181[2]). As the normal processes of repair, renovation, and new construction occur, the ADA imposes a higher standard of accessibility, seeking greater reimagination of the physical space of public accommodations.

Section 303 of the ADA requires that newly constructed facilities must be "readily accessible to and usable by" persons with disabilities except in the rare cases in which it is structurally impracticable to do so (42 U.S.C. §12183[a][1]). The act clarifies that buildings less than 3,000 square feet shall not be required to include an elevator unless the buildings contain a shopping center, shopping mall, or the professional office of a health care provider, or unless the Attorney General determines that a particular category requires the installation of an elevator (42 U.S.C. §12183[b]). The DOJ regulations add terminals, depots, and public transportation stations to the list of facilities requiring elevators (DOJ, 1992; 28 C.F.R. §36.404). The ADA also requires that new alterations ensure ready accessibility "to the maximum extent feasible" and that all alterations that affect access to an area of the facility containing a "primary function" of that facility must also ensure ready accessibility for the path of travel to the altered area and the bathrooms, telephones, and drinking fountains serving the altered area, except in cases in which such alterations are disproportionate to the overall alterations in terms of cost and scope (42 U.S.C. §12183[a][2]).

The exact meaning of these alteration and construction requirements is specified in the DOJ regulations (DOJ, 1992; 28 C.F.R. §36, Appendix A), which adopt and incorporate the ADA accessibility guidelines promulgated by the ATBCB. The DOJ standards are based in large part on the ATBCB's prior MGRAD standards, as well as planned revisions by the ANSI (ATBCB, 1991a, pp. 35410–35411). The standards are extremely detailed. Covering issues ranging from the adequacy of the number of parking spaces set aside for persons with disabilities to the design of bathrooms accessible to persons using wheelchairs, the regulations form a comprehensive basis for determining what the physical space of the public world will look like in the years to come as new buildings are built and old ones are reconstructed. The images they offer and the standards they set are those of a world in which all public spaces, from shopping centers to doctors' offices, from daycare centers to amusement parks, are radically different from what we know today.

Accommodating a Range of Disabilities

The ADA's design standards offer a hope of building, over time, a more inclusive world. Their inclusiveness, however, is not universal. The standards are designed with only some users in mind, particularly those with hearing, sight, or mobility impairments. What these standards do not disclose is what physical accessibility will mean to the many other persons with disabilities who also are entitled to protection under the ADA.

Title III employs the ADA's broad definition of disability (see Breadth of Coverage, above). Although a significant portion of persons with disabilities will have mobility, hearing, or sight impairments that are the subject of most of the ADA's construction and alteration regulations, not all will. Some will have mental disabilities, others cardiac, pulmonary, or other chronic medical conditions. What would a world designed and constructed to be physically accessible to all such persons look like?

Here the ADA and its regulations are mostly silent. That silence is understandable: There is no rich precedent for answering such a question. In addition, it is highly probable that design and construction issues most seriously affect those with vision, hearing, and mobility impairments.

It is possible, however, that individuals with other disabilities may also be excluded by public spaces that are designed and built without their particular disabilities in mind. One potential issue, which arose during the notice and comment period for the DOJ regulations, concerned individuals with so-called environmental illnesses, or multiple chemical sensitivities. During the rule-making process, individuals affected by such conditions commented to the DOJ that their conditions should be listed as examples of disabilities. The DOJ declined, noting that the determination of whether an impairment is a disability depends on whether, given the particular circumstances at issue, the impairment substantially limits one or more major life activities (DOJ, 1991, pp. 35548–35549). The Department added that some sensitivities may well cause respiratory or neurological impairments constituting disabilities (DOJ, 1991, pp. 35548–35549).

Although the Department was on solid ground in refusing to provide a blanket categorization of a varied and controversial set of conditions, its answer misses the larger point. The significant issue is not whether environmental sensitivities or a myriad of other conditions warrant wholesale inclusion as disabilities. The issue is what the accessibility and other requirements will mean to these vastly varied cases. How does one design a building to be "readily accessible" to everyone with a disability, even to those whose conditions defy global labeling? How is a building designed to be "readily accessible" to all with impairing allergies, whatever their allergies may be? To those with respiratory problems? To those with mental disabilities that are aggravated by certain environmental designs?

Neither the statute, its legislative history, nor its regulations provide clear answers to those questions, nor is it certain that universal standards can be drafted. It may well be that only time, trial and error, and a careful consideration of the particular circumstances of each public accommodation in light of the particular needs of each of its users can discern the beginnings of the answers. However, only by asking the question and beginning to consider the answer can Title III's goal of a truly inclusive public world ever be realized.

Beyond Brick and Mortar: Policies and Practices

The discussion thus far has focused largely on Title III's treatment of the physical design of public accommodations and commercial facilities. Physical barriers to access, however, are not the only impediments to creating a more inclusive world. The specific provisions of Section 302 make it clear that attitudes, practices, and policies must also be remade if the public world is to become more inclusive.

In contrast to the construction and design requirements under the title, the mandate to alter policies and practices does not allow for gradual change. As of the ADA's effective date the specific provisions of Section 302 came into effect. They require all public accommodations to make reasonable modifications in their policies and practices except where doing so would constitute an undue burden or fundamentally alter the nature of the service. They also require the provision of auxiliary aids except when that would cause an undue burden, and they prohibit standards and criteria that tend to exclude persons with disabilities.

The meaning of these provisions is developed, to some extent, in the regulations. These clarify that the term *undue burden* means "significant difficulty or expense" in light of the financial resources and type of operation at issue (DOJ, 1992; 28 C.F.R. §36.104). Moreover, the regulations are fairly specific about the requirements for auxiliary aids (DOJ, 1992; 28 C.F.R. §36.303). Most important, these provisions make clear that the neutral application of preexisting policies and criteria will not suffice. All the terms, conditions, and ways in which public accommodations go about performing their services and providing their benefits must be reconsidered in order to achieve true inclusiveness.

Ultimately, however, neither the regulations nor the statute provides a clear picture of what would be an inclusive policy or how the practices of the public world will need to be changed. Few clues are given as to what it would mean for a daycare teacher or a licensed social worker to provide equal benefits to clients with different backgrounds and different physical and psychological needs. These public accommodations, after all, are not just the transient consumer services that were the core concern of Title II of the 1964 Civil Rights Act. These are professional but, more importantly, relational services that depend on long-term understandings and relatively personal relationships between the so-called public accommodation and the person served. They are inherently evolutionary and defiant of absolute criteria. Moreover, the law's ability to control them is always limited. It is one thing to require a store to sell groceries to individuals with disabilities; it is quite another to require a daycare teacher to be sensitive to the needs of a child with mental illness. Thus Title III of the ADA is more like Title VII of the 1964 Civil Rights Act (42 U.S.C. 2000e *et seq.*), which covers employment and deals with multifaceted, long-term relationships, than like Title II of that act. And, not surprisingly, it is Title VII that has come to be the focus of controversy and litigation.

Even if the law can reach such relationships, understanding how it must do so will not be easy. In reviewing the vast number of informal, idiosyncratic, and ever-changing policies of all the nation's service providers, subtle distinctions will have to be made to determine which policies are discriminatory, which are unalterable, and which are specifically tailored responses or reasonable modifications. After all, the history of the struggle against discrimination and, in particular, the saga of affirmative action attest to the fact the lines between stigmatizing segregation and specially tailored services remain controversial. In addition, although denial of equal services is generally rejected by the ADA, the very requirement for reasonable modifications and auxiliary benefits might to some appear to endorse the provision of separate or discriminating treatment.

Title III recognizes this. The ADA states that it is discriminatory to provide a person with a "separate benefit" "unless it is necessary to provide the individual with a good, service, facility, privilege, advantage, or accommodation. . . " (42 U.S.C. §12182[b][1][A][iii]). Similarly, the ADA requires modifications unless they "fundamentally alter" or are necessary to the provision of the good itself (42 U.S.C. §12182[b][2][A]][ii]). In other words, the ADA acknowledges that, in some instances, requiring the alteration of the given nature of a service to accommodate individuals with disabilities might clash with the ADA's mandate to provide similar services to such persons.

Recognition of the clash, however, does not resolve it. Indeed, neither the ADA nor its regulations attempt to resolve it by defining what it means to "fundamentally alter" a public accommodation or what would be "necessary to provide" the good or service at issue. Those omissions, although significant, should not be surprising. Ultimately, one cannot know what is necessary for a good or what it means to fundamentally alter the good without knowing a priori what the good, benefit, or service is and what its policies ought to be. However, the only basis we have for knowing that—the pre-ADA nature of the service—is itself what is challenged by the ADA, and the ADA's recognition that the preexisting structure of the world around us may be the very structure that excludes people with disabilities.

Consider, for example, one service covered by Title III, medical services. Some applications of Title III to medical services are simple to predict. The physical and design criteria that will apply to new medical offices are relatively straightforward but also of profound importance. Moreover, there is no doubt that Title III prohibits a health care provider from refusing to provide services to a patient simply because the provider harbors a stereotypical and invidious animus toward the patient because of the patient's disability. However, other applications of Title III to the course of treatment are more problematical.

For example, the ADA does not prohibit the provider from refusing to treat the patient for economic reasons. This is no trivial omission. A large percentage of the population with disabilities is poor (U.S. House of Representatives Committee on the Judiciary, 1990, p. 50). Many are presumably either without health insurance or dependent on Medicaid, which many health care providers refuse to accept. Moreover, The ADA's exemption for certain insurance underwriting practices will allow insurers to refuse to insure certain risks, which may well leave many people with disabilities either totally uninsured or without insurance for their preexisting conditions (Parmet, 1990, p. 340).

In addition, the DOJ's commentary on its regulations states that medical specialization is acceptable and that a physician may continue to refuse a treatment beyond his or her specialty (DOJ, 1991, pp. 35564–35565). That seems sensible, although not actually required by the language of the statute. Surely the ADA does not require an obstetrician to perform cardiac surgery, but when must an obstetrician provide care to an HIV-positive patient confronting opportunistic infections? Can the obstetrician decline care of such a patient on the grounds that the doctor does not take "high-risk" cases and that the presence of the HIV infection pushes the case outside his or her area of knowledge and specialization?

The answer to those questions depends ultimately on how a specialty or "service" is defined and what is therefore necessary for the provision of the service (42 U.S.C. §12182[b][2][i]). Is the service performed "obstetrics" or "low-risk obstetrical care"? Is it "obstetrical care for all pregnant patients," or "for patients without serious compounding conditions"? Ultimately, by accepting the idea that physicians can specialize, the DOJ accepts the idea that physicians themselves, perhaps not as individuals but as a profession, can define their own services and specialties, the nature of the very benefits they give. In the case cited above, for example, medical practice may dictate that obstetricians generally do provide care for patients with HIV infection. The specialty is not defined narrowly, but the profession's understanding of its service would allow for exclusions in particular cases in which the obstetrician could show that the HIV infection does, following medical standards, present formidable complications.

The problem with this approach is that it relies for its resolution on prior definitions and conceptions of services, definitions that may themselves not take into account the ways in which they exclude people with disabilities. Although medical specialization serves critical purposes, its structure and character is the result of the profession's own development, not a process necessarily open to voices and needs of the larger community, including citizens with disabilities. To accept without question the medical profession's definition of specialization and treatment criteria, or any other profession's own definition of its service and the nature of the benefit it offers, is in some ways similar to accepting a storekeeper's assumption about the design and physical structure of the store. It is, in effect, to undermine the ADA's presumption of qualification and its mandate for universal inclusion.

Herein lies the dilemma of Title III: inclusion requires a willingness to challenge preexisting definitions, but those very definitions form hard-to-escape baselines necessary for measuring how much alteration shall be required. With respect to physical and design criteria, the dilemma is resolved not by deduction but by resort to the prior practices and regulations that have resulted from two decades of dialogue and experience in making physical structures more accessible. It is those practices and customs that enable us to know that accessible buildings have ramps but need not be limited to a single story. However, when it comes to the practices and policies of services, our history is less rich and the shared meanings not always available. The picture of the public world in which all are qualified and all are included is not yet filled in.

CONCLUSION

What does this suggest for the potential of Title III to create a more inclusive world? Title III reaches far and offers a broad challenge. In many clear and specific ways, it will affect a broad array of services and facilities and open up the public world in a way in which it has never before been open.

However, Title III may go further. It mandates the alteration and reconsideration of policies and practices that govern a wide scope of services and relationships from education to medicine, from accountancy to hair styling. In requiring the modification and redrawing of such services, however, it gives few guidelines and offers few clues. What is necessary for the provision of such services? How dramatically must they be altered? What is "fundamental"? When is the personalization of a specialized service segregation and when is it an accommodation? These are questions that are yet unanswered.

The options for the resolution of such questions are relatively few. One option is the one relied on implicitly by the DOJ regulations in accepting the fact of medical specialization. Whatever the wisdom or statutory authority for that regulation, it implicitly accepts the profession's own authority to define its services. Even if that is not objectionable, the assumption that the profession itself can define its own services may limit the extent to which the ADA actually achieves its goal of making a more inclusive public world.

The second alternative presents no more cause for optimism. If the definitions of the services and policies of public accommodations are to be challenged, the meaning of much of Title III will remain open, its application uncertain, as new definitions are debated. Ambiguity in statutes, however, traditionally invites litigation as parties struggle over contested meanings. Typically, in our common law–based system that process of litigation becomes one of evolutionary interpretation. Boundaries are challenged and redefined as cases build on precedent.

Unfortunately, leaving the uncertainties of Title III to the judicial process does not bode well for the fulfillment of the title's vision. The federal courts at the present time, led by the Supreme Court, are not sympathetic to applications of civil rights laws that challenge preexisting critiera (see Burgdorf, 1991b; *Southeastern Community College v. Davis*, 1979; *Wards Cove v. Antonio*, 1988; *Washington v. Davis*, 1976). Left to the courts, the uncertainties of Title III are apt to be resolved in favor of the status quo. The result could be that, while the physical and design features of the public world will change to comply with the statute's most specific commands and although overt invidious treatment would be illegal, the more subtle practices and policies that relegate persons with disabilities to second-class citizenship would not be greatly altered. The public world would not be changed very much at all.

The remaining option is to accept Title III's temporal view of equality and recognize that no clear answers can exist now. Only by going outside the statute, by continuing the movement and dialogue that led to its creation, can answers appear and definitions for the services and goods provided by public accommodations be developed. This option would thus seek the inclusion of the voices of individuals with disabilities in the process of defining the nature and criteria of the services provided. In the medical field, for example, this approach would require that the views and concerns of persons with disabilities be part of the formulation of medical standards. By entering into a continuing discussion with the profession, challenging its definitions and participating in its review of its own standards, those protected by Title III can give shape to the ADA's meaning.

Title III of the ADA, unfortunately, provides no vehicle or means for undertaking such a process, nor is such a task an easy one. It is, indeed, a never-ending and always indeterminate one. Any meaningful reimagining of the public world, however, requires nothing less. Only with a continuing process of questioning and reconsidering the most basic elements of the public world will Title III's goal of recreating that world be realized. Without such a daring dialogue, the remade world of Title III will not be all that more open than the public world it seeks to replace.

REFERENCES

Air Carriers Access Act of 1986, 49 U.S.C. app. §1374(c) (1986).

Alexander v. Choate, 469 U.S. 287, 295 (1985).

Burgdorf, R.L., Jr. (1991a). Equal access to public accommodations. In J. West (Ed.), *The Americans with Disabilities Act: From policy to practice* (pp. 183–213). New York: Milbank Memorial Fund.

Burgdorf, R.L., Jr. (1991b). The Americans with Disabilities Act: Analysis and implications of a second general civil rights statute. *Harvard Civil Rights–Civil Liberties Law Review, 26*, 413–522.

Civil Rights Act of 1964, 42 U.S.C. §2000a *et seq.* (1988).

Fair Housing Amendments Act of 1988, 42 U.S.C. §§3601–3619 (1988).

Gostin, L. (1991). Public health powers: the imminence of radical change. In J. West (Ed.), *The Americans with Disabilities Act: From policy to practice* (pp. 268–290). New York: Milbank Memorial Fund.

Parmet, W.E. (1987). AIDS and the limits of discrimination law. *Law, Medicine and Health Care, 15*, 61–72.

Parmet, W.E. (1990). Disability and discrimination: The challenges of the ADA. *Law, Medicine and Health Care, 18*, 331–344.

Rehabilitation Act of 1973, 29 U.S.C.A. §790 *et seq.* (1985 & Supp. 1991).

School Board of Nassau County, Fla. v. Arline, 480 U.S. 273, 288 (1987).

Severino v. North Fort Myers Fire Control District, 935 F.2d 1179 (11th Cir. 1991).

Southeastern Community College v. Davis, 442 U.S. 397 (1979).

U.S. Architectural and Transportation Barriers Compliance Board. (1991, July 26). Americans with Disabilities Act (ADA) accessibility guidelines for buildings and facilities; final guidelines. *Federal Register, 56*, 35407–35453.

U.S. Department of Health and Human Services. (1990). Nondiscrimination on the basis of handicap in programs and activities receiving federal financial assistance. In *Code of Federal Regulations* (45: Public Welfare, pp. 354–395). Washington, DC: U.S. Government Printing Office.

U.S. Department of Justice. (1992a). Appendix A to Part 36—standards for accessible design: ADA accessibility guidelines for buildings and facilities. *Federal Register, 56*, 35605–35690.

U.S. Department of Justice. (1991, July 26). Nondiscrimination on the basis of disability by public accommodations and in commercial facilities; final rule. *Federal Register, 56*, 35543–35604.

U.S. Department of Justice. (1992b). Nondiscrimination on the basis of disability by public accommodations and in commercial facilities. In *Code of Federal Regulations* (28: Judicial Administration, pp. 457–629). Washington, DC: U.S. Government Printing Office.

U.S. Department of Transportation. (1991, September 6). Transportation for individuals with disabilities; final rule. *Federal Register, 56*, 45583–45641.

U.S. House of Representatives. (1990, July 12). *House conference report no. 101-596, to accompany S. 933 (101st Congress, 2nd session)*. Washington, DC: U.S. Government Printing Office. (Reprinted in *United States Code Congressional and Administrative News, 4*, 565–600 [1990])

U.S. House of Representatives Committee on Education and Labor. (1990, May 15). *House report no. 101-485 (II), to accompany H.R. 2273 (101st Congress, 2nd session)*. Washington, DC: U.S. Government Printing Office. (Reprinted in *United States Code Congressional and Administrative News, 4*, 303–344 [1990])

U.S. House of Representatives Committee on the Judiciary. (1990, May 15). *House report no. 101-485 (III), to accompany H.R. 2273 (101st Congress, 2nd session)*. Washington, DC: U.S. Government Printing Office. (Reprinted in *United States Code Congressional and Administrative News, 4*, 445–511 [1990])

Ward's Cove v. Antonio, 490 U.S. 642 (1988).

Washington v. Davis, 426 U.S. 229 (1976).

Chapter 11

Housing and the ADA

Bonnie Milstein and Steven Hitov

As a result of the passage of the Fair Housing Amendments Act[1] of 1988 (FHAA), housing, zoning, and land use law is changing dramatically (Milstein, Pepper, & Rubenstein, 1989; Mental Health Law Project, 1990; Mental Health Law Project, 1991; Simring, 1991; Burnim, Jackson, Milstein, & Pepper, 1992). Towns and cities around the country are discovering that their attempts to exclude individuals with disabilities from their neighborhoods are being rebuffed with successful lawsuits and state Attorney General opinions. Public and private landlords are discovering that "no pets rules," arbitrary parking assignments, and assumptions about the risks involved in renting to people with visual, mental, mobility, and hearing disabilities are also being successfully challenged by housing consumers and by the federal government. Can the Americans with Disabilities Act[2] (ADA) add anything to this revolution? Yes, even though the ADA, unlike the FHAA, does not cover all types of housing.

First, where the laws do overlap, the ADA's statutory language and legislative history often articulate the promise of equal opportunity and community integration with greater specificity. Second, the ADA imposes stricter structural accessibility requirements, especially for existing housing. Third, although the goals of both statutes are similar, the breadth of the ADA demands new approaches to expanding housing opportunities for people with disabilities.

THE ADA'S COVERAGE OF HOUSING

Both Title II (Public Services) and Title III (Public Accommodations) of the ADA protect against housing discrimination in certain circumstances, with the public services title covering many more types and units of housing than fall within the category of public accommodations. The ADA defines public services to include all public entities (33,000 political jurisdictions, according to the U.S. Department of Justice (DOJ, 1991c, p. 35694, 35715) and everything that they do in their executive, legislative, and judicial capacities. This includes all housing created, developed, managed, leased, owned, and planned by every state, county, and local public entity.

---

[1]The Fair Housing Amendments Act of 1988 is codified in the *United States Code* (42 U.S.C. §§3601–3619 [1988]). References to various portions of the act within this chapter cite the specific section of the Code.

[2]The Americans with Disabilities Act of 1990 (PL 101–336) is published in *Statutes at Large* (104 Stat. 327) and codified in the *United States Code* (42 U.S.C. §§12101–12213 [Supp. II, 1990]). References to various portions of the act within this chapter cite the specific section of the Code.

Title III's coverage of housing is narrower because its primary focus is on business establishments and because the definition of "commercial facilities" specifically excludes "facilities that are covered or expressly exempted from coverage under the Fair Housing Act of 1968 (42 U.S.C. 3601 *et seq.*)" (42 U.S.C. §12181). Nonetheless, according to the DOJ regulations, this exclusion applies only to "commercial facilities" and not to "places of public accommodation" (DOJ, 1991b, pp. 35551–35552). Places of public accommodation are defined differently from public accommodations. Public accommodations refer to the entity "that owns, leases (or leases to), or operates a place of public accommodation" (28 C.F.R. §36.104).[3] The purpose of the distinction is to emphasize that the ADA's obligation rests on the person or entity, not on the place (DOJ, 1991b, p. 35553). Not all commercial facilities are places of public accommodation. Thus factories that are not open to the public and do not sell their products at the manufacturing site are not places of public accommodation (DOJ, 1991b, p. 35547).

A place of public accommodation is "a facility, operated by a private entity, whose operations affect commerce and fall within at least one of the 12 specified categories" of facilities listed in the statutory definition (DOJ, 1991b, p. 35551). Two of the categories are "places of lodging" and "social service center establishments," including inns, hotels, motels, homeless shelters, substance abuse treatment centers, rape crisis centers, and halfway houses (DOJ, 1991b, p. 35551).

According to the DOJ, the ADA may also apply to these facilities, in addition to their coverage as residences by the FHAA. First, many places of lodging include facilities for both short- and long-term stays. The former units would be covered by the ADA and the latter by both the ADA and the FHAA. Or, the facility would be covered in its entirety by both statutes if short- and long-term stay units are not distinct. Second, some places of lodging, such as single-room-occupancy hotels, provide social services to their residents regardless of the length of their stays. Thus, these facilities fall within the definition of "social service center establishment." The same analyses apply to homeless shelters, domestic violence shelters, "nursing homes, residential care facilities and other facilities where persons may reside for varying lengths of time" (DOJ, 1991b, p. 35552).

> For example, a homeless shelter that is intended and used only for long term residential stays and that does not provide social services to its residents would not be covered as a place of public accommodation. However, if this facility permitted short-term stays or provided social services to its residents, it would be covered under the ADA either as a "place of lodging" or as a "social service center establishment," or as both. (DOJ, 1991b, p. 35552)

One question that the DOJ does not answer in its regulations is whether Title II or Title III applies when the social services consist of government-funded programs in a place of lodging. Possibly Title II would apply to the program and Title III might or might not apply to the entire operation. As the preamble to the Title III regulations states, determinations such as these "will need to be made on a case by case basis" (DOJ, 1991b, p. 35552). "The receipt of government assistance by a private entity does not by itself preclude a facility from being considered as a place of public accommodation" (DOJ, 1991b, p. 35551).

Finally, even a private home may be defined as a place of public accommodation if it, or a portion of it, is used as a facility described in one of the 12 categories. In the example given in the regulations, the portion of the home that is used as a doctor's office, including the entrance to the home/office, is covered by both the ADA and the FHAA (DOJ, 1991b, p. 35551; but see the limits on FHAA coverage [42 U.S.C. §3603]).

BENEFITS OF DUAL COVERAGE

Housing consumers with disabilities benefit in at least four ways from the dual coverage provided by the ADA and the FHAA: greater architectural accessibility in both existing and new construc-

---

[3]The DOJ regulations are codified at 28 C.F.R. parts 35 and 36. References to various portions of these regulations within this chapter cite the specific section of the regulations.

tion, expanded procedural approaches, more clearly defined tenancy rights, and new bases for gaining access to integrated housing.

Accessibility Issues

The ADA requires greater structural accessibility in existing housing than does the FHAA. Under the FHAA, owners must permit tenants to make reasonable modifications to their apartments "if such modifications may be necessary to afford such person full enjoyment of the premises . . ." (42 U.S.C. §3604[f][3][A]).

Although the statute and regulations require providers to share some minimal amount of the expense to make housing accessible to tenants with disabilities, the focus of the FHAA for existing housing is on accommodations through changes in policies and practices. Owners and managers must make "reasonable accommodations in rules, policies, practices or services, when such accommodations may be necessary to afford such person equal opportunity to use and enjoy a dwelling . . ." (42 U.S.C. §3604[f][3][B]). The two examples included in the regulations of the U.S. Department of Housing and Urban Development (DHUD) explaining this requirement concern waiving a "no pets rule" for tenants using service animals and providing a parking space close to the tenant's unit if the tenant has a mobility impairment (DHUD Office of the Assistant Secretary, Equal Opportunity, 1992; 24 C.F.R. §100.204[b]).

Cases decided under Section 504 of the Rehabilitation Act and the FHAA have taken the reasonable accommodation requirement further, requiring, for example, that providers install visual buzzers and fire detectors as well as train management staff to communicate with tenants who have hearing impairments (*Peabody Properties v. Jeffries*, 1989). In *Cason v. Rochester Housing Authority* (1990) the judge ordered the public housing authority to work with DHUD to stop singling out applicants with disabilities for a determination of whether they were "capable of independent living," holding that the standard was discriminatory. (DHUD amended its *Public and Indian Housing Handbook* to reflect *Cason* [DHUD, 1991], and issued a policy memorandum on the use of capability of independent living as a criterion [DHUD Offices of Public and Indian Housing and Fair Housing and Equal Opportunity, 1990].)

The ADA also includes "reasonable accommodation" requirements and, for existing housing covered by Title II of the ADA, imposes the structural accessibility standards of Section 504 of the Rehabilitation Act (which are stricter than those of the FHAA). Following the ADA's mandate, the DOJ has issued ADA regulations for state and local government services that adopt and extend the basic premises of Section 504: that a housing "program" must be accessible, even if all of its parts are not. Furthermore, the only justification for "program accessibility" rather than total accessibility is that the necessary modifications would result in "a fundamental alteration of the nature of a service, program or activity or in undue financial and administrative burdens" (DOJ, 1992; 28 C.F.R. §35.150[a]; but cf. U.S. House of Representatives Committee on the Judiciary, 1990, p. 51).

A key element in program accessibility is integration. Thus, where undue financial and administrative burdens prevent a public services provider from making its housing structurally accessible, the ADA regulations suggest a variety of options, including reassigning services to accessible locations, assigning aides to tenants, and making home visits. Most important, however, is that the housing provider's choice must be based on integration: "In choosing among available methods for meeting the requirements of this section, a public entity shall give priority to those methods that offer services, programs, and activities to qualified individuals with disabilities in the most integrated setting appropriate" (28 C.F.R. §§35.150[b], 36.203). This requirement will reinforce the FHAA's equal opportunity and integration mandates and will expand their application for tenants living in and applying for existing housing.

The ADA regulations also echo the Section 504 responsibilities to conduct self-evaluations, develop transition plans, and designate an employee or employees responsible for responding to disability-related complaints and ensuring that the program accomplishes the accessibility modifications identified in the self-evaluation and included in the transition plan (28 C.F.R. §§35.105, 35.107, 35.150). The FHAA does not include these requirements.

Housing providers who have received federal financial assistance have had to meet more stringent financial obligations because of their coverage by Section 504 of the Rehabilitation Act of 1973. Those obligations, however, have been more theoretical than real because tenants and providers had to wait until 1988 for DHUD to issue final Section 504 regulations. Because the FHAA also was passed in 1988, DHUD has paid more attention to drafting its regulations (which were published on January 23, 1989) (DHUD, Office of the Secretary, Office of the Assistant Secretary for Fair Housing and Equal Opportunity, 1989; 24 C.F.R. pts. 14, 100, 103–106, 109, 110, 115, 121). and to developing its enforcement scheme than it has to enforcing Section 504 (DHUD, 1990; see also Citizens Commission on Civil Rights, 1989, 1991). Fortunately, the ADA rejuvenates and extends the concepts and obligations required by that statute (U.S. Senate Committee on Labor and Human Resources, 1989, pp. 44–45).

The structural access standards for existing housing defined as public accommodations are more likely to resemble those of the FHAA than of Section 504. Under the ADA, the provider is responsible for making accessibility changes that are "readily achievable . . . easily accomplishable and able to be carried out without much difficulty or expense" (42 U.S.C. §12181). Even if this standard proves to be lower than that of the FHAA, at least the FHAA will continue to apply.

For new construction, both Title II–covered and Title III–covered housing is required to meet stricter accessibility requirements than those imposed by the FHAA. Under the FHAA only new multifamily dwellings with four or more units must meet standards of universal, adaptive design (42 U.S.C. §§3604[f][3][C], 3604[f][4–8]). These include accessible public and common use areas, accessible routes into and through the building and the units, usable kitchens and bathrooms, the placement of environmental controls (e.g., light switches and thermostats) in accessible locations, and bathroom wall reinforcements to permit the later installation of grab bars (42 U.S.C. 3604[f][3][C]).

When DHUD issued its Accessibility Guidelines and its FHAA regulations, it interpreted the statute to exclude townhouses and to permit builders to build inaccessible units on floors that were not served by elevators. The ADA's Accessibility Guidelines (DOJ, 1991a; see also U.S. Architectural and Transportation Barriers Compliance Board [ATBCB], 1991) do not include these limitations; they define multifamily dwellings as "any building containing more than two dwelling units" (DOJ, 1991a, p. 35609); and they are not limited to multifamily dwellings. The DOJ regulations require that:

> each facility or part of a facility constructed [or altered] by, on behalf of, or for the use of a public entity shall be designed and constructed in such manner that the facility or part of the facility is readily accessible to and usable by individuals with disabilities, if the construction was commenced after January 26, 1992. (DOJ, 1991c, p. 35720; 28 C.F.R. §35.151)

Although the guidelines do not indicate that they apply to permanent housing (DOJ, 1991a), the Title II regulations clarify that they do (DOJ, 1991c, p. 35720; 28 C.F.R. §35.151).

Tenancy Rights

The FHAA and both the public services and public accommodations titles of the ADA are consistent in their protections of tenants' rights. However, the ADA provides helpful specifics where the FHAA speaks in broader generalizations. There are at least four issues on which the ADA provides either greater specificity or confirmation of FHAA requirements.

Direct Threat   The FHAA states that:

> Nothing in this subsection requires that a dwelling be made available to an individual whose tenancy would constitute a direct threat to the health or safety of other individuals or whose tenancy would result in substantial physical damage to the property of others. (42 U.S.C. §3604[f][9])

The legislative history of the act explains that this prohibition was added as a substitute for language that would have excluded "a category of individuals from the protection of the Act" (U.S. House of Representatives Committee on the Judiciary, 1988, p. 28). The Committee further explained that the language included in the statute was based on *School Board of Nassau County, Fla. v. Arline* (1987), and that it was to be construed as including the language "unless such threat can be eliminated by reasonable accommodations" (U.S. House of Representatives Committee on the Judiciary, 1988, p. 28). Nonetheless, the DHUD regulation implementing the act did not include this qualifying provision (24 C.F.R. §100.202[d]).

The ADA, in contrast, clarifies how Congress intended the direct threat standard to be applied:

> Nothing in this title shall require an entity to permit an individual to participate in or benefit from the goods, services, facilities, privileges, advantages and accommodations of such entity where such individual poses a direct threat to the health or safety of others. The term "direct threat" means a significant risk to the health or safety of others that cannot be eliminated by a modification of policies, practices, or procedures or by the provision of auxiliary aids or services. (42 U.S.C. §12182[b][3])

This language is a more complete and therefore more accurate reflection of the adoption of the *Arline* standard by both the FHAA and the ADA. It requires the provider to determine whether there is some action he or she can take to eliminate the threat. That requirement is intended to eliminate subjective decision making, and to encourage providers to work with the consumer to determine whether the consumer's tenancy will pose a direct threat and, if it will, to devise a modification that will satisfy both the provider and the consumer.

Right To Refuse Special or Segregated Services The FHAA permits the continued provision of "special" housing designated for use by tenants with disabilities and at the same time prohibits providers from restricting consumers only to such housing. The ADA emphasizes this prohibition by making the consumer's right to choose explicit: "[n]othing in this Act shall be construed to require an individual with a disability to accept an accommodation, aid, service, opportunity, or benefit which such individual chooses not to accept" (42 U.S.C. §12201[d]). Also, the regulations for both the public services and the public accommodations titles include the "most integrated setting" standard discussed earlier. The public services (Title II) regulations apply this concept in the context of making existing facilities, including housing, usable by people with disabilities. The regulations require the political entities to "give priority to those methods that offer services, programs, and activities to qualified individuals with disabilities in the most integrated setting appropriate" (28 C.F.R. §35.150[b][1]).

The public accommodations (Title III) regulations combine the provider's responsibility to promote integration with the prohibition that providers may not require consumers to accept a special service, program, or accommodation. Thus consumers must always have the right to participate in the service (and to apply for housing) that is provided to the general public (28 C.F.R. §36.203). Although the FHAA and ADA are consistent about this question, the ADA's statutory and regulatory language is more explicit.

Auxiliary Aids and Effective Communication Because DHUD did not issue Section 504 regulations until 1988, little case law has developed on Section 504's requirement that reasonable accommodations and "housing adjustments" be provided to ensure that applicants and tenants with disabilities are able to participate in housing programs (DHUD, Office of the Secretary, 1988; 24 C.F.R. §§8.11, 8.24, 8.33). The FHAA includes a specific requirement that providers make "reasonable accommodations in rules, policies, practices, or services when such accommodations may be necessary to afford such person equal opportunity to use and enjoy a dwelling" (42 U.S.C. §3604[f][3][B]). In the context of tenancy decisions at least one court has found that Section 504 required a landlord to provide reasonable accommodations sufficient to permit a tenant with mental disabilities to retain her apartment despite her lack of cooperation with the landlord. She had failed to verify her income, which made it impossible for the landlord to draft a valid lease that met DHUD rules, and she had repeatedly refused to give the landlord access to her apartment, unjustifiably claiming sexual harassment, assault and battery, unlawful search and seizure, and "rifling my apartment" (*CRM Management, Inc. v. Carol Day*, 1991).

The ADA clarifies the Section 504 and FHAA requirements by being more specific in its guidance. For example, the regulations implementing Title III include detailed sections on "Modifications in policies, practices, or procedures" (28 C.F.R. §36.302) and "Auxiliary aids and services" (28 C.F.R. §36.303). Both require providers to show that the modification they refuse to make would fundamentally alter the nature of whatever is being offered or that the accommodations "would result in an undue burden, i.e., significant difficulty or expense" (28 C.F.R. §36.303). Furthermore, even where those limits can be shown, the provider must find an alternative aid or service that permits the consumer to receive the goods, services, facilities, and so forth being offered in the most integrated setting possible (28 C.F.R. §36.303). The discussion in the Preamble provides helpful guidance on consulting with the consumer regarding what type of aid or service may be necessary as well as on the variety of aids and services that are available.

Public services are held to the stricter Section 504 compliance standards. Where the regulations recommend that public accommodations make certain accommodations to consumers, the public services regulations make them mandatory, at least to the point of "undue financial and administrative burden" (DOJ, 1991c, p. 35708 *passim*). The Preamble to the regulations is also helpful in its discussion, for example, of factors the provider should consider when trying to decide whether using pen and paper is sufficient for communicating with a tenant or whether, because of "the context in which the communication is taking place, the number of people involved, and the importance of the communication," hiring a qualified interpreter is required (DOJ, 1991c, p. 35712).

Maintenance of Accessible Features   Once a landlord installs an elevator, a ramp, or a visual fire alarm, maintenance is the sine qua non for satisfying the accessibility promises of the FHAA and the ADA. The ADA regulations, however, have translated this requirement into specific regulations clarifying that the installation of accessibility features, like the modifications of policies and practices, are meaningless if they are not "maintained" in such a way as to permit applicants and tenants to rely on the usability of their residences (28 C.F.R. §§35.153, 36.211).

Zoning and Land Use Issues

For housing consumers with disabilities, zoning and land use laws have posed some of the most intractable barriers to integration. Combined with the NIMBY (not in my back yard) syndrome, they have resulted in the creation of quotas in apartment buildings, distance requirements between congregate residences, exclusionary definitions of "family," and outright exclusions from all types of neighborhoods of people living with AIDS or recovering from drug and alcohol addictions.

The ADA includes zoning and land use commissions in its coverage of political entities. Because of the ADA, these commissions must now conduct self-evaluations of how their policies and practices limit the rights of individuals with disabilities. Both case law and state attorney general opinions that have incorporated the provisions of the FHAA now provide substantial guidance and information on how state, local, and county officials must incorporate regulations and practices for compliance with the mandates of the ADA into their reviews of zoning and land use laws. The Mental Health Law Project (1900) has published an Index of court decisions and state attorney general opinions on this topic that may be obtained at no cost. Prentice Hall's "Fair Housing—Fair Lending" series also publishes the majority of these materials. In addition, the Housing and Civil Enforcement Section of the Department of Justice's Civil Rights Division provides both information and litigation assistance on these matters.

INNOVATIVE APPROACHES TO HOUSING DISCRIMINATION

Homelessness, at least among people with mental illness, is an issue that public policy makers have addressed primarily as a mental health issue. The ADA suggests a new approach. Like Section 504 and the FHAA, it requires that public officials stop creating programs that address the disability rather than the person, a change of focus that has already taken place, for example, in education.

Before the enactment of Section 504 and the Individuals with Disabilities Education Act of 1992 (originally the Education for All Handicapped Children Act of 1975), school officials routinely segregated students according to their disabilities, denying them the option of attending school with their peers, and creating special classrooms and facilities to which they then were assigned. Officials acted as if the most important fact about a student with a disability was his or her disability. The result was as damning and damaging as was segregation for African-Americans (Cook, 1991, pp. 393, 409ff). In debating the ADA, members of Congress referred often to *Brown v. Board of Education* (1954) to emphasize their sense that the ADA's eradication of disability segregation was as important as eliminating racial discrimination, and for the same reasons.

By focusing only on the mental impairment of a homeless person, the person's disability is seen as the cause of his or her homelessness, and mental health treatment as his or her primary need. The result of this treatment-oriented policy has been obvious: people remain homeless and their cure-oriented politicians and health professionals remain frustrated. With the ADA it will be possible to reorient attention and resources toward integration and equal opportunity models that will include consumer-driven choices about mental and physical health treatment.

The fact that the ADA is based on and extends the coverage of Section 504 supports this conclusion. In its enactment of the ADA, Congress restated its intent that Section 504 facilitate the integration of people with disabilities and characterized the ADA as a vehicle to ensure the continued implementation of Section 504's integration mandate. The ADA prohibits discrimination against persons with disabilities by both federally funded and non–federally funded entities. For a general discussion of the history and purpose of the act, see Cook (1991). The plain language of the ADA notes the historic "isolat[ion] and segregat[ion]" of people with disabilities and characterizes these practices as "forms of discrimination that continue to be a serious and pervasive social problem" (42 U.S.C. §12101[a][2]). Congress intended the ADA "to provide a clear and comprehensive national mandate" (42 US.C. §12101[b][1]) to eliminate segregation and other forms of discrimination against individuals with disabilities, "to provide clear, strong, consistent, enforceable standards addressing discrimination" (42 U.S.C. §12101[b][2]; see also Cook, 1991, p. 417), and to "reverse . . . practices [of segregation], root and branch, and to eliminate their legacy" (U.S. House of Representatives, 1990).

The ADA's legislative history reiterates Congress's goal of full integration for people with disabilities (Cook, 1991, pp. 409–416). Congressional committees recognized segregation as "humiliating" (U.S. House of Representatives Committee on Education and Labor, 1990, p. 47) and "one of the most debilitating forms of discrimination" (U.S. Senate Committee on Labor and Human Resources, 1989, p. 6). In addition, Congress made clear that *both* Section 504 and the ADA were intended to eradicate segregation. Under Title II of the ADA, codified at 42 U.S.C. §§12131–12161, no "qualified individual with a disability" may be "excluded from participation in or . . . denied the benefits of the services, programs or activities" of state or local governments or be otherwise "subjected to discrimination" (42 U.S.C. §12132). In addressing the obligations of state and local governments under Title II of the ADA, the House Judiciary Committee stated:

> Section 504 of the Rehabilitation Act has served not only to open up public services and programs to people with disabilities but has also been used to end segregation. The purpose of Title II is to continue to break down barriers to the integrated participation of people with disabilities in all aspects of community life . . . . As with Section 504 of the Rehabilitation Act, integrated services are

essential to accomplishing the purpose of Title II . . . . [T]he goal [is to] eradicat[e] the invisibility of the handicapped. Separate-but-equal services do not accomplish this central goal and should be rejected. (U.S. House of Representatives Committee on the Judiciary, 1990, pp. 49–50)

In addition, Congress made clear that neither Section 504 nor the ADA would allow state and local governments to use administrative or financial costs as an excuse to avoid integrating people with disabilities into the community:

> The fact that it is more convenient, either administratively or fiscally, to provide services in a segregated manner, does not constitute a valid justification for separate or different services under Section 504 of the Rehabilitation Act or under this title. Nor is the fact that the separate service is equal to or better than the service offered to others sufficient justification for involuntary different treatment for persons with disabilities. While Section 504 . . . and this title do not prohibit the existence of all separate services which are designed to provide a benefit for persons with disabilities . . . the existence of such programs can never be used as a basis to exclude a person with a disability from a program that is offered to persons without disabilities, or to refuse to provide an accommodation in a regular setting. (U.S. House of Representatives Committee on the Judiciary, 1990, p. 50)

Thus both the plain language and the legislative history of the ADA demonstrate that Congress considered the unnecessary exclusion of people with disabilities as a continuing form of discrimination, that it viewed Section 504 as requiring integrated services for people with disabilities, and that it intended the ADA as an additional tool to eradicate disability segregation (see, generally, Cook, 1991).

The remainder of this section uses the Massachusetts Department of Mental Health (MDMH) as a backdrop against which to demonstrate one example of how the ADA may be used to redefine "the homeless mentally ill" as housing consumers with a mental disability. In a challenge to the MDMH, *Williams et al. v. Forsberg* (1991), a coalition of homeless Massachusetts residents and their advocates alleged that the state mental health system was violating state and federal law by precluding the existence of comprehensive community mental health services, ignoring state planning mandates, subjecting the plaintiffs to both unnecessary institutionalization and dangerous postdischarge conditions, and violating the plaintiffs' rights to meaningful integration into their communities as required by the ADA.[4] The lawsuit was based on the analysis that follows, which concludes that, by operating according to a "medical model" that attempts to "cure" its clients' mental disabilities, the MDMH has denied the plaintiffs their right to integrated housing, has perpetuated their homelessness, and has misdirected financial and human resources away from housing and maintaining them in their communities. Although this discussion is limited to events in the state of Massachusetts, the methods of operation of the MDMH do not differ significantly from those of other state mental health agencies. Thus this example may be instructive for readers in other states.

The Inside-Out Service System of the MDMH

The medical model on which the mental health system operated by the MDMH is based regularly contributes to homelessness among people with mental illness both directly and indirectly. The system has historically, conceptually, and financially always started with hospitals. Only then, almost as an afterthought, has it considered other options for allowing people with mental health problems to continue or resume functioning as contributing citizens in their communities. The results of such a hospital-centered, doctor-driven approach are, as a matter of resource allocation, quite appalling. The MDMH expends 42% of its resource (over $192 million) on inpatient care that services only 6 percent of its clients (Governor's Special Commission on Consolidation of Health and Human Services Institutional Facilities, 1991, p. 3). As of May, 1991, there were 2,156 inpa-

---

[4]The remainder of this chapter has previously appeared in Hitov, S.A. (1992, Spring/Summer). Ending homelessness: New England and beyond. *New England Journal of Public Policy*, 599–612; reprinted by permission.

tients (MDMH, 1991, p. 117); over 500 of those were people being detained solely because the MDMH had not located or developed sufficient community placements for them (Governor's Special Commission, 1991, p. 3). Thus, in addition to spending enormous amounts of money on a tiny fraction of its clients, the MDMH expends almost 25% of that sum (over $45 million) on people who it admits do not require and almost certainly do not desire such care.

Unfortunately, the misallocation of financial resources is not the only, nor even necessarily the most egregious, cost of the MDMH service delivery system. Although, pursuant to Massachusetts General Law chapter 123 (1990), Massachusetts in theory has both voluntary (§10) and involuntary (§§7, 8, 11, 12) inpatients, it is the practice of MDMH facilities not to accept purely voluntary patients. Thus a person is either brought to a facility against his or her will and admitted and retained pursuant to §§7, 8, and 12 or voluntarily seeks treatment and is admitted pursuant to §11 on a "conditional voluntary" basis. Under §11 a person is not free to leave if he or she is dissatisfied with the care but rather must give the facility 3 days' written notice of the intention to leave. During this period the facility may petition a court to have the person committed pursuant to §§7 and 8. Because the court hearing need not be, and most often is not, scheduled for 14 days after the MDMH request, a person who enters a facility "voluntarily" can be forced to remain for up to 17 days against his or her will without any opportunity for impartial review.

The hospital-centered medical model views life in the community as a privilege to be earned by those who have required hospitalization. All MDMH inpatients, regardless of their condition, start with enforced confinement on a locked ward (sometimes in seclusion) and then proceed to earn the "privilege" (so described by the MDMH Inpatient Policy Manual) of increased freedom. Initially a person may be given permission to go to unlocked parts of the facility, then onto the grounds, and ultimately to visit the community. At all times, however, even this limited freedom is subject to the person's willingness and ability to comply with all of a facility's rules, no matter how petty or seemingly unrelated to treatment. Independence, either of thought or action, is not a characteristic highly valued, or wisely exhibited, within a MDMH facility. The inpatient system is so control oriented that, regardless of treatment needs, facilities have been known to discharge people directly to the streets or to shelters, even in the dead of winter, because of perceived violations of "program" rules (e.g., taking legal but unprescribed medications). In short, the inpatient system is one in which clients are afforded only rudimentary rights and in which client choice has little or no meaningful role.

If one then views community placement, as does the MDMH, as a person's "next step" following such an inpatient experience, it is not surprising that the MDMH has chosen to develop "programs" rather than housing for those seeking to return to the community. Of the approximately 3,255 people now being served in MDMH residential settings (Governor's Special Commission, 1991, p. 3), probably fewer than 100 are residing in the MDMH's most touted independent living initiative: apartments administered by the Massachusetts Housing Finance Agency (MHFA) to which the MDMH and the Massachusetts Department of Mental Retardation (MDMR) have negotiated access (Governor's Special Commission, 1991, p. 33). This arrangement has resulted in a total of less than 140 apartments being occupied by clients of the MDMH and the MDMR. Less than 25 of those apartments are subsidized, which, given the substantial market rents charged by MHFA developments, means that the vast majority of independent living situations being provided by the MDMH are going to its wealthier clients. MHFA market-rent apartments are not a financially viable option for the homeless even if they could get accepted for occupancy at such developments. The vast majority of people who count on the MDMH for residence in the community are living not in houses but in programs.

Programs differ from housing in several critical respects in both human and financial/development terms. First and foremost, programs reflect the medical model mentality that perceives people with mental disabilities as perpetual patients, with the resultant infantilization that so often accompanies that status. Additionally, or perhaps merely as an example of that infantilization, programs often require unrelated adults to share not only their housing but even their bedrooms. Nearly 65% of the settings for MDMH residential services are located in buildings in which only other MDMH clients live (MDMH, 1991, p. 119). In nearly a third of those settings, people are forced to share their bedrooms with someone not of their choosing (MDMH, 1991, p. 119). This is not how most adults choose to live, and even the MDMH recognizes that such an arrangement is often clinically dysfunctional (MDMH, 1991, p. 119).

Groups of eight unrelated adults ordinarily do not choose to live together. Nonetheless, communal living is exactly what the MDMH demands of most of its clients in residential programs. The stress of such an environment is compounded by the fact that a person must conform not only to the norms of general tenancy but also to any treatment requirements the MDMH decides must accompany the program. In this way, programs perpetuate the control and compliance regimens of the inpatient facilities. Should a person decide that he or she does not like or no longer needs the type of treatment that is being offered in a given program, he or she is faced not only with the loss of services but also with the specter of imminent homelessness. (As a further reflection of the fact that such programs are not really housing in any meaningful sense, the MDMH—and unfortunately some courts—take the position that people living in MDMH residential settings are not entitled to the protections of Massachusetts landlord–tenant law before they can be removed from a program.) This is hardly an environment in which one is led to question the services that are being rendered. As a result, consumer choice and input and ultimately the quality of any services offered are also victims of the current MDMH system.

Conversely, but of equal importance, some persons may be quite happy with a given program and therefore flourish in it. If a person has come to consider a program of a given intensity level to be his or her home, and thrives there, he or she risks being removed for that very reason so that someone more needy can benefit from the program. The tenant, however, is likely to be distraught at the prospect of losing perhaps the first true home he or she has known. Perversely, this possibility builds in an incentive not to do too well in persons who indeed like the program in which they are placed. Thus, even when a program is apparently "successful," it may nonetheless prove in the long run to be injurious.

In a recent review of the current MDMH system, a Special Commission appointed by the Governor recognized that more community placements must be developed (Governor's Special Commission, 1991). However, the Commission identified two major problems in accomplishing the creation of those placements. Both, as it turns out, are problems that exist solely because of the limited approach to community care that is employed by the MDMH. First, because so many of the MDMH's present and projected residential settings are program oriented and congregate in nature, they require substantial lead time and money just to acquire and/or develop the property in which they operate.

Unfortunately, as the Commission Report also recognizes, the problems for the typical MDMH community residential program do not end when the money has been found to finance it. Because the programs so often create congregations of MDMH clients, the now familiar NIMBY syndrome regularly rears its provincial head. Neighborhoods and even whole cities all too frequently attempt to erect barriers to the siting of community residences. Although the law is increasingly clear that such efforts are illegal, defeating them and winning over the neighborhood is both difficult and time-consuming work. Moreover, it is work that often turns what should be a very private affair (i.e., a person's desired choice of residence) into a public if not a political debate. This process only exacerbates the already lengthy delays inherent in developing necessary community resources.

The inability of the current community residential system to respond on an "as-needed" basis has a disproportionate negative impact on homeless individuals with mental disabilities, many of whom are "pink papered" (i.e., forcibly admitted under the involuntary hospitalization provision of Massachusetts General Law chapter 123, §12) to MDMH inpatient facilities following acute psychiatric episodes on the street. Such individuals by definition enter the facilities in need of housing as well as acute care, but their inpatient stays are often quite short, varying in length from overnight to 1 or 2 weeks. As a matter of law, people admitted in this fashion are entitled to an individualized service plan (ISP) designed to assess and address both their medical and social needs (pursuant to 104 C.M.R. §16.03[2][c], anyone admitted to a MDMH inpatient facility under Massachusetts General Law chapter 123 §§10, 11, or 12 "shall be eligible for . . . an ISP . . . ." The goals of the ISP process are set forth at 104 C.M.R. §16.01[2]). In practice, however, ISPs are almost never afforded to such short-term inpatients. As a consequence, homeless individuals with mental disabilities receive virtually no assistance even in applying for the public benefit programs for which they may be eligible before they are again discharged. Furthermore, because of the chronic shortage of community placements and the inherent difficulty of creating and siting new ones of the type now most often utilized, the MDMH maintains lengthy waiting lists for such placements. As a result, homeless individuals who have been "pink papered" to MDMH facilities are regularly discharged by those facilities right back to the street or to an emergency shelter for singles. As one might easily predict, many of those so discharged quickly wind up back in the facility, often in worse condition than on their initial admission.

In summary, presumably not through malevolence but largely as a result of its outdated focus and inflexible community residential system, the MDMH has managed to create a world in which it unnecessarily detains 500 citizens in its facilities against their wishes and simultaneously discharges homeless people with mental disabilities directly back to the very environment that contributed to their admissions in the first place. It is a world that is literally and figuratively inside out. It does not assume that a citizen with a mental health problem is entitled to a place in the community just like any other citizen. Rather, its focus and starting point are the inside of a locked facility from which a person must earn his or her way "out" to the community. The present system constantly undermines independence by demanding and rewarding compliance in the guise of teaching personal responsibility and enforces that demand by tying it directly to the provision of housing. It is a system that is both enormously expensive and wasteful at least in part because it continues to elevate the perceived need for treatment above the obvious need for food and housing. In short, it is a system in need of a total overhaul if it is ever to achieve the national goal set forth in the ADA of integrating as many individuals with disabilities as possible, as fully as possible, back into the community.

Providing Housing with Desired Supports

As the Governor's Special Commission (1991) has determined, citizens with mental disabilities are both better and more efficiently served in their community. This conclusion has been embraced by the National Institute of Mental Health as a matter of public policy (Stockdill, 1987) and is now a matter of law under the ADA. The sections of the ADA that govern the provision of government services, including mental health services, took effect on January 26, 1992. The legislative history of the Act makes it clear that Congress intends services to be provided in the most integrated setting possible even if to do so is either logistically or financially less convenient for the provider (U.S. House of Representatives Committee on the Judiciary, 1990, p. 50).

The cornerstone of a functional community mental health system must be stable housing that is not conditioned on a person's willingness to participate in treatment. The separation of housing from treatment will foster the very independence that the MDMH purports to desire because it will for the first time allow services to be consumer driven. When not faced with the Hobson's choice of taking whatever services are offered in order to be housed or rejecting those services and facing homelessness, people will clearly indicate which services they find helpful by utilizing those that are and rejecting those that are not. This is not to say that persuasion should be forsaken as an option or that people should not be made aware of the possible adverse consequences of any given course of conduct. However, it will force such persuasion to be just that, and not coercion. Such an approach, in turn, will offer MDMH planners useful guidance in future program development and will offer private, not-for-profit providers a market incentive to be responsive to the perceived needs and preferences of their consumers. In short, citizens with mental disabilities will actually have a meaningful voice in meeting their needs.

If housing is to be the foundation of the community mental health system, how is it best to be provided? The answer to this question must take into consideration the problems that citizens with mental disabilities have traditionally experienced in gaining access to housing. The MDMH has realized since at least 1985 that part of the cause of homelessness among those with mental disabilities is that such people regularly lose out when competing with the general populace for any scarce resource, especially housing (MDMH, 1985, p. 130). Thus the housing provided in conjunction with a true community mental health system must be designed to afford the target population the greatest choice possible in order to redress the past and present proclivity of society (and the MDMH) to segregate those with mental health problems. Next, it must be reasonably plentiful so the MDMH can eliminate the dual shameful practices of unnecessarily detaining individuals who do not require inpatient care and discharging vulnerable people directly to the streets or to overcrowded and devitalizing homeless shelters. Finally, but of paramount importance if the system is to address the issue of homelessness among persons with mental disabilities, the housing must be affordable.

Fortunately, an option exists that would meet all of the above criteria. Rather than attempting to "develop" either residential milieus or even housing, the MDMH could immediately implement a housing subsidy program funded, if necessary, entirely with current mental health dollars. The program would operate much like the federal Section 8 Existing Housing program, which requires a person to pay no more than 30% of his or her income toward a predetermined fair market rent for private housing that already exists in the community and then pays the landlord the difference between the tenant's share and the fair market rent. The program would be available only to those eligible to receive services from the MDMH who lack an appropriate place to call home. If financially necessary, it could be further limited to the MDMH's priority population—those with a serious or long-term mental impairment. Thus there would be a finite population eligible for such a housing benefit and they would not be competing with the general population to acquire it.

Because the MDMH and its doctors believe themselves capable of defining and recognizing mental illness, a major problem in operating a general housing program is thereby overcome. In seeking to assist the general homeless population through various housing initiatives, Massachusetts has felt constrained to develop elaborate and often bizarre definitions of the "worthy" homeless in order to protect itself from what it believes would otherwise be an epidemic of voluntarily induced homelessness endured solely to gain access to affordable housing. It is highly unlikely that, even for the substantial benefit of affordable housing, someone would voluntarily seek the stigma still associated with mental illness. Even if a person were to do so, however, he or she presumably would not be able to fool a MDMH doctor. Hence quality control should not be a significant problem in the proposed program. The MDMH estimates that a maximum of 12,000 people could be eligible if affordable housing were provided to all needy MDMH clients (Governor's Special Commission, 1991, p. 28).

Included in the eligible population, whether defined broadly or narrowly, would always be those who have been admitted as inpatients at a MDMH facility. This, in conjunction with the housing search and other ISP services discussed below, should completely eliminate both the long waiting lists for placement and the discharge of homeless people to the streets or shelters. Few have claimed that there is a shortage of housing in this country; it is only claimed that there is a critical shortage of affordable housing. By operating its own subsidy program, the MDMH would gain for its clients ready access to the entire private housing market, which, especially when the rental market is soft, is only too eager to rent to those whose rent payments are government guaranteed. Because the subsidies would be mobile and would travel with the citizen with mental disabilities, the program would also accomplish community integration to the maximum extent possible while achieving the generally accepted programmatic benefit of having service dollars follow the beneficiary, not the provider. Finally, the subsidy must not be tied to the acceptance of treatment or services of any kind. Rather, it would be available to anyone who was a MDMH (priority) client and lacked a suitable place to live. Although clients might reasonably be required to hear about what other services existed, they would be entirely free to reject them all and accept only the housing subsidy.

Among the services available must be knowledgeable and flexible assistance in searching for habitable housing. Whereas such a service would assist people to find housing, it would not decide which housing a person would choose nor would it decide with whom, if anybody, the person should live. It would be acceptable if two or more people should choose to live together, but such a living arrangement would never be forced on anyone. The Massachusetts experience with using housing search workers employed by the Department of Public Welfare (MDPW) to help homeless families locate qualifying apartments is quite instructive regarding the value of this kind of assistance, as is the method utilized within the Homelessness Unit of Greater Boston Legal Services (GBLS). In the Section 8 program a housing subsidy certificate is valid for no more than 4 months. If a person is not able to find a qualifying apartment within that period, the person's right to a subsidy expires and the certificate is given to the next person on the waiting list. (There would be no purpose for such a time limit in the program run by the MDMH. Unlike in the Section 8 program, the number of eligible people is relatively small, and a subsidy would be offered to everyone who needs one. Thus there would be no need to pass the subsidy along if it were not converted into an apartment within a fixed period of time.) Before the recent softening of the housing market, only about 50% of the unassisted families with Section 8 certificates were successful in renting apartments before their certificates expired. In contrast, over 90% of the families who had housing search workers assigned by the MDPW were able to rent accommodations within the same time frame. This discrepancy in results reflects the irrational and labyrinthine nature of the country's affordable housing system and demonstrates graphically that it takes professional help for almost anyone to negotiate it successfully.

This fact has led the Homelessness Unit of GBLS to develop its own demonstration program. Once GBLS is successful in acquiring a housing subsidy for a client, it assigns a student intern from the Boston University School of Social Work to assist that person locating a qualifying apartment owned by a landlord willing to participate in the program. As interns in a law office, the students can offer their opinions to clients, but ultimately it is the client's wishes that control. If a client chooses to make a "bad" decision, that is his or her right. In fact, clients have made very few such decisions (at least in the author's opinion) and have proved to be every bit as diligent and creative in their housing search as one might expect from persons afforded the possibility of access to decent, affordable homes for perhaps the first time in their lives.

Nonetheless, the social work students play a valuable role in the process. First, they provide a nonjudgmental companion with whom the homeless person with disabilities can share any anxieties that he or she may be experiencing in the search process. They also provide a "professional" presence when the client interviews for a particular apartment, thus overcoming or easing the unfounded fears that a landlord may have about dealing with a person with mental disabilities. Finally, the students are willing "to do what it takes" to ensure a successful result (to borrow a phrase from the Vermont-based Center for Community Change Through Housing and Support, a pioneering organization in the sorts of solutions suggested here). So far, included in this category have been such endeavors as helping a client acquire and move furniture on a Saturday, purchasing two telephones for a client (one was stolen on the client's last night in a singles shelter) so that she would not feel isolated in the new apartment, and arranging to repair a broken television to provide a client with some entertainment and/or company. This is exactly the sort of hands-on approach that is sometimes necessary, that the ADA requires (28 C.F.R. §35.130 *passim*), and that the MDMH must be willing to provide.

Again, the mechanism already exists to do the sort of housing search that will ensure that the proposed MDMH subsidy system will work. The MDMH employs large numbers of (although not enough) case managers who are supposed to help plan an inpatient's smooth return to the community. In addition, the MDMH should hire ex-patients as case managers and assistants to case managers, thereby bringing a wealth of experience and understanding to the job of "doing what it takes" in a nonjudgmental manner. As one such Consumer Case Manager from New York recently (ironically) explained it, his employment has allowed him to look back on his 20 years of institutionalization not simply as a maddening waste of his life but also as on-the-job training for his new endeavors (Gelman, 1991).

Once the MDMH has, as part of its mission and raison d'être, provided affordable housing, facilitated access to public benefit programs, and/or offered employment to those who need and desire such assistance, it can begin to offer other treatment-oriented services to assist these persons to maintain and enjoy their places in the community. As discussed earlier, these services will for the first time be consumer driven and therefore will more likely exhibit the flexibility necessary to accommodate the individual needs and preferences of the people they are designed to serve.

In 1989 the Community Center for Change Through Housing and Support conducted a national survey of 378 supported housing programs (Community Center for Change Through Housing and Support, 1991). It evaluated programs using criteria that included basing housing on people's choices, using integrated regular housing, providing flexible supports, not imposing program requirements, and maintaining housing during periods of crisis or hospitalization. In other words, it looked for and found programs operated pursuant to the approaches described in this chapter. The survey discovered that individuals served in supported housing settings tended to be more, not less, disabled than those served in more traditional residential programs. Because the system is premised on stable, varied housing options buttressed by flexible service supports, the severity of the handicap that can be accommodated is limited only by the creativity of those providing support.

Nor would a model premised on the provision of a housing subsidy to each MDMH client who lacked a home cost any more than the current system. Indeed, it could operate much more effectively than the present system for less money than is now being spent. Exactly how much money the proposed model would cost in the long run is largely unknown because the calculation depends on many policy decisions concerning the nature and quality of supports that would be made along the way. The study by the Center for Community Change Through Housing and Support (1991) found that, as the severity of the impairments being accommodated increased, so did the cost of providing such accommodation. Thus this model could be made to cost as much as the one used now by the MDMH, but it would provide more complete and effective services. The Center therefore suggests that the supported model may not always be less expensive, but it will never be more expensive for any given level of care. In all cases, moreover, because of the underlying human assumptions of the model, it will provide better care for each dollar expended.

The median fair market rent (FMR) for a studio apartment in Massachusetts is $465 and that for a one-bedroom apartment is $561. This would represent the MDMH's maximum liability per person and would almost always be reduced by one or both of the following factors. First, the tenant would contribute 30% of his or her income toward the cost of the apartment. If the person were receiving, for example, Supplemental Security Income at the current rate of $520 per month, the tenant's share would be approximately $160 per month, which would reduce the cost of a one-bedroom apartment to the MDMH, even based on the full median FMR, to $401 per month. Thus, a single person could be subsidized in his or her own apartment in Massachusetts for less than $5,000 per year. This is an incredible bargain when one considers that the cost to the Commonwealth (although not the total cost) of maintaining each person in the state's largest singles shelter is $30 per night, or nearly $1,000 per month. However, especially in a soft market, apartments are almost always available for less than the FMR in any particular area. Although the 1990 one-bedroom apartment FMR for Medford (a city within 5 miles of Boston) was $739, the actual average rent of all the Section 8 one-bedroom apartments administered by the Medford Housing Authority that year was just under $510 per month. When the predictable tenant share is deducted from this figure, the cost to the MDMH is even less.

Most dramatically, however, a MDMH subsidy program would benefit the "homeless mentally ill." The medical model looks at this group and sees people with mental disabilities who happen to be homeless. Starting from this perspective, it attempts to "cure," or at least control, the illness and has little professional interest in housing those for whom treatment proves unavailing. A true community model of care based on affordable housing would view the same group as homeless people who happen to have a mental disability. Even, or perhaps especially, if their homelessness is caused by or related to their mental disabilities, it makes absolutely no sense either medically or socially to ignore the symptom (homelessness) because the infirmity cannot be corrected. A similar approach with regard to a physical disability would have doctors refusing to prescribe pain killers for a person with a chronically bad back because they could not, or the patient would not let them, diagnose or cure the cause of the pain. Each of these approaches is equally absurd, but only the former is in fact practiced. A person's mental disability may help explain why he or she is homeless if he or she has been asked to compete in the open market for housing, but it is no indication that he or she cannot live in the community if reasonable accommodation is made for his or her handicap. A subsidized housing program exclusively for those with mental disabilities is just such an accommodation.

Thus the MDMH should provide a subsidy to each of its clients who require one in order to avoid homelessness, whether or not the person is interested in any of the other services that the agency may have to offer. This is exactly the approach that has been undertaken in both Ohio and parts of New York and that is getting rave reviews from the mental health professionals responsible for administering the programs (Lewis, 1991; Meyers, 1991). Indeed, exhibiting a rationality rarely demonstrated by a bureaucracy, New York has included such assistance as a furniture grant and an emergency needs fund to ensure that those it discharges from its inpatient facilities do not end up both with mental disabilities and homeless. The essential point is that, even if the former condition is considered a given, the latter need not be. Arguing that "improved service rather than enhanced liberty should be the priority," an assistant legal counsel to the New York State Office of Mental Health has urged the mental health community to follow the example of the ADA proponents to achieve consensus and verbal support to address deficiencies in the mental health system (Haimowitz, 1991).

Equipped with the proper perspective, a targeted subsidy program, and flexible supports, the MDMH could end homelessness among the Commonwealth's population with mental disabilities almost immediately. Furthermore, it could do so without spending any more, and perhaps spending less, money than is now the case. At a time when its delivery system already is being reexamined, the MDMH should jettison its reliance on a medical model that has arguably contributed to, but unarguably failed to address, the problem of homelessness among those with mental disabilities. By adopting a subsidy system just for its clients with services developed to address their expressed needs, the MDMH would provide better care, integrate and empower persons with disabilities as the ADA now requires, and, perhaps most importantly, end homelessness among that portion of the Commonwealth's population for which the MDMH is legally responsible.

CONCLUSION

Even if long overdue, the ADA is nonetheless the broadest and noblest enactment since the Civil Rights Act of 1964, which established the machinery for the full integration of racial minorities into American society. For the first time Congress has mandated that segregation and distinctions made on the basis of disability, whether motivated by animus or the best of intentions, must be measured as are those made on the basis of race (42 U.S.C. §12101[a][7]: "individuals with disabilities are a discrete and insular minority . . ."). The language chosen in §12101(a)(7) is taken verbatim from Chief Justice Stone's famous footnote in *United States v. Carolene Products Co.* (1938) and has served universally ever since as the factor that compels a court to apply strict scrutiny to any state efforts to treat members of a given minority differently from how it treats those who do not belong to the group. As the Supreme Court recently stated in *Molzof v. United States* (1992), it is a "cardinal rule of statutory construction" that, when Congress adopts such a term of specific legal significance from the common law into one of its enactments:

> it presumably knows and adopts the cluster of ideas that were attached to each borrowed word in the learning from which it was taken and the meaning its use will convey to the judicial mind unless otherwise instructed. In such case, absence of contrary direction may be taken as satisfaction with widely accepted definitions, not as a departure from them (*Morissette v. United States*, 1952; *Molzof v. United States*, 1992, pp. 4082–4083)

As written, the ADA is a statute of breathtaking scope: one that for the first time affords people with disabilities the promise of meaningful access to virtually every nook and cranny of the community and the opportunity, finally, to make their own choices regarding where they will live, eat, work, travel, and receive any services they may need to accomplish full participation in everyday life. The ADA caps 18 years of radical developments in the rights of people with disabilities. Each of the federal and state laws that has been enacted, beginning with Section 504 of the Rehabilitation Act and including the FHAA, has succeeded in more effectively integrating people with disabilities into the mainstream of American life.

As we have tried to show, the goals and benefits achievable through the FHAA and the ADA can be used to supplement and reinforce each other. Whether or not these laws prove successful is now essentially in the hands of the courts, which will inevitably be called on by both those with disabilities seeking implementation and those intent on maintaining the status quo to interpret and enforce what Congress has written.

REFERENCES

Brown v. Board of Education, 347 U.S. 483 (1954).
Burnim, I., Jackson, S., Milstein, B., & Pepper, B. (1992, January). Developments in mental disability law in 1991. *Clearinghouse Review, 25*(9), 1218–1231.
Cason v. Rochester Housing Authority, 748 F. Supp. 1002 (W.D.N.Y. 1990).
Citizens Commission on Civil Rights. (1989). *One nation indivisible.* Washington, DC: Author.
Citizens Commission on Civil Rights. (1991). *Lost opportunities: The civil rights record of the Bush administration midterm.* Washington, DC: Author.
Civil Rights Act of 1964 (codified as amended in scattered sections of 42 U.S.C.).
Community Center for Change through Housing and Support. (1991, June). *In Community, 1,* 6.
Cook, T. (1991). The Americans with Disabilities Act of 1990; The move to integration. *Temple Law Review, 64*(2) 393–469.
CRM Management, Inc. v. Carol Day, No. 91-SP-1300, Mass. Trial Court, Hampden Div. (June 26, 1991).
Education for All Handicapped Children Act of 1975, 20 U.S.C. §§1232, 1401, 1405–1420, 1453 (1975).
Gelman, D. (1991, May 29). *Statement at the Ninth National CSP Learning Community Conference.* Washington, DC.
Governor's Special Commission on Consolidation of Health and Human Services Institutional Facilities (1991). *Actions for quality care, executive summary.* Boston: Author.
Haimowitz, S. (1991). Americans with Disabilities Act of 1990: Its significance for persons with mental illness. *Hospital and Community Psychiatry, 42,* 1200–1202.
Individuals with Disabilities Education Act of 1992, 20 U.S.C. §1400 *et seq.* (1992).

Lewis, G. (1991, May 30). Statement delivered at the Ninth National CSP Learning Community Conference, Washington, DC.

Massachusetts Department of Mental Health. (1985). *Homelessness needs assessment, executive summary* (p. 130). Boston: Author.

Massachusetts Department of Mental Health. (1991). *Comprehensive mental health service plan* (ed. 4.0, p. 117). Boston: Author.

Mental Health Law Project. (1990, January). Mental disability law developments. *Clearinghouse Review, 23*(9)1214–1221.

Mental Health Law Project. (1991, January). Developments in mental disability law—1990. *Clearinghouse Review, 24*(9)959–970.

Mental Health Law Project. (1992, February). Index of resource materials on fair housing for people with disabilities (pp. 1–22). Washington, DC: Author.

Meyers, R. (1991, May 30). *Statement delivered at the Ninth National CSP Learning Community Conference.* Washington, DC.

Milstein, B., Pepper, B., & Rubenstein, L. (1989, June). The Fair Housing Act of 1988: What it means for people with mental disabilities. *Clearinghouse Review 23*(2)128–140.

Molzof v. United States, 60 1.W. 4081, 4082–83 (January 14, 1992).

Morisette v. United States, 342 U.S. 246, 263 (1952).

Peabody Properties v. Jeffries, No. 88-SP-7613-S, Mass. Trial. Ct., Housing Ct., Hampden Div. (Feb. 13, 1989).

Rehabilitation Act of 1973, 29 U.S.C. §§791–794 (1988 & Supp. I 1989).

School Board of Nassau County, Fla. v. Arline, 107 S.Ct. 1123 (1987).

Simring, R.B., (1991, January). The impact of federal antidiscrimination laws on housing for people with mental disabilities. *George Washington Law Review 59*(2)413–450.

Stockdill, J. (1987). *Guiding principles for meeting the housing needs of people with psychiatric disabilities (Technical assistance transmittal from the National Institute of Mental Health to state mental health directors).* Bethesda, MD: National Institute of Mental Health.

United States v. Carolene Products Co., 304 U.S. 144, 153 n. 4 (1938).

U.S. Architectural and Transportation Barriers Compliance Board. (1991, July 26). Americans with Disabilities Act (ADA) accessibility guidelines for buildings and facilities; final guidelines. *Federal Register, 56,* 35407–35453.

U.S. Department of Housing and Urban Development. (1990, September 12). *The state of fair housing: Report to the Congress pursuant to section 808(e) of the Fair Housing Act.* Washington, DC: U.S. Government Printing Office.

U.S. Department of Housing and Urban Development. (1991). *Public and Indian housing handbook.* Washington, DC: U.S. Government Printing Office.

U.S. Department of Housing and Urban Development, Office of the Assistant Secretary, Equal Opportunity. (1992). Discriminatory conduct under the Fair Housing Act. In *Code of Federal Regulations* (24: Housing and Urban Development, pp. 779–795). Washington, DC: U.S. Government Printing Office.

U.S. Department of Housing and Urban Development, Office of the Secretary. (1988). Nondiscrimination based on handicap in federally assisted programs and activities of the Department of Housing and Urban Development. In *Code of Federal Regulations* (24: Housing and Urban Development, pp. 65–99). Washington, DC: U.S. Government Printing Office.

U.S. Department of Housing and Urban Development, Office of the Secretary, Office of the Assistant Secretary for Fair Housing and Equal Opportunity. (1989, January 23). Implementation of the Fair Housing Amendments Act of 1988: Final rule. *Federal Register, 54,* 3231–3317.

U.S. Department of Justice. (1991a, July 26). Appendix A to Part 36—standards for accessible design: ADA accessibility guidelines for buildings and facilities. *Federal Register, 56,* 35605–35690.

U.S. Department of Justice. (1991b, July 26). Nondiscrimination on the basis of disability by public accommodations and in commercial facilities; final rule. *Federal Register, 56,* 35543–35604.

U.S. Department of Justice. (1991c, July 26). Nondiscrimination on the basis of disability in state and local government services; final rule. *Federal Register, 56,* 35693–35723.

U.S. Department of Justice. (1992). Nondiscrimination on the basis of disability in state and local government services. In *Code of Federal Regulations* (28: Judicial Administration, pp. 417–457). Washington, DC: U.S. Government Printing Office.

U.S. House of Representatives. (1990). Debate on H.R. 2273, statement of Rep. Dellums. *Congressional Record, 136,* H2639.

U.S. House of Representatives Committee on Education and Labor. (1990, May 15). *House report no. 101-485 (II), to accompany H.R. 2273 (101st Congress, 2nd session).* Washington, DC: U.S. Government Printing Office. (Reprinted in *United States Code Congressional and Administrative News, 4,* 303–444 [1990])

U.S. House of Representatives Committee on the Judiciary. (1988). *House report no. 100-711, to accompany H.R. 1158 (Fair Housing Amendments Act of 1988) (100th Congress, 2nd session).* Washington, DC: U.S. Government Printing Office.

U.S. House of Representatives Committee on the Judiciary. (1990, May 15). *House report no. 101-485 (III), to accompany H.R. 2273 (101st Congress, 2nd session).* Washington, DC: U.S. Government Printing Office. (Reprinted in *United States Code Congressional and Administrative News, 4,* 445–511 [1990])

U.S. Senate Committee on Labor and Human Resources. (1989, August 30). *Senate report no. 101-116, to accompany S. 933 (101st Congress, 1st session).* Washington, DC: U.S. Government Printing Office.

Williams et al. v. Forsberg, Civ. No. 91-3835E (Superior Ct., Suffolk Co., filed June 10, 1991).

Chapter 12

Title IV—Telecommunications

Karen Peltz Strauss

In 1934 Congress passed the Communications Act, establishing the Federal Communications Commission (FCC) and entrusting it with the responsibility of making telephone access universally accessible to all Americans. This obligation, which has come to be known as the "universal service obligation," assigned to the FCC the responsibility of "regulating interstate and foreign commerce in communication by wire and radio so as to *make available, so far as possible, to all the people of the United States a rapid, efficient, Nation-wide, and world-wide wire and radio communication service* with adequate facilities at reasonable charges" (47 U.S.C. §151 [1988], emphasis added). More than 50 years after this obligation was established, most individuals who are deaf, hard of hearing, or have speech impairments were still denied basic telephone access. Title IV of the Americans with Disabilities Act[1] (ADA) has promised to eliminate many of the barriers to this access. By requiring local and long-distance telephone companies to provide nationwide telephone relay services by July 26, 1993, the mandate of Title IV finally will enable individuals who are deaf or hard of hearing or have speech impairments to use the telephone to communicate with anyone, anywhere, at any time.

TEXT TELEPHONES AND RELAY SERVICES: DEFINITIONS AND FUNCTIONS

Text Telephones

Individuals with hearing losses or speech impairments can conduct telephone conversations by using text telephones (TTYs). A text telephone is a device with a keyboard that uses graphic communication to send or receive coded signals over radio or wire communication systems. The messages then appear on a small light-emitting diode screen at the receiving end of the telephone conversation. The term *text telephone* is a relatively new one. It is in the process of superseding the term *telecommunications device for the deaf* (TDD), which has been used, and in large part continues to be used, to describe these telephone devices. The reason for the change in terminology stems, in part, from a shift in the population that is now beginning to use text telephones. In the past, telecommunication devices *for the deaf* were considered to be for the use of deaf individuals

---

[1]Title IV of the Americans with Disabilities Act of 1990 (PL 101-336) is published in *Statutes at Large* (104 Stat. 366–369) and codified in the *United States Code* (47 U.S.C. §§225, 611 [Supp. II, 1990]). References to various portions of Title IV within this chapter cite the specific portion of the Code.

only. The new nomenclature makes clear that other individuals, including persons who are hard of hearing and persons with speech impairments, are just as likely to use these devices. The term *text telephones* also recognizes a recent shift to the use of computers to transmit coded signals over the telephone lines. Indeed, it was this reason, or an effort to "avoid entrenching current technology," that the FCC gave for adopting the term *text telephone* in its recent relay rules (FCC, 1991, p. 3).

The creation of the text telephone is credited to an inventor named Robert Weitbrecht, who in 1964 obtained a surplus teletypewriter from AT&T. At that time, AT&T, Western Union, and other telecommunications companies were disposing of machines that utilized the Baudot format for teletype transmissions (Potomac Telecom, Inc., 1985). The Baudot format—developed around the time of the invention of the telephone itself—had been considered the international standard for telegraphic communications until the 1950s (Jensema, 1988). In 1968, a new format—the American Standard Code for Information Interchange (ASCII)—took over as the new standard for computer transmissions. The limited functions of the Baudot code simply could not survive the need for sophisticated computer transmissions of which the ASCII code was capable. Weitbrecht, deaf himself, seized the opportunity to use the otherwise obsolete Baudot machines for the deaf population. He invented an acoustic coupler to attach these outdated teletype machines to conventional telephones, enabling individuals who are deaf, for the first time, to communicate in print across telephone wires.

In 1974, an individual named Lee Brody invented a means by which text telephones could be used with braille, enabling individuals who are deaf and blind to use the text telephone network. These machines are commonly known as telebrailles. Unfortunately, the high cost of these machines—averaging several thousand dollars each—has limited their availability and put their continued existence in jeopardy.

The teletypewriter machines of the 1960s were heavy, large, and noisy. In the early 1970s a quieter, smaller machine able to display the digital readout on a screen was introduced. However, the spread of even these portable machines did not actually take place until the early 1980s, when they became more reasonably priced to meet the needs of the deaf community. Since that time, other changes have dramatically improved the capabilities of text telephones. Newer text telephones are able to send messages in the ASCII format, allowing the transmission of a greater number of computer demands at a considerably faster speed than the Baudot format permits (see, generally, Starr, 1989). Moreover, the new ASCII machines permit communication to take place in both directions of a conversation simultaneously, as compared with the Baudot format, which requires the receiving party of a message to wait until the sender finishes sending that message before being able to respond.

The advantages of the ASCII system have caused many persons who are deaf and at least two nationwide organizations—the National Association of the Deaf and Telecommunications for the Deaf, Inc.—to advocate the elimination of the Baudot code for text telephone use within the next few years. For now, however, the great majority of individuals who use text telephones still rely on Baudot machines. For this reason, as discussed below, new FCC regulations[2] implementing the relay provisions of the ADA (FCC, 1991) require that all relay services be accessible to both the Baudot and the ASCII formats (47 C.F.R. §64.604[b][1]; see U.S. House of Representatives Committee on Energy and Commerce, 1990, pp. 66–67).

Relay Services

Although the invention of the text telephone opened the pathways of communication between its users, it did not eliminate the telephone barriers that existed between text telephone users and con-

---

[2]Federal Communications Commission regulations are codified at 47 C.F.R. Part 64 (1991). References to various portions of these regulations within this chapter cite the specific section of the regulations.

ventional voice telephone users. Although text telephone users could call each other, they still could not use the telephone to access businesses, employers, and others who used conventional voice telephones. Still barred from access to the general telecommunications network, these individuals again began searching for a way to bridge this gap. Relay services offered the perfect solution.

Relay services allow TTY users to converse with voice telephone users through a third party. The individual using the text telephone makes a call into the relay center, which is then handled by a relay operator, also known as a communications assistant. The communications assistant then dials the requested voice number and acts as a go-between for the two parties, speaking the text telephone user's typewritten messages to the voice party and typing the oral messages from the voice party to the text telephone user. This process also can be performed in reverse, when a voice telephone user initiates the call.

The first relay service consisted of 20 families, each of whom contributed $2.00 for the ability to relay calls to and from voice telephone users through a home-based telephone answering service (Taylor, 1988, pp. 11, 13). The home operation was able to exist for 6 months, when it realized that it could no longer handle the unexpectedly high demand for its services.

In the years that followed numerous private relay systems were created, often staffed by volunteers or low-paid workers. In one survey conducted in the early part of 1987 through the spring of 1988, evidence of the existence of over 300 relay services was gathered (a complete list of these relay services can be found in Baquis, 1988, pp. 25, 34–43). Often these relays were funded through a variety of unstable sources. For example, at one time the relay service serving Virginia received funding though local governmental appropriations, contributions from telephone companies, employee donation campaigns, foundation grants, charitable contributions and endowments, and a dance marathon (Taylor, 1988, p. 14).

Generally, the little funding that could be collected for relay systems was insufficient to meet the high demand for these services. The result was that thousands of relay requests went unanswered. As many as 60% of these early systems were able to handle only one call at a time; 22% could handle only two calls at a time (Baquis, 1988, p. 27). (This can be compared with the ability of the existing California system to handle more than 100 calls at a time.) Moreover, many of the relays placed severe limitations on the quantity, frequency, duration, and content of calls that could be made.

In January, 1987, California became the first state to open a 24-hour, 7-day-a-week relay system to service all telephone subscribers in that state. Numerous states followed California's example, and by the time the ADA was introduced in the 101st Congress, there were approximately 17 states that had begun to operate formal, statewide relay programs. So rapid was the growth of these systems that, by the time the ADA was passed, as many as 40 states either operated relay programs or had concrete plans to develop such programs within 1 or 2 years.

Why, then, the need for the relay section of the ADA? Unfortunately, although many of the states began to mandate the provision of relay services prior to the ADA's passage, most of the states were not willing to provide sufficient funding for these services. The result was that most, if not all, of these state programs fell short of meeting the basic telephone needs of individuals with hearing and speech impairments. Funding and staff shortages caused restrictions on the number, length, and types of calls that these programs would relay.

For example, some states (e.g., Arkansas) limited the length of relayed calls and rejected all personal calls (National Center for Law and the Deaf, 1989, 1990). Other states operated their systems only during daily business hours. Until they recently began their full-service relay programs, Kansas, Massachusetts and Vermont were three states that imposed this restriction (National Center for Law and the Deaf, 1989, 1990, 1991). Still other states limited the number of relayed calls that any one person was permitted to make in a given day; for example, New Hampshire limited its callers to five calls per day (National Center for Law and the Deaf, 1989,

1990). Until very recently, almost all of the state programs also suffered from high blockage rates, resulting in excessive delays and constant busy signals for relay users. Finally, questions about jurisdictional boundaries continue to prevent many of the states (e.g., Kansas, Hawaii, and Mississippi) from relaying both outgoing and incoming interstate relay calls (National Center for Law and Deafness, 1992).

Although the shortcomings of the relay programs were many, the demand for these services was overwhelming. For example, by the end of the first year of the California Relay Service's operation in 1987, the number of calls processed had increased by 305%. Similarly, call volumes in New York state increased nearly 100% in the first year of that program's operation and 167% after 16 months of operation.

HISTORY OF FEDERAL ACTIVITY IN REDUCING TELEPHONE BARRIERS

Although the states were making steady progress in the area of telecommunications relay services, this progress was painfully slow given the urgent need for these services. Thus, at the same time individual communities of persons who are deaf were working with their state legislatures and public utility commissions to develop these systems, national consumer organizations representing the interests of individuals who are deaf and hard of hearing were working to obtain results on the federal level.

Early Federal Intervention

Until the late 1970s, federal action to expand access to telecommunications services for individuals with hearing loss had been virtually nonexistent. (For a comprehensive review of federal action to expand telecommunications access for individuals with disabilities, see Strauss & Richardson, 1991.) In 1977, an organization called the National Center for Law and the Deaf petitioned the FCC to begin its first formal inquiry into the telecommunications needs of persons who are deaf. In 1978, the FCC did, in fact, open an inquiry (FCC, 1978), but then let it sit, without ever acting on the issues the inquiry had presented. Five years after its initiation, the FCC terminated this proceeding altogether (FCC, 1983).

It was not until 1982 that Congress took the first real step to address the telecommunications needs of individuals with disabilities on a national level. At that time Congress passed the Telecommunications for the Disabled Act of 1982 (PL 97-410), which, among other things, required certain telephones—considered to be "essential" to individuals with hearing loss—to be hearing aid compatible. Congress defined "essential" telephones as coin-operated telephones, telephones for emergencies, and telephones frequently needed by individuals with hearing impairments. Hearing aid–compatible telephones have electromagnetic leakage that emits certain sound waves. The leakage blocks out background sounds and high-pitched squeals that can occur with noncompatible telephones. Unfortunately, the spread of domestic and foreign telephone equipment manufacturers in the early 1980s had brought with it the increased distribution of noncompatible telephones. The 1982 act reflected Congress's effort to reverse a manufacturing trend that was beginning to preclude access to the telephone network by hearing aid users.

The 1982 act also contained provisions expressly allowing states to subsidize the cost of providing specialized telephone equipment with revenues from other telephone services. Specialized telephone equipment includes text telephones, artificial larynxes, breath-activated telephones, telebraille machines, and other devices designed to facilitate telecommunications access for individuals with disabilities. A 1980 FCC ruling requiring telephone users to pay the full costs of their telephone equipment had put these subsidies in jeopardy (see *Second Computer Inquiry*, 1982). The FCC's action to eliminate the cross-subsidization of equipment with revenues from telephone services was intended to encourage competition in the sale of telephone equipment. As

Congress noted, however, for individuals with disabilities the ban on cross-subsidization might have meant considerable price increases on the expensive equipment that they needed for access to the telephone network (U.S. House of Representatives Committee on Energy and Commerce, 1982, p. 3). The 1982 act offered some promise to these individuals that the costs of this otherwise expensive equipment might be contained. Congress stated the goal of and rationale for its actions: "One of the most frustrating aspects of hearing impairment and deafness is the inability to use telecommunications media on which modern life has grown so dependent . . . . [M]aking the benefits of the technological revolution in telecommunications available to all Americans, including those with disabilities, *should be a priority of our national telecommunications policy*" (U.S. House of Representatives Committee on Energy and Commerce, 1982, pp. 4–5, emphasis added).

Congressional action in the 1982 act held special significance for individuals with hearing disabilities. Not only was this the first time any federal body had taken concrete action to recognize the need to address the telecommunication needs of these individuals, but also it was the first time that Congress had relied on the FCC's obligation to provide universal service to order improvements in this area (U.S. House of Representatives Committee on Energy and Commerce, 1982, p. 4).

In the years following passage of the 1982 act, individuals with hearing loss insisted that the definition of "essential" telephones in that act was far too narrow to meet the needs of hearing aid users. As a consequence, in 1988, Congress passed the Hearing Aid Compatibility Act of 1988 (PL 100-394), requiring that all telephones manufactured after August 16, 1989, be compatible for use with hearing aids. In 1990 and 1992, after more consumer demand for these telephones, the FCC again expanded the requirements for hearing aid compatibility (FCC, 1990a, FCC, 1992).

Federal Involvement in the Provision of Relay Services

Notwithstanding Congress's 1982 mandate to consider the needs of individuals with hearing disabilities in national telecommunications policy, 4 more years passed before the FCC visited this issue. It was not until December 1986 that the FCC finally called together individuals who are deaf and those with other disabilities to acquire information about their telecommunications needs (FCC Public Notice No. 0626, November 13, 1986). Information gathered at this meeting prompted the FCC to adopt, in the spring of 1987, a Notice of Inquiry, requesting further comments and factual information on the provision of telecommunications services and equipment for individuals with hearing impairments (FCC, 1987). It was this proceeding that, for the first time, formally addressed the issue of relay services. Indeed, this proceeding resulted in a Further Notice of Inquiry (FNOI) issued 1 year later, in which the FCC sought specific proposals for the implementation, administration and funding of an interstate relay system (FCC, 1988).

The response to the FCC's March 1988 FNOI was uniform; virtually all of the parties who submitted comments, including hundreds of text telephone users, spoke out in support of the establishment of an interstate telephone relay service. One month later, Congress actually passed legislation requiring limited relay services. Specifically, in the Telecommunications Accessibility Enhancement Act of 1988 (PL 100-542), Congress ordered the expansion of a federal relay system for calls made to, from, and within the federal government. (Two years earlier, in August of 1986, the Architectural and Transportation Barriers Compliance Board had created a pilot Federal Relay Service for these federal calls, but this service had been understaffed and poorly publicized. The 1988 legislation transferred authority for the program to the General Services Administration and expanded its size considerably.) Congress explained that all employers, including the federal government, have a responsibility to take steps to bring individuals with disabilities into the work force. It concluded that "[i]n the case of hearing impaired and speech impaired individuals, the costs of . . . operating the relay service are small in comparison to the resulting benefits" (U.S. Senate Committee on Commerce, Science, and Transportation, 1988, p. 2).

Although Congress's mandate for relay services was limited to the federal government, the new legislation also ordered the FCC to complete its inquiry into interstate relay services within 9 months after the law's enactment date. In compliance with this Congressional directive, on July 21, 1989, the FCC issued a proposed Order offering alternatives for the establishment and operation of an *interstate* relay service (FCC, 1989). Although pleased with this development, consumer advocates were, at the time, hopeful that a more comprehensive proposal for both *intrastate and interstate* relay services nationwide would emerge from the newly introduced ADA. Consumers saw their wishes fulfilled. Before the FCC could finalize its order implementing an interstate relay service by administrative action, on July 26, 1990, Congress directed implementation of both intrastate and interstate relay services through the ADA. One year later to the day, the FCC issued final regulations setting forth comprehensive guidelines for the establishment and operation of nationwide relay services (FCC, 1991).

IMPLEMENTATION OF TITLE IV

Fulfillment of the Universal Service Obligation

Title IV of the ADA requires all common carriers (telephone companies) to provide local and long-distance telecommunications relay services nationwide by July 26, 1993. Passage of Title IV was the logical extension of Congress's prior efforts to achieve universal telephone service for individuals with hearing and speech disabilities. Indeed, the language of Title IV itself mirrors the language of the universal service obligation (cf. 47 U.S.C. §225[b][1] with 47 U.S.C. §151). In its report on the ADA, the U.S. Senate Committee on Labor and Human Resources explained:

> The goal of universal service has governed the development of the Nation's telephone system for over fifty years. The inability of over twenty-six million Americans to access fully the Nation's telephone system poses a serious threat to the full attainment of the goal of universal service. (1989, pp. 77–78; see also U.S. House of Representatives, 1990a)

Congress's message was clear. Finally, it was time to break down the barriers that, for more than half a century, had perpetuated a second-class telephone system for individuals who are deaf or hard of hearing or have speech impairments.

Relay Administration

Under Title IV, the telephone companies themselves are responsible for providing relay services in the geographic areas in which they provide conventional telephone service. In its regulation on this issue, the FCC makes clear that virtually all common carriers engaged in voice transmission service by wire or radio, including cellular carriers, are bound by this requirement. (One-way paging services are not considered among these voice transmission telephone services [FCC, 1991, p. 9]. In addition, in a recent ruling, the FCC clarified that to the extent satellite service providers are not engaging in the provision of voice transmission services, they are not covered under Title IV [FCC, 1993].)

Telephone carriers are afforded considerable flexibility in carrying out this mandate. Specifically, they may provide relay services individually, through designees, through competitively selected vendors, or in concert with other carriers. The relay programs already in existence demonstrate the wide variety of options open to the carriers. In the various states, relay services are provided by interexchange (long-distance) telephone companies such as AT&T, MCI, and Sprint. For example, as of this writing, AT&T provides relay service for 15 states plus the District of Columbia and Sprint has been awarded relay contracts for 14 states. Together the two interexchange carriers enjoy a good majority of the relay market. In other states, relay services are provided by regional Bell companies or their affiliates or nonprofit agencies. For example, Southwestern Bell provides relay services in Kansas, and Michigan Bell is the service provider for Michigan residents. The Utah Association of the Deaf, a nonprofit organization, has provided relay services for that state for several years. Savings in the overall costs of relay staff, administration, and equipment also have caused some common carriers to join efforts in regional relay centers. At present, Delaware and Pennsylvania, Maine and New York, Alabama and Kentucky, and Texas and Colorado operate regional centers.

Title IV permits states to continue operating and enforcing their own programs so long as they receive FCC certification to do so. The FCC's rules state that, in order to obtain relay certification, a state must submit documentation to the FCC that proves that its program will:

1. Meet or exceed all of the operational, technical, and functional minimum standards contained in the FCC's regulation.
2. Provide adequate procedures and remedies to enforce the state program (at a minimum, consumers urge that these states should offer the same procedural protections for relay consumers, including equivalent complaint and hearing procedures, that are provided for other telephone customers).
3. Not conflict with federal law where the state's program exceeds the minimum standards contained in the FCC regulations (47 C.F.R. §64.605[b]).

State certification can remain in effect for 5 years, after which it may be renewed (47 C.F.R. §64.605[c]). During the latter part of 1992 and the early part of 1993, all 50 states plus the District of Columbia and Puerto Rico submitted to the FCC requests for certification to operate their own statewide relay systems. As of this writing, these applications are still pending before the FCC.

Functional Equivalency—Operational Guidelines

Although carriers and states have a good deal of leeway in the organizational structure of their relay systems, both must comply with a stringent list of minimum guidelines in the operation of those services. These guidelines, set forth in both the ADA itself and the FCC's rule on Title IV, are intended to fulfill the Congressional mandate that relay services be "functionally equivalent" to telephone services available to conventional telephone users (47 U.S.C. §225[a][3], [d][1]).

Technical Requirements First and foremost, both intrastate and interstate relay service must be provided 24 hours per day, 7 days per week (47 C.F.R. §64.604[b][4]) and must be accessible to both the Baudot and the ASCII formats (47 C.F.R. §64.604[b][1]). Moreover, telecommunications relay systems must be capable of relaying any kind of call otherwise provided by common carriers (47 C.F.R. §64.604[a][3]).[3] This means that relay providers must complete coin-sent paid, non–coin-sent paid, third-party number, calling card, collect, three-way calling, remote polling of personal answering machines, and any other calls normally handled by common carriers. To have any of these requirements waived, telephone companies bear the responsibility of proving that the completion of any of these calls through the relay system is not technologically possible.

The FCC recently ruled against petitions that had requested reconsideration of this section of the FCC's regulation with respect to the handling of coin-sent paid telephone calls (FCC, 1993). Petitioners had argued that various technological obstacles made completion of these calls through the relay very difficult. First, petitioners argued that text telephone users would not be able to hear operator requests for coins. Petitioners also argued that technological difficulties prevent the exchange of coin deposits and signaling information between the pay phone user and the relay center (as compared with a telephone service operator). Finally, they argued that communications assistants are not capable of determining the cost of a given call at the time the call is being placed. The

---

[3]Relay providers are, however, permitted to reject a call where credit authorization is denied.

FCC rejected all of these arguments, deciding that the petitioners had not presented persuasive evidence to justify a general exclusion from "providing a service readily available to voice telephone users" (FCC, 1993, p. 5). Pointing to various technological advances that already had been made in the provision of pay text telephones, the FCC concluded that to rule otherwise would impair and discourage the development of improving these technologies.

Relay providers may also not limit the length of calls and must accept and relay single or sequential calls on request (47 C.F.R. §64.604[a][3]). The right to make sequential calls is an important one to the community of relay users. It is this requirement that will allow, for example, an individual to call a variety of potential employers with one call into the relay system. In promulgating this rule, the FCC recognized that each call requested by a relay user requires a separate dialing for the communications assistant, no different from what is required of a hearing person who wishes to make multiple calls. Moreover, eliminating the need for the relay caller to hang up and call back each time he or she wishes to call a new number saves time for both the caller and the communications assistant, resulting in greater overall relay savings.

Under the FCC's regulations, communications assistants may not intentionally alter any part of a relayed conversation and, "to the extent that it is not inconsistent with federal, state or local law regarding use of telephone company facilities for illegal purposes," must relay conversations verbatim (47 C.F.R. §64.604[a][2]). Among other things, this means that communications assistants may not interject any opinions or comments into a relayed conversation. The reason for requiring relay operators to relay messages verbatim is obvious. Individuals on both ends of a telephone conversation must have 100% assurance that what they are saying is being accurately conveyed to the directed party. Mistakes made in relaying communications regarding business transactions, medical reports, or airline schedules, for example, could have significant and often detrimental consequences for relay consumers.

Notwithstanding the requirement to relay conversations verbatim, the FCC's rule does permit communications assistants to summarize portions of conversations where specifically requested to do so by a relay party. There are at least two situations in which a relay user might make this request. The first involves recorded telephone messages that are played back too quickly for communications assistants to type. For example, an individual might use a relay system to call a movie theater for show times. He or she may wish to receive information on only one of the five movie schedules played in the recorded message. Similarly, an individual may be interested in the probability of snow or the current temperature but have no interest in the other information reported in a recorded weather announcement.

The second situation in which relaying calls verbatim may not be appropriate involves calls between individuals who are deaf and use American Sign Language (ASL) and hearing individuals who use English. Because ASL differs in grammar and syntax from English, parties communicating in each of these languages may have difficulty understanding one another without some interpretation between the two. The FCC's rule allows communications assistants, when requested, to perform this interpreting function.

The ADA also requires that relay providers transmit relayed conversations simultaneously, or in "real time" (47 C.F.R. §64.604[b][4]). Although there may be some minimal lag time in relaying conversations, this requirement ensures that conversations are relayed as soon as they are received. This can be compared with what was formerly called "message relay services," in which the message given to the communications assistant was held and relayed to the receiving party at a later time.

Finally, the FCC's rules require that relay users be given their choice of interexchange carrier when relaying calls, to the same extent that voice callers have this choice (47 C.F.R. §64.604[b][3]). This is consistent with the Modified Final Judgment issued in 1982 that divested AT&T from the seven regional Bell companies and resulted in giving all telephone users their choice of long-distance carriers (*United States v. American Telephone & Telegraph Co.*, 1982). The FCC did set forth one exception to this Title IV requirement. In its Order, the FCC explained that some states have already contracted with an interexchange carrier or other entity to provide relay services. These states, the Commission explained, fear that they will need to renegotiate their relay contracts if they are required to offer a choice of carrier to relay users before these contracts have expired. The FCC has decided to allow these states to apply for a limited exemption from this requirement at the time they apply for FCC certification, so that they need not incur the costs and time involved in renegotiation exercises (FCC, 1991, pp. 11–12).

Blockage Rates   In its report on the ADA, the U.S. Senate Committee on Labor and Human Resources directed the FCC to require that "blockage rates for telecommunications relay services be no greater than standard industry blockage rates for voice telephone services" (U.S. Senate Committee on Labor and Human Resources, 1989, p. 81). Blockage rates represent the percentage of time that callers cannot access a telecommunications system because of busy signals or long delays. In the past, blockage rates for relay services tended to be excessive, causing a good deal of frustration for individuals relying on these systems. The new FCC rule, it is hoped, will put an end to high relay blockage rates. It requires relay service providers to provide staffing and network facilities that are sufficient to ensure that the probability of a busy response because of either communications assistant unavailability or loop or trunk congestion is functionally equivalent to what a voice caller would experience in attempting to reach a party through the voice telephone network (47 C.F.R. §64.604[b][2] and [4]). Also toward this end, the FCC has required that relay providers answer 85% of all incoming calls within 10 seconds. After receiving dialing information from the caller, communications assistants may allow no more than 30 seconds to pass before they dial the requested number (47 C.F.R. §64.604[b][2]). Thus for 85% of all incoming calls, the exchange of information between the TDD user and the voice telephone user must begin within 40 seconds after the relay center receives the call.

Similarly, the FCC's rule contains requirements for maintaining adequate relay service in the event of an emergency (FCC, 1991, March 3). Relay providers must make provisions for providing uninterruptible power in the event of an emergency to the same extent that these redundancy features are available in central offices for conventional telephone service (47 C.F.R. §64.604[b][4]).

Whether the FCC's regulation on call blockage will be sufficient to provide telephone service for text telephone users that is functionally equivalent to voice telephone services remains to be seen. At a minimum, however, this FCC rule promises a vast improvement over the blockage rates of most of the former relay systems.

Communications Assistant Standards   The quality of services provided by a relay center in large part turns on the abilities of the communications assistants providing those services. The FCC recognized this and issued a rule that makes relay providers responsible for ensuring that:

> [communications assistants] be sufficiently trained to effectively meet the specialized communications needs of individuals with hearing and speech disabilities; and that [they] have competent skills in typing, grammar, spelling, interpretation of typewritten ASL, and familiarity with hearing and speech disability cultures, languages and etiquette. (47 C.F.R. §64.604[a][1])

Information about and sensitivity to the cultural and linguistic differences of persons who are deaf or hard of hearing or have speech impairments is best provided by these individuals. Accordingly, text telephone user communities have strongly urged state commissions and relay providers to involve them in the training of potential relay employees. For the most part, their efforts have been successful.

The FCC defined hearing and speech disability languages to include ASL, manual English, fingerspelling, cued speech, speech amplification, and speechreading (FCC, 1991, p. 4, note 6).

Although in its proposed relay rule the FCC had gone further to propose a minimum typing speed of 35 words per minute (wpm) for communications assistants (FCC, 1990b, pp. 50037, 50046), the Commission's final rule left the responsibility of choosing an appropriate typing speed to the individual relay providers. One reason for this FCC decision may have been the adamant opposition of the deaf community to what they considered to be too slow a typing standard.

Consumers offered several arguments against the FCC's originally proposed typing speed of 35 wpm. A swift typing speed, they argued, is critical to the efficient flow of information during a relayed conversation. Where typing speeds are slow, delays result, causing conversations to be stilted and uncomfortable for both consumers who can hear and those who are deaf. Moreover, longer calls caused by slow typing result in higher toll charges for relay users and, consequently, they argued, a possible reluctance on the part of employers and businesses to use the relay system. Consumers also directed the FCC to the ADA's requirement that relay conversations be transmitted in real time. They pointed out that the real time requirement could not be met with a minimum typing speed of 35 wpm because 35 wpm is less than one third the rate of spoken telephone communications.

Finally, the text telephone user community cited the need to switch from Baudot to the ASCII format as a reason for rejecting the FCC's proposed typing speed. Specifically, although Baudot machines can transmit messages at a maximum speed of only 60 wpm, ASCII equipment can transmit messages at the speed of the fastest typist. A change to the ASCII mode for this and other reasons, they argued, will be critical to ensuring that individuals who are deaf or have speech impairments do not fall prey to second-class, substandard telephone services in the future. The more telecommunications for the general public come to rely on computer transmissions, the more text telephone users who employ the Baudot format will find themselves excluded from new advances in the telecommunications and information networks. Yet slow relay typists, these consumers concluded, offer little incentive to text telephone users to purchase higher priced, faster ASCII machines. As a consequence, although initially the hiring of slow typists may give the impression of saving money for a relay center, employment of these individuals might actually carry heavy costs later on when continued reliance on the substandard Baudot technology prevents text telephone users from benefiting from the more sophisticated technologies of the future. At a minimum, the community offered, a typing speed of 60 wpm would be needed to guarantee quality relay services and offer the necessary incentives to relay users wishing to upgrade to the ASCII mode.

The FCC rejected the 60 wpm and all other proposed typing standards. It explained its decision:

> Rather than articulate a low threshold of expectations, a safe harbor, we instead expect that [relay] providers will deliver the excellent level of service all telephone consumers demand. Competition among [relay] providers to attract customers to the service also should spur providers to achieve the highest quality service. (FCC, 1991, p. 5, note 8)

At the same time, the FCC promised to monitor the quality of relay services and added it would not hesitate to prescribe additional communications assistant standards if these became necessary to meet the level of excellence demanded by the ADA. The text telephone user community recognizes that it, too, must actively monitor the performance of relay providers to ensure that the typing speeds adopted effectively meet their telecommunication needs. Moreover, consumers should not hesitate to use the FCC's complaint process should they determine that the standards chosen fail to provide them with functionally equivalent telephone service (see Enforcement, below).

Confidentiality and Call Content Under Title IV, communications assistants may not place any restrictions on the content of a relayed call (47 C.F.R. §64.604[a][3]). In addition, communications assistants may not disclose the content of any relayed conversation, nor may they keep the records of any relayed conversation beyond the duration of the call (47 C.F.R. §64.604[a][2]). Rather, the FCC has explained that communications assistants must act as "transparent conduits relaying conversations without censorship or monitoring functions" (FCC, 1991, p. 6). It is these Title IV requirements that prohibit communications assistants from passing judgment on the conversations they are obligated to relay. Just as a hearing person can use the telephone to communicate any message without limitation, so too, as Congress made clear in the ADA, do relay users have this right (47 U.S.C. §225[d][1][E]).

The prohibition against refusing calls based on their content is critical to the proper functioning of any relay program. Without this prohibition, practices regarding call content could vary from state to state, program to program, or even operator to operator, resulting in inconsistent practices throughout the nation. One can only begin to imagine the problems were operators to be allowed to refuse calls at whim. What one operator might consider light-hearted humor, another might find extremely offensive. What one operator might consider a harmless phrase, another might mistake for clues concerning illegal behavior. Never knowing when their calls could be terminated or refused, both persons who are deaf and those who can hear would be inhibited in their communications, causing them to lose trust in the relay system.

Just as the promise to relay all calls, no matter how offensive to a particular communications assistant, is critical to an effective relay system, so too is the promise that all relayed calls remain confidential. The FCC addressed this issue at length in its recent regulation, repeatedly recognizing the critical importance of offering relay users confidence in the privacy of their conversations (FCC, 1991, p. 7).

The FCC's rule is unequivocal in its mandate that, consistent with their other obligations as common carriers, relay providers may not divulge the content of any *intrastate* relay communication. In its discussion on this issue, the Commission pointed to at least two state legislatures, Tennessee and Texas, that have already passed legislation making any such disclosure subject to a criminal penalty (Legislature of Tennessee, 1990; Legislature of Texas, 1991). The FCC explained that each of these statutes prohibits communications assistants from being compelled to disclose, through testimony or by subpoena, the contents of any conversation unless both parties to the conversation consent to the disclosure (FCC, 1991, p. 6).

Whereas the confidentiality requirement for *intrastate* conversations is absolute, the ban against disclosing message content relayed in *interstate and foreign* conversations is somewhat qualified under the FCC's new rules. Prior to the passage of the ADA, the Communications Act had already placed a prohibition on the disclosure of telephone conversations by individuals receiving or assisting in the transmission of interstate and foreign telephone communication (47 U.S.C. §605[a]). However, as the Commission explained in its recent Order, this rule of nondisclosure has always been subject to certain exceptions. Specifically, the Communications Act does, in fact, allow individuals engaged in the transmission of telephone communications to disclose interstate and foreign telephone transmissions in response to a court-issued subpoena or upon demand of a lawful authority (47 U.S.C. §605[a][5] and [6]). Because, according to the FCC, Congress did not reflect a clear intent to repeal these limited exceptions in the case of relayed conversations, the FCC has ruled that the exceptions can, in fact, be used to require disclosure of the content of interstate and foreign relay conversations. The FCC has stated, however, that the exceptions mandate disclosure only when government officials make "authorized requests . . . in connection with specific incidents of possible law violations" (FCC, 1991, p. 8, note 14). The Commission concluded that such requests are likely to be "extremely rare" (FCC, 1991, p. 8).

Moreover, the FCC has explained that the limited federal exceptions permitting disclosure of relayed interstate and foreign conversations do not permit the states to enact affirmative disclosure requirements for all relayed conversations. For example, some states routinely require all individuals with knowledge of child, spousal, or elderly abuse occurring within the state to disclose that information to law enforcement authorities. Despite the general protests of the text telephone user community, in the past most of these states refused to exempt relay providers from these disclosure laws. The FCC's rule now states, in no uncertain terms, that the affirmative disclosure requirements of these statutes come into conflict with the ADA's requirements for conversation privacy and are preempted by the FCC's rules on this issue (FCC, 1991, p. 8, note 14).

In the past, the general rule against nondisclosure of relayed conversations often presented another problem for relay providers and communications assistants. Although communications assistants wished to protect confidentiality, they feared criminal liability that could result if they were caught withholding information they suspected involved illegal activities. The FCC's Order addresses this matter, too, and states that a relay service provider will only be held liable under federal criminal statutes where it is *knowingly* involved in the exchange of the unlawful transmissions. A communications assistant, it concluded, "would generally not be deemed to have a 'high degree of involvement or actual notice of an illegal use' or be 'knowingly' involved in such illegal use" in the normal performance of his or her relay duties (FCC, 1991, pp. 8–9). Again, the FCC predicted that the actual incidents giving rise to criminal liability issues were likely to be rare.

The FCC's resolution of the issues of confidentiality and call content offers an improvement over the manner in which these issues had been handled by many of the individual state relay programs. However, even the FCC's rule may leave too much room for the disclosure of relay conversations. Relay consumers maintain that the ADA's promise of confidentiality is intended to be absolute, without any exceptions whatsoever. Just as hearing individuals cannot have their private telephone conversations reported to law enforcement officials unless a court-ordered wiretap is put into place, so too should relay users have the comfort of knowing that their conversations are not subject to open scrutiny under ordinary circumstances. The FCC has acknowledged that some ambiguity remains between the ADA's provisions and the need to comply with the exceptions to the nondisclosure rules of the Communications Act and the federal criminal code. It has argued that Congress simply did not clarify the application of these laws to communications assistants and has suggested that Congress readdress this issue (FCC, 1991, p. 9).

It will now be incumbent on the relay user community to ensure that Congress, in fact, resolves this issue to protect the total privacy of relay conversations. Until such time that relay services are automated through voice synthesis, speech-to-text, and other technologies, communications assistants must be required to provide the same degree of secrecy that these computer technologies will automatically guarantee.

Public Education and Awareness   The goal of providing relay services is to close the telecommunications gap between text telephone users and voice telephone users. Yet the only way that this gap can begin to be narrowed is through the education of individuals throughout the country about the existence and functions of a relay system. To this day the vast majority of individuals who can hear are unaware of the functions of relay systems, having had no contact with the services these systems offer. As a consequence, such individuals may be reluctant to use relay services, in part because they may be uncertain about their dependability or unaware of their general promises of confidentiality. Moreover, there are many persons such as those who are hard of hearing who might need relay services but who might otherwise not be acquainted with these and other services available to persons who are deaf. In order to educate all of these populations, the new FCC rule requires telephone companies to publish information about their relay systems, including the actual numbers of their relay centers, in telephone directories and periodic billing inserts. Additionally, common carriers must ensure that information about relay services is available through directory assistance services (47 C.F.R. §64.604[c][2]).

FUNDING ISSUES

Cost Recovery Methods

With few exceptions, the ADA leaves to the discretion of the common carriers the means by which relay services may be funded. The costs of providing relay services have been recovered in at least three ways. The first, funding through specific and general state appropriations, has proven time and again not to be sufficient to meet the needs of the relay user community. States that adopted this method in the past often ran into financial difficulties, forcing relay users to return to their legislatures year after year to argue the merits of increased funding.

A majority of the states have employed a second cost recovery method, a monthly end-user surcharge. Typically, this is a charge, totaling anywhere from 5 to 25 cents, added to the monthly telephone bills of the state's telephone subscribers. Currently approximately 33 states use this type of funding method (National Center for Law and Deafness, 1992).

In the past, some states listed this surcharge on subscriber bills in a fashion that was prejudicial to individuals with hearing loss. For example, the line item on the bills of California residents was "Communications Devices for Deaf and Disabled." In Montana, consumers received bills with a surcharge labeled "MT Telecommunications for the Handicapped." These labels have implied that relay service is a special service, provided solely for the benefit of persons with communication disabilities, when in fact relay service is intended to enable voice telephone users and text telephone users to communicate with each other. Addressing this issue, the new FCC rule allows states to use the surcharge mechanism but warns that any labels must "promote national understanding of [relay services] and . . . not offend the public" (47 C.F.R. §64.605[d]).

Members of the deaf community of persons who are deaf maintain that the most appropriate way to fund relay services is to incorporate these costs into the normal operating expenses of providing telephone service. This approach has the advantage of providing a flexible funding source for relay operations that allows the states to respond as needed to increased relay demands. The inclusion of relay expenses within general operating expenses also furthers the concept of universal telephone service. Just as the higher costs of providing rural telephone service are already rolled into general telephone rates, so too should the costs of providing equal access for individuals who are deaf, hard of hearing, or have speech impairments be recovered in the basic rates paid by all telephone subscribers. Indeed, the FCC itself recognized this point and prohibited the subscriber line charge for the recovery of these expenses for *interstate* relay services for this very reason:

> [I]n order to provide universal telephone service to [relay] users as mandated by the ADA, carriers are required to recover interstate [relay] costs as part of the cost of interstate telephone services and not as a specifically identified charge on subscribers' lines. (FCC, 1991, p. 17, note 2)

The FCC specifically directed the costs of interstate relay services to be recovered through a shared cost recovery mechanism. Under the FCC's plan, an assessment will be placed on all interstate common carriers based on their relative share of nationwide interstate revenues for common carrier services (FCC, 1993). The assessments will go into a Telecommunications Relay Service Fund, from which relay service providers will receive settlements based on the total minutes of use of their interstate relay services.

Discounted Toll Rates

Under Title IV, relay users cannot be charged rates for long distance calls that are any higher than the rates charged for voice calls of the same duration, time, and distance (47 C.F.R. §64.604[c][3]). In essence, this means that relay users need not pay the extra costs of routing a call through a relay system. However, the completion of a relay call takes much longer than does a voice-to-voice call because of the added time needed to relay text telephone transmissions. To adjust for the disparity in time needed to complete these calls, some states and telephone companies have offered discounted toll rates. For example, AT&T offers a discounted long-distance rate on text telephone calls to all of its customers who are certified as having hearing or speech disabilities when those calls are made from their residence telephone numbers. Similarly, Sprint offers across-the-board discounts to both text telephone and voice relay customers in the states for which it provides relay services.

Several organizations commenting on the FCC's proposed relay rule urged the FCC to require a nationwide rate adjustment for relayed calls. These consumers argued that the failure to require a mandated discount unfairly imposes an added expense on relay users and thereby runs against the grain of Title IV's requirement for functionally equivalent telephone service. Moreover, if discounts are not provided, they concluded, employers may be reluctant to allow their employees who are deaf, hard of hearing, or have speech impairments to use the relay system for toll calls because these calls would cost more than would the same calls made by their employees who can hear. The result again would be discrimination against individuals with disabilities, this time in violation of Title II, the employment section of the ADA.

The FCC recognized these concerns in the discussion of rates in its final rule but concluded that it did not have sufficient evidence to order toll discounts at this time. Nevertheless, the Commission stated that it encourages interexchange carriers to offer toll discounts "as a competitive feature of service" (FCC, 1991, p. 15, note 2). Whether such words of encouragement are enough to convince telephone carriers of the need to provide discounted rates remains to be seen. More likely, consumers will have to return to Congress if they wish to obtain a universal discount for relayed toll calls.

ENFORCEMENT

Because Title IV is an amendment to the Communications Act, its provisions for enforcement derive from that Act. Although the remedies and enforcement procedures contained in the Communications Act are generally applicable only to interstate carriers, the ADA specifically extends these mechanisms to intrastate carriers charged with carrying out relay obligations (47 U.S.C. §225[b]). This means that the FCC has the authority to receive and investigate relay complaints against any of these carriers (47 U.S.C. §208[a]). Under the ADA, the FCC must resolve such complaints within 180 days after the complaints are filed (47 C.F.R. §64.604[c][1]). If the Commission finds that a certain carrier has violated Title IV, it has authority to order the carrier to come into compliance immediately (47 U.S.C. §205[a]) and to pay damages to the complainant (47 U.S.C. §209). The Commission or any person seeking compliance with a Commission order may seek to enforce that order through a petition to a federal district court. Finally, willful violations of the Communications Act, including its requirements for relay service, are subject to criminal penalties including fines of up to $10,000 and imprisonment (47 U.S.C. §501 et seq.).

Where states have been certified to operate their own relay services, consumers follow a different enforcement procedure. Specifically, in these instances, consumers may file their complaints directly with the state agency charged with the responsibility of enforcing the ADA's relay requirements. If an individual files a complaint with the FCC against a relay program operating in a certified state, the FCC must refer that complaint to the certified state expeditiously (47 C.F.R. §64.604[c][5]). The state must then take final action on the complaint within 180 days after it receives the complaint or within a shorter period as prescribed by the regulations of that state (47 C.F.R. §64.604[c][5][ii]). If the state fails to act within these prescribed times, or if the FCC determines that the state is no longer qualified to receive certification, the FCC may then resume jurisdiction over the complaint (47 C.F.R. §64.604[c][5][ii]).

In addition to the above administrative remedies, Section 207 of the Communications Act gives individuals the right to bring a private suit in federal district court against a carrier that has violated Title IV. Remedies under this section include both damages and reasonable attorney's fees. Notwithstanding this private right of action, courts have often required litigants to complain initially to the FCC for complaints that involve questions within the special competence of the Commission (see, e.g., *U.S. v. Western Pacific Railroad Co.*, 1956).

THE FUTURE: THE GOAL OF FUNCTIONAL EQUIVALENCE

Monitoring Efforts

A relay system that offers telephone service that is truly functionally equivalent to conventional telephone service can only come about if two conditions are met. First, consumers, state agencies, and the FCC must aggressively monitor the performance of relay centers. In the past, the involvement of relay consumers in both designing and monitoring local relay programs has contributed significantly to the effectiveness of these programs. Advisory committees created for this purpose—with representation from individuals who are deaf, hard of hearing, or have speech impairments—have become the norm for most state relay programs. Among other things, these committees have helped to select service providers, train operators, conduct consumer outreach programs, mediate disputes, and evaluate the quality of relay performance. (For a more comprehensive discussion of the role that consumer advisory committees can play in the development and operation of relay centers, see Strauss [1991].)

Both the states and the federal government also should take an active role in the monitoring of interstate and intrastate relay services. One way to monitor services effectively is to gather information regularly on program operations, including blockage rates, average speeds of relay answers, and customer satisfaction with communications assistant performance. The states should collect this data directly from their programs; the FCC should collect this information from the states in making determinations to renew state certification. Only with careful monitoring and enforcement on all three levels—consumer, state, and federal—can relay users hope to receive truly effective relay services.

New Technology

The second way to ensure that the services provided through relay programs continue to be functionally equivalent to conventional telephone services is to require relay providers to keep abreast of current telephone technology. Congress, too, recognized the importance of improving relay services as new technologies are developed. In its Report on Title IV, the U.S. Senate Committee on Labor and Human Resources explained:

> [T]his legislation is not intended to discourage innovation regarding telecommunications services to individuals with hearing and speech impairments. The hearing- and speech-impaired communities should be allowed to benefit from advancing technology. As such, the provisions of this section do not seek to entrench technology but rather to allow for new, more advanced, and more efficient technology. (U.S. Senate Committee on Labor and Human Resources, 1989, p. 78, note 29)

Toward this end, telephone carriers must make an effort to extend to the relay network the benefits that come with the development of new technology in the general telecommunications network. An example will help to illustrate this point. Recent years have seen a shift from the use of live-voice operators to audiotext or interactive telephone services by a variety of institutions. Banks, schools, and transportation authorities are just a few of the types of entities that now routinely use this technology to provide general telephone access to their services. Yet audiotext services often require a response by the caller within a specific period of time—a period of time that may be too short for the communications assistant to respond to in a relay situation. For similar reasons, "enhanced" 900 number telephone services often are not available to relay users. Although many 900 numbers have come under attack because of their high costs and sometimes questionable practices, their rapid proliferation into legitimate information services (e.g., offering brief explanations of common medications or methods of contributing to charities) is likely to make them as attractive to text telephone users as they are to voice telephone users.

Title IV of the ADA seeks to extend *all* of the benefits of the telecommunications network to text telephone users. The failure to provide access to audiotext services through relay systems, then, comes into direct conflict with the intent of Title IV's relay requirements. The FCC's rule does address this issue for audiotext calls that are not billed to users, by directing carriers to relay all such calls (47 C.F.R. §64.604[a][3]; FCC, 1993). User-billed audiotext services are a different matter, however. On this issue, Congress had stated that "[i]f future technology can make these services available utilizing a relay service, it is our intent to ensure such access" (U.S. House of Representatives, 1990b). Notwithstanding this Congressional mandate, the FCC recently concluded that because these services are enhanced, they are not required by the ADA. At most, the FCC's new rule merely *encourages* the provision of these services by relay providers (FCC, 1993). The categorical exclusion of these services for relay consumers may force these consumers to return to Congress to obtain full access to these services.

Whereas user-billed audiotext services are currently unavailable to relay users, two other new technologies have already begun to enhance and facilitate the provision of standard relay services. The first, voice carryover (VCO)/hearing carryover (HCO), will be required of all relay services under the new FCC rule (47 C.F.R. §64.604[b][5]). VCO enables an individual who has hearing loss, but who is able to use his or her voice, to talk directly to the hearing party of a relayed telephone conversation. When this technology is in use, the communications assistant need only type the hearing party's message back to the text telephone user. A similar technology, HCO, allows individuals with speech impairments to listen to messages directly and type back their conversations using their text telephones. When HCO is used, communications assistants merely read the typed messages to the receiving party.

Both VCO and HCO have a number of advantages. First, they save time and thereby reduce the overall costs of relaying a telephone call. Second, they increase privacy in that systems using this technology typically do not allow relay operators to listen to that part of the message that does not need to be relayed. In doing so, they tailor the functions that the relay service can provide to the needs of the relay consumer, allowing for increased independence for those persons wishing to send (via VCO) or receive (via HCO) messages without any assistance from the operator. Finally, the carryover technologies are likely to increase the populations of individuals who can benefit from relay services but who might otherwise be reluctant to allow relay operators to convey their messages. In particular, this may be true of individuals who have lost their hearing later in life and who may prefer to speak for themselves in a telephone conversation.

A second technology that is relatively new is called automatic call setup. With this technology, a relay center computer makes initial inquiries to the calling party regarding the number to be called, the identity of the caller, and an initial message to the called party. An operator comes on the line only after the computer finishes receiving this information, thereby saving costly communications assistant time. It is hoped that other technologies such as speech-to-text and voice synthesis will further enhance the privacy and independence of relay users in the future.

CONCLUSION

Relay services have flourished nationwide since the passage of the ADA. By July 26, 1993, all 50 states and some of the United States territories will have comprehensive full service relay programs in operation. Already, the vast majority of these states have taken affirmative steps to ensure that their infant services will meet the recently promulgated FCC guidelines. Yet consumers must maintain a watchful eye as these services proliferate. Care must be taken to ensure that relay programs fully and effectively meet the needs of the text telephone user community so that this community can finally enjoy equal opportunities in employment, education, and recreation throughout·all facets of society.

REFERENCES

Baquis, D. (1988). TDD relay services across the United States. In J. Harkins & B. Virvan (Eds.), *Speech to Text: Today and tomorrow* (GRI Monograph Series B, No. 2, pp. 25–32). Washington, DC: Gallaudet Research Institute.

Communications Act of 1934 (codified in scattered sections of 47 U.S.C. §§151 *et. seq.*)

Federal Communications Commission. (1978). In re telecommunications services for the deaf and hearing impaired; notice of inquiry. CC Dkt. No. 78–50, 67 *F.C.C.* 2d 1602.

Federal Communications Commission. (1983, April 27). Common carrier matters; final order. CC Dkt. No. 83–177, 92 *F.C.C.* 2d 1497.

Federal Communications Commission. (1987, May 21). (In re access to telecommunications equipment and services by the hearing impaired and other disabled persons, notice of inquiry, CC Dkt. No. 87–124 [released May 14, 1987].) *Federal Register*, *52*, 19198.

Federal Communications Commission. (1988, April 15). Access to telecommunications equipment and services by the hearing impaired and other disabled persons; notice of proposed rulemaking and further notice of inquiry. *Federal Register*, *53*, 12546.

Federal Communications Commission. (1989, July 27). Access to telecommunications equipment and services by the hearing impaired and other disabled persons; order completing inquiry and providing further notice of proposed rulemaking. CC Dkt. No. 87–124, 4 *F.C.C.* Rcd. 6214.

Federal Communications Commission. (1990a, July 13). Telephones for use by the hearing impaired; final rule. *Federal Register*, *55*, 28762–28764.

Federal Communications Commission. (1990b, December 4). Telephone communication by hearing and speech impaired; notice of proposed rulemaking, CC Dkt. No. 90–571,) *Federal Register*, *55*, 50037–50047.

Federal Communications Commission. (1991, August 1). Telecommunications services for hearing and speech disabled; report and order and request for comments. CC Dkt. No. 90-571, *Federal Register*, *56*, 36729–36733.

Federal Communications Commission. (1992, June 18). Access to telecommunications equipment by hearing impaired; final rule. CC Dkt. No. 87-124, *Federal Register*, *57*, 27182–27184, codified at 47 C.F.R. §§ 68.4; 68.112.

Federal Communications Commission. (1993, March 3). Telecommunications services for hearing and speech disabled; final rules and interpretation. CC Dkt. No. 90-571, *Federal Register*, *58*, 12175–12176.

Hearing Aid Compatibility Act of 1988, 47 U.S.C. §610 (1988).

Jensema, C. (1988). *Telecommunications for the hearing impaired: An era of technological change*. Paper presented at the National Conference on Deaf and Hard of Hearing People, El Paso, TX.

Kelleher, M.F. (1991). The confidentiality of criminal conversations on TDD relay systems. *California Law Review*, *79*, 1349–1387.

Legislature of Tennessee, Oaths, Sec. 24-1-210 (July 1, 1990).

Legislature of Texas, H.B. No. 1132, Companion to S.B. No. 867, amending Sec. 1 Tit. 4 Human Resources Code, Sec. 82.001 (1991).

National Center for Law and Deafness. (1992). *Summary of state telecommunications relay services*. Washington, DC: K.P. Strauss, B. Gracer, and H. Norton.

National Center for Law and the Deaf. (1989). *Summary of state dual party relay services*. Washington, DC: K.P. Strauss and H. Norton.

National Center for Law and the Deaf. (1990). *Summary of state dual party relay services*. Washington, DC: K.P. Strauss and H. Norton.

National Center for Law and the Deaf. (1991). *Summary of state dual party relay services*. Washington, DC: K.P. Strauss and H. Norton.

Potomac Telecom, Inc. (1985). *A short history of telecommunication devices for the deaf*. Rockville, MD.

Second Computer Inquiry, 77 F.C.C. 2d 384, 446-47 (1980), *recon.* 84 F.C.C. 2d 50 (1981), *further recon.* 88 F.C.C. 2d 512 (1981), *aff'd sub nom Computer and Communications Industry Association v. Federal Communications Commission*, 693 F. 2d 19 (D.C. Cir. 1982).

Starr, S. (1989, January/February). Using a TDD to communicate with a personal computer. *SHHH Monthly Newsletter*, p. 17.

Strauss, K.P. (1991). Implementing the telecommunications provisions. In J. West (Ed.), *The Americans with Disabilities Act: From policy to practice* (pp. 238–267). New York: Milbank Memorial Fund.

Strauss, K.P., & Richardson, B. (1991). Breaking down the telephone barrier—relay services on the line. *Temple Law Review*, *64*, 583–607.

Taylor, P. (1988). Telephone relay service: Rationale and overview. In J. Harkins & B. Virvan (Eds.), *Speech to text: Today and tomorrow* (GRI Monograph Series B, No. 2, pp. 11–18). Washington, DC: Gallaudet Research Institute.

Telecommunications Accessibility Enhancement Act of 1988, 40 U.S.C. §762 (1988).

Telecommunications for the Disabled Act of 1982, 47 U.S.C. §610 (1988).

United States v. American Telephone & Telegraph Co., 552 F. Supp. 131 (D.D.C. 1982).

United States v. Western Pacific Railroad Company, 352 U.S. 59, 63–64 (1956).

U.S. House of Representatives. (1990a, May 17). Debate on H.R. 2273, statement of Rep. Dingell. *Congressional Record*, *136*, H2432.

U.S. House of Representatives. (1990b, May 17). Debate on H.R. 2273, statement of Rep. Luken. *Congressional Record*, *136*, H2434.

U.S. House of Representatives Committee on Energy and Commerce. (1982, September 28). *House report no. 97-888, to accompany H.R. 7168/S. 2355 (Telecommunications for the Disabled Act of 1982) (97th Congress, 2nd session)*. Washington, DC: U.S. Government Printing Office.

U.S. House of Representatives Committee on Energy and Commerce. (1990, May 15). *House report no. 101-485(IV), to accompany H.R. 2273 (101st Congress, 2nd session)*. Washington, DC: U.S. Government Printing Office. (Reprinted in *United States Code Congressional and Administrative News, 4*, 512–564 [1990])

U.S. Senate Committee on Commerce, Science and Transportation. (1988, August 9). *Senate report no. 100-464, to accompany S. 2221 (Telecommunications for the Hearing-Impaired) (100th Congress, 2nd session)*. Washington, DC: U.S. Government Printing Office.

U.S. Senate Committee on Labor and Human Resources. (1989, August 30). *Senate report no. 101-116, to accompany S. 933 (101st Congress, 1st session)*. Washington, DC: U.S. Government Printing Office.

PART III

INNOVATIVE AND CONTROVERSIAL ISSUES

Chapter 13

Impact of
the ADA on the Health Care System

Lawrence O. Gostin

The Americans with Disabilities Act[1] (ADA) provides a strong weapon in the fight against discrimination by prohibiting the adverse treatment of qualified persons with disabilities. Nevertheless, health care professionals do not yet recognize the impact that the ADA will have on the health care system. In this chapter I examine three areas of impact of the ADA on that system. First, I show how the ADA affects the clinical freedom of health care professionals to choose which patients to treat. Second, I explain how the ADA limits the ability of employers to require medical testing and examination. Third, I explain how the ADA provides an effective review of the government's use of communicable disease powers.

DEFINING DISABILITY AND DISCRIMINATION IN TERMS OF HEALTH CARE

Disability

Disability is defined broadly to mean "a physical or mental impairment that substantially limits one or more of an individual's major life activities," a record of such impairment, or being regarded as having such impairment. Thus, the definition of disability covers a wide range of medical conditions, including disabilities of a genetic (*Bowen v. American Hospital Association*, 1986; *Gerben v. Holsclaw*, 1988; U.S. Senate Committee on Labor and Human Resources, 1989b, p. 22) or multifactorial (U.S. Senate Committee on Labor and Human Resources, 1989b, pp. 7, 22, 24) origin and communicable diseases (*New York State Association for Retarded Children v. Carey*, 1979, *School Board of Nassau County, Fla. v. Arline*, 1987).

The ADA covers most patients who are not seen as "deserving" by some segments of society, such as persons living with HIV infection or AIDS (*Benjamin R. v. Orkin Exterminating Co.*, 1990), alcoholism (*Traynor v. Turnage*, 1988), and epilepsy (*Reynolds v. Brock*, 1987). Indeed,

Research support was provided, in part, by the Milbank Memorial Fund, Americans with Disabilities Act Implementation Project, and the National Center for Human Genome Research, National Institutes of Health. The author thanks Chai Feldblum and Wendy Parmet for their insights and discussions on the Americans with Disabilities Act.

[1]The Americans with Disabilities Act of 1990 (PL 101-336) is published in *Statutes at Large* (104 Stat. 327) and codified in the *United States Code* (42 U.S.C. §§12101–12213 [Supp. II 1990]). References to various portions of the act within this chapter cite the specific section of the code.

Congress specifically included asymptomatic infection such as HIV under the definition of disability, and this has been affirmed by the courts (*Doe v. Centinela Hospital*, 1988). However, a person who currently is using illegal drugs is not considered to have a disability, but is covered once he or she has been rehabilitated successfully and is no longer using drugs (42 U.S.C. §12213). Similarly, a range of socially disapproved behavior disorders are excluded from protection, such as most gender identity and sexual behavior disorders, compulsive gambling, kleptomania, pyromania, and psychoactive substance use disorders resulting from current illegal drug use (42 U.S.C. §12211).

A person is considered disabled if he or she has a "record" of, or is "regarded" as, being disabled even if there is no actual impairment (Southeastern Community College v. Davis, 1979). A "record" indicates that a person has a history of disability or has been misclassified as having a disability. This provision protects persons who have recovered from a disability or disease, such as cancer survivors.

The term *regarded* includes individuals who do not have disabilities but are treated as if they did. This concept protects people who are discriminated against in the false belief that they have a disability. It would be inequitable for a defendant who intended to discriminate on the basis of disability successfully to raise the defense that the person did not, in fact, have a disability. This provision is particularly important for individuals who are perceived to have stigmatic or disfiguring conditions such as HIV, leprosy, or severe burns (U.S. Senate Committee on Labor and Human Resources, 1989b, p. 24).

The fact that a perception of disability is included in the ADA is vitally important in determining whether a pure carrier of disease should be regarded as having a disability. For example, heterozygotes (persons who can pass on a genetic disease but will not have the disease themselves) for sickle cell disease, Tay-Sachs disease, or cystic fibrosis should be covered by the term *regarded* or perceived to have a disability. Carriers of recessive genetic traits thus are protected against discrimination that is motivated by the fundamental misconception that they have or will develop a disability (see Gostin, chap. 14, this volume).

Can a person who currently is healthy but who is predicted to become ill be classified as "disabled" within the meaning of the ADA? Strong reasons in law, ethics, and public policy suggest that the person should receive the same protection as those who currently have a disability. The ADA expressly protects not only individuals who actually have a disability but also those who are "regarded" or perceived to have a disability. The law, therefore, does not objectively measure the actual abilities or disabilities of the person. Rather, it judges the defendant through his or her own subjective perceptions, prejudices, and stereotypes. Those who discriminate because of a future prediction of impairment are fostering a harmful stereotype because the person currently is healthy and capable of meeting all the performance criteria for the job, benefit, or service. The discrimination is speculative and prejudicial: no sound judgment can be made regarding whether, when, and to what extent the person will lose his or her skills and capabilities, and whether reasonable accommodations could be provided. It would be inequitable for a defendant who intended to discriminate on the basis of disability to raise successfully the defense that the person did not, in fact, currently have a disability. A narrow construction of the term *regarded* as having a disability would yield an anomalous result. Persons with genetic conditions would be required to wait until they actually develop symptoms before becoming eligible for protection.

The case law on the federal Rehabilitation Act and state disability statutes also suggests that it is unlawful to discriminate on the basis of future disability. This interpretation can be found in *Kimmel v. Crowley Maritime Corporation* (1979) (knee injury that might pose a future safety risk at sea); *Dairy Equipment Company v. Department of Industry* (1980) (fear of exacerbated future injury from a fall because the individual had only one kidney); *Neeld v. American Hockey League* (1977) (future harm to player with one eye). In contrast, the court found in *Burgess v. Joseph Schlitz Brewery Company* (1979) that disability refers to present, noncorrectable loss of vision, not potentially disabling conditions, so that correctable glaucoma was not a handicap under the state statute. One court observed that it would be "ironic and insidious" if current disabilities were protected but the same protection was denied to those whom employers perceive to be predisposed to future disability (*Dairy Equipment Company v. Department of Industry*, 1980; the employee who had only one kidney was "handicapped" within the meaning of the state Fair Employment Act). The New York Court of Appeals held that obesity is a handicap even though it causes no current disability. The court aptly observed that "disabilities, particularly resulting from disease, often develop gradually. . . . An employer cannot deny employment simply because the condition has been detected before it has actually begun to produce deleterious effects" (*State Division of Human Rights v. Xerox Corporation*, 1985). An employer also may not point to future safety risks as grounds for dismissal (see *Kimmel v. Crowley Maritime Corporation*, 1979).

Discrimination

Although the specific titles of the ADA have slightly different provisions, a finding of discrimination requires adverse treatment because of a "disability" of a person who is "qualified" or who would be qualified if "reasonable accommodations" or modifications were made available. A person with a disability is "qualified" if he or she is capable of meeting the essential performance or eligibility criteria for the particular position, service, or benefit. Qualification standards can include a requirement that the person with a disability does "not pose a direct threat to the health or safety of others" (42 U.S.C. §§12113[b], 12182[b][3]). The "direct threat" standard means that persons can be excluded from jobs, public accommodations, or public services if necessary to prevent a "significant risk" to others, a risk that cannot be eliminated through reasonable accommodations (*School Board of Nassau County, Fla. v. Arline*, 1987). In order to determine that a person with mental illness, for example, poses a significant risk, evidence of specific dangerous behavior must be presented. Disability law has been thoughtfully crafted to replace reflexive actions based on irrational fears, speculation, stereotypes, or pernicious mythologies with carefully reasoned judgments based on well-established scientific information. The legislative record is replete with statements rejecting decision making based on ignorance, misconceptions, and patronizing attitudes (see, e.g., U.S. House of Respresentatives Committee on Education and Labor, 1990, p. 51; U.S. House of Representatives Committee on Energy and Commerce, 1990; U.S. House of Representatives Committee on the Judiciary, 1990; U.S. Senate Committee on Labor and Human Resources, 1989b).

Congress was acutely aware of potential risks to health and safety posed by persons with disabilities to employees or others in the workplace (see, e.g., U.S. House of Representatives and U.S. Senate, 1900, paras. no. 2 and 13; U.S. Senate Committee on Labor and Human Resources, 1989b). Although the "direct threat" criterion was limited to persons with contagious disease in the Senate bill, it was extended in conference to all individuals with disabilities (U.S. House of Representatives, 1990). In the House the standard of "direct threat" was extended by the Judiciary Committee to all individuals with disabilities, and not simply those with contagious diseases or infections (U.S. House of Representatives Committee on the Judiciary, 1990). The ADA does not override any legitimate medical standards or requirements for workplace safety established by federal, state, or local law, or by employers (U.S. House of Representatives and U.S. Senate, 1900, para. 10).

Because occupational health and safety concerns are incorporated within qualification standards, they primarily must be determined by actual workplace risks and not speculation about risks that are theoretical, remote, or distant (see *School Board of Nassau County, Fla. v. Arline*, 1987). The courts, however, are likely to uphold decisions to protect employers from foreseeable risks in the immediate future, particularly for safety or security-sensitive positions (42 U.S.C. §12113[b]). For example, clear medical evidence demonstrating a likelihood of harm or injury may disqualify a person from an inherently risky position such as airline pilot, police officer, or fire fighter (see U.S. House of Representatives and U.S. Senate, 1990, para. 10).

The ADA requires reasonable accommodations or modification for otherwise qualified individuals unless this would pose an undue hardship (42 U.S.C. §12112[b][5], 12182[b][2][A][ii]). This requires adaptation of facilities to make them accessible and modification of equipment to make it usable. Job restructuring might be necessary to provide more flexible schedules for persons who need medical treatment (42 U.S.C. §12111[9]). Although Congress was addressing primarily physical barriers to access, it also required that workplace environments be "usable" by individuals with disabilities. This could include reducing the environmental hazards to which the person with a disability is hypersusceptible. One federal district court assumed that this would include marked reductions in tobacco smoke to accommodate an employee who was hypersensitive, but did not require providing a smoke-free environment (*Vickers v. The Veteran's Administration*, 1982). To accommodate otherwise qualified persons with infectious conditions, the covered entity might have to reduce or eliminate the risk of transmission. Employers, for example, might be required to provide infection control and training to reduce nosocomial or blood-borne infections.

An employer, however, is not forced to endure an undue hardship that would alter the fundamental nature of the business or would be disproportionately costly (*Southeastern Community College v. Davis*, 1979). The Eighth Circuit Court of Appeals, for example, held that a school for persons with mental retardation was not obliged to vaccinate employees in order reasonably to accommodate a student who was an active carrier of hepatitis B virus because of the excessive cost (*Kohl v. Woodhaven Learning Center*, 1989).

HEALTH CARE PROVIDERS' DUTY TO TREAT

The HIV epidemic has revived the perennial question of whether physicians have a duty to provide care within their realm of competence for any patient in need (Jonsen, 1990). The question runs deeper than occupational fears of patients with communicable disease (Brennan, 1991). Physicians' decisions not to treat may be based on cost (e.g., refusing to take uninsured or Medicaid patients), prejudice (e.g., shunning drug users), liability concerns (e.g., refusing drug abuse treatment for pregnant women), or subtle judgments about which patients deserve scarce health care resources (e.g., rejecting an institutionalized person with schizophrenia for a transplant).

Under common law, practitioners have no absolute duty to treat patients, but they cannot abandon patients already in their care whose health would be jeopardized (Annas, 1988). Federal law also forbids "dumping" patients from the emergency room of any hospital that participates in the Medicare program (*Burditt v. U.S. Department of Health and Human Services*, 1991). The advent of civil rights legislation meant that health care services had to be rendered without discrimination based on race, sex, religion, or national origin.

The ADA prohibits health care professionals from discriminating against persons with disabilities (U.S. Department of Justice, 1992). The act specifies that "no individual shall be discriminated against in the full and equal enjoyment" of services, privileges, or advantages (42 U.S.C. §12182[a]). This requires the medical or dental practitioner to provide equivalent services to all patients consistent with their medical needs and irrespective of their disabilities. Title III of the ADA also requires newly constructed health care facilities to be "readily accessible."

The ADA resolves two significant ambiguities in earlier disability legislation. First, the ADA expressly defines public accommodations to include a professional office of a health care provider, hospital, or other service establishment (42 U.S.C. §12181[7]). Thus, the act applies to traditionally private medical and dental offices. Some state courts already had decided that private medical and dental offices as well as clinics, hospitals, and dispensaries were "public accommodations" and that the medical field was not exempt from the requirement to provide nondiscriminatory services to persons with a disability (*Hurwitz v. New York City Commission on Human Rights*, 1988). Second, the ADA expressly applies to covered entities whether or not they receive federal funds. A federal district court had held that a hospital in receipt of Medicare or Medicaid is liable for disability discrimination under the Rehabilitation Act of 1973 (*Glantz v. Vernick*, 1991, p. 981).

The ADA certainly prohibits a refusal to treat based on prejudice or irrational fear, but some medical practices are far more subtle. Practitioners are defending their decisions not to treat or refer patients with communicable conditions by arguing that this is an exercise of clinical judgment and does not constitute discrimination, and that to restrict the physician's right to decide whom to treat or when to refer is to dictate the practice of medicine. To be sure, the ADA's acceptance of selection criteria that are "necessary for the provision of services" (42 U.S.C. §12182[b][2][A][i]) appears to authorize the exercise of legitimate clinical judgment based on the practitioner's areas of skill and specialization. Thus, the ADA does not prohibit a practitioner from providing the most appropriate medical treatment in his or her judgment or from referring a person with a disability to another practitioner when clinically appropriate and when the same referral would be made for an individual without a disability. For example, a physician who specializes in treating burn victims could not refuse to treat the burns of a person who has tuberculosis, but he or she could refuse to provide other types of medical treatment outside his or her area of specialty unless he or she provides that treatment to individuals without disabilities.

Such fine distinctions may be hard to make in practice, as Parmet (1990) has observed, particularly when the "disability is directly related to the condition being treated" (*United States v. University Hospital*, 1984). In that case, the Second Circuit Court held that denial of surgery to correct myelomeningocele was not discrimination when the surgeon believed that there was an extremely high risk that the child would never interact with her environment. Is denial of orthopedic surgery justified when the surgeon claims that the insertion of a pin in an immunocompromised patient infected with HIV would be contraindicated? Would denial of a kidney transplant to a person in an advanced state of terminal cancer deny equal opportunities (Parmet, 1990)? The ADA provides no easy answers. The physician should be prepared to demonstrate that his or her decision is based on the genuine exercise of clinical judgment supported by objective medical evidence and not based on prejudice or fear.

Another reason for refusing to treat patients with dangerous infectious conditions is a concern about occupational hazards. Some physicians believe they should be excused from treating patients with infectious conditions, particularly if the treatment is elective, even cosmetic (Gostin, 1990). The physician might conceivably rely on the "direct threat" standard that is contained in Title III of the ADA and argue that the patient's infection poses a significant risk of transmission in cases of seriously invasive or particularly bloody procedures. Courts, however, are unlikely to accept occupational risks as a justification for discrimination: the risk is exceedingly low and can be kept low through the "accommodation" of strict adherence to infection control procedures; health care professionals probably will be expected to accept reasonable risks in carrying out the essential functions of their jobs in the same way that fire fighters or police officers cannot excuse themselves from particularly dangerous assignments.

The ADA does not guarantee access to health care but merely requires that the refusal to provide equal access cannot be based on a person's disability. A provider's health care decision may be based, in part, on cost. Providing health services of inferior quality or not providing services at all because of a person's inability to pay may be unethical, but it is not necessarily unlawful. The ADA does not set out to interfere in the purely financial decisions of providers. Yet, a financial decision that impacts unequally and unfairly on persons with disabilities may be challengeable. Would a decision by a hospital to provide chemotherapy for cancer, but not antiviral medication for AIDS, be a valid cost decision or pernicious discrimination? Would a state Medicaid rationing plan that refused to cover liver transplants violate the ADA? The courts would be more likely to invalidate such "cost-based" decisions if the plaintiff could demonstrate some underlying animus or improper motive against a group of persons with disabilities (*Alexander v. Choate*, 1985).

In August 1992, the Bush administration refused to provide a waiver for Oregon's Medicaid health care rationing program on the grounds that it violates the ADA. The Oregon plan would have increased the number of people eligible for Medicaid, but would have restricted certain medical services. The Bush administrtion argued that these restrictions on services, such as highly expensive treatments for incurable cancer, the final stages of AIDS, or premature infants with virtually no chance of survival, would present a disproportionate impact on persons with disabilities. The ADA, suggested the administration, would prevent the state from denying care simply because the treatment is expensive or because the person's life is not worth living.

The ADA, then, in only a limited sense tears down barriers to access to health services. It steadfastly refuses to allow a person to be turned away because of the provider's fears and biases toward the disability. However, it remains uncertain as to what extent the act will help to ensure access to health care for those who arguably need it most.

MEDICAL TESTING, EXAMINATION, AND HEALTH CARE BENEFITS PROVIDED BY EMPLOYERS

In an age when large employers pay as much or more for health care as for the raw materials of production, they have a marked economic incentive to select out employees who will develop medical illness and disease (Liebman, 1988). Payment for medical expenses has become a burdensome cost for employers, often exceeding one third of total payroll costs (Disney, 1987). The drive to stay competitive requires employers to invest heavily in worker selection at a time when the use of medical, biological, and drug tests is booming and when the use of genetic predictive tests is no longer a remote, futuristic possibility (Gostin, 1991a; Office of Technology Assessment, 1990). The overwhelming majority of large firms currently require preemployment medical examinations (Office of Technology Assessment, 1991; Rothstein, 1983, p. 1379).

Discrimination against persons with hidden disabilities has been technically unlawful since the Rehabilitation Act of 1973. However, although prior regulations under Section 504 of the Rehabilitation Act prohibited pre-offer medical examinations, most private employers, including federal contractors, were not covered by those regulations. Also, enforcement of the regulations has been exceedingly difficult because an employer did not have to disclose that the person's medical condition was the prime reason for the failure to hire. So long as employers were able to conduct extensive medical examinations before offering a job, they could effectively hide the true reason for the employment decision.

The ADA's most radical departure from the Rehabilitation Act is its proscription against pre-offer medical inquiries. (For the purposes of the ADA, drug testing is not considered a medical examination, and employers are not prohibited from taking action against a person who currently is using drugs.) Section 12112(c)(2) prohibits employers from conducting medical examinations or inquiries as to whether a job applicant has a disability or the nature or seriousness of the disability. Thus, the ADA presents a potentially irreconcilable paradox for employers: medical benefit costs make it fiscally imperative to consider current and future disease and disability, while Congress requires employers not to discriminate against qualified workers with potentially costly disabilities. Pre-offer inquiries must be limited to assessing the applicant's ability to perform job-related functions, not the future health costs to the employer.

The ADA permits an employer to require an entrance examination only after an offer of employment has been made. All entering employees must be subjected to the same examination and the medical information must be kept strictly confidential. Employers also are limited in their rights to conduct medical examinations or inquiries after a person is hired. The employer cannot compel an employee to take a medical examination or inquire as to whether the employee has a disability unless the examination or inquiry is job related and consistent with business necessity (42 U.S.C. §12112[c][3]).

Congress, in enacting the ADA, recognized that "an inquiry or medical examination that is not job-related serves no legitimate employer purpose, but simply serves to stigmatize persons with a disability (U.S. Senate Committee on Labor and Human Resources, 1989b, p. 39). The ADA promises to impede significantly the growing use of medical testing and information gathering by employers across America, thus transforming the way the business community makes employment decisions.

Health Insurance Coverage

When asked, employers cite cost benefit and greater productivity as the main reasons for medical testing (Office of Technology Assessment, 1990, pp. 171–188). Costs to employers for health care and other benefits have risen substantially in recent years (see, generally, Liebman, 1988; Rothstein, 1983, p. 1379). These costs are borne directly by employers with larger work forces, many of whom tend to be self-insurers or have experience in rating. Alternatively, increased benefits costs are passed on from insurance companies to employers.

Some astute commentators on disability law give considerable credence to employer decisions not to hire persons with current or future disabilities based on probable costs to health, disability, life, and other insurance benefits. "If a worker will become ill, and if the employer will be responsible for the medical costs as well as the output costs of the worker's absence, then the predicted illness is nothing but a future dollar cost that the employer must consider and discount" (Liebman, 1988).

Although industry certainly has made its fiscal position clear (see U.S. Senate Committee on Labor and Human Resources, 1989a), a legislative and judicial consensus has emerged that financial burdens on employee benefit programs do not justify discrimination. The Senate Labor and Human Resources Committee echoed a theme found throughout the legislative process: "An employer may not refuse to hire an individual because of fears regarding increased insurance costs attendant on hiring the individual—either because of increased costs to be incurred because of that individual's health needs or because of the health needs of that individual's family" (U.S. House of Representatives, 1990, p. H-4614, Statement of Rep. Augustus Hawkins).

Disability law is concerned only with the relationship between a person's disability and his or her ability to perform the job he or she seeks. The fact that the person may have an undesirable impact on disability, life, or health insurance programs is irrelevant (*Garner v. Rainbow Lodge*, 1989; *Shawn v. Legs Company Partnership*, 1989; *State Division of Human Rights v. Xerox Corporation*, 1985). The reasons that courts reject cost as an excuse for discrimination are that antidiscrimination is considered to have a higher social value than strict business interests and that cost incentives, if allowed, would swallow up all the protection currently conferred by disability law. Congressman Hawkins noted that: "allowing the fact of increased costs to justify employment discrimination would effectively gut the protections of the ADA for individuals with disabilities" (U.S. House of Representatives, 1990, p. H-4614).

Congress intended to afford to insurers, employers, and health care providers the same opportunities they would enjoy in the absence of the ADA to design and administer insurance products and benefit plans in a manner that is consistent with the basic principles of underwriting, classifying, and administering risks (U.S. House of Representatives Committee on Education and Labor, 1990). Thus, insurers may continue to sell to and underwrite individuals applying for life, health, or other insurance (42 U.S.C. §12201[c][1]), and employers and their agents may establish and observe the terms of employee benefit plans based on sound actuarial data. The Employee Retirement Income Security Act (ERISA) imposes no requirements on employers to provide minimal benefits for those employees covered by health plans. At the same time, ERISA preempts any state regulation of risk retention plans (commonly called *self-insurance* arrangements) provided by employers (see *Metropolitan Life Insurance v. Massachusetts*, 1985). ERISA's exemption of self-insured plans from state insurance regulation is not affected by the ADA (42 U.S.C. §12201[c][3]; see, e.g., U.S. House of Representatives Committee on the Judiciary, 1990 ["Concerns had been raised that sections 501(c)(1) and (2) could be interpreted as affecting the preemption provision of ERISA. The Committee does not intend such an implication"]). The problem with ERISA's preemption provision is that self-insured plans cannot be required by states to provide certain benefits or to contribute to risk pools. Because an estimated 60% of all covered workers are under self-insured plans, a significant limitation is placed on the states that seek to rectify inequitable coverage.

An inequitable result of ERISA's preemption of state regulation of risk retention plans is that employers apparently can severely reduce or even eliminate coverage for a particular illness *after* the employee has made a claim for an illness. Courts of Appeals in *Owens v. Storehouse* (1993) and *McGann v. H. & H. Music Company* (1991) upheld decisions by employers to reduce coverage for AIDS from one million dollars to $20,000 and $5,000 dollars, respectively, after an employee was diagnosed with HIV disease. The Supreme Court did not review the *McGann* case, in part because the Solicitor General argued that the ADA might affect the outcome of future cases. In *Terrence Donaghey, Jr., v. Mason Tenders District Council Trust Fund* (1993), the EEOC made a determination, in a case similar to *McGann* and *Owens*, that reducing coverage after a person is diagnosed with HIV disease is a violation of the ADA.

The ADA, therefore, does not restrict an insurer, health care provider, or any entity that administers benefit plans from carrying on its normal underwriting activities. This includes the use of preexisting condition clauses in health insurance contracts, the placing of caps or other limits on coverage for certain procedures or treatments, or the charging of a premium to persons with higher risks (see, e.g., U.S. Senate Committee on Labor and Human Resources, 1989). Nor can employee benefit plans be found to violate the ADA under impact analysis simply because they do not address the special needs of every person with a disability (e.g., additional sick leave or medical coverage) (U.S. House of Representatives Committee on Education and Labor, 1990; see *Alexander v. Choate*, 1985). The ADA, however, may prevent employers from reducing coverage after a person becomes ill.

The ADA's exemption of underwriting is reasonable if the industry is regarded strictly as a business. It is difficult to question the right of the insurance industry to discriminate on the basis of sound actuarial data. The very essence of underwriting is to classify people according to risk, treating those with higher risks differently. However, if health insurers are viewed as an integral part of health care policy, the ADA's exemption of underwriting becomes worrisome. The social purpose of health insurance is to spread risk across groups, enabling wider access to health care services. If health benefits become unavailable or unaffordable to those who are most likely to become ill, the social purpose of health coverage is thwarted.

The shift in many insurance schemes from community to experience or group rating is particularly troubling. Employers who can demonstrate that their workers are at lower risk of disease and disability may be able to negotiate lower cost insurance coverage. The consequence, of course, is that this experience rating places affordable insurance even further out of the reach of higher risk, typically poorer, work forces. In a barely regulated environment, inevitable competitive pressures to narrow risk and lower cost may inextricably lead to an increasing divide between those who can and those who cannot afford health insurance.

The ADA, then, may stifle the prevalent practice of employee screening and medical examination as well as prevent futuristic employee selection through genetic and biological tests. However, it will do little to solve the deeper underlying problem of who pays for health care costs and how.

EXERCISE OF GOVERNMENT'S COMMUNICABLE DISEASE POWERS

State public health departments long have had the power to order vaccination, testing, treatment, contact tracing, and isolation for those with communicable and sexually transmitted diseases (Parmet, 1989). Although these powers are exercised in the name of public health, they deprive the individual of the human rights of autonomy, privacy, and even freedom. In the past, public health departments had few constraints on the exercise of these powers. Courts often have been deferential to these departments provided their powers were not exercised in an "arbitrary, oppressive or unreasonable" manner (*Jacobson v. Massachusetts*, 1905). Certainly, modern constitutional law requires a more compelling justification when fundamental rights such as liberty are affected (Burris, 1989). However, as discussed elsewhere (Gostin, 1991b), the courts have yet to develop a cogent standard of review for public health powers (Gostin, 1987).

The ADA promises to provide an effective review of the exercise of government's public health powers. Any use of compulsory powers will have to comply with the standards provided under the ADA. The ADA may appear to be an unlikely source of law with which to regulate public health. To all appearances, disability law is concerned with the inequitable treatment of persons with disabilities as a result of bigotry or stereotype, disregarding their qualifications, skills, and experience. Regulation of communicable disease is intended to safeguard the health of the community, not to foster prejudice. Yet, Title II of the ADA applies to all public services, which are defined to include all actions by state and local governments, including those of public health departments. Public health departments now must operate under the standard of "significant risk"; that is, the department must demonstrate that the subject poses a significant risk of transmitting disease before it will be permitted to exercise compulsory powers (*School Board of Nassau County, Fla. v. Arline*, 1987).

The determination of significant risk is solely a public health inquiry. Under the ADA, significant risk must be determined on an individualized basis by means of a fact-specific inquiry. The risk, moreover, must be "significant," not speculative, theoretical, or remote (U.S. House of Representatives Committee on the Judiciary, 1990, p. 53). The Supreme Court in *School Board of Nassau County v. Arline* (1987) laid down a four-part test for determining significant risk. First, the risk should be based on a *primary mode of transmission*, not a mode that is unestablished or highly inefficient. Second, a person can be subjected to compulsory public health powers only for the *period of time of contagiousness*. The subject must continue to be currently infectious, and the conditions or activities must exist for a communication of infection. Third, the *probability of risk* of transmission must be substantial. Substantial probabilities of transmission based on firm scientific calculations provide the best justification for the exercise of public health powers. Fourth, as the *severity of potential harm* to the community increases, the level of risk needed to justify the public health power decreases. The level of risk, then, can be roughly calculated through an inverse correlation between the seriousness of harm and the probability of its occurrence: minor or inconsequential infections require a higher probability of transmission than lethal infections. Even the most serious harm should not justify public health regulation in the absence of a reasonable probability that it will occur.

The court in *Leckelt v. Board of Commissioners of Hospital District No. 1* (1990) exhibited a misunderstanding of the relationship between probability and severity of risk. The court held that, even though the probability of HIV transmission from a nurse to a patient "may be extremely low . . . there is no cure for HIV . . . and the potential for harm is extremely high." If the seriousness of harm were the conclusive consideration in all cases, it would require the courts to uphold almost any restriction on a person with a potentially lethal contagious disease, even if the risk of transmission were exceedingly low. The court in *Glover v. Eastern Nebraska Office of Retardation* (1989) recognized this in finding a violation of law when staff in a facility for persons with mental retardation were required to be tested for HIV. Even though the potential harm from HIV infection is serious, its chance of occurring in this situation "approaches zero."

The Supreme Court in *Arline* did not specifically refer to the *human rights burdens* of a public health policy. Nevertheless, the efficacy of the public health power should be weighed against the burdens on human freedom, autonomy, and privacy. Courts should balance the significance of the risk and the efficacy of the intervention (will the public health power reduce a serious health threat?) with the burdens (at what human, social, and economic cost will the public health benefit be achieved?). Wherever possible, public health officials should use the least restrictive and least invasive power capable of achieving the public health goal (Gostin, 1991b).

CONCLUSION

The ADA views health care decisions through the lens of antidiscrimination and civil rights law. Accordingly, if a physician refuses to treat a patient, an employer fires a person with a costly disease, or a public health official requires a subject to submit to testing or vaccination, the courts will inquire whether persons with disabilities were denied equal opportunities under the law. The courts will require objective evidence and careful justification for treating persons with disabilities differently. This way of conceptualizing the problem is most favorable to the person who is subject to the discrimination. The use of disability law to review decisions of physicians, employers, and public health officials provides a new way of thinking about health law.

REFERENCES

Alexander v. Choate, 469 U.S. 287 (1985).
Annas, G. (1988). Legal risks and responsibilities of physicians in the AIDS epidemic. *Hastings Center Report*, *18*, 26–31.
Benjamin R. v. Orkin Exterminating Company, 390 S.E. 2d 814 (W.Va. S.Ct. 1990).
Brennan, T. (1991). Transmission of the human immunodeficiency virus in the health care setting—time for action. *New England Journal of Medicine*, *324*, 1504–1508.
Burditt v. U.S. Department of Health and Human Services, 934 F. 2d 1362 (5th Cir. 1991).
Burris, S. (1989). Rationality review and the politics of public health. *Villanova Law Review*, *34*, 933–982.
Bowen v. American Hospital Association, 476 U.S. 619 (1986).
Burgess v. Joseph Schlitz Brewery Company, 25g S.E.2d 248 (S.Ct. N.C. 1979).
Dairy Equipment Company v. Department of Industry, 390 N.W. 2d 330 (1980).
Disney, D.M. (1987). The development and scope of employment-related health protections. (Report prepared for the Ford Foundation.) Waltham, MA: Brandeis University Press.
Doe v. Centinela Hospital, 57 USLW 2034 (CD Cal. 1988).
Employment Retirement Income Security Act of 1974, 29 U.S.C. §1140.
Garner v. Rainbow Lodge, U.S.D.C. S.D. Tex., Houston Div. H-88-1705 (1989).
Gerben v. Holsclaw, 692 F. Supp. 557, 563 (E.D. Pa. 1988).
Glantz v. Vernick, U.S.D.C. (1991). (In *Massachusetts Lawyers Weekly*, *19*, 981 [1991]).
Glover v. Eastern Nebraska Office of Retardation, 867 F.2d 461 (8th Cir. 1989).
Gostin, L. (1987). The future of public health law. *American Journal of Medicine*, *12*, 461–490.
Gostin, L. (1990). The AIDS litigation project: Part II—discrimination. *JAMA*, *263*, 2086–2093.
Gostin, L. (1991a). Genetic discrimination: The use of genetically based diagnostic and prognostic tests by employers and insurers. *American Journal of Law & Medicine*, *17*, 801–836.
Gostin, L. (1991b). Public health powers: The imminence of radical change. In J. West (Ed.), *The Americans with Disabilities Act: From policy to practice* (pp. 268–290). New York: Milbank Memorial Fund.
Hurwitz v. New York City Commission on Human Rights, 142 Misc. 2d 214 (N.Y. Sup. 1988).
Jacobson v. Massachusetts, 197 U.S. 11 (1905).
Jonsen, A. R. (1990). The duty to treat patients with AIDS and HIV infection. In L. Gostin (Ed.), *AIDS and the health care system* (pp. 155–168). New Haven, CT: Yale University Press.
Kimmel v. Crowley Maritime Corporation, 23 Wash. App. 78, 596 P.2d 1069 (1979).
Kohl v. Woodhaven Learning Center, 865 F.2d 930 (8th Cir. 1989).
Leckelt v. Board of Commissioners of Hospital District No. 1., 909, F.2d 820 (5th Cir. 1990).
Liebman, L. (1988). Too much information: Predictions of employee disease and the fringe benefit system. *University of Chicago Legal Forum, 1988*, 57–91.
McGann v. H. & H. Music Company, 946 F.2d 401 A1. 4 (5th Cir. 1991).
Metropolitan Life Insurance v. Massachusetts, 471 U.S. 724 (1985).

Neeld v. American Hockey League, 439 F.Supp. 459 (W.D.N.Y. 1977).

New York State Association of Retarded Children v. Carey, 612 F.2d 644 (2d Cir. 1979).

Office of Technology Assessment. (1990). *Genetic monitoring and screening in the workplace.* Washington, DC: U.S. Government Printing Office.

Office of Technology Assessment. (1991). *Medical monitoring and screening in the workplace.* Washington, DC: U.S. Government Printing Office.

Owens v. Storehouse, U.S. App. 1993 LEXIS 3066 (11th Cir. 1993).

Parmet, W. (1989). Legal rights and communicable disease: AIDS, the police power, and individual liberty. *Journal of Health Politics, Policy & Law, 14*, 741–771.

Parmet, W. E. (1990). Discrimination and disability: The challenges of the ADA. *Law, Medicine & Health Care, 18*, 331–334.

Rehabilitation Act of 1973, 29 U.S.C. §§791–794 (1988 & Supp. I 1989).

Reynolds v. Brock, 815 F.2d 571 (9th Cir. 1987).

Rothstein, M. (1983). Employee selection based on susceptibility to occupational illness. *Michigan Law Review, 81*, 1379–1496.

School Board of Nassau County, Fla. v. Arline, 480 U.S. 273 (1987).

Shawn v. Legs Company Partnership, Sup. Ct. NY (In *AIDS Litigation Reporter*, March 10 [1989]).

Southeastern Community College v. Davis, 442 U.S. 397 (1979).

State Division of Human Rights v. Xerox Corporation, 480 N.E. 2d 695 (1985).

Terrence Donaghey, Jr., v. Mason Tenders District Council Trust Fund, Charge No.: 160–93–0419 (Jan. 27, 1993).

Traynor v. Turnage, 485 U.S. 535 (1988).

U.S. Department of Justice. (1992). Nondiscrimination on the basis of disability by public accommodations and in commercial facilities. In *Code of Federal Regulations* (28: Judicial Administration, pp. 457–629). Washington, DC: U.S. Government Printing Office.

U.S. House of Representatives. (1990, July 12). *House conference report no. 101-596, to accompany S. 933 (101st Congress, 2nd Session).* Washington, DC: U.S. Government Printing Office. (Reprinted in *United States Code Congressional and Administrative News, 4*, 565–600 [1990]).

U.S. House of Representatives Committee on Education and Labor. (1990, May 15). *House report no. 101-485(II), to accompany H.R. 2273 (101st Congress, 2nd session).* Washington, DC: U.S. Government Printing Office, (Reprinted in *United States Code Congressional and Administrative News, 4*, 303–444 [1990]).

U.S. House of Representatives Committee on Energy and Commerce. (1990, May 15). *House report no. 101-485 (IV), to accompany H.R. 2273 (101st Congress, 2nd session).* Washington, DC: U.S. Government Printing Office. (Reprinted in *United States Code Congressional and Administrative News, 4*, 512–564 [1990]).

U.S. House of Representatives Committee on the Judiciary. (1990, May 15). *House report no. 101-485 (III), to accompany H.R. 2273 (101st Congress, 2nd session).* Washington, DC: U.S. Government Printing Office. (Reprinted in *United States Code Congressional and Administrative News, 4*, 445–511 [1990]).

U.S. House of Representatives and U.S. Senate. (1990). *Joint explanatory statement of the committee of conference.* Washington, DC: U.S. Government Printing Office.

U.S. Senate Committee on Labor and Human Resources. (1989a, May 9, 10, 16; June 22). *Hearings on S. 933, the Americans with Disabilities Act of 1989 (S. Hrg. 101-156).* Washington, DC: U.S. Government Printing Office.

U.S. Senate Committee on Labor and Human Resources. (1989b, August 30). *Senate report no. 101-116, to accompany S. 933 (101st Congress, 1st session).* Washington, DC: U.S. Government Printing Office.

United States v. University Hospital, 729 F.2d 144 (2d Cir. 1984).

Vickers v. The Veterans Administration, 549 F. Supp. 85 (W.D. Wash. 1982).

Chapter 14

Genetic Discrimination in Employment and Insurance

Lawrence O. Gostin

The Human Genome Initiative is a worldwide research effort with the goal of mapping and sequencing an estimated 100,000 human genes. Two reports published in 1988 laid the groundwork for the Genome Initiative by setting out methods and goals (National Research Council, 1988; Office of Technology Assessment, 1988a), and a report from the U.S. Public Health Service (USPHS) and U.S. Department of Energy (DOE) in 1990 updates earlier descriptions (see also Annas, 1990; Watson & Cook-Deegan, 1990). The National Center for Human Genome Research anticipates that genetic information will be the sourcebook for biomedical science in the 21st century (USPHS and DOE, 1990, p. vii). Professor Cook-Deegan, an ethicist at the Center, explains that, whereas science now conceptualizes disease in terms of biochemistry, it is possible to envision that science will move to the next stratum of reductionism, identifying and manipulating the genes that provide instructions for the biochemistry in every human cell (Cook-Deegan, 1990).

The Genome Initiative will enhance the ability of science and medicine to gather and organize information to foresee a person's future potentials and disabilities. Enormous human benefits may ensue in understanding the etiology and pathophysiology of genetic disorders, preventing disease through genetic counseling, and treating the disorders through genetic manipulation (see, e.g., Antonarakis, 1990; Goldstein & Brown, 1989). Genomic information will help clinicians to understand and eventually to treat many of the more than 4,000 genetic diseases as well as those multifactorial diseases in which there is a genetic predisposition (USPHS and DOE, 1990, p. viii).

The Human Genome Initiative also has the potential for social detriment. Imagine that employers and insurers one day will be able to obtain a genetic profile from the blood drawn from a small finger prick (Hening, 1989, p. 20; Liebman, 1988, pp. 57, 60). The genetic profile will go beyond the discrete conditions currently understood, such as Huntington disease, sickle cell anemia, cystic fibrosis, and Duchenne muscular dystrophy. The employer may delve into future probabilities for a wide range of physical conditions, such as cancer, heart disease, Alzheimer disease, and schizophrenia. Liebman observes that "suddenly the job applicant is not a member of an undifferentiated population . . . [but has] a statistically analyzable medical future" (1988, p. 60; see also Bishop & Waldholz, 1990). This chapter analyzes the law, ethics, and public policy concerning "genetic discrimination," which is defined as the denial of rights, privileges, or opportunities on the basis of information obtained from genetically based diagnostic and prognostic tests.

Prejudice, alienation, and exclusion often accompany genetically related diseases even though, by definition, the person has no control over the disorder and it is not the result of willful behavior. The fact that genetic diseases sometimes are closely associated with historically insular ethnic or racial groups such as African blacks (e.g., sickle cell disease), Ashkenazi Jews (e.g., Tay-Sachs disease, Bloom syndrome, Gaucher disease [adult form]), or Armenians (e.g., familial Mediterranean fever) only compounds the potential for invidious discrimination (Goldstein & Brown, 1989, p. 288). Preventing discrimination based on a person's health care status and providing equal opportunities for persons with disease and disability both emerge as powerful societal goals fully recognized by Congress in the Americans with Disabilities Act[1] (ADA) (42 U.S.C. §12101[2]) and the courts (*School Board of Nassau County, Fla. v. Arline*, 1987).

Genetic discrimination, however, cannot always be attributed to pernicious myths, irrational fears, or ethnic hatred. The demand for genomic information can be rational. The Genome Initiative places squarely before society a set of legitimate values that conflict with the antidiscrimination principle (Liebman, 1988, p. 57). These societal values include promoting the health of people known to have genetic predispositions to disease by excluding them from hazardous environments; ensuring that workers are fit for employment by requiring them to meet qualification standards; and saving cost by refusing to hire persons who have a high probability of disproportionately burdening company benefit plans. In an age when large employers pay as much, or more, for health and welfare benefits as for the raw materials of production, they are anxious to improve productivity and to lower personnel costs (see, generally, Rothstein, 1983). The Human Genome Initiative, therefore, poses unequalled societal conflict between the rights of individuals and the rights of institutions. The goal of the law and ethics explored in this chapter is to ensure that genomic information is used only when clearly necessary to protect a person's health or safety, or to enforce legitimate performance criteria for a job, service, or benefit.

This chapter begins with a review of genetic discrimination and its prevalence and potential, as well as arguments as to why discrimination violates fundamental human rights principles and undermines the public health goals necessary to fulfill the true promise of the Genome Initiative. The chapter then examines whether the ADA and the corpus of antidiscrimination law are sufficiently relevant and comprehensive to safeguard against genetic discrimination. As part of this examination, the chapter discusses genetic discrimination in two key sectors: employment and insurance. The chapter ends with proposals for future legislative and judicial safeguards against genetic discrimination.

PREVALENCE AND POTENTIAL FOR GENETIC DISCRIMINATION: JUSTICE AND PUBLIC HEALTH CONSEQUENCES

Amid the euphoria generated by the Human Genome Initiative, the National Institutes of Health (USPHS and DOE, 1990, App. 7) and the Congress have expressed concern that genomic information may result in stigma and discrimination. The U.S. House of Representatives noted that the human genome project may divide us into "two groups, those with pluperfect and imperfect genes. . . . Taxpayers should not be put in the position of financing government programs without protections to ensure that those programs will not in the end lead to fencing them out of jobs or reasonably priced health insurance" and that we need to develop legal and ethical safeguards "before the knowledge genie is completely out of the bottle" (1990b, H5003). Indeed, fear of the social impact of discovery of the human genome may be the most significant impediment to continued full funding of the project (U.S. House of Representatives, 1990b). Fortunately, most funders appreciate the

---

[1]The Americans with Disabilities Act of 1990 (PL 101-336) is published in *Statutes at Large* (104 Stat. 327) and codified in the *United States Code* (42 U.S.C. §§12101–12213 [Supp. II 1990]). References to various portions of the act within this chapter cite the specific section of the Code.

notion that fear of unknown medical advances does not justify stifling scientific progress, but that it does require careful ethical planning and legal safeguards.

The Social Impact

Genetic discrimination violates basic tenets of individual justice and is detrimental to the public health. Discrimination based on actual or perceived genetic characteristics denies an individual equal opportunity because of a status over which he or she has no control. Genetic discrimination is as unjust as status-based discrimination against other historically disfavored classes based on race, gender, or disability. In each case, people are treated inequitably, not because of their inherent abilities, but solely because of predetermined characteristics. The right to be treated equally and according to one's abilities in all the diverse aspects of human endeavor is a core social value.

Genetic discrimination is socially harmful not merely because it violates core social values, but also because it thwarts the creativity and productivity of human beings perhaps more than the disability itself. By excluding qualified individuals from education, employment, government services, or insurance, the marketplace is robbed of skills, energy, and imagination. Such exclusion promotes physical and economic dependency, which drains rather than enriches social institutions.

Genetic discrimination, most importantly, undercuts the fundamental purpose of the Human Genome Project, which is to promote the public health. The infusion of unprecedented human and financial resources into the Genome Initiative is justified by the promise of clinical benefits in identifying, preventing, and effectively intervening in human disease. If fear of discrimination drives people away from genetic diagnosis and prognosis, renders them less willing to confide in physicians and genetic counselors, and makes them more concerned with loss of a job or insurance than with care and treatment, the benefits cannot be fully achieved.

The public health impact of discrimination will become all the more clear as genetic technology advances. The public health justification for widespread collection and utilization of genomic data will increase as genetic diagnosis and prognosis become more accurate and less expensive, and as gene therapies become standard medical practice. The ability of society to develop and implement ambitious genetic screening and intervention strategies will depend on the adequacy of safeguards against breaches of confidence and discrimination.

Discrimination and Scientific Uncertainty

Complex and often pernicious mythologies emerge from public ignorance of genetically based diagnostic and prognostic tests. The common belief is that genetic testing, because it is generated from scientific assessment, is always accurate and highly predictive and illuminates an inevitable predestination of future disability in the individual or his or her offspring. Of course, the facts are diametrically opposite to the common belief. The precision of genetic-based diagnosis and prognosis is uncertain for many reasons. The sensitivity of genetic testing is limited by the known mutations in a target population.

For example, screening can currently detect only 75% of cystic fibrosis chromosomes in the U.S. white population. (Screening for cystic fibrosis is now very much on the public agenda, despite cautionary statements by the USPHS and professional organizations [American Society of Human Genetics, 1990; National Institutes of Health, 1990].) In addition, only 56% of at-risk couples both will be identified as carriers (National Institutes of Health, 1990; Wilford & Fost, 1990, p. 2777). Wilford and Fost (1990) calculated that one out of every two couples from the general population identified to be at risk by cystic fibrosis population screening would be falsely labeled, with the potential for increased anxiety, discrimination, and alteration of reproductive plans. Billings and his colleagues recounted a case of a family with a child who has cystic fibrosis and received care through a health maintenance organization (HMO). When a second pregnancy occurred, a prenatal DNA test was positive for two copies of the cystic fibrosis gene. The HMO considered withdrawal of coverage if the family proceeded with the pregnancy. Threats of legal action were required before the HMO agreed to continue coverage (Billings et al., 1992).

Predicting the nature, severity, and course of disease on the basis of a genetic marker also is fraught with difficulty. The date of onset of disease, the severity of symptoms, and the efficacy of treatment and management are highly variable with most genetic diseases (see generally McKusick, 1988). Some people remain virtually symptom free, whereas others progress to seriously disabling illness. A marker for Huntington chorea, for example, presents an aura of inevitability of a relentless and progressive neurological impairment but, in fact, a great deal of variability is apparent even within the same family (De Long & Moses, 1988). In a disease such as neurofibromatosis, some will suffer marked disability of the nervous system, muscles, bones, and skin, whereas others will exhibit minor pigmented spots on their bodies (McKusick, 1988, p. 287).

Many genetic-associated diseases, unlike cystic fibrosis and Huntington chorea, are not attributed to a single gene mutation or genetic marker, but are multifactorial. Their appearance can depend on a complex interaction of genetic and environmental factors that cannot be measured accurately. Current scientific assessments point to numerous, poorly understood multifactorial diseases ranging from colon cancer, heart disease, and emphysema to schizophrenia, depression, and alcoholism. Genetic-based diagnosis and prognosis, therefore, is characterized by marked heterogeneity: the reliability and predictive value of testing is limited by known mutations and prevalence in the target population; variability exists in the onset, presentation, and outcome of disease; and predictions are confounded by a multiplicity of genetic, biomedical, and environmental factors.

For all these reasons, significant scientific uncertainty surrounds much genetic testing. Genomic information may be highly beneficial for patients and health care professionals in deciding on prevention, treatment, diet, lifestyle, or reproductive choices. Employers, insurers, educators, police, and others, however, surely will come to have access to genomic information. When genomic information is used by social institutions not to prevent or treat disease, but to deny opportunity, exclude from work or benefits, remove health care coverage, or restrict liberty, a whole new dimension to the Genome Initiative becomes apparent. Adverse decisions in employment and insurance are particularly hurtful when they are rendered on the basis of false assumptions regarding the nature, accuracy, and predictability of genetic tests.

Genetic Screening and Monitoring

The Office of Technology Assessment (OTA) provides the only systematic data about the past, current, and future use of genetic screening and monitoring in the workplace (OTA, 1983, 1990). Genetic testing includes a number of technologies to detect genetic traits, changes in chromosomes, or changes in DNA. The OTA distinguishes between two different kinds of genetic testing: examining persons for evidence of induced change in their genetic material (monitoring) and identifying individuals with particular inherited traits or disorders (screening) (OTA, 1990, pp. 3–6). The OTA terminology is somewhat confusing from a public health perspective because testing usually refers to case identification of an individual, whereas screening involves more systematic application to whole populations (see generally Gostin, Curran, & Clark, 1987).

The OTA surveyed a comparable population of industrial companies, utilities, and trade unions in 1982 and 1989 in order to provide trend data. The surveys showed that relatively few companies are currently utilizing genetic screening and monitoring. The 1989 survey found that a total of 20 health officers at the 330 Fortune 500 companies responding (6%) reported the use of genetic monitoring or screening at present (12) or in the past (8) compared with 18 (6 current and 12 past) in 1982. The rate of current to past monitoring and screening was reversed from 1982 to 1989, with twice the number of companies currently using genomic information in 1989 as in 1982.

If there has been little or no real growth in the number of companies conducting genetic monitoring and screening in the workplace, what do companies foresee for the future? In 1982, 55 companies said they possibly would use genomic information in the next 5 years. The 1989 OTA report notes that fewer companies anticipate using genetic testing and monitoring. However, in a survey of 400 firms conducted in 1989 by Northwestern National Life Insurance Company, 15% of companies responded that, by the year 2000, they planned to check the genetic status of prospective employees and their dependents before making an offer of employment (Brownlee & Silberner, 1990).

The only available data from the insurance industry validate the findings of the OTA employment surveys. In 1989, the American Council on Life Insurance conducted the first study on whether insurers were beginning to perform genetic testing. The Council reported that no insurance company was performing its own tests, but some did access known genomic information in their underwriting decisions (Pokorski, 1990; Sit, 1990). The Health Insurance Association of America (HIAA) has formed its own committee and plans to survey its members on the use of genetic testing (HIAA, 1990).

The absence of expected growth in genetic testing and monitoring in industry and insurance should not provide grounds for complacency in anticipating the social impact. Employers and insurers claimed to choose genetic testing based on its predictive value, scientific consensus, and cost (OTA, 1983, p. 36). The OTA found, however, that none of the genetic tests evaluated at that time met established scientific criteria for routine use in an occupational setting. The chasm in perception between the OTA and industry appears to be the employer's willingness to assume that, if tests are sufficiently reliable for clinical use, they can be used safely in occupational settings (see also "Prediction and Prejudice," 1990).

The Human Genome Initiative certainly will promote rapid progress in human molecular genetics, which suggests increased occupational and insurance use in the future. Industry and insurers are not likely to use routinely genetic diagnosis that costs, for example, $2,000–$3,000 per test. However, as the technology becomes capable of identifying a battery of genetic conditions at a fraction of the current cost, the sheer competitive nature of industry and insurance may result in a vastly increased amount of testing. American industry is likely to turn to genetic diagnosis in the future for many of the same reasons that have driven the sharp increases in drug, polygraph, and general medical testing in the workplace. A comprehensive OTA report on testing in health insurance documents the substantial rise in testing, including prospects for genetic testing (OTA, 1988b).

In the end, market forces may be the single greatest factor in generating increased use of genetic testing. Market researchers have projected U.S. sales of genetic tests to reach several hundred million dollars before the end of the decade. The commercial appeal of genetic testing is revealed in a staff background paper to the 1990 OTA report (Hewitt & Holtzman, 1988), which cites market value estimates ranging from several million to a billion dollars ("Arthur D. Little Projects," 1987; "Disease Disposition Screening," 1986; "DNA Probes," 1988; "Market for DNA," 1986; R.S. First, Inc., 1986). *Business Week* predicted a $200 million-a-year market for genetic tests actively being pursued by prominent biotechnology companies (Carey, 1990). The emergence of commercial interests in genetic test development provides powerful incentives to lower costs of genetic testing and to place the technology within the reach of industry and insurance.

Once genetic testing gains a foothold within a particular industrial or insurance sector, the sheer competitive nature of the marketplace may require its wider adoption. Clearly, if some insurers or employers begin to make increasingly more sophisticated genetic predictions of ill health and shortened life, the pressure on others to utilize the same technology will become irresistible.

If the marketplace itself is the only restraint to the proliferation of genetic technology, once the technology comes down in price and demonstrates a cost–benefit advantage, its widespread adoption will become inevitable. The need for legal safeguards against genetic discrimination in employment and insurance is apparent.

Genetic Discrimination

The 1982 OTA survey reported that, of the 18 companies taking some action on the basis of genetic testing, 7 had transferred or dismissed the "at-risk" employee (OTA, 1983, p. 37). The 1989 OTA survey reported very few instances of negative personnel decisions as a result of genetic monitoring or screening. Only two Fortune 500 companies reported ever rejecting a job applicant or transferring an employee primarily or partly based on the results of genetic testing (OTA, 1990, p. 182).

No systematic studies of genetic discrimination in employment and/or insurance have been undertaken. Billings and his colleagues did report 29 cases of apparent genetic discrimination based on responses to an advertisement (Billings et al., 1992). Other anecdotal reports of genetic discrimination have appeared in the media (see, e.g., MacDonald, 1990). Reported cases of genetic discrimination reinforce the idea that adverse decisions often are based on mythologies and misconceptions rather than real cost or safety concerns. Adverse decisions are made because of the person's genetic status rather than actual disability, lack of qualification, or even accurate forecasting of future impairment.

A common misconception is that the presence of a genetic trait can be equated with actual disability without any need to demonstrate a cogent nexus between current impairment and inability to meet reasonable qualification standards. Genetic discrimination affects heterozygotes (unaffected carriers), "at-risk" individuals (those with a predisposition to disease), and persons who are asymptomatic or have a minor form of the disease.

Several cases of discrimination were reported involving heterozygotes of sickle cell anemia or Gaucher disease. Shapiro (1990, p. 1) reported on Dr. Bereano's testimony before a Congressional subcommittee: "The Armed Forces for many years has followed a policy of excluding carriers of sickle cell disease, despite the fact that these individuals are not themselves impaired" (see also "Air Force Rejects," 1988; Matthewman, 1984, p. 1199). Billings et al. (1992) cite the case of a government job applicant heterozygotic for Gaucher disease who was denied the job because he was a "carrier, like sickle cell." In such cases the genetic trait may affect future offspring, but not the person himself or herself. Discrimination against an unaffected carrier is particularly pernicious because the condition is irrelevant to the person's current or future health status or abilities. The discrimination is based on the mythology that a heterozygote has the disease or will develop it.

"At-risk" persons have a propensity to develop genetic disease and often encounter discrimination based on a positive DNA test result or a family history. For example, a Chicago woman was turned down for a job after her prospective employer learned that her mother was schizophrenic; the job was denied to her based on the fear that schizophrenia was an inherited trait (Shaw, 1990). Persons "at risk" also are treated as though they are currently impaired with the most severe form of the disease, even though there is great variability in the onset and severity of symptoms. Persons with the marker for Huntington chorea have been discriminated against because of this misconception: cases have involved rejection by adoption agencies, termination from a pilot's position, and rejection of life insurance coverage (Billings et al., 1992).

Persons actually affected with genetic disease often are wrongly believed to have severe symptoms, even if their impairments are relatively minor. At the worst extreme, discrimination occurs against the "healthy ill," those who test positive for a hereditary condition but are asymptomatic. Billings et al. (1992) reported the case of a person with hereditary hemochromatosis, which is characterized by an excessive absorption and storage of iron and can be controlled. This individual, despite the absence of symptoms, was consistently denied insurance (see also Brownlee & Silberner, 1990; Holtzman, 1989). In other cases, persons are discriminated against because of a genetic condition despite the fact that the symptoms do not interfere with performance. Persons with Charcot-Marie-Tooth disease, an hereditary sensorimotor neuropathy (foot weakness, particularly footdrop, foot deformity, and hand weakness are the most severe manifestations) have been rejected for life, accident, or automobile insurance (Griffith & Cornblath, 1988, pp. 1095–1096). They were apparently very mildly affected, with only a slight foot deformity. One case of discrimination occurred despite a favorable letter from the personal physician and the absence of any record of past ill health or accidents (Billings et al., 1992).

The desire to save cost is implicit in many cases of genetic discrimination. A decision to deny health or life insurance based on a diagnosis of hemochromatosis (MacDonald, 1990) or a positive fetal DNA test for cystic fibrosis (Billings et al., 1992) is based on the belief that these individuals or their offspring could burden health care and other benefit plans. Whether cost alone is ever a sufficient justification for genetic discrimination becomes an overriding public policy question.

LEGAL MECHANISMS TO REDRESS GENETIC DISCRIMINATION

Although discrimination against human beings because of their status may be morally wrong, it is not necessarily unlawful. Congress and state legislatures have proscribed discrimination against certain classes based on their inherent characteristics. These characteristics include race, gender, religion, national origin, age, and disability. Equivalent statutory safeguards do not exist in most jurisdictions to protect against inequitable treatment based on other immutable personal characteristics such as sexual orientation, intelligence, height, looks, or personality.

The distinction among these diverse human characteristics often is hard to fathom, yet the key issue in determining the lawfulness of genetic discrimination is whether it is more akin to race, gender, or disability than sexual orientation, personality, or intelligence. Certainly, genetic discrimination that disproportionately burdens particular races, religions, or genders must be examined under relevant civil rights legislation. However, before going into such obviously fertile areas of inquiry, I ask the more basic question, can a genetic condition or trait be regarded as a disability?

Applicability of Disability Law to Genetic Discrimination

Three sources of disability law emerge from federal, state, and municipal legislatures: 1) the ADA and other federal disability legislation, 2) state and municipal handicap laws, and 3) genetic-specific laws. Federal legislation provides protection to persons with disabilities in three primary areas:

1. The Fair Housing Amendments Act of 1989 is the prime legislation protecting persons with disabilities from discrimination in housing.
2. The Education for All Handicapped Children Act of 1975 gives all school-age children with disabilities the right to a free public education in the least restrictive environment appropriate to their needs. This act was renamed by Congress to follow the more progressive language of "persons with disabilities." It is now entitled the Individuals with Disabilities Education Act.
3. The Rehabilitation Act of 1973 continues to be the prime legislation affecting persons with disabilities working for the federal government.

State and municipal disability legislation stand as important supplements to federal law. All states have disability statutes, all but four of which prohibit discrimination in the private as well as public sectors (Bridgham & Rowe, 1989; National Gay Rights Advocates, 1989). Courts have reasoned that state disability statutes closely follow the federal civil rights approach and should be construed accordingly (see, e.g., *Raytheon v. Fair Employment and Housing Commission, Estate of Chadbourne*, 1989). State and local disability laws are characteristically enforced by a well-established network of experienced human rights organizations, which can be far more productive than courts in preventing and remedying discrimination. These administrative agencies initiate targeted education and use reconciliation as an effective tool. The ADA also encourages the use of alternative means of dispute resolution, including settlement negotiations, conciliation, facilitation, medication, fact finding, minitrials, and arbitration (42 U.S.C. §12212). Many agencies report that they settle 80% or more of their cases through these less costly and less adversarial methods (Steele, Karsten, Lorenz, & Ritter, 1989). State and local disability legislation will continue to be an important source of law to prevent and remedy genetic discrimination because of the existing regulatory network dedicated to education, fact finding, and alternative forms of dispute resolution.

To reinforce the importance of safeguarding persons from genetic discrimination, a few states and municipalities have enacted specific legislation. Some of these laws apply generally to hereditary disorders (see, e.g., California Health and Safety Code §150, 1990: "carriers of most deleterious genes should not be stigmatized and should not be discriminated against by any person . . ."), but most are directed to particular traits such as sickle cell anemia, Tay-Sachs disease, or Cooley anemia (see, e.g., Civil Rights Amendments in Relation to the Employment of Persons with Certain Genetic Disorders of 1990). Most state and local legislatures have thus far refrained from enacting genetic-specific antidiscrimination legislation (compare with the flood of HIV-specific antidiscrimination legislation; see Bridgham & Rowe, 1989; Gostin, 1989, p. 1621, 1990, p. 2086). So the primary source of law continues to be disability law.

A thorough search of the legislative history of the ADA reveals that little attention was given to genetic discrimination. Congressman Steny Hoyer, the Floor Manager in the House, informed the Congressional Bioethics Advisory Committee that genetic discrimination was "not raised or discussed," and that it could not, therefore, be addressed by the Conference Committees. Congressman Hoyer recognized that genetic discrimination was "improper" and "very dangerous," but left it to the courts to determine whether it was covered under the ADA (Hoyer, 1990).

Some of the legislative history of the ADA did, in fact, reflect the view that genetic discrimination was covered. Several congressmen expressed the position that "the ADA will also benefit individuals who are identified through genetic tests as being carriers of a disease associated gene" (U.S. House of Representatives, 1990a, statement of Rep. Hawkins, p. H-4614). These legislators referred to the history of genetic discrimination, particularly during the sickle cell screening programs in the 1970s (U.S. House of Representatives, 1990a, statements of Reps. Edwards, Hawkins, and Waxman).

Defining a Disability   Disability is defined broadly in the ADA to mean: 1) "a physical or mental impairment that substantially limits one or more of the major life activities," 2) "a record of such an impairment," or 3) "being regarded as having such an impairment" (42 U.S.C. §12102[2]). The term *physical or mental impairment* does not include simple physical characteristics, such as blue eyes or black hair, nor does it include environmental, cultural, and economic disadvantages in and of themselves (U.S. House of Representatives, 1990a, statement of Rep. Waxman). The question may arise as to why genetic traits for sickle cell anemia or cystic fibrosis ought to be covered in the ADA, but not the genetic determinants for blue eyes or black hair. The reason is simply that Congress has designated disability, but not general personal characteristics, under civil rights.

A person has a disability if he or she has a "record" of or is "regarded" as having a disability or is perceived to have a disability, even if there is no actual incapacity. A "record" indicates that the person has a history of impairment or has been misclassified as having an impairment. This provision is designed to protect persons who have recovered from a disability or disease that previously impaired their life activities. By including those who have a record of impairment, Congress acknowledged that people who have recovered from diseases such as cancer, or have diseases that are under control (e.g., diabetes), face discrimination based on prejudice and irrational fear.

The term *regarded* as being impaired includes individuals who do not have limitations in their major life functions but are treated as if they did. This concept protects people who are discriminated against in the false belief that they have disabilities. This provision is particularly important for individuals who are perceived to have stigmatic conditions that are viewed negatively by society.

It is the reaction of society, rather than the disability itself, that deprives the person of equal enjoyment of rights and services.

Current Genetic Disability   Persons who currently have disabilities as a result of a genetic disease are undoubtedly covered under the ADA. The legislative history of the act, as well as the prior case law, make it clear that disability is defined according to the degree of impairment of life functions and not the etiology. No distinction can be drawn between genetic and other causes of disabilities. Congress and the courts have recognized disabilities of genetic (e.g., Down syndrome, Duchenne muscular dystrophy, cystic fibrosis) or multifactorial (e.g., congenital heart disease, schizophrenia, epilepsy, diabetes mellitus, and arthritis) origin. For example, in *Bowen v. American Hospital Association* (1986), although the case turned on whether withholding of treatment for an esophageal obstruction was covered under the Rehabilitation Act, Justice White clearly saw Down syndrome as a protected handicap. The U.S. Senate Committee on Labor and Human Resources (1989a) drew attention to a New Jersey zookeeper who refused to admit children with Down syndrome because he feared they would upset the chimpanzees. This committee also mentioned Duchenne muscular dystrophy and cystic fibrosis ("A person with lung disease will have a substantial limitation in the major life activity of breathing"; U.S. Senate Committee on Labor and Human Resources, 1989a; see *Gerben v. Holsclaw*, 1988). Cystic fibrosis is "undoubtedly" a handicapped status under the Rehabilitation Act of 1973 (*Department of Education, Hawaii v. Katherine D.*, 1982) and the Education for All Handicapped Children Act of 1975. In *School Board of Nassau County, Fla. v. Arline* (1987), the court cited remarks of Senator Walter Mondale discussing a case in which a woman "crippled by arthritis" was denied a job *not* because she could not work, but because college trustees thought "normal students shouldn't see her" (U.S. Senate, 1972, p. S-36761). Mental illness qualifies as a handicap under the Rehabilitation Act of 1973 (*Doe v. Region 13 Mental Health–Mental Retardation Commission*, 1983). The question for courts is whether the person currently has a disability. It does not matter how he or she came to have the disability.

The courts require a "substantial" limitation of one or more major life activities to determine disability. Thus, a genetic condition that does not cause substantial impairment may not constitute a disability. Persons with minor or trivial impairments, such as a simple infected finger, do not have a disability within the meaning of the act (U.S. Senate Committee on Labor and Human Resources, 1989b). However, if a defendant discriminates because he or she regards or perceives the genetic condition as more serious than it actually is, the person is protected under the third prong of the definition given above. For example, if a person with neurofibrosis has only mild changes in pigmentation she may not be considered to have a disability, but if she suffers from gross disfigurement she most assuredly would be protected under the ADA. The Senate Labor and Human Resources Committee cited the example of a severe burn victim as a person with a disability under the ADA (U.S. Senate Committee on Labor and Human Resources, 1989b). Citing the example of cosmetic disfigurement, the Supreme Court said that Congress was just as concerned about the effects of impairment on others as it was about its effects on the individuals with impairments (*School Board of Nassau County, Fla. v. Arline*, 1987). (Technically, the effects of disfigurement on others could be classified under the third prong of the definition.) Although the *Arline* court was concentrating on infectious disease, its conclusion is equally applicable to genetic discrimination: "It would be unfair to allow an employer to seize upon the distinction between the effects of the disease on others and the effects of the disease on a patient, and use that distinction to justify discriminatory treatment" (p. 282).

Future or Predicted Disability (Presymptomatic)   Genetic diagnosis or prognosis creates a new category of individuals who are asymptomatic but who are predicted to develop disease in the future. These individuals sometimes are referred to as the "healthy ill" or "at risk" (see Human Genetics Committee of the Council for Responsible Genetics, 1990). The number of people in this category is small because the technology is new and has been applied only to relatively rare diseases such as Huntington chorea. Progress in DNA technology undoubtedly will increase the number of diseases that can be detected before symptoms appear.

Can a person who currently is healthy but is predicted to become ill be classified as having a disability? The issue of future disability becomes more important as the Human Genome Initiative enhances the ability of physicians to predict diseases such as a genetic propensity for Huntington chorea (Gostin, 1991). Those who discriminate because of subjective and uncertain predictions of future impairment foster harmful stereotypes because the person currently is healthy and capable of meeting all job, benefit, or service criteria.

The intention of Congress to include future disability is reflected both in the legislative history of the ADA and in the prior case law. During the Conference Report debate on the ADA, Congressman Hawkins opined that persons who are genetically at risk "may not be discriminated against simply because they may not be qualified for a job sometime in the future. The determination as to whether an individual is qualified must take place at the time of the employment decision, and may not be based on speculation regarding the future" (U.S. House of Representatives, 1990a, Statement of Rep. Hawkins). Several congressmen concurred in this reasoning, expressly stating that future disability was covered by the term *regarded* as having a disability (U.S. House of Representatives, 1990a, Statements of Reps. Edwards and Waxman).

The analogy of asymptomatic HIV infection is helpful in ascertaining the court's likely position on persons at risk for genetic disease. A positive test for HIV infection is a powerful predictor of future disease and disability. In 1986, the U.S. Department of Justice (DOJ) concluded that, although the disabling effects of AIDS may constitute a handicap, pure asymptomatic infection could not (DOJ, 1986). The Justice Department position has been thoroughly repudiated by Congress and the courts. (The Justice Department itself reversed its opinion in 1988 [DOJ, 1988].) Both the legislative (see e.g., *Civil Rights Restoration Act of 1987*, 1988; U.S. House of Representatives Committee on Education and Labor, 1990) and judicial (see, e.g., *Doe v. Centinela Hospital*, 1988) branches have made it clear that pure asymptomatic infection is protected under disability law.

It is difficult to distinguish a predictive test for AIDS and for Huntington chorea. In both cases there is no current disability, the predictive value of the test is strong, and the date of onset and severity of symptoms is uncertain. Employers might argue that persons who test positive for HIV have a current infection manifesting a clear disease process, whereas persons testing positive for Huntington chorea do not. This is not a convincing argument. A defect in a specific chromosome can be identified as the beginning of a genetic disease process in the same way as infection is identified as the beginning of a contagious disease process (Burris, 1985, p. 933; Gostin, 1987, p. 461). Public policy clearly would be skewed if it left individuals unprotected while free of symptoms and protected them only after they developed symptoms (Capron & Pelligrino, 1990). Fortunately, courts are not likely to accept this construction of the ADA.

Genetic Carriers   Carriers of recessive genetic diseases such as hemoglobin disorders (e.g., sickle cell anemia and thalassemia) and Tay-Sachs disease have only one gene that mediates the disease, whereas two genes are required in order to manifest the disease. A carrier will not develop symptoms, but his or her offspring may inherit the disease if his or her partner also is a carrier. Employers, insurers, or health care providers may discriminate against carriers because of a fundamental misconception that a recessive gene might affect a person's own health or capabilities.

The ADA's prohibition of discrimination based on a perception of disability applies to those who falsely assume that carriers have or will develop a disability. The primary purpose of disability law is to overcome such irrational fears and beliefs. A clear consensus emerges from the case law that employment decisions must be based on reasonable medical judgments showing that the person's disability prevents him or her from meeting legitimate performance criteria.

Multifactorial Diseases and Environmental Factors   The social impact of genetic diagnosis and prognosis is felt strongly in the occupational setting. The identification of persons who are hypersusceptible to occupational disease provides an ostensible health justification for employment discrimination. These persons are protected under the ADA provided the employer's decision is based on a perception that the person has or will have a disability. A federal district court, for example, held that a person who is unusually sensitive to tobacco smoke is handicapped under the federal Rehabilitation Act of 1973. The Court reasoned that this hypersensitivity limited one of the employee's major life activities—his capacity to work in an environment that is not completely smoke free (*Vickers v. The Veterans Administration*, 1982). Similarly, an athlete may have a disability if he or she has a weak heart (see "Football Player," 1988), which would make him or her susceptible to future harm or injury, or a person may be regarded as having a disability if the stresses of fire fighting would provoke a sickle cell crisis (*People v. City of Salina, Kansas*, 1990). However, employers can take action if the person's condition renders him or her unqualified for the job or would pose a direct threat to others in the workplace (42 U.S.C. §§12111[3], 12113[b]).

The promise of the ADA is to protect all individuals who have or are perceived to have disabilities in the past, present, or future. It would be a betrayal of that promise if the law did not equally protect individuals who do not, and indeed may never, have a disability but whose predictive genetic tests cast a shadow over their own future health or that of their children (Wilker & Hubbard, 1990).

Employment Discrimination under Disability Law

"Qualification Standards," Including "Direct Threat" The antidiscrimination principle in the ADA applies only to "qualified individuals." A "qualified" person must be capable of meeting all of the performance or eligibility criteria for the particular position, service, or benefit. Qualification standards under the ADA may include a requirement that an individual shall not pose a "direct threat" to health or safety in the workplace (42 U.S.C. §12113[b]). "Direct threat" means a significant risk to the health or safety of others that cannot be eliminated by reasonable accommodation (42 U.S.C. §12111[3]). There is, moreover, an affirmative obligation to provide "reasonable accommodations" (42 U.S.C. §12112[b][5]) or "reasonable modifications" (42 U.S.C. §12131) if they would enable the person to meet the performance or eligibility criteria. Employers are not required to provide reasonable accommodations if this would pose an undue hardship on the operation of the business (42 U.S.C. §12112[b][5][A]; see *Southeastern Community College v. Davis*, 1979). "Undue hardship" is carefully defined in §12111(10) as "requiring significant expense" when considered in light of many enumerated factors.

How do such terms as *qualified, direct threat, reasonable accommodation*, and *undue hardship* apply to discrimination based on a genetic prediction of future disability to the employee or to his or her offspring? Qualification standards are measured against current skills and performance. The fact that a person may become unqualified sometime in the future does not provide a justification for discrimination. As noted throughout the legislative process on the ADA, "the determination as to whether a person is qualified must be made at the time of the particular employment decision—of hiring, firing, or promotion—and may not be based upon speculation and predictions regarding the person's ability to be qualified for the job in the future" (U.S. House of Representatives, 1990a, p. H-4626; see also U.S. House of Representatives, 1990a, statements of Reps. Edwards and Hawkins).

With regard to "direct threat," the explicit language of the ADA refers to *significant* risks to the health or safety of *other* individuals in the *workplace* (42 U.S.C. §12113[b] and [d][3]). This language helps define the parameters of genetic discrimination based on current or foreseeable health and safety risks. Occupational risks must be significant, and the determination of significant risk must be based on scientific evidence (see, e.g., U.S. House of Representatives Committee on the Judiciary, 1990) and determined on a case-by-case basis, not under any type of blanket generalization about a class of persons with disabilities or assumptions about the nature of disease. This requires a fact-specific individualized inquiry resulting in a "well-informed judgment grounded in a careful and open-minded weighing of risks and alternatives" (*Hall v. United States Postal Service*, 1988, quoting *School Board of Nassau County, Fla. v. Arline* [1987]; see also *Mantolete v. Bolger*, 1985; *Strathe v. Department of Transportation*, 1983). A specific determination must be made that a person with a genetic predisposition will develop symptomatology in the immediate future leading to a real health or safety threat in the workplace.

The language of the ADA also refers to risk to "other individuals" in the "workplace." Courts might disregard risks to the health of the person with a disability on a strict reading of the act. Thus, it is conceivable that persons with disabilities may argue that they cannot be discriminated against merely because they are hypersusceptible to workplace toxins or because they pose a safety risk to themselves. Courts, however, may well take a broader view of the act and disqualify persons with disabilities if occupational exposure poses a significant and immediate threat to their health. Courts are not likely to overturn employers' decisions to terminate employees to avoid an immediate sickle cell crisis (*People v. City of Salina, Kansas*, 1990) or to avoid a likely heart attack in a vulnerable athlete. Whether or not a well-documented and serious longer term risk of cancer would justify discrimination remains to be decided (see *Jackson v. Johns-Manville Sales Corporation*, 1986, examining whether an individual exposed to asbestos but not currently symptomatic can recover now but maintain the likelihood of future cancer). The courts, however, would comply with the letter and spirit of the ADA if they did not allow discrimination based on cumulative exposure to workplace toxins over many years. This could open the door to potentially widespread genetic discrimination. As suggested earlier, it also would provide an excuse for employers to weed out hypersusceptible workers rather than reducing overall toxic levels.

The reference in the ADA to the risk to others in the "workplace" raises the question of whether employers can discriminate based on risks to future offspring. The language would not permit discrimination against genetic carriers because the risk to the fetus does not arise from the workplace environment. Risks of teratogenicity to the employee or congenital risks to the fetus in the womb stemming from occupational exposure may present sharper jurisprudential and ethical questions. This form of discrimination is more likely to be directed against women rather than persons with disabilities, so it is discussed under gender discrimination below.

"Reasonable Accommodations" and "Undue Hardship" The employer has an affirmative obligation to provide reasonable accommodations to enable a person with a disability to meet qualification standards, including the reduction of significant risks to health or safety. The ADA requires reasonable accommodations unless they would impose "undue hardship" on the operation of the business (42 U.S.C. §§12111[10], 12112[b][5][A]). Undue hardship means an action requiring significant difficulty or expense when considered against such factors as the nature and cost of the accommodation and the overall financial resources and size of the business (42 U.S.C. §12111[10][B]). Congress specifically rejected the contention of the Supreme Court in *T.W.A. v. Hardison* (1977) that an employer need not expend more than a *de minimus* amount for the accommodations (U.S. Senate Committee on Labor and Human Resources, 1989b). Employers do not have to provide accommodations that would fundamentally alter the nature of the industry (U.S. Senate Committee on Labor and Human Resources, 1989), so that a company need not stop producing batteries to eliminate lead levels. Employers that can improve the workplace environment without undue financial burden may be required to do so.

Preemployment Genetic Testing and Prognosis The ADA specifies that the prohibition of discrimination against persons with disabilities applies to medical examinations and inquiries (42 U.S.C. §12113[c]). Historically, employers gathered information concerning the applicant's physical and mental condition through application forms, interviews, and medical examinations. This information often was used to exclude persons with disabilities from employment— particularly applicants with hidden disabilities such as epilepsy, emotional illness, cancer, or HIV infection (U.S. Senate Committee on Labor and Human Resources, 1989b). Employers' abilities systematically to obtain and use medical information to predict currently hidden conditions is vastly expanding with the development of genetic testing and prognosis.

Preemployment inquiries must be limited to assessing the applicant's ability to perform job-related functions. Thus, employers may not require job applicants to undergo extensive medical examinations and screenings, including diagnosis and prognosis for genetic traits or conditions such as Huntington chorea, sickle cell anemia, or Tay-Sachs disease. This will strictly limit the employer's ability to obtain information about a person's current and future illnesses, diseases, or genetic predispositions before a job is offered.

Employer Costs: Health, Disability, Life, and Other Insurance Benefits Employers caught in the clash between economic competitiveness and antidiscrimination principles undoubtedly will search for ways to reduce their health benefit costs, and they are likely to do so by limiting health care coverage. Employers, insurers, benefit plan administrators, and health care providers are entitled to design and administer insurance and benefit plans using standard underwriting principles (42 U.S.C. §12201[c]; U.S. House of Representatives Committee on Education and Labor, 1990, pp. 136–138). They may sell to, and underwrite, individuals applying for health coverage and establish employee benefit plans based on sound actuarial data (*Alexander v. Choate*, 1985). Employers and insurers can use creative methods to reduce their costs without violating the ADA. They can insert preexisting condition clauses in health benefit contracts, place caps or other limits on coverage for certain treatments, and charge higher premiums or copayments to persons with higher risks.

Employers and insurers, however, may not use underwriting as a "subterfuge" for invidious discrimination (42 U.S.C. §12201[c]). Any clear evasion of the principles of antidiscrimination, whether malicious, purposeful, or inadvertent, is unlawful. Congress rejected the Supreme Court's restrictive reading of the term *subterfuge* in *Public Employment Retirement Systems of Ohio v. Betts* (1989), in which the Court held that subterfuge required some malicious or purposeful intent to evade (see, e.g., U.S. House of Representatives, 1990a, statements of Reps. Hawkins and Waxman). Thus an employer cannot deny a qualified applicant a job either because the employer's insurance plan does not cover that individual's disability or because of the increased cost. Differences in health coverage for persons with disabilities must be justified on the basis of actuarial data demonstrating a heightened risk of future illness.

People with genetic traits, conditions, or predispositions for illness must not be denied a job or promotion based on their perceived or future disabilities: "An employer could not discriminate against a carrier of a disease-associated gene because such individual may be at higher risk of having a child with a genetic disease whose care would increase costs for the patient's employer" (U.S. House of Representatives, 1990a, statement of Rep. Waxman, p. H-4626). Also, they must have equal access to health and other insurance coverage provided to all employees. Agencies required to promulgate regulations under the ADA should carefully consider the interaction of unlawful employment decisions with lawful underwriting decisions, to ensure that the latter are not used to circumvent the overriding antidiscrimination principles under the act. Employers, however, have greater opportunities to circumvent antidiscrimination principles when they are acting as self-insurers, as the following section demonstrates.

The Employee Retirement Income Security Act (ERISA) of 1974 may provide an additional source of law to remedy discrimination based purely on cost factors. Section 510 of ERISA makes it unlawful for an employer to "discriminate against a participant or beneficiary for exercising any right to which he is entitled under the provisions of any employer benefit plan . . . or any right to which such participant may become entitled." Although ERISA does not require employers to provide benefit plans at all, it does prohibit employers from discriminating against employees because they may disproportionately burden a benefits plan now or in the future. The terms *participant* and *beneficiary* suggest that persons are eligible for relief under ERISA only after they have been hired. The purpose of ERISA is to protect "employees" and the "employment relationship" (*West v. Butler*, 1980). Indeed, courts thus far have restricted entitlement under ERISA to current or discharged employees (see Liebman, 1988). Thus, ERISA may provide a remedy for persons with genetic conditions or predispositions once they are hired.

Insurance Discrimination under Disability Law The major limitation of the ADA on insurers, including self-insurers, is to prevent them from using underwriting as a subterfuge for invidious discrimination (42 U.S.C. §12201[c]). Thus, insurers could not completely deny health insurance coverage on the basis of a genetic predisposition, and employers could not deny a qualified applicant a job because their insurance plans do not cover the genetic disability or because of the increased cost (U.S. House of Representatives Committee on Education and Labor, 1990; U.S. House of Representatives Committee on the Judiciary, 1990). The sharp distinction drawn by the ADA is that any discrimination among applicants with disabilities for insurance or employment must be justified on the basis of actuarial data demonstrating a heightened risk of future illness.

The very essence of underwriting is to classify people according to risk and to treat those with higher risks differently. The adverse impact of underwriting for persons with genetic predispositions is significant. The social purpose of insurance is to spread risk across groups, enabling wider access to health care services. It may not be too far in the future before a person's genome becomes a template for identifying a wide array of diseases. Once each person's medical future can be predicted with specificity, the conceptual foundations of the industry are turned around. If insurers have actuarial data demonstrating a likelihood of future illness, they can limit coverage.

Seen through the eyes of the insurance industry, no rational distinction could be drawn between genetic prognosis and smoking, hypertension, high serum cholesterol, or HIV infection. In each case, the health data can provide powerful predictions of future health and longevity. Worse still from the insurer's perspective is "adverse selection," whereby the buyer has access to genomic information that is denied to the company. Perhaps the greatest fear of insurers is that genetic testing will become common in clinical medicine and they will be barred from obtaining that information.

More worrisome, from the point of view of the buyer, would be a decision by an insurer to view a genetic predisposition as a preexisting condition. The greater the predictive value of the genetic test, the more likely it is that insurers will regard the condition as uninsurable or preexisting. This process became clear in the reaction of insurance companies to HIV infection. As epidemiological evidence demonstrated the inexorable course of HIV infection, insurers began insisting on having access to serological information, and now much of the industry conducts its own HIV testing. HIV infection almost universally is regarded as an uninsurable condition. As genetic tests begin to demonstrate the inevitability of future illness, we can expect insurers to follow the same course as has occurred with HIV infection. If insurers choose to utilize genomic information to make sound actuarial predictions of disease, the ADA may not be effective in placing any restrictions on the industry.

Genetic Discrimination: Disparate Impact on Race, Ethnicity, and Gender

Genetic prognosis, by its very nature, often disproportionately impacts vulnerable classes based on race, ethnicity, national origin, or gender. Sickle cell anemia is associated with persons of African heritage, Tay-Sachs disease and Gaucher disease (adult form) with Ashkenazi Jews, and familial Mediterranean fever with Armenians. Risks of teratogenicity or congenital risks to the fetus often are focused on women or pregnant women, setting up a class based on gender.

Title VII of the Civil Rights Act of 1964 (42 U.S.C. §2000e *et seq.*) prohibits job discrimination based on race or gender unless the discriminatory practice is related to job performance. Lack of discriminatory purpose is irrelevant (see *Smith v. Olin Chemical Corporation*, 1977). Supreme Court Justice O'Connor explained that the intention behind Title VII was "to prohibit an employer from singling out an employee by race or sex for the purpose of imposing a greater burden or denying an equal benefit because of a characteristic statistically identifiable with the group but empirically false in many individual cases" (*Arizona Governing Committee v. Norris*, 1983 [O'Connor J., Concurring]).

The outcome of Title VII lawsuits often is dependent on whether the racial or gender discrimination is intentional or not. If the class is explicitly based on race or gender or if the discrimination is intentional, the employer is required to meet the more exacting standard that the action is based on a "bona fide occupational qualification." Title VII also allows lawsuits based on the disparate impact of a facially neutral policy. Once discriminatory effect is shown, the employer must only demonstrate that there was "business necessity" for the employment practice (*Hayes v. Shelby Memorial Hospital*, 1984; *Wright v. Olin Corporation*, 1982). The Supreme Court in *Wards Cove Packing Company v. Antonio* (1989) said that the plaintiff has the ultimate burden of proof, and the employer need not demonstrate that the challenged practice is "essential" or "indispensable" to show business necessity. Congress has been trying, so far unsuccessfully, to repudiate the holding in *Wards*.

Surprisingly little court litigation has focused on the burden of genetic testing on racial minorities or women. Sickle cell anemia lawsuits have been brought under many other theories that are not germane to employment discrimination. In *Williams v. Treen* (1982) the court found that, if state prison officials had denied treatment to persons with sickle cell anemia, it would raise a constitutional issue. *Ross v. Bounds* (1974) presented a complaint by black inmates seeking injunctive relief requiring that all black inmates be routinely examined to determine if they had sickle cell anemia or trait; the court found that the plaintiffs did not state a cognizable claim under the Civil Rights Act. In *Taylor v. Flint Osteopathic Hospital* (1983) the court found against plaintiff who argued that black patients were discriminated against by being denied reimbursement for "unnecessary" medical treatments especially helpful for typically black problems. An immediate problem is that a genetic prognosis represents a facially neutral policy that does not expressly discriminate on the basis of race or gender. For example, in *Equal Employment Opportunity Commission v. Greyhound Lines* (1980), an African-American employee sued under Title VII alleging that a no-beard policy adversely impacted black workers. The employee had a skin condition particular to African-Americans. It is far more likely that Title VII litigation to remedy genetic discrimination will be based on disparate impact theory—that is, that the genetic trait or condition disqualifies proportionately more racial minorities or women.

Sickle Cell Classification: A Form of Race Discrimination?   Some courts have said *in dicta* that a job classification based on sickle cell anemia or trait would create a disparate impact on African-Americans. For example, in *Narragansett Electric Co. v. Rhode Island Commission for Human Rights* (1977) the court found that a sickle cell screen clearly would be discriminatory because a nonracial explanation was not possible. Again, in *General Electric Company v. Gilbert* (1977) Justices Brennan and Marshall in dissent argued that, under the majority opinion, the employer could exclude sickle cell–related disabilities from its disability benefits plan and not violate Title VII. Yet no lawsuit has been successful under this theory. In *Smith v. Olin Chemical Corporation* (1977) an African-American employee brought a Title VII claim when he was fired because of current and future bone degeneration, which is characteristic of sickle cell anemia. The Fifth Circuit Court rejected his claim that he was dismissed because of his race, stating that the category of "bone degeneration" was racially neutral. The court also rejected arguments based on disparate impact because of the "manifest job-relatedness of the requirement that a manual laborer have a good back" (*Smith v. Olin Chemical Corporation*, 1977). In *People v. City of Salina, Kansas* (1990) the court rejected the claim of racial discrimination when a fire fighter with sickle cell anemia was dismissed because of the heightened risk of sickle cell crisis because in fact he was not qualified for the position.

Employment decisions based on sickle cell *trait* may well violate Title VII. Such a class disproportionately impacts African-Americans. Because the existence of a genetic trait usually does not indicate any current or future illness, it is difficult to conceive how employers would justify the discrimination as a business necessity.

Fetal Protection Policies: A Form of Gender Discrimination?   An employer's decision not to hire women of child-bearing age based on the risk of teratogenicity or harms to the fetus in utero from occupational exposure may be easier to challenge because of a more direct gender classification and less obvious job relatedness. Fetal protection policies, in one form or another, have a long history. Earlier in this century, the Supreme Court upheld exclusion of women from hazardous employment to protect the "future well-being of the race" (*Muller v. Oregon*, 1908). Since that time, however, a series of federal statutes set standards for employers to reduce toxic levels and other hazards to both men and women (e.g., the Fair Labor Standards Act; the Occupational Safety and Health Act). The Pregnancy Discrimination Act of 1978 amended Title VII to clarify that the statute prohibits "discrimination [against working women] on the basis of their childbearing capacity." Women affected in pregnancy, childbirth, or related medical conditions shall be treated the same as others who are "similar in their ability or inability to work."

The Supreme Court is about to decide whether fetal protection policies are allowed under Title VII. *International Union, United Automobile, Aerospace and Agricultural Implement Workers of America v. Johnson Controls* (1989), currently before the court, concerns the policy of a battery manufacturer that bars any woman from working in a job that exposes her to amounts of lead that exceed preset levels unless she presents medical evidence of sterility. The preset levels are: 1) where any employee recorded a blood lead level exceeding 30 μg/dl during the preceding year, or 2) the work site yielded an air sample during the preceding year in which lead was measured in excess of 30 μg/m^3. The Seventh Circuit Court found no violation of Title VII in this case. It reasoned that the fetal protection policy constituted a gender-neutral rule that had a disparate impact on a protected group as found in *Wright v. Olin Corporation*, 1982 ("the problem presented by a fetal protection policy involved motivations and consequences most closely resembling a disparate impact case"; *Hayes v. Shelby Memorial Hospital*, 1984). The policy was justified by the "business necessity" of preventing a "substantial health risk" to the children of female, but not male, workers (following *Hayes v. Shelby Memorial Hospital*, 1984).

The threshold question for the Supreme Court is whether fetal protection policies present a case of intentional or facial discrimination that can be justified only if sex were shown to be a "bona fide occupational qualification." If this stricter standard were adopted, it would be difficult to hold that sterility is necessary to the business of making batteries, or any other business for that matter. Even if the Court uses disparate impact analysis, it still has to find that the "moral imperative" of protecting children from their parents' mistakes represents a business necessity and whether substantial harm to the fetus is empirically likely. The "moral" quality of the policy of Johnson Controls was emphasized by its legal counsel in the oral argument before the Supreme Court (Greenhouse, 1990).

Perhaps more important, the question for the Court is whether the company or the woman should be permitted to make the choice between continuing to work and a small risk to an as yet unborn, perhaps even unplanned, child. If one compares a pregnant unemployed or underemployed woman with no health benefits to one who is "exposed to an indeterminant lead risk but well fed, housed, and doctored, whose fetus is at greater risk? Whose decision is this to make?" (*International Union, United Automobile, Aerospace and Agricultural Implement Workers of America v. Johnson Controls*, 1989). Ultimately, the resolution to this ethical and legal dilemma is to reduce environmental hazards that harm both men and women, rather than excluding a class of persons deemed hypersusceptible. By allowing employers to "fix the worker, not the job," courts would harm the public health (Bertin, 1989). The Occupational Safety and Health Act already mandates that employers maintain a workplace "free from recognized hazards that are causing or are likely to cause death or serious physical harm," and it requires the Secretary of Labor to promulgate health and safety standards, to the extent feasible, "that no employee will suffer material impairment of health or functional capacity" (OSHA, para 655[b][5]). The act provides statutory authority to protect the fetuses of lead-exposed working mothers. (Harm to fetuses is a material impairment of the reproductive systems of parents," *United Steelworkers of America v. Marshall*, 1981.) Private employers should not be permitted to make determinations about what is "safe" for whole sub-classes of the employed population. Employers' fetal protection policies, by focusing on excluding workers rather than reducing hazards, provide less protection to workers than federal regulators and public health experts regard as necessary (see Mayer & Taub, 1989).

The fetal protection policy in *Johnson Controls* is directed more toward risks in utero than to genetic risks. Suppose an employer were to discriminate against women based on the teratogenicity of workplace toxins. That case would raise squarely the issue of whether teratogenic risks fall exclusively, or even predominantly, on women. Medical evidence that toxic exposure causes de-formed sperm leading to birth defects would surely result in a finding of intentional gender discrim-ination. In such circumstances, Title VII would not tolerate consigning women to a class of employ-ment with lower pay and potential based strictly on the possibility that they could become pregnant.

Genetic-Specific Antidiscrimination Statutes

A minority of states have enacted statutes that specifically apply to persons with hereditary condi-tions (e.g., California, Florida, Illinois, Louisiana, Maryland, Missouri, New Jersey, New York, and Virginia). The most progressive of these statutes recognize that disease-specific legislation might prove too rigid as scientific understanding of the human genome progresses (e.g., California Health and Safety Code, 1990). These statutes have broad application to any hereditary disorder (see, e.g., New Jersey Statutes, 1987; New Jersey Annotated Code, 1988), and they draw the dis-tinction between carriers and those who experience manifestations of the disease (California Health and Safety Code, 1990). Other statutes are directed more narrowly to specific conditions or traits such as sickle cell anemia (the Florida Statutes Annotated, 1981, prohibits testing for sickle cell anemia but no other genetic trait or disease; the Florida Statutes, 1989, single out sickle cell and hemophilia for medical care grants; and in the Louisiana Revised Statutes Annotated, 1982, pro-hibition on employment discrimination only includes sickle cell anemia), phenylketonuria, hemo-philia, cystic fibrosis, Tay-Sachs disease, and Cooley anemia (e.g., 191 Revised Statutes of Mis-souri, 1989, which is limited to cystic fibrosis, hemophilia, and sickle cell anemia; and the New York Laws 900, 1990, which is limited to sickle cell anemia, Tay-Sachs disease, and Cooley anemia).

Genetic-specific statutes around the country do not appear to follow any coherent policy or pattern. Only a few genetic-specific statutes ban discrimination. California adopted a general anti-discrimination policy that includes penalties for violating the Hereditary Disorders Act of 1990. The California statute is comprehensive and prohibits "stigmatization" and "discrimination" against "carriers of most deleterious genes." It also proscribes mandated state restrictions on child-bearing decisions regardless of the genetic purpose (California Health and Safety Code, 1990).

Statutes in Florida, Illinois, Louisiana, New Jersey, New York, and North Carolina are pat-terned after disability law and prohibit employment discrimination against persons with any "atypi-cal hereditary or blood trait" (New Jersey Annotated Code, 1988) or particular genetic conditions or traits (see, e.g., Florida Statutes, 1981: "No person, firm, corporation, state agency, . . . or any public or private entity shall deny or refuse employment to any person or discharge any person from employment solely because such person has the sickle cell trait"). In some cases the statutes have more general application beyond employment discrimination, including disparate impact on racial or ethnic minorities (Illinois Public Act 86-1028, 1990), or discrimination on the basis of familial status when in the process of securing legal custody (Illinois Public Act 86-1028, 1990).

The remainder of the genetic-specific statutes prohibit certain types of screening (e.g., Florida Statutes Annotated, 1981, prohibiting testing for sickle cell); provide funding for research or treatment (e.g., Florida Statutes, 1989; Iowa Code, 1989); or require mandatory information on genetic disorders to be given to marriage applicants (Illinois Public Act 86-1028, 1990). Others are concerned with genetic counseling and confidentiality (191 Revised Statutes of Missouri, 1989).

A review of current state statutes reveals a patchwork of provisions that are incomplete, even inconsistent, and that fail to follow a coherent vision for genetic screening, counseling, treatment, and nondiscrimination.

CONCLUSION: FUTURE LEGAL
SAFEGUARDS AGAINST GENETIC DISCRIMINATION

The course currently being charted by the Human Genome Initiative is filled with the promise of unimagined medical advancement for humankind. Unfortunately, the potential to harm human beings by rendering them virtually unemployable or uninsurable is just as real (see, generally, Nelkin & Tancredi, 1989). Policymakers should be considering several legal strategies to safeguard against genetic discrimination. Although the ADA emerges as a mighty tool to remedy genetic discrimination, it would be preferable not to leave its construction to the vagaries of future adjudication. The ADA specifically redresses discrimination based on past disability ("record of impairment"), current disability ("impairment"), or perception of disability ("regarded" as impaired). The ADA, however, is silent about discrimination based on future disability. This chapter has presented a number of legal, ethical, and public policy arguments to suggest that future disability is covered, but a simple amendment to Section 3 (42 U.S.C. §12102[2]) of the ADA would remove any uncertainty. A new subsection "D" would amend the definition of disability to include: "having a genetic or other medically identified potential of, or predisposition toward, such an impairment." Such language would ensure that discrimination against currently asymptomatic persons based on a future prediction of disease would be covered by the ADA.

There remains in the ADA one major gap in coverage that is not so easily rectified. That is the exclusion of underwriting from the coverage of the act. Future regulations on the ADA should seek to ensure that employers do not use this underwriting exclusion to discriminate against applicants or employees on the basis of financial burden. Employers may well turn to imaginative actuarial justifications for invidious discrimination. Employers need not take the drastic measure of not employing a person. Rather, employers may make the benefits plan so unattractive and unaffordable as to erect a formidable barrier to persons with disabilities.

Strict regulations preventing employers from evading the principles of the ADA are only a stopgap remedy. Ultimately, a political choice will have to be made by Congress as to whether insurance and self-insurance is merely a business, or whether it has a wider social purpose. If insurance discrimination rises to a truly unconscionable level as the genome is mapped, society may have to confront the issue of access to health care.

Gaps in the coverage of disability law also need to be addressed at the state level. State disability laws also should be amended to make it clear that they cover future disability. The continued importance of state disability law cannot be underestimated given the much more efficient administrative structures, and greater resources, available to combat discrimination.

Policymakers also will have to confront the philosophical and pragmatic issue of whether genetic-specific legislation is necessary or desirable. The great majority of state legislatures have enacted HIV-specific legislation (see Gostin, 1989, p. 1621), so the precedent is set for the concept of separately addressing particularly vexing public health problems. The National Human Genome Initiative should give careful consideration to developing a set of legislative guidelines for future genetic-specific statutes. In the absence of such guidelines, the prospect for rational legislation appears low.

Model guidelines on the law and ethics of genetic screening, confidentiality, and discrimination ought to go hand-in-hand with the scientific advances. Funding, original thinking, and carefully crafted policy on the legal and ethical dimensions of the Human Genome Project are as essential as the science itself.

REFERENCES

Air Force rejects cadets with sickle cell trait. (1988, February 6). *New York Times*, p. C-10.

Alexander v. Choate, 469 U.S. 287 (1985).

The American Society of Human Genetics. (1990). Statement on cystic fibrosis screening. *American Journal of Human Genetics, 46*, 393.

Annas, G.J. (1990). Mapping the human genome and the meaning of monster mythology. *Emory Law Journal, 39*, 629–719.

Antonarakis, S.E. (1990). The mapping and sequencing of the human genome. *Southern Medical Journal, 83*, 876–878.

Arizona Governing Committee v. Norris, 463 U.S. 1073, 1108 (1983).

Arthur D. Little projects a $5.7 billion clinical diagnostic market in 1990. (1987, March). *Genetic Engineering News*, p. 13.

Bertin, J.B. (1989, November 27). Fix the job, not the worker. *L.A. Times*, p. B7.

Billings, P., Kohn, M.A., de Cuevas, M., & Beckwith, J. (1992). Discrimination as a consequence of genetic testing. *American Journal of Human Genetics, 50*, 476–482.

Bishop, J.E., & Waldholz, M. (1990). *Genome*. New York: Simon & Schuster.

Bowen v. American Hospital Association, 476 U.S. 610 (1986).

Bridgham, B., & Rowe, M. (1989). AIDS and discrimination—a review of state laws that affect HIV infections 1983–1988.

Brownlee, S., & Silberner, J. (1990, July 23). The assurances of genes. *U.S. News and World Report*, p. 57.

Burris, S. (1985). Rationality review and the politics of public health. *Villanova Law Review, 34*, 933–982.

California Health and Safety Code, §150 (1990).

Capron, A.M., & Pelligrino, E. (1990, June 25). *Fact sheet accompanying letter to Senator Thomas Harkin*.

Carey, J. (1990, May 23). The genetic age. *Business Week*, p. 18.

Civil Rights Act of 1964, codified as amended in scattered sections of 42 U.S.C. (1988).

Civil Rights Amendments in Relation to the Employment of Persons with Certain Genetic Disorders of 1990, N.Y. ALS 900, N.Y. Laws 900, N.Y. A.N. 9437 (1990).

Civil Rights Restoration Act of 1987, 20 U.S.C. §168 *et seq.* 29 U.S.C. §706, 42 U.S.C. §2000 (1988).

Cook-Deegan, R.M. (1990). Social and ethical implications of advances in human genetics. *Southern Medical Journal, 83*, 879–882.

Cronan v. New England Telephone, 41 FEP 1273 (Mass 1986).

De Long, M.R., & Moses, H. (1988). Disorders of movement. In A.M. Harvey, R.J. Johns, V.A. McKusick, A.H. Owens, & R.S. Ross (Eds.), *Principles and practice of medicine* (22nd ed., pp. 1057–1065). Norwalk, CT: Appleton & Lange.

Department of Education, Hawaii v. Katherine D., 531 F. Supp. 517 (D. Hawaii 1982).

Disease disposition screening. (1986, December 11). *Biomedical Business International*, pp. 230–232.

DNA probes nudge monoclonals in the race to export the medical diagnostic market. (1988, September). *Genetic Engineering News*, pp. 1, 12, 13, 21.

Doe v. Centinela Hospital, 57 U.S.L.W. 2034 (CD Cal. 1988).

Doe v. Region *13* Mental Health–Mental Retardation Commission, 704 F.2d 1402 (5th Cir. 1983).

Education for All Handicapped Children Act of 1975, 20 U.S.C. §§1232, 1401, 1405–1420, 1453 (1975).

Equal Employment Opportunity Commission v. Greyhound Lines, 635 F.2d 188 (3d Cir. 1980).

Fair Housing Amendments Act of 1988, 42 U.S.C. §§3601–3619 (1988).

Fair Labor Standards Act of 1938, 29 U.S.C. §201 *et. seq.* (1938).

Football player sues to be permitted to play. (1988, October 5). *USA Today*.

General Electric Company v. Gilbert, 429 U.S. 125 (1977).

Gerben v. Holsclaw, 692 F. Supp. 557 (E.D. Pa. 1988).

Goldstein, J.L., & Brown, M.S. (1989). Genetic aspects of disease. In E. Braunwald, K.J. Isselbacher, R.G. Petersdorf, J.D. Wilson, J.B. Martin, & A.S. Fauci (Eds.), *Harrison's principles of internal medicine* (11th ed., pp. 585–597). New York: McGraw Hill.

Gostin, L. (1987). The future of public health law. *American Journal of Law & Medicine, 12*, 461–490.

Gostin, L. (1989a). Public health strategies for confronting AIDS: Legislative and regulatory policy in the United States. *JAMA, 261*, 1621–1630.

Gostin, L. (1990). The AIDS litigation project: A national review of court and human rights commission decisions, part II: Discrimination. *JAMA, 263*, 2086–2093.

Gostin, L. (1991). Genetic discrimination: The use of genetically based diagnostic and prognostic tests by employers and insurers. *American Journal of Law & Medicine, 17*, 801–836.

Gostin, L., Curran, W.J., & Clark, M.E. (1987). The case against compulsory casefinding in controlling AIDS: Testing, screening and reporting. *American Journal of Law & Medicine*, *12*, 7–53.

Griffin, J.W., & Cornblath, D.R. (1988). Peripheral neuropathies. In A.M. Harvey, R.J. Johns, V.A. McKusick, A.H. Owens, & R.S. Ross (Eds.), *Principles and practice of medicine* (22nd ed., pp. 1092–1096). Norwalk, CT: Appleton & Lange.

Hall v. United States Postal Service, 857 F.2d 1073, 1979 (6th Cir. 1988).

Hayes v. Shelby Memorial Hospital, 726 F.2d 1543 (11th Cir. 1984).

Health Insurance Association of America. (1990). *Working group on genetic testing*. Washington, DC: Author.

Hening, R.M. (1989, December 24). Body and mind: High-tech fortunetelling. *New York Times*, p. 20.

Hewitt, M., & Holtzman, N.A. (1988). [Commercial development of tests for human genetic disorders.] Unpublished document.

Holtzman (1989). *Proceed with caution: Predicting risks in the recombinant DNA era*. Baltimore: Johns Hopkins University Press.

Hoyer, S.H. (1990, August 1). *Letter from Congressman Steny H. Hoyer (5th Dist. Maryland) to Alexander M. Capron, Chairman of the Biomedical Ethics Advisory Committee*.

Human Genetics Committee of the Council for Responsible Genetics. (1990). Position paper on genetic discrimination. *Genewatch*, *3*.

International Union, United Automobile, Aerospace and Agricultural Implement Workers of America v. Johnson Controls, No. 88-1308 (7th Cir. 1989).

Jackson v. Johns-Manville Sales Corporation, 781 F.2d 394 (5th Cir. 1986).

Liebman, L. (1988). Too much information: Predictions of employee disease and the fringe benefit system. *University of Chicago Legal Forum*, 57–92.

MacDonald, X. (1990, July 15). Ethical eye on insurers' genetic tests. *Daily Telegraph*, p. 9.

Mantolete v. Bolger, 757 F.2d 1416 (9th Cir. 1985).

Market for DNA probe tests for genetic diseases. (1986, November). *Genetic Technology News*, pp. 6–7.

Matthewman, W. (1900). Title VII and genetic testing: Can your genes screen you out of a job? *Howard Law Journal*, *27*, 1185–1220.

Mayer, S., & Taub, N. (1900). Petition for writ or certiorari to the U.S. Supreme Court in *International UAW v. Johnson Controls*.

McKusick, V.A. (1988). The Mendelian disorder. In A.M. Harvey, R.J. Johns, V.A. McKusick, A.H. Owens, & R.S. Ross (Eds.), *Principles and practice of medicine* (22nd ed., pp. 281–303). Norwalk, CT: Appleton & Lange.

Mosby v. Joe's Westlake Rest., Cal. Super. Ct., San Fran. Cty, No. 865045.

Muller v. Oregon, 208 U.S. 412, 422 (1908).

Narragansett Electric Co. v. Rhode Island Commission for Human Rights, 118 R.I. 457, 374 A.2d 1022, 1026 (1977).

National Gay Rights Advocates. (1989). *Protection against discrimination under state handicap laws: A fifty state analysis*. San Francisco: Author.

National Institutes of Health. (1990). Statement of the Workshop on Population Screening for the Cystic Fibrosis Gene. *New England Journal of Medicine*, *323*, 70.

National Research Council. (1988). *Mapping and sequencing the human genome*. Washington, DC: U.S. Government Printing Office.

Nelkin, D., & Tancredi, L. (1989). *Dangerous diagnostics*. New York: Basic Books, Inc.

Occupational Safety and Health Act, 29 U.S.C. §655(b)(5) (1988).

Office of Technology Assessment. (1983). *The role of genetic testing in the prevention of occupational disease*. Washington, DC: U.S. Government Printing Office.

Office of Technology Assessment. (1988a). *Mapping our genes: Genome projects: How big, how fast?* Washington, DC: U.S. Government Printing Office.

Office of Technology Assessment. (1988b). *Medical testing and health insurance*. Washington, DC: U.S. Government Printing Office.

Office of Technology Assessment. (1990). *Genetic monitoring and screening in the workplace*. Washington, DC: U.S. Government Printing Office.

People v. City of Salina, Kansas, 1990 U.S. Dist. LEXIS 4070 (March 20, 1990).

Pokorski, R. (1990). *The potential role of genetic testing in risk classification*. City: American Council of Life Insurance.

Prediction and prejudice: Forging a new underclass. (1990). *Consumer Reports*, *55*, 483.

Pregnancy Discrimination Act of 1978, 42 U.S.C. §2000e(k) (1978).

Public Employment Retirement Systems of Ohio v. Betts, 109 S.Ct. 256 (1989).

Raytheon v. Fair Employment and Housing Commission, Estate of Chadbourne, 261 Cal Rptr. 197 (Cal. App. 2d Dist. 1989).

Rehabilitation Act of 1973, 29 U.S.C. §§791–794 (1988 & Supp. I 1989).

Ross v. Bounds, 373 F. Supp. 450 (E.D. N.C. 1974).

Rothstein, M.A. (1983). Employee selection based upon susceptibility to occupational illness. *Michigan Law Review*, *81*, 1379–1496.

R.S. First, Inc. (1986). *Genetic testing in the USA 1986–1990*. In M. Hewitt & N.A. Holtzman (Eds.). [Commercial development of tests for human genetic disorders.] Unpublished document.

School Board of Nassau County, Fla. v. Arline, 107 S.Ct. 1123, 480 U.S. 273 (1987).

Shannon v. Charter Red Hospital, Admin. Complaint, Dallas, Tex., April 28, 1986.

Shapiro, E.D. (1990, January). Dangers of DNA: It ain't just fingerprints. *New York Law Journal*, p. 1.

Shaw (1990, November 23). Genetic gains raise fear of a new kind of bias. *Philadelphia Inquirer*, pp. 1-A, 10-A.

Sit, M. (1990, August 21). Will genetic mapping threaten worker's privacy? August 21. *Boston Globe*, p. 23.

Smith v. Olin Chemical Corporation, 555 F.2d 1283 (5th Cir. 1977).

Southeastern Community College v. Davis, 442 U.S. 397 (1979).

Steele, R., Karsten, S., Lorenz, B., & Ritter, J. (1989). *Identification and assessment of state and local strategies to prevent discrimination*. DHHS, Washington, DC.

Strathe v. Department of Transportation, 716 F.2d 227 (3d Cir. 1983).

T.W.A. v. Hardison, 432 U.S. 63 (1977).

Taylor v. Flint Osteopathic Hospital, 561 F. Supp. (1983).

U.S. Department of Justice. (1986, June 23). *Opinion of Charles J. Cooper, Assistant Attorney General, Office of Legal Counsel, for Ronald E. Robertson, General Counsel, Department of Health and Human Services.*

U.S. Department of Justice. (1988, September 27). Memorandum from Douglas W. Kamiec, Acting Assistant Attorney General, Office of Legal Counsel, to Arthur B. Calvahouse, Jr., Counsel to the President, *re* Application of Section 504 of the Rehabilitation Act to HIV-Infected Individuals.

U.S. House of Representatives. (1990a, July 12). *House conference report no. 101-596, to accompany S. 933 (101st Congress, 2nd session)*. Washington, DC: U.S. Government Printing Office. (Reprinted in *United States Code Congressional and Administrative News, 4*, 565–600 [1990]).

U.S. House of Representatives. (1990b, July 19). Departments of Labor, Health and Human Services, and Education, and Related Agencies Appropriations Act (H.R. 4996) (101st Congress, 2nd session). *Congressional Record, 136*, H5003.

U.S. House of Representatives Committee on Education and Labor. (1990, May 15). *House report no. 101-485(II), to accompany H.R. 2273 (101st Congress, 2nd session)*. Washington, DC: U.S. Government Printing Office. (Reprinted in *United States Code Congressional and Administrative News, 4*, 303–444 [1990]).

U.S. House of Representatives Committee on the Judiciary. (1990a, May 15). *House report no. 101-485(III), to accompany H.R. 2273 (101st Congress, 2nd session)*. Washington, DC: U.S. Government Printing Office. (Reprinted in *United States Code Congressional and Administrative News, 4*, 445–511 [1990]).

U.S. Public Health Service and U.S. Department of Energy. (1990). *Understanding our genetic inheritance: The U.S. human genome project: The first five years FY 1991–1995*. Washington, DC: U.S. Government Printing Office.

U.S. Senate. (1972). Statement of Sen. Mondale. *Congressional Record, 118*, S36761.

U.S. Senate Committee on Labor and Human Resources. (1989a, May 9, 10, 16; June 22). *Hearings on S. 933, the Americans with Disabilities Act of 1989 (S. Hrg. 101-156)*. Washington, DC: U.S. Government Printing Office.

U.S. Senate Committee on Labor and Human Resources. (1989b, August 30). *Senate report no. 101-116, to accompany S. 933 (101st Congress, 1st session)*. Washington, DC: U.S. Government Printing Office.

United Steelworkers of America v. Marshall, 647 F.2d 1189, 1256 n. 96 (D.C. Cir. 1980), *cert. denied*, 453 U.S. 913 (1981).

Vickers v. The Veterans Administration, 549 F. Supp. 85 (W.D. Wash. 1982).

Wards Cove Packing Company v. Antonio, 109 S.Ct. 2115 (1989).

Watson, J.D., & Cook-Deegan, R.M. (1990). The human genome project and international health. *JAMA, 263*, 3322–3324.

Wilford, B.S., & Fost, N. (1990). The cystic fibrosis gene: Medical and social implications for heterozygote detection. *JAMA, 263*, 2777–2783.

Wilker, N.L., & Hubbard, R. (1990, June 27). *Letter from Nachama L. Wilker and Ruth Hubbard of the Council for Responsible Genetics to the Honorable Steny H. Hoyer, U.S. House of Representatives.*

Williams v. Treen, 671 F.2d. 892 (5th Cir. 1982).

Wright v. Olin Corporation, 697 F.2d 1172 (4th Cir. 1982).

Chapter 15

Mental Disorder and the ADA

Leonard S. Rubenstein

The Americans with Disabilities Act[1] (ADA) is mostly thought of as a law about the rights of people with physical disabilities. Its pages of details concern removal of physical barriers to transportation, communication, buildings, and the like. The multiple hearings, reports, analyses, and celebrations similarly focus principally on the physical and attitudinal barriers society has erected to equality and inclusion for people with physical disabilities.

The largest number of people affected by the ADA, however, either have mental disorders[2] or have been treated for emotional or psychological problems. The law has profound consequences for them, with the potential not only to change many social practices, and with them many lives, but also in the long term to change patterns of thought.

However, the inclusion of people with mental disorders within the ADA was, like AIDS, drug addiction, and alcoholism, controversial. In the Senate, Senator Armstrong offered an amendment to exclude conditions with a "moral component" and later succeeded in excluding people with some specific psychiatric diagnoses from the law's coverage (see Mental Disorders Excluded by the ADA, below). After the bill was enacted in the Senate, he complained that, "if the ADA is enacted the private sector will be swamped with mental disability litigation (U.S. Senate, 1989b). In the House, the Energy and Commerce Committee floated a draft amendment that would have excluded people with mental disorders entirely from the ADA.

By and large, these attacks failed, but they reflected common and highly ambivalent attitudes toward persons with mental disorders in American society. Popular culture encourages acknowledgment of emotional problems and seems to find a support group for all of them. Guests on confessional talk shows elbow each other onto the set to reveal how some childhood trauma has rendered them dysfunctional as adults. Private hospitals prey on the concerns of anxious parents by suggesting their children's troubles are the result of psychiatric disorders.

Yet prejudice against people with mental disorders runs very deep. They are devalued, mar-

---

[1]The Americans with Disabilities Act of 1990 (PL 101-336) is published in *Statutes at Large* (104 Stat. 327) and codified in the *United States Code* (42 U.S.C. §§12101–12213 [Supp. II 1990]). References to various portions of the act within this chapter cite the specific section of the code.

[2]The language to describe the people who are the subject of this chapter is both controversial and very political. I use the term *mental disorders* rather than mental illness to convey that these conditions are not well understood and, furthermore, that their relation to physical illness is distinctly unclear. These disorders may have genetic or biological components but are in other respects quite different from physical diseases. They certainly are not "brain diseases" in the same sense that we speak of liver disease. People with mental retardation and with substance abuse or alcohol problems are not covered in this chapter.

ginalized, loathed, and feared, even offered as scapegoats for crime and homelessness (there is a vast literature on this subject; see, e.g., Perlin, 1991). As recent political campaigns have demonstrated, the mere disclosure of treatment for psychiatric conditions creates an "issue" that requires "explanation." Even those who have intimate knowledge of these conditions share these feelings. A recent survey revealed that, although half of the individuals questioned said they or a family member suffered from depression, 43% believed depression to be a sign of emotional or personal weakness ("Many View Depression," 1991).

These attitudes are reflected as well in social practices and rules. People who have been treated for psychiatric problems are discriminated against in employment (Combs & Omvig, 1986; Farina & Felner, 1973), higher education, the professions, and activities of civic life. People routinely are expected to waive their right to privacy in mental health treatment when applying for employment, admission to the bar, and much else because of the assumption that seeking help bespeaks a disqualifying deficiency.

For people with more severe forms of mental disorder, particularly schizophrenia, the image is even worse. These are among the few groups in society who respectable people will openly try to keep out of their neighborhoods and about whom they will tell offensive jokes. The media devote little attention to this group unless a patient released from a psychiatric hospital shoots a gun in a shopping center or someone calls for institutionalizing homeless people. In the same way we treat other devalued people, we feel more comfortable distancing ourselves by exaggerating their difference, attributing to them fearful characteristics they do not possess, or putting a label on them, such as "brain diseased."

This chapter explores how, in the face of these prejudices, the ADA's antidiscrimination and reasonable accommodation requirements can change practices and ultimately attitudes about people with mental disorders. It begins with an analysis of who is covered by the ADA and then looks at how the ADA dramatically changes the law's approach to the rights of persons with mental disorders. At that point, rather than engage in a summary of the ADA's effect on people with mental disorders (see Milstein, Rubenstein, & Cyr, 1991; Parry, 1993) I examine two areas of the ADA's concern in some depth: employment in Title I and governmental decisions premised on mental disorder in Title II. Needless to say, this approach necessarily leaves some subjects untouched, such as the ADA's impact on public accommodations ranging from dentists to restaurants.

SCOPE OF THE MANDATE: WHO IS COVERED

Congress found that there are 43 million or more people with disabilities in the United States (42 U.S.C. §1210[a][1]), but there are at least that many people who either have a condition that can be diagnosed as a mental disorder using the American Psychiatric Association's (1987) *Diagnostic and Statistical Manual of Mental Disorders* (third edition, revised; DSM-III-R) or seek treatment for emotional problems but do not fit into any diagnostic category. Estimating the number of people affected by the ADA as a result of mental disorder is tricky business because even defining mental disorder is a political as much as a scientific endeavor. However, existing data suggest that the number is very high. Epidemiological prevalence studies conducted by the Epidemiological Catchment Area Program of the National Institute of Mental Health concluded that in 1980, about 35.1 million people were affected by a nonaddictive mental disorder. These included about 15.1 million Americans who suffered from depression, 20 million people with anxiety disorders, and 1.7 million people diagnosed with schizophrenia (Regier et al., 1993). Not all of these individuals have disabilities severe enough to meet the ADA's first definition of an individual with a disability—that the impairment substantially limits one or more major life activities (42 U.S.C. §12103[2]). Those who do, however, comprise a substantial group, especially when interpreted in light of the broad remedial purpose likely to be given this definition (Burgdorf, 1991, pp. 445–446). A recent survey estimated that about 3.3 million Americans living in noninstitutional settings have mental disorders that seriously interfere with one or more aspects of daily life, and that 2.6 million of these are currently limited in one or more functional areas (Barker et al., 1992).

The ADA also guarantees protection against discrimination to two additional and even larger groups of people: those who have a "record" of having an impairment that substantially limits a major life activity and those who are "regarded as having such an impairment" (42 U.S.C. §12102[2][C]). The last definition follows the approach taken in implementation of Section 504 of the Rehabilitation Act of 1973 and the Fair Housing Amendments Act of 1988 in defining disability by the conduct of others: if another person discriminates against an individual on the basis of a (mis)perceived disability, that individual is protected. In view of the number of people who seek help for some emotional or mental problem and who suffer discrimination as a result, this group is enormous.

CONCEPT OF EQUALITY IN MENTAL HEALTH LAW

For centuries the law has taken account of mental disorder: in the insanity defense, in guardianship and competency proceedings, and in state-compelled institutionalization. Since the early 1970s, mental disability law has taken a dramatic turn, with an explosion of litigation concerning the rights of people with mental disorders and mental retardation.

Yet most mental disability litigation framed rights as a matter of due process, not equality. The principal substantive concerns have been the permissable extent of state coercion imposed on persons with mental disorders in the name of treatment (e.g., *Donaldson v. O'Connor,* 1975; *Washington v. Harper,* 1990), the procedures needed to protect the individual against unwarranted coercion (e.g., *Addington v. Texas,* 1979), and the extent of the state's obligation to provide treatment and protection from harm to someone in state custody (e.g., *Youngberg v. Romeo,* 1981).

Equal treatment and nondiscrimination did not play a significant role in the evolution of this law. (An exception, but applicable only to children, was the Education for All Handicapped Children Act of 1975.) The more pressing concern was fundamental fairness and the extent of state obligations in proceedings that applied to a group considered to be different and unequal. Indeed, the very posing of the questions concerning institutionalization and coerced treatment undercut an equality-based approach to the law because these questions presumed that people with mental disabilities could be treated differently by the state.

Predecessors to the ADA: The Rehabilitation Act and Fair Housing Amendments Act

Passage of Sections 503 and 504 of the Rehabilitation Act of 1973 did not much affect this approach despite their mandate of nondiscrimination by federal contractors and recipients of federal financial assistance against all persons with disabilities. Agencies were slow to adopt regulations (see *Cherry v. Mathews,* 1976, regarding U.S. Department of Health, Education and Welfare [DHEW] rules). The U.S. Department of Housing and Urban Development (DHUD) did not adopt rules enforcing Section 504 until 1988 (DHUD, 1988, p. 20216; see Simring, 1991). Private enforcement was restricted; only recipients of federal financial assistance, not federal contractors, could be sued in court. The Supreme Court narrowly intepreted the statutory trigger for coverage (the requirement that a program or activity receive federal financial assistance) in *Grove City College v. Bell* (1984). (Congress subsequently overruled the Supreme Court's interpretation in the Civil Rights Restoration Act of 1987.) In addition, judicial decisions involving people with mental disorders have been discouraging.

Courts rejected efforts to enforce the nondiscrimination and reasonable accommodation mandates of Section 504 on behalf of people with mental disabilities, both in individual cases of exclusion (e.g., *Doe v. New York University,* 1981) and in attacks on segregated services (Cook, 1991).

The idea of equality for people with mental disorders simply failed to take hold, largely because of deeply held prejudices: equality becomes problematic in the face of difference (Minow, 1990). In legal terms, people with mental disorders were not considered "similarly situated" to others, so that the typical nondiscrimination analysis could not apply at all (Rubenstein & Milstein, 1993). It has been difficult for society to accept that a person may be impaired, even severely, in some life functions but still be able to make decisions, engage in competitive employment, and otherwise become involved in the community. In the face of deeply entrenched prejudice against people with mental disorders, it has been even more difficult to convince judges that people with emotional problems or mental disorders can perform productively in the workplace, be acceptable parents, make medical decisions, or participate appropriately in civic life. As a result, scholars have considered Section 504 virtually a dead letter for people with mental disabilities, as illustrated by the single paragraph devoted to the Rehabilitation Act in a major three-volume treatise on mental disability law (Perlin, 1989).

The concept of equality for people with mental disabilities broke through in only one area, housing, where discrimination has been so virulent and so openly expressed that, even before enactment of the Fair Housing Amendments Act of 1988, it was difficult for courts to turn away. Group home providers battling neighborhood associations convinced courts either to redefine the concept of "family" in local zoning codes to allow the homes in (Kanter, 1984, 1986) or to find exclusionary land-use rules a violation of the Constitution's equal protection clause (see *City of Cleburne v. Cleburne Living Center,* 1985). When the latter issue reached the Supreme Court, the Court held that prejudice, stereotypes, and even seemingly benign concerns may not be used to exclude (*Cleburne,* 1985).

In 1988 passage of the Fair Housing Amendments Act reinforced and expanded this trend. The Fair Housing Amendments Act for the first time brought people with disabilities—mental disorder included—within the nondiscrimination provisions of a mainstream civil rights law. It began the reorientation of mental disability law as well by insisting on equal treatment. Furthermore, it obligates landlords and local government to alter their rules in order to promote and achieve integration and equality (Milstein, Pepper, & Rubenstein, 1989). That requirement is embodied in the concept of reasonable accommodation, designed to make differences between persons with and without disabilities irrelevant.

The ADA's Approach to Equality

The ADA applies the ideas contained in fair housing law to all other aspects of civic life, including private employment. It carries two fundamental messages about nondiscrimination and inclusion: first, that common prejudices against people with a diagnosis or history of treatment for a mental disorder can no longer be a reason to keep a person out of a job, a dentist's office, a restaurant, or a government program; and second, that other institutions must adjust their practices—albeit within the limitations of "reasonable accommodation" or "reasonable modification"—to meet the needs of people.

It also challenges some of the most deeply held prejudices against people with mental disorders, particularly the idea that they can be excluded because they are threatening or dangerous. The employment and public accommodations titles of the law prohibit discrimination or exclusion unless the person is shown to be a "direct threat" to the health or safety of others. That phrase is defined to mean "a significant risk to the health or safety of others that cannot be eliminated by reasonable accommodation (42 U.S.C. §12111[3]; see also 42 U.S.C. §12182[b][3]).

The legislative history carefully assures that a determination of significant risk must be based on objective criteria and, when appropriate, medical standards. It warns against the use of stereotypes or preconceptions, particularly in the case of people with mental disorders. Rather, the determination that a person poses a direct threat must be an individualized assessment based on "objective evidence from the person's behavior that the person has a recent history of committing overt acts or making threats which cause harm or which directly threatened harm (U.S. House of Representatives Committee on the Judiciary, 1990, pp. 44–45). An accompanying footnote specifically warns employers not to "presume that the person poses a threat to the health or safety of others" because of his or her mental illness (cf. *School Board of Nassau County, Fla. v. Arline*, 1987, dealing with direct threat in infectious disease cases). So the common perception that people with schizophrenia or other psychotic conditions are dangerous and hence excludable, if not stamped out, is at least neutralized because it can no longer be the basis of a decision to discriminate. Rather, a person can be excluded only if he or she has engaged in overt behavior that reasonably leads to the conclusion that he or she is dangerous.

Mental Disorders Excluded by the ADA

The prejudice against people with mental disorders did not go totally unheeded in the legislative process leading to enactment of the ADA. Rather, it forced the ADA's backers in the Senate to compromise with Senator Armstrong when he proposed an amendment to exclude mental impairments "with a moral component" (U.S. Senate, 1989a). His amendment defined these to include, among others, any "impulse control disorder," any sexual disorder, and, for children, conduct or disruptive behavior disorders (thus excluding most emotionally disturbed children). The amendment was never offered formally, so there is no official record of it. After it was floated, a compromise with the ADA's Senate sponsors led to the amendment that became Section 511 of the ADA (42 U.S.C. §12211).

One could simply laugh at this combination of moral confusion and 19th-century medicine, but the Armstrong amendment led to categorical exclusion of a laundry list of Senator Armstrong's "morally objectionable disorders," mostly involving compulsive behavior or sexual disorders. The list includes, among others, exhibitionism, voyeurism, pedophilia, "sexual behavior disorders," compulsive gambling, kleptomania, and pyromania (42 U.S.C. §12211[b]). These are the only recognized disabilities not involving unlawful use of controlled substances to be excluded from the ADA (Milstein et al., 1991); even AIDS survived efforts to carve out exceptions.

So the ADA is imperfect. Like racial minorities after the Civil Rights Act of 1964, people with mental disorders face discontinuity between law and many prevailing social attitudes. The Civil Rights Act rested on strongly held moral beliefs about racial equality and integration but faced a deeply entrenched racism. Similarly, the ADA is premised on the idea that people with disabilities can and must be treated equally, but at the same time is far ahead of contemporary thinking about people with mental disorders. It imposes requirements many people and judges may have a great deal of trouble accepting. Indeed, the courts on which the law relies to enforce the ADA themselves engage in practices that probably violate the ADA. For example, lawyers licensed by court systems typically must disclose any psychiatric treatment, counseling, or the like from birth together with a blanket release of all medical information relating to that treatment. No similar disclosure is typically required for any physical problem. The ADA's highly specific rules against discrimination challenge the widely held assumptions on which these rules are based.

THE ADA IN PRACTICE: EMPLOYMENT

Employment is a means to self-worth and to escape from dependence but is frequently denied to people who have mental disorders or have had psychiatric treatment in the past. Irrespective of ability or job performance, people commonly are denied employment if they disclose prior psychiatric treatment or fired if "found out." For example, in *Finney v. Baylor Medical Center Grapevine* (1990), the employee had been dismissed as soon as the employer learned of the existence of a bipolar (manic–depressive) disorder. Also, despite the growth of employee assistance programs in the workplace, few employers attempt to accommodate the situations of people whose emotional or psychiatric problems may interfere with their productivity.

Now, this discrimination in employment against persons with mental disorders on the basis of their disability is prohibited, and reasonable accommodation to enable them to work is required. Three employment issues are particularly relevant to people with mental disorders under the ADA: blanket inquiries into an applicant's medical history; the employer's setting of a job qualification standards; and reasonable accommodation.

Pre-offer Inquiry into Psychiatric History

For generations employment-related decisions have presumed a connection between a diagnosis of mental disorder and the needs of competitive work, such as productivity, reliability, and emotional stability. As a result, written employment applications have typically asked whether the person has been hospitalized or treated for a psychiatric or emotional condition and, if so, for the details. The presumption was so strong and the use of these standard questions so commonplace that even the federal government demanded answers to these questions for a decade after the law prohibited them.

That "commonsense" presumption, it turns out, is wrong. Even for people with the most serious psychotic diagnoses, such as schizophrenia, researchers have found only a tenuous connection between psychiatric diagnosis and capacity to withstand the stresses of a job (Anthony & Jansen, 1984). Rather, as Anthony and his colleague have shown, the critical indicators for working are functional strengths such as getting along with others, doing the job, and being dependable (Anthony, Howell, & Danley, 1982). Particular jobs may have additional requirements that also can be expressed in functional terms, such as capacity to deal with the public, ability to make decisions without supervision, and ability to get along with co-workers (Mancuso, 1990).

The ADA gives legal protection against ill-considered stereotypes. It prohibits employers from using psychiatric history as a surrogate for the determination of the person's ability to do the job. It accomplishes this through the simple device of prohibiting preoffer inquiries as to whether the applicant has a disability or the "nature or severity of the disability" (42 U.S.C. §12113[c][2][A]). Hence the standard inquiry on employment forms as to whether a person has had psychiatric treatment is forbidden. As a result the ADA will, if taken seriously, alter the hiring practices of all employers covered by the act.

For the millions of people who have sought psychiatric treatment or counseling for emotional problems in the past and who are able to work, the significance of the change extends beyond nondiscrimination. The ADA amounts to a significant privacy protection because these people no longer will be subject to the stigma and humiliation of having to explain or justify their private lives in order to obtain a job. Because these inquiries now are carried out quietly and an applicant's risk in challenging the procedures has been so great, it is difficult to gauge how many people will gain employment who are denied or discouraged from seeking work now. In any event, the feelings of humiliation at having to disclose treatment felt by these millions of people will become a thing of the past.

The privacy protection feature of the ADA, however, ends at the offer stage. After that the ADA contains no limit on the medical information the employer may obtain from the employee (other than that, with a few exceptions, it must be kept confidential) so long as the employer subjects all employees to the same rules requiring medical examinations and disclosure of medical history (42 U.S.C. §12112[c][3]). The law contains no requirement that the postoffer inquiry be job related, and the Equal Employment Opportunity Commission (EEOC, 1992), explicitly eschews such a rule (29 C.F.R. §1630.14[b][3]).[3]

---

[3]EEOC regulations are codified at 29 C.F.R. part 1630 (1992). References to various portions of these regulations within this chapter cite the specific section of the regulations.

One might conclude that the limitation on pre-offer inquiries is only a Pyrrhic victory because the employer can demand the information after an offer is made. After the job offer is made, however, the employer's interest in obtaining the information significantly recedes. Furthermore, the employer likely will be restrained in seeking (and acting on) this information because rejection after the disclosure of prior treatment of a now certifiably qualified applicant is likely to create a clear case of discrimination. Thus the danger of postoffer revelation and discrimination appears slight.

Employment Standards and Psychiatric Condition

Blanket inquiries into medical history are prohibited at the pre-offer stage, but the ADA does not hinder the employer from relevant inquiry into the applicant's ability to meet the "essential functions" (42 U.S.C. §12111[8]) of the job. Functional criteria in job selection are, of course, not new. They have long been part of personnel practice, ranging from minimum typing speeds to lifting requirements in jobs requiring physical labor. Their use was expanded by claims of gender-based employment discrimination in police, fire fighting, and other jobs. That litigation forced the development of functional job criteria such as physical strength and stamina and also led to challenges to other employer-established functional requirements as not job related.

The ADA can have a similar impact on the emotional or psychological dimensions of work. It amounts to an invitation to set highly specific and precise job qualification standards instead of drawing inferences from a medical inquiry. These could include job criteria such as the ability to get along with co-workers, to come to work every day on time, to concentrate on tasks, and to complete tasks in a timely way. In other words, instead of finding out whether a person has been treated for depression, the employer will have to ask whether the person is able to meet these qualification standards. One consequence of these rules is to increase the level of inquiry for all job applicants, so the employer can make a reasonable judgment about the person's capacity to concentrate, to get along, to complete tasks, and the like. Everyone will feel the intrusion in order to prevent discrimination.

The ADA allows the employer leeway in determining these job qualification standards; they must be "job-related and consistent with business necessity" (42 U.S.C. §12113). The employer has considerable discretion in inquiring whether the applicant meets standards for job-related functions (42 U.S.C. §12112[c][2][B]). Furthermore, an amendment adopted in the House grants substantial, albeit not absolute, deference to the employer's own determination of what an "essential function" of a job is, particularly if it is presented in writing (42 U.S.C. §12111[8]). Although the House rejected an amendment creating a presumption in favor of the employer's determination of essential functions, it is likely that in the usual case the employer's view will prevail, especially since the EEOC regulations (1992) appear to give significant weight to the employer's view of an essential function (29 C.F.R. §1630.2[n][3]).

Nevertheless, the change from a diagnosis to a functional approach is likely to benefit people with mental disorders substantially. The shift in assessment of the work capacity of a person with a mental disorder from diagnosis to job-based functional criteria already has taken place in disability benefit procedures. In the 1970s the Social Security Administration adopted disability assessment standards for persons with mental impairments that were diagnosis and symptom driven rather than based on the person's capacity to work (Rubenstein, 1985). By the 1980s it had become apparent that this approach was inconsistent with acceptable standards for assessing the capacity to work, and it was successfully challenged in the courts as impermissible under the Social Security Act (*Bowen v. City of New York*, 1986; *Mental Health Association of Minnesota v. Heckler*, 1984). In 1984 Congress required reforms in the standards for determining disability, demanding that disability standards specifically relate to the vocational capacity of a person with a mental impairment (Security Disability Benefits Reform Act of 1984, §5). The standards issued by the Social Security Administration (1992) focus on four essential mental requirements of work: appropriate functioning in one's own daily life; social skills; the ability to concentrate on, persist at, and complete specific tasks; and the ability to carry on work without exacerbation of symptoms (20 C.F.R. pt. 404[P] app. 1, §12.00 *et seq.*). Generally, the system has worked well.

The analogy is, of course, imperfect. The Social Security Administration uses these standards to determine whether a person cannot work; under the ADA a similar approach is required by employers to decide whether a person with a disability can work. The Social Security Administration is attempting to assess whether the applicant can perform any competitive work, not whether he or she can perform a particular job. Furthermore, it is trying to use a single standard nationwide. Nevertheless, the underlying, functional approach is the same, and diagnosis-based decisions are unlawful. Under the ADA employers will be forced to follow the same approach.

One qualification standard, however, may prove more troublesome than it need be. As indicated above, Congress allowed employers not to hire persons who pose a "direct threat to the health or safety of others in the workplace" (42 U.S.C. §12113[6]). The very narrow meaning of the "direct threat" provision, however, enlarges rather than contracts employment opportunities and enables employers to gain a fair picture of potential employees with or without a mental disorder. Yet the EEOC has issued a highly questionable interpretation of the ADA's "direct threat" provision by expanding it to permit exclusion of persons who pose a threat to *themselves* as well as to others (EEOC, 1991a, p. 35736; 29 C.F.R. §1630.2[r]).

In response to criticism from disability advocates that the proposal both was inconsistent with the ADA and represented a resurrection of paternalism in discrimination law, the EEOC hedged but did not eliminate the employer's defense that it was seeking to protect employees. Instead, the EEOC required that the employer's decision be based on an "individualized assessment," be supported by "reasonable medical judgment that relies on the most current medical knowledge and/or on the best available objective evidence," and consider four factors: the duration of the risk, the nature and severity of the potential harm, the likelihood that the potential harm will occur, and the imminence of the potential harm (EEOC, 1991a, p. 35736; 29 C.F.R. §1630.2[r]).

All the qualifications hardly suffice. In the first place, the business of the employer is to get the job done and allow employees to watch out for themselves; the employee should decide what level of risk he or she is willing to endure. Second, it places far more faith in the predictive powers of mental health professionals than is warranted. The EEOC's interpretive guidance is unhelpful and even troubling. It opines that a law firm cannot exclude a person with a history of mental illness because of a "generalized fear" that the person's work might "trigger a relapse under the stress of trying to make partner" (EEOC, 1991b, p. 35745; 29 C.F.R. pt. 1630 app.). Suppose, however, that the person has had experiences in the past of exacerbations under stress so that the fear is not "generalized" but specific and individualized. Would that justify a failure to hire? How far can the employer go? The EEOC's approach leaves far too much room for employer discretion.

These EEOC guidelines, although likely to face a legal challenge, are important symbolically. They signify the continuing attitudinal hurdles employees with a history of mental disorder are likely to face despite the ADA's mandate.

Reasonable Accommodations

If the ADA fundamentally alters personnel practice by substituting a functional approach to employment decisions rather than exclusion based on diagnosis or treatment, the reasonable accommodation rules will have an even greater impact. Once an employee (or potential employee) self-identifies or is identified through permissible inquiries, the employer has the obligation to attempt reasonable accommodation that will enable the person to perform the essential functions of the job, so long as the accommodation does not impose an undue hardship on the employer. That subject is discussed elsewhere in this volume (see Parry, chap. 5), but little attention has been paid to its relevance to persons with mental disorders. As Parry has shown, neither the government's

Handbook of Job Analysis for Reasonable Accommodation nor the Job Accommodation Network operated by the President's Committee on the Employment of People with Disabilities gives more than passing attention to accommodating people with mental disorders in the workplace (Mancuso, 1990).

For them, reasonable accommodation is very different from the physical changes in the work environment needed to enable people with physical or sensory impairments to perform productively. Accommodations are likely to involve adjustments such as flexible use of leave time, assignment (or reassignment) to positions in which productivity requirements are consistent with the employee's ability to handle stress, and scheduling work (Mancuso, 1990).

Despite the new requirements, employers do not face the law in a sea of ignorance. Many employers have accommodated people with emotional problems for generations. Accommodations such as altering work schedules to allow for attending therapy sessions, reassignment to tasks that lessen contact with the public, and additional leave time hardly are uncommon even in the absence of legal requirements. Indeed, one could argue that most employers have far more experience in this form of accommodation than in any other. Because the accomodations required are judged by a reasonableness and undue hardship test and the ADA does not excuse lack of employee productivity once an accommodation is made, employers' fears of this unknown, like those of landlords (Simring, 1991), largely should be unfounded. Furthermore, common types of accommodations such as flexibility in scheduling and job shifting frequently are inexpensive (Mancuso, 1990, p. 14) and not especially difficult to analyze. For example, in a case concerning a machinist with serious migraine headaches, a court found that, in the particular circumstances of the case, the employer was not obligated to allow the employee to work on his own after hours to make up for lost time because the safety risk was too great, but it held that granting a leave of absence to the employee was reasonable (*Kimbro v. Atlantic Richfield Company,* 1989).

Still, there remains a great deal of new terrain because not every employer is so understanding and because the variety of possible accommodations likely exceeds current practices. The Rehabilitation Act cases offer virtually no guidance in applying the concept of reasonable accommodation. Moreover, employers easily are drawn to some coercive "accommodations" such as a "firm choice" between discharge or therapy. Requiring an employee to undergo therapy as a condition of working may seem an attractive option, but it raises many problems even beyond its coercive nature. These include interference with the confidentiality of medical treatment and the practical problem of an employee becoming stuck between an unwanted therapist and the need to keep the job. The concept of an accommodation is based on helping the employee perform his or her job. It is not at all clear that accommodations can be compulsory.

Here, the EEOC regulations (1992) are helpful because they mandate a collaborative rather than a coercive approach to reasonable accommodation. They call for an "informal, interactive process with the qualified individual with a disability" (29 C.F.R. §1630.2[o][3]). This means that reasonable accommodation should be seen as a method as well as end: a means of arriving at a solution as well as the solution itself.

THE ADA IN PRACTICE:
LIMITS TO EXCLUSION AND COERCION UNDER STATE LAW

Taking the ADA's principles of integration and nondiscrimination seriously has even more intriguing effects in the operation of government than in the private sector. Title II, Subtitle A of the ADA can change dramatically the manner in which people with mental disorders are treated by government and law. Hundreds of state laws governing marriage, the family, driver's licenses, medical treatment, and much else use distinctions based on mental disability. They all now are subject to challenge.

The nondiscrimination provisions of Title II, Subtitle A, which apply to state and local governments, are not new. Congress sought to apply the 1977 DHEW regulations (DHEW, 1991) interpreting Section 504 of the Rehabilitation Act to all state and local governments, not simply those receiving federal financial assistance. It appears at first glance that, because virtually all state and local governments now receive federal financial assistance, Title II will offer little that was not there before.

Yet it offers much that is new. Title II must be read in light of the law's purpose, to provide a "clear and comprehensive national mandate for the elimination of discrimination against individuals with disabilities" (42 U.S.C. §12101[b][2]). Cook has argued that, when considered as a whole, the ADA prohibits all segregation in services for people with disabilities, including institutional rather than community-based care (Cook, 1991). I consider here whether the ADA would permit challenges to a host of laws and other forms of state-authorized coercion and punishment that are premised on the existence of a mental disorder.

These amount to categorical exclusions, limitations, and legally sanctioned discrimination based on mental disorder. The most obvious of these are categorical exclusions based explicitly on mental disorder or a history of psychiatric treatment or hospitalization. Many states still prohibit marriage of persons who are identified as "lunatics" or "insane" (Brackel, Parry, & Weiner, 1985, pp. 508, 532–538). These statutes by and large have fallen into desuetude, but others, particularly those governing childrearing, have not. For example, the majority of states permit adoption without parental consent if the parents have one or another mental disability (Brackel et al., 1985, p. 517); many states explicitly consider mental disability as a ground for termination of parental rights (Hayman, 1990).

In other arenas as well, discrimination against persons with a history of mental disorder, however remote in time, is legally mandated. Federal law, for example, prohibits the sale of a gun to various categories of persons deemed undesirable, such as felons, illegal aliens, and dishonorably discharged veterans, but also to any person who "has been committed to any mental institution" (18 U.S.C. §922[d][4]). Legally sanctioned discrimination even extends to medical treatment. In some jurisdictions the state has assumed the authority to force psychiatric patients competent to make their own decisions to take medication, supposedly for their own good. Needless to say, other competent patients are not subject to such compulsion. A number of courts have held that the practice is consistent with a patient's right to due process of law (*Dautremont v. Broadlawns Hospital*, 1987), but even if so, is not the practice plainly discriminatory?

In these cases decisions are based on the person's diagnosis or label together with the presumption that mental disorder gives the state license to act where it otherwise would be restrained. However, the discrimination goes even deeper. Even in jurisdictions where state authorities, especially courts, do not explicitly premise their decisions on a finding of mental disorder *de jure,* they are heavily—and often inappropriately—influenced by the finding. As Stefan (1989) has shown, courts in child custody and termination of parental rights cases almost always rule, often reflexively, against the party with such a disorder. If they cannot categorically exclude based on a person's mental disorder, they apply standards such as "best interests of the child" that discriminate against the person. These decisions mirror social prejudices against and myths and stereotypes about people with mental disorders, a pattern so entrenched as often to go unnoticed and unquestioned.

These laws and practices raise fundamental questions of equality. It is plainly discriminatory to single out one group of people for differential and less beneficial consideration in these central areas of civic and personal life because of prevailing attitudes about their diagnoses or labels. As in employment, the ADA should require decisions based on people's abilities and behavior rather than on diagnosis, label, or, worse, prejudicial attitudes about a disability. For example, it means that a court must make its decision to terminate parental rights based on the person's behavior, without infection by prejudicial attitudes about the person's mental disorder. It also means that, in medical treatment, decision-making authority cannot be taken away simply because the person has a particular diagnosis.

Litigation under Section 504 has rarely been brought to effect these changes. In *United States Department of the Treasury v. Galioto* (1986), the plaintiffs challenged, on equal protection grounds, a total ban on purchase of firearms by anyone who had been hospitalized for psychiatric treatment. Felons, by contrast, were permitted to petition for authority to purchase. (The case was rendered moot by statutory change.) The question is whether the ADA can do better to get at this patent but heretofore tolerated discrimination. Congress's extraordinarily visionary statement of purpose—to eliminate discrimination based on disability (42 U.S.C. §12101[b][1])—and the ADA's requirement of reasonable modification of existing, and presumably neutral, rules, practices, and policies that tend to discriminate (42 U.S.C. §12131[2]) certainly suggests that it was intended to apply here.

To reach that conclusion, however, it is necessary to reconcile some of the ADA's apparently confusing language. It certainly covers, as Section 504 did, the existence of a government service or benefit program. However, does it cover the frequent use of state power arguably outside a government service or benefit program, such as in court-ordered child custody determinations, termination of parental rights cases, or authorization of unwanted medical treatment?

The portion of Title II of the ADA that covers state and local government actions (Subtitle A) is the most cryptic of all the law's titles. It protects only "qualified individuals with a disability," defined in Section 201 as:

> an individual who, with or without reasonable modifications in rules, policies or practices, the removal of architectural, communications, or transportation barriers, or the provision of auxiliary aids and services, meets the essential requirements for the *receipt of services or the participation in programs or activities provided by a public entity.* (42 U.S.C. §12131[2]), emphasis added)

This section, then, appears to relate only to "receipt of services" or "participation in programs or activities." We would not ordinarily perceive a mother with schizophrenia who seeks to maintain parental rights over her child against the state's petition, for example, as "participating" in any "program" or "activity," nor is she "receiving" any "services" in any conventional sense. (In certain circumstances, of course, persons with mental disorders are discriminated against by being denied services to promote family preservation. This discrimination clearly is prohibited by the ADA.) Although one could argue that she is participating in the court system or the child welfare system, that seems a bit farfetched. She wants no participation and desires no service; she simply wants to resist state interference in her life and avoid discrimination in the use of coercive state power against her. The question is whether she and others who are discriminated against by operation of state law or practice by courts or officials that do not relate to the "receipt of services" or "participation in" a program or activity nevertheless are covered by Title II of the ADA.

Section 202 of Title II, the provision that declares the right to be free from discrimination, solves the problem. It prohibits not only exclusion from receipt of services or participation in programs or activities, but also "discrimination by any such entity" (42 U.S.C. §12132). This phrase, of course, is not the least bit limited: it covers discrimination by the entity in any context in which it acts.

Clearly, a lack of harmony exists between these two sections of the ADA because the definition of "qualified individuals with a disability" seems to require receipt of services or participation in programs or activities. However, it is unlikely that Congress meant to limit the broad prohibition on discrimination in Section 202 by the definitional language in Section 201. If that were the case, the phrase "discrimination by any such entity" would add nothing to the preceding phrases in the section that refer to receipt of services or participation in programs.

The legislative history also supports the application of the ADA to the government's use of coercion. One illustration of the application of Title II of the ADA offered by the House Judiciary Committee was the inappropriate arrest and jailing of persons with epilepsy because police officers are not trained to recognize its manifestations (U.S. House of Representatives Committee on the Judiciary, 1990, p. 50). Such a person is not excluded from a particular program or activity or denied a particular service; rather, the person is the victim of discrimination in the state's otherwise legitimate use of force against citizens.

The U.S. Department of Justice (DOJ) regulations[4] fleshing out the broad but opaque language of the ADA as applied to public entities also support this view (DOJ, 1992). One provision prohibits a public entity from using "criteria or methods of administration" that discriminate on the basis of disability (DOJ, 1991, p. 35718; 28 C.F.R. §35.130[b][3]). The DOJ has stated that the phrase "criteria or methods of administration" refers to "official written policies of the public entity and to the actual practices of the public entity" (1991, p. 35704). It also prohibits practices that "perpetuate the discrimination of another public entity if both public entities are subject to the common administrative control of the state" (DOJ, 1991, p. 35718; 28 C.F.R. §35.130[b][3][iii]). These provisions certainly apply to situations beyond the operation of a service or a benefit.

As a result, the ADA can become an extremely powerful tool to challenge the way courts as well as other institutions of society deal with people who have a history of or currently are receiving psychiatric treatment. One can envision facial challenges to statutes governing marriage, divorce, custody, and parental rights that permit decisions based on mental disorder. Laws or regulations permitting forced medication of competent psychiatric patients (but imposing no similar rules on nonpsychiatric patients) similarly run afoul of the ADA.

The most profound influence of the ADA on state law, however, is likely to appear in day-to-day practice, where the validity of state law is not at issue but where prejudice against people with mental disorders infects the proceedings. The ADA is a vehicle to question stereotypes and assumptions and to preclude easy inferences and predictions about capacity and behavior from the mere existence of a psychiatric diagnosis. As importantly, these issues will be raised in the most exquisitely rich factual settings where judges will be forced to confront their own prejudices and assumptions. The open-ended provisions of Title II, then, can be a means to expose discrimination and challenge it. The task is difficult because the same judges can mask their prejudices by citing facts other than a person's disability, but the tool, at least, is there.

CONCLUSION

The ADA is a law of vast application and possibilities. Despite its qualifications, exclusions, limitations, and defenses, it can affect dramatically social practices toward people with mental disorders. Its predecessor, Section 504 of the Rehabilitation Act, had the same potential, but for people with mental disabilities that potential was never realized. Neither society nor the judiciary was prepared to accept its implications.

One could profitably ask whether we are in a better position now. We certainly cannot take encouragement from public attitudes toward people with mental disorders, but much else has changed. There is more than a technical difference between the Rehabilitation Act's few sentences, passed without national debate or attention, and a law with both sweeping and comprehensive language and the attention accompanying a Rose Garden signing ceremony. It is one thing to challenge deeply entrenched social practices by invoking regulations based on a cryptic statute far ahead of contemporary thinking; it is quite another to rely on a powerful congressional statement like the ADA. Furthermore, the idea of civil rights for people with mental disabilities is far more

---

[4]DOJ regulations are codified at 28 C.F.R. part 35 (1992). References to various portions of these regulations within this chapter cite the specific section of the regulations.

accepted, however grudgingly, now than in the past. For example, courts have been willing to enforce the Fair Housing Amendments Act in claims brought by people with mental (and other) disabilities against strong and vocal opposition from neighborhood associations.

This is all speculation, of course. Over the next decade we shall discover whether the law will challenge our prejudices or be a casualty of them.

REFERENCES

Addington v. Texas, 441 U.S. 418 (1979).

American Psychiatric Association. (1987). *Diagnostic and statistical manual of mental disorders* (3rd ed., rev.). Washington, DC: American Psychiatric Press.

Anthony, W., Howell, J., & Danley, K. (1982). *The vocational rehabilitation of the severely psychiatrically disabled.* Boston: Center for Rehabilitation Research and Training in Mental Health.

Anthony, W., & Jansen, M. (1984). Predicting the vocational capacity of the chronically mentally ill. *American Psychologist, 39,* 537–544.

Barker, P.R., Manderscheid, R.W., Hendershot, G.E., Jack, S.S., Schoenborn, C.A., Goldstrom, I.D. (1992). Serious mental illness in the adult household population: United States, 1989. In R.W. Manderscheid & M.A. Sonnenschein (Eds.), *Mental health: The move to integration.* Washington, DC: Center for Mental Health Services & National Institute of Mental Health (DHHS Publication No. [SMA] 92–1942).

Bowen v. City of New York, 476 U.S. 467 (1986).

Brackel, S., Parry, J., & Weiner, B. (1985). *The mentally disabled and the law.* Chicago: American Bar Foundation.

Burgdorf, R. (1991). The Americans with Disabilities Act: Analysis and implications of a second-generation civil rights statute. *Harvard Civil Rights–Civil Liberties Law Review, 26,* 413–522.

Cherry v. Mathews, 419 F. Supp. 922 (D.D.C. 1976).

City of Cleburne v. Cleburne Living Center, 473 U.S. 432 (1985).

Civil Rights Act of 1964, codified as amended in scattered sections of 42 U.S.C. (1988).

Civil Rights Restoration Act of 1987, 20 U.S.C. §168 *et seq.,* 29 U.S.C. §706, 42 U.S.C. §2000 (1900).

Combs, I.H., & Omvig, C.P. (1986). Accommodation of disabled people into employment: Perceptions of employers. *Journal of Rehabilitation, 52,* 42–45.

Cook, T.M. (1991). The Americans with Disabilities Act: The move to integration. *Temple Law Review, 64,* 393–469.

Dautremont v. Broadlawns Hospital, 827 F.2d 291 (8th Cir. 1987).

Doe v. New York University, 666 F.2d 761 (2d Cir. 1981).

Donaldson v. O'Connor, 442 U.S. 563 (1975).

Education for All Handicapped Children Act of 1975, 20 U.S.C. §§1232, 1401, 1405–1420, 1453 (1975).

Equal Employment Opportunity Commission. (1991a, July 26). Equal employment opportunity for individuals with disabilities; final rule (29 C.F.R. pt. 1630). *Federal Register, 56,* 35725–35739.

Equal Employment Opportunity Commission. (1991b, July 26). Interpretive guidance on Title I of the Americans with Disabilities Act (29 C.F.R. pt. 1630 app.). *Federal Register, 56,* 35739–35753.

Equal Employment Opportunity Commission. (1992). Regulations to implement the equal employment provisions of the Americans with Disabilities Act. In *Code of Federal Regulations* (29: Labor, pp. 395–404). Washington, DC: U.S. Government Printing Office.

Fair Housing Amendments Act of 1988, 42 U.S.C. §§3601–3619 (1988).

Farina, A., & Felner, R.D. (1973). Employer interviewer reactions to former mental patients. *Journal of Abnormal Psychology, 82,* 268–272.

Finney v. Baylor Medical Center Grapevine, 792 S.W. 2d 859 (Texas 1990).

Grove City College v. Bell, 465 U.S. 555 (1984).

Hayman, R. (1990). Presumptions of justice: Law, politics and the mentally retarded parent. *Harvard Law Review, 103,* 1201–1271.

Kanter, A. (1984). Recent zoning cases uphold establishment of group homes for the mentally disabled. *Clearinghouse Review, 18,* 515–518.

Kanter, A. (1986). Homeless mentally ill people: No longer out of sight and out of mind. *New York Law School Human Rights Annual, 3,* 331–357.

Kimbro v. Atlantic Richfield Co., 889 F.2d 869 (9th Cir. 1989).

Mancuso, L. (1990). Reasonable accommodation for workers with psychiatric disabilities. *Psychosocial Rehabilitation Journal, 14,* 3–19.

Many view depression as weakness. (1991, December 11). *New York Times,* p. C16.

Mental Health Association of Minnesota v. Heckler, 720 F.2d 965 (8th Cir. 1984).

Milstein, B., Pepper, B., & Rubenstein, L. (1989). The Fair Housing Amendments Act of 1988: What it means for people with mental disabilities. *Clearinghouse Review, 23,* 128–140.

Milstein, B., Rubenstein, L., & Cyr, R. (1991). The Americans with Disabilities Act: A breathtaking promise for people with mental disabilities. *Clearinghouse Review, 24,* 1240–1249.

Minow, M. (1990). *Making all the difference: Inclusion, exclusion and American law.* Ithaca, NY: Cornell University Press.

Parry, J. (1993). Mental disabilities under the ADA: A difficult path to follow. *Mental and Physical Disability Law Reporter, 17,* 100–110.

Perlin, M. (1989). *Mental disability law, civil and criminal.* Charlottesville, VA: Michie.

Perlin, M. (1991). Competency, deinstitutionalization and homelessness: A study in marginalization. *Houston Law Review, 28,* 63–142.

Regier, D.A, Narrow, W.E., Rae, D.S., Manderscheid, R.W., Locke, B.Z., & Goodwin, F.K. (1993). The defacto U.S. mental and addictive disorders service system. *Archives of General Psychiatry, 50,* 85–94.

Rubenstein, L. (1985). Science, law and psychiatric disability. *Psychosocial Rehabilitation Journal, 9,* 7–19.

Rubenstein, L.S., & Milstein, B. (1993). Redefining equality through the ADA. In P. Wehman (Ed.), *The ADA mandate for social change* (pp. 3–18). Baltimore: Paul H. Brookes Publishing Co.

School Board of Nassau County, Fla. v. Arline, 480 U.S. 273 (1987).

Security Disability Benefits Reform Act of 1984, 00 U.S.C. §0000 (1900).

Simring, R.B. (1991). The impact of federal antidiscrimination laws on housing for people with mental disabilities. *George Washington Law Review, 59,* 413–450.

Social Security Administration, Department of Health and Human Services. (1992). Federal old-age survivors and disability insurance (1950). Subpart P—determining disability and blindness, Appendix 1—listing of impairments. In *Code of Federal Regulations* (20: Employee's Benefits, pp. 376–426). Washington, DC: U.S. Government Printing Office.

Stefan, S. (1989). Whose egg is it anyway? Reproductive rights of incarcerated, institutionalized and incompetent women. *Nova Law Review, 13,* 405–456.

U.S. Department of Health, Education and Welfare. (1991). Nondiscrimination on the basis of handicap in programs and activities receiving federal financial assistance. In *Code of Federal Regulations* (45: Public Welfare, pp. 354–395). Washington, DC: U.S. Government Printing Office.

U.S. Department of Housing and Urban Development. (1988, June 2). Nondiscrimination based on handicap in federally assisted programs and activities; final rule. *Federal Register, 53,* 20216–20252.

U.S. Department of Justice. (1991, July 26). Nondiscrimination on the basis of disability in state and local government services; final rule. *Federal Register, 56,* 35693–35723.

U.S. Department of Justice. (1992). Nondiscrimination on the basis of disability in state and local government services. In *Code of Federal Regulations* (28: Judicial Administration, pp. 417–457). Washington, DC: U.S. Government Printing Office.

United States Department of the Treasury v. Galioto, 477 U.S. 556 (1986).

U.S. House of Representatives Committee on the Judiciary. (1990, May 15). *House report no. 485(III), to accompany H.R. 2273 (101st Congress, 1st session).* Washington, DC: U.S. Government Printing Office. (Reprinted in *United States Code Congressional and Administrative News, 4,* 445–511 [1990]).

U.S. Senate. (1989a, September 7). Debate on amendment no. 722 to S. 933, statements of Sen. Armstrong and Sen. Harkin. *Congressional Record, 135,* S10785–S10786.

U.S. Senate. (1989b, September 14). Debate on S. 933, statement of Sen. Armstrong. *Congressional Record, 135,* S11176.

Washington v. Harper, 110 S. Ct. 1028 (1990).

Youngberg v. Romeo, 451 U.S. 982 (1981).

Chapter 16

Psychiatric Disabilities
and the ADA

An Advocate's Perspective

Judi Chamberlin

There is little doubt that the Americans with Disabilities Act (ADA) was conceived and promoted with the idea of aiding people with physical disabilities, and that its implications have been most clearly thought through with regard to those disabilities. Although the bill was enlarged during the legislative process to cover people with mental and emotional disabilities, it is much more difficult to conceptualize how the law will be implemented in ways that will benefit these populations.

Covering people with mental disabilities was controversial, and the bill was rewritten several times as it neared final passage, with psychiatric disabilities (or specific diagnoses) excluded from coverage. During this debate, much stigmatizing language was used; one senator referred to "schizophrenics, pyromaniacs and pedophiles" as people who should not be covered under the law.

As a former mental patient (who now prefers to use the term *psychiatric survivor*) who has been active for many years in the movement to develop self-help and empowerment, I have seen the crippling effect that stigma has on people who carry the mental illness label. Few people would dare to say in public about persons with physical disabilities the things that they feel free to say about "mental patients, who are frequently presumed to be dangerous, unreliable, and incapable of knowing their own best interests." Indeed, this prejudice may be the most powerful barrier that persons with psychiatric labels face, keeping us out of the mainstream in the same way that the lack of ramps hampers people in wheelchairs from fully participating in community life.

On March 16, 1990, as the ADA was being debated in Congress, Representative Chuck Douglas of New Hampshire sent out a "Dear Colleague" letter headed, "Berserkers: Time Bombs in the Workplace—How can we protect ourselves from an apparently growing menace?" He then answered this question, "Certainly not by passing the Americans with Disabilities Act in its present form that protects people *who do not have physical disabilities*" (emphasis added). The congressman then went on to state that, because the ADA does not "limit itself to physical disabilities, it can lead to the situation described on the back of this letter where an employee with manic depression was reinstated after a disability discrimination suit brought under state law in Kentucky. He then went on to kill seven fellow employees last September." This is an example of the kind of prejudice former mental patients face when we try to work, to find an apartment, or merely to live our lives.

On March 22, 1990, Don Feder, a columnist for the *Boston Herald,* wrote a column called "Now we can all be persecuted minorities." Once again, the stereotypes were trotted out. Feder did not just oppose adding former mental patients to the ADA; he opposed the whole bill, making such statements as, "Failure to hire, promote or serve the handicapped, whether justified or not, will result in costly litigation," and "The Utopian scheme will be a shyster's bonanza." However, he reserved his most egregious insults for one segment of the population with disabilities:

> The real fun begins when one contemplates the mental disabilities which might be encompassed by the law. The Diagnostic and Statistical Manual of the American Psychiatric Association, standard reference of the shrink industry, lists all sorts of ailments which could be included. Besides "telephone scatologia" (making obscene phone calls), "anti-social personality disorders" covers a panoply of so-called disabilities, including "forcing someone into sexual activity" (that's rape, to you) and "spouse or child-beating."
>
> Almost any personality quirk or character flaw can be classified as a mental disorder. Do you have a "preoccupation with fear of having . . . a serious disease?" Then you suffer from "hypochondriasis." Do you often get angry, lose control? Clearly you are afflicted by an "intermittant [sic] explosive disorder."
>
> Once upon a time, slow work, poor performance and resentment to authority were prime causes for dismissal. Soon they may be a passport to lifetime job tenure. You see, the lucky worker so beset is severely disabled, having a "passive-aggressive personality disorder."

On April 3, 1990, an editorial cartoon appeared in the Colorado Springs *Gazette Telegraph* that pictured a man in a hockey mask carrying a chain saw (a clear reference to a murderous character in a series of horror movies). He is walking into an office through a door labeled "Personnel Department" while one worker, pointing to a paper labeled "Americans With Disabilities Act," explains to another, "I HAD to hire him!"

The fact remains that the ADA, as passed into law, *does* cover psychiatric disabilities, making clear that what has been called "the civil rights law for the disabled" is a civil rights law that includes current and former mental patients. The psychiatric survivor movement, which has as one of its key goals the establishment of basic civil rights for people labeled "mentally ill," has been excited to find itself provided with this new tool for enforcing rights.

COMMONALITIES AMONG PERSONS
WITH PSYCHIATRIC AND PHYSICAL DISABILITIES

Almost all of the problems that persons with physical disabilities face are shared by persons with psychiatric labels (e.g., difficulty in accessing housing, employment, and community services). Another major result of being included in the purview of the ADA is that we have drawn closer to the disability community and discovered the commonalities that we share. In the beginning this was difficult for both communities because there were mutual levels of mistrust and of feeling that we did not have the same problems. Many people with physical disabilities feared being lumped in with "crazy" people, while many former mental patients took the position that "We're not disabled, we're just oppressed." The opportunities to work together with a cross-disability focus have served as major learning experiences for us all.

Both communities find themselves oppressed by a medical model that puts doctors in charge of many decisions about our lives that have nothing to do with medicine but are in fact personal, economic, or social. What has happened has been a process of mutual unlearning in which persons with both physical and psychiatric disabilities have learned to undo stereotypes and myths and to see each other as the individuals we are.

One of my most powerful learning experiences was a conference I attended in January 1989—sponsored by the Office of Special Education and Rehabilitative Services (OSERS) and the U.S. Department of Education—that brought together a small group of activists with disabilities and disability advocates for 2 days of focused discussion on the concept of "self-determination." With a cross-disability focus, we examined self-determination on the individual, community, and public policy levels. I was the only person among approximately 50 participants who had had experience with psychiatric disability, and I found that people were eager to learn from me, just as I was able to learn from others about the problems of having mental retardation, cerebral palsy, deafness, blindness, or any of a number of other disabilities.

Even in the brief period we were together, a feeling of community developed. Each of us, of course, knew the most about his or her own disability, and little or nothing about some of the others (or, perhaps even worse, had assimilated misinformation). I remember most clearly a woman with mental retardation who had spent much of her life in an institution but who now lived in the community and had become an active advocate. She spoke passionately about how living in an institution was the worst thing that could ever happen to anyone and how hard she worked to help other people get out of the institution that she had lived in for so long. For me and for everyone there who had experienced the dehumanization that accompanies life in an institution, we saw what a powerful bond we shared.

Society is all too willing to believe that a person with a disability (*any* disability) is a source of difficulty and should accept being treated as a second-class citizen. The ADA is one of the forces working to change that image, but it would not have come about without a strong activist community of persons with disabilities themselves demanding change.

REASONABLE ACCOMMODATIONS FOR PERSONS WITH A PSYCHIATRIC DISABILITY

At the heart of the ADA is the concept of "reasonable accommodation," the means by which a person with a disability will be able to access facilities. Whereas it is relatively straightforward to conceptualize reasonable accommodation for various physical disabilities (e.g., a ramp to enable a person in a wheelchair to enter a building, or a signer to enable a deaf person to participate in a public meeting), it is more difficult to determine how the concept applies to a person with a psychiatric disability.

In an unpublished paper entitled "A Crazy Folks' Guide to Reasonable Accommodation and 'Psychiatric Disability,'" Howie the Harp, one of the leaders of the ex-patients' movement, stated that a reasonable accommodation in employment for people with psychiatric disabilities

> is a service provided, a modification in job duties, hours or work environment, extra training, a personnel policy modification and patience and tolerance. It is reasonable in that it does not cause a major hardship to the work of the agency or company, or its budget. It is a recognition that everyone has the right to work, and that disabled employees are valued. (n.d., p. 4)

He then went on to list a number of accommodations that have been utilized at his agency—the Oakland Independence Support Center, a self-help service center run by and for people who are both homeless and mentally ill—including peer counseling, acceptance of volunteer work experience in lieu of education or paid work experience requirements, allowance of "mental health leave," flexible work hours, flexibility in the assignment of duties, and flexibility of workspaces, including provision of distraction-free space or a place where an employee can converse easily with other employees, depending on individual need. Most importantly, he emphasized that reasonable accommodation *must* be voluntary and not based on something that the employer does unilaterally in the belief that a person with a psychiatric disability should be assumed to be less capable than a person without disabilities in knowing what he or she wants or needs.

Mancuso conducted a thorough search of the literature on reasonable accommodation in employment and found very little referring to psychiatric disability. She identified four factors that constitute reasonable accommodation for this disability—changes in interpersonal communication, modifications to the physical environment, job modification, and schedule modification—and went on to point out that "accommodations such as these are relatively easy to undertake and can be of significant assistance to persons with psychiatric disabilities for whom competitive employment may be otherwise inaccessible" (Mancuso, 1990, pp. 15–16).

Mancuso also discussed the use of job coaches as a reasonable accommodation:

> After developing a strong and trusting relationship with the worker and employer, then carefully selecting the job match, the final steps to successful employment may be made possible by job coaches through the creative development of accommodations. Of course, reasonable accommodations will never take the place of a good job match and should never be used to pressure an employer to hire an unqualified applicant. But reasonable accommodations can be a powerful tool in efforts to assist consumers to achieve the economic and personal empowerment of competitive employment. (1990, p.16)

It is important to emphasize that, because of the image of persons with psychiatric disabilities as incompetent and unable to define their own best interests, there is enormous potential for misuse of the concept of reasonable accommodation to justify involuntary psychiatric interventions. One of the goals of the psychiatric survivor movement is to end *all* involuntary aspects of the psychiatric system; it would be ironic indeed if the ADA were to be used in direct contradiction to that goal. Howie the Harp described a situation in which a college-educated former mental patient was successfully holding down a responsible job, but after several years was found by his supervisor to be edgy, talking too loudly, and using poor judgment. The supervisor, rather than discussing this situation with the employee (which would have disclosed that this behavior was related to mistreatment by a fellow employee), assumed that it was a manifestation of disability and ordered an involuntary leave of absence. The employee was forced to file a complaint of discrimination on the basis of disability in order to regain his job. Howie the Harp pointed out that, by not discussing the situation with the employee or giving him the choice of going on leave, the action was *not* an accommodation, but was instead punitive and disempowering (Howie the Harp, n.d., p. 3).

Similarly, *requiring* an employee to attend therapy sessions or monitoring an employee's medication compliance are not reasonable accommodations, although adjusting work hours for the employee to go to therapy or assisting an employee who requests assistance with medication may well be. The key element is that the accommodation is something that is mutually acceptable to the employer and the employee, not something that is imposed.

DISCRIMINATION AGAINST PERSONS WITH A PSYCHIATRIC DISABILITY

As stated earlier, perhaps the most difficult barrier that people with psychiatric disabilities face is the negative image that others have of them and the discriminatory acts that result from that image. People whose behavior is nondangerous and nonthreatening but considered odd may be discriminated against if they have (or are perceived to have) psychiatric disabilities; the same behavior may be tolerated if the person is seen as being simply eccentric or unusual. It is a common misconception that persons with psychiatric disabilities look different as a result of their disability. If such people *do* look different, usually it is because of factors such as poverty, which causes them to be dressed poorly, or the result of psychiatric drug treatment, which often causes unusual body postures and movements. It is common for former mental patients to be deemed in need of further psychiatric treatment when they engage in behavior that would be considered quite normal in other people, such as getting angry (which may be perfectly justifiable when taken in context).

In the psychiatric survivor movement, as in the disability movement in general, we have engaged in endless speculation as to just what the ADA means and how it will be implemented. It is quite likely that the field of psychiatric disability will require more litigation than other disabilities to clarify just what the ADA means and what activities are covered. It also is quite likely, unfortunately, that the prejudice and stigma against people with psychiatric labels that was so evident as the ADA neared passage will continue to affect implementation for this population. The ADA alone is not a panacea; it will require continued activism to ensure that its provisions make a real difference in the lives of persons with psychiatric disabilities.

INVOLUNTARY COMMITMENT AND THE ADA

I have been told by legal experts that one of my personal dreams of how the ADA might be implemented is totally unrealistic, but I continue to hope that the ADA might be useful in achieving our ultimate goal of ending involuntary commitment. "Mental illness" is the only medical diagnosis that is linked to the legal power to order incarceration and "treatment" (except, perhaps, for communicable diseases). Whereas, in theory at least, the diagnosis needs to be linked to concepts such as "dangerousness to self or others" or "inability to care for oneself" (the exact requirements vary from state to state), in reality, once a person has a psychiatric history, virtually any unusual behavior can serve to trigger involuntary commitment. As I interpret the ADA, this constitutes a situation of people being treated differently *because of their disability.*

If a person without a psychiatric history is seen as "merely annoying" or is treated as a minor criminal offender when engaging in behavior such as yelling in the street, whereas a person with a psychiatric label is civilly committed for engaging in the same behavior, does that not constitute discrimination because of disability? If so, why cannot the ADA be used to challenge the legal basis for involuntary commitment? The legal question then becomes: "Is the person a 'direct threat' to others?" At the very least, the state must prove that the person with a psychiatric disability poses a significant risk of substantial harm to himself or herself or to others.

Although I have been told that the ADA is unlikely to be used to review civil commitment, I hope it will encourage disability advocates to look at the whole question of involuntary incarceration and treatment and understand why this issue is such a pressing one for psychiatric survivors.

CONCLUSION

I was one of the thousands of guests on the White House lawn when President Bush signed the ADA into law, and I joined in the jubilant celebration that followed. It was truly inspiring to see so many people with so many different disabilities enjoying the triumph that resulted from so much hard work over so many years. Now the celebration is over, and more hard work lies ahead as we try to translate words on paper into real changes in the lives of millions of people. We have much to do to bring people with disabilities into mainstream society, and it is essential to continue to recognize the differing needs of various disability groups. We with psychiatric disabilities face many unique problems, but there is no reason why the ADA cannot be a big part of bringing us into the community and helping us lead better lives.

REFERENCES

Douglas, C. (1990, March 16). U.S. House of Representatives. *"Dear Colleague" letter: "Berserkers: Time bombs in the workplace."*

Feder, D. (1990, March 22). Now we can all be persecuted minorities. *Boston Herald,* p. 43.

Howie the Harp. (n.d.). *A crazy folks' guide to reasonable accommodation and "psychiatric disability."* Manuscript available from Howie the Harp, c/o OLSC, P.O. Box 70010-Sta. D, Oakland, CA 94612-0010.

Mancuso, L.L. (1990). Reasonable accommodation for workers with psychiatric disabilities. *Psychosocial Rehabilitation Journal, 14*(2), 3–19.

Chapter 17

The ADA
in International and Developmental
Disabilities Perspectives

Stanley S. Herr

This chapter seeks to place the Americans with Disabilities Act[1] (ADA) in both international and developmental disabilities perspectives. Part one suggests that the ADA is an international as well as national milestone in human rights and effectuates a long line of international declarations. Part two explores the act's implications for the field of developmental disabilities and the lessons to be drawn from related litigation under Section 504 of the Rehabilitation Act of 1973.

The ADA has international significance for a variety of reasons. First, it is consistent with a series of international human rights standards and provides effective legal protection for the equal rights of persons with developmental disabilities. Indeed, two key international declarations highlighted the rights of persons with mental retardation and proved to be significant building blocks for the more inclusive human rights documents that followed. Second, the ADA offers a legislative model for defining the rights and remedies to achieve nondiscrimination. Third, this sweeping law represents a political statement by a leading nation that persons with disabilities are moving from the margins to the mainstreams of society. Fourth, the principles recognized as legitimate legal claims in the ADA may have extraterritorial effects as multinational corporations, U.S. government installations overseas, and U.S.-backed foreign aid programs are influenced by domestic norms. (Regarding the application of certain federal laws to U.S. employers abroad, see *Mahoney v. Radio Free Europe/Radio Liberty, Inc.* [1992], covering specifically the Age Discrimination in Employment Act, and to federally aided projects abroad, see *Lujan v. Defenders of Wildlife* [1991],

This chapter is a revised and fuller version of the chapter that originally appeared as "Nondiscrimination and Integration: International Standards and National Legislation," in *Gezondheidschrecht in Perspectief* (Lochem, The Netherlands: De Tijdstroom, 1993). The De Tijdstroom b.v. Publishing Company has kindly given permission to Paul H. Brookes Publishing Co. for this publication.

This chapter is dedicated to Dr. Rosemary Dybwad and Professor Gunnar Dybwad, whose visions of equal rights for all persons have inspired changes around the world. Although Rosemary saw this chapter in draft form, she did not survive to see its ultimate publication. The author fully joins in the dedication of this volume to the cherished memory of Rosemary and to Gunnar. The author also expresses his thanks to Professor Dybwad for his valuable research consultation and to Lynn Edwards and Roberta Cepko for their research assistance.

[1]The Americans with Disabilities Act of 1990 (PL 101-336) is published in *Statutes at Large* (104 Stat. 327) and codified in the *United States Code* (42 U.S.C. §§12101–12213 [Supp. II 1990]). References to various portions of the act within this chapter cite the specific section of the Code.

covering specifically the Endangered Species Act.) Fifth, foreign visitors and trainees observing U.S. practices and policies and U.S. visitors, exchange workers, and trainees abroad can carry the message of the ADA to distant places, conveying the legal and social reform experiences from one nation to another. Finally, the ADA can be improved by knowledge of other countries' laws and practices that strive to include persons with disabilities in egalitarian societies.

The ADA also is significant for its inclusiveness. Its goal is to eliminate discrimination against *all* persons with disabilities (U.S. Senate, 1989a). Persons with mental retardation and other developmental disabilities (referred to in this chapter simply as "persons with developmental disabilities"), long overlooked in antidiscrimination laws, clearly are protected by the ADA. This inclusion is not surprising given the prominent role of advocacy groups such as the Association for Retarded Citizens (now renamed The Arc) and the National Association of Protection and Advocacy Systems among the 133 national organizations who lobbied for the act's passage (U.S. Senate, 1989a). (Other groups aligned with this coalition included the American Association on Mental Retardation, the American Association of University Affiliated Programs, the Autism Society of America, the Epilepsy Foundation of America, and the National Association of Developmental Disabilities Councils.) Large segments of the American public, however, still may be surprised to learn that the act exists, let alone that such persons are entitled to its guarantees of nondiscriminatory treatment. A Louis Harris and Associates survey in 1991 showed that only 18% of Americans claimed to be aware of the ADA, with 82% not aware of "any laws passed recently to give more protection to disabled people." Less than half of the 18% could describe properly the components of the ADA, with 49% of this subgroup incorrectly stating that employers are required to accommodate a qualified person with a disability regardless of cost (Louis Harris and Associates, Inc., 1991, pp. 60, 63). Furthermore, the media's coverage of the ADA spotlights architectural and other barriers confronting persons in wheelchairs (see, e.g., Holmes, 1992, p. 1), doing little to explain the ways in which persons with nonphysical disabilities may benefit from the new law. Nonetheless, persons with developmental disabilities certainly have much to gain from the promise of the ADA.

The views presented here are necessarily preliminary ones. With the ADA only in its first months of enforcement at the time of this writing, it remains to be seen whether practical consequences follow from the political rhetoric of mainstreaming and full participation that accompanied the act's passage (e.g., President Bush's statement: "I am going to do whatever it takes to make sure that the disabled are included in the mainstreams. For too long the disabled have been left out of the mainstream, but they're not going to be left out anymore"; U.S. Senate, 1989b). The Clinton Administration now has the opportunity to make good on its campaign pledges that the ADA is "fully implemented and aggressively enforced—to empower people with disabilities to make their own choices and to create a framework for independence and self-determination (Clinton & Gore, 1992, p. 82).

INTERNATIONAL PERSPECTIVES ON THE ADA

The ADA should not be viewed in a parochial manner. It is consistent with a long line of human rights declarations and draws on concepts validated by international organs. In addition to its unique features that may influence laws and practices abroad, the act also can be compared to the innovative laws of other nations.

Universal Declaration of Human Rights

The ADA gives legal effect to universal norms of equality and the inherent dignity of every individual, with or without disabilities. Those norms of equal rights and nondiscrimination are central to the U.N. Universal Declaration of Human Rights (1948). The Declaration forcefully recognizes in its Preamble "the equal and inalienable rights of all members of the human family." Article 1 solemnly declares that "[a]ll human beings are born free and equal in dignity and rights."

The Declaration's semantic structure is that "everyone is entitled" or "everyone has the right to" enumerated basic rights. Persons with disabilities clearly have a status that entitles them to "all the rights and freedoms set forth in this Declaration, *without distinction of any kind,* such as race, color, sex . . . , birth or other status (Article 2, emphasis added). Those broadly defined rights include the "right to recognition everywhere as a person before the law" (Article 6), the right to "equal protection of the law" and against any discrimination (Article 7), and the right to "work, to free choice of employment, to just and favorable conditions of work" (Article 23[1]), including the "right to equal pay for equal work" (Article 23[2]). Access to leisure and cultural activities is also guaranteed through the "right to rest and leisure" (Article 24) and the "right freely to participate in the cultural life of the community, to enjoy the arts" and similar public accommodations (Article 27[1]).

In addition to evoking international action, the Declaration is intended to have indirect legal effects through the actions of the U.N.'s member states. For example, courts and other "national tribunals" must assure that "everyone has the right to an effective remedy" for violations of fundamental rights under constitutional or other national law (Article 8). As an authoritative yardstick for progressive national and international action, the Declaration's provisions frequently have been adopted in national legislation. Indeed, Article 21[2] declares that everyone has the "right of equal access to public service in his country," a right now legally protected under the ADA for persons in the United States with disabilities (42 U.S.C.§§12131–12165).

Such indirect effects are not the only method of applying human rights declarations (see Luard, 1967, pp. 132, 154). Although not legally binding on its own, the Universal Declaration is recognized as an "authoritative guide" to the U.N. Charter and as an element of the "law of the United Nations" (Brownlie, 1981, p. 21). Adopted unanimously by the General Assembly, the Universal Declaration embodies a consensus on standards of human rights that has been reaffirmed and made more specific (and in some instances legally binding) in subsequent international instruments. (For commentary on the legal and indirect effects of the Universal Declaration, see Drost [1965, pp. 32–38] and Sohn and Buergenthal [1973, pp. 518–522, 936–947].) According to Harvard Law Professor Louis B. Sohn, the Declaration is "a part of the constitutional law of the world community" that, together with the U.N. Charter, has "achieved the character of a world law superior to all other international instruments and to domestic laws" (Sohn, 1967, pp. 17, 26; cited in Carey, 1970, p. 13).

A number of U.S. courts have either discussed or cited the Universal Declaration as a standard in adjudicating certain human rights cases. In *Zemel v. Rusk* (1965) the court upheld the Secretary of State's refusal to grant a passport to travel to Cuba. The court in *Huynh Thi Anh v. Levi* (1978), in a habeas corpus action by a grandmother to obtain custody of her children placed in foster care in America from Vietnam, held that international treaties and the U.N. Declaration of Human Rights do not create a private right of action for aliens in federal court. (However, in *Nguyen Da Yen v. Kissinger* [1975], it was found that babylifting of Vietnamese children may constitute a tort committed in violation of the law of nations, including the U.N. Declaration of Human Rights.) In *Filartiga v. Pena-Irala* (1980) the court found that an act of torture committed by a state official against a person held in detention "violates established norms of the international law of human rights and hence the law of nations," including the U.N. Charter, the Universal Declaration of Human Rights, and the U.N. Declaration Against Torture, and thus offends the customary international law of human rights. In *Fernandez v. Wilkinson* (1981), a Cuban refugee detained in a federal prison was ordered released because such detention violated international law as exemplified by the U.N. Declaration of Human Rights and the American Convention of Human Rights because, "while not technically binding, those documents establish broadly recognized standards." This caselaw demonstrates that international human rights can be effectively applied by U.S. judges.

International Declarations on Disability Rights

The United Nations and nongovernmental organizations (NGOs) have turned to declaration making for more specific human rights for persons with disabilities. In 1968, the Jerusalem Declaration on the General and Special Rights of Mentally Retarded Persons was promulgated by the International League of Societies for the Mentally Handicapped (ILSMH, 1969). Article 1 of the ILSMH Declaration states unequivocally that a person with mental retardation has "the same basic rights as other citizens of the same country and the same age." This pioneering declaration, with its strong egalitarian themes, served as the inspiration and model for two U.N. human rights declarations concerning disabilities.

In 1971, the U.N. Declaration on the Rights of Mentally Retarded Persons, in terms nearly identical to those of the ILSMH text, was unanimously adopted by the General Assembly. It proclaims that such persons have "the same rights as other human beings," including the "right to perform productive work" and the right to be able to participate in normal modes of life (Articles 1, 3, and 4, p. 99). The rights stated in this Declaration have been incorporated almost verbatim in the laws of Tennessee (Tennessee Code Annotated, §33-5-201 [1984]) and Delaware (Delaware Code Annotated title 16, §§5501–5507 [1983] ["Subchapter I. Declaration of General and Special Rights of the Mentally Retarded"]) and have elsewhere influenced statutes and court decisions that affirm principles of equality and normalization (Ohio Revised Code Annotated §5123.67 [Baldwin, 1991]; Florida Statutes Chapter 393.062, 393.066[1] [1990]; Idaho Code §67–6701 [1989]; see ADA as Legislative Model for Equal Rights, below).

Building on these principles and the Universal Declaration, the U.N. Declaration on the Rights of Disabled Persons (1975) called for international and national action to advance the rights of all persons with physical or mental disabilities. Like the ADA, these rights were inclusive and granted regardless of the degree, origin, or type of disability. Emphasizing principles of egalitarianism and normalization, the 1975 U.N. Declaration affirms that persons with disabilities have "the same fundamental rights as their fellow-citizens of the same age, which implies first and foremost the right to enjoy a decent life, as normal and full as possible (Article 3, p. 92). Other equality provisions proclaim rights to nondiscrimination, equal civil and political rights, and the broadly defined "inherent right to respect for their human dignity" (Articles 2, 3, and 4).

The 1975 Declaration also is notable for conferring access to affirmative social and economic rights. Rights to treatment, rehabilitation, education, vocational education, training, counseling, placement services, economic security, social security, family living, and participation in recreational and cultural activities are some of the measures enumerated to "develop their capabilities and skills to the maximum" and to speed "their social integration or reintegration" (Articles 6, 7, and 9). The Declaration also prohibits discriminatory, abusive, or degrading treatment and regulations. It bars unnecessary "differential treatment" in housing and requires living conditions in specialized facilities that are as "close as possible to those of normal life of a person of his or her own age" (Articles 10 and 11). Persons with disabilities are entitled to measures to "enable them to become as self-reliant as possible" (Article 5). In outlawing employment discrimination, the Declaration refers to the rights of persons with disabilities, "according to their capabilities, to secure and retain employment or to engage in a useful, productive and remunerative occupation and to join trade unions" (Article 7). These impressive standards offer a foundation for further human rights activism.

Six years later, the United Nations Educational, Scientific, and Cultural Organization (UNESCO) Declaration of the World Conference on Actions and Strategies for Education, Prevention and Integration ("Sundberg Declaration") reaffirmed the need to "ensure full observance" of the prior U.N. declarations (Preamble, paragraph 5). In November 1981, representatives of 103 nations and 15 NGOs unanimously and solemnly affirmed measures aimed at full access, participation, and integration of persons with disabilities in their communities. Article 1 insists that every disabled person "must be able to exercise his fundamental right to have full access to education, training, culture and information." Other articles specify that such education programs be designed to integrate "disabled persons into the ordinary working and living environments," that such integration begin "as early as possible" in the person's life, and that all urban development and housing projects should "facilitate the integration and participation of disabled persons in all community activities" (Articles 6 and 12). The Sundberg Declaration concludes with a call for nations to implement it through "all possible legislative, technical and fiscal measures" (Article 16). To hasten these steps, its framers urged that persons with disabilities and their organizations be ensured active participation in defining the terms of such legislation. The ADA certainly exemplifies legislation framed with such participation to achieve full access and integration in the community.

United Nations Decade of Disabled Persons

"Full Participation and Equality" was the central theme of the 1981 International Year of Disabled Persons. To implement the Year's objectives, the United Nations urged member states to review their existing legislation and to "eliminate possible discriminatory practices regarding the education and employment of disabled persons (U.N. Secretary General, 1979, p. 19). Commentators viewed the International Year as a seed to "dismantling . . . barriers to education, employment and civil life" and to raising the "public's awareness of the rights and aspirations of disabled people" (Schuster-Herr & Herr, 1980, p. 19). That seed took root in the U.N. World Programme of Action concerning Disabled Persons (1982) and now has blossomed with the ADA and other national laws.

As a long-term plan of action, the World Programme emphasized the responsibility of national governments to assure equal rights for persons with disabilities and equalization of opportunities, a concept broadly defined as "the process through which the general system[s] of society, such as the physical and cultural environment, housing and transportation, social and health services, educational and work opportunities and cultural and social life, including sports and recreational facilities, are made accessible to all" (paragraphs 12, 22–26). The World Programme viewed legislation and advocacy by persons with disabilities for "their own integration into the mainstream of society" as desirable forms of political action to achieve this equalization (paragraphs 60–62).

The United Nations acknowledged that the conditions prevailing in 1982 were a far cry from these equality goals. Persons with disabilities were the last hired and first fired, and many such persons not only were excluded from normal communal life but were confined in institutions without justification (World Programme, paragraphs 63, 69, 75). For example, paragraph 75 of the World Programme states that, "While the leper colonies of the past have been partly done away with and large institutions are not as numerous as they once were, far too many people are today institutionalized when there is nothing in their condition to justify it."

Comprehensive remedies were sought as part of the United Nations Decade of Disabled Persons (1983–1992). Member states were called on to adopt legislation granting such persons "equal opportunities with other citizens" and prohibiting "any discriminatory practices with respect to disability" (World Programme, paragraphs 108–110). The World Programme urged that, as a part of this legislative review, the rights to work, education, and equal protection be given specific attention (paragraphs 110–111). The General Assembly adopted these recommendations, requesting member states to develop "plans for the equalization of opportunities" for persons with disabilities that would ensure the Programme's early implementation (U.N. General Assembly, 1983). The international stage thus was primed for concrete forms of nondiscrimination lawmaking.

Convention on the Rights of the Child

The U.N. Convention on the Rights of the Child (1989) is a human rights treaty that reinforces the rights of minors with disabilities. It entered into force on September 2, 1990, and defined a child as "every human being below the age of eighteen years" (Article 1). Like the ADA, it stresses integration and access to a full continuum of aids, benefits, and services. Article 23, for instance, identifies the rights of children with mental and physical disabilities to a wide spectrum of rehabilitation services and special care. It recognizes that such a child "should enjoy a full and decent life," with conditions promoting the child's dignity, self-reliance, and "active participation in the community" (Article 23[1]). Ratifying nations agree that each child's program for care and assistance "shall be designed to ensure that the disabled child has effective access to receive education, training, health care services, rehabilitation services, preparation for employment and recreation opportunities in a manner conducive to the child's achieving the fullest possible social integration and individual development (Article 23[3]). Under other relevant articles, States Parties to the Convention recognize the child's right to education (Article 28), right to health and treatment facilities (Article 24), and right to the nondiscriminatory enjoyment of declared rights irrespective of the child's disability or other ascribed status (Article 2).

The Convention calls for strong protection for the institutionalized child. States Parties shall ensure that such a child receives services meeting established standards of health, safety, supervision and staffing, protection, and care to ensure his or her well-being and protective measures against all forms of abuse and maltreatment (Articles 3[2], 3[3], 19). Like the U.N. Declaration on the Rights of Disabled Persons, the Convention reflects a strong presumption against out-of-home institutional treatment and a preference for "a family environment" when residential treatment is required (Preamble, Articles 18[1] and 20[3]). Only when subject to judicial review can a child be placed away from parents against their will (Article 9[1]).

The United States has not joined the over 156 nations in ratifying or signing the Convention on the Rights of the Child. As of February 23, 1993, 129 nations had become States Parties to the Convention by ratification or by accession, and 27 additional nations have only signed but not ratified it. However, the Convention may encourage the United States, along with other nations, to reform laws and practices inconsistent with this human rights consensus. For now the United States is in odd company with Iraq, Libya, Oman, and a handful of other states that have neither signed nor become States Parties to the Convention. As of January 29, 1993, even South Africa—long a human rights pariah nation—has signed the children's rights convention (M. Hamed, personal communication February 23, 1993, with UNICEF Public Affairs officer, New York City).

ADA as Legislative Model for Equal Rights

Although the United States may draw criticism for its reluctance to join the world community in signing certain documents on fundamental human rights, it may claim in its defense to have national laws and national tribunals sensitive to the very rights embodied in those international documents. For instance, Federal Judge Frank M. Johnson, Jr., in the landmark case of *Wyatt v. Stickney* (1972), cited with approval the U.N. Declaration on the Rights of Mentally Retarded Persons in upholding the habilitation rights of state institutional residents. In reaching that conclusion, Judge Johnson noted that the "Court's decision with regard to the right of the mentally retarded to habilitation is supported not only by applicable legal authority, but also by a resolution adopted on December 27, 1971, by the General Assembly of the United Nations." The principles embodied in *Wyatt* have influenced not only case law, but regulatory and legislative standards in the developmental disabilities field.

Like *Wyatt,* the ADA also has the potential for such ripple effects. Its supporters have touted it as the "world's first comprehensive civil rights law for persons with disabilities" (citation on plaque awarded by Task Force for Rights and Empowerment for People with Disabilities in 1990 to Christy Boswell, Executive Director, Maryland Arc, for efforts in securing the ADA's passage). However, New South Wales, Australia, can lay claim to an earlier antidiscrimination law (New South Wales Anti-Discrimination Act, 1977 [amended 1982]; for a critical discussion of Australian legislation, see Astor, 1990). Discrimination based on intellectual disability also is prohibited in the states of Victoria and Western Australia. In addition, France has unique enforcement mechanisms for its statute barring discrimination by reason of the individual's state of health or handicap (Sick and Handicapped Persons [Discrimination] Act, 1990). In this statute, penal sanctions are provided (§§1, 2), and associations for the sick and handicapped (§7) and for the relief of the poor (§8) can appear as a civil party to assist the victimized individual. Finally, Canada has the distinction of specific constitutional language on equal protection for persons with physical or mental disabilities (Canadian Constitution [Constitution Act, 1982], part I [Canadian Charter of Rights and Freedoms], §15[1]). This provision states, "Every individual is equal before and under the law and has the right to the equal protection and equal benefit of the law without discrimination and, in particular, without discrimination based on race, national or ethnic origin, colour, religion, sex, age or mental or physical disability" (see Vickers & Endicott, 1985).

Nevertheless, the United States can be justly proud of the ADA's scope and generous remedies. Activists in other nations and NGOs such as the International League of Societies for Persons with Mental Handicap (formerly known as ILSMH) have begun to study the ADA and to weigh the need for comparable laws elsewhere (see Lachwitz [1991] report planning comparative study of antidiscrimination laws in the United States, France, Canada, Australia, and elsewhere). For example, in the Czech and Slovak Republics habilitation professionals have examined the ADA in detail and urged their governments to take effective actions to prevent discrimination in employment, education, community living, and other spheres of life affecting persons with disabilities.[2] Thus, this influential statute is likely to have far-reaching effects in distant places.

DEVELOPMENTAL DISABILITIES IMPLICATIONS OF THE ADA

Given the importance of the U.N. Declaration on the Rights of Mentally Retarded Persons to subsequent human rights milestones, it is entirely fitting that persons with mental retardation and other developmental disabilities should share in the promise of the ADA. Moreover, they form a significant segment of the nation's 43,000,000 citizens with disabilities (42 U.S.C. §12101[a][1]).

Until recently, they were "the new clients" who had no legal redress in the face of discrimination and lack of access to justice (42 U.S.C. §12101[a][4]; Herr, 1979). Despite the Supreme Court's majority opinion in *Cleburne Living Center v. City of Cleburne* (1985) refusing to treat mental retardation as a suspect classification, Congress has made findings in the ADA that persons with disabilities meet the criteria for strict scrutiny of disadvantaging classifications (42 U.S.C. §12101[a][7]). Their status as a discrete and insular minority now is recognized on the basis of "a history of purposeful unequal treatment" and the continuing "stereotypic assumptions" that impose unfair restrictions (42 U.S.C. §12101[a][7]). The ADA takes an inclusive approach to righting such discriminatory wrongs and therefore does not place disability groups at odds with each other.

Coverage

Without question, persons with developmental disabilities are covered by the ADA. Under the act, the term *disability* is broadly defined to include not only a person with a mental or physical impair-

---

[2]The AJ JDC-IDP "Training Institute/Model Community Living Arrangements Project" is organized, implemented, and funded by the American Jewish Joint Distribution Committee, Inc.–International Development Program, funded in part by the U.S. Agency for International Development, and implemented in partnership with Charles University and the Czech ministries of health and of social affairs.

ment that "substantially limits one or more . . . major life activities," but a person with a history of such an impairment or a person who simply is regarded as having such an impairment (42 U.S.C. §12102[2]). In contrast, the Developmental Disabilities Assistance and Bill of Rights Act of 1975, as amended in 1978, defines persons with developmental disabilities as a far narrower subset of persons with current and actual disabilities. That five-part definitional test refers to a severe, chronic disability attributable to a mental or physical impairment (or combination of impairments) limiting major life activities such as learning, language, or economic self-sufficiency, manifested before age 22, likely to continue indefinitely, and requiring coordinated and individualized services (42 U.S.C. §6001[5]). Under the ADA, even persons with mild mental retardation qualify for coverage because, by definition, mental retardation is a "significantly subaverage general intellectual functioning" that limits major life activities such as learning (American Psychiatric Association, 1980, p. 25).

Legislative history confirms that the ADA covers persons with mental retardation and other developmental disabilities. Ironically, Senator Helms, in colloquy with Senator Harkin, the act's chief Senate sponsor, put any such question to rest. In testing whether the act's definition of an individual with disabilities was intended to be "all-encompassing," Senator Helms first asked if "pedophiles," "schizophrenics," or "kleptomania" were included. He then squarely asked whether persons with mental retardation were protected by the ADA.

> **Mr. Helms:** People with intelligence levels, as measured on standardized tests such as the IQ test, which are so far below standard average levels as to limit substantially one or more major life activities, but who do not have any identifiable mental disease?
> **Mr. Harkin:** It is my understanding that they would be covered in this bill. If I understood the Senator correctly to say that it was so low that it did limit one or more, I do think I heard the Senator say that. I did hear the Senator say the IQ is so low that it limited one or more life activities.
> **Mr. Helms:** Correct.
> **Mr. Harkin:** Yes; in that case. (U.S. Senate, 1989c)

Relevance

The ADA has considerable relevance and resonance for persons with developmental disabilities. All of its provisions can apply because such persons may have both physical and mental disabilities. On a political level, the act's cross-disability approach encouraged coalition building as persons with all types of disabilities testified and lobbied together and celebrated the ADA's passage (Baffuto & Boggs, 1990–1991). As a coalition, they accommodated each other's concerns, such as the preservation of paratransit systems as a complement to fixed route services, a major concern of advocates for persons with mental retardation (42 U.S.C. §12143; P. Marchand, Director of Governmental Affairs, The Arc, personal communication, January 15, 1992). In addition to public transportation, as discusssed below, access to other public services, employment, and public accommodations in the private sector are of central importance to persons with such disabilities.

Public Accommodation

Some of the most glaring examples of discrimination cited in the legislative history to the ADA involved denials of public accommodation to persons with mental retardation. In one particularly egregious case, the owner of a private zoo refused to "admit children with Down's Syndrome because he feared they would upset his chimpanzees" (U.S. Senate Committee on Labor and Human Resources, 1989, p. 7). One bank even went so far as to refuse to open a bank account for a person with mental retardation because he "did not fit the image that the bank wanted to project" (Tucker, 1989, quoting Owens, 1989). The record demonstrated that persons with developmental disabilities often were the victims of exclusion based on their physical appearance alone and the degrading claims that others would find them "nauseating" or "disgusting to look at" (U.S. Senate Committee on Labor and Human Resources, 1989, p. 7).

The ADA prohibits such discrimination by restaurants, retail stores, child care centers, and similar commercial places of public accommodation (42 U.S.C. §§12181[7], 12182[a]). A public accommodation cannot use eligibility criteria that screen out or otherwise deny persons with disabilities the "full and equal enjoyment" of its goods and services (42 U.S.C. §12182[a], [b][2][A][i]). For example, this statutory and regulatory requirement could be violated if a store required presentation of a driver's license as the sole method of identification when presenting a check, because many persons with developmental disabilities may be ineligible to receive a driver's license (Equal Opportunity Employment Commission [EEOC] and U.S. Department of Justice [DOJ], 1992, p. III-73). Unnecessary separation of patrons with disabilities from other persons would also violate the ADA and its clear mandate that "accommodations shall be afforded to an individual with a disability in the most integrated setting appropriate to the needs of the individual" (42 U.S.C. §12182[b][12][B]). Thus, a person with Down syndrome could not be forced to sit in particular areas of a restaurant, and the wishes of other customers would not justify any discriminatory segregation (EEOC and DOJ, 1991, p. III-71, analyzing Final Rule 36.301).

Enforcement of these requirements, however, can present serious hurdles. The ADA provides very general defenses (e.g., standards of necessity, reasonable modifications that do not result in "undue burden" or fundamentally alter the nature of the service, and the removal of architectural or communication barriers only if "readily achievable") (42 U.S.C. §12182[b][2][A][i-v]). In addition, a public accommodation may limit access based on "legitimate safety requirements" that are grounded in actual risks, not stereotypes, generalizations, or speculations (EEOC and DOJ, 1991, p. III-71, §36.301[b]). Regulations offer an analytical framework rather than a precise road map to the types of changes businesses will have to undertake to accommodate patrons with developmental disabilities. Furthermore, case-by-case determinations possibly will yield inconsistent outcomes.

The media and consultants to business also focused heavily on physical changes and physical disabilities as the deadlines for Title III (public accommodations and services operated by private entities) compliance approached (e.g., Spayd, 1992a). The first lawsuits only heightened this emphasis on physical accessibility. One week after these provisions went into effect, New York's Empire State Building was sued, and a Washington lawyer who uses a wheelchair unleashed separate suits against a hotel, a clothing store, and a movie complex for keeping him from using their services and for inflicting "inconvenience, embarrassment, humiliation, emotional distress and the indignity and stigma of discrimination" (Spayd, 1992b). Predictably, in the "multimillion-dollar scramble to make the renovations and repairs" to assure access to persons with physical disabilities (Spayd, 1991), the less obvious needs of persons with mental disabilities were overlooked.

The U.S. Department of Justice recognized the need for some specific exploration of the public accommodation problems facing persons with mental retardation. Under a grant to The Arc, it sought to promote voluntary compliance with the act. The Arc is to provide technical assistance to businesses and other public accommodations in order to encourage "access and usability by people with mental retardation and other disabilities (The Arc, 1992). The Arc's "Access ADA" project is an effort to define concepts of cognitive accessibility and to help businesses recognize and act sensitively to persons whose disability may not be physically apparent, and to assist them to respond with changes in customer service, communication, signs, and other methods of making their environments meaningfully accessible and usable to individuals with mental retardation. To bolster the incentives for those changes, The Arc suggests that those changes will benefit not only its constituents, but the 72 million Americans described as functionally illiterate and the many older Americans and non–English-speaking persons who may have some difficulties with hurried or complex transactions (The Arc, 1992).

These are obviously complicated but important issues. In the past, an individual's differences from the norm have sometimes been blurred under concepts of mainstreaming. In contrast, this analysis calls for a nuanced recognition of the ways in which persons with mental retardation may be limited in langauge, cognition, memory, and learning characteristics. In a society in which the written word is crucial, the ADA challenges museums, amusement parks, restaurants, and other businesses to supplement those communications not only with the spoken word but with pictures, color codes, demonstrations, and personal assistance.

Achieving this access will require a massive training effort for the leadership and customer service staff of these establishments. To help its own members and others to apply the ADA, The Arc is training its 1,200 state and local chapters in practical strategies for overcoming access barriers and persuasive strategies for convincing business that such efforts are cost beneficial.[3] For example, depending on the nature of their service, restaurants might choose to provide a pictorial menu or sign board in a fast-food chain or to have waiters read the menus in a patient manner. Whether the issue is of child care centers that unduly limit the enrollment of preschoolers with disabilities or banks that have not taken the time to train its front-line representatives to aid their customers with mental retardation, the ADA requires such issues be addressed now.

Employment

Employment discrimination against persons with developmental disabilities raises more familiar legal issues. Section 504 of the Rehabilitation Act of 1973 is the source of the ADA's concepts of qualified individual with a disability, reasonable accommodation, and undue hardship. The ADA, however, embellishes those concepts and defines discrimination and defenses to such a charge in considerable statutory detail. For example, reasonable accommodation is defined to include job restructuring, changing work schedules, modifying training materials or policies, providing qualified readers, making existing facilities readily accessible, and other accommodations for individuals with disabilities (42 U.S.C. §12111[9]). Clearly, these types of accommodations will assist qualified individuals with developmental disabilities to be hired, promoted, paid, and treated on a fair, nondiscriminatory basis.

Workplace accommodations for persons with mental retardation often are inexpensive and straightforward (Baffuto & Boggs, 1990–1991, pp. 12–14). To perform effectively, such persons may need more time to learn the job, more reminders, adequate training opportunities, or perhaps a job coach. Interpretive guidance under Title I regulations notes that a temporary job coach— defined as an outside professional to assist in job training—may be required on a case-by-case basis "to assist in the training of a qualified individual with a disability as a reasonable accommodation" (EEOC and DOJ, 1991, p. I-59, Regulation §1630.9). This interpretive guidance also notes that modified training materials also may be required. Reasonable accommodation also might entail job restructuring by exchanging assignments with other employees, the use of checklists or picture cases, simple jigs in assembly jobs, and patience in uncovering the reasons for an employee's failure or mistake (Baffuto & Boggs, 1990–1991, pp. 12–14). Baffuto and Boggs cited the example of a new employee who did not show up on the job after his first week of diligent work because he felt cheated by paycheck deductions that no one had explained to him (1990–1991, p. 14).

Individuals with mild or no impairments may be able to invoke legal remedies if they can show that the employer mistakenly believes that they are more limited than they actually are. Employment decisions based on myth, fear, or stereotype, rather than an individualized determination of ability, are actionable (EEOC and DOJ, 1991, pp. I-35–I-36, §1630.2[k], Interpretive Guidance). This is a significant legal protection for persons who are mislabeled as having mental retardation or who have a degree of impairment that does not justify prejudiced assumptions of global incompetence. Fur-

---

[3]As part of its dissemination and technical assistance efforts, The Arc has a toll-free information service (1-800-433-5255) to help its own members, businesses, and others in the community to understand their rights and responsibilities under the ADA. For those using telecommunications devices for deaf persons, this service can be dialed (1-800-855-1155) and then the operator asked to call collect to 817-277-0553.

thermore, neither the existence of fears or prejudices on the part of the employer's workforce nor claims that reasonable accommodations reduce their morale will support an "undue hardship" defense (EEOC and DOJ, 1991, p. I-80, §1630.15[d], Interpretive Guidance).

The families and friends of persons with mental retardation also enjoy protection from job discrimination. Employers may not exclude or otherwise deny equal employment benefits to a qualified individual "because of the known disability of an individual with whom the qualified individual is known to have a relationship or association" (42 U.S.C. §12112[b][4]). Thus, the employer's fears concerning the burdens of raising a child with a disability cannot in themselves be used to justify denying the parent equal employment opportunities.

Will persons with mental retardation actually bring complaints of employment discrimination? The ADA (42 U.S.C. §12117[a]) incorporates the remedies and procedures found in the Civil Rights Act of 1964, including the power of the EEOC to receive complaints from individuals, to attempt conciliation, and to file a civil action in meritorious cases that have not settled (42 U.S.C. §§2000e-4 to 2000e-6, 2000e-8, 2000e-9). Evan J. Kemp, Jr., the chair of the EEOC, has predicted "not 'a lot of lawsuits,'" but expects 12,000–15,000 new administrative complaints, amounting to a 20%–25% increase in the agency's caseload (LaFraniere, 1992). Nationwide computer searches of past EEOC cases referring to mental retardation suggest that cases involving claimants with that disability are infrequent and often unsuccessful.

In a search for case law, only 42 EEOC cases referring to mental retardation were discovered from January 1984 to May 1990. For example, in *Wilkins v. Austin, General Services Administration, Acting Administrator* (1989), the right of administrative appeal was denied an employee with mild mental retardation who sought to reopen a settlement agreement on the unsupported grounds that he was deceived and misled into signing it. In *McKoy v. Stone, Secretary of the Army* (1990), a request to reopen determination of no discrimination was denied an employee with a learning disability who failed to demonstrate a nexus between his handicap and his removal. In addition, the EEOC denied his attempt to recharacterize his handicap as mental retardation, noting that "his discrimination complaint was brought and has proceeded only on the basis of his learning disabilities, which is a condition distinct from mental retardation" (p. 4).

Judicial cases under the Rehabilitation Act are even rarer. As one federal appellate court observed, plaintiffs in such job discrimination actions must overcome the "'Catch-22' implicit in virtually all Section 504 actions": that they can prove they are disabled enough to be covered by the act but not so disabled as to be unqualified to do the job (*Doe v. Region 13 Mental Health–Mental Retardation Commission* [1983]). Courts may give considerable deference to the employer's decisions where there is a risk of harm to third parties and there is no showing of discriminatory animus. For example, in *Doe v. Region 13*, a jury had found for Ms. Doe, but the Fifth Circuit Court upheld a ruling not on the verdict in which the defendant, an administrator of a program for mental health and mental retardation clients, showed that Ms. Doe, a therapist with an exemplary record, had suffered psychiatric deterioration to the point where suicidal tendencies might somehow affect her clients (p. 1410). Furthermore, workers with disabilities who may be insecure of their acceptance in the workplace may find it psychologically difficult to challenge adverse job decisions even when they are performing routine assembly jobs without safety risks (see *Doe v. Region 13*, 1983, p. 1410 ["This is not a case involving whether an employee is able to screw nuts and bolts onto a widget with sufficient speed."]. (But see *Drennen v. Philadelphia General Hospital* [1977] [colorable claim under Section 504 stated by a person with epilepsy].)

State and Local Government Services

One area of the ADA with particularly significant litigation potential is Title II, Subtitle A, dealing with public services by any state or local government. It prohibits discrimination by such entities and their instrumentalities in the same way that Section 504 of the Rehabilitation Act bars the federal government and programs receiving federal financial assistance from disability discrimination. As a result, the case law under Section 504 will prove a source of prediction and precedent for claims under the ADA filed by persons with developmental disabilities against state and local governments in their administration of services, programs, and activities. Title II reaches not only executive agencies but also the judicial and legislative branches of these levels of government (DOJ, 1992; see 28 C.F.R. §35.102[a] and comments to the federal rule).[4] Thus, all governmental activities are covered, even those activities performed by contractors to public services that have been "privatized," as, for example, a privately managed jail or juvenile reformatory institution (28 C.F.R. §35.102, comments).

Public Services Claims   Section 504 litigation has produced mixed results for plaintiffs with mental retardation who bring public services claims. In the field of special education, this provision led to an injunction against the State of New Mexico when it was the lone holdout among the 50 states in declining to accept the funds—and the equal opportunity mandate—attached to PL 94-142, the Education for All Handicapped Children Act (EAHCA) of 1975 (*New Mexico Association for Retarded Citizens v. New Mexico* [1982], in which the court found that failure to provide free appropriate public education to children with disabilities may violate Section 504). Although New Mexico subsequently returned to the fold, the Supreme Court in *Smith v. Robinson* (1984) severely limited Section 504 remedies when a claim under the EAHCA could be made. The Court found that "a plaintiff may not circumvent or enlarge the remedies available under the [EAHCA] by resort to Section 504" and did not reach the question of use of Section 504 where the EAHCA is not available or Section 504 would offer greater substantive rights than the EAHCA. (For citations to pre-*Smith* Section 504 decisions enforcing the right to a free appropriate public education, see *Gladys J. v. Pearland Independent School District* [1981].)

Then, with the Handicapped Children's Protection Act in 1986, Congress restored the rights of children with disabilities to enforce the complementary safeguards of both the Rehabilitation Act and the EAHCA. Administrative remedies under Section 504 to correct discrimination by school systems against students with disabilities are readily accessible (see, e.g., U.S. Dept. of Education, OCR, Reg. 1, *Berliner v. Putnam Board of Education, Connecticut,* No. 01-91-1034, Findings of Fact, April 19, 1991, regarding the failure to provide free appropriate public education and obtain and document parental consent to evaluation and placement). However, in *Eva N. v. Brock* (1991), under Section 504, the Kentucky School for the Blind was not required to admit a multiply handicapped and severely retarded student because it would not have been a reasonable accommodation if the institution's mission would have to be modified and new faculty hired to accommodate students with this combination of disabilities.

Life-Saving Medical Treatment Cases   The Supreme Court also took a restrictive view of Section 504's application to disputes on the withdrawal or withholding of life-saving medical treatments. In *American Hospital Association v. Bowen* (1986), the Court held that the decision involving the treatment of so-called Baby Doe patients did not involve discrimination against "otherwise qualified handicapped individuals" because their parents, and not the hospitals, had refused to authorize treatment. The Court also found a lack of evidence of discrimination in the administrative record used to justify the Department of Health and Human Services regulation of treatment decisions concerning children with disabilities and a correctable life-threatening condition. In a related case, the U.S. Court of Appeals flatly held that Section 504 did not apply to medical treatment decisions involving "defective newborn infants" because such decisions entail difficult questions of distinguishing bona fide medical judgment from discriminatory action, and because of the absence

---

[4]DOJ regulations are codified at 28 C.F.R. part 35 (1992). References to various portions of these regulations within this chapter cite the specific section of the regulations.

of legislative history that Congress intended the Rehabilitation Act provisions to apply to these situations (*United States v. University Hospital*, 1984).

Deinstitutionalization and Least Restrictive Placement Cases Institutional conditions and less restrictive placement cases have enjoyed a greater degree of success. In part, this may be explained by the fact that the Supreme Court has not yet reviewed Section 504 claims in this context. One high water mark was reached in *Halderman v. Pennhurst State School and Hospital* (1977), in which Federal District Judge Broderick held that the segregation of persons with mental retardation in an isolated institution like Pennhurst without minimally adequate habilitation constituted "unnecessarily separate and minimally inadequate services" in violation of Section 504 (pp. 1323–1324). The court interpreted Section 504 as a codification of the constitutional right to equal protection, and linked its holding that the Pennhurst residents' equal protection rights had been violated to the parallel Section 504 holding. In its analysis of what it termed a federal statutory right to nondiscriminatory habilitation, Judge Broderick cited legislative history expressing concern that the majority of "the Nation's institutionalized mentally retarded" were isolated from society and consigned to "terminal" care rather than enjoying rights in the community (p. 1323, quoting Sen. Humphrey). Because alternative legal theories were seen as supporting the lower court's remedies of adequate habilitation and massive deinstitutionalization, the Third Circuit Court never reached either the equal protection or Section 504 theories advanced in *Pennhurst*.

Other lower courts have divided on whether Section 504 will remedy a claim for deinstitutionalization. Some decisions have rejected this remedy as a general matter on the theory that, for some persons with profound retardation, the institution may be the least restrictive alternative (*Kentucky Association for Retarded Citizens v. Conn*, 1982), or on the somewhat confusing rationale that the resident was restrictively placed "not because of any particular aspect [or level] of her handicap, but simply because she is handicapped" (*Clark v. Cohen*, 1986). In contrast, federal courts have upheld relief under Section 504 where institutional residents with mental retardation were denied equal educational opportunities compared to other citizens (*Association for Retarded Citizens of North Dakota v. Olson*, 1983; Section 504 was not addressed on appeal given the alternative legal basis for the right to equal educational opportunities), or where those residents with more severe retardation were not provided educational, recreational, or other habilitation programs on the blanket assumption that such individuals cannot benefit from such services (*Garrity v. Gallen*, 1981).

More recently and dramatically, in *Homeward Bound v. Hissom* (1987), the federal court held that Section 504 prohibits unnecessarily segregated services for persons institutionalized as mentally retarded and ordered sweeping relief to close this Oklahoma institution and transfer its residents to community living arrangements. (Although an appeal was filed, the case was ultimately settled by the parties and the court-ordered relief is being implemented.) The *Hissom* court found four types of discrimination: the perpetuation of a segregated institution when effective services could have been delivered in more integrated settings; the denial of therapy and habilitation on the basis of severity of handicap; the consignment of persons with severe retardation or with retardation and physical or behavioral disabilities only to segregated settings; and the denial of vocational rehabilitation services to residents with severe disabilities (p. 20). In *Lelsz v. Kavanagh* (1987), the court also concluded that Section 504 violations resulted from substandard institutional care, approving a remedial agreement to upgrade habilitation services and to assure quality community placements for the class plaintiffs to "live, work, learn and recreate in environments which are or approximate ordinary homes and workplaces and afford each the opportunity to interact with and participate in the community" (paragraph 26 of implementation agreement).

This use of antidiscrimination law to open up community living arrangements to institutionalized persons is evident in another southwestern state. In *Jackson by Jackson v. Fort Stanton*

Hospital & Training School (1990), New Mexico's community service system for persons with developmental disabilities was held to violate Section 504 by relegating some 500 of the state's citizens with the most severe disabilities to the two public institutions for persons with developmental disabilities. (The respective institutions housed 345 and 149 residents, despite a statutory "preference for community based care" [p. 1250].) The case also is significant to this discussion because the plaintiffs brought one of the first claims under the ADA. However, because that claim was raised after a trial that was spread over 2½ years and long before the applicable provisions of the ADA came into effect, the plaintiffs' motion for leave to amend the complaint was denied as untimely (p. 1249, note 3). Instead, the crux of the Section 504 holding of discrimination was that New Mexico had designed a system that denied the institutions' residents access to community programs based on their physical and mental disabilities. In a broad interpretation of reasonable accommodation, the state was required to offer the appropriate services and additional supports to enable individuals recommended for community settings to be accepted and maintained in such settings that already served residents with less severe disabilities. For individuals with such recommended placements, the state was obligated to plan and carry out within a prescribed time frame "the full scope of community programs and services to be provided to support an effective community placement" (p. 1316). Thus, the early promise of *Pennhurst* and its little-discussed Section 504 holding has been redeemed in a region of the country—New Mexico, Texas, and Oklahoma—where the replacement of institutional models once would have seemed unlikely.

Individual placement cases have yielded less encouraging results, largely because of the evidentiary problems of demonstrating that the individual was excluded from the desired program "solely by reason of his handicap" (29 U.S.C. §794). For instance, when the parents of a man with mental retardation unilaterally placed him in a geriatric facility, sought to have the state pay the bill, and rejected the state's preferred placement in an adult foster care home, the court ruled that Section 504 was not violated when the state declined to pay (*Dempsey v. Ladd,* 1987). Among the many nondiscriminatory reasons cited by the court were the state's policy decision generally to offer separate facilities for elderly persons and persons with mental retardation, the possibility of exceptions to that policy, and factors of economy, morale, security, and menu planning justifying specialized treatment facilities. The court also was troubled by the circumvention of the state's need-based placement procedures, and the plaintiff's attempts to "unilaterally evade those processes and resort to judicial placement" (p. 640). (See also *Plummer by Plummer v. Branstad,* 1984, in which the court found that it was not a violation of Section 504 for a state to offer parallel, but mutually exclusive, adult day care services for persons with disabilities.)

Relief under Section 504 has been denied where proof of discrimination is missing. For instance, a trial court ruled that a lack of funds appropriated by the legislature to support transfers from a particular institution to community living arrangements can defeat a Section 504 claim (*Daniel B. v. White,* 1991, in which transfers to community living arrangements were upheld on other grounds on preliminary injunction). The U.S. Court of Appeals for the Sixth Circuit also found no discrimination when the state moved adults with mental retardation to state mental institutions when the private facility in which they lived had closed with only 24 hours' notice to the state, they had "no other place to live" on such short notice, and they failed to claim that because of their disabilities they were denied access to community residential living afforded to other Illinois citizens (*Phillips v. Thompson,* 1983). The First Circuit Court similarly found a lack of evidence to support a Section 504 claim for the failure to provide adequate services to a young man with mild retardation when there was no proof that more suitable accommodations were available but not offered or that he suffered discrimination compared to some defined class of individuals (*P.C. v. McLaughlin,* 1990). The plaintiff's assaultive behavior had contributed to his restrictive institutional placement. However, after the litigation was initiated, he was moved to a professional foster home and provided with special education services. The appellate court permitted this injunctive relief to stand, but dismissed claims for compensatory damages for alleged past inappropriate services.

Educational Placement Cases The struggle to escape inferior, unreasonably separate, and stigmatizing settings occurs as well in public schools and day vocational programs. It is reflected in court opinions that outlaw disparities in the classroom space and facilities allotted to children with disabilities and their peers without disabilities, relegating those with disabilities to basement classes, mobile class trailers, separate wings of regular schools, or long bus rides to classes far from their homes (e.g., *Hendricks v. Gilhool,* 1989, noting violations of Section 504 regulations to educate children with handicaps to the maximum extent appropriate to such children's needs). It is captured in the vortex of emotions and tangled assessments of acceptable risks when the individual with mental retardation also is the carrier of an infectious disease.

In the Willowbrook class action, for instance, a courageous district court judge saved deinstitutionalized school-age children from being placed in separate public school classes on the basis of their hepatitis B status, reasoning that other accommodations could be made without the stigmatizing effect of separating these Willowbrook children from other children (*New York State Association for Retarded Children v. Carey,* 1979). In contrast, a divided panel of the U.S. Court of Appeals for the Eighth Circuit held that a single carrier of hepatitis B was not otherwise qualified for admission to a day adult educational and vocational program because of the asserted undue financial burden of inoculating staff, the added risks of the individual's aggressive behavior, and the inoculation plan's potential disruption of the program (*Kohl v. Woodhaven Learning Center,* 1989).

Finally, and most heartening, there is the case of Eliana Martinez, age 7, IQ of 41, who was diagnosed as having AIDS-related complex. First consigned to homebound instruction and later ordered by a federal judge to be taught in a separate room to be "constructed in the TMH classroom with a large glass window and sound system," she was rescued from this sealed environment by an appellate court that applied the tests of Section 504, the EAHCA, and *School Board of Nassau County, Fla. v. Arline* (1987) with care and compassion (*Martinez v. School Board of Hillsborough County,* 1988). There the U.S. Court of Appeals for the Eleventh Circuit reasoned that, under Section 504, a "remote theoretical possibility" of transmission of AIDS by tears, saliva, or urine did not constitute a significant risk to justify exclusion, and that a reasonable accommodation must also take into account the psychological and educational effects of isolating Eliana from the rest of her classmates. On remand, the lower court found that Eliana was "otherwise qualified" to attend a Trainable Mentally Handicapped classroom and that the overall risk of transmission was not significant to bar her integration in that classroom (*Martinez by Martinez v. School Board,* 1989). As the cases described above suggest, the tools crafted under Section 504 can be sensitively applied to the ADA's purpose of nondiscrimination in public services.

Additional Judicial Applications of the ADA The ADA can build on the judiciary's experience over the last 20 years in dispelling the myths and correcting the injustices rooted in faulty generalizations. As one federal court observed, "[n]o longer are mentally retarded persons shackled by notions that they cannot learn and grow, that they are eternal children, that they have no ability to care for themselves or that they cannot live dignified and productive lives" (*Lelsz v. Kavanaugh,* 1987). As a comprehensive piece of legislation and with its extensive legislative history, the ADA, unlike Section 504 of the Rehabilitation Act, can better reach coercive and differential treatment that is discriminatory.

Title II bars discrimination by any public entity, and this may include the actions of courts and administrative agencies (see Rubenstein, chap. 15, this volume [pp. 219–221]). As a result, the ADA could be invoked to challenge child custody awards that did not give individualized consideration to the abilities of a parent but instead viewed his or her disability as "prima facie evidence of the person's unfitness as a parent or of probable detriment to the child" (*In re Marriage of Carney,*

1979; see Hayman, 1990, stating that classification of a parent labeled as "mentally retarded" reduces "individualized adjudications to formalities and foregone conclusions" [p. 1269]). In 1992, a Maryland court was presented with such ADA-based arguments, and awarded the child's custody to the mother with disabilities.

The ADA could, along with other legal theories, be raised to question behavioral intervention practices that cause physical pain or regulations of such practices that are insufficiently protective of students with disabilities, perhaps comparing such regulations to regulations that bar corporal punishment for their peers without disabilities (see, e.g., *Lacayo v. Honig,* 1991, containing a consent decree that requires school system regulations to ensure compliance with least restrictive environment requirements and to prohibit "[a]ny intervention that is designed to, or likely to, cause physical pain" and to prohibit "[r]eleasing noxious, toxic or otherwise unpleasant sprays, mists or substances in proximity to the pupil's face" [summarized by Pike Institute, Boston University School of Law, 1991, pp. 21–22]). The ADA also might serve as a basis for reviewing the dwindling number of statutes or circumstances under which the involuntary sterilization of a person with mental retardation is proposed (see, e.g., *North Carolina Association for Retarded Children v. North Carolina,* 1976; see generally Herr & van Melle, 1992). These and other possible applications can be considered carefully when agencies begin the self-study evaluation procedures that the ADA regulations require (DOJ, 1992; 28 C.F.R. §35.105).

NEXT STEPS

Training Self-Advocates and Others

Formidable training tasks lie ahead to turn theoretical rights into realities. Persons with developmental disabilities, their families, and their friends should be offered simple and straightforward explanations of what the ADA can mean to them. Self-advocacy groups and their advisors are prime audiences for training modules and audiovisual packages that clearly teach people how to recognize violations of their ADA rights and how to correct them. Developmental Disabilities Councils and consumer organizations also can fund and publish state-specific brochures, pamphlets, and manuals that summarize ADA provisions and compare those provisions and remedies to Section 504 and state antidiscrimination laws.

Judges and court administrators have a dual stake in becoming familiar with this corpus of antidiscrimination and disability law. First, the judicial system should become a model of accessibility and remove attitudinal and other barriers that have limited persons with disabilities from using that system as litigants, court personnel, job applicants, jurors, witnesses, and members of the public (American Bar Association and National Judicial College, 1991, pp. 3, 7). State courts clearly are covered under Title II, and courts that failed to comply with the ADA, whether out of lack of knowledge or lack of funds, would send a poor message to the rest of the community. Second, the ADA may stimulate awareness of disability discrimination and produce a wave of new complaints under related laws and regulations. To equip judges and other court personnel for these added challenges, the National Judicial College has developed a curriculum and engaged a faculty to conduct training sessions on the ADA, other disability rights, and the human services concepts that underlie normalized habilitation. At the time of this writing, training sessions have been conducted for representatives of the judicial systems of Connecticut, Delaware, Maryland, New Jersey, and Pennsylvania, as well as sessions for a national audience of judges.

Informing the Community

As previously discussed, public opinion polls reveal that most of the public remains unaware of, or misinformed about, the ADA and its requirements (Louis Harris and Associates, 1991). Unless more effective information campaigns are mounted, several negative consequences can follow. Obviously, an uninformed public will not be a compliant public. Furthermore, selective and politically biased accounts of claimed burdensome and excessively costly implementation of the ADA can fuel a backlash against not only the ADA but the entire disability rights movement. For example, a Maryland legislator in floor debate on the state budget claimed that only 37 persons with a disability used the Mass Transit Administration buses on any given day, thus casting ADA requirements and the expense of adding lifts to buses as wasteful. A few hours later, when the same House of Delegates debated a proposed constitutional amendment on equal rights for persons with disabilities, the amendment failed by a two-vote margin in a debate colored by references to the presumed effects of the ADA (author's personal observation).

Creative public relations and public information campaigns are needed to counter negative images and knowledge gaps about the ADA. For instance, such campaigns can emphasize how reducing cognitive accessibility barriers benefits not only persons with mental retardation but persons who are illiterate or non-English speakers as well. Similarly, eliminating physical barriers helps not only persons in wheelchairs but parents pushing strollers, persons recovering from short-term illness or injury, and frail elderly persons. Specific information campaigns also can focus attention on the ADA's applications to persons with developmental disabilities and the accommodations that will benefit them.

State Constitutional Amendments

Advocates for persons with disabilities should not be complacent that the ADA is a panacea to end discrimination and should consider the adequacy of state law remedies. In particular, state constitutions can be an important source of legal protection that is beyond the reach of the U.S. Supreme Court to review and weaken. In calling for new state court activism resting on state constitutional grounds, then–Associate Justice William J. Brennan argued that state constitutions are "a font of individual liberties, their protections often extending beyond those required by the Supreme Court's interpretation of federal law" and that without the "independent protective force of state law . . . the full realization of our liberties cannot be guaranteed" (Brennan, 1977, p. 491). As significant as the ADA is, it does not cover all areas (e.g., the omission of the insurance industry; 42 U.S.C. §12201[c]), contains numerous political compromises, and could be subject to legislative amendments and weakening interpretations by the courts and administrative agencies (Cook, 1991, p. 469).

In contrast, a state constitutional amendment could be broader in application than the ADA or other state or federal law, and is less susceptible to repeal than ordinary legislation. A constitutional amendment offers a clear and succinct statement of public policy, the promise of a long-term commitment to equal rights, and the possibility of strict scrutiny of challenged forms of discrimination. Because such an amendment requires referendum approval by a state's voters and the state constitution has a higher visibility than a mere statute, this type of legal change can have significant educational effects. It can raise the awareness, sensitivity, and knowledge of a state's citizens about the facts of disability discrimination and the legal means to remedy it.

To date, the states of Massachusetts and Connecticut have adopted constitutional amendments specifically prohibiting discrimination based on physical or mental disability (Massachusetts Constitution, article 114 [amended 1980]; Connecticut Constitution, article 1, §20 [amended 1984]). Such provisions have served as a reference point for further legal and practical reforms. Canada also has adopted a constitutional provision guaranteeing equality before and under the law for persons with physical or mental disabilities, while stipulating that this does not preclude any "law, program or activity" of affirmative action for such persons (Canadian Constitution [Constitution Act, 1982], part I [Canadian Charter of Rights and Freedoms], §15[2]). Maryland also has come close to passing an amendment that "equality of rights under the law shall not be abridged or denied because of physical or mental disability." The proposed Article 47 to the Maryland Declaration of Rights was unanimously passed in the Senate but defeated by a two-vote margin in the House of Delegates when it fell two votes short of the 60% super-majority required for a constitutional change (Maryland State House of Delegates, 1992; Maryland State Senate, 1992). As a result of this activism in Maryland, The Arc has resolved to encourage all the states to enact similar constitutional mandates (Resolution No. 9: Enactment of Constitutional Provisions to Prohibit Discrimination against Persons with Disabilities, adopted on November 10, 1990).

International Information Exchange Strategies

As previously noted, the United States and other nations can benefit from exchanging information on their legal and social reform experiences in moving toward integration. Although there is a growing body of legal literature on the ADA, such as this book and law review commentaries (e.g., Murphy, 1991; Stuhlbard, 1991; Temple Symposium, 1991), there is an absence of comparative legal studies in this field. Organizations such as the World Institute on Disability and the International Exchange of Experts in Rehabilitation might wish to undertake a series of such studies that would place such laws in sociolegal and particular disability contexts. Nongovernmental organizations such as the International League of Societies for Persons with Mental Handicap and the International Association for the Scientific Study of Mental Deficiency also have a stake in sponsoring surveys, position papers, and conferences that critically evaluate the ADA and its overseas counterparts.

The issues go beyond sharing technical and legal solutions to problems of reasonable accommodation. Instead, at their core the deeper issues are how a society musters the political will not only to declare the equality norm but to practice it. As Senator Harkin, the ADA's chief sponsor, wrote, the act "sends a clear message that people with disabilities are now legally entitled to be treated with dignity. They are to be judged on the basis of their abilities and not with fear, ignorance, prejudice or patronization. Segregation and exclusion are now illegal" (Law, 1991, p. 113, quoting Harkin, 1990, p. 61). Audiences in this country and abroad are waiting to see if this message is heeded.

CONCLUSION

The ADA represents a radical and historic opportunity to bring unjustified segregation to an end for persons with developmental disabilities. Its intellectual foundations rest on over 40 years of domestic and international pledges of equal rights for persons with disabilities (see International Perspectives on the ADA, above, and Weicker, 1991, p. 387, on the pathbreaking Civil Service Act Amendment of 1948, prohibiting employment discrimination on the basis of physical handicap in the U.S. Civil Service). The political strength of the ADA is the breadth of the coalition that insisted on inclusiveness.

Persons with developmental disabilities and their advocates strongly believe that the ADA's ultimate goal and vision is to transform social attitudes and power relations, "to create a society in which both the physical and social norms are more broadly defined, where diversity is celebrated and where stigmatizing or discomforting differences are minimized, not only in the work place but in all aspects of a person's life" (Baffuto & Boggs, 1990–1991, p. 14).

Section 504 of the Rehabilitation Act also was accompanied by high hopes. To many commentators, it stands as a reminder that bold statutes can be nullified by grudging judicial interpretations and inconsistent executive enforcement. However, this glass is also half full, as a reading of the cases in this chapter confirms. The ADA is a chance to get it right this time. Through systematic training of advocates and constituency groups, campaigns of information and outreach to the general public, and disciplined strategies of legal advocacy, the ADA can create real and positive changes.

The outcome of this struggle will be closely watched in countries with far fewer resources and less developed civil rights infrastructures than the United States. If the ADA succeeds, other countries may choose to reevaluate the adequacy of their own laws and nonlegal approaches to combatting discrimination. If the ADA falters, the lessons drawn from that experience also may have international reverberations. In the United States, the ADA can be a catalyst to actions at state and local levels to enable persons with disabilities, regardless of the nature and seriousness of those disabilities, to have the "right to enjoy a decent life, as normal and full as possible" (U.N. Declaration on the Rights of Disabled Persons, 1975, article 3). The ADA is a necessary but not sufficient step toward realizing those values and human rights.

REFERENCES

American Bar Association and National Judicial College. (1991). *Court-related needs of the elderly and persons with disabilities: A blueprint for the future*. Washington, DC: American Bar Association.

American Hospital Association v. Bowen, 476 U.S. 610 (1986).

American Psychiatric Association. (1980). *Quick reference to the diagnostic criteria from DSM-III* (3rd ed.). Washington, DC: American Psychiatric Press, Inc.

The Arc. (1992). *Access ADA: Free assistance to help your business comply with Title III of the Americans with Disabilities Act* [brochure]. Arlington, Texas: Author.

Association for Retarded Citizens of North Dakota v. Olson, 561 F. Supp. 473, 493 (D.N.D. 1982), aff'd, 713 F.2d 1384, 1394 (8th Cir. 1983).

Astor, H. (1990). Antidiscrimination legislation and physical disability: The lessons of experience. *Australian Law Journal, 64*, 113–128.

Baffuto, T., & Boggs, E. (1990–1991, Winter). What ADA has meant and what it can mean for people with mental retardation. *American Rehabilitation*, pp. 10–14.

Brennan, W.J., Jr. (1977). State constitutions and the protection of individual rights. *Harvard Law Review, 90*, 489–504.

Brownlie, I. (Ed.). (1981). *Basic documents on human rights* (2nd ed.). Oxford, England: Clarendon Press.

Carey, J. (1970). *U.N. protection of civil and political rights*. Syracuse, NY: Syracuse University Press.

Civil Rights Act of 1964, codified as amended in scattered sections of 42 U.S.C. (1988).

Civil Service Act Amendment of 1948, Pub. L. No. 617, 62 Stat. 351 (1948).

Clark v. Cohen, 613 F. Supp. 684, 694 (E.D. Pa. 1985), aff'd, 794 F.2d 79 (3d Cir. 1986), cert. denied, 479 U.S. 962 (1986).

Cleburne Living Center v. City of Cleburne, 473 U.S. 432 (1985).

Clinton, B., & Gore, A. (1992). *Putting people first: How we can all change America*. New York: Times Books.

Cook, T.M. (1991). The Americans with Disabilities Act: The move to integration. *Temple Law Review, 64*, 393–469.

Daniel B. v. White, No. 79-4088, 1991 WL 58494 (E.D. Pa. April 11, 1991).

Dempsey v. Ladd, 840 F.2d 638 (9th Cir. 1987).

Developmental Disabilities Assistance and Bill of Rights Act of 1975, 42 U.S.C. §§6000–6081 (1988).

Doe v. Region 13 Mental Health–Mental Retardation Commission, 704 F.2d 1402 (5th Cir. 1983).

Drennen v. Philadelphia General Hospital, 428 F. Supp. 809 (E.D. Pa. 1977).

Drost, P. (1965). *Human rights as legal rights: The realization of individual human rights in positive international law*. Leyden, The Netherlands: A.W. Sijthoff.

Education for All Handicapped Children Act of 1975, 20 U.S.C. §§1232, 1401, 1405–1420, 1453 (1975).

Equal Opportunity Employment Commission and U.S. Department of Justice. (1991). *Americans with Disabilities Act handbook*. Washington, DC: U.S. Government Printing Office.

Eva N. v. Brock, 741 F. Supp. 626 (E.D. Ky. 1990), aff'd 943 F.2d 51 (6th Cir. 1991).

Fernandez v. Wilkinson, 505 F. Supp. 787 (D. Kan. 1980), aff'd 654 F.2d 1382 (10th Cir. 1981).

Filartiga v. Pena-Irala, 630 F.2d 876 (2d Cir. 1980).

Garrity v. Gallen, 522 F. Supp. 171 (D.N.H. 1981).

Gladys J. v. Pearland Independent School District, 520 F. Supp. 869 (S.D. Tex. 1981).

Halderman v. Pennhurst State School and Hospital, 446 F. Supp. 1295 (E.D. Pa. 1977), aff'd on other grounds, 612 F.2d 84 (3d Cir. 1979) (en banc), rev'd on other grounds, 451 U.S. 1 (1981), on remand 673 F.2d 647 (3d Cir. 1982) (en banc), rev'd on other grounds, 465 U.S. 89 (1984).

Handicapped Children's Protection Act of 1986, 20 U.S.C.A. §1415 (1990).

Harkin, T. (1990). Our Newest Civil Rights Law: The A.D.A. *Trial Magazine, December*, 56.

Hayman, R.L., Jr. (1990). Presumptions of justice: Law, politics, and the mentally retarded parent. *Harvard Law Review, 103*, 1201–1271.

Hendricks v. Gilhool, 709 F. Supp. 1362 (E.D. Pa. 1989).

Herr, S. (1979). The new clients: Legal services for mentally retarded persons. *Stanford Law Review, 31,* 553–611.

Herr, S.S., & van Melle, M. (1992). Reproductive choices: Sterilization, abortion and the rights of persons with mental handicap. In S.M. Nemeth & A.F. Felix (Eds.), *European workshop on bio-ethics—mental handicap.* Utrecht, The Netherlands: Bishop Bekkers Institute.

Holmes, S.A. (1992, January 27). Sweeping U.S. law to help disabled goes into effect. *New York Times,* p. 1.

Homeward Bound v. Hissom, No. 85-C-437-E, slip op. at 14-18, 20–21, 32-34 (N.D. Okla. July 24, 1987). (Available in Westlaw, 1987, WL 27104)

Huynh Thi Anh v. Levi, 586 F.2d 625 (6th Cir. 1978).

In re Marriage of Carney, 157 Cal. Rptr. 383, 598 P.2d 36 (1979).

International League of Societies for the Mentally Handicapped. (1969). Jerusalem declaration on the general and special rights of mentally retarded persons. In *Charity to rights* (pp. 160–161). Brussels: Author.

Jackson by Jackson v. Fort Stanton Hospital & Training School, 757 F. Supp. 1243 (D.N.M. 1990).

Kentucky Association for Retarded Citizens v. Conn, 510 F. Supp. 1233 (W.D. Ky. 1980), aff'd, 674 F.2d 582 (6th Cir.), *cert. denied,* 459 U.S. 1041 (1982).

Kohl v. Woodhaven Learning Center, 865 F.2d 930 (8th Cir. 1989), *cert. denied,* 493 U.S. 892 (1989).

Lacayo v. Honig, No. S90-0947 LKK JFM, slip op. at 23-24 (E.D. Cal. May 22, 1991). (Summarized in Disability Advocates Bulletin, 7, 21–22 [1991, December 2])

Lachwitz, K. (1991, November 15). *Report to the Committee on Rights and Advocacy.* Brussels: International League of Societies for Persons with Mental Handicap.

LaFraniere, S. (1992, January 24). For the disabled, a question of dignity. *Washington Post,* p. A21.

Law, S.K. (1991). The Americans with Disabilities Act of 1990: Burden on business or dignity for the disabled? *Duquesne Law Review, 30,* 99–114.

Lelsz v. Kavanagh, 673 F. Supp. 828 (N.D. Tex. 1987).

Louis Harris and Associates, Inc. (1991). *Public attitudes towards people with disabilities.* Washington, DC: Author.

Luard, E. (1967). Promotion of human rights by UN political bodies. In E. Luard (Ed.), *The international protection of human rights* (pp. 132–159). London: Thames and Hudson.

Lujan v. Defenders of Wildlife, 112 S.Ct. 2130 (1992).

Mahoney v. Radio Free Europe/Radio Liberty Inc., No. 91-1842-LFO, 61 U.S.L.W. 2354 (D.D.C. November 24, 1992).

Martinez v. School Board of Hillsborough County, 861 F.2d 1502 (11th Cir. 1988).

Martinez by Martinez v. School Board, 711 F. Supp. 1066 (M.D. Fla. 1989).

Maryland State House of Delegates. (1992, March 23). Vote on H.B. 1248, proposed article 47 to the Maryland Declaration of Rights.

Maryland State Senate. (1992, March 19). Vote on S.B. 526, proposed article 47 to the Maryland Declaration of Rights, Appendix 1, Senate Journal, p. 391 (1992).

McKoy v. Stone, Secretary of the Army, No. 01892408 (EEOC May 4, 1990).

Murphy, R. K. (1991). Reasonable accommodation and employment discrimination under Title I of the Americans with Disabilities Act. *Southern California Law Review, 64,* 1607–1644.

New Mexico Association for Retarded Citizens v. New Mexico, 495 F. Supp. 391 (D.N.M. 1980), rev'd and remanded, 678 F.2d 847 (10th Cir. 1982).

New South Wales Anti-Discrimination Act of 1977, No. 48 (amended 1982).

New York State Association for Retarded Children v. Carey, 612 F.2d 644 (2d Cir. 1979).

Nguyen Da Yen v. Kissinger, 528 F.2d 1194 (9th Cir. 1975).

North Carolina Association for Retarded Children v. North Carolina, 420 F. Supp. 451 (M.D.N.C. 1976).

Owens, M. (1989, November 15). *Owens says disability rights bill is a victory for all Americans* [press release]. Washington, DC: Author.

P.C. v. McLaughlin, 913 F.2d 1033 (1st Cir. 1990).

Phillips v. Thompson, 715 F.2d 365 (7th Cir. 1983).

Pike Institute on Law and Disability, Boston University School of Law. (1991, December 2). *Disability Advocates Bulletin, 7,* 21–22.

Plummer by Plummer v. Branstad, 731 F.2d 574 (8th Cir. 1984).

Rehabilitation Act of 1973, 29 U.S.C. §791–794 (1988).

School Board of Nassau County, Fla. v. Arline, 480 U.S. 273 (1987).

Schuster-Herr, R., & Herr, S. (1980, January/February). Human rights and disabled persons: An international perspective. *Amicus, 5,* 14–19.

Sick and Handicapped Persons (Discrimination) Act of 1990, Law No. 90-602 (1990), J.O.R.F. 8272.

Smith v. Robinson, 468 U.S. 992 (1984).

Sohn, L. (1967). The Universal Declaration of Human Rights. *Journal of the International Commission of Jurists, 8,* 7–26.

Sohn, L.B., & Buergenthal, T. (1973). *International protection of human rights.* New York: Bobbs-Merrill.

Spayd, L. (1991, November 11). As deadline nears, barriers fall for disabled. *Washington Post,* p. A1.

Spayd, L. (1992a, January 24). Business faces $2 billion overhaul to lower the barriers; entrepreneurs see dollars and sense in ADA. *Washington Post,* p. A21.

Spayd, L. (1992b, February 4). Disabilities act sparks lawsuits; D.C. businesses cited by local lawyer. *Washington Post,* p. A13.

Stuhlbard, S.F. (1991). Reasonable accommodation under the Americans with Disabilities Act: How much must one do before hardship turns undue? *University of Cincinnati Law Review, 59,* 1311–1348.

Temple Symposium. The Americans with Disabilities Act symposium: A view from within. (1991). *Temple Law Review, 64,* 371–628.

Tucker, B. (1989). An overview of the Americans with Disabilities Act. *University of Illinois Law Review, 1989,* 923–939.

U.N. Convention on the Rights of the Child of 1989, 28 I.L.M. 1456 (1989).

U.N. Declaration on the Rights of Disabled Persons of 1975, U.N. G.A. Res. 3447, U.N. GAOR, 30th Sess., Supp. No. 34, U.N. Doc. A/10034 (1975).

U.N. Declaration on the Rights of Mentally Retarded Persons of 1971, U.N. G.A. Res. 2856, U.N. GAOR, 26th Sess., Supp. No. 29, U.N. Doc. A/8429 (1971).

U.N. Educational, Scientific, and Cultural Organization. (1981). Declaration of the World Conference on Actions and Strategies for Education, Prevention and Integration (Sundberg Declaration).

U.N. General Assembly. (1983). *Implementation of the World Programme of Action Concerning Disabled Persons* (U.N. G.A. A/RES/37/53). New York: United Nations.

U.N. Secretary General. (1979). *Report to the meeting of the Advisory Committee for the International Year for Disabled People* (U.N. Doc. A/34/158). New York: United Nations.

U.N. Universal Declaration of Human Rights, U.N. G.A. Res. 217, U.N. Doc. A/810 (1948).

U.N. World Programme of Action Concerning Disabled Persons, U.N. G.A. A/37/351/Add. 1, Annex, Sect. VIII (Dec. 3, 1982).

U.S. Department of Education, Office of Civil Rights (1991, April 19). Region 1, *Berliner v. Putnam Board of Education, Connecticut,* No. 01-91-1034, Findings of Fact.

U.S. Department of Justice. (1992). Nondiscrimination on the basis of disability in state and local government services. In *Code of Federal Regulations* (28: Judicial Administration, pp. 417–457). Washington, DC: U.S. Government Printing Office.

U.S. Senate. (1989a, September 8). Debate on S. 933, letter of September 5, 1989, from Consortium for Citizens with Disabilities to Sen. Kennedy. *Congressional Record, 135,* S10770–S10771.

U.S. Senate. (1989b, September 8). Debate on S. 933, statement of President Bush. *Congressional Record, 135,* S10770.

U.S. Senate. (1989c, September 8). Debate on S. 933, statements of Sen. Helms and Sen. Harkin. *Congressional Record, 135,* S10765.

U.S. Senate Committee on Labor and Human Resources. (1989, August 30). *Senate report no. 101-116, to accompany S. 933 (101st Congress, 1st session).* Washington, DC: U.S. Government Printing Office.

United States v. University Hospital, 729 F.2d 144 (2d Cir. 1984).

Vickers, D., & Endicott, O. (1985). Mental disability and equal rights. In A. Bayefsky & M. Eberts (Eds.), *Equality and the Canadian Charter of Rights and Freedoms* (pp. 381–410). Toronto: Carswell.

Weicker, L.P., Jr. (1991). Historical background of the Americans with Disabilities Act. *Temple Law Review, 64,* 387–392.

Wilkins v. Austin, General Services Administration, Acting Administrator, No. 01890321 (EEOC Oct. 27, 1989).

Wyatt v. Stickney, 344 F. Supp. 387 (M.D. Ala. 1972), *aff'd sub nom.,* Wyatt v. Aderholt, 503 F.2d 1305 (5th Cir. 1974).

Zemel v. Rusk, 381 U.S. 1 (1965).

Chapter 18

Building Our Own Boats

A Personal Perspective on Disability Policy

Judith E. Heumann

Throughout the world disability policy is of a very piecemeal nature. This is readily apparent in a study initiated by the World Health Organization (WHO), in which progress in health and social legislation for disabled people[1] in 25 U.N. member states was evaluated. The introduction to the study explains that:

> The interests of the severely disabled are not easily acknowledged in the political process that leads towards laws and administrative practices. They are a minority group with few advantages and few to speak for them, especially in times of economic difficulty . . . . Too little is known about the effects of legislative changes on the quality of life of those for whom the laws are passed in the first place. The legislation concerning disabled persons is vast and complex because its development has been piecemeal, including reactions to acute situations such as great wars. (Pinet, 1990, p. vii)

From this it can be inferred that policy, at least in the 25 countries included in the survey, tends to be created in response to political situations, not in response to the needs of disabled people. Generally policy design and fund allocation are based on the origin of a person's disability. For example, why do we distinguish between a person who became a quadriplegic in Vietnam and a person who became a quadriplegic as the result of an injury in an automobile crash in Des Moines, Iowa? The disabled veteran receives at least enough benefits to ensure that his basic needs are met, whereas someone who becomes disabled in a crash must pursue litigation to try to attain a reasonable level of financial security to cope with his or her new needs.

Leaving aside the issues of litigation and war in our society, the situation can be viewed as an attempt to identify culpability for disability. The government, considering itself responsible for those who serve in its military forces, agrees to pay for veterans' disability benefits. The insurance

This project was partially supported under a grant from the National Institute on Disability and Rehabilitation Research, Office of Special Education and Rehabilitative Services (NIDRR #H133B00006-90). The contents do not necessarily reflect the policies of these agencies and endorsement by the federal government should not be assumed.

I would also like to thank the publisher for being willing to pay for PAS related to the writing of this chapter. Special thanks to Susan Brown, my personal assistant and research associate during the writing of this chapter, and to Barbara Duncan, of Rehabilitation International, for editorial assistance.

[1]The usage of such terms by the author differs from the form generally used throughout this book; see Terminology, later in this chapter.—*ed*

company of the driver at fault, if forced to, assumes responsibility for the disability-related costs of the person injured in an automobile crash. However, this idea of culpability leaves many of us out in the cold. Those of us with early-onset or progressive disabilities, for example, have no one to sue and no single governmental agency to petition for disability assessment or financial supports. We have no one to blame for our disabilities, and in fact we have no wish to blame. We want our needs to be addressed without regard for how our disability occurred. We do not want to receive benefits because we are perceived as victims, but rather because it is recognized that our needs are legitimate and must be addressed for full integration to become reality.

I believe this is the rethinking that must take place in terms of disability policy and that underlies much of this chapter: that policy should be determined by our needs, not by political expedience, prejudice, or pity. We, as disabled people, must be proactive instead of reactive, defining our own agendas and creating change on our own terms.

POLICY VERSUS PATCHWORK

Policy in the United States is piecemeal as well. As Edward Berkowitz stated in his groundbreaking work *Disabled Policy: America's Programs for the Handicapped*, "In disability, as in social welfare in general, the only avenue of fundamental reform is to add another program to existing programs and to cope with the resulting confusion" (1987, p. 227).

There has never been a clear articulation of the goals and underlying values of policy affecting disabled people. This lack of a framework for policy development and implementation is in large part responsible for the patchwork nature of disability policy. Problems resulting from a piecemeal approach are manifold. The incremental nature of legislation makes change an incredibly slow process. The lives of untold numbers of disabled people are being squandered, despite legislative advances, as a result of this patchwork approach to policy. Although incremental change may be a reality, there is too little recognition of the long-term negative effects of such policy development on the lives of disabled people, their families, and society as a whole.

Historically, policymakers were constrained not just by economics, but by a prejudice that disabled people could not be productive members of society. As disabled people began to protest such stereotypes, attitudes began to change. These changes in part led to advances in policy, but the process continues to be far too slow. The vision we as disabled people have of how our lives should and could be is not generally consistent with that of policymakers and general society. The articulation of our goal of full participation for all of society's members, regardless of cost or comfort level, must take place in order for change to occur more rapidly. The need for a framework cannot be overemphasized.

There are many examples of the patchwork nature of disability-related legislation. In the 1970s policymakers, convinced by the transit industry that the vast majority of disabled individuals could not use mass transit, refused to legislate the design of accessible public transit despite the fact that all major disabled-run groups throughout the United States supported such an initiative. This situation continued until the passage of the Americans with Disabilities Act (ADA) in 1990, so that there are today thousands of inaccessible buses and trains because of the lack of a clear-cut policy of inclusion. The effects of such short-term, prejudicial thinking will be felt for years to come because the ADA does not require retrofitting. Yet another patch has been put in place that does not completely address our needs.

Another example can be found in the area of education. The requirement that disabled children be given the same educational opportunities as nondisabled children did not occur until 1975 with the passage of the Education for All Handicapped Children Act. During the intervening years, as more disabled people and their allies fought for inclusion in the educational system, more pieces of legislation were added, each addressing part of the larger problem. There are many children who have benefitted from the legislation; however, children with more significant needs are still too frequently underserved or segregated. As it currently stands, the school district is responsible for all educational disability-related expenses. Funds are tight; a child with more significant needs is likely not to receive needed services for many reasons. For one, the federal and state educational agencies responsible for enforcing the law are not doing an adequate job. Therefore fighting for an appropriate education becomes the family's responsibility. The amount of time and energy necessary to be an advocate is often too much for the typical family to expend, and the government has failed to provide funding for the needed number of paid advocates. This in one of the greatest failings of the "special" education system in this country. Until this situation is remedied, I fear that large numbers of children with significant disabilities will continue to be denied the educational opportunities guaranteed them by law. As these children grow older they will join the swelling ranks of Americans who are unemployable or, at best, underemployed. So the educational "patch" is also full of holes.

These few examples should serve to illustrate problems in existing legislation. It is also true, however, that there are entire pieces of the quilt still missing—that is, needs for which no, or completely inadequate, legislative redress exists. The passage of the Rehabilitation Act of 1973, which includes the well-known Section 504 prohibiting discrimination against disabled people in programs receiving federal financial assistance, was extremely important to the disability civil rights movement. Section 504 was a radical step, but there is still a long way to go.

I do not mean to deny that there has been great progress in the last 2 decades, only to emphasize that the legislative quilt still has many missing pieces. If we are truly committed to the needs of disabled people, we must prioritize our work on essential patches without losing sight of our long-term goal of full and complete participation.

PERSONAL ASSISTANCE SERVICES

One of the most important patches missing from the quilt is personal assistance services (PAS). These are services that provide for the assistance of another person in tasks individuals would normally do for themselves if they did not have disability. These tasks include personal maintenance and hygiene, such as dressing, bathing, and catheter care; mobility needs, such as getting in and out of bed or a wheelchair; household responsibilities, including cooking, cleaning, and child-rearing; cognitive tasks, such as money handling and budget planning; and communications access, such as interpreting and reading.

For the 9.6 million people who need PAS, how can the dream of the ADA become a reality? Those of us with significant disabilities know that it cannot. If I am unable to pay someone to help me get out of bed in the morning, what good does being protected from employment discrimination do me? If a deaf person is allocated funds for an on-the-job sign language interpreter only for group meetings, how can he or she fully participate in the activities of the work site? If a blind person cannot pay a driver and happens to live in an area with little or no public transportation, how can he or she participate in general community activities? All too frequently people with significant needs are forced to rely on inadequate volunteer assistance or even to be institutionalized.

Nondisabled people do not have to think about how often they go to the bathroom. They drink what they want as often as they want. Disabled people should be able to do the same thing. If we need assistance, it becomes a matter of scrambling to find money to pay someone to assist us or relying on our friends and relations to help for free. For millions of disabled people the failure to receive adequate PAS results in a loss of control over their own lives and an inability to participate equally in society.

For these issues to be addressed, a comprehensive PAS policy must be created and implemented. I use the term *comprehensive* to mean policy that mandates a single-point-of-entry system with at least the following characteristics: need is determined on a 24-hour-a-day, 7-day-a-week basis; no limits are placed on the types of services available or the type of provider used; and the disabled person's needs and desires are the driving force behind services (i.e., the services are consumer controlled).

WEAKNESSES OF THE ADA

I have always seen the ADA as another piece of the patchwork quilt of legislation concerning disabled people. I do not deny its importance, but, just as one ornate patch in a quilt will not keep out the cold, neither is the ADA *the* piece of legislation that will provide true equality for all disabled people. It is important to be realistic about the weaknesses in the ADA in order to address necessary additional legislation honestly.

Accessibility

One area in which the ADA could be stronger is accessibility. The ADA addresses the issue, of course, but will not solve all of our structural access problems. The far-thinking ideal behind much of the ADA was to create an atmosphere in which accessibility is no longer "special" but the norm. Unfortunately, in many respects the ADA falls far short of such a goal; many aspects of society will continue to deny disabled people equal access for years to come.

For example, the ADA does not require certain new buildings of less than three stories or less than 3,000 square feet to install elevators, as long as there are not certain types of facilities in the building. This is problematic in two major ways: first, because it attempts to allow inaccessibility for certain types of facilities, and, second, because it is contrary to the concept of universal access and "accessibility as a standard." The first problem seems to be a loophole for elevator construction. How can it be assured that, throughout the life of the building, there will never be one of the "elevator-required" types of facilities (i.e., a doctor's office) in the structure? Who decided which small facilities do not need to be accessible?

The second problem is a larger issue, in that it does not reflect the far-thinking goals of the ADA. What happens if a qualified wheelchair rider wants to apply for a position in a "non–elevator-required" facility? I believe that the law should have required that all new buildings be 100% accessible. I also believe that retrofitting should be required. I know that until that happens, I am not valued as an equal human being. I believe that most people think that I should simply accept the fact that I am excluded from many buildings, bathrooms, and private homes in this country because I was born at the wrong time.

Because it is highly improbable that Congress ever will mandate that all buildings be retrofitted to be made accessible, all new buildings that are not covered by the ADA will remain forever closed to many disabled people.

Universal Access Versus Percentages

Another such example can be found in the ADA regulations concerning hotel rooms. If "universal access" ever is to become the norm, how will requiring only a small percentage of newly built hotel rooms to be completely accessible possibly push that agenda forward? These standards were accepted by disability rights advocates in the spirit of compromise, but to some degree what actually was compromised was our rights. Cost should not be considered as paramount when the issue is civil rights: "the very idea of a right is that it should be recognized without view to inconvenience, competing priorities or disruptive effect" (Scotch, 1984, p. 75), or, I would argue, cost. Too frequently lack of resources is used as an easy excuse to do nothing.

These discriminatory barriers, which could have been legislated out of existence, instead remain for people with disabilities for generations to come to accept as reality. Society has not been willing to accept responsibility for structural problems such as steps or a lack of elevators. Our society, although perhaps willing to acknowledge that disabled people historically have been discriminated against, has been unwilling to accept that redressment of these wrongs must include the principle of retrofitting in order for integration to take place.

Financial Supports

Yet another area of policy in which the patchwork approach has failed many disabled people is income supports. Disabled people have legitimate additional expenses, often called disability-related expenses, such as PAS, home and vehicle modifications, assistive technology, and health care. The way the system now stands, disability is too frequently equated with inability to work. If a disabled person does not happen to be independently wealthy, there are generally two options for survival available: work and spend a disproportionate amount of one's salary on disability-related expenses, or stay on welfare.

I am fortunate in that I have had a decent education and receive a reasonable salary. Even so, my standard of living is far lower than it would be if I were nondisabled. My disability-related expenses are approximately $18,000 per year. I cannot afford to buy a home; to purchase the amount of PAS I need; to pay for my durable medical equipment (i.e., my wheelchair) because my health insurance does not cover such expenses. I cannot afford to purchase a new van when my current one, which was purchased under a Self Support Plan when I was receiving Supplemental Security Income and is now 13 years old, finally gives out. Again, I am expected to accept that I never will achieve the same standard of living as my nondisabled friends and neighbors, simply because I am disabled. Remember, I am one of the lucky ones. Too many disabled people do not even have a choice to make. Lacking an adequate education, they cannot afford to work because the salary they could make would not even begin to make up for the loss of their benefits.

It is even harder to accept these conditions when the limited benefit programs that exist have unnecessary costs built in. Federal programs in the area of PAS are an excellent example of this. Title XIX Personal Care Option PAS programs require that services be prescribed by a physician and that a nurse supervise the services, with no exceptions. States implement the rule differently, and some also require that all individuals go through home care agencies, so costs vary widely. However, even the most efficient of these Title XIX programs have inflated costs, and this is only one example. The medical model, with its monitoring requirements, is extremely expensive and is not required for the PAS used by most disabled people.

Exactly how much money is being wasted with such requirements is unknown, but I am sure that the figures are extraordinary. I believe it would be better to enable more of the people who need these benefits to receive them than to have paternalistic, choice-reducing requirements. I am not arguing that all forms of supervision are unnecessary—if individuals need supervisory services they should certainly be able to receive them—but requiring this for most people is inappropriate and results in necessary dollars being unavailable.

I envision a rethinking of benefits policy similar to the system under which disabled veterans are compensated. In this system the degree of financial support is determined by the extent of the disability. These programs typically are not means tested, which means that I would be able to improve my standard of living without having to forgo meeting basic needs. Programs like that for disabled veterans also should be offered to civilians. Instead of separating us into small disability categories and forcing us to fight for limited funds, it would be much more efficient to address our needs and funnel available monies into direct benefits.

It seems that whenever a serious discussion of benefits takes place, it always comes down to a chorus of opponents, calling themselves realists, chanting, "We don't have the money, where will the money come from, what about the costs involved?" All I know is that if we as a society are unwilling to meet the needs of all our members, we should stop the rhetoric that we do take care of our own and admit that we only support rich, white, heterosexual, nondisabled men. I for one do not want to believe that, by refusing to recognize my unique needs and assist me in meeting them, my country does not want me to have the opportunity to be equal.

Madness or Wisdom   I agree that:

> Depending on your point of view, it is either madness or wisdom to suggest an increase in our social welfare benefits to people with disabilities when the federal budget deficit has reached staggering proportions. It is madness if you view the problem of disability and aging in a fractionated and short-term manner. However, it is wisdom if you view the problem from a systems and long-term point of view. (Trieschmann, 1987, p. 134)

The long-term view shows that disabled people, if given the supports we need and the chance to succeed, will more than pay back such costs. Once we are given the chance to work, we can prove ourselves to be excellent workers. Our taxes support our nation and communities and, once we can enter our local businesses, we will be able to support them. Integration and adequate supports will elevate all of society along with us.

The concept of acknowledging additional needs and accepting ongoing support for them is uncommon to the thinking of most Americans. As Berkowitz said:

> the handicapped may need continuous assistance from the government, but that does not mean that the assistance has to be at the expense of their participation in the labor force. Instead, this assistance might enable handicapped people to hold a job or to remain outside a costly custodial institution. Such a policy would require a more sophisticated approach to the corrective response to disability than is embodied by vocational rehabilitation programs and other first-generation disability programs. To emerge from the political arena, a program would require much more than a simple appeal to saving welfare costs, for it would *posit no contradiction between being independent and receiving government aid.* (1987, p. 185, emphasis added)

In many other countries the provision of financial supports is not necessarily viewed as a welfare payment that is no longer needed once the recipient is educated and employed. Some women are beginning to accept a similar premise in the fight for available and affordable daycare. This argument, that the government has a responsibility to provide financial supports on a long-term basis for there to be true equal opportunity, must receive greater attention if we are to end discrimination against all disabled people.

Technical Aids

Another missing piece of the patchwork is technical aids. Longmore addressed the issue from the point of view of the historian:

> adaptive devices and services (e.g., wheelchairs and sign language interpreters) had been considered special benefits to those who were fundamentally dependent and incapacitated. Section 504 moved beyond these social welfare notions by viewing such devices and services as simply different modes of functioning and departed from traditional civil rights concepts by defining them as legitimate permanent differential treatment necessary to achieve and maintain equal access. This perspective was the heart of the emerging disability rights ideology. (1987, p. 363)

Defining assistance with our unique needs as "legitimate permanent differential treatment" that is necessary for equality is, of course, an underlying theme of the rethinking of disability policy posited in this chapter. This is perhaps easier to conceptualize in terms of technical aids. In an accessible environment, a wheelchair allows someone with a mobility impairment to function at the same level as someone without a mobility impairment. The wheelchair cannot be taken away without the result being a lack of equality.

Although this seems to have become clear for wheelchairs and a few other familiar services and devices, it does not seem to have become clear for more advanced aids. Even when the concept of equality is understood in these terms, there is no commitment to assistance in finding and purchasing needed aids. Again, in other countries technical aids for disabled people are considered a right, provided by the government, with no means testing. There seems to be an acceptance of the legitimacy of such "preferential" treatment.

Disabled people continue to struggle to find and purchase appropriate technical aids, from the simplest sort, such as a speaker telephone, to the most advanced technology-driven applications. Until the government accepts that providing assistance in these endeavors is an important part of ensuring equality, technical aids will remain a missing piece of the quilt.

IMPACT OF THE INDEPENDENT LIVING MOVEMENT

The key force behind a rethinking of policy toward persons with disabilities has been the independent living movement. This movement, which was given its name in the early 1970s, is a political movement of disabled people that has been evolving for more than 100 years. Starting at least that long ago, people with various kinds of disability formed organizations representing specific disability groups. Until the 1960s most of these organizations did not work in coalition but rather worked to address the specific concerns of their constituency. Organizations of deaf and blind people, for example, had national voices of their own before people with other disabilities were represented.

The term itself, *independent living movement*, has evolved over the past 20 years. I believe the term was born at the Center for Independent Living (CIL) in Berkeley, California, which was founded in 1972. The Berkeley CIL was started primarily by people with physical disabilities who became disabled in their late teens. It was formed with the belief that we as disabled people have the answers to our needs.

Direct services, such as assistance with finding accessible housing, making home renovations, moving through the bureaucratic maze of benefit systems, and finding quality PAS, were designed to be the core of the organization. Early on, the CIL also began to see the need to fight for systemic change at local, state, and national levels. The Berkeley CIL was one of the first places in the country to show that the removal of physical and attitudinal barriers resulted in disabled people becoming more empowered. This empowerment led to more vocal demand for change and a refusal to accept the professionals' view that we were not capable of becoming integrated, contributing members of society.

In 1975 Ed Roberts, one of the founders of the CIL, became the State Director of the Department of Rehabilitation. Roberts, who himself had been denied services from the Department, quickly utilized federal dollars to help create 10 new independent living centers in California. Although there were a few other centers in Massachusetts and Michigan, California, because of the larger number of centers, began to see improvements occurring in the lives of disabled people throughout the state. In the mid-1970s the CIL also became committed to a more cross-disability approach. Cross-disability means encompassing persons with all types of disabilities, including but not limited to deafness, blindness, psychiatric disabilities, cognitive disabilities, physical disabilities, and hidden disabilities such as environmental illness, drug and alcohol abuse, epilepsy, diabetes, and AIDS.

As the CIL began to have a profound effect on the thinking of persons with physical disabilities and some professionals and policymakers, the CIL model began to take hold in the U.S. disability community. Centers slowly began to develop on their own, and then in 1979 Congress authorized the funding of centers for independent living across the United States.

As this was unfolding, the Rehabilitation Act of 1973 was passed, with the previously mentioned landmark Section 504. The fight that ensued over the promulgation of regulations was probably the first major cross-disability activity in the United States. This was when the term *independent living movement* emerged, and it has been utilized ever since.

Defining Our Own Agendas

It was necessary for us to create our own groups after we realized that nondisabled-controlled groups did not have the same motivation for change that we did. How hard could these groups fight for us when we had insignificant representation on their staffs and boards? We saw that we could never begin to fight for our real needs until we gained control of our own groups.

As one of the more recent political movements to emerge in this country, the independent living civil rights movement of disabled people is still in the process of defining its goals. One of these goals, I believe, is for disabled people to expand the discussion of civil rights to include the acknowledgment and fulfillment of our unique needs:

> Organisations of disabled people, on the other hand, reject the charity and the medical models of disability, asserting that the services we require should be provided as a civil right and that it is society which disables us rather than our physical condition. (Morris, 1991, p. 176)

Unique Issues

We face oppression that is similar to that faced by other minority groups, but we also have unique issues. In order for persons with more significant disabilities to achieve equality, we need supports that many other people do not need. We are learning no longer to be ashamed of these needs, but rather to express them honestly, in an atmosphere of expectation that they will be adequately met:

> I want to get out. I really do. I want to prove that I can hold a job. I want to prove that I can live alone. I'm waiting for society to change some more, for it to fix itself up and be okay for people like me. A friend of mine came up with an analogy of my life, and I guess it's not that far off base. He said I was like a shipwrecked sailor on a deserted island. I know the ships are coming for me, but I don't know when. So I just wait. I just wait for the ships to come. (Kleinfeld, 1977, p. 205)

There was a time when the majority of disabled people felt this way about our needs. Today, however, we are refusing to wait for the ships; we are building boats of our own.

> Historically it has been proven that powerless groups are not given recognition until they demand and fight for it. Likewise I am not asking for my rights and humanity, to be given a place in this society, which like it or not I belong to, I demand it. (Hannaford, 1985, p. 12)

We are learning to speak for ourselves, and we are becoming more emphatic in our demands.

Another important goal for the independent living movement is control over our own lives, our own groups, and our movement. One important way in which this is beginning to occur is in our new understanding and articulation of the failure of existing policies. Examining these policies from our own point of view and addressing our concerns from the perspective of civil rights instead of charity, we have moved into a paradigm of doing for ourselves: our own research, our own agendas, and our own policy recommendations. Disabled-controlled groups, such as the World Institute on Disability, Independent Living Research Utilization, the National Council on Independent Living, and the Disability Rights Education and Defense Fund are leading the way in this paradigm.

Yet another goal of the Independent Living Movement is that we become even more of a cross-disability movement. Slowly we are meeting with success. This will take a long time to achieve because we as disabled people need to learn about each other and to develop respect and understanding for one another in a pervasive social environment that insists that we are inferior and have nothing in common. "There is a great deal of pressure from society to keep us from recognizing that we are disabled and to keep us hidden from the world and each other. Despite the established barriers we seek each other out" (Browne, Connors, & Stern, 1985, p. 330). As we learn together what we share, we are able to make more progress toward our goal.

The independent living movement of disabled people is producing stronger disabled people with greater self-esteem. These new strengths are helping to combat discrimination. We have achieved a level of political sophistication that did not exist in past decades. Our task now is to continue to refine this sophistication, work toward our self-defined goals, and to bring forward policy issues that must be addressed in order for us to achieve equality.

OBSTACLES TO CHANGE

It is essential that the policy issues outlined above (e.g., income supports, PAS) be addressed. There are many obstacles to the radical changes I have proposed, some of which I would like to discuss in more depth.

Insufficient Accessibility

> By accessibility we mean access to the same choices accorded able-bodied people. Attitudinal and functional barriers work in concert. Both must be eliminated. Our requirements should be built into the fabric of society and considered routine. (Browne, Connors, & Stern, 1985, p. 13)

Many disabled Americans also define access in this way, refusing to accept the general societal view of it as special and responsive to the occasion.

A frequently utilized analogy compares the discrimination against people of color to that faced by disabled people. Historically denied equal access to schools, toilets, restaurants, and transportation, people of color eventually began to protest such discrimination. The courts finally agreed that separate was not equal and mandated that people of color could not be denied the opportunity to use these facilities alongside white people. In the case of public transportation, it meant that African-Americans could no longer be required to sit in the back of a bus or in a separate car. The removal of such barriers began to accord people of color the same choices as white people.

Here, however, the analogy begins to break down. In the first place, merely legislating barriers away has by no means solved the problem of racial discrimination. Second, and more important in terms of the point I am trying to make, the barriers themselves are of a fundamentally different nature.

If all people in the United States swore that they would stop discriminating against disabled people today, many of our problems would not change. For unlike ethnic minorities, disabled people face a bias in the very structure of society. Whereas African-Americans were not allowed to sit in the front of the bus, many disabled Americans have been denied the right even to *board* the bus. It was not until the passage of the ADA that a national requirement that all new buses must be built to be accessible existed. This was in spite of the fact that disabled people had been fighting since the 1960s for all new transit systems to be accessible.

This blatant structural discrimination has resulted in thousands of inaccessible buses all across this country. The transit authority fought accessible buses at every juncture, even after the technology existed, and today we are told that existing buses cannot be retrofitted because of the cost involved. This structural bias effectively shuts disabled people out of everyday society. It makes us all too aware of the fact that, although the rhetoric says we are equal, we are not as equal as non-disabled people.

I believe that the only solution to structural discrimination is mandatory accessibility. As I have argued earlier, until all aspects of society are completely accessible to all disabled people, we are not really considered equal members and cannot be equal participants. Because integration takes place primarily in social settings, allowing private homes and a large number of public housing units to be built inaccessible sends a clear-cut message to disabled people: stay home, do not have friends, do not socialize, do not attempt to form peer relationships. Although we have numerous pieces of legislation requiring certain new construction to be accessible, there is no mandate that private housing be accessible. My nondisabled friends cannot take a tax deduction to make their homes accessible, as many businesses are now allowed to do. Such policies are essential if our goals include true equality.

Negative Societal Attitudes

The difficulty of reaching such a goal is compounded by the fact that structural bias is firmly supported by negative societal attitudes. If we truly wish to provide the same choices for everyone, we must examine these damaging attitudes more closely. Longmore wrote:

> the underlying concept of disability remained constant: disability was a defect residing in the individual and therefore requiring individual medical rehabilitation, special education, and vocational training to improve employment prospects. In the 1960s and 1970s, a civil rights movement of people with physical and sensory disabilities and some rehabilitation professionals began to espouse a major new conceptualization of disability: handicaps result from the interaction of individuals with the social and built environment; "disability" is primarily a socially constructed and stigmatized role. (1987, p. 362)

As clear as this articulation of such a role may be to many of us now, at the time it was a radically new proposition.

Today there are still too many people who do not believe that disabled people, particularly those with more significant disabilities, can make contributions to our society. Too many people still are influenced strongly by the charity model of disability. Telethons continue to ask people for money to prevent disabilities instead of focusing on how life with a disability could be made "no big deal." Why hire disabled people or learn to overcome your prejudices when all you know of us is the "tragic" lives the stereotypes tell you we lead? The continual negative descriptions scarcely are countered by the occasional positive depiction of a disabled person in an advertisement.

We have been taught to feel ashamed of ourselves and more ashamed of anyone whose disability was more significant than our own. The only thing we were encouraged to do was work toward a cure of whatever caused our disability; to pray and give money so that no more disability occurred. Any rejection of the cure model on our part was seen as denial, an act of hostility:

> That image became and has remained the preferred, even required, mode of self-presentation for people with physical and sensory (not mental) disabilities. It involved an implicit bargain in which the nonhandicapped majority extended provisional and partial tolerance of the public presence of handicapped individuals so long as they demonstrated continued cheerful striving toward normalization. This arrangement defined disability as a private physical and emotional tragedy to be managed by psychological adjustment, rather than a stigmatized social condition, and it disallowed collective protests against prejudice and discrimination, permitting at most efforts to educate away "attitudinal barriers." (Longmore, 1987, p. 361)

There are many interrelating forces behind the attitudes of most nondisabled people in our society: fear, pity, ignorance, and prejudice. They work to perpetuate the charity model, which says "Give to others that we may not become like them." In giving, may we never have to face the fact of our own vulnerabilities, our own differences. Society also has placed a value on denying that these attitudes exist: "I don't treat my wheelchair friends any differently."; "I admire her so much, she's had such a difficult life." We don't want admiration for simply doing what nondisabled people do every day—living our lives as fully as possible.

It is difficult to confront such sentiments when no one will admit to having them. This denial, partly due to societal pressures to be "polite," suffocates a natural desire to know. Being told not to look at, or not to ask questions of, people with visible disabilities results in nondisabled people trying to ignore our very existence. Yes, frequently there are things about us that are different, and denying that truth is ridiculous, but neither should it be pretended that only our differences are unusual or special. This widespread invisibility only adds to the problem. How are attitudes that cannot be confronted going to change?

KEYS TO CHANGE

Confrontation is the key to change in this arena. The only way that it can take place is for non-disabled and disabled people to be together. In an inaccessible environment this cannot happen, so it is easy to see how the self-perpetuating cycle feeds itself: inaccessibility shuts disabled people out, so society does not confront its attitudes, which compounds the ignorance and discrimination, which leads to a further desire to shut disabled people out, and so on. As change begins to occur in both structural policy and attitudes, we hope the cycle can be reversed. Such a reversal will, over the years, result in millions of people who previously lived outside the system becoming integral members of society.

Sometimes when I reflect on the attitudinal changes that have taken place in my lifetime, I get discouraged. The prejudice is so pervasive, so deep seated. Unless we reach people when they are very young, they already will have formed negative opinions about disabled people. After childhood, the research seems to say that only sustained, peer-level interaction with disabled people can change nondisabled people's attitudes. So as more segments of society become fully integrated, attitudes will improve. We hope the next generation of disabled people will have more opportunities as a result of the work we have already done.

In the meantime we must develop a strong sense of ourselves to combat our internalized oppression. We must work on improving our self-esteem so that we can be strong when we confront the stereotypes of society. We are recognizing that many of the ways we were told to achieve equality are not ways we would choose for ourselves. Valuing ourselves for who we are and what we can offer and learning to feel pride in being disabled is critical. Role models are essential to this process. Disabled children must have significant exposure to and interaction with other disabled children and disabled adults. Working in coalition for change, learning to be self-advocates, also will help us to be strong.

As disabled people, we also have discriminated against our own. Too often we have tried to fit into the nondisabled world on its terms. Those whose disability made them more unacceptable to nondisabled people frequently were more stigmatized by other disabled people as well. Confronting our own prejudices about one another while we build our self-esteem is important.

We should feel proud of the great strides we have made. We are attempting to pull ourselves out of the thick webs of discrimination and isolation and survive. It is no easy task. These webs were created over the years by a society that has tried to convince us that we have nothing in common with one another. We have not been encouraged to see ourselves as a discriminated group:

> It is a challenge and a struggle for us to face ourselves and each other in depth. Entering this process gives us strength. We become more powerful. Finding each other is a way to say, "We are here. This is what we need. This is what we want." (Browne, Connors, & Stern, 1985, p. 330)

TERMINOLOGY

Another important aspect of attitudes I would like to address is language. As our movement has evolved, we have been plagued by people, almost always not themselves disabled, attempting to change what we call ourselves. If we are "victims" of anything, it is of such terms as *physically challenged*, *able–disabled*, *differently abled*, *handi-capables*, and *people with differing abilities*, to offer just a few. Nondisabled people's discomfort with reality-based terms such as *disabled* led them to these euphemisms. I believe these euphemisms have the effect of depoliticizing our own terminology and devaluing our own view of ourselves as disabled people.

Disabled people also are involved in the discussion of terminology, but for our part the discussion centers around what will empower us and what will have the most positive impact on our movement. Nondisabled people think they also are promoting empowerment, but, to return to an earlier analogy, I wonder how far a group of white people would get by trying to determine the most empowering term for African-American people.

I have a physical disability that results in my inability to walk and perform a number of other significant tasks without the assistance of another person. This cannot be labeled away and I am not ashamed of it. I feel no need to change the word "disabled." For me, there is no stigma. I am not driven to call myself a "person with a disability." I know I am a person; I do not need to tell myself that I am. I also do not believe that being called "a person with a disability" results in my being treated any more like a human being. Maybe putting the word "disabled" first makes people stop and look at what, as a result of society's historical indifference and/or hatred of people like me, is a critical part of my existence. I know that "disabled" is not a noun, as in "the disabled want . . . ."

Purists should maybe just call me a cripple. In Germany in the early 1980s, there was a separatist group that called itself the Cripple Movement. They said people treated them like cripples, so, knowing how uncomfortable people felt with the term, they took it as their own and were empowered by it. There are certainly some disabled people in the United States who are talking about taking back the word "cripple."

As a disabled woman from Britain put it: "For myself, I do not want to have to try to emulate what a nondisabled woman looks like in order to assert positive things about myself. I want to be able to celebrate my difference, not hide from it" (Morris, 1991, p. 184). Respect for my rights as a person, as well as the rights of other disabled people, will be achieved when laws and policies are drafted in a way that enables us to go when and where we want with whom we want; when we have an equal chance at quality education and employment, quality health care, and housing; and when the ultimate success in the area of disability is no longer to do away with our very existence.

Let the disabled people who are politically involved and personally affected determine our own language. May we please have no more $50,000 contests to select the best new word for people like me. A suggestion to those of you who do not know what to call me: ask! I frequently ask other disabled people what they call themselves and then respect their language.

Until we receive the respect due us as the experts on ourselves in terms of our terminology, our needs, and our movement, we cannot believe that in general society shares our goal of equal participation. Adolf Ratzka, a disabled user of PAS from Sweden, has said:

> Our message is that disability is a normal part of life, that we have the same basic human needs and life aspirations as everybody else. Disability is not a medical, technical or humanitarian issue but a political one, an issue of unequal distribution of resources and political power. In working for our human rights we help to make this world a better place for everybody. (1992)

REFERENCES

Berkowitz, E.S. (1987). *Disabled policy: America's programs for the handicapped.* Cambridge, England: Cambridge University Press.

Browne, S.E., Connors, D., & Stern, N. (Eds.). (1985). *With the power of each breath: A disabled women's anthology.* Pittsburgh: Cleis Press.

Education for All Handicapped Children Act of 1975, 20 U.S.C. §§1232, 1401, 1405–1420, 1453 (1975).

Hannaford, S. (1985). *Living outside inside: A disabled woman's experience: Towards a social and political perspective.* Berkeley: Canterbury Press.

Kleinfeld, S. (1977). *The hidden minority: A profile of handicapped Americans.* Boston: Little, Brown.

Longmore, P.K. (1987, September). Uncovering the hidden history of people with disabilities. *Reviews in American History*, p. 363.

Morris, J. (1991). *Pride against prejudice: A personal politics of disability*. London: The Women's Press.

Pinet, G. (Coord.). (1990). *Is the law fair to the disabled?: A European survey*. Copenhagen: WHO Regional Publications.

Ratzka, A. (1992, April). Abstract presented at "Independence '92," the International Congress and Exposition on Disability, Vancouver.

Rehabilitation Act of 1973, 29 U.S.C. §§791–794 (1973).

Scotch, R.K. (1984). *From good will to civil rights: Transforming federal disability policy*. Philadelphia: Temple University Press.

Trieschmann, R.B. (1987). *Aging with a disability*. New York: Demos Publications.

APPENDIX

THE AMERICANS WITH DISABILITIES ACT OF 1990

Editors' Note: As a service to our readers, we have chosen to reproduce the complete Americans with Disabilities Act of 1990 (PL 101-336), including revisions. The Civil Rights Act of 1991 (PL 102-166) made several changes in the provisions of the ADA for the purpose of clarifying the Act's applicability to U.S. employers and workers in foreign countries and its coverage of the U.S. Congress and agencies of the legislative branch. These revisions are incorporated and identified by footnotes on respective pages of this Appendix.

The Americans with Disabilities Act of 1990, PL 101-336. (July 26, 1990). Title 42, U.S.C. 12101 et seq: *U.S. Statutes at Large*, *104*, 327-378.
The Civil Rights Act of 1991, PL 102-166. (November 21, 1991). 42 U.S.C. 1981, *U.S. Statutes at Large*, *105*, 1071.

An Act

July 26, 1990
[S. 933]

Americans with
Disabilities Act
of 1990.

42 USC 12101
note.

To establish a clear and comprehensive prohibition of discrimination on the basis of disability.

Be it enacted by the Senate and House of Representatives of the United States of America in Congress assembled,

SECTION 1. SHORT TITLE; TABLE OF CONTENTS.

(a) SHORT TITLE.—This Act may be cited as the "Americans with Disabilities Act of 1990".

(b) TABLE OF CONTENTS.—The table of contents is as follows:

SEC. 2. FINDINGS AND PURPOSES.   42 USC 12101.

(a) FINDINGS.—The Congress finds that—

(1) some 43,000,000 Americans have one or more physical or mental disabilities, and this number is increasing as the population as a whole is growing older;

(2) historically, society has tended to isolate and segregate individuals with disabilities, and, despite some improvements, such forms of discrimination against individuals with disabilities continue to be a serious and pervasive social problem;

(3) discrimination against individuals with disabilities persists in such critical areas as employment, housing, public accommodations, education, transportation, communication, recreation, institutionalization, health services, voting, and access to public services;

(4) unlike individuals who have experienced discrimination on the basis of race, color, sex, national origin, religion, or age, individuals who have experienced discrimination on the basis of disability have often had no legal recourse to redress such discrimination;

(5) individuals with disabilities continually encounter various forms of discrimination, including outright intentional exclusion, the discriminatory effects of architectural, transportation, and communication barriers, overprotective rules and policies, failure to make modifications to existing facilities and practices, exclusionary qualification standards and criteria, segregation, and relegation to lesser services, programs, activities, benefits, jobs, or other opportunities;

(6) census data, national polls, and other studies have documented that people with disabilities, as a group, occupy an inferior status in our society, and are severely disadvantaged socially, vocationally, economically, and educationally;

(7) individuals with disabilities are a discrete and insular minority who have been faced with restrictions and limitations, subjected to a history of purposeful unequal treatment, and relegated to a position of political powerlessness in our society, based on characteristics that are beyond the control of such individuals and resulting from stereotypic assumptions not truly indicative of the individual ability of such individuals to participate in, and contribute to, society;

(8) the Nation's proper goals regarding individuals with disabilities are to assure equality of opportunity, full participation, independent living, and economic self-sufficiency for such individuals; and

(9) the continuing existence of unfair and unnecessary discrimination and prejudice denies people with disabilities the opportunity to compete on an equal basis and to pursue those opportunities for which our free society is justifiably famous, and costs the United States billions of dollars in unnecessary expenses resulting from dependency and nonproductivity.

(b) PURPOSE.—It is the purpose of this Act—

(1) to provide a clear and comprehensive national mandate for the elimination of discrimination against individuals with disabilities;

(2) to provide clear, strong, consistent, enforceable standards addressing discrimination against individuals with disabilities;

(3) to ensure that the Federal Government plays a central role in enforcing the standards established in this Act on behalf of individuals with disabilities; and

(4) to invoke the sweep of congressional authority, including the power to enforce the fourteenth amendment and to regulate commerce, in order to address the major areas of discrimination faced day-to-day by people with disabilities.

42 USC 12102.

SEC. 3. DEFINITIONS.

As used in this Act:

(1) AUXILIARY AIDS AND SERVICES.—The term "auxiliary aids and services" includes—

(A) qualified interpreters or other effective methods of making aurally delivered materials available to individuals with hearing impairments;

(B) qualified readers, taped texts, or other effective methods of making visually delivered materials available to individuals with visual impairments;

(C) acquisition or modification of equipment or devices; and

(D) other similar services and actions.

(2) DISABILITY.—The term "disability" means, with respect to an individual—

(A) a physical or mental impairment that substantially limits one or more of the major life activities of such individual;

(B) a record of such an impairment; or

(C) being regarded as having such an impairment.

(3) STATE.—The term "State" means each of the several States, the District of Columbia, the Commonwealth of Puerto Rico, Guam, American Samoa, the Virgin Islands, the Trust Territory of the Pacific Islands, and the Commonwealth of the Northern Mariana Islands.

TITLE I—EMPLOYMENT

42 USC 12111.

SEC. 101. DEFINITIONS.

As used in this title:

(1) COMMISSION.—The term "Commission" means the Equal Employment Opportunity Commission established by section 705 of the Civil Rights Act of 1964 (42 U.S.C. 2000e-4).

(2) COVERED ENTITY.—The term "covered entity" means an employer, employment agency, labor organization, or joint labor-management committee.

(3) DIRECT THREAT.—The term "direct threat" means a significant risk to the health or safety of others that cannot be eliminated by reasonable accommodation.

(4) EMPLOYEE.—The term "employee" means an individual employed by an employer. With respect to employment in a foreign country, such term includes an individual who is a citizen of the United States.*

(5) EMPLOYER.—

(A) IN GENERAL.—The term "employer" means a person engaged in an industry affecting commerce who has 15 or more employees for each working day in each of 20 or more calendar weeks in the current or preceding calendar year, and any agent of such person, except that, for two years following the effective date of this title, an employer means a person engaged in an industry affecting commerce who has 25 or more employees for each working day in each of 20 or more calendar weeks in the current or preceding year, and any agent of such person.

(B) EXCEPTIONS.—The term "employer" does not include—

(i) the United States, a corporation wholly owned by the government of the United States, or an Indian tribe; or

(ii) a bona fide private membership club (other than a labor organization) that is exempt from taxation under section 501(c) of the Internal Revenue Code of 1986.

(6) ILLEGAL USE OF DRUGS.—

(A) IN GENERAL.—The term "illegal use of drugs" means the use of drugs, the possession or distribution of which is unlawful under the Controlled Substances Act (21 U.S.C. 812). Such term does not include the use of a drug taken under supervision by a licensed health care professional, or other uses authorized by the Controlled Substances Act or other provisions of Federal law.

(B) DRUGS.—The term "drug" means a controlled substance, as defined in schedules I through V of section 202 of the Controlled Substances Act.

(7) PERSON, ETC.—The terms "person", "labor organization", "employment agency", "commerce", and "industry affecting commerce", shall have the same meaning given such terms in section 701 of the Civil Rights Act of 1964 (42 U.S.C. 2000e).

(8) QUALIFIED INDIVIDUAL WITH A DISABILITY.—The term "qualified individual with a disability" means an individual with a disability who, with or without reasonable accommodation, can perform the essential functions of the employment position that such individual holds or desires. For the purposes of this title, consideration shall be given to the employer's judgment as to what functions of a job are essential, and if an employer has prepared a written description before advertising or interviewing applicants for the job, this description shall be considered evidence of the essential functions of the job.

(9) REASONABLE ACCOMMODATION.—The term "reasonable accommodation" may include—

(A) making existing facilities used by employees readily accessible to and usable by individuals with disabilities; and

(B) job restructuring, part-time or modified work schedules, reassignment to a vacant position, acquisition or modification of equipment or devices, appropriate adjustment or modifications of examinations, training materials or poli-

---

*The last sentence of (4) has been inserted in accordance with the *Civil Rights Act of 1991* (PL 102-166. [November 21, 1991]. Title I, 42 U.S.C. 1981: *U.S. Statutes at Large, 105*, 1077).

cies, the provision of qualified readers or interpreters, and other similar accommodations for individuals with disabilities.

(10) UNDUE HARDSHIP.—

(A) IN GENERAL.—The term "undue hardship" means an action requiring significant difficulty or expense, when considered in light of the factors set forth in subparagraph (B).

(B) FACTORS TO BE CONSIDERED.—In determining whether an accommodation would impose an undue hardship on a covered entity, factors to be considered include—

(i) the nature and cost of the accommodation needed under this Act;

(ii) the overall financial resources of the facility or facilities involved in the provision of the reasonable accommodation; the number of persons employed at such facility; the effect on expenses and resources, or the impact otherwise of such accommodation upon the operation of the facility;

(iii) the overall financial resources of the covered entity; the overall size of the business of a covered entity with respect to the number of its employees; the number, type, and location of its facilities; and

(iv) the type of operation or operations of the covered entity, including the composition, structure, and functions of the workforce of such entity; the geographic separateness, administrative, or fiscal relationship of the facility or facilities in question to the covered entity.

42 USC 12112.

SEC. 102. DISCRIMINATION.

(a) GENERAL RULE.—No covered entity shall discriminate against a qualified individual with a disability because of the disability of such individual in regard to job application procedures, the hiring, advancement, or discharge of employees, employee compensation, job training, and other terms, conditions, and privileges of employment.

(b) CONSTRUCTION.—As used in subsection (a), the term "discriminate" includes—

(1) limiting, segregating, or classifying a job applicant or employee in a way that adversely affects the opportunities or status of such applicant or employee because of the disability of such applicant or employee;

(2) participating in a contractual or other arrangement or relationship that has the effect of subjecting a covered entity's qualified applicant or employee with a disability to the discrimination prohibited by this title (such relationship includes a relationship with an employment or referral agency, labor union, an organization providing fringe benefits to an employee of the covered entity, or an organization providing training and apprenticeship programs);

(3) utilizing standards, criteria, or methods of administration—

(A) that have the effect of discrimination on the basis of disability; or

(B) that perpetuate the discrimination of others who are subject to common administrative control;

(4) excluding or otherwise denying equal jobs or benefits to a qualified individual because of the known disability of an individual with whom the qualified individual is known to have a relationship or association;

(5)(A) not making reasonable accommodations to the known physical or mental limitations of an otherwise qualified individ-

ual with a disability who is an applicant or employee, unless
such covered entity can demonstrate that the accommodation
would impose an undue hardship on the operation of the business of such covered entity; or

(B) denying employment opportunities to a job applicant or
employee who is an otherwise qualified individual with a
disability, if such denial is based on the need of such covered
entity to make reasonable accommodation to the physical or
mental impairments of the employee or applicant;

(6) using qualification standards, employment tests or other
selection criteria that screen out or tend to screen out an
individual with a disability or a class of individuals with disabilities unless the standard, test or other selection criteria, as used
by the covered entity, is shown to be job-related for the position
in question and is consistent with business necessity; and

(7) failing to select and administer tests concerning employment in the most effective manner to ensure that, when such
test is administered to a job applicant or employee who has a
disability that impairs sensory, manual, or speaking skills, such
test results accurately reflect the skills, aptitude, or whatever
other factor of such applicant or employee that such test
purports to measure, rather than reflecting the impaired sensory, manual, or speaking skills of such employee or applicant
(except where such skills are the factors that the test purports to
measure).

*(c) COVERED ENTITIES IN FOREIGN COUNTRIES. —

"(1) IN GENERAL. — It shall not be unlawful under this section
for a covered entity to take any action that constitutes discrimination under this section with respect to an employee in a workplace in a foreign country if compliance with this section would
cause such covered entity to violate the law of the foreign country
in which such workplace is located.

"(2) CONTROL OF CORPORATION. —

(A) PRESUMPTION. — If an employer controls a corporation whose place of incorporation is a foreign country, any practice that constitutes discrimination under this section and is engaged in by such corporation shall be presumed to be engaged in
by such employer.

(B) EXCEPTION. — This section shall not apply with respect
to the foreign operations of an employer that is a foreign person
not controlled by an American employer.

(C) DETERMINATION. — For purposes of this paragraph, the
determination of whether an employer controls a corporation
shall be based on—

"(i) the interrelation of operations;

"(ii) the common management;

"(iii) the centralized control of labor relations; and

"(iv) the common ownership or financial control,

of the employer and the corporation."

(d) MEDICAL EXAMINATIONS AND INQUIRIES. —

(1) IN GENERAL. — The prohibition against discrimination as referred to in subsection (a) shall include medical examinations and
inquiries.

(2) PREEMPLOYMENT. —

(A) PROHIBITED EXAMINATION OR INQUIRY. —Except as provided in paragraph (3), a covered entity shall not conduct a
medical examination or make inquiries of a job applicant as
to whether such applicant is an individual with a disability
or as to the nature or severity of such disability.

---

*This material has been inserted in accordance with the *Civil Rights Act of
1991* (PL 102-166. [November 21, 1991]. Title I, 42 U.S.C. 1981: *U.S. Statutes at
Large, 105,* 1077). "Medical Examinations and Inquiries" has been changed to (d)
to accommodate the insertion.

(B) ACCEPTABLE INQUIRY.—A covered entity may make preemployment inquiries into the ability of an applicant to perform job-related functions.

(3) EMPLOYMENT ENTRANCE EXAMINATION.—A covered entity may require a medical examination after an offer of employment has been made to a job applicant and prior to the commencement of the employment duties of such applicant, and may condition an offer of employment on the results of such examination, if—

(A) all entering employees are subjected to such an examination regardless of disability;

(B) information obtained regarding the medical condition or history of the applicant is collected and maintained on separate forms and in separate medical files and is treated as a confidential medical record, except that—

(i) supervisors and managers may be informed regarding necessary restrictions on the work or duties of the employee and necessary accommodations;

(ii) first aid and safety personnel may be informed, when appropriate, if the disability might require emergency treatment; and

(iii) government officials investigating compliance with this Act shall be provided relevant information on request; and

(C) the results of such examination are used only in accordance with this title.

(4) EXAMINATION AND INQUIRY.—

(A) PROHIBITED EXAMINATIONS AND INQUIRIES.—A covered entity shall not require a medical examination and shall not make inquiries of an employee as to whether such employee is an individual with a disability or as to the nature or severity of the disability, unless such examination or inquiry is shown to be job-related and consistent with business necessity.

(B) ACCEPTABLE EXAMINATIONS AND INQUIRIES.—A covered entity may conduct voluntary medical examinations, including voluntary medical histories, which are part of an employee health program available to employees at that work site. A covered entity may make inquiries into the ability of an employee to perform job-related functions.

(C) REQUIREMENT.—Information obtained under subparagraph (B) regarding the medical condition or history of any employee is subject to the requirements of subparagraphs (B) and (C) of paragraph (3).

42 USC 12113.   SEC. 103. DEFENSES.

(a) IN GENERAL.—It may be a defense to a charge of discrimination under this Act that an alleged application of qualification standards, tests, or selection criteria that screen out or tend to screen out or otherwise deny a job or benefit to an individual with a disability has been shown to be job-related and consistent with business necessity, and such performance cannot be accomplished by reasonable accommodation, as required under this title.

(b) QUALIFICATION STANDARDS.—The term "qualification standards" may include a requirement that an individual shall not pose a direct threat to the health or safety of other individuals in the workplace.

(c) RELIGIOUS ENTITIES.—

(1) IN GENERAL.—This title shall not prohibit a religious corporation, association, educational institution, or society from giving preference in employment to individuals of a particular religion to perform work connected with the carrying on by

such corporation, association, educational institution, or society of its activities.

(2) RELIGIOUS TENETS REQUIREMENT.—Under this title, a religious organization may require that all applicants and employees conform to the religious tenets of such organization.

(d) LIST OF INFECTIOUS AND COMMUNICABLE DISEASES.—

(1) IN GENERAL.—The Secretary of Health and Human Services, not later than 6 months after the date of enactment of this Act, shall—

(A) review all infectious and communicable diseases which may be transmitted through handling the food supply;

(B) publish a list of infectious and communicable diseases which are transmitted through handling the food supply;

(C) publish the methods by which such diseases are transmitted; and

(D) widely disseminate such information regarding the list of diseases and their modes of transmissability to the general public.

Public information.

Such list shall be updated annually.

(2) APPLICATIONS.—In any case in which an individual has an infectious or communicable disease that is transmitted to others through the handling of food, that is included on the list developed by the Secretary of Health and Human Services under paragraph (1), and which cannot be eliminated by reasonable accommodation, a covered entity may refuse to assign or continue to assign such individual to a job involving food handling.

(3) CONSTRUCTION.—Nothing in this Act shall be construed to preempt, modify, or amend any State, county, or local law, ordinance, or regulation applicable to food handling which is designed to protect the public health from individuals who pose a significant risk to the health or safety of others, which cannot be eliminated by reasonable accommodation, pursuant to the list of infectious or communicable diseases and the modes of transmissability published by the Secretary of Health and Human Services.

SEC. 104. ILLEGAL USE OF DRUGS AND ALCOHOL.

42 USC 12114.

(a) QUALIFIED INDIVIDUAL WITH A DISABILITY.—For purposes of this title, the term "qualified individual with a disability" shall not include any employee or applicant who is currently engaging in the illegal use of drugs, when the covered entity acts on the basis of such use.

(b) RULES OF CONSTRUCTION.—Nothing in subsection (a) shall be construed to exclude as a qualified individual with a disability an individual who—

(1) has successfully completed a supervised drug rehabilitation program and is no longer engaging in the illegal use of drugs, or has otherwise been rehabilitated successfully and is no longer engaging in such use;

(2) is participating in a supervised rehabilitation program and is no longer engaging in such use; or

(3) is erroneously regarded as engaging in such use, but is not engaging in such use;

except that it shall not be a violation of this Act for a covered entity to adopt or administer reasonable policies or procedures, including but not limited to drug testing, designed to ensure that an individual described in paragraph (1) or (2) is no longer engaging in the illegal use of drugs.

(c) AUTHORITY OF COVERED ENTITY.—A covered entity—

(1) may prohibit the illegal use of drugs and the use of alcohol at the workplace by all employees;

(2) may require that employees shall not be under the influence of alcohol or be engaging in the illegal use of drugs at the workplace;

(3) may require that employees behave in conformance with the requirements established under the Drug-Free Workplace Act of 1988 (41 U.S.C. 701 et seq.);

(4) may hold an employee who engages in the illegal use of drugs or who is an alcoholic to the same qualification standards for employment or job performance and behavior that such entity holds other employees, even if any unsatisfactory performance or behavior is related to the drug use or alcoholism of such employee; and

(5) may, with respect to Federal regulations regarding alcohol and the illegal use of drugs, require that—

(A) employees comply with the standards established in such regulations of the Department of Defense, if the employees of the covered entity are employed in an industry subject to such regulations, including complying with regulations (if any) that apply to employment in sensitive positions in such an industry, in the case of employees of the covered entity who are employed in such positions (as defined in the regulations of the Department of Defense);

(B) employees comply with the standards established in such regulations of the Nuclear Regulatory Commission, if the employees of the covered entity are employed in an industry subject to such regulations, including complying with regulations (if any) that apply to employment in sensitive positions in such an industry, in the case of employees of the covered entity who are employed in such positions (as defined in the regulations of the Nuclear Regulatory Commission); and

(C) employees comply with the standards established in such regulations of the Department of Transportation, if the employees of the covered entity are employed in a transportation industry subject to such regulations, including complying with such regulations (if any) that apply to employment in sensitive positions in such an industry, in the case of employees of the covered entity who are employed in such positions (as defined in the regulations of the Department of Transportation).

(d) DRUG TESTING.—

(1) IN GENERAL.—For purposes of this title, a test to determine the illegal use of drugs shall not be considered a medical examination.

(2) CONSTRUCTION.—Nothing in this title shall be construed to encourage, prohibit, or authorize the conducting of drug testing for the illegal use of drugs by job applicants or employees or making employment decisions based on such test results.

(e) TRANSPORTATION EMPLOYEES.—Nothing in this title shall be construed to encourage, prohibit, restrict, or authorize the otherwise lawful exercise by entities subject to the jurisdiction of the Department of Transportation of authority to—

(1) test employees of such entities in, and applicants for, positions involving safety-sensitive duties for the illegal use of drugs and for on-duty impairment by alcohol; and

(2) remove such persons who test positive for illegal use of drugs and on-duty impairment by alcohol pursuant to paragraph (1) from safety-sensitive duties in implementing subsection (c).

SEC. 105. POSTING NOTICES.

42 USC 12115.

Every employer, employment agency, labor organization, or joint labor-management committee covered under this title shall post notices in an accessible format to applicants, employees, and members describing the applicable provisions of this Act, in the manner prescribed by section 711 of the Civil Rights Act of 1964 (42 U.S.C. 2000e-10).

SEC. 106. REGULATIONS.

42 USC 12116.

Not later than 1 year after the date of enactment of this Act, the Commission shall issue regulations in an accessible format to carry out this title in accordance with subchapter II of chapter 5 of title 5, United States Code.

SEC. 107. ENFORCEMENT.

42 USC 12117.

(a) POWERS, REMEDIES, AND PROCEDURES.—The powers, remedies, and procedures set forth in sections 705, 706, 707, 709, and 710 of the Civil Rights Act of 1964 (42 U.S.C. 2000e-4, 2000e-5, 2000e-6, 2000e-8, and 2000e-9) shall be the powers, remedies, and procedures this title provides to the Commission, to the Attorney General, or to any person alleging discrimination on the basis of disability in violation of any provision of this Act, or regulations promulgated under section 106, concerning employment.

(b) COORDINATION.—The agencies with enforcement authority for actions which allege employment discrimination under this title and under the Rehabilitation Act of 1973 shall develop procedures to ensure that administrative complaints filed under this title and under the Rehabilitation Act of 1973 are dealt with in a manner that avoids duplication of effort and prevents imposition of inconsistent or conflicting standards for the same requirements under this title and the Rehabilitation Act of 1973. The Commission, the Attorney General, and the Office of Federal Contract Compliance Programs shall establish such coordinating mechanisms (similar to provisions contained in the joint regulations promulgated by the Commission and the Attorney General at part 42 of title 28 and part 1691 of title 29, Code of Federal Regulations, and the Memorandum of Understanding between the Commission and the Office of Federal Contract Compliance Programs dated January 16, 1981 (46 Fed. Reg. 7435, January 23, 1981)) in regulations implementing this title and Rehabilitation Act of 1973 not later than 18 months after the date of enactment of this Act.

Regulations.

SEC. 108. EFFECTIVE DATE.

42 USC 12111 note.

This title shall become effective 24 months after the date of enactment.

TITLE II—PUBLIC SERVICES

Subtitle A—Prohibition Against Discrimination and Other Generally Applicable Provisions

SEC. 201. DEFINITION.

42 USC 12131.

As used in this title:

(1) PUBLIC ENTITY.—The term "public entity" means—

(A) any State or local government;

(B) any department, agency, special purpose district, or other instrumentality of a State or States or local government; and

(C) the National Railroad Passenger Corporation, and any commuter authority (as defined in section 103(8) of the Rail Passenger Service Act).

(2) QUALIFIED INDIVIDUAL WITH A DISABILITY.—The term "qualified individual with a disability" means an individual with a disability who, with or without reasonable modifications to rules, policies, or practices, the removal of architectural, communication, or transportation barriers, or the provision of auxiliary aids and services, meets the essential eligibility requirements for the receipt of services or the participation in programs or activities provided by a public entity.

42 USC 12132.

SEC. 202. DISCRIMINATION.

Subject to the provisions of this title, no qualified individual with a disability shall, by reason of such disability, be excluded from participation in or be denied the benefits of the services, programs, or activities of a public entity, or be subjected to discrimination by any such entity.

42 USC 12133.

SEC. 203. ENFORCEMENT.

The remedies, procedures, and rights set forth in section 505 of the Rehabilitation Act of 1973 (29 U.S.C. 794a) shall be the remedies, procedures, and rights this title provides to any person alleging discrimination on the basis of disability in violation of section 202.

42 USC 12134.

SEC. 204. REGULATIONS.

(a) IN GENERAL.—Not later than 1 year after the date of enactment of this Act, the Attorney General shall promulgate regulations in an accessible format that implement this subtitle. Such regulations shall not include any matter within the scope of the authority of the Secretary of Transportation under section 223, 229, or 244.

(b) RELATIONSHIP TO OTHER REGULATIONS.—Except for "program accessibility, existing facilities", and "communications", regulations under subsection (a) shall be consistent with this Act and with the coordination regulations under part 41 of title 28, Code of Federal Regulations (as promulgated by the Department of Health, Education, and Welfare on January 13, 1978), applicable to recipients of Federal financial assistance under section 504 of the Rehabilitation Act of 1973 (29 U.S.C. 794). With respect to "program accessibility, existing facilities", and "communications", such regulations shall be consistent with regulations and analysis as in part 39 of title 28 of the Code of Federal Regulations, applicable to federally conducted activities under such section 504.

(c) STANDARDS.—Regulations under subsection (a) shall include standards applicable to facilities and vehicles covered by this subtitle, other than facilities, stations, rail passenger cars, and vehicles covered by subtitle B. Such standards shall be consistent with the minimum guidelines and requirements issued by the Architectural and Transportation Barriers Compliance Board in accordance with section 504(a) of this Act.

42 USC 12131 note.

SEC. 205. EFFECTIVE DATE.

(a) GENERAL RULE.—Except as provided in subsection (b), this subtitle shall become effective 18 months after the date of enactment of this Act.

(b) EXCEPTION.—Section 204 shall become effective on the date of enactment of this Act.

Subtitle B—Actions Applicable to Public Transportation Provided by Public Entities Considered Discriminatory

PART I—PUBLIC TRANSPORTATION OTHER THAN BY AIRCRAFT OR CERTAIN RAIL OPERATIONS

SEC. 221. DEFINITIONS.

42 USC 12141.

As used in this part:

(1) DEMAND RESPONSIVE SYSTEM.—The term "demand responsive system" means any system of providing designated public transportation which is not a fixed route system.

(2) DESIGNATED PUBLIC TRANSPORTATION.—The term "designated public transportation" means transportation (other than public school transportation) by bus, rail, or any other conveyance (other than transportation by aircraft or intercity or commuter rail transportation (as defined in section 241)) that provides the general public with general or special service (including charter service) on a regular and continuing basis.

(3) FIXED ROUTE SYSTEM.—The term "fixed route system" means a system of providing designated public transportation on which a vehicle is operated along a prescribed route according to a fixed schedule.

(4) OPERATES.—The term "operates", as used with respect to a fixed route system or demand responsive system, includes operation of such system by a person under a contractual or other arrangement or relationship with a public entity.

(5) PUBLIC SCHOOL TRANSPORTATION.—The term "public school transportation" means transportation by schoolbus vehicles of schoolchildren, personnel, and equipment to and from a public elementary or secondary school and school-related activities.

(6) SECRETARY.—The term "Secretary" means the Secretary of Transportation.

SEC. 222. PUBLIC ENTITIES OPERATING FIXED ROUTE SYSTEMS.

42 USC 12142.

(a) PURCHASE AND LEASE OF NEW VEHICLES.—It shall be considered discrimination for purposes of section 202 of this Act and section 504 of the Rehabilitation Act of 1973 (29 U.S.C. 794) for a public entity which operates a fixed route system to purchase or lease a new bus, a new rapid rail vehicle, a new light rail vehicle, or any other new vehicle to be used on such system, if the solicitation for such purchase or lease is made after the 30th day following the effective date of this subsection and if such bus, rail vehicle, or other vehicle is not readily accessible to and usable by individuals with disabilities, including individuals who use wheelchairs.

(b) PURCHASE AND LEASE OF USED VEHICLES.—Subject to subsection (c)(1), it shall be considered discrimination for purposes of section 202 of this Act and section 504 of the Rehabilitation Act of 1973 (29 U.S.C. 794) for a public entity which operates a fixed route system to purchase or lease, after the 30th day following the effective date of this subsection, a used vehicle for use on such system unless such entity makes demonstrated good faith efforts to purchase or lease a used vehicle for use on such system that is readily accessible to and usable by individuals with disabilities, including individuals who use wheelchairs.

(c) REMANUFACTURED VEHICLES.—

(1) GENERAL RULE.—Except as provided in paragraph (2), it shall be considered discrimination for purposes of section 202 of this Act and section 504 of the Rehabilitation Act of 1973 (29

U.S.C. 794) for a public entity which operates a fixed route
system—

(A) to remanufacture a vehicle for use on such system so
as to extend its usable life for 5 years or more, which
remanufacture begins (or for which the solicitation is made)
after the 30th day following the effective date of this subsection; or

(B) to purchase or lease for use on such system a remanufactured vehicle which has been remanufactured so as to
extend its usable life for 5 years or more, which purchase or
lease occurs after such 30th day and during the period in
which the usable life is extended;

unless, after remanufacture, the vehicle is, to the maximum
extent feasible, readily accessible to and usable by individuals
with disabilities, including individuals who use wheelchairs.

(2) EXCEPTION FOR HISTORIC VEHICLES.—

(A) GENERAL RULE.—If a public entity operates a fixed
route system any segment of which is included on the
National Register of Historic Places and if making a vehicle
of historic character to be used solely on such segment
readily accessible to and usable by individuals with disabilities would significantly alter the historic character of such
vehicle, the public entity only has to make (or to purchase
or lease a remanufactured vehicle with) those modifications
which are necessary to meet the requirements of paragraph
(1) and which do not significantly alter the historic character of such vehicle.

(B) VEHICLES OF HISTORIC CHARACTER DEFINED BY REGULA-
TIONS.—For purposes of this paragraph and section 228(b), a
vehicle of historic character shall be defined by the regulations issued by the Secretary to carry out this subsection.

42 USC 12143.

SEC. 223. PARATRANSIT AS A COMPLEMENT TO FIXED ROUTE SERVICE.

(a) GENERAL RULE.—It shall be considered discrimination for purposes of section 202 of this Act and section 504 of the Rehabilitation
Act of 1973 (29 U.S.C. 794) for a public entity which operates a fixed
route system (other than a system which provides solely commuter
bus service) to fail to provide with respect to the operations of its
fixed route system, in accordance with this section, paratransit and
other special transportation services to individuals with disabilities,
including individuals who use wheelchairs, that are sufficient to
provide to such individuals a level of service (1) which is comparable
to the level of designated public transportation services provided to
individuals without disabilities using such system; or (2) in the case
of response time, which is comparable, to the extent practicable, to
the level of designated public transportation services provided to
individuals without disabilities using such system.

(b) ISSUANCE OF REGULATIONS.—Not later than 1 year after the
effective date of this subsection, the Secretary shall issue final
regulations to carry out this section.

(c) REQUIRED CONTENTS OF REGULATIONS.—

(1) ELIGIBLE RECIPIENTS OF SERVICE.—The regulations issued
under this section shall require each public entity which operates a fixed route system to provide the paratransit and other
special transportation services required under this section—

(A)(i) to any individual with a disability who is unable, as
a result of a physical or mental impairment (including a
vision impairment) and without the assistance of another
individual (except an operator of a wheelchair lift or other
boarding assistance device), to board, ride, or disembark
from any vehicle on the system which is readily accessible
to and usable by individuals with disabilities;

(ii) to any individual with a disability who needs the assistance of a wheelchair lift or other boarding assistance device (and is able with such assistance) to board, ride, and disembark from any vehicle which is readily accessible to and usable by individuals with disabilities if the individual wants to travel on a route on the system during the hours of operation of the system at a time (or within a reasonable period of such time) when such a vehicle is not being used to provide designated public transportation on the route; and

(iii) to any individual with a disability who has a specific impairment-related condition which prevents such individual from traveling to a boarding location or from a disembarking location on such system;

(B) to one other individual accompanying the individual with the disability; and

(C) to other individuals, in addition to the one individual described in subparagraph (B), accompanying the individual with a disability provided that space for these additional individuals is available on the paratransit vehicle carrying the individual with a disability and that the transportation of such additional individuals will not result in a denial of service to individuals with disabilities.

For purposes of clauses (i) and (ii) of subparagraph (A), boarding or disembarking from a vehicle does not include travel to the boarding location or from the disembarking location.

(2) SERVICE AREA.—The regulations issued under this section shall require the provision of paratransit and special transportation services required under this section in the service area of each public entity which operates a fixed route system, other than any portion of the service area in which the public entity solely provides commuter bus service.

(3) SERVICE CRITERIA.—Subject to paragraphs (1) and (2), the regulations issued under this section shall establish minimum service criteria for determining the level of services to be required under this section.

(4) UNDUE FINANCIAL BURDEN LIMITATION.—The regulations issued under this section shall provide that, if the public entity is able to demonstrate to the satisfaction of the Secretary that the provision of paratransit and other special transportation services otherwise required under this section would impose an undue financial burden on the public entity, the public entity, notwithstanding any other provision of this section (other than paragraph (5)), shall only be required to provide such services to the extent that providing such services would not impose such a burden.

(5) ADDITIONAL SERVICES.—The regulations issued under this section shall establish circumstances under which the Secretary may require a public entity to provide, notwithstanding paragraph (4), paratransit and other special transportation services under this section beyond the level of paratransit and other special transportation services which would otherwise be required under paragraph (4).

(6) PUBLIC PARTICIPATION.—The regulations issued under this section shall require that each public entity which operates a fixed route system hold a public hearing, provide an opportunity for public comment, and consult with individuals with disabilities in preparing its plan under paragraph (7).

(7) PLANS.—The regulations issued under this section shall require that each public entity which operates a fixed route system—

(A) within 18 months after the effective date of this subsection, submit to the Secretary, and commence implementation of, a plan for providing paratransit and other special transportation services which meets the requirements of this section; and

(B) on an annual basis thereafter, submit to the Secretary, and commence implementation of, a plan for providing such services.

(8) PROVISION OF SERVICES BY OTHERS.—The regulations issued under this section shall—

(A) require that a public entity submitting a plan to the Secretary under this section identify in the plan any person or other public entity which is providing a paratransit or other special transportation service for individuals with disabilities in the service area to which the plan applies; and

(B) provide that the public entity submitting the plan does not have to provide under the plan such service for individuals with disabilities.

(9) OTHER PROVISIONS.—The regulations issued under this section shall include such other provisions and requirements as the Secretary determines are necessary to carry out the objectives of this section.

(d) REVIEW OF PLAN.—

(1) GENERAL RULE.—The Secretary shall review a plan submitted under this section for the purpose of determining whether or not such plan meets the requirements of this section, including the regulations issued under this section.

(2) DISAPPROVAL.—If the Secretary determines that a plan reviewed under this subsection fails to meet the requirements of this section, the Secretary shall disapprove the plan and notify the public entity which submitted the plan of such disapproval and the reasons therefor.

(3) MODIFICATION OF DISAPPROVED PLAN.—Not later than 90 days after the date of disapproval of a plan under this subsection, the public entity which submitted the plan shall modify the plan to meet the requirements of this section and shall submit to the Secretary, and commence implementation of, such modified plan.

(e) DISCRIMINATION DEFINED.—As used in subsection (a), the term "discrimination" includes—

(1) a failure of a public entity to which the regulations issued under this section apply to submit, or commence implementation of, a plan in accordance with subsections (c)(6) and (c)(7);

(2) a failure of such entity to submit, or commence implementation of, a modified plan in accordance with subsection (d)(3);

(3) submission to the Secretary of a modified plan under subsection (d)(3) which does not meet the requirements of this section; or

(4) a failure of such entity to provide paratransit or other special transportation services in accordance with the plan or modified plan the public entity submitted to the Secretary under this section.

(f) STATUTORY CONSTRUCTION.—Nothing in this section shall be construed as preventing a public entity—

(1) from providing paratransit or other special transportation services at a level which is greater than the level of such services which are required by this section,

(2) from providing paratransit or other special transportation services in addition to those paratransit and special transportation services required by this section, or

(3) from providing such services to individuals in addition to those individuals to whom such services are required to be provided by this section.

SEC. 224. PUBLIC ENTITY OPERATING A DEMAND RESPONSIVE SYSTEM.

42 USC 12144.

If a public entity operates a demand responsive system, it shall be considered discrimination, for purposes of section 202 of this Act and section 504 of the Rehabilitation Act of 1973 (29 U.S.C. 794), for such entity to purchase or lease a new vehicle for use on such system, for which a solicitation is made after the 30th day following the effective date of this section, that is not readily accessible to and usable by individuals with disabilities, including individuals who use wheelchairs, unless such system, when viewed in its entirety, provides a level of service to such individuals equivalent to the level of service such system provides to individuals without disabilities.

SEC. 225. TEMPORARY RELIEF WHERE LIFTS ARE UNAVAILABLE.

42 USC 12145.

(a) GRANTING.—With respect to the purchase of new buses, a public entity may apply for, and the Secretary may temporarily relieve such public entity from the obligation under section 222(a) or 224 to purchase new buses that are readily accessible to and usable by individuals with disabilities if such public entity demonstrates to the satisfaction of the Secretary—

(1) that the initial solicitation for new buses made by the public entity specified that all new buses were to be lift-equipped and were to be otherwise accessible to and usable by individuals with disabilities;

(2) the unavailability from any qualified manufacturer of hydraulic, electromechanical, or other lifts for such new buses;

(3) that the public entity seeking temporary relief has made good faith efforts to locate a qualified manufacturer to supply the lifts to the manufacturer of such buses in sufficient time to comply with such solicitation; and

(4) that any further delay in purchasing new buses necessary to obtain such lifts would significantly impair transportation services in the community served by the public entity.

(b) DURATION AND NOTICE TO CONGRESS.—Any relief granted under subsection (a) shall be limited in duration by a specified date, and the appropriate committees of Congress shall be notified of any such relief granted.

(c) FRAUDULENT APPLICATION.—If, at any time, the Secretary has reasonable cause to believe that any relief granted under subsection (a) was fraudulently applied for, the Secretary shall—

(1) cancel such relief if such relief is still in effect; and

(2) take such other action as the Secretary considers appropriate.

SEC. 226. NEW FACILITIES.

42 USC 12146.

For purposes of section 202 of this Act and section 504 of the Rehabilitation Act of 1973 (29 U.S.C. 794), it shall be considered discrimination for a public entity to construct a new facility to be used in the provision of designated public transportation services unless such facility is readily accessible to and usable by individuals with disabilities, including individuals who use wheelchairs.

SEC. 227. ALTERATIONS OF EXISTING FACILITIES.

42 USC 12147.

(a) GENERAL RULE.—With respect to alterations of an existing facility or part thereof used in the provision of designated public transportation services that affect or could affect the usability of the facility or part thereof, it shall be considered discrimination, for purposes of section 202 of this Act and section 504 of the Rehabilitation Act of 1973 (29 U.S.C. 794), for a public entity to fail to make such alterations (or to ensure that the alterations are made) in such a manner that, to the maximum extent feasible, the altered portions of the facility are readily accessible to and usable by individuals with disabilities, including individuals who use wheelchairs, upon the completion of such alterations. Where the public entity is undertaking an alteration that affects or could affect usability of or access to an area of the facility containing a primary function, the entity shall also make the alterations in such a manner that, to the maximum extent feasible, the path of travel to the altered area and the bathrooms, telephones, and drinking fountains serving the altered area, are readily accessible to and usable by individuals with disabilities, including individuals who use wheelchairs, upon completion of such alterations, where such alterations to the path of travel or the bathrooms, telephones, and drinking fountains serving the altered area are not disproportionate to the overall alterations in terms of cost and scope (as determined under criteria established by the Attorney General).

(b) SPECIAL RULE FOR STATIONS.—

(1) GENERAL RULE.—For purposes of section 202 of this Act and section 504 of the Rehabilitation Act of 1973 (29 U.S.C. 794), it shall be considered discrimination for a public entity that provides designated public transportation to fail, in accordance with the provisions of this subsection, to make key stations (as determined under criteria established by the Secretary by regulation) in rapid rail and light rail systems readily accessible to and usable by individuals with disabilities, including individuals who use wheelchairs.

(2) RAPID RAIL AND LIGHT RAIL KEY STATIONS.—

(A) ACCESSIBILITY.—Except as otherwise provided in this paragraph, all key stations (as determined under criteria established by the Secretary by regulation) in rapid rail and light rail systems shall be made readily accessible to and usable by individuals with disabilities, including individuals who use wheelchairs, as soon as practicable but in no event later than the last day of the 3-year period beginning on the effective date of this paragraph.

(B) EXTENSION FOR EXTRAORDINARILY EXPENSIVE STRUCTURAL CHANGES.—The Secretary may extend the 3-year period under subparagraph (A) up to a 30-year period for key stations in a rapid rail or light rail system which stations need extraordinarily expensive structural changes to, or replacement of, existing facilities; except that by the last day of the 20th year following the date of the enactment of this Act at least ⅔ of such key stations must be readily accessible to and usable by individuals with disabilities.

(3) PLANS AND MILESTONES.—The Secretary shall require the appropriate public entity to develop and submit to the Secretary a plan for compliance with this subsection—

(A) that reflects consultation with individuals with disabilities affected by such plan and the results of a public hearing and public comments on such plan, and

(B) that establishes milestones for achievement of the requirements of this subsection.

42 USC 12148.

SEC. 228. PUBLIC TRANSPORTATION PROGRAMS AND ACTIVITIES IN EXISTING FACILITIES AND ONE CAR PER TRAIN RULE.

(a) PUBLIC TRANSPORTATION PROGRAMS AND ACTIVITIES IN EXISTING FACILITIES.—

(1) IN GENERAL.—With respect to existing facilities used in the provision of designated public transportation services, it shall be considered discrimination, for purposes of section 202 of this Act and section 504 of the Rehabilitation Act of 1973 (29 U.S.C. 794), for a public entity to fail to operate a designated public transportation program or activity conducted in such facilities so that, when viewed in the entirety, the program or activity is readily accessible to and usable by individuals with disabilities.

(2) EXCEPTION.—Paragraph (1) shall not require a public entity to make structural changes to existing facilities in order to make such facilities accessible to individuals who use wheelchairs, unless and to the extent required by section 227(a) (relating to alterations) or section 227(b) (relating to key stations).

(3) UTILIZATION.—Paragraph (1) shall not require a public entity to which paragraph (2) applies, to provide to individuals who use wheelchairs services made available to the general public at such facilities when such individuals could not utilize or benefit from such services provided at such facilities.

(b) ONE CAR PER TRAIN RULE.—

(1) GENERAL RULE.—Subject to paragraph (2), with respect to 2 or more vehicles operated as a train by a light or rapid rail system, for purposes of section 202 of this Act and section 504 of the Rehabilitation Act of 1973 (29 U.S.C. 794), it shall be considered discrimination for a public entity to fail to have at least 1 vehicle per train that is accessible to individuals with disabilities, including individuals who use wheelchairs, as soon as practicable but in no event later than the last day of the 5-year period beginning on the effective date of this section.

(2) HISTORIC TRAINS.—In order to comply with paragraph (1) with respect to the remanufacture of a vehicle of historic character which is to be used on a segment of a light or rapid rail system which is included on the National Register of Historic Places, if making such vehicle readily accessible to and usable by individuals with disabilities would significantly alter the historic character of such vehicle, the public entity which operates such system only has to make (or to purchase or lease a remanufactured vehicle with) those modifications which are necessary to meet the requirements of section 222(c)(1) and which do not significantly alter the historic character of such vehicle.

SEC. 229. REGULATIONS.

42 USC 12149.

(a) IN GENERAL.—Not later than 1 year after the date of enactment of this Act, the Secretary of Transportation shall issue regulations, in an accessible format, necessary for carrying out this part (other than section 223).

(b) STANDARDS.—The regulations issued under this section and section 223 shall include standards applicable to facilities and vehicles covered by this subtitle. The standards shall be consistent with the minimum guidelines and requirements issued by the Architectural and Transportation Barriers Compliance Board in accordance with section 504 of this Act.

SEC. 230. INTERIM ACCESSIBILITY REQUIREMENTS.

42 USC 12150.

If final regulations have not been issued pursuant to section 229, for new construction or alterations for which a valid and appropriate State or local building permit is obtained prior to the issuance of final regulations under such section, and for which the construction or alteration authorized by such permit begins within one year of the receipt of such permit and is completed under the terms of such permit, compliance with the Uniform Federal Accessibility Standards in effect at the time the building permit is issued shall suffice to satisfy the requirement that facilities be readily accessible to and usable by persons with disabilities as required under sections 226 and 227, except that, if such final regulations have not been issued one year after the Architectural and Transportation Barriers Compliance Board has issued the supplemental minimum guidelines required under section 504(a) of this Act, compliance with such supplemental minimum guidelines shall be necessary to satisfy the requirement that facilities be readily accessible to and usable by persons with disabilities prior to issuance of the final regulations.

42 USC 12141 note.

SEC. 231. EFFECTIVE DATE.

(a) GENERAL RULE.—Except as provided in subsection (b), this part shall become effective 18 months after the date of enactment of this Act.

(b) EXCEPTION.—Sections 222, 223 (other than subsection (a)), 224, 225, 227(b), 228(b), and 229 shall become effective on the date of enactment of this Act.

PART II—PUBLIC TRANSPORTATION BY INTERCITY AND COMMUTER RAIL

42 USC 12161.

SEC. 241. DEFINITIONS.

As used in this part:

(1) COMMUTER AUTHORITY.—The term "commuter authority" has the meaning given such term in section 103(8) of the Rail Passenger Service Act (45 U.S.C. 502(8)).

(2) COMMUTER RAIL TRANSPORTATION.—The term "commuter rail transportation" has the meaning given the term "commuter service" in section 103(9) of the Rail Passenger Service Act (45 U.S.C. 502(9)).

(3) INTERCITY RAIL TRANSPORTATION.—The term "intercity rail transportation" means transportation provided by the National Railroad Passenger Corporation.

(4) RAIL PASSENGER CAR.—The term "rail passenger car" means, with respect to intercity rail transportation, single-level and bi-level coach cars, single-level and bi-level dining cars, single-level and bi-level sleeping cars, single-level and bi-level lounge cars, and food service cars.

(5) RESPONSIBLE PERSON.—The term "responsible person" means—

(A) in the case of a station more than 50 percent of which is owned by a public entity, such public entity;

(B) in the case of a station more than 50 percent of which is owned by a private party, the persons providing intercity or commuter rail transportation to such station, as allocated on an equitable basis by regulation by the Secretary of Transportation; and

(C) in a case where no party owns more than 50 percent of a station, the persons providing intercity or commuter rail transportation to such station and the owners of the station, other than private party owners, as allocated on an equitable basis by regulation by the Secretary of Transportation.

(6) STATION.—The term "station" means the portion of a property located appurtenant to a right-of-way on which intercity or commuter rail transportation is operated, where such portion is used by the general public and is related to the provision of such transportation, including passenger platforms, designated waiting areas, ticketing areas, restrooms, and, where a public entity providing rail transportation owns the property, concession areas, to the extent that such public entity exercises control over the selection, design, construction, or alteration of the property, but such term does not include flag stops.

42 USC 12162

SEC. 242. INTERCITY AND COMMUTER RAIL ACTIONS CONSIDERED DISCRIMINATORY.

(a) INTERCITY RAIL TRANSPORTATION.—

(1) ONE CAR PER TRAIN RULE.—It shall be considered discrimination for purposes of section 202 of this Act and section 504 of

the Rehabilitation Act of 1973 (29 U.S.C. 794) for a person who provides intercity rail transportation to fail to have at least one passenger car per train that is readily accessible to and usable by individuals with disabilities, including individuals who use wheelchairs, in accordance with regulations issued under section 244, as soon as practicable, but in no event later than 5 years after the date of enactment of this Act.

(2) NEW INTERCITY CARS.—

(A) GENERAL RULE.—Except as otherwise provided in this subsection with respect to individuals who use wheelchairs, it shall be considered discrimination for purposes of section 202 of this Act and section 504 of the Rehabilitation Act of 1973 (29 U.S.C. 794) for a person to purchase or lease any new rail passenger cars for use in intercity rail transportation, and for which a solicitation is made later than 30 days after the effective date of this section, unless all such rail cars are readily accessible to and usable by individuals with disabilities, including individuals who use wheelchairs, as prescribed by the Secretary of Transportation in regulations issued under section 244.

(B) SPECIAL RULE FOR SINGLE-LEVEL PASSENGER COACHES FOR INDIVIDUALS WHO USE WHEELCHAIRS.—Single-level passenger coaches shall be required to—

(i) be able to be entered by an individual who uses a wheelchair;

(ii) have space to park and secure a wheelchair;

(iii) have a seat to which a passenger in a wheelchair can transfer, and a space to fold and store such passenger's wheelchair; and

(iv) have a restroom usable by an individual who uses a wheelchair,

only to the extent provided in paragraph (3).

(C) SPECIAL RULE FOR SINGLE-LEVEL DINING CARS FOR INDIVIDUALS WHO USE WHEELCHAIRS.—Single-level dining cars shall not be required to—

(i) be able to be entered from the station platform by an individual who uses a wheelchair; or

(ii) have a restroom usable by an individual who uses a wheelchair if no restroom is provided in such car for any passenger.

(D) SPECIAL RULE FOR BI-LEVEL DINING CARS FOR INDIVIDUALS WHO USE WHEELCHAIRS.—Bi-level dining cars shall not be required to—

(i) be able to be entered by an individual who uses a wheelchair;

(ii) have space to park and secure a wheelchair;

(iii) have a seat to which a passenger in a wheelchair can transfer, or a space to fold and store such passenger's wheelchair; or

(iv) have a restroom usable by an individual who uses a wheelchair.

(3) ACCESSIBILITY OF SINGLE-LEVEL COACHES.—

(A) GENERAL RULE.—It shall be considered discrimination for purposes of section 202 of this Act and section 504 of the Rehabilitation Act of 1973 (29 U.S.C. 794) for a person who provides intercity rail transportation to fail to have on each train which includes one or more single-level rail passenger coaches—

(i) a number of spaces—

(I) to park and secure wheelchairs (to accommodate individuals who wish to remain in their wheelchairs) equal to not less than one-half of the number of single-level rail passenger coaches in such train; and

(II) to fold and store wheelchairs (to accommodate individuals who wish to transfer to coach seats) equal to not less than one-half of the number of single-level rail passenger coaches in such train, as soon as practicable, but in no event later than 5 years after the date of enactment of this Act; and

(ii) a number of spaces—

(I) to park and secure wheelchairs (to accommodate individuals who wish to remain in their wheelchairs) equal to not less than the total number of single-level rail passenger coaches in such train; and

(II) to fold and store wheelchairs (to accommodate individuals who wish to transfer to coach seats) equal to not less than the total number of single-level rail passenger coaches in such train, as soon as practicable, but in no event later than 10 years after the date of enactment of this Act.

(B) LOCATION.—Spaces required by subparagraph (A) shall be located in single-level rail passenger coaches or food service cars.

(C) LIMITATION.—Of the number of spaces required on a train by subparagraph (A), not more than two spaces to park and secure wheelchairs nor more than two spaces to fold and store wheelchairs shall be located in any one coach or food service car.

(D) OTHER ACCESSIBILITY FEATURES.—Single-level rail passenger coaches and food service cars on which the spaces required by subparagraph (A) are located shall have a restroom usable by an individual who uses a wheelchair and shall be able to be entered from the station platform by an individual who uses a wheelchair.

(4) FOOD SERVICE.—

(A) SINGLE-LEVEL DINING CARS.—On any train in which a single-level dining car is used to provide food service—

(i) if such single-level dining car was purchased after the date of enactment of this Act, table service in such car shall be provided to a passenger who uses a wheelchair if—

(I) the car adjacent to the end of the dining car through which a wheelchair may enter is itself accessible to a wheelchair;

(II) such passenger can exit to the platform from the car such passenger occupies, move down the platform, and enter the adjacent accessible car described in subclause (I) without the necessity of the train being moved within the station; and

(III) space to park and secure a wheelchair is available in the dining car at the time such passenger wishes to eat (if such passenger wishes to remain in a wheelchair), or space to store and fold a wheelchair is available in the dining car at the time such passenger wishes to eat (if such passenger wishes to transfer to a dining car seat); and

(ii) appropriate auxiliary aids and services, including a hard surface on which to eat, shall be provided to ensure that other equivalent food service is available to individuals with disabilities, including individuals who use wheelchairs, and to passengers traveling with such individuals.

Unless not practicable, a person providing intercity rail transportation shall place an accessible car adjacent to the end of a dining car described in clause (i) through which an individual who uses a wheelchair may enter.

(B) BI-LEVEL DINING CARS.—On any train in which a bi-level dining car is used to provide food service—

(i) if such train includes a bi-level lounge car purchased after the date of enactment of this Act, table service in such lounge car shall be provided to individuals who use wheelchairs and to other passengers; and

(ii) appropriate auxiliary aids and services, including a hard surface on which to eat, shall be provided to ensure that other equivalent food service is available to individuals with disabilities, including individuals who use wheelchairs, and to passengers traveling with such individuals.

(b) COMMUTER RAIL TRANSPORTATION.—

(1) ONE CAR PER TRAIN RULE.—It shall be considered discrimination for purposes of section 202 of this Act and section 504 of the Rehabilitation Act of 1973 (29 U.S.C. 794) for a person who provides commuter rail transportation to fail to have at least one passenger car per train that is readily accessible to and usable by individuals with disabilities, including individuals who use wheelchairs, in accordance with regulations issued under section 244, as soon as practicable, but in no event later than 5 years after the date of enactment of this Act.

(2) NEW COMMUTER RAIL CARS.—

(A) GENERAL RULE.—It shall be considered discrimination for purposes of section 202 of this Act and section 504 of the Rehabilitation Act of 1973 (29 U.S.C. 794) for a person to purchase or lease any new rail passenger cars for use in commuter rail transportation, and for which a solicitation is made later than 30 days after the effective date of this section, unless all such rail cars are readily accessible to and usable by individuals with disabilities, including individuals who use wheelchairs, as prescribed by the Secretary of Transportation in regulations issued under section 244.

(B) ACCESSIBILITY.—For purposes of section 202 of this Act and section 504 of the Rehabilitation Act of 1973 (29 U.S.C. 794), a requirement that a rail passenger car used in commuter rail transportation be accessible to or readily accessible to and usable by individuals with disabilities, including individuals who use wheelchairs, shall not be construed to require—

(i) a restroom usable by an individual who uses a wheelchair if no restroom is provided in such car for any passenger;

(ii) space to fold and store a wheelchair; or

(iii) a seat to which a passenger who uses a wheelchair can transfer.

(c) USED RAIL CARS.—It shall be considered discrimination for purposes of section 202 of this Act and section 504 of the Rehabilitation Act of 1973 (29 U.S.C. 794) for a person to purchase or lease a used rail passenger car for use in intercity or commuter rail transportation, unless such person makes demonstrated good faith efforts to purchase or lease a used rail car that is readily accessible to and usable by individuals with disabilities, including individuals who use wheelchairs, as prescribed by the Secretary of Transportation in regulations issued under section 244.

(d) REMANUFACTURED RAIL CARS.—

(1) REMANUFACTURING.—It shall be considered discrimination

for purposes of section 202 of this Act and section 504 of the Rehabilitation Act of 1973 (29 U.S.C. 794) for a person to re-manufacture a rail passenger car for use in intercity or commuter rail transportation so as to extend its usable life for 10 years or more, unless the rail car, to the maximum extent feasible, is made readily accessible to and usable by individuals with disabilities, including individuals who use wheelchairs, as prescribed by the Secretary of Transportation in regulations issued under section 244.

(2) PURCHASE OR LEASE.—It shall be considered discrimination for purposes of section 202 of this Act and section 504 of the Rehabilitation Act of 1973 (29 U.S.C. 794) for a person to purchase or lease a remanufactured rail passenger car for use in intercity or commuter rail transportation unless such car was remanufactured in accordance with paragraph (1).

(e) STATIONS.—

(1) NEW STATIONS.—It shall be considered discrimination for purposes of section 202 of this Act and section 504 of the Rehabilitation Act of 1973 (29 U.S.C. 794) for a person to build a new station for use in intercity or commuter rail transportation that is not readily accessible to and usable by individuals with disabilities, including individuals who use wheelchairs, as prescribed by the Secretary of Transportation in regulations issued under section 244.

(2) EXISTING STATIONS.—

(A) FAILURE TO MAKE READILY ACCESSIBLE.—

(i) GENERAL RULE.—It shall be considered discrimination for purposes of section 202 of this Act and section 504 of the Rehabilitation Act of 1973 (29 U.S.C. 794) for a responsible person to fail to make existing stations in the intercity rail transportation system, and existing key stations in commuter rail transportation systems, readily accessible to and usable by individuals with disabilities, including individuals who use wheelchairs, as prescribed by the Secretary of Transportation in regulations issued under section 244.

(ii) PERIOD FOR COMPLIANCE.—

(I) INTERCITY RAIL.—All stations in the intercity rail transportation system shall be made readily accessible to and usable by individuals with disabilities, including individuals who use wheelchairs, as soon as practicable, but in no event later than 20 years after the date of enactment of this Act.

(II) COMMUTER RAIL.—Key stations in commuter rail transportation systems shall be made readily accessible to and usable by individuals with disabilities, including individuals who use wheelchairs, as soon as practicable but in no event later than 3 years after the date of enactment of this Act, except that the time limit may be extended by the Secretary of Transportation up to 20 years after the date of enactment of this Act in a case where the raising of the entire passenger platform is the only means available of attaining accessibility or where other extraordinarily expensive structural changes are necessary to attain accessibility.

(iii) DESIGNATION OF KEY STATIONS.—Each commuter authority shall designate the key stations in its commuter rail transportation system, in consultation with individuals with disabilities and organizations representing such individuals, taking into consideration such factors as high ridership and whether such station serves as a transfer or feeder station. Before the final designation of key stations under this clause, a commuter authority shall hold a public hearing.

(iv) PLANS AND MILESTONES.—The Secretary of Transportation shall require the appropriate person to develop a plan for carrying out this subparagraph that reflects consultation with individuals with disabilities affected by such plan and that establishes milestones for achievement of the requirements of this subparagraph.

(B) REQUIREMENT WHEN MAKING ALTERATIONS.—

(i) GENERAL RULE.—It shall be considered discrimination, for purposes of section 202 of this Act and section 504 of the Rehabilitation Act of 1973 (29 U.S.C. 794), with respect to alterations of an existing station or part thereof in the intercity or commuter rail transportation systems that affect or could affect the usability of the station or part thereof, for the responsible person, owner, or person in control of the station to fail to make the alterations in such a manner that, to the maximum extent feasible, the altered portions of the station are readily accessible to and usable by individuals with disabilities, including individuals who use wheelchairs, upon completion of such alterations.

(ii) ALTERATIONS TO A PRIMARY FUNCTION AREA.—It shall be considered discrimination, for purposes of section 202 of this Act and section 504 of the Rehabilitation Act of 1973 (29 U.S.C. 794), with respect to alterations that affect or could affect the usability of or access to an area of the station containing a primary function, for the responsible person, owner, or person in control of the station to fail to make the alterations in such a manner that, to the maximum extent feasible, the path of travel to the altered area, and the bathrooms, telephones, and drinking fountains serving the altered area, are readily accessible to and usable by individuals with disabilities, including individuals who use wheelchairs, upon completion of such alterations, where such alterations to the path of travel or the bathrooms, telephones, and drinking fountains serving the altered area are not disproportionate to the overall alterations in terms of cost and scope (as determined under criteria established by the Attorney General).

(C) REQUIRED COOPERATION.—It shall be considered discrimination for purposes of section 202 of this Act and section 504 of the Rehabilitation Act of 1973 (29 U.S.C. 794) for an owner, or person in control, of a station governed by subparagraph (A) or (B) to fail to provide reasonable cooperation to a responsible person with respect to such station in that responsible person's efforts to comply with such subparagraph. An owner, or person in control, of a station shall be liable to a responsible person for any failure to provide reasonable cooperation as required by this subparagraph. Failure to receive reasonable cooperation required by this subparagraph shall not be a defense to a claim of discrimination under this Act.

SEC. 243. CONFORMANCE OF ACCESSIBILITY STANDARDS.   42 USC 12163.

Accessibility standards included in regulations issued under this part shall be consistent with the minimum guidelines issued by the Architectural and Transportation Barriers Compliance Board under section 504(a) of this Act.

42 USC 12164.

SEC. 244. REGULATIONS.

Not later than 1 year after the date of enactment of this Act, the Secretary of Transportation shall issue regulations, in an accessible format, necessary for carrying out this part.

42 USC 12165.

SEC. 245. INTERIM ACCESSIBILITY REQUIREMENTS.

(a) STATIONS.—If final regulations have not been issued pursuant to section 244, for new construction or alterations for which a valid and appropriate State or local building permit is obtained prior to the issuance of final regulations under such section, and for which the construction or alteration authorized by such permit begins within one year of the receipt of such permit and is completed under the terms of such permit, compliance with the Uniform Federal Accessibility Standards in effect at the time the building permit is issued shall suffice to satisfy the requirement that stations be readily accessible to and usable by persons with disabilities as required under section 242(e), except that, if such final regulations have not been issued one year after the Architectural and Transportation Barriers Compliance Board has issued the supplemental minimum guidelines required under section 504(a) of this Act, compliance with such supplemental minimum guidelines shall be necessary to satisfy the requirement that stations be readily accessible to and usable by persons with disabilities prior to issuance of the final regulations.

(b) RAIL PASSENGER CARS.—If final regulations have not been issued pursuant to section 244, a person shall be considered to have complied with the requirements of section 242 (a) through (d) that a rail passenger car be readily accessible to and usable by individuals with disabilities, if the design for such car complies with the laws and regulations (including the Minimum Guidelines and Requirements for Accessible Design and such supplemental minimum guidelines as are issued under section 504(a) of this Act) governing accessibility of such cars, to the extent that such laws and regulations are not inconsistent with this part and are in effect at the time such design is substantially completed.

42 USC 12161
note.

SEC. 246. EFFECTIVE DATE.

(a) GENERAL RULE.—Except as provided in subsection (b), this part shall become effective 18 months after the date of enactment of this Act.

(b) EXCEPTION.—Sections 242 and 244 shall become effective on the date of enactment of this Act.

TITLE III—PUBLIC ACCOMMODATIONS AND SERVICES OPERATED BY PRIVATE ENTITIES

42 USC 12181.

SEC. 301. DEFINITIONS.

As used in this title:

(1) COMMERCE.—The term "commerce" means travel, trade, traffic, commerce, transportation, or communication—

(A) among the several States;

(B) between any foreign country or any territory or possession and any State; or

(C) between points in the same State but through another State or foreign country.

(2) COMMERCIAL FACILITIES.—The term "commercial facilities" means facilities—

(A) that are intended for nonresidential use; and

(B) whose operations will affect commerce.

Such term shall not include railroad locomotives, railroad freight cars, railroad cabooses, railroad cars described in section 242 or covered under this title, railroad rights-of-way, or facilities that are covered or expressly exempted from coverage under the Fair Housing Act of 1968 (42 U.S.C. 3601 et seq.).

(3) DEMAND RESPONSIVE SYSTEM.—The term "demand responsive system" means any system of providing transportation of individuals by a vehicle, other than a system which is a fixed route system.

(4) FIXED ROUTE SYSTEM.—The term "fixed route system" means a system of providing transportation of individuals (other than by aircraft) on which a vehicle is operated along a prescribed route according to a fixed schedule.

(5) OVER-THE-ROAD BUS.—The term "over-the-road bus" means a bus characterized by an elevated passenger deck located over a baggage compartment.

(6) PRIVATE ENTITY.—The term "private entity" means any entity other than a public entity (as defined in section 201(1)).

(7) PUBLIC ACCOMMODATION.—The following private entities are considered public accommodations for purposes of this title, if the operations of such entities affect commerce—

(A) an inn, hotel, motel, or other place of lodging, except for an establishment located within a building that contains not more than five rooms for rent or hire and that is actually occupied by the proprietor of such establishment as the residence of such proprietor;

(B) a restaurant, bar, or other establishment serving food or drink;

(C) a motion picture house, theater, concert hall, stadium, or other place of exhibition or entertainment;

(D) an auditorium, convention center, lecture hall, or other place of public gathering;

(E) a bakery, grocery store, clothing store, hardware store, shopping center, or other sales or rental establishment;

(F) a laundromat, dry-cleaner, bank, barber shop, beauty shop, travel service, shoe repair service, funeral parlor, gas station, office of an accountant or lawyer, pharmacy, insurance office, professional office of a health care provider, hospital, or other service establishment;

(G) a terminal, depot, or other station used for specified public transportation;

(H) a museum, library, gallery, or other place of public display or collection;

(I) a park, zoo, amusement park, or other place of recreation;

(J) a nursery, elementary, secondary, undergraduate, or postgraduate private school, or other place of education;

(K) a day care center, senior citizen center, homeless shelter, food bank, adoption agency, or other social service center establishment; and

(L) a gymnasium, health spa, bowling alley, golf course, or other place of exercise or recreation.

(8) RAIL AND RAILROAD.—The terms "rail" and "railroad" have the meaning given the term "railroad" in section 202(e) of the Federal Railroad Safety Act of 1970 (45 U.S.C. 431(e)).

(9) READILY ACHIEVABLE.—The term "readily achievable" means easily accomplishable and able to be carried out without much difficulty or expense. In determining whether an action is readily achievable, factors to be considered include—

(A) the nature and cost of the action needed under this Act;

(B) the overall financial resources of the facility or facilities involved in the action; the number of persons employed at such facility; the effect on expenses and resources, or the impact otherwise of such action upon the operation of the facility;

(C) the overall financial resources of the covered entity; the overall size of the business of a covered entity with respect to the number of its employees; the number, type, and location of its facilities; and

(D) the type of operation or operations of the covered entity, including the composition, structure, and functions of the workforce of such entity; the geographic separateness, administrative or fiscal relationship of the facility or facilities in question to the covered entity.

(10) SPECIFIED PUBLIC TRANSPORTATION.—The term "specified public transportation" means transportation by bus, rail, or any other conveyance (other than by aircraft) that provides the general public with general or special service (including charter service) on a regular and continuing basis.

(11) VEHICLE.—The term "vehicle" does not include a rail passenger car, railroad locomotive, railroad freight car, railroad caboose, or a railroad car described in section 242 or covered under this title.

42 USC 12182.

SEC. 302. PROHIBITION OF DISCRIMINATION BY PUBLIC ACCOMMODATIONS.

(a) GENERAL RULE.—No individual shall be discriminated against on the basis of disability in the full and equal enjoyment of the goods, services, facilities, privileges, advantages, or accommodations of any place of public accommodation by any person who owns, leases (or leases to), or operates a place of public accommodation.

(b) CONSTRUCTION.—

(1) GENERAL PROHIBITION.—

(A) ACTIVITIES.—

(i) DENIAL OF PARTICIPATION.—It shall be discriminatory to subject an individual or class of individuals on the basis of a disability or disabilities of such individual or class, directly, or through contractual, licensing, or other arrangements, to a denial of the opportunity of the individual or class to participate in or benefit from the goods, services, facilities, privileges, advantages, or accommodations of an entity.

(ii) PARTICIPATION IN UNEQUAL BENEFIT.—It shall be discriminatory to afford an individual or class of individuals, on the basis of a disability or disabilities of such individual or class, directly, or through contractual, licensing, or other arrangements with the opportunity to participate in or benefit from a good, service, facility, privilege, advantage, or accommodation that is not equal to that afforded to other individuals.

(iii) SEPARATE BENEFIT.—It shall be discriminatory to provide an individual or class of individuals, on the basis of a disability or disabilities of such individual or class, directly, or through contractual, licensing, or other arrangements with a good, service, facility, privilege, advantage, or accommodation that is different or separate from that provided to other individuals, unless such action is necessary to provide the individual or class of individuals with a good, service, facility, privilege, advantage, or accommodation, or other opportunity that is as effective as that provided to others.

(iv) INDIVIDUAL OR CLASS OF INDIVIDUALS.—For purposes of clauses (i) through (iii) of this subparagraph, the term "individual or class of individuals" refers to the clients or customers of the covered public accommodation that enters into the contractual, licensing or other arrangement.

(B) INTEGRATED SETTINGS.—Goods, services, facilities, privileges, advantages, and accommodations shall be afforded to an individual with a disability in the most integrated setting appropriate to the needs of the individual.

(C) OPPORTUNITY TO PARTICIPATE.—Notwithstanding the existence of separate or different programs or activities provided in accordance with this section, an individual with a disability shall not be denied the opportunity to participate in such programs or activities that are not separate or different.

(D) ADMINISTRATIVE METHODS.—An individual or entity shall not, directly or through contractual or other arrangements, utilize standards or criteria or methods of administration—

(i) that have the effect of discriminating on the basis of disability; or

(ii) that perpetuate the discrimination of others who are subject to common administrative control.

(E) ASSOCIATION.—It shall be discriminatory to exclude or otherwise deny equal goods, services, facilities, privileges, advantages, accommodations, or other opportunities to an individual or entity because of the known disability of an individual with whom the individual or entity is known to have a relationship or association.

(2) SPECIFIC PROHIBITIONS.—

(A) DISCRIMINATION.—For purposes of subsection (a), discrimination includes—

(i) the imposition or application of eligibility criteria that screen out or tend to screen out an individual with a disability or any class of individuals with disabilities from fully and equally enjoying any goods, services, facilities, privileges, advantages, or accommodations, unless such criteria can be shown to be necessary for the provision of the goods, services, facilities, privileges, advantages, or accommodations being offered;

(ii) a failure to make reasonable modifications in policies, practices, or procedures, when such modifications are necessary to afford such goods, services, facilities, privileges, advantages, or accommodations to individuals with disabilities, unless the entity can demonstrate that making such modifications would fundamentally alter the nature of such goods, services, facilities, privileges, advantages, or accommodations;

(iii) a failure to take such steps as may be necessary to ensure that no individual with a disability is excluded, denied services, segregated or otherwise treated differently than other individuals because of the absence of auxiliary aids and services, unless the entity can demonstrate that taking such steps would fundamentally alter the nature of the good, service, facility, privilege, advantage, or accommodation being offered or would result in an undue burden;

(iv) a failure to remove architectural barriers, and communication barriers that are structural in nature, in existing facilities, and transportation barriers in existing vehicles and rail passenger cars used by an establishment for transporting individuals (not including barriers that can only be removed through the retrofitting of vehicles or rail passenger cars by the installation of a hydraulic or other lift), where such removal is readily achievable; and

(v) where an entity can demonstrate that the removal of a barrier under clause (iv) is not readily achievable, a failure to make such goods, services, facilities, privileges, advantages, or accommodations available through alternative methods if such methods are readily achievable.

(B) FIXED ROUTE SYSTEM.—

(i) ACCESSIBILITY.—It shall be considered discrimination for a private entity which operates a fixed route system and which is not subject to section 304 to purchase or lease a vehicle with a seating capacity in excess of 16 passengers (including the driver) for use on such system, for which a solicitation is made after the 30th day following the effective date of this subparagraph, that is not readily accessible to and usable by individuals with disabilities, including individuals who use wheelchairs.

(ii) EQUIVALENT SERVICE.—If a private entity which operates a fixed route system and which is not subject to section 304 purchases or leases a vehicle with a seating capacity of 16 passengers or less (including the driver) for use on such system after the effective date of this subparagraph that is not readily accessible to or usable by individuals with disabilities, it shall be considered discrimination for such entity to fail to operate such system so that, when viewed in its entirety, such system ensures a level of service to individuals with disabilities, including individuals who use wheelchairs, equivalent to the level of service provided to individuals without disabilities.

(C) DEMAND RESPONSIVE SYSTEM.—For purposes of subsection (a), discrimination includes—

(i) a failure of a private entity which operates a demand responsive system and which is not subject to section 304 to operate such system so that, when viewed in its entirety, such system ensures a level of service to individuals with disabilities, including individuals who use wheelchairs, equivalent to the level of service provided to individuals without disabilities; and

(ii) the purchase or lease by such entity for use on such system of a vehicle with a seating capacity in excess of 16 passengers (including the driver), for which solicitations are made after the 30th day following the effective date of this subparagraph, that is not readily accessible to and usable by individuals with disabilities (including individuals who use wheelchairs) unless such entity can demonstrate that such system, when viewed in its entirety, provides a level of service to individuals with disabilities equivalent to that provided to individuals without disabilities.

(D) OVER-THE-ROAD BUSES.—

(i) LIMITATION ON APPLICABILITY.—Subparagraphs (B) and (C) do not apply to over-the-road buses.

(ii) ACCESSIBILITY REQUIREMENTS.—For purposes of subsection (a), discrimination includes (I) the purchase or lease of an over-the-road bus which does not comply with the regulations issued under section 306(a)(2) by a private entity which provides transportation of individuals and which is not primarily engaged in the business of transporting people, and (II) any other failure of such entity to comply with such regulations.

(3) SPECIFIC CONSTRUCTION.—Nothing in this title shall require an entity to permit an individual to participate in or benefit from the goods, services, facilities, privileges, advantages and accommodations of such entity where such individual poses a direct threat to the health or safety of others. The term "direct threat" means a significant risk to the health or safety of others that cannot be eliminated by a modification of policies, practices, or procedures or by the provision of auxiliary aids or services.

SEC. 303. NEW CONSTRUCTION AND ALTERATIONS IN PUBLIC ACCOMMODATIONS AND COMMERCIAL FACILITIES.

42 USC 12183.

(a) APPLICATION OF TERM.—Except as provided in subsection (b), as applied to public accommodations and commercial facilities, discrimination for purposes of section 302(a) includes—

(1) a failure to design and construct facilities for first occupancy later than 30 months after the date of enactment of this Act that are readily accessible to and usable by individuals with disabilities, except where an entity can demonstrate that it is structurally impracticable to meet the requirements of such subsection in accordance with standards set forth or incorporated by reference in regulations issued under this title; and

(2) with respect to a facility or part thereof that is altered by, on behalf of, or for the use of an establishment in a manner that affects or could affect the usability of the facility or part thereof, a failure to make alterations in such a manner that, to the maximum extent feasible, the altered portions of the facility are readily accessible to and usable by individuals with disabilities, including individuals who use wheelchairs. Where the entity is undertaking an alteration that affects or could affect usability of or access to an area of the facility containing a primary function, the entity shall also make the alterations in such a manner that, to the maximum extent feasible, the path of travel to the altered area and the bathrooms, telephones, and drinking fountains serving the altered area, are readily accessible to and usable by individuals with disabilities where such alterations to the path of travel or the bathrooms, telephones, and drinking fountains serving the altered area are not disproportionate to the overall alterations in terms of cost and scope (as determined under criteria established by the Attorney General).

(b) ELEVATOR.—Subsection (a) shall not be construed to require the installation of an elevator for facilities that are less than three stories or have less than 3,000 square feet per story unless the building is a shopping center, a shopping mall, or the professional office of a health care provider or unless the Attorney General determines that a particular category of such facilities requires the installation of elevators based on the usage of such facilities.

SEC. 304. PROHIBITION OF DISCRIMINATION IN SPECIFIED PUBLIC TRANSPORTATION SERVICES PROVIDED BY PRIVATE ENTITIES.

42 USC 12184.

(a) GENERAL RULE.—No individual shall be discriminated against on the basis of disability in the full and equal enjoyment of specified public transportation services provided by a private entity that is primarily engaged in the business of transporting people and whose operations affect commerce.

(b) CONSTRUCTION.—For purposes of subsection (a), discrimination
includes—

(1) the imposition or application by a entity described in
subsection (a) of eligibility criteria that screen out or tend to
screen out an individual with a disability or any class of individuals with disabilities from fully enjoying the specified public
transportation services provided by the entity, unless such criteria can be shown to be necessary for the provision of the
services being offered;

(2) the failure of such entity to—

(A) make reasonable modifications consistent with those
required under section 302(b)(2)(A)(ii);

(B) provide auxiliary aids and services consistent with the
requirements of section 302(b)(2)(A)(iii); and

(C) remove barriers consistent with the requirements of
section 302(b)(2)(A) and with the requirements of section
303(a)(2);

(3) the purchase or lease by such entity of a new vehicle (other
than an automobile, a van with a seating capacity of less than 8
passengers, including the driver, or an over-the-road bus) which
is to be used to provide specified public transportation and for
which a solicitation is made after the 30th day following the
effective date of this section, that is not readily accessible to and
usable by individuals with disabilities, including individuals
who use wheelchairs; except that the new vehicle need not be
readily accessible to and usable by such individuals if the new
vehicle is to be used solely in a demand responsive system and if
the entity can demonstrate that such system, when viewed in its
entirety, provides a level of service to such individuals equivalent to the level of service provided to the general public;

(4)(A) the purchase or lease by such entity of an over-the-road
bus which does not comply with the regulations issued under
section 306(a)(2); and

(B) any other failure of such entity to comply with such
regulations; and

(5) the purchase or lease by such entity of a new van with a
seating capacity of less than 8 passengers, including the driver,
which is to be used to provide specified public transportation
and for which a solicitation is made after the 30th day following
the effective date of this section that is not readily accessible to
or usable by individuals with disabilities, including individuals
who use wheelchairs; except that the new van need not be
readily accessible to and usable by such individuals if the entity
can demonstrate that the system for which the van is being
purchased or leased, when viewed in its entirety, provides a
level of service to such individuals equivalent to the level of
service provided to the general public;

(6) the purchase or lease by such entity of a new rail passenger car that is to be used to provide specified public transportation, and for which a solicitation is made later than 30 days
after the effective date of this paragraph, that is not readily
accessible to and usable by individuals with disabilities, including individuals who use wheelchairs; and

(7) the remanufacture by such entity of a rail passenger car
that is to be used to provide specified public transportation so as
to extend its usable life for 10 years or more, or the purchase or
lease by such entity of such a rail car, unless the rail car, to the
maximum extent feasible, is made readily accessible to and
usable by individuals with disabilities, including individuals
who use wheelchairs.

(c) HISTORICAL OR ANTIQUATED CARS.—

(1) EXCEPTION.—To the extent that compliance with subsection (b)(2)(C) or (b)(7) would significantly alter the historic or

antiquated character of a historical or antiquated rail passenger car, or a rail station served exclusively by such cars, or would result in violation of any rule, regulation, standard, or order issued by the Secretary of Transportation under the Federal Railroad Safety Act of 1970, such compliance shall not be required.

(2) DEFINITION.—As used in this subsection, the term "historical or antiquated rail passenger car" means a rail passenger car—

(A) which is not less than 30 years old at the time of its use for transporting individuals;

(B) the manufacturer of which is no longer in the business of manufacturing rail passenger cars; and

(C) which—

(i) has a consequential association with events or persons significant to the past; or

(ii) embodies, or is being restored to embody, the distinctive characteristics of a type of rail passenger car used in the past, or to represent a time period which has passed.

SEC. 305. STUDY.

42 USC 12185.

(a) PURPOSES.—The Office of Technology Assessment shall undertake a study to determine—

(1) the access needs of individuals with disabilities to over-the-road buses and over-the-road bus service; and

(2) the most cost-effective methods for providing access to over-the-road buses and over-the-road bus service to individuals with disabilities, particularly individuals who use wheelchairs, through all forms of boarding options.

(b) CONTENTS.—The study shall include, at a minimum, an analysis of the following:

(1) The anticipated demand by individuals with disabilities for accessible over-the-road buses and over-the-road bus service.

(2) The degree to which such buses and service, including any service required under sections 304(b)(4) and 306(a)(2), are readily accessible to and usable by individuals with disabilities.

(3) The effectiveness of various methods of providing accessibility to such buses and service to individuals with disabilities.

(4) The cost of providing accessible over-the-road buses and bus service to individuals with disabilities, including consideration of recent technological and cost saving developments in equipment and devices.

(5) Possible design changes in over-the-road buses that could enhance accessibility, including the installation of accessible restrooms which do not result in a loss of seating capacity.

(6) The impact of accessibility requirements on the continuation of over-the-road bus service, with particular consideration of the impact of such requirements on such service to rural communities.

(c) ADVISORY COMMITTEE.—In conducting the study required by subsection (a), the Office of Technology Assessment shall establish an advisory committee, which shall consist of—

(1) members selected from among private operators and manufacturers of over-the-road buses;

(2) members selected from among individuals with disabilities, particularly individuals who use wheelchairs, who are potential riders of such buses; and

(3) members selected for their technical expertise on issues included in the study, including manufacturers of boarding assistance equipment and devices.

The number of members selected under each of paragraphs (1) and (2) shall be equal, and the total number of members selected under paragraphs (1) and (2) shall exceed the number of members selected under paragraph (3).

(d) DEADLINE.—The study required by subsection (a), along with recommendations by the Office of Technology Assessment, including any policy options for legislative action, shall be submitted to the President and Congress within 36 months after the date of the

President of U.S.

enactment of this Act. If the President determines that compliance with the regulations issued pursuant to section 306(a)(2)(B) on or before the applicable deadlines specified in section 306(a)(2)(B) will result in a significant reduction in intercity over-the-road bus service, the President shall extend each such deadline by 1 year.

(e) REVIEW.—In developing the study required by subsection (a), the Office of Technology Assessment shall provide a preliminary draft of such study to the Architectural and Transportation Barriers Compliance Board established under section 502 of the Rehabilitation Act of 1973 (29 U.S.C. 792). The Board shall have an opportunity to comment on such draft study, and any such comments by the Board made in writing within 120 days after the Board's receipt of the draft study shall be incorporated as part of the final study required to be submitted under subsection (d).

42 USC 12186.

SEC. 306. REGULATIONS.

(a) TRANSPORTATION PROVISIONS.—

(1) GENERAL RULE.—Not later than 1 year after the date of the enactment of this Act, the Secretary of Transportation shall issue regulations in an accessible format to carry out sections 302(b)(2) (B) and (C) and to carry out section 304 (other than subsection (b)(4)).

(2) SPECIAL RULES FOR PROVIDING ACCESS TO OVER-THE-ROAD BUSES.—

(A) INTERIM REQUIREMENTS.—

(i) ISSUANCE.—Not later than 1 year after the date of the enactment of this Act, the Secretary of Transportation shall issue regulations in an accessible format to carry out sections 304(b)(4) and 302(b)(2)(D)(ii) that require each private entity which uses an over-the-road bus to provide transportation of individuals to provide accessibility to such bus; except that such regulations shall not require any structural changes in over-the-road buses in order to provide access to individuals who use wheelchairs during the effective period of such regulations and shall not require the purchase of boarding assistance devices to provide access to such individuals.

(ii) EFFECTIVE PERIOD.—The regulations issued pursuant to this subparagraph shall be effective until the effective date of the regulations issued under subparagraph (B).

(B) FINAL REQUIREMENT.—

(i) REVIEW OF STUDY AND INTERIM REQUIREMENTS.—The Secretary shall review the study submitted under section 305 and the regulations issued pursuant to subparagraph (A).

(ii) ISSUANCE.—Not later than 1 year after the date of the submission of the study under section 305, the Secretary shall issue in an accessible format new regulations to carry out sections 304(b)(4) and 302(b)(2)(D)(ii) that require, taking into account the purposes of the study under section 305 and any recommendations resulting from such study, each private entity which uses an over-the-road bus to provide transportation to individuals to provide accessibility to such bus to individuals with disabilities, including individuals who use wheelchairs.

(iii) EFFECTIVE PERIOD.—Subject to section 305(d), the regulations issued pursuant to this subparagraph shall take effect—

(I) with respect to small providers of transportation (as defined by the Secretary), 7 years after the date of the enactment of this Act; and

(II) with respect to other providers of transportation, 6 years after such date of enactment.

(C) LIMITATION ON REQUIRING INSTALLATION OF ACCESSIBLE RESTROOMS.—The regulations issued pursuant to this paragraph shall not require the installation of accessible restrooms in over-the-road buses if such installation would result in a loss of seating capacity.

(3) STANDARDS.—The regulations issued pursuant to this subsection shall include standards applicable to facilities and vehicles covered by sections 302(b)(2) and 304.

(b) OTHER PROVISIONS.—Not later than 1 year after the date of the enactment of this Act, the Attorney General shall issue regulations in an accessible format to carry out the provisions of this title not referred to in subsection (a) that include standards applicable to facilities and vehicles covered under section 302.

(c) CONSISTENCY WITH ATBCB GUIDELINES.—Standards included in regulations issued under subsections (a) and (b) shall be consistent with the minimum guidelines and requirements issued by the Architectural and Transportation Barriers Compliance Board in accordance with section 504 of this Act.

(d) INTERIM ACCESSIBILITY STANDARDS.—

(1) FACILITIES.—If final regulations have not been issued pursuant to this section, for new construction or alterations for which a valid and appropriate State or local building permit is obtained prior to the issuance of final regulations under this section, and for which the construction or alteration authorized by such permit begins within one year of the receipt of such permit and is completed under the terms of such permit, compliance with the Uniform Federal Accessibility Standards in effect at the time the building permit is issued shall suffice to satisfy the requirement that facilities be readily accessible to and usable by persons with disabilities as required under section 303, except that, if such final regulations have not been issued one year after the Architectural and Transportation Barriers Compliance Board has issued the supplemental minimum guidelines required under section 504(a) of this Act, compliance with such supplemental minimum guidelines shall be necessary to satisfy the requirement that facilities be readily accessible to and usable by persons with disabilities prior to issuance of the final regulations.

(2) VEHICLES AND RAIL PASSENGER CARS.—If final regulations have not been issued pursuant to this section, a private entity shall be considered to have complied with the requirements of this title, if any, that a vehicle or rail passenger car be readily accessible to and usable by individuals with disabilities, if the design for such vehicle or car complies with the laws and regulations (including the Minimum Guidelines and Requirements for Accessible Design and such supplemental minimum guidelines as are issued under section 504(a) of this Act) governing accessibility of such vehicles or cars, to the extent that such laws and regulations are not inconsistent with this title and are in effect at the time such design is substantially completed.

42 USC 12187.

SEC. 307. EXEMPTIONS FOR PRIVATE CLUBS AND RELIGIOUS ORGANIZATIONS.

The provisions of this title shall not apply to private clubs or establishments exempted from coverage under title II of the Civil Rights Act of 1964 (42 U.S.C. 2000-a(e)) or to religious organizations or entities controlled by religious organizations, including places of worship.

42 USC 12188.

SEC. 308. ENFORCEMENT.

(a) IN GENERAL.—

(1) AVAILABILITY OF REMEDIES AND PROCEDURES.—The remedies and procedures set forth in section 204(a) of the Civil Rights Act of 1964 (42 U.S.C. 2000a-3(a)) are the remedies and procedures this title provides to any person who is being subjected to discrimination on the basis of disability in violation of this title or who has reasonable grounds for believing that such person is about to be subjected to discrimination in violation of section 303. Nothing in this section shall require a person with a disability to engage in a futile gesture if such person has actual notice that a person or organization covered by this title does not intend to comply with its provisions.

(2) INJUNCTIVE RELIEF.—In the case of violations of sections 302(b)(2)(A)(iv) and section 303(a), injunctive relief shall include an order to alter facilities to make such facilities readily accessible to and usable by individuals with disabilities to the extent required by this title. Where appropriate, injunctive relief shall also include requiring the provision of an auxiliary aid or service, modification of a policy, or provision of alternative methods, to the extent required by this title.

(b) ENFORCEMENT BY THE ATTORNEY GENERAL.—

(1) DENIAL OF RIGHTS.—

(A) DUTY TO INVESTIGATE.—

(i) IN GENERAL.—The Attorney General shall investigate alleged violations of this title, and shall undertake periodic reviews of compliance of covered entities under this title.

(ii) ATTORNEY GENERAL CERTIFICATION.—On the application of a State or local government, the Attorney General may, in consultation with the Architectural and Transportation Barriers Compliance Board, and after prior notice and a public hearing at which persons, including individuals with disabilities, are provided an opportunity to testify against such certification, certify that a State law or local building code or similar ordinance that establishes accessibility requirements meets or exceeds the minimum requirements of this Act for the accessibility and usability of covered facilities under this title. At any enforcement proceeding under this section, such certification by the Attorney General shall be rebuttable evidence that such State law or local ordinance does meet or exceed the minimum requirements of this Act.

(B) POTENTIAL VIOLATION.—If the Attorney General has reasonable cause to believe that—

(i) any person or group of persons is engaged in a pattern or practice of discrimination under this title; or

(ii) any person or group of persons has been discriminated against under this title and such discrimination raises an issue of general public importance,

the Attorney General may commence a civil action in any appropriate United States district court.

(2) AUTHORITY OF COURT.—In a civil action under paragraph (1)(B), the court—

(A) may grant any equitable relief that such court considers to be appropriate, including, to the extent required by this title—

(i) granting temporary, preliminary, or permanent relief;

(ii) providing an auxiliary aid or service, modification of policy, practice, or procedure, or alternative method; and

(iii) making facilities readily accessible to and usable by individuals with disabilities;

(B) may award such other relief as the court considers to be appropriate, including monetary damages to persons aggrieved when requested by the Attorney General; and

(C) may, to vindicate the public interest, assess a civil penalty against the entity in an amount—

(i) not exceeding $50,000 for a first violation; and

(ii) not exceeding $100,000 for any subsequent violation.

(3) SINGLE VIOLATION.—For purposes of paragraph (2)(C), in determining whether a first or subsequent violation has occurred, a determination in a single action, by judgment or settlement, that the covered entity has engaged in more than one discriminatory act shall be counted as a single violation.

(4) PUNITIVE DAMAGES.—For purposes of subsection (b)(2)(B), the term "monetary damages" and "such other relief" does not include punitive damages.

(5) JUDICIAL CONSIDERATION.—In a civil action under paragraph (1)(B), the court, when considering what amount of civil penalty, if any, is appropriate, shall give consideration to any good faith effort or attempt to comply with this Act by the entity. In evaluating good faith, the court shall consider, among other factors it deems relevant, whether the entity could have reasonably anticipated the need for an appropriate type of auxiliary aid needed to accommodate the unique needs of a particular individual with a disability.

SEC. 309. EXAMINATIONS AND COURSES.

42 USC 12189.

Any person that offers examinations or courses related to applications, licensing, certification, or credentialing for secondary or post-secondary education, professional, or trade purposes shall offer such examinations or courses in a place and manner accessible to persons with disabilities or offer alternative accessible arrangements for such individuals.

SEC. 310. EFFECTIVE DATE.

42 USC 12181 note.

(a) GENERAL RULE.—Except as provided in subsections (b) and (c), this title shall become effective 18 months after the date of the enactment of this Act.

(b) CIVIL ACTIONS.—Except for any civil action brought for a violation of section 303, no civil action shall be brought for any act or omission described in section 302 which occurs—

(1) during the first 6 months after the effective date, against businesses that employ 25 or fewer employees and have gross receipts of $1,000,000 or less; and

(2) during the first year after the effective date, against businesses that employ 10 or fewer employees and have gross receipts of $500,000 or less.

(c) EXCEPTION.—Sections 302(a) for purposes of section 302(b)(2) (B) and (C) only, 304(a) for purposes of section 304(b)(3) only, 304(b)(3), 305, and 306 shall take effect on the date of the enactment of this Act.

TITLE IV—TELECOMMUNICATIONS

SEC. 401. TELECOMMUNICATIONS RELAY SERVICES FOR HEARING-IMPAIRED AND SPEECH-IMPAIRED INDIVIDUALS.

(a) TELECOMMUNICATIONS.—Title II of the Communications Act of 1934 (47 U.S.C. 201 et seq.) is amended by adding at the end thereof the following new section:

State and local
governments.
47 USC 225.

"SEC. 225. TELECOMMUNICATIONS SERVICES FOR HEARING-IMPAIRED AND SPEECH-IMPAIRED INDIVIDUALS.

"(a) DEFINITIONS.—As used in this section—

"(1) COMMON CARRIER OR CARRIER.—The term 'common carrier' or 'carrier' includes any common carrier engaged in interstate communication by wire or radio as defined in section 3(h) and any common carrier engaged in intrastate communication by wire or radio, notwithstanding sections 2(b) and 221(b).

"(2) TDD.—The term 'TDD' means a Telecommunications Device for the Deaf, which is a machine that employs graphic communication in the transmission of coded signals through a wire or radio communication system.

"(3) TELECOMMUNICATIONS RELAY SERVICES.—The term 'telecommunications relay services' means telephone transmission services that provide the ability for an individual who has a hearing impairment or speech impairment to engage in communication by wire or radio with a hearing individual in a manner that is functionally equivalent to the ability of an individual who does not have a hearing impairment or speech impairment to communicate using voice communication services by wire or radio. Such term includes services that enable two-way communication between an individual who uses a TDD or other nonvoice terminal device and an individual who does not use such a device.

"(b) AVAILABILITY OF TELECOMMUNICATIONS RELAY SERVICES.—

"(1) IN GENERAL.—In order to carry out the purposes established under section 1, to make available to all individuals in the United States a rapid, efficient nationwide communication service, and to increase the utility of the telephone system of the Nation, the Commission shall ensure that interstate and intrastate telecommunications relay services are available, to the extent possible and in the most efficient manner, to hearing-impaired and speech-impaired individuals in the United States.

"(2) USE OF GENERAL AUTHORITY AND REMEDIES.—For the purposes of administering and enforcing the provisions of this section and the regulations prescribed thereunder, the Commission shall have the same authority, power, and functions with respect to common carriers engaged in intrastate communication as the Commission has in administering and enforcing the provisions of this title with respect to any common carrier engaged in interstate communication. Any violation of this section by any common carrier engaged in intrastate communication shall be subject to the same remedies, penalties, and procedures as are applicable to a violation of this Act by a common carrier engaged in interstate communication.

"(c) PROVISION OF SERVICES.—Each common carrier providing telephone voice transmission services shall, not later than 3 years after the date of enactment of this section, provide in compliance with the regulations prescribed under this section, throughout the area in which it offers service, telecommunications relay services, individually, through designees, through a competitively selected vendor, or in concert with other carriers. A common carrier shall be considered to be in compliance with such regulations—

"(1) with respect to intrastate telecommunications relay services in any State that does not have a certified program under subsection (f) and with respect to interstate telecommunications relay services, if such common carrier (or other entity through which the carrier is providing such relay services) is in compliance with the Commission's regulations under subsection (d); or

"(2) with respect to intrastate telecommunications relay services in any State that has a certified program under subsection (f) for such State, if such common carrier (or other entity through which the carrier is providing such relay services) is in compliance with the program certified under subsection (f) for such State.

"(d) REGULATIONS.—

"(1) IN GENERAL.—The Commission shall, not later than 1 year after the date of enactment of this section, prescribe regulations to implement this section, including regulations that—

"(A) establish functional requirements, guidelines, and operations procedures for telecommunications relay services;

"(B) establish minimum standards that shall be met in carrying out subsection (c);

"(C) require that telecommunications relay services operate every day for 24 hours per day;

"(D) require that users of telecommunications relay services pay rates no greater than the rates paid for functionally equivalent voice communication services with respect to such factors as the duration of the call, the time of day, and the distance from point of origination to point of termination;

"(E) prohibit relay operators from failing to fulfill the obligations of common carriers by refusing calls or limiting the length of calls that use telecommunications relay services;

"(F) prohibit relay operators from disclosing the content of any relayed conversation and from keeping records of the content of any such conversation beyond the duration of the call; and

"(G) prohibit relay operators from intentionally altering a relayed conversation.

"(2) TECHNOLOGY.—The Commission shall ensure that regulations prescribed to implement this section encourage, consistent with section 7(a) of this Act, the use of existing technology and do not discourage or impair the development of improved technology.

"(3) JURISDICTIONAL SEPARATION OF COSTS.—

"(A) IN GENERAL.—Consistent with the provisions of section 410 of this Act, the Commission shall prescribe regulations governing the jurisdictional separation of costs for the services provided pursuant to this section.

"(B) RECOVERING COSTS.—Such regulations shall generally provide that costs caused by interstate telecommunications relay services shall be recovered from all subscribers for every interstate service and costs caused by intrastate telecommunications relay services shall be recovered from the intrastate jurisdiction. In a State that has a certified program under subsection (f), a State commission shall permit a common carrier to recover the costs incurred in providing intrastate telecommunications relay services by a method consistent with the requirements of this section.

"(e) ENFORCEMENT.—

"(1) IN GENERAL.—Subject to subsections (f) and (g), the Commission shall enforce this section.

"(2) COMPLAINT.—The Commission shall resolve, by final order, a complaint alleging a violation of this section within 180 days after the date such complaint is filed.

"(f) CERTIFICATION.—

"(1) STATE DOCUMENTATION.—Any State desiring to establish a State program under this section shall submit documentation to the Commission that describes the program of such State for implementing intrastate telecommunications relay services and the procedures and remedies available for enforcing any requirements imposed by the State program.

"(2) REQUIREMENTS FOR CERTIFICATION.—After review of such documentation, the Commission shall certify the State program if the Commission determines that—

"(A) the program makes available to hearing-impaired and speech-impaired individuals, either directly, through designees, through a competitively selected vendor, or through regulation of intrastate common carriers, intrastate telecommunications relay services in such State in a manner that meets or exceeds the requirements of regulations prescribed by the Commission under subsection (d); and

"(B) the program makes available adequate procedures and remedies for enforcing the requirements of the State program.

"(3) METHOD OF FUNDING.—Except as provided in subsection (d), the Commission shall not refuse to certify a State program based solely on the method such State will implement for funding intrastate telecommunication relay services.

"(4) SUSPENSION OR REVOCATION OF CERTIFICATION.—The Commission may suspend or revoke such certification if, after notice and opportunity for hearing, the Commission determines that such certification is no longer warranted. In a State whose program has been suspended or revoked, the Commission shall take such steps as may be necessary, consistent with this section, to ensure continuity of telecommunications relay services.

"(g) COMPLAINT.—

"(1) REFERRAL OF COMPLAINT.—If a complaint to the Commission alleges a violation of this section with respect to intrastate telecommunications relay services within a State and certification of the program of such State under subsection (f) is in effect, the Commission shall refer such complaint to such State.

"(2) JURISDICTION OF COMMISSION.—After referring a complaint to a State under paragraph (1), the Commission shall exercise jurisdiction over such complaint only if—

"(A) final action under such State program has not been taken on such complaint by such State—

"(i) within 180 days after the complaint is filed with such State; or

"(ii) within a shorter period as prescribed by the regulations of such State; or

"(B) the Commission determines that such State program is no longer qualified for certification under subsection (f).".

(b) CONFORMING AMENDMENTS.—The Communications Act of 1934 (47 U.S.C. 151 et seq.) is amended—

(1) in section 2(b) (47 U.S.C. 152(b)), by striking "section 224" and inserting "sections 224 and 225"; and

(2) in section 221(b) (47 U.S.C. 221(b)), by striking "section 301" and inserting "sections 225 and 301".

SEC. 402. CLOSED-CAPTIONING OF PUBLIC SERVICE ANNOUNCEMENTS.

47 USC 611.

Section 711 of the Communications Act of 1934 is amended to read as follows:

"**SEC. 711. CLOSED-CAPTIONING OF PUBLIC SERVICE ANNOUNCEMENTS.**

"Any television public service announcement that is produced or funded in whole or in part by any agency or instrumentality of Federal Government shall include closed captioning of the verbal content of such announcement. A television broadcast station licensee—

"(1) shall not be required to supply closed captioning for any such announcement that fails to include it; and

"(2) shall not be liable for broadcasting any such announcement without transmitting a closed caption unless the licensee intentionally fails to transmit the closed caption that was included with the announcement.".

TITLE V—MISCELLANEOUS PROVISIONS

SEC. 501. CONSTRUCTION.

42 USC 12201.

(a) IN GENERAL.—Except as otherwise provided in this Act, nothing in this Act shall be construed to apply a lesser standard than the standards applied under title V of the Rehabilitation Act of 1973 (29 U.S.C. 790 et seq.) or the regulations issued by Federal agencies pursuant to such title.

(b) RELATIONSHIP TO OTHER LAWS.—Nothing in this Act shall be construed to invalidate or limit the remedies, rights, and procedures of any Federal law or law of any State or political subdivision of any State or jurisdiction that provides greater or equal protection for the rights of individuals with disabilities than are afforded by this Act. Nothing in this Act shall be construed to preclude the prohibition of, or the imposition of restrictions on, smoking in places of employment covered by title I, in transportation covered by title II or III, or in places of public accommodation covered by title III.

(c) INSURANCE.—Titles I through IV of this Act shall not be construed to prohibit or restrict—

(1) an insurer, hospital or medical service company, health maintenance organization, or any agent, or entity that administers benefit plans, or similar organizations from underwriting risks, classifying risks, or administering such risks that are based on or not inconsistent with State law; or

(2) a person or organization covered by this Act from establishing, sponsoring, observing or administering the terms of a bona fide benefit plan that are based on underwriting risks, classifying risks, or administering such risks that are based on or not inconsistent with State law; or

(3) a person or organization covered by this Act from establishing, sponsoring, observing or administering the terms of a bona fide benefit plan that is not subject to State laws that regulate insurance.

Paragraphs (1), (2), and (3) shall not be used as a subterfuge to evade the purposes of title I and III.

(d) ACCOMMODATIONS AND SERVICES.—Nothing in this Act shall be construed to require an individual with a disability to accept an accommodation, aid, service, opportunity, or benefit which such individual chooses not to accept.

SEC. 502. STATE IMMUNITY.

42 USC 12202.

A State shall not be immune under the eleventh amendment to the Constitution of the United States from an action in Federal or State court of competent jurisdiction for a violation of this Act. In any action against a State for a violation of the requirements of this Act, remedies (including remedies both at law and in equity) are available for such a violation to the same extent as such remedies are available for such a violation in an action against any public or private entity other than a State.

42 USC 12203.

SEC. 503. PROHIBITION AGAINST RETALIATION AND COERCION.

(a) RETALIATION.—No person shall discriminate against any individual because such individual has opposed any act or practice made unlawful by this Act or because such individual made a charge, testified, assisted, or participated in any manner in an investigation, proceeding, or hearing under this Act.

(b) INTERFERENCE, COERCION, OR INTIMIDATION.—It shall be unlawful to coerce, intimidate, threaten, or interfere with any individual in the exercise or enjoyment of, or on account of his or her having exercised or enjoyed, or on account of his or her having aided or encouraged any other individual in the exercise or enjoyment of, any right granted or protected by this Act.

(c) REMEDIES AND PROCEDURES.—The remedies and procedures available under sections 107, 203, and 308 of this Act shall be available to aggrieved persons for violations of subsections (a) and (b), with respect to title I, title II and title III, respectively.

42 USC 12204.

SEC. 504. REGULATIONS BY THE ARCHITECTURAL AND TRANSPORTATION BARRIERS COMPLIANCE BOARD.

(a) ISSUANCE OF GUIDELINES.—Not later than 9 months after the date of enactment of this Act, the Architectural and Transportation Barriers Compliance Board shall issue minimum guidelines that shall supplement the existing Minimum Guidelines and Requirements for Accessible Design for purposes of titles II and III of this Act.

(b) CONTENTS OF GUIDELINES.—The supplemental guidelines issued under subsection (a) shall establish additional requirements, consistent with this Act, to ensure that buildings, facilities, rail passenger cars, and vehicles are accessible, in terms of architecture and design, transportation, and communication, to individuals with disabilities.

(c) QUALIFIED HISTORIC PROPERTIES.—

(1) IN GENERAL.—The supplemental guidelines issued under subsection (a) shall include procedures and requirements for alterations that will threaten or destroy the historic significance of qualified historic buildings and facilities as defined in 4.1.7(1)(a) of the Uniform Federal Accessibility Standards.

(2) SITES ELIGIBLE FOR LISTING IN NATIONAL REGISTER.—With respect to alterations of buildings or facilities that are eligible for listing in the National Register of Historic Places under the National Historic Preservation Act (16 U.S.C. 470 et seq.), the guidelines described in paragraph (1) shall, at a minimum, maintain the procedures and requirements established in 4.1.7 (1) and (2) of the Uniform Federal Accessibility Standards.

(3) OTHER SITES.—With respect to alterations of buildings or facilities designated as historic under State or local law, the guidelines described in paragraph (1) shall establish procedures equivalent to those established by 4.1.7(1) (b) and (c) of the Uniform Federal Accessibility Standards, and shall require, at a minimum, compliance with the requirements established in 4.1.7(2) of such standards.

42 USC 12205.

SEC. 505. ATTORNEY'S FEES.

In any action or administrative proceeding commenced pursuant to this Act, the court or agency, in its discretion, may allow the prevailing party, other than the United States, a reasonable attorney's fee, including litigation expenses, and costs, and the United States shall be liable for the foregoing the same as a private individual.

SEC. 506. TECHNICAL ASSISTANCE.

(a) PLAN FOR ASSISTANCE.—

(1) IN GENERAL.—Not later than 180 days after the date of enactment of this Act, the Attorney General, in consultation with the Chair of the Equal Employment Opportunity Commission, the Secretary of Transportation, the Chair of the Architectural and Transportation Barriers Compliance Board, and the Chairman of the Federal Communications Commission, shall develop a plan to assist entities covered under this Act, and other Federal agencies, in understanding the responsibility of such entities and agencies under this Act.

(2) PUBLICATION OF PLAN.—The Attorney General shall publish the plan referred to in paragraph (1) for public comment in accordance with subchapter II of chapter 5 of title 5, United States Code (commonly known as the Administrative Procedure Act).

(b) AGENCY AND PUBLIC ASSISTANCE.—The Attorney General may obtain the assistance of other Federal agencies in carrying out subsection (a), including the National Council on Disability, the President's Committee on Employment of People with Disabilities, the Small Business Administration, and the Department of Commerce.

(c) IMPLEMENTATION.—

(1) RENDERING ASSISTANCE.—Each Federal agency that has responsibility under paragraph (2) for implementing this Act may render technical assistance to individuals and institutions that have rights or duties under the respective title or titles for which such agency has responsibility.

(2) IMPLEMENTATION OF TITLES.—

(A) TITLE I.—The Equal Employment Opportunity Commission and the Attorney General shall implement the plan for assistance developed under subsection (a), for title I.

(B) TITLE II.—

(i) SUBTITLE A.—The Attorney General shall implement such plan for assistance for subtitle A of title II.

(ii) SUBTITLE B.—The Secretary of Transportation shall implement such plan for assistance for subtitle B of title II.

(C) TITLE III.—The Attorney General, in coordination with the Secretary of Transportation and the Chair of the Architectural Transportation Barriers Compliance Board, shall implement such plan for assistance for title III, except for section 304, the plan for assistance for which shall be implemented by the Secretary of Transportation.

(D) TITLE IV.—The Chairman of the Federal Communications Commission, in coordination with the Attorney General, shall implement such plan for assistance for title IV.

(3) TECHNICAL ASSISTANCE MANUALS.—Each Federal agency that has responsibility under paragraph (2) for implementing this Act shall, as part of its implementation responsibilities, ensure the availability and provision of appropriate technical assistance manuals to individuals or entities with rights or duties under this Act no later than six months after applicable final regulations are published under titles I, II, III, and IV.

(d) GRANTS AND CONTRACTS.—

(1) IN GENERAL.—Each Federal agency that has responsibility under subsection (c)(2) for implementing this Act may make grants or award contracts to effectuate the purposes of this section, subject to the availability of appropriations. Such grants and contracts may be awarded to individuals, institu-

tions not organized for profit and no part of the net earnings of which inures to the benefit of any private shareholder or individual (including educational institutions), and associations representing individuals who have rights or .duties .under this Act. Contracts may be awarded to entities organized for profit, but such entities may not be the recipients or grants described in this paragraph.

(2) DISSEMINATION OF INFORMATION.—Such grants and contracts, among other uses, may be designed to ensure wide dissemination of information about the rights and duties established by this Act and to provide information and technical assistance about techniques for effective compliance with this Act.

(e) FAILURE TO RECEIVE ASSISTANCE.—An employer, public accommodation, or other entity covered under this Act shall not be excused from compliance with the requirements of this Act because of any failure to receive technical assistance under this section, including any failure in the development or dissemination of any technical assistance manual authorized by this section.

42 USC 12207.

SEC. 507. FEDERAL WILDERNESS AREAS.

(a) STUDY.—The National Council on Disability shall conduct a study and report on the effect that wilderness designations and wilderness land management practices have on the ability of individuals with disabilities to use and enjoy the National Wilderness Preservation System as established under the Wilderness Act (16 U.S.C. 1131 et seq.).

(b) SUBMISSION OF REPORT.—Not later than 1 year after the enactment of this Act, the National Council on Disability shall submit the report required under subsection (a) to Congress.

(c) SPECIFIC WILDERNESS ACCESS.—

(1) IN GENERAL.—Congress reaffirms that nothing in the Wilderness Act is to be construed as prohibiting the use of a wheelchair in a wilderness area by an individual whose disability requires use of a wheelchair, and consistent with the Wilderness Act no agency is required to provide any form of special treatment or accommodation, or to construct any facilities or modify any conditions of lands within a wilderness area in order to facilitate such use.

(2) DEFINITION.—For purposes of paragraph (1), the term "wheelchair" means a device designed solely for use by a mobility-impaired person for locomotion, that is suitable for use in an indoor pedestrian area.

42 USC 12208.

SEC. 508. TRANSVESTITES.

For the purposes of this Act, the term "disabled" or "disability" shall not apply to an individual solely because that individual is a transvestite.

42 USC 12209.

SEC. 509. COVERAGE OF CONGRESS AND THE AGENCIES OF THE LEGISLATIVE BRANCH.

(a) COVERAGE OF THE SENATE.—

(1) COMMITMENT TO RULE XLII.—The Senate reaffirms its commitment to Rule XLII of the Standing Rules of the Senate which provides as follows:

"No member, officer, or employee of the Senate shall, with respect to employment by the Senate or any office thereof—

"(a) fail or refuse to hire an individual;

"(b) discharge an individual; or

"(c) otherwise discriminate against an individual with

respect to promotion, compensation, or terms, conditions, or privileges of employment
on the basis of such individual's race, color, religion, sex, national origin, age, or state of physical handicap.''.

*(2) MATTERS OTHER THAN EMPLOYMENT.—

(A) IN GENERAL.—The rights and protections under this Act shall, subject to subparagraph (B), apply with respect to the conduct of the Senate regarding matters other than employment.

(B) REMEDIES.—The Architect of the Capitol shall establish remedies and procedures to be utilized with respect to the rights and protections provided pursuant to subparagraph (A). Such remedies and procedures shall apply exclusively, after approval in accordance with subparagraph (C).

(C) PROPOSED REMEDIES AND PROCEDURES.—For purposes of subparagraph (B), the Architect of the Capitol shall submit proposed remedies and procedures to the Senate Committee on Rules and Administration. The remedies and procedures shall be effective upon the approval of the Committee on Rules and Administration.

(3) EXERCISE OF RULEMAKING POWER.—Notwithstanding any other provision of law, enforcement and adjudication of the rights and protections referred to in paragraph (2) and (6)(A) shall be within the exclusive jurisdiction of the United States Senate. The provisions of paragraph (1), (3), (4), (5), (6)(B), and (6)(C) are enacted by the Senate as an exercise of the rule-making power of the Senate, with full recognition of the right of the Senate to change its rules, in the same manner, and to the same extent, as in the case of any other rule of the Senate.

(b) COVERAGE OF THE HOUSE OF REPRESENTATIVES.—

(1) IN GENERAL.—Notwithstanding any other provision of this Act or of law, the purposes of this Act shall, subject to paragraphs (2) and (3), apply in their entirety to the House of Representatives.

(2) EMPLOYMENT IN THE HOUSE.—

(A) APPLICATION.—The rights and protections under this Act shall, subject to subparagraph (B), apply with respect to any employee in an employment position in the House of Representatives and any employing authority of the House of Representatives.

(B) ADMINISTRATION.—

(i) IN GENERAL.—In the administration of this paragraph, the remedies and procedures made applicable pursuant to the resolution described in clause (ii) shall apply exclusively.

(ii) RESOLUTION.—The resolution referred to in clause (i) is House Resolution 15 of the One Hundred First Congress, as agreed to January 3, 1989, or any other provision that continues in effect the provisions of, or is a successor to, the Fair Employment Practices Resolution (House Resolution 558 of the One Hundredth Congress, as agreed to October 4, 1988).

(C) EXERCISE OF RULEMAKING POWER.—The provisions of subparagraph (B) are enacted by the House of Representatives as an exercise of the rulemaking power of the House

---

*Original items (2)–(5) have been deleted in accordance with the *Civil Rights Act of 1991* (PL 102-166 [November 21, 1991]. Title III, 42 U.S.C. 1981. *U.S. Statutes at Large, 105*, 1095). Original items (6) and (7) have been renumbered as (2) and (3) to accommodate the deletion.

of Representatives, with full recognition of the right of the House to change its rules, in the same manner, and to the same extent as in the case of any other rule of the House.

(3) MATTERS OTHER THAN EMPLOYMENT.—

(A) IN GENERAL.—The rights and protections under this Act shall, subject to subparagraph (B), apply with respect to the conduct of the House of Representatives regarding matters other than employment.

(B) REMEDIES.—The Architect of the Capitol shall establish remedies and procedures to be utilized with respect to the rights and protections provided pursuant to subparagraph (A). Such remedies and procedures shall apply exclusively, after approval in accordance with subparagraph (C).

(C) APPROVAL.—For purposes of subparagraph (B), the Architect of the Capitol shall submit proposed remedies and procedures to the Speaker of the House of Representatives. The remedies and procedures shall be effective upon the approval of the Speaker, after consultation with the House Office Building Commission.

(c) INSTRUMENTALITIES OF CONGRESS.—

(1) IN GENERAL.—The rights and protections under this Act shall, subject to paragraph (2), apply with respect to the conduct of each instrumentality of the Congress.

(2) ESTABLISHMENT OF REMEDIES AND PROCEDURES BY INSTRUMENTALITIES.—The chief official of each instrumentality of the Congress shall establish remedies and procedures to be utilized with respect to the rights and protections provided pursuant to paragraph (1). Such remedies and procedures shall apply exclusively except for the employees who are defined as Senate employees in section 301(c)(1) of the Civil Rights Act of 1991.*

(3) REPORT TO CONGRESS.—The chief official of each instrumentality of the Congress shall, after establishing remedies and procedures for purposes of paragraph (2), submit to the Congress a report describing the remedies and procedures.

(4) DEFINITION OF INSTRUMENTALITIES.—For purposes of this section, instrumentalities of the Congress include the following: the Architect of the Capitol, the Congressional Budget Office, the General Accounting Office, the Government Printing Office, the Library of Congress, the Office of Technology Assessment, and the United States Botanic Garden.

(5) CONSTRUCTION.—Nothing in this section shall alter the enforcement procedures for individuals with disabilities provided in the General Accounting Office Personnel Act of 1980 and regulations promulgated pursuant to that Act.

42 USC 12213

SEC. 510. ILLEGAL USE OF DRUGS.

(a) IN GENERAL.—For purposes of this Act, the term "individual with a disability" does not include an individual who is currently engaging in the illegal use of drugs, when the covered entity act. on the basis of such use.

(b) RULES OF CONSTRUCTION.—Nothing in subsection (a) shall be construed to exclude as an individual with a disability an individual who—

---

*The last portion of the last sentence in (2) has been added in accordance with the *Civil Rights Acts of 1991* (PL 102-166 [November 21, 1991]. Title I, 42 U.S.C. 1981. *U.S. Statutes at Large, 105,* 1080).

(1) has successfully completed a supervised drug rehabilitation program and is no longer engaging in the illegal use of drugs, or has otherwise been rehabilitated successfully and is no longer engaging in such use;

(2) is participating in a supervised rehabilitation program and is no longer engaging in such use; or

(3) is erroneously regarded as engaging in such use, but is not engaging in such use;

except that it shall not be a violation of this Act for a covered entity to adopt or administer reasonable policies or procedures, including but not limited to drug testing, designed to ensure that an individual described in paragraph (1) or (2) is no longer engaging in the illegal use of drugs; however, nothing in this section shall be construed to encourage, prohibit, restrict, or authorize the conducting of testing for the illegal use of drugs.

(c) HEALTH AND OTHER SERVICES.—Notwithstanding subsection (a) and section 511(b)(3), an individual shall not be denied health services, or services provided in connection with drug rehabilitation, on the basis of the current illegal use of drugs if the individual is otherwise entitled to such services.

(d) DEFINITION OF ILLEGAL USE OF DRUGS.—

(1) IN GENERAL.—The term "illegal use of drugs" means the use of drugs, the possession or distribution of which is unlawful under the Controlled Substances Act (21 U.S.C. 812). Such term does not include the use of a drug taken under supervision by a licensed health care professional, or other uses authorized by the Controlled Substances Act or other provisions of Federal law.

(2) DRUGS.—The term "drug" means a controlled substance, as defined in schedules I through V of section 202 of the Controlled Substances Act.

SEC. 511. DEFINITIONS.

42 USC 12211.

(a) HOMOSEXUALITY AND BISEXUALITY.—For purposes of the definition of "disability" in section 3(2), homosexuality and bisexuality are not impairments and as such are not disabilities under this Act.

(b) CERTAIN CONDITIONS.—Under this Act, the term "disability" shall not include—

(1) transvestism, transsexualism, pedophilia, exhibitionism, voyeurism, gender identity disorders not resulting from physical impairments, or other sexual behavior disorders;

(2) compulsive gambling, kleptomania, or pyromania; or

(3) psychoactive substance use disorders resulting from current illegal use of drugs.

SEC. 512. AMENDMENTS TO THE REHABILITATION ACT.

(a) DEFINITION OF HANDICAPPED INDIVIDUAL.—Section 7(8) of the Rehabilitation Act of 1973 (29 U.S.C. 706(8)) is amended by redesignating subparagraph (C) as subparagraph (D), and by inserting after subparagraph (B) the following subparagraph:

"(C)(i) For purposes of title V, the term 'individual with handicaps' does not include an individual who is currently engaging in the illegal use of drugs, when a covered entity acts on the basis of such use.

"(ii) Nothing in clause (i) shall be construed to exclude as an individual with handicaps an individual who—

"(I) has successfully completed a supervised drug rehabilitation program and is no longer engaging in the illegal use of drugs, or has otherwise been rehabilitated successfully and is no longer engaging in such use;

"(II) is participating in a supervised rehabilitation program and is no longer engaging in such use; or

"(III) is erroneously regarded as engaging in such use, but is not engaging in such use;

except that it shall not be a violation of this Act for a covered entity to adopt or administer reasonable policies or procedures, including but not limited to drug testing, designed to ensure that an individual described in subclause (I) or (II) is no longer engaging in the illegal use of drugs.

"(iii) Notwithstanding clause (i), for purposes of programs and activities providing health services and services provided under titles I, II and III, an individual shall not be excluded from the benefits of such programs or activities on the basis of his or her current illegal use of drugs if he or she is otherwise entitled to.such services.

"(iv) For purposes of programs and activities providing educational services, local educational agencies may take disciplinary action pertaining to the use or possession of illegal drugs or alcohol against any handicapped student who currently is engaging in the illegal use of drugs or in the use of alcohol to the same extent that such disciplinary action is taken against nonhandicapped students. Furthermore, the due process procedures at 34 CFR 104.36 shall not apply to such disciplinary actions.

"(v) For purposes of sections 503 and 504 as such sections relate to employment, the term 'individual with handicaps' does not include any individual who is an alcoholic whose current use of alcohol prevents such individual from performing the duties of the job in question or whose employment, by reason of such current alcohol abuse, would constitute a direct threat to property or the safety of others.".

(b) DEFINITION OF ILLEGAL DRUGS.—Section 7 of the Rehabilitation Act of 1973 (29 U.S.C. 706) is amended by adding at the end the following new paragraph:

"(22)(A) The term 'drug' means a controlled substance, as defined in schedules I through V of section 202 of the Controlled Substances Act (21 U.S.C. 812).

"(B) The term 'illegal use of drugs' means the use of drugs, the possession or distribution of which is unlawful under the Controlled Substances Act. Such term does not include the use of a drug taken under supervision by a licensed health care professional, or other uses authorized by the Controlled Substances Act or other provisions of Federal law.".

(c) CONFORMING AMENDMENTS.—Section 7(8)(B) of the Rehabilitation Act of 1973 (29 U.S.C. 706(8)(B)) is amended—

(1) in the first sentence, by striking "Subject to the second sentence of this subparagraph," and inserting "Subject to subparagraphs (C) and (D),"; and

(2) by striking the second sentence.

42 USC 12212.

SEC. 513. ALTERNATIVE MEANS OF DISPUTE RESOLUTION.

Where appropriate and to the extent authorized by law, the use of alternative means of dispute resolution, including settlement negotiations, conciliation, facilitation, mediation, factfinding, minitrials, and arbitration, is encouraged to resolve disputes arising under this Act.

SEC. 514. SEVERABILITY.   42 USC 12213.

Should any provision in this Act be found to be unconstitutional by a court of law, such provision shall be severed from the remainder of the Act, and such action shall not affect the enforceability of the remaining provisions of the Act.

Approved July 26, 1990.

LEGISLATIVE HISTORY—S. 933 (H.R. 2273):

HOUSE REPORTS: No. 101-485, Pt. 1 (Comm. on Public Works and Transportation), Pt. 2 (Comm. on Education and Labor), Pt. 3 (Comm. on the Judiciary), and Pt. 4 (Comm. on Energy and Commerce) all accompanying H.R. 2273; and No. 101-558 and No. 101-569 both from (Comm. of Conference).
SENATE REPORTS: No. 101-116 (Comm. on Labor and Human Resources).
CONGRESSIONAL RECORD:
  Vol. 135 (1989): Sept. 7, considered and passed Senate.
  Vol. 136 (1990): May 17, 22, H.R. 2273 considered and passed House; S. 933 passed in lieu.
      July 11, Senate recommitted conference report.
      July 12, House agreed to conference report.
      July 13, Senate agreed to conference report.
WEEKLY COMPILATION OF PRESIDENTIAL DOCUMENTS, Vol. 26 (1990):
  July 26, Presidential remarks and statement.

Index